PERSPECTIVES ON THE HISTORY
OF ANCIENT NEAR EASTERN STUDIES

Perspectives on the History of Ancient Near Eastern Studies

EDITED BY AGNÈS GARCIA-VENTURA
AND LORENZO VERDERAME

EISENBRAUNS | University Park, Pennsylvania

Library of Congress Cataloging-in-Publication Data

Names: Garcia-Ventura, Agnès, editor. | Verderame, L. (Lorenzo), editor.

Title: Perspectives on the History of Ancient Near Eastern Studies / edited by Agnès
Garcia-Ventura and Lorenzo Verderame.

Description: University Park, Pennsylvania : Eisenbrauns, [2020] | Includes bibliographical
references and index.

Summary: "A collection of essays that encompass the two principal approaches to the history
of ancient Near Eastern studies: descriptive historiography and intellectual history"—Provided by publisher.

Identifiers: LCCN 2020011867 | ISBN 9781575068367 (hardback)

Subjects: LCSH: Assyriology—History. | Assyriology—Historiography. | Middle East—Study
and teaching—History. | Middle East—Study and teaching—Historiography.

Classification: LCC DS61.8 .P47 2020 | DDC 935/.03—dc23

LC record available at https://lccn.loc.gov/2020011867

Copyright © 2020 The Pennsylvania State University
All rights reserved
Printed in the United States of America
Published by The Pennsylvania State University Press,
University Park, PA 16802-1003

Eisenbrauns is an imprint of The Pennsylvania State University Press.

The Pennsylvania State University Press is a member of the Association of University
Presses.

It is the policy of The Pennsylvania State University Press to use acid-free paper. Publications on uncoated stock satisfy the minimum requirements of American National Standard for
Information Sciences—Permanence of Paper for Printed Library Material, ANSI Z39.48–1992.

TABLE OF CONTENTS

Perspectives on the History of Ancient Near Eastern Studies: An Introduction vii
Lorenzo Verderame and Agnès Garcia-Ventura

PART I. THE EDGE OF THE ABYSS:
THE STUDY OF ANTIQUITY UNDER TOTALITARIAN THREAT

CHAPTER 1. Hittite Studies at the Crossroads: Albrecht Goetze's and
Hans Gustav Güterbock's Flight from Nazi Germany 3
Silvia Alaura

CHAPTER 2. Language and Race in Assyriology:
From Benno Landsberger to Wolfram von Soden 25
Sebastian Fink

CHAPTER 3. Assyriology in Nazi Germany: The Case of Wolfram von Soden . . 44
Jakob Flygare

CHAPTER 4. Carthage the Deceitful and Perfidious Albion:
The Phoenicians and the British in Fascist Italy 61
Pietro Giammellaro

CHAPTER 5. The Sharing Out of Antiquities in Syria During the Interwar
Period: Sir Leonard Woolley's Excavation at Tell Sheikh Yusuf (Al-Mina) 77
Patrick Maxime Michel

CHAPTER 6. "Die Assyriologie nicht weiter unberücksichtigt bleiben
dürfte": On the (Non-)Existence of Assyriology at the German University
in Prague (1908–1945) 87
Luděk Vacín and Jitka Sýkorová

vi   *Table of Contents*

PART II. INTELLECTUAL HISTORY AND ANCIENT NEAR EASTERN STUDIES: SOME CASE STUDIES

CHAPTER 7. Notes on the History of the Historiography of Cuneiform Mathematics 147
Carlos Gonçalves

CHAPTER 8. Feudalism and Vassalage in Twentieth-Century Assyriology 172
Emanuel Pfoh

CHAPTER 9. Nation Building in the Plain of Antioch from Hatti to Hatay 190
Eva von Dassow

PART III. FROM OUR STORIES TO THE HISTORY OF ANCIENT NEAR EASTERN STUDIES

CHAPTER 10. The Historiography of Assyriology in Turkey: A Short Survey . . 211
Selim Ferruh Adalı and Hakan Erol

CHAPTER 11. Ancient Near Eastern Studies and Portuguese Academia: A Love Affair Under Construction 222
Isabel Gomes de Almeida

CHAPTER 12. Near Eastern Archaeology and the Czech-Speaking Lands . . . 237
Petr Charvát

CHAPTER 13. Tintin in Mesopotamia: The Story of Belgian Assyriology (1890–2017) 252
Katrien De Graef

CHAPTER 14. Assyriology in Iran? 266
Parsa Daneshmand

CHAPTER 15. Assyriology in China 283
Changyu Liu

CHAPTER 16. Looking for a Tell: The Beginnings of Ancient Near Eastern Archaeology at the University of Barcelona 289
Jordi Vidal

PART IV. CURRENT PROSPECTIVES, FUTURE PERSPECTIVES

CHAPTER 17. Big Data, Big Deal: Use of Google Books Ngram Viewer and JSTOR *Data for Research* for Charting the Rise of Assyriology 299
Steven W. Holloway

CHAPTER 18. The Future of the Past: How the Past Contributes to the Construction of Syrian National Identity 326
Ahmed Fatima Kzzo

Perspectives on the History of Ancient Near Eastern Studies: An Introduction

Lorenzo Verderame and Agnès Garcia-Ventura

From January to May 2016 the editors of the present volume organized at "Sapienza," Università degli Studi di Roma, a series of lectures and workshops under the title *Storia degli studi sul Vicino Oriente Antico*.[1] In that occasion we used "storia degli studi" in a broad sense, as a label encompassing a myriad of perspectives and topics of study, sharing as common denominator a reflexive approach toward the study of the past and, more specifically in our case, the study of the ancient Near East.

As a result of this broad scope, the series included about thirty lectures and presentations dealing with four main topics: first, the reception of the ancient Near East in popular culture; second, the reconstruction of the Near Eastern past through archaeology; third, the historiography of ancient Near Eastern studies; fourth and last, approaches to intellectual history through a selection of issues and topics most commonly discussed in ancient Near Eastern studies. The essays dealing with the first and second topics, those linked to the so-called reception studies, have been collected and edited by the present writers in the volume *Receptions of the Ancient Near East in Popular Culture and Beyond*.[2] Those dealing with the third and fourth topic, those linked with the history of ancient Near Eastern studies, are the ones collected and edited in the present volume. Before summarizing the structure and content of the book, a few words are in order about how we understand the relationship between historiography and intellectual history, as well as about the way the diverse authors approach their topics of study in this collection of essays.

As mentioned above, the common denominator of "storia degli studi" understood in a broad sense is the reflexive approach to the disciplines and to the research devoted to the study of the past. This reflexive approach includes what we may define as several research branches or even, in some cases, as several stages of the same (at least potentially) research perspectives. On the one hand, there is the research about the history of a given academic discipline. This research, at least in its first stages, has a more descriptive character, as it aims at collecting the basic data about who developed certain studies, and about the years, conditions, and institutions in which this research was developed. This first descriptive approach is often devoted to the reconstruction of the way a discipline, ancient Near Eastern studies in our case, has been founded

---

1. The initiative has been funded by a grant program organized at "Sapienza" Università degli Studi di Roma ("Giornate di storia degli studi sul Vicino Oriente Antico"; C26C157SL3). For a detailed program with titles and participants, see http://lorenzoverderame.site.uniroma1.it/attivita-1/2016storiastudi (accessed 15 September 2018).

2. Verderame and Garcia-Ventura 2020.

vii

and developed in a specific country or in a specific academic tradition. In this direction there is a quite long tradition of research, carried on since the first decades of the twentieth century in the Great Britain, France, and Germany.[3] Solid proof of this early interest in historiography was the publication in 1904 of C. Fossey's *Manuel d'assyriologie*, or the monograph by E. A. Wallis Budge, *Rise and Progress of the Assyriology* (1925).

On the other hand, another branch or stage of the research, often following the previous one, has an eminently analytical character. This branch is included as well within the "storia degli studi" we used as framework for our series of seminars, even though it is distinct from the more descriptive research just reported and is often labelled as "storia delle idee" or "intellectual history" in the English-speaking traditions. Intellectual history can take as its framework a specific country or a specific academic tradition, as the more descriptive historiography usually does. When it happens, this research may work as a synthesis of the previous descriptive work as it often takes as a starting point this previous collection of data. In other cases, intellectual history does not restrict analysis to the research produced in a specific territory, but it develops it, taking into account a transnational point of view that aims at identifying the *Zeitgeist* shared by contemporary researchers who do necessarily share the same academic tradition. A good example of this line of research is the one developed by Mario Liverani, as can be seen in his collection of essays translated into English and published in 2004 under the title *Myth and Politics in Ancient Near Eastern Historiography*. All in all, despite the differences between intellectual history ("storia delle idee") and the more descriptive histories of the specific disciplines ("storia degli studi" in a strict sense), we decided to include both in the same volume, thus considering both as complementary one to the other. As a consequence of this choice, in this volume we present together elaborate analytical approaches to topics recurring in ancient Near Eastern studies, as well as descriptive essays laying the foundation for further analyses in countries and academic traditions never considered as research topics up to this point.

The volume you have in your hands brings together eighteen essays dealing with the history of ancient Near Eastern studies, understood in this broad sense previously described. Preliminary versions of six of the essays were presented at the seminars held in Rome in 2016,[4] and they are offered here alongside papers from other guest contributors. Among the authors there are colleagues who have been dealing with historiography and intellectual history as one of their main lines of research in recent years, while others kindly accepted our invitation to contribute to the volume, giving us the possibility to include first hand studies from academic traditions, like Chinese or Portuguese ancient Near Eastern studies, not common in the historiographical debates. To all of them we owe gratitude for their willingness to cooperate and to be part of this editorial project.

---

3. On this early interest of ancient Near Eastern scholars to reflect on the discipline and on their own careers, see, among others, Vita 2012. However, despite this early interest, there is also a clear lack of tradition of historiographical research in our field of study. For some thoughts in this direction and discussion of previous publications, see Vidal 2015.

4. These are the essays by the following authors (by alphabetical order): Silvia Alaura, Eva von Dassow, Sebastian Fink, Pietro Giammellaro, Ahmed Fatima Kzzo, and Jordi Vidal.

Perspectives on the History of Ancient Near Eastern Studies   ix

The eighteen essays are grouped in four sections, preceded by this introductory chapter, each section being an example of the different possible developments of the study of the history of our discipline. The first section, titled "The Edge of the Abyss: The Study of Antiquity Under Totalitarian Threat," includes the chapters by Silvia Alaura, Sebastian Fink, Jakob Flygare, Pietro Giammellaro, Patrick Maxime Michel, and Luděk Vacín and Jitka Sýkorová, who co-author their contribution. All these contributions have in common, on the one hand, the chronological framework chosen, that is the first half of the twentieth century CE roughly speaking. On the other hand, they have in common the particular attention devoted to the way the political context affects and shapes research. In this case, they discuss the influence totalitarian regimes and wars had on the way the discipline was taught and developed, but also commenting on the way material culture was managed and displayed. The essays included in this section cover a rich array of territories (Italy, Germany, UK, current Czech Republic, and Syria), as well as some of the most outstanding characters of ancient Near Eastern studies such as Albrecht Goetze, Hans Gustav Güterbock, Benno Landsberger, Wolfram von Soden, and Leonard Woolley. Moreover, it is worth highlighting the richness of the specialties discussed in these essays, including Hittitology and Phoenician studies, among others, offering a picture more varied than the usual one, which often restricts the debates to ancient Mesopotamian sources.

The second section, titled "Intellectual History and Ancient Near Eastern Studies: Some Case Studies," includes the chapters by Carlos Gonçalves, Emanuel Pfoh, and Eva von Dassow. They discuss concepts and research topics as complex as mathematics, feudalism, ethnic identity, and nation-building. Each topic is approached from a broad chronological perspective, which traces in all cases the course of their use throughout the history of ancient Near Eastern studies. Unlike the previous section, these chapters do not circumscribe themselves to a specific chronology or to a specific country but try to see through diachronic analysis how certain topics and concepts have been discussed in the discipline and how in each case the cultural and the social context potentially influenced research.

The third section, titled "From our Stories to the History of Ancient Near Eastern Studies," includes the chapters by Selim Ferruh Adalı and Hakan Erol (a joint contribution), Isabel Almeida, Petr Charvát, Katrien De Graef, Parsa Daneshmand, Changyu Liu, and Jordi Vidal. This section is devoted to the history of the discipline in diverse geographical areas, focusing on academic traditions in ancient Near Eastern studies only seldomly considered as topics of study, or even as territories never before considered as such. All of them, then, aim to lay the foundations for future research on the history of ancient Near Eastern studies in academic traditions often considered "peripheral" in the field of study. In this section the following territories are considered (listed following the chapter order): Turkey, Portugal, the Czech-speaking lands, Belgium, Iran, China, and Spain. All of them are authored by colleagues who developed (or are still developing) their research in these countries and, in some cases, they offer the reader firsthand data about the development of the discipline there. However, while some of them offer a panoramic view result of the work with archival materials, others are examples of oral history.

The fourth and last section of the present volume is titled "Current Prospectives, Future Perspectives," and it includes the chapters authored by Steven W. Holloway and Ahmed Fatima Kzzo. As we tried to convey with the title, these two chapters offer not only a glance into the past, but especially a glance into the way this past may influence or may be studied in the future. The potential of internet resources, heritage management, and schoolbooks are main features discussed here as tools which mediate between the past and us, but also as tools which transform the past itself and its reception thanks to this mediation.

The final editing of the volume was completed during the burst of the COVID-19 pandemic. The editors would like to thank both the authors and the Pennsylvania State University Press's project manager, Matthew Williams, for keeping pace with the circumstances. Without their effort, we could not complete the present volume.

REFERENCES

Budge, E. A. W. 1925. *The Rise and Progress of Assyriology*. London: M. Hopkinson & Co.

Fossey, C. 1904. *Manuel d'assyriologie*. Paris: Ernest Leroux.

Liverani, M. 2004. *Myth and Politics in Ancient Near Eastern Historiography*. Sheffield: Equinox.

Verderame, L., and A. Garcia-Ventura. 2020. *Receptions of the Ancient Near East in Popular Culture and Beyond*. Atlanta: Lockwood Press.

Vidal, J. 2015. "Reflexiones historiográficas sobre el Orientalismo Antiguo." Pages 25–36 in *Descubriendo el Antiguo Oriente. Pioneros y arqueólogos de Mesopotamia y Egipto a finales del s. XIX y principios del s. XX*. Edited by R. Da Riva and J. Vidal. Barcelona: Bellaterra arqueología.

Vita, J.-P. 2012. "La Asiriología según los asiriólogos." *Cadmo. Revista de História Antiga* 22:9–18.

PART I

The Edge of the Abyss: The Study of Antiquity Under Totalitarian Threat

CHAPTER I

Hittite Studies at the Crossroads: Albrecht Goetze's and Hans Gustav Güterbock's Flight from Nazi Germany

Silvia Alaura

FROM 1933 ONWARDS, the German scientific system was undermined by the removal of many outstanding scholars because of their Jewish origins or because they were politically opposed to the National Socialist regime. This affected all disciplines, including the still young science of ancient Near Eastern studies and its even younger "offshoot," Hittitology. This was a period of fundamental significance, which made these studies what they are today and which is only now beginning to be studied and reflected upon.

The event of central importance for Hittite studies in this period is undoubtedly the departure from Germany of Albrecht Götze/Goetze (1897–1971)[1] and Hans Gustav Güterbock (1908–2000),[2] universally acknowledged as two of the greatest scholars of the ancient Near East. Both Goetze and Güterbock were forced to leave Germany at the beginning of the Nazi period.

In 1933 Goetze left Marburg, where he had been teaching Semitic languages and comparative linguistics as a tenured professor, to emigrate to the United States of America, where he was to teach at Yale University for over thirty years. Goetze was dismissed from his post by the Nazi regime in November 1933, not on racial grounds but because he was deemed "politically unreliable" (*politisch unzuverlässig*).[3] Indeed, he had been supporting the Jewish socialist Emil J. Gumbel, professor of mathematical statistics at Heidelberg, one of the most important figures in the German pacifist movement.[4] Goetze arrived at Yale as a visiting professor in 1934 thanks to the support

1. The surname Götze was spelled Goetze after his immigration to the United States of America in 1934. Throughout the present article I shall employ the Americanized surname. For a biographical sketch of Goetze see the obituaries in Edzard 1972, Finkelstein 1972, Jacobsen 1972, Laroche 1972, and Güterbock 1973; see also Foster 1999 and 2012, Oberheid 2007, 368–72 and 447, Maas 2013, and Maier-Metz 2015.

2. For a biographical sketch of Güterbock see, besides the obituaries in Hoffner 1999–2000, Melchert 1999–2000, Renger 2001a, Wilhelm 2001, and Reiner 2002, the autobiographical memoir in Güterbock 1995 and the posthumous publication of the autobiography of Güterbock's mother (Auer 1995). Furthermore, see Doğan-Alparslan 2001, 76–85, Renger 2001b, 256–58, Oberheid 2007, 375–77 and 447, Klinger 2012a, and Maas 2014. Also note the symposium and photographic exhibition "A Tribute to Hans Gustav Güterbock: A Pioneer of Hittitology," organized in November 2014 by the Departments of Archaeology and History at Bilkent University in Ankara, as well as the monograph in preparation by P. Raulwing, Th. van den Hout, and L. Petersen, *Hans Gustav Güterbock. Ein Leben für die Hethitologie. Berlin, Ankara, Uppsala, Chicago* (working title); I wish to thank the authors for generously making their work available to me and for the stimulating exchange of information and opinions.

3. See Maier-Metz 2015 and the review article by Raulwing 2018. I wish to thank the author for kindly making his work available to me.

4. Gumbel had been his colleague at the University of Heidelberg, where Goetze had taught until 1930 before moving to Marburg; see Maier-Metz 2015.

3

4   Silvia Alaura

of the linguist Edgar Howard Sturtevant (1883–1952),[5] and in 1936 he obtained the William M. Laffan Professorship of Assyriology and Babylonian Literature.[6] Goetze's departure from Germany made Yale a leading center of Hittite studies and set back the discipline at Marburg,[7] for several years at least. The damage done to German Hittitology was far more extensive than that, however, since over time the "List of Harmful and Undesirable Publications" (*Liste des schädlichen und unerwünschten Schrifttums*) of the "Reich Chamber of Publications" (*Reichsschrifttumskammer-Reichskulturkammer*) came to include not only two works that Goezte had published in Germany at the end of the 1920s—*Das Hethiter-Reich. Seine Stellung zwischen Ost und West* and *Madduwattaš*[8]—but also his two groundbreaking monographs of the 1930s, which he completed in Scandinavia during the brief period before his departure for America. These were *Muršilis Sprachlähmung. Ein hethitischer Text mit philologischen und linguistischen Erörterungen*, written in collaboration with the Danish linguist Holger Pedersen and published in Copenhagen, and *Hethiter, Churriter und Assyrer. Hauptlinien der vorderasiatischen Kulturentwicklung im 2. Jahrtausend v. Chr*, published in Oslo.[9] As a result, the dissemination of Goetze's books in public libraries and through any kind of trade (publishers, bookstores, mail order, and lending libraries) was forbidden.[10]

Similarly, in 1935, the departure from Berlin of Güterbock, who had recently defended in Leipzig his dissertation "Die historische Tradition und ihre literarische Gestaltung bei Babyloniern und Hethitern bis 1200,"[11] had far-reaching consequences for the development of Hittitological studies. Güterbock, barred from employment in Germany by Nazi racial laws for being of Jewish heritage, decided to follow his Leipzig teacher and close friend Benno Landsberger (1890–1968)[12] to Turkey, where

---

5. On Sturtevant see Hahn 1952, Emeneau 1953, Wyatt 1994, and Falk 2005; also Hill 1963.

6. See Finkelstein 1972, 197 and the remarks in Hahn 1952, 420–21: "Through Sturtevant's instrumentality, Yale also acquired, in 1934, the services of the well-known German Hethitologist and Semitist, Albrecht Goetze; a lesser man than Sturtevant might have hesitated to introduce a scholar outstanding precisely in his own specialty, but he worked indefatigably to bring this about, and thus placed Yale in the forefront of Hittite studies in general. The association of these two men proved a source of mutual enrichment, to which Goetze pays generous tribute in the preface to his edition of Tunnawi" (i.e. Goetze in cooperation with Sturtevant 1938). On the fruitful collaboration between Goetze and Sturtevant see also Güterbock 1995, 2769.

7. Indeed, Goetze was replaced by the art historian Friedrich Wachtsmuth, who was explicitly charged with the study of the Aryans in the ancient Near East; see Maier-Metz 2015, 161. Hittitology at Marburg was resumed by Heinrich Otten, who from the winter semester of 1958–1959 had a teaching assignment for ancient Near Eastern Languages and Cultures, and in September 1959 became a full professor of Oriental Studies.

8. Goetze 1928a and 1928b.

9. Goetze and Pedersen 1934, and Goetze 1936.

10. Maier-Metz 2015, 180; Lemberg 2001, 2, 177; in general, Lewy 2016.

11. Güterbock recalls this event in his autobiographical memoir "Resurrecting the Hittites" as follows: "I handed in my dissertation three days before Hitler seized power and passed my oral examination in the spring of 1933" (Güterbock 1995, 2765). His dissertation was then published in the *Zeitschrift für Assyriologie* (Güterbock 1934 and 1938).

12. When Landsberger was dismissed from his post in Leipzig in 1935, he emigrated to Turkey and found employment at the University of Ankara. He left Ankara in 1948 to take up a position at the University of Chicago. For Landsberger see, among others, Kienast 1970, Oelsner 2006 and 2012, and Sallaberger 2007; also Schmidt 2014, 8–9 and n. 15. The Commemoration of the Centenary of Benno Landsberger, held by the American Oriental Society in Atlanta in March 1990, in which H. G. Güterbock also took part, is available online at http://discoverarchive.vanderbilt.edu/handle/1803/4342. I am grateful to David I. Owen for bringing this to my attention.

many German scholars who fell afoul of Nazi racial laws found a home and position, as an alternative to emigrating to America.[13] The good relations between Turkey and Germany had their roots in Wilhelmine and Ottoman politics and in the subsequent alliance between the two countries during the First World War. In the mid 1930s, Atatürk, who was reorganizing the Turkish higher education system, encouraged the inclusion of scholars of various disciplines escaping the Nazi regime in the newly founded institutions.[14] Because of the central role played by the history of the ancient Anatolian civilizations in the so-called Turkish history thesis (*Türk Tarih Tezi*), which was promoted by the activities of the Turkish Historical Society (*Turk Tarih Kurumu*),[15] scholars of the ancient Near East were made especially welcome.[16]

As recently pointed out by Luděk Vacín, a significant role in Landsberger's relocation to Ankara was played by Bedřich Hrozný, the Czech orientalist and linguist who had contributed to the decipherment of Hittite, identifying it as an Indo-European language and laying the groundwork for the development of Hittitology.[17] In the mid-1930s Hrozný was regarded by Turkish academics and politicians, including Atatürk himself, as the most prominent cuneiformist and scholar of Hittite studies.[18]

Güterbock taught Hittitology and Landsberger Assyriology (formally Sumerology) in the Faculty of Linguistics, History, and Geography at the newly founded University of Ankara.[19] Güterbock remained in Turkey until 1948 when, at the invitation of Thorkild Jacobsen, he moved to Chicago and became Visiting Associate Professor of Hittitology at the university's Oriental Institute, having first served for a year in Sweden as a guest lecturer at the University of Uppsala.

Thus, as a consequence of the Nazi persecution of political opponents and Jews and their dismissal from public positions, the scholarship of the German cuneiformists further strengthened Hittite studies in the United States and spread them into Kemalist Turkey.

During these years, the fates of Goetze and Güterbock intersected, not face-to-face but through the written word, as is documented by their unpublished correspondence, which spans the period from 1931 to 1970, until shortly before Goetze's death. Today it is kept in the Deutsche Nationalbibliothek, Deutsches Exilarchiv 1933–1945,

---

13. Emigration to the United States was harder to achieve because of restrictive laws on immigration and difficult procedures involved in acquiring visas. Furthermore, the United States was viewed as a point of no return. The exile of Germans to Turkey, and particularly of academics, although on a relatively small scale compared with other countries (little more than a thousand individuals, of whom only 144 were academics), has been the subject of numerous studies, including recent ones. On the German academics who emigrated in the 1930s and 1940s from Nazi Germany to Turkey see, among others Widmann 1973, Grothusen 1981, Bozay 2001, Reisman 2006 and 2009, Guttstadt 2008, Kubasek and Seufert 2008, Ergin 2009 and 2017, esp. 162–63, Tomenendal, Doğuş Özdenir, and Mercan 2010.

14. Ellinger 2006, 206–8, Strohmeier 2008.

15. For this aspect see, among others, Shaw 2006, Atakuman 2008, Erimtan 2008, Francia 2014, and Dressler 2017.

16. See Renger 2008, 494, Ergin 2009, esp. 116 and 119, Schmidt 2010 and various contributions in Kubaseck and Seufert 2008, particularly Strohmeier 2008, 72.

17. See Vacín 2018, 67–70 with fig. 18.

18. See Hrozný 1935.

19. Both Güterbock and Landsberger appear in the report on the German academics employed in Turkish universities prepared by Herbert Scurla during his stay in Turkey in May 1939, known as the "Scurla Bericht"; see Grothusen 1987 and Şen and Halm 2007.

6   Silvia Alaura

Frankfurt am Main, and in the Yale University Library, Manuscripts and Archives, New Haven.[20]

Both Goetze and Güterbock often retained carbon copies of the letters they sent to their colleagues together with those they received, so that in some cases the copies fill in the gaps in the originals. Equally, it is not unusual to find the same letter in each of the two archives. The letters of both men are written in German or English (after his dismissal from Marburg, Goetze preferred to write in English to his German-speaking colleagues). Some of the letters are handwritten, while others are typewritten.

Of course, further information is supplied by the correspondence the two scholars engaged in with other colleagues, so that the Goetze–Güterbock epistolary exchange is just a fragment of a much broader picture. And, as one might expect, the two men have many correspondents in common, including Walter Andrae, Richard D. Barnett, Kurt Bittel, Hans Ehelolf, Johannes Friedrich, Ignace J. Gelb, Hans Krahe, Fritz R. Kraus, Benno Landsberger, Piero Meriggi, Heinrich Otten, Bernhard Rosenkranz, Ferdinand Sommer, and Ernst F. Weidner.[21] The correspondence of foreign scholars living in Ankara such as Güterbock and Landsberger serve as an extraordinary "counterbalance" to the recently published collection of letters of the German Assyriologist Fritz Rudolf Kraus (1910–1991), who lived in exile in Istanbul between 1937 and 1949.[22] Güterbock's correspondence also augments what is already documented in the memoirs of German exiles living in Ankara, such as those of the legal scholar Ernst Eduard Hirsch (who, having been dismissed by the University of Frankfurt, went first to Istanbul and then to Ankara), in which both Güterbock and Landsberger are referred to.[23] Hirsch's memoirs show the close relationships that existed between German academics of diverse disciplines in Turkey. Further sources for the reconstruction of this intellectual milieu are the memoirs written by Turks who studied with or knew exiled German academics, including Güterbock, such as the Assyriologist Muazzez Cığ (1914–),[24] the sociologist Niyazi Berkes (1908–1988),[25] and the historian Halil İnalcık (1916–2016).[26]

In the Goetze–Güterbock correspondence of the thirties and forties, which is the focus of the present article, we see the real, dramatic impact on the two men's lives of tragic political events and war, and the effects they had on the future of Hittite studies and, more generally, of ancient Near Eastern scholarship. The main subject

---

20. I would like to express my deepest thanks to Katrin Kokot for her kind assistance and for permitting me to consult the documents of the Deutsches Exilarchiv 1933–1945, Frankfurt am Main. I am also deeply indebted to Benjamin Foster for the valuable information he gave me concerning Goetze's papers and for his indispensable help in accessing the materials of the Yale University archives. Furthermore, I wish to offer my warmest thanks to Hans Gustav's sons, Thomas† and Walter Güterbock, for permitting me to study and publish their father's correspondence.

21. As regards the link between Güterbock and Landsberger, important complementary information will no doubt be provided by the publication of Landsberger's letters to Goetze, which are also kept at Yale. It is also possible that further information will be found in the set of Landsberger documents that was discovered in the Hebrew University of Jerusalem in April 2012, the publication of which will be handled by Michael Streck and Nathan Wasserman.

22. See Schmidt 2014.

23. See Hirsch 2008, 220, 224 for Güterbock and Landsberger.

24. Çığ 1988 and 2006.

25. Berkes 1997, 466–68 for references to Güterbock and Landsberger.

26. Çaykara 2009, 53, 57, 74, 398 for references to Güterbock and Landsberger.

of the Goetze–Güterbock correspondence in this crucial twenty-year period is the advancement of cuneiform studies, particularly with regard to Anatolian issues. The correspondence also deals with practical aspects of research and teaching, including publications, conferences, and archaeological expeditions.

The second half of the 1930s saw Goetze promptly immersing himself in his new American working environment. Of great significance was his collaboration with the archaeological expedition at Gözlü-Kule/Tarsus (Cilicia), conducted by Hetty Goldman and sponsored jointly by Bryn Mawr College, the Archaeological Institute of America, and the Fogg Museum of Harvard University.[27] A major focus of the Goetze–Güterbock correspondence of this period is the interpretation of the extraordinary epigraphic finds from the Gözlü-Kule/Tarsus excavations.[28] The discussion between the two scholars mainly deals with the controversial dating of the Hittite land deed tablet known as Tarsus 1, discovered by Goldman in a sealed refuse pit together with a bulla exhibiting the seal of the queen Puduḫepa.

Throwing light on the remarkably stimulating exchanges of views on philological matters between Goetze and Güterbock, which reflects their depth of skill and breadth of knowledge, these letters include lengthy discussions of problems in the transcription, translation and interpretation of Tarsus 1. At the end of 1936, Goetze, who was working on photographs at Yale, asked Güterbock to collate the Tarsus finds, but this had to be postponed for a year because of Güterbock's various commitments during 1937. As Güterbock writes from Ankara on 8 January 1938:

> Hochverehrter Herr Professor! Endlich bin ich dazu gekommen, die Tarsustafeln durchzusehen; zuerst dauerte es ziemlich lange, bis sie von Tarsus hierhergeschafft und mir übergeben wurden, von Ende Juni bis Anfang Oktober war ich unterwegs, und vorher und nachher stark mit anderen Arbeiten in Anspruch genommen. Nun sehe ich zu meinem Schrecken aus dem Datum Ihres Briefes, das schon über ein Jahr vergangen ist seit Sie mir Ihre Kopien geschickt haben.[29]

Of particular importance among Güterbock's commitments in 1937 was his participation, together with Landsberger, in the Second Congress of the Turkish Historical Society (İkinci Türk Tarih Kongresi), a large-scale international conference dedicated to the classification and documentation of Turkish history.[30] The Congress, held in Istanbul, tried to provide concrete arguments supporting historical continuities between Republican Turkey, the Sumerians, and the ancient Anatolian civilizations, and more particularly, to recognize the Hittites as the predecessors of modern Turks (known as the Turkish history thesis, referred to above).[31] A central role was played

---

27. Excavations at Gözlü-Kule/Tarsus began in 1935 and continued until January 1939, when fieldwork was interrupted due to financial difficulties and then halted during the Second World War. Work resumed in 1947 and came to an end in 1949.

28. The letters are published in Alaura forthcoming.

29. Letter from H. G. Güterbock to A. Goetze, Ankara, 8 January 1938 (Yale University Library, Manuscripts and Archives, Albrecht Goetze Papers MS 648: box 8, folder 194).

30. On the congress see Tanyeri-Erdemir 2006, 385–88 and Atakuman 2008, 225–28. See also Schmidt 2014, 81 n. 45, 94, 97–98, and 115–16.

31. For this aspect see, among others, Shaw 2006, Atakuman 2008, Erimtan 2008, Francia 2014, and Dressler 2017.

8   Silvia Alaura

in this by the excavations at Alaca Höyük, in Çorum Province, conducted by Remzi Oğuz Arık and Hamit Zübeyr Koşay from 1935 onwards, under the personal instructions of Atatürk, who contributed from his own budget.[32] In the paper they delivered at the Istanbul Congress, the two archaeologists presented the culture of Alaca Höyük as the direct antecedent of Turkish culture.[33] In his own paper, devoted to the writing of history among the Hittites, Güterbock emphasized the differences between the Hittite and the Sumero-Akkadian cultures.[34]

In those same years, the exchange of letters between Goetze and Güterbock on what were then highly topical Hittitological subjects also deals with the seals from Boğazköy, the site of the Hittite capital Ḫattuša whose excavation was directed by Kurt Bittel (1907–1991).[35] Remarkably, shortly after the Gözlü-Kule/Tarsus sealings had begun to be excavated in 1935 and published in annual preliminary reports, Güterbock himself was entrusted with the publication of the large closed deposit of Hittite seal impressions discovered in 1936 in the palace complex of Büyükkale in Boğazköy.[36] The prompt preliminary publication of the Tarsus material by Goldman and by Goetze,[37] together with the publication of seals and sealings excavated between 1927 and 1932 by the Oriental Institute of Chicago in Alişar Höyük,[38] provided Güterbock with a point of departure for his two groundbreaking volumes on the Boğazköy glyptic.[39] The Goetze–Güterbock correspondence also conveys a sense of their concern about the continuation of the excavations at Boğazköy.

In addition to his teaching, Güterbock continued to devote himself in Turkey to studying the cuneiform texts from Ḫattuša. He had copied them in Germany, producing two volumes of the official series of the Berlin Museum, the *Keilschrifturkunden aus Boghazköi* (KUB).[40] However, since he was no longer permitted to join the official staff of the excavations, he could not gain access to the tablets that were being found and taken to the recently established Archaeological Museum of Ankara.[41] On several occasions, the Goetze–Güterbock correspondence documents Goetze's disapproval of

32. For the role played by archaeology in the ideological framework of Kemalist Turkey see, among others, Özdoğan 1998, Tanyeri-Erdemir 2006, and Çınaroğlu and Çelik 2010.

33. Koşay 1943, 31–32.

34. Güterbock 1943, 178 and 181. More generally for the linguistic theories connected with the Turkish history thesis and their rejection by foreign scholars see, among others, Aytürk 2004.

35. For Bittel see, among others, Boehmer 1991–1992, Çambel 1991, Naumann 1991, Otten 1991, Güterbock 1992, and Klinger 2012b. See also Bittel 1998.

36. For a preliminary report see Bittel 1937 and Güterbock 1937. The importance of the work being done by Güterbock was immediately pointed out in Goetze 1938, 150 ("Since the publication of the Kg [i.e. Goetze's *Kulturgeschichte des Alten Orients*, 1933] the decipherment of the so-called Hittite hieroglyphs has reached a decisive stage. After the waste of so much energy [Kg 167] with no result had almost created an atmosphere of despair, the problem yielded finally to the efforts of P. Meriggi, H. Th. Bossert, E. Forrer, I. J. Gelb, B. Hrozný and H. G. Güterbock. Two books that are promised for the immediate future will presumably bring this pioneering period to a close: B. Hrozný's 4th volume of interpretations which, it is announced, will contain also an up-to-date presentation of the known grammatical facts, and H. G. Güterbock's treatment and evaluation of the 280 bullae, many of them bilingual, which are the most spectacular find of the campaign of 1936 at Boğazköy").

37. The preliminary reports were published by Goldman and Goetze in the *American Journal of Archaeology* from 1935 onwards.

38. Schmidt 1931.

39. Güterbock 1940 and 1942.

40. Güterbock 1930 and 1935.

41. On the establishment of this museum see Güterbock 1939–1941 and Karasu 2017.

the restrictions imposed on Güterbock and of the slow publication of the recently discovered tablets, which at Berlin was being handled by the Hittitologist Hans Ehelolf:

> Ueber das Faktum, dass der Professor für Hethitologie in Ankara an der Publikation der Ankara gehörigen Bo[ğazköy] Tafeln nicht mitarbeiten darf, kann ich nur den Kopf schütteln. Dank auch für Ihre Mitteilungen über Boğazköy. Ich habe an Bittel lange vor zu schreiben. Wir sind uns ein wenig in die Haare geraten.[42]

As the restrictions did not apply to the texts found during the first period of excavations at Boğazköy-Ḫattuša by Hugo Winckler at the beginning of the twentieth century (1905–1912), which were kept in the Museum of Istanbul, Güterbock dedicated himself to publishing those texts that remained as yet unpublished (i.e. the tablets that had stayed all along in Istanbul, and those that had been sent back there from Berlin in 1939 and 1942).[43] Güterbock worked in Istanbul with his own and Landsberger's pupils, including the aforementioned Muazzez Çığ, with whom his friendship endured even after his departure from Turkey. Thus, the letters written by Güterbock to Goetze also document the rise of cuneiform studies as an academic specialization in Kemalist Turkey.

After the interruption in the correspondence between the two scholars caused by the Second World War, Güterbock's long letter to Goetze dated 22 February 1946, together with Goetze's reply dated 29 April of the same year, marked the re-establishment of their epistolary contact.[44] The beginning of 1946 was a time of general, widespread resumption of contacts between scholars, who exchanged news about their own fates and circumstances and those of their colleagues. Indeed, Güterbock's letter is very similar to, for example, the one sent by Alfred Pohl in Rome to Fritz Rudolf Kraus in Istanbul, dated 17 January 1946.[45]

Güterbock's letter contains a detailed update on his scientific activity and the publications resulting from it. One is struck by the richness of information on the gestation of new works—not only his own, but also those of colleagues. However, philological research is not the only topic Güterbock deals with. He also discusses the planned foundation of a French institute at Ankara (together with the resumption of the excavations at Arslantepe) and the progress of the construction of the new Archaeological Museum in the old *bedestan*, and he asks about the fate of the Berlin Museum and its cuneiform tablets. Furthermore, the pages are punctuated by sober but dramatic

---

42. Letter from A. Goetze to H. G. Güterbock, Yale, 5 November 1938 (Deutsche Nationalbibliothek, Deutsches Exilarchiv 1933–1945, Frankfurt am Main, Teilnachlass H. G. Güterbock EB 2008/002, Korrespondenz Goetze; carbon copy at Yale). Shortly before, during the Haverford Symposium on Archaeology and the Bible, Goetze had publicly expressed his disappointment at the slowness of the publication of the texts from Boğazköy (see Goetze 1938, 148–49: "Large numbers of Bogazkoy tablets are still unpublished . . . Also the translation of important texts has been lagging").

43. In order to publish the Boğazköy tablets kept in the Istanbul Museum, a new series was started, *İstanbul Arkeoloji Müzelerinde Bulunan Boğazköy Tabletlerinden Seçme Metinler* (IBoT). It includes four volumes published between 1944 and 1988. Güterbock co-authored the first two volumes: Bozkurt, Çığ, and Güterbock 1944 and 1947.

44. Both mentioned in Maier-Metz 2015, 202–4 and published in Alaura 2017, 9–14.

45. Schmidt 2014, 1099–1100.

reports of what became of many colleagues. These include the Jewish philologist Leonie Zuntz, who died at the age of 32 in England after escaping from Nazi Germany.[46] Zuntz's death was regarded by Goetze and Güterbock as a great loss to Hittite studies. In 1934–1935 she had introduced Oliver R. Gurney to Hittite, and her study "Un testo ittita di scongiuri," which was translated into Italian by Giacomo Devoto, was regarded by Goetze as a *Pionierleistung*.[47]

Among the themes of Güterbock's letter, there are also very personal references to his life and career in Turkey:

> Dass die Arbeit in diesem Lande auch ihre weniger erfreulichen Seiten hat und man, besonders auch in allgemein-geistiger Beziehung, hier oft ein gewisses Gefühl von Stagnation hat, ist dabei nicht zu leugnen. So hat man oft den Wunsch, von hier wegzukönnen, und da Deutschland für uns doch nicht mehr in Frage kommt, so träumt man dabei immer mehr oder weniger von den Staaten. Aber ich sehe keine rechten Möglichkeiten für mich dort, und vor allem habe ich das Gefühl der Verpflichtung, die hier begonnenen Aufgaben erst fertig zu machen; nicht so sehr als Verpflichtung den hiesigen Leuten, als vielmehr unserem Fach gegenüber. Das ist vor allem die Einrichtung des heth. Museums und die Ankurbelung der Textveröffentlichungen. So hoffe ich im Moment nur, dass die Politik in diesem Weltteil mir keinen Strich durch die Rechnung macht![48]

In his letter of response, Goetze not only promptly addresses the topics raised by Güterbock but expands on them to introduce new themes. Further topics of interest are found in the lively, free, and unfettered exchanges of information about the handling of institutional matters, about colleagues and about the chairs of universities. Goetze's letter reveals his new areas of interest. Starting from the mid-forties, in addition to his continuing Hittitological output, Goetze produced an extraordinary body of Assyriological work. Indeed, during these years at Yale, Goetze devoted himself above all to publishing the texts of the Babylonian Collection, consisting of thousands of uncatalogued, and largely unpublished, tablets.[49] He therefore resumed the production of cuneiform copies, as he had done energetically in Germany (but with Hittite texts) between 1926 and 1933, a fertile period that saw the publication of some five volumes of copies of Hittite texts in the official series of the excavations at Boğazköy-Ḫattuša[50] and of a further volume of Hittite tablets scattered throughout the world, published under his own imprint and at his own expense.[51] Goetze described his coming to the

---

46. Zuntz emigrated to England in 1934 after she had obtained her doctorate. She settled in Oxford where she taught German and worked for Oxford University Press. She committed suicide in London in 1942. For a biographical sketch of Zuntz, see Maas 2018.

47. Goetze 1938. During the period from 1937 to 1939 Zuntz exchanged letters with Kraus, see Schmidt 2014, 8, 103, 132–35, 212, 220, 243, 274, 285, 312, 314, 419. Zuntz's unpublished lexicographical notes and cards on Hittite vocabulary are now kept in the Manuscripts Collection of the Griffith Institute Archive, Oxford.

48. H. G. Güterbock to A. Goetze, Ankara, 22 February 1946 (Yale University Library, Manuscripts and Archives, Albrecht Goetze Papers MS 648: box 8, folder 194; carbon copy at Frankfurt am Main).

49. See Finkelstein's list of Goetze's publications in Finkelstein 1974, 1–15.

50. KUB XIV, 1926; KUB XIX, 1927; KUB XXI, 1928; KUB XXIII, 1929; KUB XXVI, 1933.

51. *Verstreute Boghazköi-Texte* (VBoT), Marburg a.d. Lahn, 1930.

United States as the beginning of a new chapter in his career, which he himself designated his "Akkadian Period," in contrast to the previous phase of his life and career in Germany, which he liked to call his "Hittite Period."[52]

Goetze devotes part of his letter to announcing the launch of a new specialized US-based periodical devoted to philological studies, the *Journal of Cuneiform Studies* (*JCS*). The idea of the new journal is to be seen in the framework of the American post-war effort to replace the facilities that Germany had provided in the past but was no longer in a position to offer.[53] During Goetze's directorship of *JCS*, Güterbock often contributed to the journal with seminal Hittitological papers, beginning with "The Song of Ullikummi. Revised Text of the Hittite Version of a Hurrian Myth I–II," published in the 1951 and 1952 issues.

From this same letter we also learn of Goetze's refusal of the professorship in Marburg, motivated by the same intellectual and moral principles that had compelled him to leave Germany during the thirties:

> The professorship in Marburg was offered to me! I wrote a letter to the faculty in Marburg which my wife says is better than Thomas Mann and which numerous people have urged me to publish. Until I have their (I mean Marburg's) reaction, I have decided to do nothing with it. Needless to say that it is impossible for me to consider myself one of theirs.[54]

On 9 February 1946, just a few days before receiving Güterbock's letter, Goetze in fact had sent the letter to Marburg in which he turned down the invitation to return to the university that he had received from the Indologist Johannes Nobel in early December 1945:

> Ich habe mein personliches Schicksal im vollen Bewusstsein meiner Handlungsweise 1933 von dem des Volkes gelöst, in das ich geboren worden bin. Vielleicht können Sie heute verstehen, warum ich damals nicht anders handeln konnte. Auf der einen Seite stand das natürliche Gefühl der Verbundenheit mit dem Lande, das mich geformt hat. Auf der anderen die schmerzliche Einsicht, das dasselbe Land diejenigen Dinge aufgegeben hatte, die allein das Leben für mich lebenswert machten: Freiheit des Individuums und Freiheit der Forschung. Mehr noch, dieses Volk proklamierte seine eigene Überlegenheit, und begann sie zum leitendem Gesichtspunkt seiner inneren und äusseren Politik zu machen. In dem Konflikte, den all dies in mir hervorbrachte, hatte ich zwischen zwei Dingen zu wählen: Vaterland oder geistige und ethische Freiheit. Ich wählte das zweite.[55]

52. Finkelstein 1972, 198.

53. To the documents of the Yale archive gathered by Benjamin Foster in his article devoted to the history of the *JCS* (Foster 2013) we can now add this letter, of which Goetze evidently did not retain a carbon copy: only the original exists in the Deutsches Exilarchiv 1933–1945 at Frankfurt am Main.

54. Letter from A. Goetze to H. G. Güterbock, Yale, 29 April 1946 (Deutsche Nationalbibliothek, Deutsches Exilarchiv 1933–1945, Frankfurt am Main, Teilnachlass H. G. Güterbock EB 2008/002, Korrespondenz Goetze).

55. A. Goetze to the Philosophical Faculty of Marburg University, dated 9 February 1946 (Yale University Library, Manuscripts and Archives, Albrecht Goetze Papers MS 648: box 14, folder 350), quoted after

12 Silvia Alaura

The Goetze–Güterbock correspondence of the forties retrospectively sheds light on the relationships between the Germans exiled in Turkey and those who worked there while maintaining close contacts with the German institutions during the thirties.[56] Indeed, the Nazi government sought to maintain the long-standing German links with Turkey. The situations of the scholars aligned with the Nazi regime were very varied, however, and sometimes rather ambiguous, as particularly shown in an extraordinary letter from Güterbock dated 11 May 1946.[57] In a previous letter, Goetze had asked Güterbock for information on Bittel, whom he had known personally in Marburg in 1933.[58] Indeed, during the thirties Bittel had been *Wissenschaftlicher Hilfsarbeiter*, *Referent*, and then (1938) *Erster Direktor* of the Abteilung Istanbul of the *Deutsches Archäologisches Institut* (DAI) and, as already mentioned, from 1931 director of the excavations at Boğazköy-Ḫattuša (1931–1939). Bittel was able to continue to direct the dig by joining the National Socialist Party in 1937.[59] It is interesting to note that at the end of August 1938, Walter Andrae, *Schriftführer* of the *Deutsche Orient-Gesellschaft* (DOG), had turned directly to the Reich Minister Hans Heinrich Lammers to request financing for the excavations in the Hittite capital, stressing the importance of the history of an Indo-European civilization.[60] The archaeological works there were suspended in 1939, however. From 1942 to 1944 Bittel was a professor at the University of Istanbul, and he resumed direction of the Boğazköy-Ḫattuša excavations when they recommenced in 1952.

This passage from Güterbock's letter to Goetze refers to Bittel's peculiar situation:

> Damit bin ich bei dem Kapitel Deutsches Archäologisches Institut, Bittel und—damit zusammenhängend—Bossert, nach dem Sie fragen. Es liegt mir vor allem daran, festzustellen und offen auszusprechen, dass sich Bittel, der die letzten Jahre Direktor der Abteilung Istanbul war, alle die Jahre hindurch als treuer Freund mir gegenüber bewahrt hat und, wie ich aus vielen, offenen und eingehenden Gespräche weiss, in keiner Weise Nazi war. Wir dürfen nicht in den Fehler verfallen, den wir nach 1933 so vielen Kollegen leider mit Recht vorwerfen mussten, zu verallgemeinern und aus Feigheit Leute zu verleugnen, damals, weil sie Juden, jetzt, weil Sie Deutsche sind. Dank Bittel Einstellung war das Institut in Istanbul auch keine Naziagentur etwa in dem Sinne wie das in Athen, dessen Direktor Wrede gleichzeitig "Landesgruppenleiter" war![61]

Maier-Metz 2015, 206, 225–26. Landsberger also declined the invitation to return to Marburg. The position was then taken by Heinrich Otten; see n. 7 above.

56. The refugees belonged to what was called "Colony B," to distinguish themselves from their compatriots in "Colony A," who were aligned with the National Socialist regime. The Jewish refugees in Turkey were in any case victimized using well-known stereotypes, as may be seen from the numerous caricatures that appeared during this period in the two main Turkish satirical newspapers, *Akbaba* and *Karikatür*. See Tomenendal, Doğuş Özdenir, and Mercan 2010, 78–80.

57. H. G. Güterbock to A. Goetze, Ankara, 11 May 1946 (Yale University Library, Manuscripts and Archives, Albrecht Goetze Papers MS 648: box 8, folder 194; carbon copy at Frankfurt am Main).

58. Their meeting is described in some detail in Bittel 1998, 378–79.

59. For Bittel's adherence to National Socialism see Ellinger 2006, 37–38 , 40, 99, 112, 196, 207, 242, 307, 468–69.

60. Ellinger 2006, 99–100, with n. 387.

61. H. G. Güterbock to A. Goetze, Ankara, 11 May 1946, see n. 57 above.

Many years later, the same ideas were reiterated by Güterbock in his obituary of Bittel in 1992:

> Bittel had his roots in his homeland, Swabia. His philosophy was determined by the old democratic liberalism of Württemberg. As a result, he detested National Socialism. As director of the Istanbul Institute he kept it apolitical, which demanded some courage at the time. His upright behavior earned him the friendship of many Turks in the administration as well as in the university.[62]

Another passage from Güterbock's letter dated 11 May 1946 refers to the archaeologist and Hittitologist Helmuth Theodor Bossert (1889–1961), who in 1934 had moved from Berlin to Istanbul.[63] He became Professor of Ancient Languages and Near Eastern Archaeology at the University of Istanbul—which, in line with the aforementioned reform of education under Atatürk, had replaced the *Dārülfünūn* ("House of Sciences")[64]—and excavated Karatepe-Aslantaş from 1947 to 1957. From Güterbock's letter we learn that Bossert tried to demonstrate that he only came under the influence of the Nazis but then quickly grew disenchanted and became a pacifist:

> Was nun Bossert betrifft, so liegt sein Fall gerade umgekehrt, und auch da scheint es mir wichtig zu sein, einmal offen auszusprechen, um was für einen Charakter es sich handelt, auch den man mir dann vielleicht "üble Nachrede über einen Fachkollegen" nach sagen könnte. Bossert ist 1933 in die Partei eingetreten und hat, als er als Gast der Expedition 1933 in Boğazköy war, mächtig aufgetrumpft, was jetzt alles "anders werden" werde. Seine erster Tat war dann, zusammen mit seinem damaligen Freund Eckhard Unger, den damaligen Direktor des Stambuler Instituts, Schede, und Bittel, der die Stelle des "Referenten" hatte, bei der Partei zu denunzieren, weil sie zu wenig Nazi seien! Natürlich hofften die beiden sauberen Brüder auf die zwei Pöstchen! Seine weitere Tätigkeit in Istanbul weist noch mehr Heldentaten dieser Art auf. Aus der Partei wurde er dann hinausgeworfen, aber nicht etwa, weil er—wie er es darstellt—zu viel mit den Emigranten-Professoren verkehrt hätte, sondern im Gegenteil, weil er bei einer Denunziation zu ungeschick vorging—für schlechte Denunzianten hat man bekanntlich keine Verwendung. Leider hat er es verstanden, sich mit seinem türkischen Dekan sehr gut zu stellen, und das hat ihn vor der Internierung gerechtet. Dadurch dass er 1944 nicht mit den offiziellen Transporten nach Deutschland ging, sondern hierblieb, hat er zwar zuletzt noch offiziell mit dem Nazi-Deutschland gebrochen und die Eigenschaft eines "Emigranten" erworben, aber diese Absprüngen von einem sinkenden Schiff kann man natürlich nicht ernst nehmen. Jetzt erklärt er urbi et orbi, das er nie Nazi war und 1933

62. Güterbock 1992, 582.

63. For Bossert see Weidner 1963, Alkım 1965, and Doğan-Alparslan 2017.

64. Planned by the Swiss pedagogist Albert Malche, this radical overhaul had led to the dismissal of numerous Turkish professors considered politically unreliable, see Strohmeier 2008, 70–72 and Doğan-Alparslan 2017, 148–49.

14 Silvia Alaura

sogar habe herausgehen müssen, weil er vorher—anonyme (man kann es also nicht kontrollieren!)—pazifistische Broschüren veröffentlicht habe.[65]

A number of subsequent letters exchanged by Goetze and Güterbock allow us to follow the development of Güterbock's "American dream." During this period, beginning with the death of Atatürk in 1938, Turkey was undergoing a great many changes. The deterioration in political relations between Germany and Turkey, which in 1945 led to Turkey's declaration of war on Germany, put the émigré German professors in a delicate position. As Turkish nationalism grew at the beginning of the 1940s, and was duly reflected in university life, an ever-greater hostility was seen toward the German professors, accompanied by a desire to replace them with Turkish academics.[66]

The topic of a concrete American future for Güterbock appears several times in his correspondence with Goetze, beginning with a letter from the latter dated 7 December 1946, where again we see the strategic mentality of the great scholar and his constant commitment to promoting Hittite studies:

I may tell you in this connection that I have tried to do something for Hittitology in this country. Besides myself there is nobody else who counts (Sturtevant is retired and around 70 years of age, Bechtel has forsaken science altogether). The Oriental Institute in Chicago would be the logical place. But they too are fighting a defensive battle. You may know that Wilson has resigned as director (to devote himself to his Egyptological professorship); the new director is Thorkild Jacobsen. I shall put the case before him, as soon as I shall see him (probably in January); by politics and persistence he might be able to do something eventually. However, there is no reason for being overly optimistic.[67]

In his reply, dated 3 January 1947, Güterbock expressed his fear that Ignace J. Gelb (1907–1985), who was mainly working on the decipherment of the Hittite hieroglyphs, might be an obstacle to his employment at the Oriental Institute at Chicago:

Auch Ihre Ausführungen über die Lage der Hethitologie in den Staaten haben mich sehr interessiert und ich danke Ihnen besonders für das Interesse an meinem Weiterkommen, das Sie damit bekundet haben. Zufällig war dieser Tage Kramer hier, er blieb zwei Tage in Ankara auf dem Wege von Istanbul nach

65. H. G. Güterbock to A. Goetze, Ankara, 11 May 1946, see nn. 57 and 61 above. See also the description of Bossert in a letter from Güterbock addressed to Kraus on 29 October 1947 (Schmidt 2014, 1340–41) and in the so-called "Güterbock-Liste" (discussed in the monograph by Raulwing, van den Hout, and Petersen mentioned above, n. 2). For Bossert's involvement with National Socialism see Bittel 1998, 380–85. Conversely, his student Muhibbe Darga maintains that Bossert was not involved with National Socialism; see Darga 2001, 45.

66. See, among others, Ergin 2009, 121–22, and Tomenendal, Doğuş Özdenir, and Mercan 2010.

67. Letter from A. Goetze to H. G. Güterbock, Yale, 7 December 1946 (Deutsche Nationalbibliothek, Deutsches Exilarchiv 1933–1945, Frankfurt am Main, Teilnachlass H. G. Güterbock EB 2008/002, Korrespondenz Goetze). See also Goetze's letter to Güterbock dated 21 December 1946, also kept at Frankfurt am Main: "The Oriental Institute in Chicago has been reorganized. Wilson resigned as Director in order to devote himself again to Egyptology. The new director is Thorkild Jacobsen. It is good to have a man like him in that position. On the other hand, it is a great pity that his abilities (and I think very highly of him) should go to waste in an administrative position. One can only hope that he will be relieved in due time by someone else."

Baghdad. Er sprach mit Landsberger und mir über die gleiche Sache und in dem gleichen Sinne. Hinsichtlich des Oriental Institute war er sogar eher noch pessimistischer, indem er meinte, dass Gelb, obwohl er selbst nicht auf dem Gebiet des Keilschrift-hethitischen arbeitet, doch kaum einen anderen Hethiter-Spezialisten haben sich wünschen würde.[68]

From Goetze's letter of 16 March 1947 we learn of Güterbock's attempt to move to the United States of America by means of the intervention of the American psychologist and musicologist Carroll C. Pratt, who from 1946–1947 was visiting professor at the University of Ankara, where he personally met Güterbock. In this circumstance, Goetze recommended Princeton, clearly with the aim of countering the dominance there of the modern Near Eastern scholars, such as the Arabist Philip Khuri Hitti:

> The Dean of Yale College sent me a letter that Professor Pratt had written him on your behalf and asked me for my reaction. I have reacted immediately in the most favorable terms. It is good propaganda. But Princeton would be by far more promising for you than Yale. It is a shame that Princeton has done so little for the Ancient Near East. They are going in there for the modern Near East. But, between us, Hitti whose name you may or may not know is more of a political propagandist than a scholar. A Christian Syrian by birth he has his fingers in the Jewish-Arabic controversy ... By the way you are mistaken that Gelb would be an obstacle to bringing a Hittitologist to Chicago. Gelb, I am informed, wants to turn to Akkadian exclusively and he will certainly be connected with the [Assyrian] Dictionary project.[69]

In his letter of response dated 22 March 1947, Güterbock reiterated what he had already written a year ago to Goetze. He was counting on staying a few more years in Ankara, but at the same time he hoped that eventually he could find a position in an American university:

> Last not least danke ich Ihnen herzlich für Ihre Mitteilung über den Brief von Pratt an Ihren Dekan und Ihre Reaktion darauf. Dafür, dass Sie in so positivem Sinne darauf eingegangen sind, bin ich Ihnen sehr dankbar. Pratt selbst geht in Juni nach Princeton. Sicher geht so etwas nicht so schnell, und in einem Hinsicht ist mir das recht, denn, wie ich Ihnen so schrieb, möchte ich erst noch hier das Museum und die Bearbeitung der Boğazköy-Tafeln etwas voran bringen, da ich das für meine wichtigste Aufgabe halte. Andererseits möchte ich nicht ewig in diesem Lande bleiben, und deshalb bin ich sehr froh, wenn sich für eine weitere Zukunft in Ihrem Lande etwas anbauten lässt. Sehr gefreut hat mich auch, was Sie über Chicago geschrieben haben.[70]

---

68. Letter from H. G. Güterbock to A. Goetze, Ankara, 3 January 1947 (Yale University Library, Manuscripts and Archives, Albrecht Goetze Papers MS 648: box 8, folder 194; carbon copy at Frankfurt am Main).

69. Letter from A. Goetze to H. G. Güterbock, Yale, 16 March 1947 (Deutsche Nationalbibliothek, Deutsches Exilarchiv 1933–1945, Frankfurt am Main, Teilnachlass H. G. Güterbock EB 2008/002, Korrespondenz Goetze).

70. Letter from H. G. Güterbock to A. Goetze, Ankara, 22 March 1947 (Yale University Library, Manuscripts and Archives, Albrecht Goetze Papers MS 648: box 8, folder 194; carbon copy at Frankfurt am Main).

16   Silvia Alaura

No less intriguing are the letters written to Güterbock in 1948 by Goetze, at the beginning of his directorship of the American School for Oriental Research in Baghdad, which placed him at the center of efforts to obtain research opportunities for Americans not only in Iraq but also in Turkey. Among the important topics covered in these letters, one finds his plan for a Yale-based "Hittite Dictionary."[71] In a letter dated 2 January 1948 Goetze writes:

> The present schedule calls for a stay in Iraq from January till about May. It was my intention to come to Turkey for about eight weeks afterward. Purpose: seeing the museums in Ankara and Istanbul and to learn on the spot of the progress Anatolian archaeology has made during the last fifteen or twenty years. Of course, I hope to see you then and to talk with you extensively on scientific and personal matters. Among the scientific plans is that of a Hittite Dictionary which I hope can be init[i]ated on a cooperative basis and for which I have asked the "American Council of Learned Societies" (a kind of "Notgemeinschaft") for financial support. I am enclosing a memorandum which I have submitted on this subject. At this end it looks hopeful.[72]

Güterbock's approval of the Hittite dictionary planned by Goetze is documented by his reply dated 14 February 1948, which already contains specific observations regarding crucial aspects of its implementation:

> Lieber Herr Goetze! Für Ihren Brief aus New Haven mit dem Memorandum über den Wörterbuchplan danke ich Ihnen erst heute, nachdem ich auch Ihnen Brief vom 6. d.M. aus Bagdad erhalten habe. Willkommen in Nahen Osten! ... Ihr Wörterbuchplan ist an sich sehr schön, und ich wünsche Ihnen allen Erfolg dazu. Ich zeigte Ihren Brief und den Plan auch Landsberger und Alp. Wenn Sie hier sind, können wir uns ausführlich darüber unterhalten. Es gibt noch allerlei Punkte zu besprechen und zu überlegen. Eine davon ist, dass, wie ich kürzlich von Otten erfuhr, die offiziellen Wörterbuchzettel nur bis KUB XXIV reichen, man also zunächst eine grosse Anzahl von Texten erst noch zu verzetteln hätte! Aber darüber noch mündlich![73]

A major change occurred in the summer of 1948, when the Faculty of Ankara University decided to cancel some professorships, including those of Güterbock and Landsberger, supposedly for budgetary reasons.[74] In a new climate of political hostility and

---

71. A Hittite dictionary had already been planned at Berlin during the twenties, see Oberheid 2007, 83–87.

72. Letter from A. Goetze to H. G. Güterbock, Yale, 2 January 1948 (Deutsche Nationalbibliothek, Deutsches Exilarchiv 1933–1945, Frankfurt am Main, Teilnachlass H. G. Güterbock EB 2008/002, Korrespondenz Goetze).

73. Letter from H. G. Güterbock to A. Goetze, Ankara, 14 February 1948 (Yale University Library, Manuscripts and Archives, Albrecht Goetze Papers MS 648: box 8, folder 194; carbon copy at Frankfurt am Main).

74. For the details of Güterbock's and Landsberger's dismissal see Widmann 1973, 170–71, Reisman 2006, 66, Strohmeier 2008, 74–75, Schmidt 2014, 34 and the memoirs of Niyazi Berkes (1997, 466–67) and of Ekrem Akurgal (2013, 133). See also the letter from Fritz R. Kraus to Jacob Johann Stamm, Istanbul,

xenophobia, both men were instantly compelled to leave Turkey. At the beginning of 1949, after some months at the University of Uppsala, the concrete prospect opened up for Güterbock to move to the University of Chicago, following Landsberger. Goetze announced to Güterbock the imminent arrival of good news from Jacobsen, who had personally met Güterbock during his visit to Ankara in summer 1948: "From a letter of Jacobsen's that came in this morning I gather that he is very hopeful about your affair. He is always very guarded with his hints. And the fact alone that he promises 'news' 'before too long' augurs well."[75]

Goetze also urged Güterbock not to delay, as shown in the following passage from his letter of 22 February 1949:

> I have been to Chicago over the weekend on business of the American Schools and had an opportunity to see Landsberger in action and to talk with almost everybody including Jacobsen. Secrets are being well kept in Chicago. But I know that you received an invitation to come over here. Now, for heaven's sake grab it, and do not disappoint all those who have worked patiently and steadily toward this climax. The conditions which one is offering you may not be the best. But don't forget two things, firstly that they will certainly improve and probably soon, and secondly that this is your only chance of getting to the States. If you prefer some other offer now (should there be such a thing), it will mean that you have decided in favor of Europe for the rest of your life. Keep these things in mind. Furthermore, prices have been falling in this country. The industrialists cry "recession" etc., all those with a fixed salary hope for a bettering of their standard of living. This is the folly of "capitalistic" economy.[76]

This passage also makes it clear that Goetze's satisfaction with the freedom of American universities did not extend to financial matters—a subject on which he expressed himself whenever the opportunity arose.

In April 1949, Güterbock finally accepted the position of Visiting Associate Professor of Hittitology at the Oriental Institute. Goetze's satisfaction is palpable in his letter

---

5 October 1948: "Die beiden Herren sind bei der Diskussion des Budgets der Universität Ankara in skandalöser Weise mit erlogenen oder an den Haaren herbeigezogenen Vorwürfen seitens einiger nazistisch "denkender" und Demagogie treibender, chauvinistischer Abgeordneter überhäuft worden, ohne daß der Minister, ihr früherer kleiner Kollege, oder besser informierte Abgeordnete es für nötig gehalten hätten, diese Anwürfe zurückzuweisen, und sind daraufhin in offenkundig illegaler Weise "im Verzuge von Sparmaßnahmen" mit Wirkung 15. Oktober gekündigt worden. Der wirkliche Grund ist eine seit Jahren geduldig getriebene Wühlarbeit ehrgeiziger Stellenhascher, an deren Spitze leider der frühere Leipziger Student Sedat Alp stand, der seine Intrigen aber geschickt zu verbergen wußte. Als diese ehrgeizigen "Jungen" sich mit persönlichen Feinden Landsbergers verbanden, war es um unsere Freunde geschehen. Sachlich denkende Türken verurteilen und beklagen diese Entlassung ebenso wie wir und erkennen, daß dem sogenannten Geistesleben des Landes durch sie ein Schlag versetzt worden ist, den man nicht wieder gutmachen kann" (published in Schmidt 2014, 1475–76).

75. Letter from A. Goetze to H. G. Güterbock, Yale, 27 January 1949 (Deutsche Nationalbibliothek, Deutsches Exilarchiv 1933–1945, Frankfurt am Main, Teilnachlass H. G. Güterbock EB 2008/002, Korrespondenz Goetze).

76. Letter from A. Goetze to H. G. Güterbock, Yale, 22 February 1949 (Deutsche Nationalbibliothek, Deutsches Exilarchiv 1933–1945, Frankfurt am Main, Teilnachlass H. G. Güterbock EB 2008/002, Korrespondenz Goetze).

dated 16 April 1949, from which we learn of the difficulties experienced by Güterbock and his family, which reminded Goetze of the events of the thirties:

Dear Gueterbock: It was nice to receive a letter from you. I admit that I had grown a little nervous some time ago. But the birds had told me soon afterward that you had accepted the offer from Chicago. I am terribly sorry that your wife is not too well and that you yourself had an accident. All such things come in batches. It reminds me of the deepest point in my life curve when I suffered from the "Privatdozenten Krankheit" and my wife suffering from "nervous exhaustion" had to be sent to Lugano for a few weeks. Perhaps you will find a nice place in Sweden where to spend your vacation. The dream place for us is Lekvatnet in Wärmland [*sic*] where we spent some weeks in 1934 between Copenhagen and Oslo. It is a Hotel in the woods near the Norvegian [*sic*] border. For our children it was the next to the paradise (loafing, swimming, boating, hiking, and—not to forget—eating).—Of course, your wife has every reason for being exhausted: The second child, the uncertainty in Turkey, the break-up in Ankara, again the waiting for the news from Chicago, the care of two small children in limited conditions, etc.—As things are nowadays $5200 is not overwhelming, but on the other side it shows an honest effort on Jacobsen's part to give you as much as he can squeeze out of his budget. When I first came here, in 1933, I got $5000 as a full professor (of course today that would be about $7500) and we felt rich. Don't forget prices are at present going down; you may find yourself better of[f] than you thought when you arrive. At any event it should be enough to allow for modest comfort. Did they give you some allowance for travelling expenses? (That was a great headache for me. Had it not been for the generosity of the Norvegians [*sic*] I do not know how I could have managed). You will now have to face the question of the visa. You may remember that I tried to help Landsberger with his. The experience is that the officials reading that you have a "visiting appointment" say that they can give you only a "visitor's visa." I do not know of what kind your appointment is. If it is a "visiting" one, just forget about the "visiting." Professors can get a "non-quota visa" provided they go to the states to continue their teaching profession. You can also have a "quota visa" (the German quota is certainly not filled). In your case, I judge it will not make a difference. A "non quota" visa entitles you only to teaching; with a regular "quota" visa you may accept any job after entry into the States. A quota immigrant is not allowed to have a job prior to his entry.—In my days the consulate only prepared the necessary papers. The case was decided in a hearing before an immigration commissioner who served for all three Scandinavian countries at the same time and spend [*sic*] his time travelling around on a certain schedule. You will have to pass a medical examination because sufferers from certain illnesses are excluded from immigration.—The consul in Copenhagen was quite cool until (on my request) a letter from the Yale president arrived. That changed the picture. A letter from Jacobsen may be useful, should any difficulties arise. As to my help: the simple truth is that one can help people who are something. In the opposite case there is nothing much one can do. In other words: what helped you in the first place are you own accomplishments. Once and a while [*sic*] one is able to push a little.[77]

The close relationship of scientific collaboration between Goetze and Güterbock endured even after Güterbock's relocation to Chicago. The two scholars' intense epistolary exchange shows how much and in how many ways Goetze continued to contribute to Hittite studies during his "Akkadian Period."

REFERENCES

Akurgal, E. 2013. *Erinnerungen eines Archäologen: Einige bedeutende Kapitel aus der Kulturgeschichte der Republik Türkei*. Peleus 57. Ruhpolding: Verlag Franz Philipp Rutzen.

Alaura, S. 2017. "The Fate of Hittitologists in the 1946 Correspondence between Hans Gustav Güterbock and Albrecht Goetze." *News from the Lands of the Hittites: Scientific Journal for Anatolian Research* 1:7–13.

———. Forthcoming. "Insights into the Correspondence between Hans Gustav Güterbock and Albrecht Goetze 1931–1939." In *Digging in the Archives: From the History of Oriental Studies to the History of Ideas*. Documenta Asiana XI. Edited by S. Alaura. Roma: Quasar.

Alkım, U. B. 1965. "Prof. Dr. H. Th. Bossert (11. IX. 1889–5. XI. 1961). Pages ix–xiii in *Helmuth Theodor Bossert'in hatirasina armağan. In memoriam Helmuth Theodor Bossert*. İstanbul: İstanbul Üniversitesi/Edebiyat Fakültesi.

Atakuman, Ç. 2008. "Cradle or Crucible: Anatolia and Archaeology in the Early Years of the Turkish Republic (1923–1938)." *Journal of Social Archaeology* 8(2):214–35.

Auer, G. 1995. *Wenn ich mein Leben betrachte . . . Wien—Bern—Marokko—Berlin. Erinnerungen*. On behalf of Hans Gustav Güterbock. Edited by H. von Herzeleide. Berlin: Stapp Verlag.

Aytürk, İ. 2004. "Turkish Linguists against the West: The Origins of Linguistic Nationalism in Atatürk's Turkey." *Middle Eastern Studies* 40(6):1–25.

Berkes, N. 1997. *Unutulan Yıllar (Forgotten Years)*. Edited by R. Sezer. Istanbul: İletişim.

Bittel, K. 1937. "Vorläufiger Bericht über die Ausgrabungen in Boğazköy 1936. 2. Büyükkale. C. Das Magazin in l-q/12-16 und der große Siegelfund." *Mitteilungen der Deutschen Orient-Gesellschaft* 75:27–34.

———. 1998. *Reisen und Ausgrabungen in Ägypten, Kleinasien, Bulgarien und Griechenland 1930–1934*. Akademie der Wissenschaften und der Literatur Mainz. Abhandlungen der Geistes- und Sozialwissenschaftlichen Klasse. Jg. 1998, Nr. 5. Stuttgart: Steiner Verlag.

Boehmer, R. M. 1991–1992. "Kurt Bittel (5.7.1907–30.1.1991)." *Archiv für Orientforschung* 38–39:259–60.

Bozay, K. 2001. *Exil Türkei. Ein Forschungsbeitrag zur deutschsprachigen Emigration in der Türkei (1933–1945)*. Fremde Nähe: Beiträge zur interkulturellen Diskussion 15. Münster: Lit Verlag.

Bozkurt, H., M. Çığ, and H. G. Güterbock. 1944. *İstanbul Arkeoloji Müzelerinde bulunan Boğazköy tabletlerinden seçme metinler—Ausgewählte Texte aus den Boğazköy-Tafeln in den Istanbuler Archäologischen Museen*. IBoT I. İstanbul: Maarif Matbaası.

———. 1947. *İstanbul Arkeoloji Müzelerinde bulunan Boğazköy Tabletleri II—Boğazköy-Tafeln im Archäologischen Museum zu Istanbul II*. IBoT II. İstanbul: Millî Eğitim Basımevi.

---

77. Letter from A. Goetze to H. G. Güterbock, Yale, 16 April 1949 (Deutsche Nationalbibliothek, Deutsches Exilarchiv 1933–1945, Frankfurt am Main, Teilnachlass H. G. Güterbock EB 2008/002, Korrespondenz Goetze).

Çambel, H. 1991. "In memoriam Kurt Bittel, 5.7.1907–30.1.1991." *Istanbuler Mitteilungen* 41:5–12.

Çaykara, E., ed. 2009. *Tarihçilerin Kutbu "Halil İnalcık Kitabı"* (*Most Eminent of Historians, "The Book of Halil İnalcık"*). 9th ed. Istanbul: Türkiye İş Bankası Kültür Yayınları.

Çığ, M. İ. 1988. "Atatürk and the Beginnings of Cuneiform Studies in Turkey." *Journal of Cuneiform Studies* 40(2):211–16.

———. 2006. *Çivi çiviyi söker. "Muazzez İlmiye Çığ Kitabı"* (*One Nail Drives Out the Other: "The Book of Muazzez İlmiye Çığ"*). Edited by S. Öztürk. 4th ed. Istanbul: Türkiye İş Bankası Kültür Yayınları.

Çınaroğlu, A., and D. Çelik. 2010. *Atatürk & Alaca Höyük*. Ankara: Yuksel.

Darga, M. 2001. "İstanbul Üniversitesi'nde Hititologji'nin ilk yılları" (The First Years of Hittitology at the University of Istanbul). Pages 44–61 in *Boğazköy'den Karatepe'ye. Hititbilim ve Hitit Dünyasının Keşfi* (*From Boğazköy to Karatepe: Hittitology and the Discovery of the Hittite World*). Edited by E. Jean et al. Istanbul: Yapı Kredi Yayınları.

Doğan-Alparslan, M. 2001. "İki Başkent, İki Serüven: Ankara ve Hattuşa" (Two Capitals, Two Adventures: Ankara and Hattusha). Pages 72–85 in *Boğazköy'den Karatepe'ye. Hititbilim ve Hitit Dünyasının Keşfi* (*From Boğazköy to Karatepe: Hittitology and the Discovery of the Hittite World*). Edited by E. Jean et al. Istanbul: Yapı Kredi Yayınları.

———. 2017. "The Foundation of Hittitology in the Istanbul University." Pages 147–56 in *The Discovery of an Anatolian Empire: A Colloquium to Commemorate the 100th Anniversary of the Decipherment of the Hittite Language* (*November 14th and 15th, 2015; Istanbul Archaeological Museum and Library*). Edited by M. Doğan-Alparslan, A. Schachner, and M. Alparslan. Beyoğlu-İstanbul: Türk Eskiçağ Bilimleri Enstitüsü.

Dressler, M. 2017. "Mehmed Fuad Köprülü and the Turkish History Thesis." Pages 245–53 in *Ölümünün 50. Yılında Uluslararası M. Fuad Köprülü Türkoloji ve Beşeri Bilimler Sempozyumu Bildirileri*. Edited by F. Turan, E. Temel, and H. Korkmaz. Istanbul: Kültür Sanat.

Edzard, D. O. 1972. "Albrecht Goetze. 11.1.1897–15.8.1971." *Zeitschrift für Assyriologie* 62(2):163–64.

Ellinger, E. 2006. *Deutsche Orientalistik zur Zeit des Nationalsozialismus, 1933–1945*. Thèses IV. Edingen-Neckarshausen: deux mondes Verlag.

Emeneau, M. B. 1953. "Edgar Howard Sturtevant (1875–1952)." *The American Philosophical Society Yearbook* 1952:339–43.

Ergin, M. 2009. "Cultural Encounters in the Social Sciences and Humanities: Western Émigré Scholars in Turkey." *History of the Human Sciences* 22(1):105–30.

———. 2017. *Is the Turk a White Man? Race and Modernity in the Making of Turkish Identity*. Studies in Critical Social Sciences 95. Leiden: Brill.

Erimtan, C. 2008. "Hittites, Ottomans and Turks: Ağaoğlu Ahmed Bey and the Kemalist Construction of Turkish Nationhood in Anatolia." *Anatolian Studies* 58:141–71.

Falk, J. S. 2005. "Sturtevant, Edgar Howard." Pages 542–43 in *American National Biography.* Supplement 2. Edited by M. C. Carnes. Oxford: Oxford University Press.

Finkelstein, J. J. 1972. "Albrecht Goetze, 1897–1971." *Journal of the American Oriental Society* 92(2):197–203.

———. 1974. "Bibliography of Albrecht Goetze (1897–1971)." *Journal of Cuneiform Studies* 26(1):1–15.

Foster, B. R. 1999. "Albrecht Goetze." Pages 166–67 in *American National Biography*. Vol. 9. Edited by J. A. Garraty and M. C. Carnes. Oxford: Oxford University Press.

———. 2012. "Goetze Albrecht." Pages 479–80 in *Geschichte der Altertumswissenschaften. Biographisches Lexikon. Der Neue Pauly*. Supplement vol. 6. Edited by P. Kuhlmann and H. Schneider. Stuttgart: Metzler.

———. 2013. "Journal of Cuneiform Studies, the Early Years." *Journal of Cuneiform Studies* 65:3–12.

Francia, R. 2014. "Gli Ittiti e la loro riscoperta nella Turchia Repubblicana." *Vicino Oriente* 18:15–24.

Goetze, A. 1928a. *Das Hethiter-Reich. Seine Stellung zwischen Ost und West*. Der Alte Orient. Gemeinverständliche Darstellungen 27/2. Leipzig: Hinrichs.

———. 1928b. *Madduwattaš*. Mitteilungen der Vorderasiatisch-Ägyptischen Gesellschaft 32/1. Hethitische Texte 3. Leipzig: Hinrichs.

———. 1936. *Hethiter, Churriter und Assyrer. Hauptlinien der vorderasiatischen Kulturentwicklung im 2. Jahrtausend v.Chr*. Instituttet for Sammenlignende Kulturforskning, Serie A: Forelesninger XVII. Oslo: Aschehoug.

———. 1938. "The Present State of Anatolian and Hittite Studies." Pages 136–57 in *The Haverford Symposium on Archaeology and the Bible*. Biblical and Kindred Studies 6. Edited by E. Grant. New Haven: The American Schools of Oriental Research.

Goetze, A., and H. Pedersen. 1934. *Muršilis Sprachlähmung. Ein hethitischer Text mit philologischen und linguistischen Erörterungen*. Historisk-filologiske meddelelser 21/1. Copenhagen: Levin & Munksgaard.

Goetze, A., in cooperation with E. H. Sturtevant. 1938. *The Hittite Ritual of Tunnawi*. American Oriental Series 14. New Haven: American Oriental Society.

Grothusen, K.-D. 1981. "1933 Yılından Sonra Alman Bilim Adamlarının Türkiye'ye Göçü" (The Immigration of German Scientists to Turkey after 1933). *Belleten. Türk Tarih Kurumu, Turkish Historical Society Review* 45:537–50.

———, ed. 1987. *Der Scurla-Bericht: Bericht des Oberregierungsrates Dr.rer.pol. Herbert Scurla von der Auslandsabteilung des Reichserziehungsministeriums in Berlin über seine Dienstreise nach Ankara und Istanbul vom 11.–25. Mai 1939: Die Tätigkeit deutscher Hochschullehrer an türkischen wissenschaftlichen Hochschulen*. Schriftenreihe des Zentrums für Türkeistudien 3. Frankfurt: Dağyeli.

Güterbock, H. G. 1930. *Keilschrifturkunden aus Boghazköi 25 (Festrituale)*. KUB XXV. Berlin: Akademie-Verlag.

———. 1934. "Die historische Tradition und ihre literarische Gestaltung bei Babyloniern und Hethitern bis 1200 (1. Teil: Babylonier)." *Zeitschrift für Assyriologie* 42 (NF 8):1–91.

———. 1935. *Keilschrifturkunden aus Boghazköi 28 (Chattische Texte)*. KUB XXVIII. Berlin: Akademie-Verlag.

———. 1937. "Vorläufiger Bericht über die Ausgrabungen in Boğazköy 1936. 3. Schrifturkunden. A. Die Siegel." *Mitteilungen der Deutschen Orient-Gesellschaft zu Berlin* 75:52–60.

———. 1938. "Die historische Tradition und ihre literarische Gestaltung bei Babyloniern und Hethitern bis 1200 (2. Teil: Hethiter)." *Zeitschrift für Assyriologie* 44 (NF 10):45–149 (supplement in *Archiv für Orientforschung* 13:49–50 [1939–1941]).

———. 1939–1941. "Die Neuaufstellung der hethitischen Denkmäler in Ankara." *Archiv für Orientforschung* 13:345–48.

———. 1940. *Siegel aus Boğazköy 1. Teil: Die Königssiegel der Grabungen bis 1938*. Archiv für Orientforschung Beiheft 5. Berlin: Printed by the editor.

———. 1942. *Siegel aus Boğazköy 2. Teil: Die Königssiegel von 1939 und die übrigen Hieroglyphensiegel*. Archiv für Orientforschung Beiheft 7. Berlin: Printed by the editor.

———. 1943. "Etilerde Tarih Yazıcılığı." Pages 177–81 in *İkinci Türk Tarih Kongresi (İstanbul, 20–25 Eylül 1937), Kongrenin Çalışmaları ve Kongreye Sunulan Tebliğler*. İstanbul: Kenan Matbaası.

———. 1973. "Albrecht Goetze (11.I.1897–15.VIII.1971)." *Archiv für Orientforschung* 24:243–45.

———. 1992. "Kurt Bittel (5 July 1907–30 January 1991)." *Proceedings of the American Philosophical Society* 136:579–83.

———. 1995. "Resurrecting the Hittites." Pages 2765–777 in *Civilizations of the Ancient Near East*. Vol. 4. Edited by J. Sasson. New York: Scribner.

Guttstadt, C. 2008. *Die Türkei, die Juden und der Holocaust*. Berlin: Assoziation A. Verlag.

Hahn, E. A. 1952. "Edgar Howard Sturtevant." *Language* 28(4):417–34.

Hill, A. A. 1963. "History of the Linguistic Institute." *Bulletin of the Indiana University Linguistic Institute* 1969:16–32. ERIC Document ED 018172.

22   Silvia Alaura

Hirsch, E. E. 2008. *Als Rechtsgelehrter im Lande Atatürks*. Berlin: Berliner Wissenschafts-Verlag.

Hoffner, H. A., Jr. 1999–2000. "Hans Gustav Güterbock: May 27, 1908–March 29, 2000." *Archiv für Orientforschung* 46–47:490–92.

Hrozný, B. 1935. "Report on Hrozný's Five-Month Archaeological Trip in 1934 to Turkey and Syria Held on December 11, 1934 During the Member's Meeting of the Research Department of the Oriental Institute." *Archiv Orientální* 7:208–10.

Jacobsen, T. 1972. "Albrecht Goetze, 1897–1971." *Bulletin of the American Schools of Oriental Research* 206:1, 3–6.

Karasu, C. 2017. "Ankara Anadolu Medeniyetleri Müzesi: Bir Eti Müzesi." Pages 202–22 in *The Discovery of an Anatolian Empire: A Colloquium to Commemorate the 100th Anniversary of the Decipherment of the Hittite Language (November 14th and 15th, 2015; Istanbul Archaeological Museum and Library)*. Edited by M. Doğan-Alparslan, A. Schachner, and M. Alparslan. Beyoğlu-İstanbul: Türk Eskiçağ Bilimleri Enstitüsü.

Kienast, B. 1970. "Benno Landsberger 1890–1968." *Zeitschrift für Assyriologie* 60:1–7.

Klinger, J. 2012a. "Güterbock, Hans Gustav." Pages 520–22 in *Geschichte der Altertumswissenschaften. Biographisches Lexikon. Der Neue Pauly*. Supplement vol. 6. Edited by P. Kuhlmann and H. Schneider. Stuttgart: Metzler.

———. 2012b. "Bittel, Kurt." Pages 108–10 in *Geschichte der Altertumswissenschaften. Biographisches Lexikon. Der Neue Pauly*. Supplement vol. 6. Edited by P. Kuhlmann and H. Schneider. Stuttgart: Metzler.

Koşay, H. Z. 1943. "Türk Tarih Kurumu Tarafından Alacahöyükte yaptırılan Hafriyatta elde edilen Neticeler" (Results of the Alacahöyük Excavations Conducted by Turkish Historical Association). Pages 21–32 in *İkinci Türk Tarih Kongresi (İstanbul, 20–25 Eylül 1937), Kongrenin Çalışmaları ve Kongreye Sunulan Tebliğler*. İstanbul: Kenan Matbaası.

Kubaseck, C., and G. Seufert, eds. 2008. *Deutsche Wissenschaftler im türkischen Exil: Die Wissenschaftsmigration in die Türkei 1933–1945*. Istanbuler Texte und Studien 12. Würzburg: Ergon.

Laroche, E. 1972. "Albrecht Goetze (1897–1971)." *Syria* 49:278–80.

Lemberg, M. 2001. *Verboten und nicht verbrannt*. Vol. 1, *Die Universitätsbibliothek Marburg und ihre Bücher von 1933 bis 1946*. Vol. 2, *Katalog der von 1933 bis 1945 in der Universitätsbibliothek Marburg sekretierten Bücher*. Schriften der Universitätsbibliothek Marburg 110. Marburg: Universitätsbibliothek Marburg.

Lewy, G. 2016. *Harmful and Undesirable: Book Censorship in Nazi Germany*. New York: Oxford University Press.

Maas, U. 2013. "Goetze (Götze), Albrecht." In *Verfolgung und Auswanderung deutschsprachiger Sprachforscher 1933–1945*. https://www.esf.uni-osnabrueck.de/index .php/module-styles/g/223-goetze-goetze-albrecht (accessed 13 September 2017).

———. 2014. "Güterbock, Hans Gustav." In *Verfolgung und Auswanderung deutschsprachiger Sprachforscher 1933–1945*. https://www.esf.uni-osnabrueck.de/index .php/module-styles/g/236-gueterbock-hans-gustav (accessed 13 September 2017).

———. 2018. "Zuntz, Leonie." In *Verfolgung und Auswanderung deutschsprachiger Sprachforscher 1933–1945*. http://zflprojekte.de/sprachforscher-im-exil/index.php/catalog/z/498 -zuntz-leonie (accessed 4 May 2018).

Maier-Metz, H. 2015. *Entlassungsgrund: Pazifismus. Albrecht Götze, der Fall Gumbel und die Marburger Universität 1930 bis 1946*. Academia Marburgensis 13. Münster: Waxmann.

Melchert, H. C. 1999–2000. "In Memoriam. Hans Gustav Güterbock. 27 May 1908–29 March 2000." Pages 5–7 in *Oriental Institute 1999–2000 Annual Report*. https://oi.uchicago.edu /sites/oi.uchicago.edu/files/uploads/shared/docs/ar/91-00/99-00/99-00_Memoriam _Guterbock.pdf.

Naumann, R. 1991. "Kurt Bittel." *Gnomon* 63:663–65.

Oberheid, R. 2007. *Emil O. Forrer und die Anfänge der Hethitologie: Eine wissenschaftshistorische Biografie*. Berlin: de Gruyter.

Oelsner, J. 2006. "Der Altorientalist Benno Landsberger. Wissenschaftstransfer Leipzig–Chicago via Ankara." Pages 269–85 in *Bausteine einer jüdischen Geschichte der Universität Leipzig.* Leipziger Beiträge zur jüdischen Geschichte und Kultur 4. Edited by S. Wendehorst. Leipzig: Universitätsverlag.

———. 2012. "Landsberger, Benno." Pages 694–96 in *Geschichte der Altertumswissenschaften. Biographisches Lexikon. Der Neue Pauly*. Supplement vol. 6. Edited by P. Kuhlmann and H. Schneider. Stuttgart: Metzler.

Otten, H. 1991. "Nachruf auf Kurt Bittel." *Akademie der Wissenschaften und der Literatur Mainz - Jahrbuch* 42:102–4.

Özdoğan, M. 1998. "Ideology and Archaeology in Turkey." Pages 111–24 in *Archaeology Under Fire: Nationalism, Politics and Heritage in the Eastern Mediterranean and Middle East*. Edited by L. Meskell. London: Routledge.

Raulwing, P. 2018. "The Dismissal of Albrecht Goetze (1897–1971) from Marburg University in November 1933 as 'Politically Unreliable' and the Years in Exile until 1946." *Bibliotheca Orientalis* 75(3/4):247–72.

Reiner, E. 2002. "Hans Gustav Güterbock." *Proceedings of the American Philosophical Society* 146(3):291–96.

Reisman, A. 2006. *Turkey's Modernization. Refugees from Nazism and Atatürk's Vision.* Washington, D.C.: New Academia Publishing.

———. 2009. "Turkey's Invitation to Nazi-Persecuted Intellectuals *Circa* 1933: A Bibliographic Essay on History's Blind Spot, Modernization. Refugees from Nazism and Atatürk's Vision." *Covenant: The Global Jewish Magazine* 3(1):31–46.

Renger, J. 2001a. "In Memoriam. Hans Gustav Güterbock." *Istanbuler Mitteilungen* 51:7–11.

———. 2001b. "Altorientalistik und jüdische Gelehrte in Deutschland: Deutsche und österreichische Altorientalisten im Exil." Pages 247–61 in *Jüdische Intellektuelle und die Philologien in Deutschland 1871–1933*. Marbacher Wissenschaftsgeschichte 3. Edited by W. Barner and Ch. König. Göttingen: Wallstein Verlag.

———. 2008. "Altorientalistik." Pages 469–502 in *Kulturwissenschaften und Nationalsozialismus*. Historische Mitteilungen im Auftrage der Ranke-Gesellschaft 72. Edited by J. Elvert and J. Nielsen-Sikora. Stuttgart: Steiner Verlag.

Sallaberger, W. 2007. "Benno Landsbergers 'Eigenbegrifflichkeit' in wissenschaftsgeschichtlicher Perspektive." Pages 63–82 in *Das geistige Erfassen der Welt im Alten Orient. Sprache, Religion, Kultur und Gesellschaft*. Edited by C. Wilcke. Wiesbaden: Harrassowitz.

Schmidt, E. 1931. *Anatolia Through the Ages: Discoveries at the Alishar Mound, 1927–1929*. Oriental Institute Communication 11. Chicago: University of Chicago Press.

Schmidt, J. 2010. "Kraus in Istanbul (1937–1949) and the Development of Ancient Near Eastern Studies in Turkey." *Bibliotheca Orientalis* 67(1/2):6–21.

———, ed. 2014. *Dreizehn Jahre Istanbul (1937–1949). Der deutsche Assyriologe Fritz Rudolf Kraus und sein Briefwechsel im türkischen Exil*. 2 vols. Leiden: Brill.

Şen, F., and D. Halm, eds. 2007. *Exil unter Halbmond und Stern. Herbert Scurlas Bericht über die Tätigkeit deutscher Hochschullehrer in der Türkei während der Zeit des Nationalsozialismus*. Essen: Klartext.

Shaw, W. M. K. 2006. "Whose Hittites, and Why? Language, Archaeology and the Quest for the Original Turks." Pages 131–53 in *Archaeology Under Dictatorship*. Edited by M. L. Galaty and C. Watkinson. Boston: Springer.

Strohmeier, M. 2008. "Der zeitgeschichtliche und politische Rahmen der türkischen Universitätsreform und die Rolle der deutschen Wissenschaftsmigranten." Pages 67–75 in *Deutsche Wissenschaftler im türkischen Exil: Die Wissenschaftsmigration in die Türkei 1933–1945*. Istanbuler Texte und Studien 12. Edited by C. Kubaseck and G. Seufert. Würzburg: Ergon.

Tanyeri-Erdemir, T. 2006. "Archaeology as a Source of National Pride in the Early Years of the Turkish Republic." *Journal of Field Archaeology* 31:381–93.

Tomenendal, K., F. Doğuş Özdemir, and F. Ö. Mercan. 2010. "German-Speaking Academic Émigrés in Turkey of the 1940s." *Österreichische Zeitschrift für Geschichtswissenschaften* 21(3):69–99.

Vacín, L., in collaboration with J. Sýkorová. 2018. *The Unknown Benno Landsberger: A Biographical Sketch of an Assyriological* Altmeister*'s Development, Exile, and Personal Life.* Leipziger Altorientalische Studien 10. Wiesbaden: Harrassowitz.

Weidner, E. 1963. "Helmuth Theodor Bossert (11. September 1889 bis 5. Februar 1961)." *Archiv für Orientforschung* 20:305–6.

Widmann, H. 1973. *Exil und Bildungshilfe. Die deutschsprachige akademische Emigration in die Türkei nach 1933. Mit einer Bio-Bibliographie der emigrierten Hochschullehrer im Anhang.* Bern: Herbert Lang; Frankfurt am Main: Peter Lang.

Wilhelm, G. 2001. "Hans Gustav Güterbock. 27.5.1908–29.3.2000." *Zeitschrift für Assyriologie* 91:161–64.

Wyatt, W. F., Jr. 1994. "Sturtevant, Edgar Howard." Pages 617–19 in *Biographical Dictionary of North American Classicists.* Edited by W. W. Briggs Jr. London: Greenwood Press.

CHAPTER 2

Language and Race in Assyriology:
From Benno Landsberger to Wolfram von Soden

Sebastian Fink

> Therefore, all these facts taken together allow the conclusion that science, in the strict sense of the word, is something that could only be created by the Indo-Germans as determined by northern race.
>
> Wolfram von Soden, 1936

THIS ARTICLE INVESTIGATES THE CONNECTION of language and race in selected writings of Benno Landsberger and Wolfram von Soden and could be understood as a "genealogical" investigation in the birth of the sentence above. Therefore, I will first give an overview on language and race outside Assyriology and then move on to a discussion of Landsberger's and von Soden's works.

Language and Race Outside Assyriology: A (Very) Short Introduction

Race was a main category in scientific[1] thought at least until the end of the Second World War, but there were always voices that opposed the idea of clear and distinguishable human races.[2] Especially in historical subjects, one has to deal with the problem of historical change, and historians want to give good answers to questions

---

Author's note: I thank Lorenzo Verderame and Agnès Garcia-Ventura for the invitation to read this paper in an inspiring atmosphere in Rome as well as for their comments on this article. Additionally, I thank Kerstin Droß-Krüpe and Malte Gasche for their comments on earlier drafts of this text and Florian Krüpe for providing me with hard-to-find literature. Gina Konstantopoulos was kind enough to correct my English and to provide me with additional references to literature. I am most grateful for Jakob Flygare's comments and corrections.

1. When I use the term scientific, I do not use it in any relation to truth in an absolute sense. Here my usage of scientific just implies that these statements were believed to be scientific by quite a number of researchers at a given time and consequently also by broad parts of the population. Hutton (1999, 206–61), in his book on linguistics in the Third Reich, formulates this in the following way: "But both linguistics and race theory have been associated with chauvinism, group narcissism, cultural solipsism; each was implicated in the cultural politics of Nazi Germany. Both have adopted the mantle of modern science, with the avowed aim of improving upon the vague and imprecise categories that ordinary people construct. It is hard to see why a science of linguistic classification should be respectable, while a science of racial classification is viewed with suspicion. Either both are scientific activities, or neither is."

2. See for example Franz Boas. On Boas see the contributions in Pöhl and Tilg 2011. Baker 1998 states that Boas and his school were the main driving forces behind the changing views on race in the United States.

25

like "why did this empire collapse?" or "why did a new material culture emerge?" An easy answer can always be because "waves" of foreign people arrived, destroyed the old culture, and brought or created their own new culture. In explicit racial theories, these "waves" of new people were able to conquer another people's territory because the race of the defeated people had already degenerated due to the influx of foreign blood or foreign spirit.[3] In the first, a straightforward biological case, the result was a degeneration of the biological race. The second, a less biological approach, is seen in the contamination of the national spirit, mostly thought to be represented by the national language. This contamination of the national language with foreign thoughts and words was seen as a crime against the "spiritual and intellectual goods of a nation."[4] The materialization of this language-based approach was the foundation of language societies or academies that aimed to keep the national language, and in a further step the "national spirit," "pure and clean," as for example the *Allgemeiner Deutscher Sprachverein* founded in 1885.[5] Especially Huston Stewart Chamberlain with his widely read *Grundlagen des 19. Jahrhunderts*, which was first published in 1899 and reprinted in many editions, popularized racist thinking and antisemitism as a scientific and intuitively understandable worldview.

The eminently biological approach to race that was finally taken in Germany and ended in the monstrosities that we know all too well, found a firm basis in the works of Chamberlain and earlier race theorists, but at that time racial thinking was not only a German phenomenon.[6] Racial thinking was seen as scientific thinking based on the results of exact sciences in many countries. Also, in the United States, scientific racism flourished in the decades before the end of World War II. After that, the crimes of Nazi Germany that were justified with "scientific racism" ended or at least altered the scientific discourse about biological race. Still, we have to keep in mind that also in the United States the segregation of races was abolished by law only in 1964.[7]

---

3. Race theorists always saw the mixture of races as a great danger, as they thought a mixture would lead to the loss of the positive attributes of the original races. See Pöhl 2018. A great number of examples can be found in philosophical and historical works; here I quote a characteristic passage from Chamberlain 1899, 266, "Wie bald hat nicht die eifersüchtige Feindschaft zwischen den einzelnen Städten des kleinen Griechenland jedem Teilchen seine eigene scharf ausgeprägte Individualität innerhalb des eigenen Familientypus gespendet! Wie schnell ward sie wieder verschwischt, als Makedonier und Römer mit ihrer nivellierenden Hand über das Land hinwegfuhren! Und wie entfloh nach und nach alles, was dem Wort 'hellenisch' ewigen Sinn verliehen hatte, als von Norden, von Osten und Westen immer neue Scharen unverwandter Völker ins Land zogen und mit echten Hellenen sich vermengten! ... die schöne hellenische Persönlichkeit jedoch, ohne die wir alle noch heute nur mehr oder weniger civilisierte Barbaren wären,—sie war verschwunden, auf ewig verschwunden." The English translation reads: "How quickly has the jealous hostility between the different cities of the small country of Greece given each part its sharply defined individuality within its own family type! How quickly this was blurred again, when Macedonians and Romans with their leveling hand swept over the land! And how everything which had given an everlasting significance to the word 'Hellenic' gradually disappeared when from North, East and West new bands of unrelated peoples kept flocking to the country and mingled with genuine Hellenes! ... but the beautiful Hellenic personality, but for which all of us would to-day be merely more or less civilized barbarians, had disappeared, disappeared forever" (Chamberlain 1913, 262).

4 See Hermann Riegel, the founder of the Allgemeiner Deutscher Sprachverein. Translation of the quote in Simon 2017, 1.

5 See Simon 2017.

6 For a new approach based on an analysis of *Weltanschauungskultur* and characterology in regard to the development of German racism and especially anti-Semitism, see Leo 2013. Liverani 1998 provides an investigation of the use of racial theories in Wooley's publications.

7 See Baker 1998 for an in-depth analysis of the discourse on race in the United States from 1896–1954.

What made the race theories that seem so odd to us today such an attractive theory for many historians and archaeologists? To cut a long story short, they provide us with easy explanations. Through the use of racial reasoning, pieces of a new type of pottery can be explained by the arrival of a new people that expressed their innate spirit— *Volksgeist*[8]—in this new type of pottery.[9] This *Volksgeist* was seen as the ultimate explanation of all types of culture, as all cultural artifacts, including the language, could be interpreted as a materialization of the *Volksgeist*.[10] Here, I do not want to touch on the complicated question of how *Volksgeist* was based on race but just hint at the two main solutions to that question. The connection of race with blood was the most popular one; according to this theory, the *Volksgeist* was something innate.[11] The other, less popular theory in Nazi Germany, hinted at an interdependence between race, language, and *Volksgeist*. Some proponents of the latter approach, like Georg Schmidt-Rohr, even claimed that a language makes up a nation, with the result that everybody who is in more or less perfect command of a foreign language (or, so to say, has become native) becomes part of its people and shares in its *Volksgeist* due to their common language, and they strongly argued against race theory.[12] The connection of race with a nation is evident: every race constitutes or should constitute a nation. Obviously, the connection between race and language is a very tricky one, as Hutton demonstrates on the example of the idea of an Indo-European race:

> Even the most superficial look at the problem makes it clear that ideas about an Indo-European (Indo-Germanic, Aryan) people (or race or tribe) derive from linguistics; race science took its lead from the study of language.... Linguistics is both the parent and the child of race theory. It is the parent, in the sense that nineteenth-century physical anthropologists took their lead from linguistics and linguistic categories. It is the child, in the sense that linguistics has reclaimed its role as the premier science in the classification of human diversity, elaborating a "characterology" or "typology" of the world's languages, and therefore of the world's ethnic groups.[13]

If we try to reconstruct a certain *Volksgeist*, the character of an ancient culture, we have to rely on the artifacts of this culture. In some cases, we only have potsherds available for

---

8. On the usage of the terms *Volk, völkisch*, etc. see Gasche 2014, 21–31.

9. So, for example, by Wolfram von Soden (1937, 14) in his infamous "Der Aufstieg des Assyrerreichers als geschichtliches Problem" when he concludes that the Assyrians are a mixture of at least three races, the oriental race, the aralic ("aralisch") race and the painted-pottery-people ("Buntkeramiker"). Apparently, the race of painted-pottery-people is deduced from the existence of painted pottery.

10. Trimborn 1936 provides a short example of the methodological discussion regarding the interconnection of ceramics and people.

11. The "Five Cardinal Laws" given by Chamberlain 1913, 275–89 with their eminently biological vocabulary provide a good example for this. Also, the continuous references to animal breeding makes Chamberlain's biological approach clear (1913, 283): "Here again the clearest and least ambiguous examples are furnished by animal breeding. The mixture of blood must be strictly limited as regards time, and it must, in addition, be appropriate; not all and any crossings, but only definite ones can form the basis of ennoblement." An in-depth analysis of Chamberlain's language is provided by Lobenstein-Reichmann 2008, 113–23, where the term race is discussed.

12. On Schmidt-Rohr see Simon 1986 and Hutton 1999, 289–94. Schmidt-Rohr stresses several times that the biggest disaster for the German nation was the loss of more than 20 million speakers to the United States, where those former Germans first lost their language and subsequently their German identity.

13. Hutton 1999, 3.

the reconstruction, but in the case of Mesopotamia we fortunately have more than this. We have many texts in Sumerian and Akkadian that enable us to reconstruct the ancient world in a more appropriate and informed manner. According to the theories mentioned above, and to our commonsense understanding, a language is a main indicator for a nation or race. We therefore conclude that the Sumerians and Akkadians were the main actors in Mesopotamian history, the so-called acting subjects of Mesopotamian history.

In earlier days, the Mesopotamian evidence was mostly interpreted as follows:[14] first, we have the Sumerians,[15] and then—at some point in the third millennium— people with a Semitic language show up, consequently conquer the Sumerian lands, and constitute the first dynasty of Akkad (ca. 2350–2200). The downfall of this dynasty leads to a Sumerian Renaissance that culminates in the Ur III Empire (ca. 2100–2000). The catastrophic end of Ur III delivered the final blow to the Sumerians and so the Sumerian culture/race died out at some point after the end of Ur III (around 2000).[16] After that, new waves of Semites arrived from somewhere in the west and repopulated the deserted lands. Since this time Mesopotamian culture remains primarily Semitic but still has some Sumerian overtones.

Benno Landsberger and the Conceptual Autonomy of the Babylonian World

Benno Landsberger (1890–1968) was one of the most influential Assyriologists. He was born in Friedek, Austria-Hungary, and studied in Leipzig. During World War I he served in the Austro-Hungarian army. After the war, he finished his *Habilitation* in Leipzig and in 1928 received a professorship in Marburg, which he left only one year later in order to take the vacant chair of his teacher Zimmern in Leipzig. Because he was considered a Jew by Nazi Germany's racial legislation, Landsberger was forced to give up this position, and until 1945 he taught in Ankara. After 1945, Landsberger held a position at the Oriental Institute in Chicago until his retirement.[17]

In 1925 Landsberger gave an inaugural lecture in Leipzig entitled "The Conceptual Autonomy of the Babylonian world."[18] In this lecture, he hints at the great wealth of

14. This view of Sumerians and Akkadians as two distinct entities was opposed by Fritz Rudolf Kraus. See especially Kraus 1970. For an overview regarding the so-called Sumerian Problem see the contributions in Jones 1969 and Rubio 1999, 1–2 and Rubio 2016. Biggs 1966, 77 hints at the fact that already in very early texts from Abū Ṣalābīkh, dating to the middle of the third millennium, scribes with Semitic personal names were quite frequent, clearly showing that the situation was more complex than described by the old "wave" theories.

15. The Sumerian question is also treated by Jerrold Cooper (2016, 14), who concludes: "I have asserted elsewhere that the Sumerians as a people are in some sense the invention of modern Assyriologists, who are more comfortable with discrete categories than with messy realities. The messy reality, as I have argued above, is that the only detectable assertion of Sumerian identity is based upon and found in the curriculum of the Babylonian school. . . . National identity, beginning at the time of the archaic texts at the end of the fourth millennium, when detectable, was a Babylonian identity, geographic but not linguistic."

16. On the end of the Sumerian language, see Michalowski 2007 with further references.

17. See Oelsner 2006, 269–85.

18. The German title was "Die Eigenbegrifflichkeit der babylonischen Welt." On the importance of this text for Assyriology, see Sallaberger 2007, 63. Sallaberger also lists the publications of this text. First, it was printed in the *Festschrift* of A. Fischer (Landsberger 1926), an Arabist from Leipzig, then reprinted two times, together with an article of Wolfram von Soden (Landsberger and von Soden 1965 [2nd ed. 1974]). Finally, it was translated into English by Thorkild Jakobsen et al. (Landsberger 1976).

material that Assyriologists had deciphered and edited in the last eighty years and discusses the possibilities and aims of future Assyriology. What should Assyriologists—beside their never-ending tasks of editing and translating texts—do with their material? He states:

> Today may, therefore, well be the first time that an attempt is made to bring nearer to its solution the problem: To what extent is it possible to reconstruct *vividly* and *faithfully* an ancient, alien civilization by philological means, without the help of a tradition continuing down to the present day?[19]

Landsberger further argues that Mesopotamian scholarship "seems abstruse to us, their religion in most of its forms barren superstition, their legal system primitive. Thus the scholar faces his own subject unmoved and aloof, and precisely those men to whom our science owes most look for more rewarding research problem outside their field."[20]

However, how can we enter this "alien civilization?" According to Landsberger "all understanding consists first of all in establishing some link between the alien world and our own."[21] The first step is to make "links" between our own and the alien language by means of dictionaries. In their entries, equations between words are given. Obviously, at least for a philologist, many of these equations are only partial because it is quite seldom that words in different languages have exactly the same range of meaning. However, these equations are, to use Landsberger's words, "only the simple algebra of comprehension. A grammar or lexicon thus organized does not tell us the slightest thing about the characteristics of the Babylonian mind."[22] At this point Landsberger introduces the term "conceptual autonomy."

> Rather, if we are not to deprive ourselves of the most important key to understanding, we seek out the conceptual autonomy [*Eigenbegrifflichkeit*] of a *particular* civilization, and it is to this task that my own work has been devoted for the last few years, some results of which I am here presenting in brief.[23]

Landsberger describes his method as *heuristic*, "that is to say, it does not approach the alien mind from a *fixed* system of *conceptual referents* in order to find out to what extent this alien civilization can be related to it."[24] Once we have found these autonomous concepts, they should be connected to systems, "the first of which is the system of autonomous grammatical concepts, which will immediately lead us on to the concept of the so-called 'inner form' of language. This may be followed by the system

---

19. Landsberger 1976, 5.

20. Landsberger 1976, 5–6. This might be a side blow toward his teacher Heinrich Zimmern, who had a strong tendency to compare and connect Mesopotamian religion with Christian religion. See also the obituary, written by Landsberger in 1931, where he stresses the importance of Zimmern's contribution to Assyriology but also stresses his evolutionary perspective and his special interest in Mesopotamia as a predecessor of our own culture (Landsberger 1931, 133–34).

21. Landsberger 1976, 6.

22. Landsberger 1976, 6.

23. Landsberger 1976, 6.

24. Landsberger 1976, 6.

of concepts relating to the apprehension of space, then we move on and on to more specific features we may finally reach the closed systems of certain special disciplines or profession as for instance those of law and culture. Only by way of constructing the system of concepts can we find our way into the nature of a civilization."[25]

At this point, we should summarize Landsberger's ideas: the way to understand an ancient foreign culture starts with deciphering and creating an understanding of the texts by relating them to our own languages. The result of this work is presented in grammars and dictionaries. The necessity of this first step is obvious. Nevertheless, as necessary as these equations are, they also conceal the differences between languages. If we put all the terms of Language A into a clear relationship with Language B by means of a dictionary, we might forget that differences do exist. The same holds true for the field of grammar. Therefore, Landsberger proposes to use autonomous grammatical concepts and to stop structuring the grammar of Akkadian with the well-known patterns of Greek grammar.

In his lecture, Landsberger refers to Wilhelm von Humboldt[26] and paraphrases him in the following way:

> Once we have understood the linguistic structure we have obtained immediate access to the structure of the people's mind as well and with it one of the most important determinants of civilization, in so far as it is a creation of mind.[27]

Walther Sallaberger discussed Landsberger's conceptual autonomy and tried to identify potential sources for his ideas.[28] In this article he argued that Wilhelm Wundt, who wrote the monumental *Völkerpsychologie* was of some importance for Landsberger. He also claimed that Wolfram von Soden's statement that Landsberger relied on the work of the German Linguist Leo Weisgerber should be doubted because Weisgerber had only published his widely read book entitled *Muttersprache und Geistesbildung* in 1929.[29] Wolfram von Soden himself was surely influenced by Weisgerber, at least indirectly, as he intensively read the works of Weisgerber's pupil Helmut Gipper and tried to use Gipper's works as a new theoretical basis for analyzing Sumerian and Akkadian.[30] Besides the quite possible influence of Wundt—Sallaberger does not provide any "hard" evidence of a connection such as a citation in Landsberger's notes or letters—I have identified two further possible sources of Landsberger's ideas.

The strange term *Eigenbegrifflichkeit* (conceptual autonomy) and my own work on the German Philosopher Oswald Spengler (1880–1936),[31] lead me to suspect that

---

25. Landsberger 1976, 7.

26. He refers to an idea that is formulated several times by Humboldt and quotes the following: "Die Geisteseigenthümlichkeit und die Sprachgestaltung eines Volkes stehen in solcher Innigkeit und Verschmelzung in einander, daß, wenn die eine gegeben wäre, die andere müßte vollständig aus ihr abgeleitet werden können" (von Humboldt 1998, 171).

27. Landsberger 1976, 11.

28. Sallaberger 2007.

29. Sallaberger 2007, 69. But one should also mention that there are also earlier articles by Weisgerber touching the same topic. See Hutton 1999, 107–22.

30. Von Soden 1973.

31. Fink 2014, and Fink and Rollinger 2018.

Language and Race in Assyriology   31

Landsberger might have been influenced somehow by Spengler's concept of autonomous cultures. Spengler was extremely popular after his book *The Decline of the West* appeared in 1919. Additionally, he was also in close contact with some of the most important German Assyriologists and ancient historians of his time.[32] In *Decline of the West* Spengler argues that there are eight completely autonomous cultures. Each of these cultures provides a world of its own: each has its own intrinsic value and has to be understood from within and cannot be compared to other cultures; on the other hand, all cultures follow the same fundamental laws of rise and decline.[33]

When I found out that Spengler himself gave a lecture in Leipzig in 1921,[34] and also that the influential Arabist C. H. Becker spoke on the "Magic Culture of Oswald Spengler" in 1923 for the Deutsche Morgenländische Gesellschaft in Leipzig, my suspicion gained additional weight. In his lecture, Becker uses the term *Eigenbedeutung* and paraphrases Spengler as follows: "Spengler harshly argues against the conventional approach to history that estimates only what is still important to us or still alive. The Orientalist is immune to such criticism. We always have judged the periods of oriental culture in their intrinsic importance [*Eigenbedeutung*]."[35]

In a list of lectures I also discovered that Walter Porzig, who held a position in Leipzig from 1922–1925 and is often described as the founder of the Neo-Humboldtian school, gave a lecture in this DMG series on 29 January 1924 with the title "Linguistics and the History of Religion."[36] In exactly the same lecture series Landsberger had given a lecture on "Semitic languages"[37] on 23 June 1923 and Zimmern had spoken on "Empire and Culture of the Hittites"[38] on 14 December 1923. Therefore, it seems quite possible that they attended each other's lectures and exchanged ideas. The main document of Porzig's revival of Humboldt's ideas is an article on "The Term Inner Form of Language,"[39] which he published in 1923.[40] Furthermore, the Humboldt quote used by Landsberger is found on the first page of Porzig's paper. If we take a look at the formulation of the aims of Porzig's new approach to language via the *innere Sprachform*, we can see many similarities with Landsberger's text.[41] Therefore, it seems quite convincing that Porzig played a role in the development of Landsberger's ideas.

---

32. See Fink 2014. Spengler exchanged quite a number of letters with Alfred Jeremias, who was also working in Leipzig until his death in 1935, and also some with Heinrich Zimmern, who was Landsberger's teacher. So, despite the non-mentioning of Spengler's name in Landsberger's notes (I have to thank Michael Streck, who has seen all the available material, for this information), it seems quite probable that Landsberger was aware of Spengler's work. Unfortunately, the notes and letters of Landsberger are not easily available, but today at least some of them are accessible at https://sites.google.com/site/landsbergerarchive/.

33. See Farrenkopf 2001.

34. Koktanek 1968, 354.

35. "Spengler polemisiert stark gegen die übliche Geschichtsbetrachtung, die an der Vergangenheit nur wertet, was heute noch nachwirkt oder lebt. Der Orientalist ist gegen diesen Vorwurf gefeit. Wir haben die orientalischen Geschichtsperioden immer in ihrer Eigenbedeutung gewertet" (Becker 1923, 269–70).

36. "Sprachwissenschaft und Religionsgeschichte."

37. "Die semitschen Sprachen."

38. The date and title of Zimmern's lecture is recalled in the *Zeitschrift der Deutschen Morgenländischen Gesellschaft* 78 (1924), page LXXXVI, about the conferences of Leipzig's DMG.

39. "Der Begriff der inneren Sprachform."

40. Porzig 1923.

41. "Vergegenwärtigen wir uns noch einmal, was der Begriff der inneren Sprachform leisten soll: Er soll erstens den sprachlichen Erscheinungen ihre Einheit geben, d.h. all die mannigfaltigen und äußerlich scheinbar gar nicht zusammenhängenden Einzelheiten, als die sich das Bild einer Sprache dem Betrachter zunächst darstellt, sollen durch exakte Interpretation als Ausfluß einer einheitlichen Anschauungsweise

32   Sebastian Fink

However, as in the case of Wundt, the lack of documentation and references in Lands-berger's work provides us with no opportunity to give undeniable proof of the influence of Spengler, Becker, and Porzig on the development of Landsberger's *Eigenbegrifflichkeit*. For now, I will leave this topic of the contextualization of Landsberger's ideas aside and turn to his analysis of the inner form of Sumerian and Akkadian.

Landsberger analyzes the Akkadian language and comes to the following conclusions:

1. The Akkadian verbal system is governed by the dualism between *momentary/punctual (ikšud)* and *durative (kašid, ikaššad)*.
2. Akkadian has a rigid character (compared to Hebrew), from this "follows further the fact of the *objectivity* of the statement, that is to say the occurrence of state is viewed as such, independent of the standpoint of the speaker."[42]
3. Akkadian verbs are not very abstract; in addition, many generic terms are missing.
4. He states that "to the early Semite, however, only the bearer of invariable, lasting characteristics is an object."[43] Therefore, Akkadian only has few "real" nouns.

Here, one should mention that points 1 and 2 are more or less outdated today, because newer investigations[44] have shown that Landsberger's views regarding the Akkadian verb are not tenable thanks to their generality. From points 1, 2, and 3 Landsberger concludes the following:

> If we want to draw conclusions from this linguistic structure concerning the intellectual assets of the Babylonians, no way leads from the logical disordering of the concepts of being to theoretical knowledge. On the other hand, all becoming and having become is structured in an imaginative, graphic, vivid manner and therein lies a means for artistic formative activity. Thus, with the power of realistic reproduction and the art of keen observation the distinctiveness of the Akkadian mind is in fact exhausted, and along with it presumably the Semitic one. In the fact, though, that the Akkadian reflects keenly and well, and also observers the sequence of occurrences lies a germ for a theoretical understanding of the phenomena of nature.[45]

He further concludes that due to the small number of real nouns and the impossibility of establishing firm relationships between nouns that would lead to a new concept, e.g., by a compound, "a firm connection between two atoms of language is

---

aufgewiesen werden. Diese Anschauungsweise ist ebenso durch die vorhandene Sprache bedingt, wie die künftige Entwicklung der Sprache von ihr bedingt ist. Es handelt sich also um ein der Sprache immanentes Prinzip. Zweitens aber soll der Begriff der inneren Sprachform das Verhältnis klarlegen, in dem die Sprache als objektives Geisteserzeugnis zu anderen Erzeugnissen gleicher Art, also z. B. Kunst, Religion und anderen, steht" (Porzig 1923, 164).

42. Landsberger 1976, 11.
43. Landsberger 1976, 9.
44. Streck 2003.
45. Landsberger 1976, 12.

impossible."[46] In other words, Akkadian makes it hard to structure and analyze the order of things or events.

But—and this is critical for Landsberger's understanding of language and race—he thinks that this language spirit (*Sprachgeist*) was hampered in its evolution by the presence of the Sumerians:

> Now this language spirit [*Sprachgeist*] could never unfold independently as a civilization; there is no purely Semitic civilization in Babylonia. The civilization of that country is an amalgamation of the Semitic spirit, not—to be sure, easily put in alien fetters—with the Sumerian, which is characterized by a fundamentally different language form.[47]

What Landsberger presents to us here is an idea very similar to what was labeled "pseudomorphosis," a term taken from mineralogy by Spengler.[48] Spengler used this term to describe his idea that one culture can develop in the forms of a preceding culture. Besides the Russian culture, molded by Western influence, his most prominent example is the "magical (Arab) culture," which was heavily influenced by classical antiquity.[49]

The idea behind this reasoning of Spengler, and most probably also of Landsberger, is that there is something like a telos, an innate aim in every language community, race, or culture that can only develop in its innate way when it is not hindered by an overpowering older culture. In the case of Spengler, culture is therefore seen as a *Wesenheit*, a substance and even as an individual, and Landsberger's approach does not seem to be very different. The result of a pseudomorphosis is that the inner form does not agree with the outer appearance, and this gives a culture a certain instability or contradictoriness. Nevertheless, let's have a look at Landsberger's conclusions and see how he evaluates this pseudmorphosis.

First, he gives a description of Sumerian as a language completely contrary to Akkadian, with the most typical characteristics of Sumerian as the following:

1. Sumerian is extremely poor in roots.
2. Therefore, an important task of Sumerian is the combination of roots (compounds do exist in Sumerian).
3. The roots are mostly abstract; their meaning is "varied through local exponents."

Landsberger concludes that "*isolating* Akkadian stands therefore over against [sic!] *combinatory* Sumerian."[50] He further explains that "at the time when the Sumerians came into contact with the Akkadians, however, they had not *only* their language, but a supra-linguistic order of things as well, an order which itself, however, was born of the spirit of the language."[51] Landsberger refers to abstract concepts formed with the par-

46. Landsberger 1976, 12.
47. Landsberger 1976, 12.
48. On pseudomorphosis in Spengler see Farrenkopf 2001, 41–43.
49. The idea of pseudomorphosis was discussed in detail in Becker 1923.
50. Landsberger 1976, 12.
51. Landsberger 1976, 12.

34 Sebastian Fink

ticle *nam-* that, according to his views, played a major role in ordering and structuring the world for the Sumerians. The Akkadians took over these concepts enthusiastically:

> Semitic peoples, who have nothing but the realism represented by their language, seized enthusiastically upon the idea of a world order but this new active numen always remains for them a concept of a higher order, which is without influence upon the understanding of the empirical world and only becomes operative when man devotes himself to emotively emphasized religious thinking.[52]

Nevertheless, despite their eagerness to understand the Sumerian concepts, the Akkadians were not able to develop "systematic theoretical thinking; for they lacked the verbs required for connecting the new concepts of order. Thus all theoretical science is without sentences."[53]

At this point, I have summarized the most important points of Landsberger's approach to language and race. Landsberger proposes a relativistic approach to the Mesopotamian culture and insists at understanding it from within. Like in Spengler's *Decline of the West* (1926/1928) each culture represents a value of its own, is a unique expression of the possibilities of human beings and should not be reduced to a mere stage of development. Like Spengler, Landsberger argues against an evolutionary approach and insists on the conceptual autonomy of each culture. Now I will turn to his pupil Wolfram von Soden, who further developed Landsberger's theories in three articles.

Wolfram von Soden

Wolfram von Soden was one of the most productive Assyriologists of the twentieth century.[54] He was a pupil of Landsberger, who was forced to leave Germany due to racial legislation in 1935.[55] Maybe because of his prominence and productivity he, as Flygare has put it, "is the Assyriologist who has most often be identified as a Nazi."[56] Other, today more or less forgotten Assyriologists, as for example Viktor Christian, whose work is full of race theory, didn't receive much attention in Assyriological circles.[57] Von Soden joined the Sturmabteilung (SA) in 1934. According to Borger, he never actively joined the NSDAP and only became a party member in

---

52. Landsberger 1976, 13.

53. Landsberger 1976, 123–24. Here we can see the first formulation of what von Soden later called *Listenwissenschaft*.

54. See for example the obituary by Röllig 1997, who hints at the fundamental tools for Assyriologists that von Soden had created, the *Akkadisches Syllabar*, the *Grundriss der akkadischen Grammatik*, and finally his *Akkadisches Handwörterbuch*.

55. Oelsner 2006.

56. Flygare 2006, 5. See now also Flygare in this volume.

57. On Christian, see Leitner 2010. Flygare (2006, 20–21) mentions Carl Frank as another example and concludes: "Finally, I wish to emphasize that the Ariocentricity in von Soden's representations of ancient Near Eastern history was far less radical than it was in earlier studies by French and English scholars; i.e., this kind of racial scholarship rooted in the Aryan myth was not limited to Nazi Germany but rather has affected other researchers in other countries."

1944, when all SA members automatically became party members.[58] This view was proven wrong by documentary evidence, as shown by Joachim Renger and Jakob Flygare: von Soden actively applied for membership and joined the party in 1937.[59] Here we should also state that even party membership was in some cases only a safety precaution or a careerist's move, not necessarily connected to political views.[60] Unfortunately, the history of Assyriology is still in its infancy, at least compared to neighboring subjects,[61] so it is hard to judge von Soden's attitudes toward National Socialism and especially his attitude toward racial thinking without comparative studies.[62] Therefore, we will simply look at three papers of von Soden that took up and further developed ideas of his teacher regarding language and race. These are

1. "Leistung und Grenze sumerischer und babylonischer Wissenschaft" (1936)[63]
2. "Die Zweisprachigkeit in der geistigen Kultur Babyloniens" (1960)[64]
3. "Sprache, Denken und Begriffsbildung im Alten Orient" (1973)[65]

"Leistung und Grenze sumerischer und babylonischer Wissenschaft" (1936)

Interestingly the first edition of this text appeared in *Die Welt als Geschichte. Eine Zeitschrift für Universalgeschichte.* This journal was founded by Hans Erich Stier,[66] whose teacher was the famous ancient historian Eduard Meyer, who tried to overcome the classical barriers of ancient history and integrated the Near East and Egypt in his influential *Geschichte des Altertums.*[67] The foundation of this journal was inspired by Spengler, who himself published articles on the history of the second millennium BCE there. As neither Stier nor Spengler were National Socialists—on the contrary, were rather seen as "political unreliable" from a National Socialist point of view—we can be sure that von Soden would have found better places for this text if he wanted to present himself as a proponent of a modern, National Socialist science.[68] Unfortunately, I do not have any information why von Soden chose this somewhat

---

58. Borger 1997–1998, 589.

59. Renger 2006 and Flygare in this volume.

60. See Flygare 2006, 16–17 and also Flygare in this volume.

61. Vidal 2013 provides a good overview on the work that has been carried out so far. Already in 1977, Volker Losemann published a monograph on National Socialism and ancient history in Germany. See now also his collected writings in Deglau, Reinard, and Ruffing 2017.

62. Borger 1997–1998, 589 remarks that in three works, namely von Soden 1936, 1937, and 1938, he had shown "besondere Sympathie für die Indogermanen" (special sympathy for the Indo-Germans). These works and their context are analyzed by Flygare 2005 and 2006, which are now partly outdated by Flygare in this volume. Borger, who openly states his deep admiration for his teacher von Soden in his obituary, adds that in the forty-four years he had known von Soden he had never heard or read anything from him that could be interpreted as anti-Semitic (Borger 1997–1998, 591).

63. "Accomplishments and Limits of Sumerian and Babylonian Science."

64. "Bilingualism in the Intellectual Culture of Babylonia."

65. "Language, Thought and Concept Formation in the Ancient Near East."

66. On Stier, see Gauger 2007. After the war, Stier was one of the founding members of the CDU, the Christian Democratic Party of Germany.

67. This work was published in five volumes from 1884–1902 and has seen many reprints. On Eduard Meyer see Calder and Demandt 1990.

68. See Rebenich 2013, 303. Spengler's continued hesitation to contribute to Nazi propaganda and his published critique of National Socialism earned him the scorn of the minister for Propaganda, Joseph Goebbels, who gave the instruction not to mention Spengler's name in the press anymore.

36   Sebastian Fink

exotic journal for an important Assyriological contribution. In addition, the fact that von Soden decided to republish this text in 1965 might indicate that he himself could still accept most of a text he wrote 30 years prior, even if he states in the epilogue of the book that he did not republish it without worries.[69]

The long article can be seen as a commentary to Landsberger's *Eigenbegrifflichkeit* and it is quite famous in Assyriological circles—perhaps not because every Assyriologist has read this long text carefully but rather because von Soden coined the term *Listenwissenschaft* within it.[70] According to him, *Listenwissenschaft* characterizes the Sumerian approach to science, laying the base for all future "scientific" endeavors in Mesopotamia.[71] Unfortunately, only the Sumerians were able to understand *Listenwissenschaft* completely, and all later Babylonian adoptions were described as a "degeneration" (*Entartung*). The original Sumerian "meaningful inner coherency" (*sinnerfüllte innere Einheit*) was lost.[72]

Von Soden explicitly tries to approach Mesopotamian science from an evolutionary account (*Begriff der Vorstufe*), finally concluding that this approach should be completely abandoned from the "History of Ideas" (*Geistesgeschichte*) because it does not help us to understand ancient science properly but rather focuses on its shortcomings. Therefore, von Soden faithfully sticks to his teacher's approach. In the last paragraph, he concludes that

> if we [...] ask ourselves what might be the cause of the deep differences of the inner form of Sumerian and Akkadian "Science," that both sprang from the same cultural soil, only one answer remains: that these differences are based on the different natural disposition of both people.[73]

Concluding this article, von Soden looks at sciences outside of Mesopotamia. He explicitly states that since "external factors" (*äußere Umstände*) had not caused the big difference between Mesopotamian and Egyptian "science," the decisive factor is rather "racial/national character" (*die völkische Eigenart*) of the Egyptians.[74] Here von Soden also emphasizes that we should get rid of the idea of a uniform "ancient Near East," a term that, especially in German, also includes Egypt—clearly a reference to Landsberger's *Eigenbegrifflichkeit*.

Then he turns to Indian science and, to our absolute surprise, it turns out that Indian science does not need quotation marks. Indian science is a *vollwertige Wissenschaft*, a real science in our sense.[75] The reader might already suspect that this might have something to do with race and in fact, we can read the following: "If we ask ourselves

---

69. See von Soden in Landsberger and von Soden 1965, 132–33.

70. See Hilgert 2009.

71. Von Soden 1936, 424–25.

72. Von Soden 1965, 117.

73. Von Soden 1965, 118 (my translation): "Wenn wir dann in Rückwendung zu unserem Sonderfall weiter fragen, worin denn die tiefen Unterschiede der Eigengesetzlichkeiten sumerischer und akkadischer "Wissenschaft," die doch beide dem gleichen Kulturboden entwachsen sind, begründet sind, so bleibt uns nur eine Antwort, daß diese in der Verschiedenheit der natürlichen Anlagen beider Völker begründet sind."

74. Von Soden 1965, 120–21. The term *völkisch* is rather vague and can comprise racial as well as cultural aspects.

75. Von Soden 1965, 121.

for the reasons of this phenomenon, we immediately think of the close linguistic and racial relation between the Arian Indians, us and the Greeks."[76] In a footnote, he adds that the reason for the differences between Greek and Indian science "can surely be attributed to the strong influence of non-Arian Indians on Indian culture."[77] He finally concludes that "science, in the strict sense of the word, is something that could only be created by the Indo-Germans as determined by northern race."[78]

I think we can end our discussion of this text here and conclude that von Soden was deeply involved in the scientific racism of his time that attributed different characters to nations much as we attribute particular character to individual persons. As far as I can see, von Soden only quoted "serious" literature. Serious, that is, in my point of view, about avoiding the usual proponents of a racial theory that gave the murderous politics in Nazi Germany a scientific justification, like, for example, Hans F. K. Günther.[79] In one of his last commentaries to the text that he wrote for the reprint, he states, somewhat apologetically, that

> Some time-bound formulations of this summary are corrected in "Zweispr." p. 32f. An important factor for the special intellectual richness of the cohabitation of the entirely different Sumerians and Akkadians and their distinct languages, is the fact that these two nations, despite all differences and fights, did not negate each other but always stayed open-minded for each other.[80]

It is clear that von Soden developed his views over time and that he was honest enough to see and openly confess the "time bound formulations" of his original text, a fact that is quite remarkable. Most historians never openly criticized their older work, even when it was deeply founded in racial theories. Many even maintained these theories, which were based on a biological racism deeply rooted in national socialist ideology.[81]

"Die Zweisprachigkeit in der geistigen Kultur Babyloniens" (1960)

This paper is quite interesting in several aspects. Not only because an Assyriologist was a forerunner in a now booming field—the investigation of both bilingualism and

76. Von Soden 1965, 121–22 (my translation): "Fragen wir uns auch hier wieder nach dem Grund dieser Erscheinung, so denken wir sofort an die nahe sprachliche und rassische Verwandtschaft, die die arischen Inder mit uns und den Griechen verbindet."

77. Von Soden 1965, 122 n. 85.

78. Flygare drew my attention to the fact that the text was changed in von Soden 1965, 122. There we can read that "Wissenschaft im strengen Sinn des Wortes nur unter den bei den indogermanischen Griechen und Indern gegebenen besonderen Voraussetzungen Gestalt gewinnen konnte." The 1937 original (the basis for the translation above) reads instead that "Wissenschaft im strengen Sinn des Wortes etwas ist, das nur von den durch die nordische Rasse bestimmten Indogermanen geschaffen werden konnte."

79. On Günther and his importance for the development of race theory in the German nationalist movement, see Breuer 2010.

80. Von Soden 1965, 132–33 (my translation), "Einige zeitgebundende Formulierungen dieser Zusammenfassung sind in "Zweispr.," besonders S. 32f., zurechtgerückt. Eine wichtige Ursache für die besondere geistige Fruchtbarkeit des Zusammenlebens der in ihren Anlagen, schon nach Ausweis der Sprachen, so grundverschiedenen Sumerer und Akkader, lag wohl in der Tatsache, daß sich beide Völker trotz aller Gegensätze und Kämpfe nicht verneint haben, sondern immer füreinander aufgeschlossen blieben."

81. To quote just one example, Fritz Schachermayer, one of the most prominent ancient historians in Austria after World War II, never gave up his biological/racial views on history. See Pesditschek 2009.

multilingualism—but also because von Soden revised his older view of two stable entities: the Sumerians and the Babylonians in Mesopotamia. He now criticizes this idea of two distinct entities because he thinks it is too difficult to talk about the influence of one language on Babylonian intellectual life—elites of Mesopotamia were bilingual since 2000 BCE, at the latest.

In this article, von Soden still characterizes Sumerian and Akkadian as Landsberger would have done, and the main thoughts of the text can be seen as a development of Landsberger's elaborations that Mesopotamian culture can only be properly understood if we take the "amalgamation"[82] of Sumerians and Akkadians into account. Interestingly, von Soden gives this idea a very positive turn and emphasizes the importance of Assyriological research for the present age (1960), a time when many nations outside of Europe, the former colonies, faced the challenge of finding a positive way to deal with the "western" impact. In the following lines, von Soden inverts Landsberger's rather negative judgment of this mixture of cultures and even states that it was only this mixture that enabled them to achieve important cultural accomplishments:

> The most important, but still preliminary, result of our examination of the characteristic of Babylonian thought is the insight that the encounter of two completely different mentalities—like that of the Sumerians and Akkadians—in *one* area can trigger important intellectual achievements that none of the involved people could have achieved alone.[83]

"Sprache, Denken und Begriffsbildung im Alten Orient" (1973)

This is the last text in which von Soden exclusively deals with the topic of language and thought. He refers to Landsberger's works once more and states that the decisive motivation for his work on this topic goes back to the influence of his teacher. In the introduction, he also refers to Helmut Gipper, one of the most influential proponents of the so-called *Sprachinhaltsforschung* and states in passing that Landsberger was influenced by the ideas and early writings of Leo Weisgerber, Gipper's teacher.[84]

Again, von Soden informs us about lacking general terms that hampered the further development of Mesopotamian science and elaborates on Mesopotamian *Listenwissenschaft*.[85] Once more, Akkadian is a language with the "power of realistic reproduction," but it lacks the linguistic means for argumentation. He concludes that texts of Greek, Roman, or Indian thinkers could not be translated into Akkadian or other older Semitic languages.[86] Again, we see the opposition of the Semitic versus the Indo-Germanic languages, and von Soden also hints at the problems the Arabs had with translating Greek authors.[87] Finally, we should also mention that the Arabs finally

---

82. Landsberger 1976, 12.

83. Von Soden 1960, 33: "Das grundsätzlich Bedeutsamste an dem, was wir von der Eigenart des babylonischen Denkens schon zu verstehen meinen, ist wohl die Erkenntnis, daß das Zusammentreffen ganz verschiedener Denkweisen wie der der Sumerer und Semiten in einem Raum bedeutende geistige Leistungen auslösen kann, Leistungen, die keines der beteiligten Völker allein hätte vollbringen können."

84. Von Soden 1973, 7–8. On Weisgerber, see Hutton 1999, 106–43.

85. See the analysis of this concept in Hilgert 2009 with further references.

86. Von Soden 1973, 27.

87. For a more detailed analysis of this text, see Fink 2015, 156–63.

overcame these problems because they adapted their language to make the translation possible, a phenomenon that also occurred when the Romans tried to translate Greek philosophers.[88]

Conclusion

It is obvious that Landsberger's *Eigenbegrifflichkeit* established the fundamentals for the work of von Soden and that von Soden's view regarding language and race changed over time. Trying to summarize the ideas of these two authors expressed in four articles, we can describe them in the following way:

- For Landsberger, language was the "only available determinant of a national culture,"[89] and in his lecture on the conceptual autonomy, he stated that the mixture of languages hampered the development of a "purely Semitic culture."
- In "Leistung und Grenze sumerischer und babylonischer Wissenschaft" (1936), von Soden's views seem to have a tendency toward more biological thinking—for example, when he speaks of natural dispositions of a people. The idea of Indo-Germans as the cultural heroes of humankind is a central axiom of this article, when he considers that even Chinese science is a product of a contact with Indo-Germans.
- In "Zweisprachigkeit" (1960), he develops a more positive attitude toward the contact between the Sumerians and Akkadians, concluding that the contact between those two peoples lead to achievements they could not have achieved alone, and he tries to promote the understanding among nations. Here we have no explicit statements about the concept of a race; von Soden even suggests that it is not very promising to analyze these two closely intertwined entities in isolation.
- In "Begriffsbildung" (1973), von Soden seems to avoid the topic of race, but in a lengthy footnote he argues against the approach of Fritz Kraus, himself also a pupil of Landsberger, who stated that he can only find different languages, but no different entities of Sumerians and Akkadians in the Mesopotamian evidence. This clearly demonstrates that von Soden did not want to go as far as Kraus and give up the distinction of a "Sumerian" and "Akkadian" culture or people at all.

To conclude: neither of the two authors discussed here was a radical proponent of race ideology. But in his 1936 lecture, von Soden points out that European science is something special[90] and tries to explain this with a special northern Indo-Germanic

---

88. See Kainz 1972, 226 who discusses the example of the influence of the article on Platonic philosophy and the problems of Cicero transferring Greek concepts into Latin.

89. Güterbock 1968–1969, 204. "die einzig greifbare Determinante einer nationalen Kultur." Landsberger himself (1976, 15) formulates this thought in the closing words of his lecture in the following way: "Only the language discloses to the scholar the riches of the alien world of ideas; without it any kind of real understanding is impossible."

90. David Pingree attacked this still widely unchallenged conviction in a seminal paper with the title "Helenophilia versus the History of Science" (Pingree 1992). See Rochberg 2002 for an analysis of the ways the historiography of science managed to get around the Mesopotamian evidence.

40   Sebastian Fink

approach to science.[91] However, as he formulates himself, "some time-bound formulations" play a role in this paper. He obviously refers to the racial reasoning concerning the origin of "real" science, which he exclusively connected with the northern Indo-Germans. Nevertheless, von Soden ended his paper with an appeal, which seemed so relativistic to me, that I checked the original edition from 1936 in order to see if it was a later addition, but it was not.[92] I will quote von Soden's final verdict in length and finally it seems that von Soden's statements regarding real science, which seem so harsh and racist to us, might only be the result of a consequent application of Landsberger's principle of the conceptual autonomy:[93]

> Therefore, all these facts taken together allow the conclusion that science, in the strict sense of the word, is something that could only be created by the Indo-Germans as determined by northern race.... If our science or that what we—despite the danger of a confusion of ideas—must call Sumerian, Babylonian or Chinese "science," is the greater intellectual achievement, it is not for us to judge, because by no stretch of imagination are we able to fully appreciate these foreign achievements. To the contrary, the uniqueness of our science can only be fully understood in all its richness when we take the achievements of other peoples completely serious and spare no effort to better and better understand their intrinsic laws (*Eigenbedeutung*). Apart from that, we would do a disservice to our own cause if we can only provide proof of the right of the existence of our kind of science[94] by degrading foreign kinds of science![95]

91. His 1937 text *Der Aufstieg des Assyrerreiches als geschichtliches Problem* (a detailed analysis of this text is provided by Flygare in this volume) does not touch the issue of language and therefore was not included here. There von Soden takes race theory seriously and tries to explain Assyrian history by making use of racial theories.

92. As noted above (thanks to an observation by Flygare), the first sentence was changed in the later edition.

93. What von Soden basically says here—and what is somehow obscured by the use of "science in the strict sense of the word" instead of "Indo-German science"—is the quite relativistic statement that every culture has its own kind of science and that we have to take all of them seriously.

94. Here the text is somewhat tricky, as the term "Art" could refer to "kind of science," as well as to "kind/race/nature," but I am quite convinced that "kind of science" is what von Soden means. See Fink 2019, 91 for a short introduction and further references to such a rather relativistic understanding of science by Thomas Kuhn and Paul Feyerabend.

95. Von Soden 1936, 556–57 (my translation). The original reads: "So erlauben alle diese Tatsachen zusammen gewiß den Schluß, daß Wissenschaft im strengen Sinn des Wortes etwas ist, das nur von den durch die nordische Rasse bestimmten Indogermanen geschaffen werden konnte.... Ob unsere Wissenschaft oder das, was wir trotz der Gefahr der Begriffsverwirrung sumerische, babylonische und chinesische "Wissenschaft" nennen müssen, die höhere geistige Leistung ist, steht uns zu beurteilen schließlich nicht zu, da wir die fremden Leistungen auch beim besten Willen nicht in ihrem vollen Werte würdigen können. Im Gegenteil, die Einzigartigkeit unserer Wissenschaft erschließt sich uns erst dann in ihrem ganzen Reichtum, wenn wir auch die Leistungen anderer Völker restlos Ernst nehmen und uns keine Mühe verdrießen lassen, ihre Eigengesetzlichkeit immer besser zu erfassen; wir erwiesen uns im übrigen auch ja auch selbst einen sehr schlechten Dienst, wenn wir die Daseinsberechtigung unserer Art nur durch Herabziehen fremder Art beweisen könnten!"

REFERENCES

Baker, L. 1998. *From Savage to Negro: Anthropology and the Construction of Race, 1896–1954*. Los Angeles: University of California Press.

Becker, C. H. 1923. "Spenglers Magische Kultur." *Zeitschrift der Deutschen Morgenländischen Gesellschaft* 77:255–71.

Biggs, R. D. 1966. "The Abū Ṣalābīkh Tablets: A Preliminary Survey." *Journal of Cuneiform Studies* 20:73–88.

Borger, R. 1997–1998. "Wolfram von Soden (Obituary)." *Archiv für Orientforschung* 44–45:588–94.

Breuer, S. 2010. "Der Streit um den 'nordischen Gedanken' in der völkischen Bewegung." *Zeitschrift für Religions und Geistesgeschichte* 62:1–27.

Calder, W. M., III, and A. Demandt, eds. 1990. *Eduard Meyer. Leben und Leistung eines Universalhistorikers*. Mnemosyne Supplementa 112. Leiden: Brill.

Chamberlain, H. S. 1899. *Die Grundlagen des neunzehnten Jahrhunderts*. Munich: Bruckmann.

———. 1913. *Foundations of the Nineteenth Century*. London: John Lane.

Cooper, J. S. 2016. "Sumerian Literature and Sumerian Identity." Pages 1–18 in *Problems of Canonicity and Identity Formation in Ancient Egypt and Mesopotamia*. CNI Publications 43. Edited by K. Ryholt and G. Barjamovic. Copenhagen: Museum Tusculanum Press.

Deglau, C., P. Reinard, and K. Ruffing, eds. *Klio und die Nationalsozialisten. Gesammelte Schriften zur Wissenschafts- und Rezeptionsgeschichte*. Philippika 106. Wiesbaden: Harrassowitz.

Farrenkopf, J. 2001. *Prophet of Decline: Spengler on World History and Politics*. Louisiana: LSU Press.

Fink, S. 2014. "Oswald Spengler, Atlantis und der Plan eines 'Atlas antiquus.'" *Orbis Terrarum. Internationale Zeitschrift für historische Geographie der Alten Welt* 12:77–86.

———. 2015. *Benjamin Whorf, die Sumerer und der Einfluss der Sprache auf das Denken*. Philippika 70. Wiesbaden: Harrassowitz.

———. 2019. "The Neo-Assyrian Empire and the History of Science: Western Terminology and Ancient Near Eastern Sources." Pages 91–108 in *Writing Neo-Assyrian History: Sources, Problems and Approaches*. State Archives of Assyria Studies 29. Edited by G. B. Lanfranchi, R. Mattila, and R. Rollinger. Helsinki: University of Helsinki.

Fink, S., and R. Rollinger, eds. 2018. *Oswald Spenglers Kulturmorphologie. Eine multiperspektivische Annäherung*. Wiesbaden: Springer.

Flygare, J. 2005. "Assyriologi under nazismen: En kontekstuel undersøgelse af tre tekster af Wolfram von Soden fra 1936–38." PhD diss., University of Copenhagen (http://www.opgavebank.dk/opgaver/793.pdf).

———. 2006. "Assyriology under Nazism: A Contextual Analysis of Three Texts by Wolfram von Soden from 1936–38." *Journal of Associated Graduates in Near Eastern Studies* 11:3–42.

Gasche, M. 2014. *Der "Germanische Wissenschaftseinsatz" des "Ahnenerbes" der SS 1942–1945*. Studien zur Archäologie Europas 20. Bonn: Habelt.

Gauger, J.-D. 2007. "Hans-Erich Stier (1902–1997)—Althistoriker, Mitgründer der CDU, Kulturpolitiker." *Archiv für Christlich-Demokratische Politik* 14:187–212.

Güterbock, H. G. 1968–1969. "Benno Landsberger (Obituary)." *Archiv für Orientforschung* 22:203–06.

Hilgert, M. 2009. "Of 'Listenwissenschaft' and 'Epistemic Things': Conceptual Approaches to Ancient Mesopotamian Epistemic Practices." *Journal for General Philosophy of Science* 40:277–309.

Humboldt, W. von. 1998. *Über die Verschiedenheit des menschlichen Sprachbaues*. Paderborn: Ferdinand Schöningh.

Hutton, C. M. 1999. *Linguistics and the Third Reich: Mother-tongue Fascism, Race and the Science of Language*. London: Routledge.

Jones, T., ed. 1969. *The Sumerian Problem*. New York: John Wiley & Sons.

42   Sebastian Fink

Kainz, F. 1972. *Über die Sprachverführung des Denkens*. Erfahrung und Denken: Schriften zur Förderung der Beziehungen zwischen Philosophie und Einzelwissenschaften 38. Berlin: Humblodt.

Koktanek, M. 1968. *Oswald Spengler in seiner Zeit*. Munich: Beck.

Kraus, F. R. 1970. *Sumerer und Akkader, ein Problem der altmesopotamischen Geschichte*. Amsterdam: North Holland Publishing.

Landsberger, B. 1926. "Die Eigenbegrifflichkeit der babylonischen Welt." *Islamica* 2:355–72.

———. 1931. "Heinrich Zimmern (Obituary)." *Zeitschrift für Assyriologie* 40:133–43.

———. 1976. *The Conceptual Autonomy of the Babylonian World*. Sources and Monographs on the Ancient Near East 1/4. Translated by T. Jacobsen, B. Foster, and H. von Siebenthal. Malibu: Undena Publications.

Landsberger, B., and W. von Soden. 1965. *Die Eigenbegrifflichkeit der babylonischen Welt/ Sumerische und babylonische Wissenschaft*. Darmstadt: Wissenschaftliche Buchgesellschaft.

Leitner, I. M. 2010 "'Bis an die Grenzen des Möglichen': Der Dekan Viktor Christian und seine Handlungsspielräume an der Philosophischen Fakultät 1938–1943." Pages 49–78 in *Geisteswissenschaften im Nationalsozialismus*. Edited by M. G. Ash, W. Nieß, and R. Pils. Göttingen: Vandenhoeck and Ruprecht.

Leo, P. 2013. *Der Wille zum Wesen. Weltanschauungskultur, charakterologisches Denken und Judenfeindschaft in Deutschland 1890–1940*. Berlin: Matthes & Seitz.

Liverani, M. 1998. "L'immagine dei Fenici nella storiografia occidentale." *Studi Storici* 39:6–22.

Lobenstein-Reichmann, A., and H. S. Chamberlain. 2008. *Zur textlichen Konstruktion einer Weltanschauung*. Studia Linguistica Germanica 95. Berlin: de Gruyter.

Losemann, V. 1977. *Nationalsozialismus und Antike. Studien zur Entwicklung des Faches Alte Geschichte 1933–1945*. Hamburg: Hoffmann und Kampe.

Michalowski, P. 2007. "The Lives of the Sumerian Language." Pages 163–88 in *Margins of Writing, Origins of Culture*. Oriental Institute Seminars 2. Edited by S. Sanders. Chicago: Oriental Institute.

Oelsner, J. 2006. "Der Altorientalist Benno Landsberger (1890–1968): Wissenschaftstransfer Leipzig–Chicago via Ankara." Pages 269–85 in *Bausteine einer jüdischen Geschichte der Universität Leipzig*. Edited by S. Wendehorst. Leipzig: Universitätsverlag.

Pingree, D. 1992. "Hellenophilia versus the History of Science." *Isis* 83:554–63.

Pesditschek, M. 2009. *Barbar, Kreter, Arier. Leben und Werk des Althistorikers Fritz Schachermeyr*. Saarbrücken: Südwestdeutscher Verlag für Hochschulschriften.

Pöhl, F. 2018. "Oswald Spenglers Rassebegriff im Kontext seiner Zeit: Boas, Chamberlain, Lenz, Rosenberg, Sombart." Pages 643–74 in *Oswald Spenglers Kulturmorphologie. Eine multiperspektivische Annäherung*. Studies in Universal and Cultural History 1. Edited by S. Fink and R. Rollinger. Wiesbaden: Springer.

Pöhl, F., and B. Tilg, eds. 2011. *Franz Boas—Kultur, Sprache, Rasse. Wege einer antirassistischen Anthropologie*. 2nd ed. Ethnologie: Forschung und Wissenschaft 19. Berlin: LIT.

Porzig, W. 1923. "Der Begriff der inneren Sprachform." *Indogermanische Forschungen* 41:150–69.

Rebenich, S. 2013. *C. H. Beck 1763–2013: Der kulturwissenchaftliche Verlag und seine Geschichte*. Munich: C. H. Beck.

Renger, J. 2008. "Altorientalistik." Pages 469–502 in *Kulturwissenschaft und Nationalsozialismus*. Edited by J. Elvert and J. Nielsen-Sikora. Stuttgart: Franz Steiner.

Rochberg, F. 2002. "A Consideration of Babylonian Astronomy within the Historiography of Science." *Studies in History and Philosophy of Science* 33:661–84.

Röllig, W. 1997. "Wolfram von Soden (Obituary)." *Die Welt des Orients* 28:5–6.

Rubio, G. 1999. "On the Alleged 'Pre-Sumerian Substratum.'" *Journal of Cuneiform Studies* 51:1–16.

———. 2016. "The Inventions of Sumerian: Literature and the Artifacts of Identity." Pages 231–57 in *Problems of Canonicity and Identity Formation in Ancient Egypt and*

Mesopotamia. CNI Publication 43. Edited by K. Ryholt and G. Barjamovic. Copenhagen: Museum Tusculanum.

Sallaberger, W. 2007. "Benno Landsbergers 'Eigenbegrifflichkeit' in wissenschaftsgeschichtlicher Perspektive." Pages 63–82 in *Das geistige Erfassen der Welt im Alten Orient*. Edited by C. Wilcke. Wiesbaden: Harrassowitz.

Simon, G. 1986. *Wissenschaft und Wende 1933. Zum Verhältniss von Wissenschaft und Politik am Beispiel des Sprachwissenschaftlers Georg Schmidt-Rohr*. https://homepages.uni-tuebingen.de/gerd.simon/wende1933.pdf (accessed 22 August 2017).

———. 2017. *Muttersprache und Menschenverfolgung*. https://homepages.uni-tuebingen.de/gerd.simon/muttersprache1.pdf (accessed 22 August 2017).

Soden, W. von. 1936. "Leistung und Grenze sumerischer und babylonischer Wissenschaft." *Die Welt als Geschichte* 2:411–64, 509–57. Reprinted in B. Landsberger and W. von Soden, *Die Eigenbegrifflichkeit der babylonischen Welt/Sumerische und babylonische Wissenschaft*. Darmstadt: Wissenschaftliche Buchgesellschaft, 1965, 21–123).

———. 1937. *Der Aufstieg des Assyrerreichs als geschichtliches Problem*. Der Alte Orient 37/1–2. Leipzig: Hinrichs.

———. 1938. "Neue Untersuchungen über die Bedeutung der Indogermanen für den Alten Orient." *Göttingische Gelehrte Anzeigen* 200:195–216

———. 1960. *Zweisprachigkeit in der geistigen Kultur Babyloniens*. Sitzungsberichte der Österreichische Akademie der Wissenschaften, Philosophisch-Historische Klasse 235, 1. Abhandlung. Vienna: H. Böhlaus Nachf.

———. 1973. "Sprache, Denken und Begriffsbildung im Alten Orient." *Akademie der Wissenschaften und der Literatur, Mainz, Abhandlung der geistes- und sozialwissenschaftlichen Klasse* 6:5–41.

Spengler, O. 1926/1928. *The Decline of the West*. New York: Alfred A. Knopf.

Streck M. P. 2003. "Sprache und Denken im Alten Mesopotamien am Beispiel des Zeitausdrucks." Pages 424–31 in *Festschrift Alexander Yu. Militarev*. Studia Semitica 3. Edited by L. Kogan. Moskow: Russian State University for the Humanities.

Trimborn, H. 1936. "Spengler contra Keramik." *Anthropos* 31:935–37.

Vidal, J. 2013. "Nazismo, Egiptología y Asiriología." *Historiae* 10:131–39.

CHAPTER 3

Assyriology in Nazi Germany:
The Case of Wolfram von Soden

Jakob Flygare

Assyriology in Nazi Germany

Studies of the past can serve the needs of the present: by representing an identity in the past, it can be imported to construct an identity in the present and projected to visions of the future. An extreme example of this is the deformed scholarship produced in Nazi Germany. An example from the field of Assyriology is provided by three texts written between 1936 and 1938 by Wolfram von Soden. The texts reflect the idea in Nazi ideology of "the superiority of the Nordic race" and their purpose is to provide it with a scholarly basis by studying the ancient Near East.

The Nazi regime in Germany from 1933 to 1945 caused great damage to German Assyriology. After the Nazis seized power in 1933 Jews and political opponents were removed from German universities, the number of teachers was reduced heavily, institutes, libraries, and research materials were destroyed, international contacts were cut off, access to sources was blocked, and many Assyriologists were killed during World War II.

After the war, the German Assyriologist Adam Falkenstein wrote:

> Die schweren personellen Verluste nach 1933 haben sie stärker als andere Fächer betroffen. Die Feindselichkeit der damaligen "Kulturpolitik" gegenüber der Orientalistik und ihre Folgen, die Lücken, die der Krieg besonders in den Reihen des wissenschaftlichen Nachwuchses schlug, die Zerstörung vieler Seminar- und Universitätsbibliotheken ... bestimmten die Jahre seit der Wiedereröffnung der westdeutschen Universitäten.[1]

The 12 years of the Third Reich had a significant impact on Assyriology and its practitioners. Benno Landsberger may serve as an example of an Assyriologist who was forced to leave Nazi Germany because he was Jewish.

In 1933, only two months after Adolf Hitler seized power, the Nazi regime passed the *Gesetz zur Wiederherstellung des Berufsbeamtentums*. It forced civil servants of "non-Aryan descent" to leave their civil positions. However, Landsberger, who at that time was a professor at the University of Leipzig, was not expelled. This was because President Paul von Hindenburg added an amendment to the law that excluded veterans who had served at the front during World War I from expulsion. However, the

---

1. Falkenstein 1960, 2.

44

following year Hindenburg died and Landsberger was expelled from the University of Leipzig in April 1935.[2] Landsberger accepted a professorship at the new University of Ankara and immigrated to Turkey, which was inviting Nazi-persecuted intellectuals as part of Kemal Atatürk's modernization efforts. In 1945 Landsberger was appointed to the Oriental Institute of Chicago, which became an important center for Assyriology.

The German universities were subjected to the unification of the Nazi Party and the German state, which began in 1934 after the death of Hindenburg. The universities lost their autonomy, pro-Nazis were placed in central positions, and opponents were removed. Nazism became a way for opportunists to advance their careers by becoming members of the Nazi Party or one of its organizations such as the SA, but also by subjecting their research and teaching to Nazi ideology.

Wolfram von Soden was one of Landsberger's students. Like many other scholars who stayed in Germany during the Nazi regime his research reflected Nazi ideology. Von Soden joined the SA in 1934 and the Nazi Party in 1937.[3] He advanced his career quickly. In 1934 he was elected reader at the University of Göttingen, which was heavily infected by the Nazis.[4] In 1936 von Soden was appointed Extraordinary Professor at the university at the age of 28.

Von Soden wrote three papers during the Nazi era, which clearly reflect a belief in "the superiority of the Nordic race."

The three texts by von Soden investigated in this paper are:

1. "Leistung und Grenze sumerischer und babylonischer Wissenschaft" (1936)
2. *Der Aufstieg des Assyrerreichs als geschichtliches Problem* (1937)
3. "Neue Untersuchungen über die Bedeutung der Indogermanen für den Alten Orient" (1938).

These three texts have been chosen because they reflect Nazi ideology. Von Soden has been chosen because his reputation within Assyriology was damaged a great deal because of his Nazi past. Also, von Soden was an eminent Assyriologist, which makes him an interesting subject.

2. Landsberger was expelled from the University of Leipzig by order of Martin Mutschmann, Prime Minister of Saxonia and district leader of the Nazi Party. Several professors, including Werner Heisenberg, Nobel Prize winner in Physics in 1932, protested unsuccessfully before the dean against Landsberger's dismissal. Furthermore, the expulsion by Mutschmann was regarded by Bernhard Rust, Minister of Science, Education and National Culture, as an infringement of his jurisdiction; it was only later that year that the *Reichbürgergesetz* of the Nuremberg racial laws was passed and the *Frontkampfprivileg* was cancelled. Rust appealed to Hitler in order to rescind Mutschmann's action, but Hitler upheld Mutschmann's decision (Renger 2008, 475).

3. Borger 1997–1998, 589 claims that von Soden first joined the Nazi Party in 1944. However, it can be seen from several sources at the Bundesarchiv in Berlin that von Soden joined the Nazi Party in 1937. See also Renger 2008, 481, who similarly states that von Soden joined the Nazi Party in 1937 and not in 1944. The application to the Nazi Party (R 9361 VII-KARTEI) and the Nazi Party membership card (R 9361 IX-KARTEI) are reproduced in this article as fig. 3.1 and fig. 3.2. An assessment of von Soden from 1939 states, "Professor Dr. von Soden ist Parteigenosse seit dem 1.5.1937 unter der Mitgl.Nr.4 238 289, ausserdem ist er Angehöriger der SA. und Mitglied der NSV. und des NS.-Dozentenbundes. Er ist regelmässiger Besucher von Parteiveranstaltungen und kommt auch seinen Verpflictungen bei Sammlungen gern und seinen Verhältnissen entsprechend nach. Sein allgemeiner Leumund ist gut. Die politische Zuverlässigkeit wird seitens der Kreisleitung Göttingen bejaht" (VBS1-1110062678).

4. Becker et al. 1987.

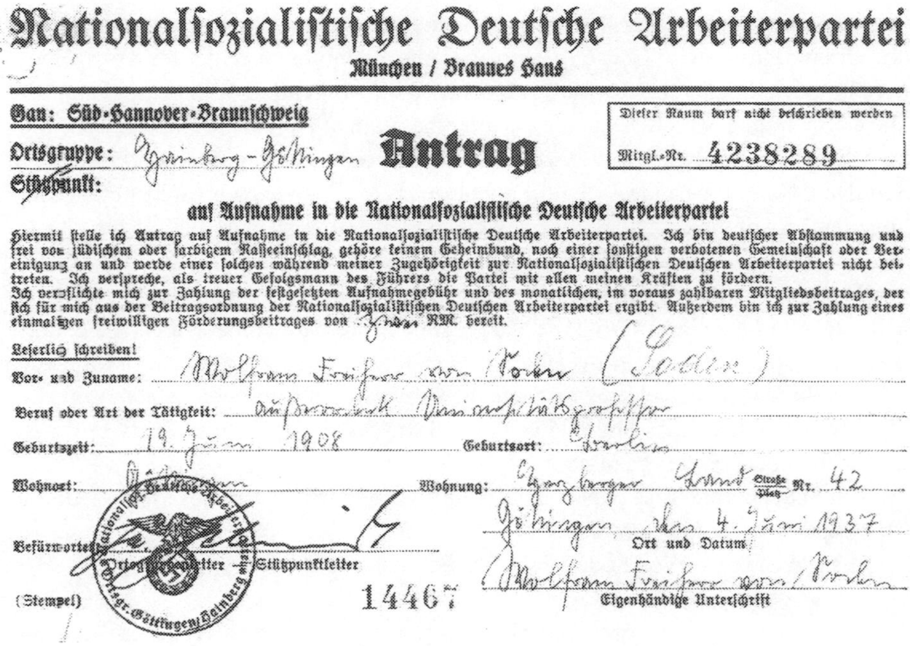

Nationalsozialistische Deutsche Arbeiterpartei
München / Braunes Haus

Gau: Süd-Hannover-Braunschweig

Dieser Raum darf nicht beschrieben werden
Mitgl.-Nr. 4238289

Ortsgruppe: Hainberg-Göttingen
Stützpunkt:

Antrag

auf Aufnahme in die Nationalsozialistische Deutsche Arbeiterpartei

Hiermit stelle ich Antrag auf Aufnahme in die Nationalsozialistische Deutsche Arbeiterpartei. Ich bin deutscher Abstammung und frei von jüdischem oder farbigem Rasseeinschlag, gehöre keinem Geheimbund, noch einer sonstigen verbotenen Gemeinschaft oder Vereinigung an und werde einer solchen während meiner Zugehörigkeit zur Nationalsozialistischen Deutschen Arbeiterpartei nicht beitreten. Ich verspreche, als treuer Gefolgsmann des Führers die Partei mit allen meinen Kräften zu fördern.
Ich verpflichte mich zur Zahlung der festgesetzten Aufnahmegebühr und des monatlichen, im voraus zahlbaren Mitgliedsbeitrages, der sich für mich aus der Beitragsordnung der Nationalsozialistischen Deutschen Arbeiterpartei ergibt. Außerdem bin ich zur Zahlung eines einmaligen freiwilligen Förderungsbeitrages von zehn RM. bereit.

Leserlich schreiben!

Vor- und Zuname: Wolfram Freiherr von Soden (Soden)

Beruf oder Art der Tätigkeit: außerordentl. Universitätsprofessor

Geburtszeit: 19. Juni 1908 Geburtsort: Berlin

Wohnort: Göttingen Wohnung: Herzberger Land Straße Nr. 42

Göttingen, den 4. Juni 1937
Ort und Datum

Befürwortet:
Ortsgruppenleiter — Stützpunktleiter

(Stempel) 14467

Wolfram Freiherr von Soden
Eigenhändige Unterschrift

FIGURE 3.1. Application to the Nazi Party (R 9361 VII-KARTEI)

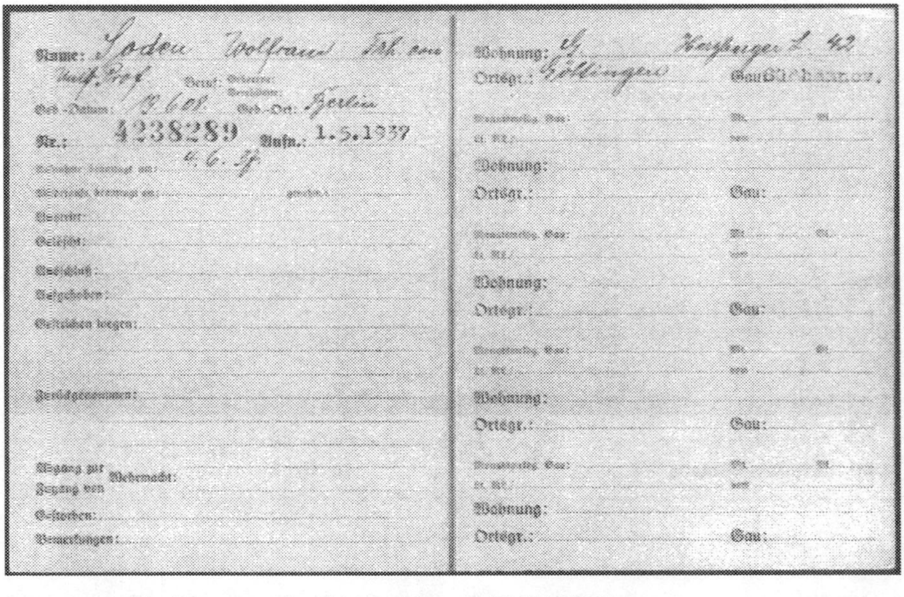

Name: Soden Wolfram Frh. von
Univ. Prof. Beruf:
Geb.-Datum: 19.6.08 Geb.-Ort: Berlin
Nr.: 4238289 Aufn.: 1.5.1937
4.6.37

Wohnung: G. Herzberger L. 42
Ortsgr.: Göttingen Gau Süd-Hannov.

Wohnung:
Ortsgr.: Gau:
Wohnung:
Ortsgr.: Gau:
Wohnung:
Ortsgr.: Gau:
Wohnung:
Ortsgr.: Gau:

Gestrichen wegen:
Zurückgenommen:
Abgang zur Wehrmacht:
Zugang von
Gestorben:
Bemerkungen:

FIGURE 3.2. Nazi Party membership card (R 9361 IX-KARTEI)

"Leistung und Grenze sumerischer und babylonischer Wissenschaft" (1936)

"Leistung und Grenze sumerischer und babylonischer Wissenschaft" (1936) addresses the question of whether or not the Sumerians, and later the Babylonians, had a science in "our" sense of the word. After a long investigation, von Soden dismisses it. Instead, he concludes that "our" science is a creation of "the Nordic race": "daß Wissenschaft im strengen Sinn des Wortes etwas ist, das nur von den durch die nordische Rasse bestimmten Indogermanen geschaffen werden konnte."[5]

According to *Ex septentrione lux* (i.e., "Light from the North"), which dominated much of German historiography at that time, the blond and blue-eyed Northerners were the "racially purest form of the Aryans" because they had remained in their northern primeval abode from which "the light of civilization" was thought to have spread. This kind of thinking was instrumental to Nazism because it served as an argument for racial imperialism. When von Soden claims that "our" science (i.e., the science of "the Nordic race") is the only real science, he simply repeats this racial ideological belief and disguises it as a scholarly deduction.

Furthermore, von Soden places the roots of "our" science in ancient Greece. This claim reflects a modern ethnocentric origin myth that misrepresents ancient Greece as the origin of an exclusively "Aryan/Western" phenomenon, which appeared after the invasion of "Aryans" from the north. This "aryanization" is claimed to have caused a "Greek miracle," which brought something completely new into the world (e.g., philosophy, democracy, freedom) and thereby separating "us" ("the Aryans") from "them/ the Other" ("the Semites").

Martin Bernal distinguishes two types of models for representing the origins of ancient Greece:[6] the "Ancient Model," which dominated until about 1800, and the "Aryan Model," which became dominant after the Greek War of Independence from the Ottomans in the 1820s. The difference between the two models is that the former, *Ex oriente lux* (i.e., "Light from the East"), places the cultural roots of ancient Greece in the ancient Near East, whereas the latter, *Ex nihilo* (i.e., "From nothing"), separates the cultural roots of ancient Greece from the ancient Near East by making its origins autochthonous. Von Soden's conclusion is bound to be given in advance because the premise of his study is the "Aryan Model."[7]

Von Soden presents a historiographic demarcation of "our" science by placing its roots of origin in "Aryan Greece." Furthermore, he separates it from non-sciences and from pre-science: The Egyptian, Sumerian, and Babylonian sciences are claimed

---

5. Von Soden 1936, 556.

6. Bernal 1997.

7. There is no need to consider the second of Bernal's theses, which is much more political and problematic. It has rightly been criticized for being too Afrocentric, because it tries to move the origins of the West from ancient Greece to ancient Egypt. Bernal's "Ancient Model" represents ancient Egypt as European proto-history, and Liverani (1996, 425) has therefore correctly pointed out that both models are Eurocentric: "Both models, *Ex oriente lux* (adopted by Bernal) and "The Greek Miracle" (refused by Bernal) are Eurocentric: the first model only values Oriental (Near Eastern) cultures for their perceived contribution to Western civilization; the second suggests that civilization began positively to evolve only with the intervention of Western people, who either modified and appropriated or dismissed Oriental contributions."

48 Jakob Flygare

to be non-sciences[8] because of the lack of "Aryan" influence. Indian science is claimed to have reached an initial state in ancient India due to "Aryans," but not to have advanced beyond this state due to the influence of "non-Aryans."[9] Similarly, von Soden claims that Arabic and Chinese sciences are the result of "Aryan" influence. In other words, von Soden sees the appearance of science throughout the world as the result of "Aryan" influence, whereas a lack or a low level of science is seen as the result of "non-Aryan" influence. This represents an Ariocentric hyperdiffusionism, which claims that all major cultural innovations are diffused from "superior Aryans."

"Leistung und Grenze sumerischer und babylonischer Wissenschaft" is described by von Soden as a contribution to the clarification of the historical foundations of "our" science. By "our" science he clearly means the Western scientific tradition, which he equates with "the science of the Aryan race." Furthermore, von Soden claims that his study shows the richness of this science by comparing it to other peoples' achievements: "die Einzigartigkeit unserer Wissenschaft erschließt sich uns erst dann in ihrem ganzen Reichtum, wenn wir auch die Leistungen anderer Völker restlos ernst nehmen und uns auch keine Mühe verdrießen lassen, ihre Eigengesetzlichkeiten immer besser zu erfassen."[10] According to von Soden the *raison d'être* for the study of Mesopotamian science was that it could assist in the self-revelation of "Aryan science" by relating it to an "Other." Hereby, von Soden based his study on a binary us/them division of "our Aryan science" and "their non-Aryan non-science," which predetermined the study's conclusion.

The utility of von Soden's conclusion for Nazi ideology can be seen by its incorporation into *Kriegseinsatz der Deutschen Geisteswissenschaft* (also known as *Aktion Ritterbusch*). This program served from 1940 to 1945 with the purpose of scientifically proving German "superiority" and hence "natural domination." As part of the program various orientalists met in Berlin from 30 September to 3 October 1942.[11] The meeting was headed by the Indologist Walther Wüst who joined the Nazi Party in 1933 and the SS in 1936. In 1937 he became the head of Heinrich Himmler's *Ahnenerbe*. In fact, Wüst thanked Himmler in the closing speech for allowing him to show the notorious SS film *Geheimnis Tibet*.

The Indologist Erich Frauwallner participated in the meeting. He had become a member of the Nazi Party in 1932 and his contribution "Die Bedeutung der indischen Philosophie"[12] served to support the purpose of *Aktion Ritterbusch*. Frauwallner concluded that philosophy was a specific "Aryan" creation. Sheldon Pollock made an interesting comment on Frauwallner's contribution:

> What interests me particularly in this scholarly convention of orientalists contributing to the mission of empire is the contribution of Erich Frauwallner,

---

8. Von Soden places the word science in quotation marks when referring to what he believes to be a non-science.

9. "Fragen wir auch hier wieder nach dem Grund dieser Erscheinung, so denken wir sofort an die nahe sprachliche und rassische Verwandtschaft, die die arischen Inder mit uns und den Griechen verbindet" (von Soden 1936, 555–56). "Daß uns trotz aller Verwandtschaft von Indien eine weit tiefere Kluft trennt als von Griechenland, darf gewiß als Folge des außerordentlich starken Einflusses der nichtarischen Inder auf die Kultur Indiens werden" (von Soden 1936, 556 n. 85).

10. Von Soden 1965, 556–57.

11. For the *Kriegseinsatz der Deutschen Geisteswissenschaft* in general, see Hausmann 1998.

12. Schaeder 1944, 158–69.

Professor of Sanskrit at the University of Vienna, who is widely regarded as the preeminent authority on Indian philosophy of his generation (and member of the National Socialist German Workers Party [NSDAP] since 1932, when the party was still illegal in Austria). In his presentation, Frauwallner argued that the special meaning of Indian philosophy lay in its being "a typical creation of an Aryan people," that its similarities with Western philosophy derived from "the same racially determined talent," and that it was a principal scholarly task of Indology to demonstrate this fact.[13]

Frauwallner's and von Soden's studies are governed by the same Ariocentric ideology, for which they try to provide a scholarly basis. Frauwallner adds to his conclusion that the advanced state of not only Indian philosophy but also Indian science can only be explained by an "Aryan factor."

> Reiterating an axiom of NS doctrine, that "Wissenschaft in the strict sense of the word is something that could be created only by nordic Indo-Germans," Frauwallner adds, "From the agreement in scientific character of Indian and European philosophy, we can draw the further conclusion that philosophy as an attempt to explain the world according to scientific method is likewise a typical creation of the Aryan mind." ... Indian knowledge, again, is meaningful to the degree that it assists in the self-revelation of "Aryan" identity. The very raison d'être of Indology for Frauwallner, as it seems to have been for so many scholars of the period, is fundamentally conditioned by this racialism. The ideology of objective "science," moreover, not only governs Frauwallner's presentation; his whole purpose is to demonstrate that this science exists in a realm beyond ideology—that it is a fact of biology. What alone enables him to do this, I think, is "orientalist" knowledge production.[14]

To both von Soden and Frauwallner the purpose of Assyriology and Indology, respectively, is to contribute to the creation of an "Aryan" identity. Frauwallner presented von Soden's investigation as an example of a similar conclusion:

> Vor wenigen Jahren hat W. v. Soden im zweiten Jahrgang der Zeitschrift "Die Welt als Geschichte" einer beachtenswerte Arbeit über "Leistung und Grenze sumerischer und babylonischer Wissenschaft" veröffentlicht, in der er den Charakter der sumerischen und babylonischen Wissenschaft genauer zu bestimmen sucht und schließlich zu der Folgerung kommt, "daß Wissenschaft im strengen Sinn des Wortes etwas ist, das nur von den durch die nordische Rasse bestimmten Indogermanen geschafen werden konnte" (S. 556). Wir können dieser Behauptung auf Grund unserer bisherigen Betrachtungen beistimmen.[15]

Von Soden's conclusion fit the purpose of the meeting and of *Aktion Ritterbusch* very well: von Soden's work allegedly provided evidence for "Aryan superiority" within

13. Pollock 2000, 93.
14. Pollock 2000, 93–94.
15. Schaeder 1944, 168.

50   Jakob Flygare

the field of science, just as Frauwallner's work allegedly provided evidence for "Aryan superiority" within the field of philosophy. Both served to create "an Aryan identity" in the present by representing it in the past.

The introduction and the conclusion of "Leistung und Grenze sumerischer und babylonischer Wissenschaft" (1936) are clearly biased by Ariocentrism; these parts of the text have no scholarly value, except as an example of how self-defined "racial groups" can construct an "Other." However, the main part presents a comprehensive overview of the Mesopotamian lexical tradition, which, despite new information and advances in our understanding, has scholarly value even today. As such, it is the most valuable of the three texts under consideration.

It was reprinted in 1965. However, the conclusion was altered: "daß Wissenschaft im strengen Sinn des Wortes nur unter den bei den indogermanischen Griechen und Indern gegebenen besonderen Voraussetzungen Gestalt gewinnen konnte."[16] The conclusion was no longer that science was the creation of the Indo-Germans of the "Nordic race," but by Indo-Germanic Greeks and Indians. This meant that *Ex septentrione lux*, which is commonly associated with the Nazis, was removed.

"Leistung und Grenze sumerischer und babylonischer Wissenschaft" was reprinted together with Landsberger's "Die Eigenbegrifflichkeit der babylonischen Welt" (1926), which clearly inspired von Soden. Landsberger was influenced by Wilhelm von Humboldt and romantic hermeneutics, and he stated in "Die Eigenbegrifflichkeit der babylonischen Welt" that the cognitive abilities of different people were determined by its *Sprachgeist*. This idea is also present in "Leistung und Grenze sumerischer und babylonischer Wissenschaft," but to von Soden it was not only a question of *Sprachgeist* but of biology.[17]

The anti-universalist idea of a plurality of sciences is based on the concept that an ethnic group has hereditary predispositions that completely determine its abilities and talents. Von Soden expresses this as "naturgegebenen Anlagen bestimmen sowohl das kulturelle Wollen wie das Können und seine Grenzen, wobei wir es gewiß als erweisen ansehen dürfen, daß auf die Dauer kein Volk leisten will, das es nach seinen Anlagen schlechthin nicht leisten kann."[18]

---

16. Von Soden 1965, 122.

17. The identification of language with race was criticized by Gordon Childe in *Is Prehistory Practical?* from 1933: "In the light of the foregoing summary, it should be easy to dispel the popular confusion between race and culture or race and language-a confusion involved for instance in the phrase 'Aryan race,' and in legislation using that expression" (Childe 1933, 416). Childe also criticized the nationalistic abuse of history in Nazi Germany: "In an official invitation received by the writer to the opening of a certain museum last June the organizers explained that they had gathered together a representative collection of prehistoric Teutonic art and industry and 'hoped thereby to establish that Germanic art was the highest art of all time.' In other words handmade clay-pots, rather poorly baked and incised, not painted, are to be exalted over Attic vases and Chinese porcelain; the barbaric carvings on a pirate galley must excel the sculptures of the Parthenon! That is hardly the verdict of scientific Prehistory. Objectively studied Prehistory will rather emphasize how much more precious and vital is the growth of the common tradition that leads up to civilization than the idiosyncrasies and divagations of any separate groups, however brilliant. To attempt to cut oneself or one's community off from this lifegiving tradition is to commit spiritual suicide. To admit as good only what is Celtic, or Germanic or Indian, as exclusive nationalism would demand, is unscientific and unhistorical" (Childe 1933, 418). See also Fink's article in this volume on the language–race connection in selected writings of Landsberger and von Soden.

18. Von Soden 1936, 552.

According to von Soden, the Akkadians had a particularly practical mind and strong perceptive abilities, the Sumerians had a particular "will to order"[19] which completely dominated their worldview, and "the Nordic race" of the Indo-Germanic (or "Aryan") group had such abilities and talent that it formed the basis for the appearance of science with logical conclusions, fundamental explanations, and regular definitions.

Der Aufstieg des Assyrerreichs als geschichtliches Problem *(1937)*

Der Aufstieg des Assyrerreichs als geschichtliches Problem (1937) presents an investigation of the reason for the rise and fall of the Assyrian Empire. This is an interesting research question, but the answer it presents is highly ideological. The text is far less scholarly than "Leistung und Grenze sumerischer und babylonischer Wissenschaft" (1936), and its only value to Assyriology today is as a warning against scholarship deformed by ideology.

In a review from 1939, William F. Albright writes:

> While the reviewer (see below) considers the racial philosophy of history as purely factitious, he cheerfully admits that one's cultural background has very profound influence on one's intellectual orientation. The well-known polarity of German intellectual activity, which combines sober, slightly pedestrian patience in research (whether philological or experimental) with a tendency to indulge in far-reaching speculations in a transmundane metaphysical sphere, is nowhere better illustrated than in the sharply defined, relatively insignificant field of Assyriology. German Assyriology has not only given us Delitzsch and Landsberger (both accidentally non-Aryan) but also Winckler and A. Jeremias (both accidentally Aryan). The reviewer earnestly hopes that the author remains in the first group and does not shift to the second (which is by no means restricted to members of the now extinct pan-Babylonian school). Certain tendencies in the present study make one hesitate to predict what will happen.[20]

In the first part of the investigation von Soden presents a racial history of the Assyrians. This leads him to conclude that at around 2000 BCE the Assyrians were mostly of the "Oriental-Semitic race."[21] However, he accredits the rise of the Assyrian Empire to "Aryan influences."

---

19. The idea that the Sumerians had a particular "will to order" gave rise the description of the Sumerian science as a *Listenwissenschaft*, which was used for a long time in Assyriology; i.e., the belief that Sumerian science was limited to the desire to classify and systematize the world in lists. Mogens Trolle Larsen commented that "the early studies of these lists by Landsberger and especially von Soden concluded that the lists must be seen as evidence of a very special Sumerian attitude towards the world, as explained by von Soden in a famous passage: 'Diese (Listen) erweisen sich dann als nur eine der vielen eigenartigen Schöpfungen des den Sumerern seit alters in ganz einzigartiger Weise eigenen **Ordnungswillens**, der alles, Sichtbares und Unsichtbares, in einer höheren Ordnung zusammenzufassen und zusammenzudenken sich bemüht.' It seems to me that the Sumerian 'will to order' is less unique than von Soden wants us to believe. Rather, it appears as an example of a general phenomenon which has been found in societies around the Globe" (Larsen 1987, 210).

20. Albright 1939, 120.

21. Albright (1939, 122) rightly notes: "to speak of the early Semites as 'sicher' belonging to an 'Oriental' race (pp. 13f.) is obviously a political act of faith, not a scholarly deduction."

52   Jakob Flygare

Von Soden's racialist view on history[22] resonates claims already presented at the turn of the nineteenth century, for example, by Friedrich Delitzsch:

> Delitzsch gave his lectures as a new ideological trend was gaining momentum: racism. Race-based thinking had already informed, in the later decades of the nineteenth century, a debate among scholars of the ancient Near East about the Semites and Sumerians, with anti-Semitic zealots generalizing about the cultural sterility of the Semitic Babylonians and Assyrians, who had taken over civilization—and most prominently, the art of writing—from the non-Semitic Sumerians. Delitzsch himself was not free of such prejudice; in fact, his anti-Semitism had an ever-increasing impact on his historical perception. To reconcile this resentment with his positive view of the Assyrian Empire, Delitzsch had to downplay the Semitic character of Assyrians and to claim that the Assyrian people had received significant Indo-European infusions. . . . Since Mesopotamian texts did not provide any evidence for an Indo-European background of the Assyrians, Delitzsch turned to the completely unfounded and rather desperate argument that Assurbanipal's wife was depicted, on a stone relief from Nineveh, with Aryan features and blond hair.[23]

At the time of von Soden's article, the ancient state of Mitanni had been discovered. Mitanni was frequently characterized as "Aryan Mitanni" in Nazi Germany due to the presence of *marjannu* (charioteers) who were thought to constitute an "Aryan" upper class of Mitanni.[24] Von Soden similarly characterized Mitanni as "Aryan": "eine sehr weitgehende Vermischung zwischen den Assyrern und den Churriern vorderasiatischer Rasse sowie in geringem Umfang wohl auch den arischen Mitanni."[25] Von Soden speculates that Mitanni's downfall provided the Assyrians with infusions of "Nordic blood": "Eine gewisse Auffrischung des von der Mitannizeit her in Assyrien noch in geringem Umfang wirksamen nordischen Blutes mag mit solchen Verpflanzungen

---

22. The belief in a racial conflict between the "Sumerian race" and the "Semitic race" is present in von Soden's text and was in fact long-lived in Assyriology; an example from 1910: "The early history of Sumer and Akkad is dominated by the racial conflict between Semites and Sumerians, in the course of which the latter were gradually worsted. The foundation of the Babylonian monarchy marks the close of the political career of the Sumerians as a race, although, as we have seen, their cultural achievements long survived them in later civilizations of Western Asia" (King 1910, ix). It was only in 1939 in the article "The Assumed Conflict Between Sumerians and Semites in Early Mesopotamian History," by Thorkild Jacobsen, that the belief in a racial conflict between Sumerians and Semites was rejected: "Semites and Sumerians lived thus, according to all the texts teach us, peacefully side by side in Mesopotamia. The wars which shook that country and the aims for which its rulers fought had nothing to do with differences of race; the issues were purely political and were determined solely by social and economic forces" (Jacobsen 1939, 495). Cf. Cooper 1991.

23. Frahm 2006, 83–84. This is arguably an overinterpretation which is based exclusively on Delitzsch's absurd statement about a drawing of Assurbanipal's queen: "augenscheinlich ist diese Gemahlin Sardanapals eine Prinzessin arischen Geblüts ist und blondhaarig zu denken" (1902, 19–20). Although this statement does leave space for imagination, Delitzsch neither states that the Assyrian people had received significant Indo-European infusions nor does he use the drawing as evidence thereof. The drawing referred to by Delitzsch was made by a German officer, Billerbeck, who visited the British Museum in 1867. In the drawing Billerbeck portrayed the queen as he imagined her based on the famous banquet scene of Assurbanipal. In 1902 Billebeck wrote to Delitzsch who reproduced both the scene and the drawing in *Babel und Bibel* (1902): "Auch ich kann mir die Dame nur blond denken" (Delitzsch 1905, 58).

24. Carena 1989, 124.

25. Von Soden 1937, 17.

natürlich gelegentlich verbunden gewesen sein."[26] In order to strengthen his case, von Soden claims that "Nordic blood" can also have found its way into Assyria due to the movement of people.

According to von Soden the infusion of "Nordic blood" created a racially new type of Assyrian that became the terror of the surrounding peoples for centuries: "Erst durch diese neue Rassenüberlagerung wurde der Typ des Assyrers geschaffen, wie er jahrhundertlang zum Schrecken der umwohnenden Völker wurde."[27] The rise of the Assyrian Empire is accredited by von Soden to the presence of "Nordic blood," which he thinks gave the Assyrians "an Aryan joy in battle." Von Soden believed he had found an example of this in the Middle Assyrian Epic of Tukulti-Ninurta I. This inference is rightly rejected by Albright: "the author's view that the joy in battle shown by the poem can only be explained by assuming Aryan influence is most extraordinary, and might lead to equally remarkable inferences with regard to the warlike zest exhibited by American Indians or tribes of Africa, to say nothing of medieval Turks and Mongolians. Would von Soden explain the warlike passages in the *mu'al-laqah* of 'Anraeah b. Shaddâd (sixth century A.D.) or the joy in combat shown monotonously often in the *sîrat 'Antar* (cir. thirteenth century A.D.) as due to Aryan infiltration?"[28]

Just as the reason for the rise of the Assyrian Empire, according to von Soden, was the infusion of "Nordic blood," the reason for the sudden fall of the Assyrian Empire, according to von Soden, is that the presence of "Nordic blood" had become exhausted, whereby the Assyrians are thought to have become more "Semitic," thus losing the idea of building an empire: "die ungeheuren Blutopfer der vielen Kriege und die rassische Zersetzung die Zahl derer, die aus dem Erleben der Idee heraus die Organisation des Staates mit Leben erfüllen konnten, immer kleiner wurde."[29]

The alleged mixing of races is thought by von Soden to have diluted the "racial power" of the Assyrian people who, according to him, became more and more "Semitic" and less and less "Aryan." This constitutes the internal reason for the fall of the Assyrian Empire. The external reason, according to von Soden, was that Babylonia had allied with the Medes to defeat Assyria. However, Sennacherib is applauded by von Soden for his destruction of Babylon. In 1945 Edith Porada made the following comment:

> Wolfram von Soden comments on the destruction of Babylon by Sennacherib in words which recall the vocabulary of the Ministry of Propaganda: "This feat has so far been unilaterally regarded as the destruction of irreparable cultural values and has been accordingly censured, but it constitutes, politically speaking, an incredibly courageous attempt not only to destroy an external enemy but also to counteract the interior disintegration of the empire which was being brought about by the Assyro-Babylonian cultural counterpoint." Further along in the article he suggests that warlike traits in the Assyrians which he greatly admires should be ascribed to Indo-Aryan racial influence.[30]

26. Von Soden 1937, 17.
27. Von Soden 1937, 40.
28. Albright 1939, 122–23.
29. Von Soden 1937, 38.
30. Porada 1945, 48.

54   Jakob Flygare

Von Soden's answer to the question about the reason for the rise and fall of the Assyrian empire can be subsumed as follows. Regarding the rise of the Assyrian Empire, Assyria changed from a Semitic mercantile society to a warlike empire because the "racial composition" of the Assyrians changed decisively from "Semitic" to "Nordic"; i.e., the rise of the Assyrian Empire was a result of the influx of "Nordic blood." Concerning the fall of the Assyrian Empire, the Assyrian Empire lost its military power and suddenly fell to comparatively weak opponents because the "racial composition" of the Assyrians changed decisively from "Nordic" to "Semitic;" i.e., the fall of the Assyrian Empire was a result of the loss of "Nordic blood."

The basic problem for von Soden clearly was that we are dealing with an empire whose population primarily spoke a Semitic language, and the subtext of von Soden's investigation is the binary opposition "Aryan" as warlike and active and "Semitic" as mercantile and passive. A shift between these two is claimed, by von Soden, to be the reason for the rise and the fall of the Assyrian Empire. Initially the mixing of races is claimed to have made the Assyrians stronger because it made them more "Aryan" and less "Semitic," but later it is thought to have weakened them because it made them more "Semitic" and less "Aryan."

The dichotomy "Aryan"/"Semitic" is projected by von Soden onto the representation of the relationship between Assyria and Babylonia, which he describes as "der Herrschaftswille Assyriens"[31] and "händlerischen Gewinnstrebens"[32] respectively.[33] Babylonia is given a crucial role in connection with the fall of the Assyrian Empire, because it is identified with "cultural degeneration" due to its alleged "Semiticness." In contrast, Mitanni is given a crucial role in connection with the rise of the Assyrian Empire, because it is identified with "cultural generation" due to its alleged "Aryanness."

Der Aufstieg des Assyrerreichs als geschichtliches Problem expounds the hyperdiffusionism of *Ex septentrione lux*, or "Nordic thinking," according to which the North was seen as the place of origin for the spread of civilization by "Nordic Aryans."

Furthermore, it constructs an "Aryan" identity in contrast to a "Semitic" identity. These elements in the text were in line with much of the historiography in Nazi Germany, which based its arguments on racial ideology and served to make Nazi ideology appear as rooted in science.

"Neue Untersuchungen über die Bedeutung der Indogermanen für den Alten Orient" (1938)

"Neue Untersuchungen über die Bedeutung der Indogermanen für den Alten Orient" (1938) is a review article of three studies of Indo-Germans: *Die Ruinen von Boğazköy, der Hauptstadt des Hethiterreiches* (1937) by Kurt Bittel, *Die ersten Arier im Alten Orient* (1938) by Hartmut Schmökel, and *Altindogermanisches Kulturgut in Nordmesopotamien* (1938) by Eckhard Unger. The stated purpose of the article is to attempt to

---

31. Von Soden 1937, 20.
32. Von Soden 1937, 42.
33. Von Soden repeats old stereotypes about the "Aryan"/"Semitic" polarity; *La France Juive* (1886) by Édouard Drumont offers an example: "the Semite, mercantile, greedy, devious and the Aryan, enthusiastic, heroic, chivalrous, disinterested, frank, trusting" (quoted in Cooper 1991, 52 n. 42).

evaluate the significance of the Indo-Germanic group for the ancient Near East with special reference to the pitfalls and perspectives of the topic.

Von Soden makes the observation that many such studies on Indo-Germans in the ancient Near East appeared at the time of writing, such as Hans F. K. Günther's *Die nordische Rasse bei den Indogermanen Asiens* (1934). Günther, or *Rassegünther* as he was also known, was one of the founders of Nazi racial ideology. In fact, the subject of von Soden's article is closely connected with the radical Ariocentricity in Nazi Germany, where the myth of a "glorious Aryan past" was dominant in studies of history, which thereby participated in the creation of a collective racial identity and "naturalized" the Nazis' ideology and expansionism.[34]

In the introduction to the article, von Soden claims that it is a scholarly duty to search for manifestations of the Indo-Germans, not only among the high cultures in Europe and India, but also outside these regions in order to widen and deepen the knowledge of "die Wurzeln unserer völkischen Art."[35] Ancient Near Eastern studies, according to von Soden, share this responsibility and should be concerned with the Indo-Germans in the ancient Near East accordingly.

This kind of self-fashioning enterprise is obviously biased, and von Soden warns that the Indo-Germans will now be ascribed all kinds of achievements without a sufficient scholarly basis. But even though he criticizes Eckhard Unger and Otto Reche for superficially jumping to conclusions,[36] he cannot himself escape the ideological basis that blinds his own research. Even though he could not find convincing evidence, he thought it was solely due to the poverty of the sources and only a matter of time before the significance of the "Nordic race" for the ancient Near East would be demonstrated.

Von Soden's critique of Unger led to a controversy between them. Unger joined the Nazi Party in 1932, wrote several articles on the swastika,[37] and criticized von Soden for his dependence on Landsberger because he was a Jew.[38] In a letter from 1939 to Unger, von Soden wrote that he felt it was necessary to respond to his publication *Altindogermanisches Kunstempfinden* (1939) because it offered an ideal opportunity for opponents of the Nazis to ridicule Nazi ideology and thereby harm Germany.

---

34. Carena (1989) presents various examples of representations of the ancient Near East that developed dangerously into the Indo-Germanic mania in Nazi Germany. Carena comments (1989, 122): "I do not think that I contravene historical common sense when affirming that the interest in the Hittites and the Hurrians would not have been so great if they had not been Indo-Germanic and if Indo-Germanism-Aryanism in the thirties and forties had not had more than enthusiastic supporters: and not only in the scientific field!"

35. Von Soden 1938, 195.

36. Reche's claim in *Rasse und Heimat der Indogermanen* (1936) that the upper class of the Sumerians and Akkadians were of "the Nordic race" is rejected by von Soden: "Bei einem Rassenkundler noch erstaunlicher ist die etwas primitive Art, wie aus dem Vorkommen von Langschädeln in sumerischen und akkadischen Gräbern ohne weiteres auf eine Oberschicht nordischer Rasse geschlossen wird, als ob Langschädel nur der nordischen Rasse eigneten" (von Soden 1938, 196–97). At the time craniometry was used as an archaeological method for the identification of different races, although it had already been denounced around 1900. Von Soden not only used the inference cranial shape indicates race, but also language indicates race, and material culture indicates race.

37. Unger 1935, 1936a, 1936b, and 1937.

38. The Nazi Assyriologst Carl Frank similarly criticized von Soden for unworthily depending on an east-Jewish translation proposition of the Akkadian word *kirimmu*. Frank did not mention Landsberger because he followed the Nazi practice not to cite Jews and, if necessary, then to add <Jd.> after the name in question. Von Soden did not follow this practice (Borger 1997–1998, 591).

56   Jakob Flygare

He felt it was necessary that another Nazi responded before a Jew or an Ultramontane could seize the opportunity:

> Die Formulierung dieser Schrift sollte und musste nämlich bei Nichtnationalsozialisten den Anschein einer Arbeit aus nationalsozialistischem Geist erwecken; sie bot damit allen Gegnern der Bewegung eine geradezu ideale Gelegenheit, das Gedankengut der Bewegung lächerlich zu machen und damit Deutschland zu schaden. Ehe nun ein Jude oder Ultramontaner diese Gelegenheit ergreifen konnte, musste eine öffentliche Antwort durch einen als Nationalsozialist auch im Ausland bekannten deutschen Forscher erfolgen; ich habe mich diese undankbare Aufgabe auf mich genommen und, wenn ich rechtsehe, damit auch wirklich der Gefahr die Spitze abgebrochen. In der neuen Anm. behaupten Sie nun, diese Abwehr sei im Geist meines früheren akademischen Lehrers B. Landsberger (durch Vermittlung der nationalsozialistischen Regierung seit 1935 in Ankara) erfolgt, also im Geist eines Juden. Eine Verteidigung gegen diese Behauptung habe ich nicht nötig. Wenn sie von einem ehrenhaften Deutschen ausgesprochen worden wäre, würde ich nicht zögern, die für einen ehrbewussten Deutschen einzig mögliche Antwort darauf zu geben, da es dann eine schwere Beleidigung wäre; bei Ihnen genügt die schärfste Zurückweisung dieser Anwurfes als bewusste Lüge und infame Ehrabschneidung. Zur Begründung dieser meiner Haltung Ihnen gegenüber noch ein paar Bemerkungen, die vor einer z.T. ausländischen Öffentlichkeit nicht gemacht werden konnten. Ihre von mir besprochene Schrift steht im Dienst der Reklame für den Ihnen befreundeten Max Freiherr von Oppenheim, also im Dienst eines allgemein als jüdischer Mischling bekannten Mannes.[39]

Von Soden chose to limit his investigation to the Indo-Germans among the Kassites, the Hurrians, and the Hittites. He admits that he is not able (1) to identify elements of "Aryan blood" among the Kassites, nor (2) to discern the specific Indo-German element from its mixture with the Hurrian people in Mitanni, nor (3) to trace a pure Indo-German people among the Hittites. Nonetheless, he still purports that the cultural and political achievements of the later states of the ancient Near East, especially Assyria, cannot be understood without referring to an Indo-German contribution: "die späteren nichtindogermanischen Staaten des Alten Orients, unter ihnen voran das Assyrerreich als der bei weitem bedeutsamste, sind in ihrer politischen und kulturellen Leistung nicht wirklich zu verstehen, ohne daß wir der aus der Hethiter- und Mitannizeit lebendig gebliebenen indogermanischen Antriebe gedenken."[40] The reason for the lack of evidence, according to von Soden, is that the "Aryans" became "racially mixed" and therefore lost their "racial identity": "Ob in der uns allein geschichtlich faßbaren späteren Zeit des Mitannireiches (nach 1500) die wenigen arischen Familien, die damals blutmäßig sicher nicht mehr ganz unvermischt geblieben waren, überhaupt noch das Bewußtsein hatten, etwas ganz anderes als die Churrier zu sein, erscheint nach dem bisherigen Quellenbefund mehr als fraglich."[41] This racialist idea of the decay of a

---

39. HU UA, UK Personalia U 016, Bd. 2, Bl. 51. Cf. Renger 2008, 491.
40. Von Soden 1938, 218.
41. Von Soden 1938, 203.

"superior race" due to mixture with an "inferior race" recalls the notorious chapter "Volk und Rasse" in Adolf Hitler's *Mein Kampf*. Also, it shows that the text reflects the context in which it was produced.

Contextual Reflections

Von Soden's three texts all clearly demonstrate how the racial ideology of "a superior Nordic race," or *Ex septentrione lux*, was reflected upon his perception of the ancient Near East and deformed his scholarship. The tension between scholarship and ideology becomes especially apparent in the third text. Here, von Soden, on the one hand, consistently insists on professionalism and a sufficient scholarly basis, while on the other hand his own scholarly character is subsumed by ideology.

The texts reflect the Nazi construction of an "Aryan" identity. Particular examples of the texts' reflexivity are speculations (1) about a separation of "inferior Assyrians" from "superior Aryans" in the Middle Assyrian Laws; (2) about a particularly "Aryan" faithfulness between leader and followers among the Hittites; and (3) about a particularly "Aryan joy in war" among the Assyrians. Von Soden's representations of "Aryans" in ancient Near Eastern history is an example of how historiography can be abused to import a constructed identity from the past into the present with visions for the future.

The "Aryan myth" underlines von Soden's three texts; i.e., the idea of "an Aryan master race" which is the bearer of civilization but loses its "racial power" due to the mixing of blood with "inferior races." Von Soden reproduced the themes of this myth in his Assyriological research. The "Aryan myth" was fundamental to Nazism, because it served as an origin myth that legitimized the Nazi regime and constructed a special "German-Aryan" racial identity with long spiritual roots far back into a distant mythical past (*Geisteswelt*). The important point to make is that not only did von Soden's texts reflect Nazi ideology, they also contributed to it.

The Monster from Münster

In 1940, active war duty prevented von Soden from becoming an ordinary professor at the University of Berlin. Von Soden participated in World War II, first in the infantry and later in the intelligence service. Here he served as a teacher for interpreters because of his knowledge of Arabic. However, this became less important when Germany suffered a devastating defeat in the desert at El Alamein in October 1942. Von Soden later served as a reserve lieutenant in the East.

After the war, von Soden was captured by the Russians, but he fled from a prisoner transport to Thüringen and surrendered to the Americans, who had captured that city in April 1945. When Thüringen was given in exchange for West Berlin in July 1945, he was transferred to the American occupation zone. In November 1945 he was released from war captivity.

Von Soden was dismissed from his position in Berlin due to his membership of the Nazi Party. Consequently, he left Berlin and went back to his home in Göttingen.

58   Jakob Flygare

On the way he went to Marburg, where it was not known if he had survived the war. He wanted to visit his parents but learned that his father had passed away one month earlier. Their relationship had suffered because his father criticized the regime and had therefore been expelled in 1934, whereas von Soden was enraptured by the Nazi regime and its ideology, joining the SA in 1934 and the Nazi Party in 1937.[42]

Von Soden lived in poverty after the war and received CARE packages from Albright, who had reviewed *Der Aufstieg des Assyrerreichs als geschichtliches Problem* in 1939 and expressed concern for what path he would choose. In September 1950 von Soden was allowed to take an unpaid position at the University of Göttingen, although a professorship had become vacant as early as 1949.

Landsberger recommended reinstating von Soden in 1952; he found it unworthy, unnatural, and detrimental to Assyriology that because of von Soden's politically uncritical past the most capable, the most knowledgeable, and the most productive Assyriologist had not been reinstated but left on the sideline.[43] In 1954 von Soden was reinstated as an extraordinary professor at the University of Vienna. He had by then published two of his most important works within the field of Assyriology: *Akkadisches Syllabar* (1948) and *Grundriß der akkadischen Grammatik* (1952).

In 1961 von Soden became a professor in Münster. He retired in 1976 and died in Münster in 1996 at the age of 88. He was called "the monster from Münster," an alliterative pun due to his massive stature.

Some colleagues saw von Soden as a terrible Nazi who you would not shake hands with and referenced his works without mentioning his name.[44] Two years before his death von Soden told a former student of his, Rykle Borger, that he had participated in a SA demonstration against a notary who had criticized the totalitarian regime.[45] Borger speculated that this episode had developed into the rumor that he participated in the pogroms in 1938. Also, he pointed out that von Soden's twenty-nine years of work on a dictionary is an exceedingly hard punishment.[46]

Von Soden was an eminent Assyriologist who contributed greatly to his field, particularly in lexicography and grammar. The three texts discussed here are interesting for the historiography of Assyriology as a reminder of scholars' reflexivity and as a warning against ideologically deformed scholarship.

REFERENCES

Albright, W. F. 1939. "Wolfram Freiherr von Soden. Der Aufstieg des Assyrerreichs als geschichtliches Problem." *Orientalia* 8:120–23.

Becker, H., et al., eds. 1987. *Die Universität Göttingen unter dem Nationalsozialismus: Das verdrängte Kapitel ihrer 250 jährigen Geschichte*. München: K. G. Saur.

Bernal, M. 1997. "The Image of Ancient Greece as a Tool for Colonialism and European Hegemony." Pages 119–28 in *Social Construction of the Past: Representation as Power*. Edited by G. C. Bond and A. Gilliam. London: Routledge.

42. Borger 1997–1998, 590.
43. Borger 1997–1998, 592.
44. Borger 1997–1998, 592–93.
45. Borger 1997–1998, 591.
46. Borger refers to *Akkadisches Handwörterbuch*, another important work in Assyriology by von Soden. It was published in installments from 1959 to 1981.

Bittel, K. 1937. *Die Ruinen von Boğazköy, der Hauptstadt des Hethiterreiches*. Berlin: de Gruyter.

Borger, R. 1997–1998. "Wolfram von Soden (19.6.1908–6.10.1996)." *Archiv für Orientforschung* 44–45:588–94.

Carena, O. 1989. *History of the Near Eastern Historiography and Its Problems: 1852–1985*. Alter Orient und Altes Testament 218/1. Neukirchen-Vluyn: Neukirchener.

Childe, V. G. 1933. "Is Prehistory Practical?" *Antiquity* 7(28):410–18.

Cooper, J. S. 1991. "Posing the Sumerian Question: Race and Scholarship in the Early History of Assyriology." *Aula Orientalis* 9:47–66.

Delitzsch, F. 1902. *Babel und Bibel. Ein Vortrag*. Leipzig: Hinrichs.

———. 1905. *Babel und Bibel. Erster Vortrag*. Leipzig: Hinrichs.

Drumont, E. 1886. *La France juive*. Paris: Flammarion.

Falkenstein, A., ed. 1960. *Denkschrift zur Lage der Orientalistik*. Wiesbaden: Franz Steiner.

Frahm, E. 2006. "Images of Assyria in Nineteenth- and Twentieth-century Western Scholarship." Pages 74–94 in *Orientalism, Assyriology and the Bible*. Edited by S. W. Holloway. Sheffield: Sheffield Phoenix.

Günther, H. F. K. 1934. *Die nordische Rasse bei den Indogermanen Asiens*. Munich: Lehmanns.

Hausmann, F.-R. 1998. *"Deutsche Geisteswissenschaft" im Zweiten Weltkrieg: Die "Aktion Ritterbusch" (1940–1945)*. Dresden: Dresden University Press.

Hitler, A. 1925. *Mein Kampf*. Munich: Verlag Franz Eher.

Jacobsen, T. 1939. "The Assumed Conflict Between Sumerians and Semites in Early Mesopotamian History." *Journal of the American Oriental Society* 59:485–95.

King, L. W. 1910. *A History of Sumer and Akkad*. London: Chatto & Windus.

Larsen, M. T. 1987. "The Babylonian Lukewarm Mind: Reflections on Science, Divination and Literacy." Pages 203–25 in *Language, Literature and History: Philological and Historical Studies Presented to Erica Reiner*. Edited by F. Rochberg-Halton. New Haven: American Oriental Society.

Liverani, M. 1996. "The Bathwater and the Baby." Pages 421–27 in *Black Athena Revisited*. Edited by M. R. Lefkowitz and G. M. Rogers. Chapel Hill: University of North Carolina Press.

Pollock, S. 2000. "Indology, Power, and the Case of Germany." Pages 302–23 in *Orientalism: A Reader*. Edited by A. L. Macfie. Edinburgh: Edinburgh University Press.

Porada, E. 1945. "The Assyrians in the Last Hundred Years." *The Metropolitan Museum of Art Bulletin* NS 4(1):38–48.

Reche, O. 1936. *Rasse und Heimat der Indogermanen*. Munich: Lehmanns.

Renger, J. 2008. "Altorientalistik." Pages 469–502 in *Kulturwissenschaften und Nationalsozialismus*. Edited by J. Elvert and J. Nielsen-Sikora. Stuttgart: Franz Steiner.

Schaeder, H. H., ed. 1944. *Der Orient in Deutscher Forschung. Vorträge der Berliner Orientalistentagung Herbst 1942*. Leipzig: Harrassowitz.

Schmökel, H. 1938. *Die ersten Arier im Alten Orient*. Leipzig: Rabitsch.

Soden, W. von. 1936. "Leistung und Grenze sumerischer und babylonischer Wissenschaft." *Die Welt als Geschichte* 2:411–64, 509–57.

———. 1937. *Der Aufstieg des Assyrerreichs als geschichtliches Problem*. Der Alte Orient 37/1–2. Leipzig: Hinrichs.

———. 1938. "Neue Untersuchungen über die Bedeutung der Indogermanen für den Alten Orient." *Göttingische Gelehrte Anzeigen* 200:195–216.

———. 1948. *Akkadisches Syllabar*. Rome: Pontificium Institutum Biblicum.

———. 1952. *Grundriß der akkadischen Grammatik*. Rome: Pontificium Institutum Biblicum.

———. 1959–1981. *Akkadisches Handwörterbuch*. Wiesbaden: Harrassowitz.

———. 1965. *Die Eigenbegrifflichkeit der babylonischen Welt/Sumerischer und babylonischer Wissenschaft*. Darmstadt: Wissenschaftliche Buchgesellschaft.

Unger, E. 1935. "Das sumerische Hakenkreuz als Wirbelsturm." *Forschungen und Fortschritte* 11:153–55.

60   Jakob Flygare

———. 1936. "Hakenkreuz und Thorshammer als Sturmsymbol des Wettergottes." *Forschungen und Fortschritte* 12:73–75.

———. 1936. "Zur Entwicklung des sumerischen Hakenkreuzsymbols." *Forschungen und Fortschritte* 12:153–55.

———. 1937. *Das antike Hakenkreuz als Wirbelsturm*. Berlin: Verlag Herbert Witting.

———. 1938. *Altindogermanisches Kulturgut in Nordmesopotamien*. Leipzig: Harrasowitz.

———. 1939. *Altindogermanisches Kunstempfinden*. Berlin: Witting.

CHAPTER 4

Carthage the Deceitful and Perfidious Albion: The Phoenicians and the British in Fascist Italy

Pietro Giammellaro

THE COMPARISON BETWEEN CARTHAGINIAN POWER and the British Empire has been a recurring *topos* in classical studies since the nineteenth century. The matter was first discussed by Mariella Cagnetta in her excellent book *Antichisti e impero fascista*, published in 1979.[1] However, the state-like features of this analogy in British, French, and German historiography have been studied more recently by Martin Bernal[2] and then by Luigi Loreto, Timoty Champion, and Corinne Bonnet.[3]

The focus of this paper is the British–Phoenician analogy in Italian historiography and propaganda during fascism. Italian studies have shown a peculiar position on this subject—there is a common identification of modern Italy with the ancient Roman Empire. This ideological exploitation would justify fascist colonial ambitions around the Mediterranean Sea and serve many other propaganda goals.

Academic Historiography

According to scholars from the other European countries, the ancient Carthaginians were not necessarily considered unkind, cruel people. Even Hitler had no biased dislike for the North African metropolis.[4] In German historiography the final defeat of Carthage was often compared to the situation of post–First World War Germany.

On the contrary, in Italy even pro-Semitic historians did not conceal their deep disdain (racial as well as political) for the Phoenician and Punic civilization. In their writings they often emphasized the similarity between ancient Semitic people and modern British society.

Among these scholars, important historian Gaetano De Sanctis (1870–1957),[5] a catholic, moderate man, considered the military collapse of Carthage as the essential circumstance for Roman Africa to enter the civilized progress of antiquity.[6] In an essay written in 1935, Sicilian scholar Emanuele Ciaceri (1869–1944) defines Phoenicians

---

1. Cagnetta 1979, 89–95; see also Cagnetta 1977, 202–4 and Perelli 1977, 215–16.

2. Bernal 1987, 350–55.

3. Loreto 2000, Champion 2001, Bonnet 2000. More broadly on the image of Phoenicians in Western historiography, see Bernal 1987, 337–99 and Liverani 1998.

4. Loreto 2000, 825.

5. Treves 1991 with previous bibliography.

6. De Sanctis 1964, 75. About the De Sanctis's attitude toward Carthage, see Canfora 1977, 98 and Cagnetta 1990, 215

62   Pietro Giammellaro

as retailers or greedy pirates. He describes Carthage as a big industrial city, devoted to fraud and deceit.[7] Just one year later, Mario Attilio Levi (1902–1998) explicitly compares Carthage with modern Britain, while, however, ascribing a more temperate mercantilism to the British Empire.[8]

More examples could be quoted among the many authors of the time. During fascism, nearly all the attempts of Italian classical studies glorify ancient Rome as an ideal paragon for Mussolini's Italy.[9] This ideological agenda inevitably involves the undervaluation of the Phoenicians and the Carthaginians and, with them, the British.

However, the fiercest enemy of the Punics and the British Empire was Ettore Pais (1856–1939), a respected classicist, who trained at the philological school of Theodore Mommsen and quickly rose to the higher levels of academic and political institutions.[10]

The parallel between Phoenico-Punic civilization and Great Britain can be found between the lines in almost every writing by Pais. This comparison is explicit in two of his works, which were ten years apart in publication. Thus, Pais's balance between scientific reasoning and political bias is very different in each one. The two volumes are *Storia di Roma durante le guerre puniche*, first printed in 1927, and *Roma dall'antico al nuovo impero*, published in 1938.

The heavy 1927 essay, in the author's intention, is a sequel of two other previous writings: *Storia dell'Italia antica* (1925) and *Storia di Roma dalle origini alle guerre puniche* (1926–1928). The propagandistic aim of the book is undeniable—the dedication to "S. E. Benito Mussolini capo del governo (His Eminence Benito Mussolini, chief of the Government)" and the passionate statements about "il nuovo assetto politico che Voi date all'Italia (the new political order You give to Italy)" clearly testify to this ideological purpose.[11] Nevertheless, the 1927 book is written with a scientific method. Ancient sources are quoted, graphic and photographic documents are shown, bibliographical and explicative notes are well organized. Overall a certain temperance can be observed when discussing the features of Phoenician and Punic civilizations. Thus, Pais's political stances are expressed through a recursive and persistent comparison between Carthage and the British Empire.

The first reason of such a comparison lies in the mutual aptitude—typical of mercantilist people—to solve political conflicts not on the military ground but via the subtle and sly deceptions of diplomacy: "Throughout the powerful Punic Nation's history, the Carthaginian warrior showed his will to die for his homeland. Like the modern Briton, when the need arises he turns from merchant to lion, the careful

---

7. Ciaceri 1935, 31. On Ciaceri see Pace 1947. About Ciaceri's attitude toward Semitic civilizations in ancient Mediterranean, see Giammellaro 2008, 66–73.

8. Levi 1936, 60–64. About Levi see Musti 1993.

9. Cagnetta 1979 and, more recently, Giardina and Vauchez 2000, 212–96 with a wider bibliography.

10. He was also one of the favorite ghost writers of Mussolini. The life and work of Pais are deeply analyzed in Polverini 2002.

11. Pais 1927, IX. In these very pages, Pais quotes a famous lecture given by Mussolini in the Università per Stranieri di Perugia on 5 October 1926, entitled *Roma antica sui mari* (*Ancient Rome on the Sea*). At the beginning of this conference, published three years later, Mussolini declares the text's bibliographical references, among which he mentions two writings by Pais. The careful analysis and the wealth of argumentations imply a sharper interference, as the structure of the lecture betrays a direct involvement of Pais in the composition.

Carthaginian prefers the subtle and effective means of commerce and diplomacy."[12] In other words, the Carthaginian Empire was only an empire of merchants, "obtained not with the inherent vigor of a warlike race, such as the Romans, but through expedients and political tricks, that resemble the tricks used by other powerful maritime nations of modern times."[13]

Another theme of comparison is the Punic army, made up of mercenary soldiers: "Just like modern Britain, Carthage knew that with gold it would always find people willing to spill their own blood for its safety."[14] According to Pais, the natural tendency to "spill other people's blood rather than its own"[15] is a product of the plutocratic nature of the Carthaginian "Nation," whose sole purpose was increasing its profits. In fact, Carthage had seized all the critical places of maritime trade in the Mediterranean, not unlike the British Colonial Empire.

> Even today, after so many centuries of history, the nations encircling the Mediterranean are subservient to the commercial interests of Great Britain, which imposes its maritime supremacy and commercial politics everywhere with ships, just like the Punic state. Carthage, like modern Britain, monopolized and distributed all its raw materials and industrial goods all over the world in its own interest. A vessel headed to distant shores does not risk being sunk nowadays as it would at the time of Carthaginians. Yet, the Suez Canal and the Straits of Gibraltar would be precluded for any nation who would dare to resist the interests and the will of the British nation, ruler of the sea waves.[16]

In Pais's discourse, British supremacy over the Mediterranean is a real obsession; in this regard, the comparison with Carthage is nothing but an excuse. Throughout the entire discussion, whenever the author argues about Punic thalassocracy, he always highlights the dangerous analogy with Britain.[17]

---

12. Pais 1927, 1.48: "Il guerriero Cartaginese, in tutto il corso della storia della potente Nazione punica, mostrò di saper morire per la patria, ma simile al moderno Britanno, che da abile mercante si trasforma, occorrendo, in leone, l'accorto Cartaginese preferiva i fini e penetranti mezzi della diplomazia e del commercio."

13. Pais 1927, 1.47: "conseguito non per vigoria intrinseca di una stirpe guerriera, quale era la romana, ma con accorgimenti ed astuzie politiche, che fanno ripensare a quelle ben note di cui si valgono potenti Nazioni marittime dell'età moderna."

14. Pais 1927, 2.361–62: "Simile all'odierna Inghilterra, Cartagine bene sapeva che con l'oro avrebbe sempre e dovunque trovato altre genti che per la sua sicurezza versassero il proprio sangue."

15. Pais 1927, 1.47.

16. Pais 1927, 1.64: "Anche oggi, dopo tanti secoli di vita storica le Nazioni che circondano il Mediterraneo sono subordinate agli interessi commerciali della grande Britannia che, a somiglianza dello Stato punico, con le sue squadre navali impone dovunque la sua supremazia marittima e la sua politica commerciale. La potenza dell'antica Cartagine al pari dell'inglese fu mantenuta dal rapido accorrere su ogni costa mediterranea di flotte, costitute da navi superiori per costruzione e per abilità di ciurme a quelle delle altre Nazioni. Anche Cartagine, come la moderna Inghilterra si assunse l'ufficio di monopolizzare e di distribuire nel mondo, a seconda dei suoi interessi nazionali, materie prime e prodotti industriali. Se ai giorni nostri una nave diretta verso lidi lontani non corre più rischio, come ai tempi cartaginesi, di venir affondata, il canale di Suez e lo stretto di Gibilterra sarebbero inesorabilmente chiusi per tutte le nazioni del Mediterraneo, che osassero opporsi agli interessi ed al volere della potente Nazione britannica 'che governa le onde del mare.'"

17. Only by way of example, see Pais 1927, 1.90, 138–39, 182, 2.256.

64   Pietro Giammellaro

Eleven years after *Storia di Roma durante le guerre puniche*, Pais returned to the Carthage–Britain connection. 1938 is a significant year regarding racial policies in Italy. In July the daily newspaper *Il Giornale d'Italia* (supporter of fascist regime), published anonymously the *Manifesto of Racist Scientists*, which was re-published in August in the new magazine *La difesa della razza*, endorsed by some of the most important academics in the country. Between September and November 1938, the first racial measures against the Jews entered into force.

The essay by Pais has a meaningful title, *Roma dall'antico al nuovo impero* (*Rome, from the Ancient to the New Empire*). But this time the political and ideological work is in plain sight. The book is propaganda disguised as academic writing. The author begins by paying tribute to the "overwhelming enthusiasm of fascist revolution,"[18] recalling "the favorable days when—after having conquered the Ethiopian Empire, thanks to the genius and the inexhaustible energy of Mussolini—Italy reaffirms the virtues that immortalized the name of ancient Rome among civilized European people."[19]

The grimness of the academic prose disappears, giving way to a less restrained, intense approach. The style is direct, effective and with a main purpose: "the historical education of people and youth."[20] In such a context, the arguments against Carthage and the ones against Britain overlap in every respect. In Pais' historiographic outline, the two countries embody a single, meta-historical enemy of Italy—an enemy who needs to be destroyed in the present just as it was in the past.

In reaction to a positive comparison between the Roman and British legal systems,[21] Pais gives a violent lecture, where he implies harsh judgments and openly uses racist expressions: "Let me clarify the features of the British Empire when compared with an ancient civilization such as the Latins. The analogy between ancient Rome and England is not as fitting as is one between Britannia and Carthage. Unlike Rome and just like Britannia, Carthage was moved by selfish feelings. Plutocratic, mercantilistic classes and the urban plebs only cared about commercial and financial gains to the colonies' detriment. Therefore, as soon as the Romans offered better conditions to the Cadice and Utica Colonies, they betrayed their political metropolis in favor of their nation's enemies."[22]

Once again, the closest connection between the Phoenicians and the British lies in the unscrupulous plutocratic mercantilism, which, according to Pais, is not ascribable

---

18. Pais 1938, 9: "impeto travolgente della rivoluzione fascista."

19. Pais 1938, XV: "i fausti giorni in cui, conseguita—grazie al genio e all'inesauribile energia di Benito Mussolini—la conquista dell'Impero Etiopico, l'Italia riafferm—tra i popoli dell'Europa civile—quelle virtù che resero immortale il nome dell'antica Roma."

20. Pais 1938, XIV: "educazione storica del popolo e della gioventù."

21. A hypothesis proposed by, among others, the law historian Giovanni Pacchioni (1867–1946). Cf. Pacchioni 1937 (in particular Chapter 9, entitled *Organizzazione imperiale romana e britannica* [*Roman and British Imperial Organization*]).

22. Pais 1938, 430: "Per chiarire le caratteristiche dell'Impero britannico di fronte alla civiltà antica e particolarmente latina, ancor più che il confronto tra l'opera dell'antica Roma e quella posteriore dell'Inghilterra, giova notare i punti di analogia e di contatto tra la Moderna Britannia e l'antica Cartagine. In modo affatto analogo a quello tenuto dalla gente inglese, e ben diverso dal romano, Cartagine, mossa da sentimenti egoistici, rivolse soprattutto le sue cure agli interessi commerciali e finanziari, sfruttati dapprima dalle plutocratiche classi mercantili, più tardi anche dalla plebe urbana, a danno delle colonie. Perciò queste, come Cadice e Utica, abbandonata la loro metropoli politica si unirono ai nemici della propria nazione, ai Romani, allorché questi offrirono loro migliori condizioni."

to Roman civilization. But this is not the only link. From the economic policies to the attitude toward allies, nearly every aspect of the two countries' institutional life helps to substantiate the thesis that the British are nothing but modern Carthaginians.[23] There is no shortage of references to the proverbial *fides punica*, which the author ascribes *tout court* also to the *perfida Albione*:

> Naval and financial policies, as well as diplomatic relations with other countries, may be used to compare the political and social history of modern Britain, with Carthage. Then and now, the Punics and modern Britain share a constant concern—the pursuit and exclusive ownership of all the harbors and mines to collect gold, the primary means of empowerment and bribery. To achieve this goal, Carthage was always ruthless and unscrupulous. The "punica fides" became proverbial, not unlike the common saying "Perfidious Albion." With mistrust and slyness, Carthage would forbid any other state from sailing to its harbors or colonies. The British, just like Carthage, took possession of all the strategic spots, like Gibraltar and Malta, and seized the Suez Canal in an effort to rule the entire African continent.[24]

With such reasoning, Pais does not hold back his fierce criticism of the British colonial policies, denouncing the use of weapons—especially in the Boer Wars and in the so-called Opium Wars—and stigmatizing the British penchant for overpowering even neighboring people and civilizations, like the Irish.

This direct attack results in a genuine threat to Britain, and once again it seeps through the filter of Carthage.

> Excessive wealth leads to an irrational selfishness on one hand and, on the other, it awakens the envy of those states who were deprived of their basic livelihood. In antiquity, selfishness and excessive wealth caused the defeat of Carthage.... Mussolini had the courage to look Britain in the eye, assess its intentions, its faith, and its real power. And now, in the aftermath of the Abyssinia conquest, Italy shall no longer suffer any other nation's domination over the Mediterranean, since our government has expressed its intention to monitor and defend its interests in all the oceans.[25]

23. See also Pais 1938, 430–31.

24. Pais 1938, 431: "Fra tutti i tratti che associano la storia politica e sociale dell'Inghilterra a quella dell'antica Cartagine, sono caratteristici quelli che si riferiscono alla politica navale e finanziaria e alle relazioni diplomatiche con i vari popoli. Preoccupazione costante dei Puni fu, e lo è tutt'ora per la moderna Inghilterra la ricerca e il possesso esclusivo di tutti i porti, di tutte le miniere che permettono l'accumulo dell'oro, strumento precipuo di potenza e di corruzione. Per raggiungere tali fini, Cartagine non conobbe scrupoli. La "fede punica" divenne proverbiale, come più tardi il detto "Perfida Albione." La diffidenza e l'astuzia con cui Cartagine impediva agli altri stati la navigazione verso i suoi porti e le sue colonie, fan ripensare ai mezzi coi quali la gente britannica si impadronì di punti strategici, ad esempio di Gibilterra e di Malta, e si rese di fatto padrona del Canale di Suez, e aspira oggi a dominare su tutto quanto il Continente africano."

25. Pais 1938, 435–36: "se da un lato l'eccessiva ricchezza conduce ad un irrazionale egoismo, eccita d'altra parte l'invidia degli Stati defraudati dei loro mezzi essenziali di sussistenza. L'egoismo e l'eccessiva ricchezza produssero, nell'antichità, la perdita dei Cartaginesi.... Mussolini ha avuto il coraggio di guardare fisso negli occhi l'Inghilterra, di valutarne le intenzioni, la fede e la reale potenza; ed ormai, dopo

FIGURE 4.1. Cover page of the first issue of *La difesa della razza* I 1 (5 August 1938)

Propaganda

With such tones in academic historiography, it is not hard to imagine the level of debate in the propaganda literature. The style becomes rougher, the assaults more violent, the discourse even weaker. On the propaganda side, the battle against the Anglo-Punic enemy is tackled by many regime journalists and intellectuals. The radio host Mario Appelius (1892–1946),[26] in his *Requisitoria contro l'Inghilterra*, describes the British Empire as "a gigantic conglomerate of colonial properties and territorial conquests, built by a people of pirates and merchants," a "monstrous empire of Phoenician essence, camped out with its mass in the five continents."[27]

But the most aggressive onslaughts come from the periodical *La difesa della razza* (*Defense of the Race*; Figure 4.1) [28] eagerly advocated by Mussolini and edited by journalist Telesio Interlandi (1894–1965).[29]

La difesa della razza was published twice a month between 1938 and 1944 and it hosted the articles of those journalists, scientists, and intellectuals who supported Italian racism in its various schools of thought.[30] The juxtaposition of the Phoenician and British maintains, at least in its first stage, the same elements identified by academic historiography (Figure 4.2).

---

la conquista dell'Abissinia, l'Italia non sopporterà più una ostile preponderanza di qualsiasi altra Nazione nel Mediterraneo, chè anzi in questi giorni il nostro Governo ha enunciato il proposito di sorvegliare e difendere i suoi interessi su tutti gli Oceani."

26. About Mario Appelius cf. De Caro 1961.

27. Appelius 1999, 153, "Un gigantesco conglomerato di possedimenti coloniali e di conquiste territoriali, costituito da un popolo di pirati e di mercanti.... Un mostruoso impero d'essenza fenicia accampato con la sua massa nei cinque continenti."

28. *La difesa della razza* has been recently the subject of two essays: the book by Pisanty 2006–2007 is basically a thematic anthology from the journal; the excellent monograph by Cassata 2008 is considerably more scientific and has a rich and useful iconographic apparatus.

29. About Telesio Interlandi, see Canali 2004 with a wider bibliography and Cassata 2008, 5–55.

30. About the different tendencies in Italian fascist racism, see the enlightening essay by Raspanti 1994.

FIGURE 4.2. *L'Inghilterra allo specchio* (*Britain in the Mirror*), in *La difesa della razza* IV 18 (20 July 1941); the comic strip *Times-Semit*, by O. Garvens, is taken from the satirical German magazine *Kladderadatsch* 93(2) (7 January 1940)

Plutocratic mercantilism is still the most controversial issue, and it always involves the usual bad-faith claims (Figure 4.3). That is what correspondent Giuseppe Grieco says about this, in a letter entitled *L'Inghilterra e l'onore*: "History is replete with evidence of British bad faith.... For a mercantilist people such as the British, there is no rule but selfish interest.... Merchant and pirate, here is the true face of the British, when the centuries old facade of hypocrisy and politics drops away. This second and more vicious Carthage—now on his last legs—got its claws out in a last-ditch effort to resist. In vain. The new Europe built by Mussolini and Hitler wields the sword of justice upon it. And justice will be served."[31]

Predictably, another reason for the identification of the British with the Phoenicians is the colonization process, as a consequence of their comparable mercantilistic policies. The colonial activity of both peoples is considered par excellence as a mere form of exploitation of human and material resources, without any civilization goal.[32]

A recurring theme, in the writings of these authors, is the discussion on army structures. Both military forces mostly consist of mercenaries and are thus destined to perish in the fight against their enemies. Once again, Grieco, in a letter from Ethiopia, emphasizes the value of Italian soldiers compared to the "blond sons of pale Albion":

31. *La difesa della razza* III 19 (5 August 1940), *Questionario*, 44–45: "La storia è piena di documenti della malafede britannica.... Per un popolo mercantile come l'inglese, non può valere che la legge dell'interesse egoistico.... Mercante e pirata, ecco il vero volto dell'inglese, quando cade la maschera sovrappostavi da secoli di 'ipocrisia' e di 'politica.' Questa seconda e più feroce Cartagine, ora che è ridotta agli estremi, scopre gli artigli in un ultimo disperato tentativo di resistenza. Invano. La nuova Europa creata da Mussolini e da Hitler le sta sopra brandendo la spada della giustizia. E giustizia sarà fatta."
32. Cf. for instance the article by A. Petrucci entitled "Il fallimento della colonizzazione britannica in Africa" ("The failure of British colonization in Africa") in *La difesa della razza* II 20 (20 August 1939), 19–21.

FIGURE 4.3. Title page of the article by A. Tosti, *Atavismi Psichici della razza inglese* (*Mental Atavisms of the British Race*), in *La difesa della razza* IV,8 (20 February 1941). 13

In comparison to the fierce spirits of our legionnaires, what are the blond sons of the pale Albion worth? They who demanded to subject the world to their heavy cape of merchants? The answer is in arms, not words.... Isn't there something fated in the fact that we ourselves, the Italians, are being asked to strike the deadly blow against the biggest merchant empire risen after Carthage? The war was long and bloody, at the time. But at the end Carthage fell. Britain will fall as well. Soon. These soldiers give us an unfailing certainty.[33]

Similarly, in the following issue of the magazine, another journalist says that "each people is just like its army; Carthage was a mercantilist and plutocratic nation, so it couldn't count on its own army, just like the present day plutocratic nations, Britain and the United States of America. So, it was forced to employ a ragtag, mercenary rabble, with a lot of colored troops. Next to a suntanned Numidian knight, next to a black frizzy-haired snub-nosed Ethiopian soldier, also a slinger from the Baleares would fight."[34]

33. *La difesa della razza* III 23 (5 October 1940), *Questionario*, 47: "Che cosa valgono, a confronto di queste fiere tempre di legionari, i biondi figli della pallida Albione, che hanno preteso di imporre in eterno al mondo la loro pesante cappa di mercanti? La risposta è alle armi, non alle parole.... Ma non c'è forse qualcosa di fatale nel fatto che proprio noi italiani siamo chiamati a vibrare il colpo mortale al più gigantesco impero di mercanti sorto dopo quello di Cartagine? Lunga e sanguinosa fu allora la guerra. Ma poi Cartagine cadde. Anche l'Inghilterra cadrà. E presto. Questi soldati ce ne danno la certezza infallibile."
34. A. Guerrieri, "Il Mediterraneo e la civiltà ariana," in *La difesa della razza* IV 15 (5 June 1941), 11–15: "poiché tali sono i popoli, tali i loro eserciti, Cartagine, nazione puramente mercantile, o plutocratica che dir si voglia, non poteva avere, come non possono averlo le moderne nazioni plutocratiche, Inghilterra e

FIGURE 4.4. Title page of *La difesa della razza* VI 6 (20 January 1943)

FIGURE 4.5. Title page of *La difesa della razza* VI 9 (5 March 1943)

As time goes by, new reasons to connect the British and Phoenicians start to occur. The image of oriental debauchery and sexual wildness—which was propagandized in the history books as well as in successful novels[35]—begins to be compared and connected to the lust and immorality of the British race. This issue is addressed in several articles (with meaningful pictures, bordering the ridiculous, e.g., Figure 4.4), and this subject is even the subject of a whole dossier (Figure 4.5).[36]

The exploitation of colonized people and slavery become a regular matter of concern, especially with reference to colonial Africa (see Figure 4.6).[37] This process peaks with the identification of Protestantism (and Anglicanism specifically) with the ancient Semitic religions. In this regard, it is worth mentioning the answer of journalist Massimo Lelj[38] to a reader's complaint (the reader is a certain Francesco Jemma) about an article against the Protestant religion:

Stati Uniti d'America, un esercito proprio, ma era obbligata a servirsi di un'accozzaglia raccogliticcia e mercenaria, dove non mancavano le truppe di colore, perché a lato al cavaliere numida abbronzato dal sole e all'etiope nero dai capelli crespi e dal naso camuso vi combatteva il fromboliere delle Baleari."

35. Said 1979, 166–97.

36. *La difesa della razza* VI 9 (5 March 1943). In the title page is written, "In questo fascicolo si documenta l'immoralità della razza inglese" (In this issue is documented the immorality of the British race).

37. The whole issue 7 of the year VI (5 February 1943) is devoted to this subject; as stated in the title page, "Questo fascicolo documenta gli orrori dell'Inghilterra schiavista" (this dossier shows the horrors of the slaver Britain). See also, among the others, the article by F. Graziani entitled "Delitti di Albione contro le razze: la tratta dei negri d'America" (Albion's Crimes Against the Races: The Negro Slave Trade in America) in *La difesa della razza* IV 15 (5 June 1941), 18–20.

38. Lelj was the editor of *La Difesa della razza's Questionario* (a selection of readers' letters and editors' answers) from the beginning up to December 1940. On his biography and the peculiar features of the *Questionario* see Cassata 2008, 315–40.

70   Pietro Giammellaro

The Italian kernel is Catholic.... Can't you see right before your eyes that the
European empires' goal is to ration peoples' livelihood by their blackmail over
raw materials? Wars break out in the name of a materials' empire, not for honor.
And these wars are fought with the aim of keeping people subjected to the need
of materials. And the Protestant laboremus has helped to build the assets of the
billionaires. The assets? A Carthaginian spirit of the Europeans. Didn't Marx
tell you? ... Who better than him? He, a European. He, a Jew, someone with
mercantilistic and Semite blood, just like the Carthaginians.... And it's certain
that Carthage's god isn't Catholic, and Carthage is a matter of life and death for
Rome.[39]

And then, in one of the subsequent numbers of the periodical:

Jemma has to consider what Catholic means for us, and what Protestant means
for the British, and generally for Europe. And he has to look for this meaning
not in the field of economics or in political doctrines, but rather in the different
concept of life (different than Catholic) suggested by Protestantism. Jemma
needs to ask himself whether a society born from English and European revolutions doesn't remind him of other societies—although very ancient—like the
Carthaginian. And he needs to find the meaning of that question—is it Rome or
Carthage? Does it mean nothing to him that Carthage was destroyed and Rome
blazed to victory? Is this not the triumph of a different way of life (different
from the Carthaginian one)? Did revolutions rebuild Rome or Carthage? Was
Rome a mercantile matriarchy? Or rather its backbone was in bravery and in the
disclosure of omina to the plebs? And what's the difference between a society
based on plebeian heroism and a society based on commerce?"[40]

These are harsh words, which project an *ante litteram* contrast between Catholicism and Protestantism into an imaginary past. On this religious basis, it is easy to

39. *La difesa della razza* III 3 (5 December 1939), *Questionario*, 44–45, "La midolla italiana è catto-
lica.... Non lo vedete sotto i vostri occhi che l'ideale degli imperi europei è quello di dosare la sussistenza
dei popoli, con il ricatto delle cosiddette materie prime? Abbiamo gli imperi della materia, e per l'impero
della materia si fanno guerre, non per altro onore. Guerre per tener soggetti i popoli alla materia. Quanto
non ha lavorato anche il laboremus protestante.... a costruire il patrimonio dei miliardari? Il patrimonio?
Lo spirito cartaginese degli europei. Di questo si tratta. Non ve lo ha detto Marx? ... Chi meglio di lui ve
lo poteva dire? Egli europeo. Egli ebreo, cioè di sangue mercantile o semita, come i cartaginesi. Ora ...
è certo che il Dio di Cartagine non è cattolico, e che Cartagine è una questione di vita e di morte per Roma."
40. *La difesa della razza* III 7 (5 February 1939), *Questionario*, 46: "Bisogna che Jemma consideri che
cosa significhi per noi cattolico, che cosa protestante per gli inglesi e generalmente per l'Europa. Ma che
non cerchi questo significato nell'economia o nelle dottrine politiche, ma nel diverso concetto della vita,
diverso dal cattolico, in cui consiste ancora, all'atto pratico, il protestantesimo. Bisogna che Jemma si
decida a considerare se la società, quale è nata dalle rivoluzioni inglesi ed europee, non gli possa ricordare
altre società, per quanto antichissime, come per esempio la cartaginese. E si decida a cercare il significato di
quella alternativa, che diceva: o Roma o Cartagine. Gli sembra forse indifferente che scomparisse Cartagine
e Roma vincesse? Non gli sembra questo il trionfo di un diverso modo di vivere, diverso dal cartaginese?
E le rivoluzioni hanno riedificato Roma o Cartagine? Roma era un matriarcato mercantile o invece ebbe
la spina dorsale nell'eroismo e nella comunicazione degli auspici alla plebe? E che differenza c'è tra una
società fatta d'eroismo plebeo e un'altra fondata nel commercio?"

FIGURE 4.6. Cover page of *La difesa della razza* VI 7 (5 February 1943)

make a double equivalence: British is to Phoenico-Punics as Phoenico-Punics are to Jews. And according to such an idea, the authors of *La difesa della razza* begin to proclaim the third, resulting equation: Britons are equal to Jews.

Titles like "I due popoli eletti (The Two Chosen Peoples)" (Figure 4.7),[41] "Il dilagare dell'influsso ebraico in Inghilterra (The Spread of Jewish Influence in Great Britain),"[42] "Giudaismo fomentatore del Protestantesimo (Judaism, Instigator of Protestantism),"[43] "Nobiltà anglosassone oppure nobiltà anglo-giudaica? (Anglo-Saxon Nobility or Anglo-Jewish nobility?),"[44] "Somiglianze tra il Giudaismo e la religione degli Inglesi (Parallels Between Judaism and the British Religions),"[45] and many more, are nothing but the most visible and surface sign of a widespread propaganda exuding from every column of *La difesa della razza* (see Figure 4.7–9).

Such a propaganda will lead to an offensive against Great Britain, launched at a purely racial level, as shown by the many single-subject issues of the journal focused on the racial inferiority of the Anglo-Saxons (e.g., Figure 4.10).[46]

41. Article by T. Interlandi, in *La difesa della razza* IV 7 (5 February 1941), 6–8.
42. Article by A. Attili, in *La difesa della razza* II 11 (5 April 1939), 29–30.
43. Article by A. M. De Giglio in *La difesa della razza* III 17 (5 July 1940), 42–44.
44. Article by G. Lupi, in *La difesa della razza* IV 7 (5 February 1941), 28–30.
45. Article by G. Dell'Isola, in *La difesa della razza* IV 2 (5 November 1940), 28–30.
46. Issues 5–9, 11, and 13 published in 1943.

FIGURE 4.7. Title pages of the article "I due popoli eletti," in *La difesa della razza* IV 7 (5 February 1941), 6–7

FIGURE 4.8. Title page of the article "Il giudaismo fomentatore del protestantesimo," in *La difesa della razza* III 17 (5 July 1940), 42–43

FIGURE 4.9. (*above*) Title pages of the article "Nobiltà anglosassone oppure nobiltà anglo-giudaica?" in *La difesa della razza* IV 7 (5 February 1941), 28–29

FIGURE 4.10. (*left*) Title page of one of the several articles by A. Modica entitled "Inferiorità razziale degli anglo-sassoni (Racial inferiority of the Anglo-Saxons)," in *La Difesa della razza* VI 6 (20 January 1943), 9

74   Pietro Giammellaro

Conclusion

A review of academic historiography is now appropriate. Among the many scholars who supported the connection between the Phoenicians and British, there is a remarkable exception. Archaeologist Biagio Pace (1889–1955) was a strong follower of fascist doctrines, who signed the infamous *Manifesto della razza* and held important institutional roles during Mussolini's regime. Pace was a scholar of ancient Mediterranean civilizations who wrote a massive work (in some ways still valuable) about ancient Sicily.[47] Such an intellectual was definitely supposed to endorse the theory of the overlap between the ancient Semitic civilization and the modern British Empire. On the contrary, in his several writings (which are not immune to fascist nationalism or the myth of ancient Rome) there is no mention of this comparison. The reason of this omission may lie in his brief but intense archaeological fieldwork during the first excavation campaigns on the island of Mozia.

Pace was the first Italian scholar to study the Phoenician civilization in Sicily, which he undertook at the invitation of Joseph Whitaker, a British businessman keen on archaeology. On that occasion, Pace also became close with the other members of the Whitaker family. These relations lasted throughout his whole life, as did his interest in Phoenician and Punic civilization (which resulted in a great number of important essays).[48] As a consequence of this first-hand (and in some respects simultaneous) experience of Phoenician and British cultural heritage—and despite his full support to the ideology of fascist Rome—Pace avoided the trap of a misleading game of mirrors, designed to demonize a political enemy on the basis of race.

There is no shortage in Pace's work of critical judgments on "the spirit of the British people." But his criticism goes hand-in-hand with a certain (almost unintentional) esteem, and it is tempered by the direct contact with an English family.[49]

As is always the case with totalitarian regimes, intolerance grows in the soil of ignorance. A lack of knowledge of other cultures, whether contemporary or from the past, often induces dogmatism, xenophobia, and racism. Maybe the study of this kind of cultural representations—typical of European dictatorships in the first half of twentieth century—is a useful debunking exercise, an antidote against similar cultural representations of our own times.

Nowadays, when newspapers, social, and mass media describe the global migrations in Europe as an "Islamic invasion," they are implementing the very same methodology used by fascist scholars and propaganda—they stigmatize migrants as dangerous enemies. As such, they spread unjustified fear among the public, fueling the notion that the otherness of foreigners is incompatible with the European way of life. This approach, I believe, is remarkably closer to *La difesa della razza* than to the free press of Western democracies.

---

47. These are the four volumes of *Arte e civiltà della Sicilia antica* (*Art and Civilization of Ancient Sicily*), published between 1935 and 1949.

48. To mention but a few, see Pace 1915, 1925, and 1930, in addition to the archaeological map of Carthage drawn up in collaboration with R. Lanier, and to part of the entry *Cartagine* in the *Enciclopedia Italiana* (cf. Cagnetta 1990).

49. On the relationship between Pace and the Whitaker family, see Giammellaro 2019. More generally on Pace's biographical and intellectual profile, see Giammellaro 2016.

REFERENCES

Appelius, M. 1999. *Parole dure e chiare*. 2nd ed. Milan: M&B Publishing.

Bernal, M. 1987. *Black Athena. The Afroasiatic Roots of Classical Civilization*. Vol. 1, *The Fabrication of Ancient Greece, 1785–1985*. New Brunswick: Rutgers University Press.

Bonnet, C. 2000. "Carthage, l' 'autre nation' dans l'historiographie ancienne et moderne." *Anabases* 1:139–60.

Cagnetta, M. 1977. "Appunti su guerra coloniale e ideologia imperiale 'romana.'" Pages 185–207 in *Matrici culturali del fascismo*. Bari: Università di Bari.

———. 1979. *Antichisti e impero fascista*. Bari: Dedalo.

———. 1990. *Antichità classiche nell'enciclopedia italiana*. Rome: Laterza.

Canali, M. 2004. "Interlandi, Telesio." Pages 519–21 in *Dizionario Biografico degli Italiani*. Vol. 62. Rome: Istituto dell'Enciclopedia Italiana.

Canfora, L. 1977. "Classicismo e fascismo." Pages 85–111 in *Matrici culturali del fascismo*. Bari: Università di Bari.

Cassata, F. 2008. *"La difesa della razza." Politica, ideologia e immagine del razzismo fascista*. Turin: Einaudi.

Champion, T. 2001. "The Appropriation of the Phoenicians in British Imperial Ideology." *Nations and Nationalism* 7:451–65.

Ciaceri, E. 1935. "La conquista romana dell'Africa." Pages 29–48 in *Africa Romana*. Milan: Hoepli.

De Caro, G. 1961. "Appelius, Mario." Pages 613–14 in *Dizionario Biografico degli Italiani*. Vol. 3. Rome: Istituto dell'Enciclopedia Italiana.

De Sanctis, G. 1964. *Storia dei Romani. Volume IV La fondazione dell'impero. Parte III Dalla battaglia di Pidna alla caduta di Numanzia*. Florence: La Nuova Italia Editrice.

Giammellaro, P. 2008. "Religione e religioni della Sicilia antica nell'opera di Emanuele Ciaceri." *Studi e Materiali di Storia delle Religioni* 74:49–76.

———. 2016. "Biagio Pace (1889–1955)." Pages 237–50 in *Lebensbilder—Klassische Archäologen und der Nationalsozialismus*. Vol. 2/2. Edited by G. Brands and M. Maischberger. Berlin: Deutsches Archäologisches Institut.

———. 2019. "Biagio Pace, the Whitakers and the First Steps of Archaeological Investigation in Motya." *Rivista di Studi Fenici* 47:39–52.

Giardina, A., and A. Vauchez. 2000. *Il mito di Roma da Carlo Magno a Mussolini*. Bari: Laterza.

Levi, M. A. 1936. *La politica imperiale di Roma*. Turin: Paravia.

Liverani, M. 1998. "L'immagine dei Fenici nella storiografia occidentale." *Studi Storici* 39:5–22.

Loreto, L. 2000. "L'idea di Cartagine nel pensiero storico tedesco da Weimar allo 'Jahr 0.'" *Studi Storici* 41:825–70.

Musti, D. 1993. "Levi, Mario Attilio." Pages 189–90 in *Enciclopedia Italiana 1979–1992*. Rome: Istituto dell'Enciclopedia Italiana.

Pacchioni, G. 1937. *L'impero britannico e l'Europa continentale*. Milan: Istituto per gli Studi di Politica Internazionale.

Pace, B. 1915. "Prime note sugli scavi di Mozia." *Notizie degli Scavi di Antichità* 1915(12):431–46.

———. 1925. "Ricerche cartaginesi." *Monumenti Antichi* 1925:129–208.

———. 1930. "Le fortificazioni di Cartagine." Pages 262–72 in *Atti del II Congresso Nazionale di Studi Romani*. Rome: Paolo Cremonese Editore.

———. 1931. "Cartagine—La cultura cartaginese." Pages 215–17 in *Enciclopedia Italiana IX (care-chia)*. Rome: Istituto dell'Enciclopedia Italiana.

———. 1935–1949. *Arte e Civiltà della Sicilia Antica*. 3 vols. Rome: Società Editrice Dante Alighieri.

———. 1947. "Commemorazione del corrispondente Emmanuele Ciaceri." *Rendiconti dell'Accademia Nazionale dei Lincei* 8(2):417–22.

Pais, E. 1927. *Storia di Roma durante le guerre puniche.* 2 vols. Roma: Casa Editrice Optima.

―――. 1938. *Roma dall'antico al nuovo impero.* Milan: Hoepli.

Perelli, L. 1977. "Sul culto fascista della 'Romanità' (una silloge)." *Quaderni di storia* 5:197–224.

Pisanty, V. 2006–2007. *La difesa della razza. Antologia 1938–1943.* Milan: Bompiani.

Polverini, L., ed. 2002. *Aspetti della storiografia di Ettore Pais.* Perugia: Edizioni Scientifiche Italiane.

Raspanti, M. 1994. "I razzismi del fascismo." Pages 73–89 in *La menzogna della razza.* Bologna: Grafis.

Said, E. 1979. *Orientalism.* 2nd ed. New York: Vintage Books.

Treves, P. 1991. "De Sanctis, Gaetano." Pages 297–309 in *Dizionario Biografico degli Italiani.* Vol. 39. Rome: Istituto dell'Enciclopedia Italiana.

CHAPTER 5

The Sharing Out of Antiquities in Syria During the Interwar Period: Sir Leonard Woolley's Excavation at Tell Sheikh Yusuf (Al-Mina)

Patrick Maxime Michel

FOLLOWING THE GREAT WAR (1914–1918), France was the mandatory power in Syria. As the Département des antiquités orientales of the Musée du Louvre (Paris) explains regarding the history of its collections, France consequently organized "l'exploitation et la conservation des monuments, suscitant une activité archéologique importante dont le site de Ras Shamra, l'antique Ugarit sur la côte syrienne, près de Lattaquié, fouillé à partir de 1929 par la mission française dirigée par Claude Schaeffer, ce qui valut au Louvre des monuments attribuées par partage jusqu'en 1939."[1]

Therefore, a sharing out of archaeological findings after excavations was indeed taking place between the Syrian state and the excavator. However, before discussing a concrete case of antiquity sharing, we must retrace the history of French presence in Syria and the history of the creation of the Services des antiquités au Levant.

It was only after the Covenant of the League of Nations in Versailles in 1919 that France's position in Syria was clarified. Article 22 of the Covenant allowed France its tutelage over Syria as a mandate: "Le 6 janvier 1920, Fayçal signe avec Clémenceau l'accord qui aboutit à la définition du mandat de la France sur la Syrie et à l'établissement d'un régime constitutionnel." King Faisal "reconnaît l'indépendance et l'intégrité du Liban, fait de Damas sa capitale," while "le Haut-Commissaire représentant la France aura sa résidence à Alep."[2]

In July 1920, French troops became engaged in conflict with King Faisal's army, took Damascus, and drove out the king. The end of the "royaume arabe"[3] made way for the establishment of Greater Lebanon. It was in this context that General Gouraud laid down the principles of archaeology in Syria and in Lebanon to ensure French presence in the region.[4]

The Levant of the French mandate, which consisted in fact of Lebanon and Syria, was however considered as a single political entity under the charge of the Haut-Commissariat de la République française, the seat of which was in Beirut. When Gouraud resigned in 1922, he was succeeded by General Weygand. Gouraud, meanwhile, had set up the

---

1. See http://www.louvre.fr/departments/antiquités-orientales (accessed 9 February 2017).
2. Gran-Aymerich 2007, 404.
3. Gran-Aymerich 2007, 405.
4. Gran-Aymerich 2007, 405.

Service des antiquités de Syrie as early as 1920,[5] attaching it to the administration of the Instruction publique.[6]

Charles Virolleaud (1879–1968) was the first director of the Service des antiquités (1920–1929) before Henri Seyrig[7] (1895–1973) succeeded him. Maurice Dunand[8] (1898–1987) inherited the position from 1940 to 1945.

The established organization was intended to ensure equality, for the French and British mandatory powers, between French, British, and American scholars. "En effet, les autorités française et anglaise collaborent étroitement pour la surveillance et la protection des antiquités du Levant, qui, au regard du patrimoine archéologique, est divisé en trois zones, confiées à des officiers appartenant aux deux nations mandataires et faisant office d'inspecteurs des antiquités."[9] The west zone was comprised of Lebanon and the coast, the east zone extended beyond Lebanon to the Euphrates, and the south zone corresponded to Palestine.

It was in this context, then, that the rules which would govern the sharing of antiquities between the mandatory powers and the Syrian state were set in place:

> Les objets découverts sur le sol syrien sont acquis à l'Etat syrien et forment, après partage avec les institutions qui assurent les recherches, les collections des musées créées à Damas pour les antiquités arabes, à Beyrouth pour l'art antique, la conservation de ces établissements est confiée aux émirs Djafar Abd el-Khader et Maurice Chéhab, tous deux anciens élèves de l'Ecole du Louvre. Par la suite, un musée est ouvert à Alep pour recevoir les sculptures et les objets découverts par M. von Oppenheim à Tell Halaf et par F. Thureau-Dangin à Arslan–Tash et Tell Ahmar. Des dépôts d'antiquités sont envisagés sur certains sites, à Antioche, Palmyre, Mishrifé, Baalbeck ou Lattaquié.[10]

In this contribution, I will attempt to present the case of the sharing out of antiquities after Sir Leonard Woolley's excavations at the site of Tell Sheik Yusuf Al Gharib (Al-Mina) in 1936. The tell was given its name by Woolley himself, who was aware of the existence of an Alawite saint's tomb onsite.[11] The tell, excavated by Woolley in March 1936 and later in 1937, is located in close proximity to the village of Suadiye (in Turkish, Samandağ or St Simeon Mountain). Later on, the site took on the name Al-Mina, "the port" in Arabic, for although the site no longer lies by the sea, Woolley had understood that it was once located in the estuary of the Orontes.[12] This excavation is perfectly documented in the private archives of Maurice Dunand, kept in the

---

5 "La législation syrienne sur le patrimoine archéologique et artistique, conçue et instaurée par le Haut-Commissariat et le Service des antiquités, est inspirée de celle en vigueur en Egypte, et mise en place en Tunisie à l'initiative d'A. Merlin" (Gran-Aymerich 2007, 405).

6. Gran-Aymerich 2007, 405.

7. For various studies on Seyrig, see Kienle 2012.

8. Michel 2008.

9. Gran-Aymerich 2007, 407.

10. Gran-Aymerich 2007, 407.

11. Lane Fox 2008, 97.

12. Lane Fox 2008, 98; see also Graham 1986.

patrimonial archives of the University of Geneva.[13] Dunand intervened in the matter as an expert mandated by Seyrig.

Chronologically, Woolley's work at Al-Mina took place soon after his extraordinary discoveries in the royal tombs of Ur, and before the beginning of his work at Tell Atchana, ancient Alalakh, situated in the Amuq Valley (in the Sanjak of Alexandretta) in modern Turkey.[14]

Woolley's findings at the site of Al-Mina are mainly characterized by Greek ceramics.[15] As Elayi noted, "le site d'Al-Mina, sur la rive droite de l'estuaire de l'Oronte, est considéré depuis sa découverte comme la plaque-tournante du commerce grec en Méditerranée orientale. Toutefois, si le caractère grec du site est généralement admis, il n'est pas conçu de la même façon par tous les auteurs."[16]

Following the excavations of March 1936, Woolley wrote a first letter (20 June 1936) to the director of the Service des antiquités, Seyrig, in which he mentioned his disapproval of the choices regarding the sharing out made by the expert Dunand (the excavator of Byblos), delegated by the Service des antiquités.

The episode of the sharing out of Al-Mina's antiquities unfolds in our archives as follows.[17] Woolley had prepared two lots of ceramics termed "attique à figures rouges,"[18] between which the Service des antiquités was to choose. As it happened, it was Dunand who had been delegated to choose between both lots. The Mutassarif[19] or Mohafez[20] was then to collect the remaining lot intended for the Syrian state, destined, as it was, for the new museum of Antioch.[21] However, Woolley disagreed with Dunand's decision and expressed his stance to the Mohafez, who then revoked the decision. But the Direction des antiquités in Beirut, through the intermediation of its director, Seyrig, was not willing to accept this reversal so easily.

In approaching the task, Woolley had considered which objects seemed better suited to the museum of Antioch and which would be more useful to the British Museum. However, as Seyrig points out,

la difficulté me paraît venir d'un malentendu sur le principe même du partage. La loi oblige très formellement le fouilleur à faire deux parts égales, entre

13. Michel 2008.

14. The excavation of Alalakh would later by undertaken by Woolley before and after the Second World War. The first dig took place between 1937 and 1939, and the second between 1946 and 1948.

15. Woolley 1937, 1938, 1953; Beazley 1939, and more recently, with bibliography, see Lehmann 1996.

16. Elayi 1987, 249.

17. Inventory reference of the file CH UNIGE/aap/65/2011/21.

18. Letter from Woolley to Robert Parr (23 July 1936), the British consul in Aleppo at the time.

19. Governor of the Sanjak of Alexandretta, a term used by Woolley in his correspondence.

20. Prefect or governor, a term used by Seyrig in his correspondence. At the time, the Mohafez of Alexandretta was Hysni Barazi, from whom we also have a letter addressed to the *délégué général* of the administration of the Service des antiquités in Alexandretta, Mr Meyrier, dated 8 July 1936.

21. The various excavations undertaken around Antioch and in the Amuq Valley motivated the creation of a museum as early as 1939. This museum opened in Antioch on 23 July 1948, on the tenth anniversary of the Hatay Province's integration into the Turkish Republic. See http://www.hatayarkeolojimuzesi.gov.tr /HatayMuzeWeb/faces/jsp/layouts/about.jsp?place=5 (accessed 9 February 2017). The Republic of Hatay (Antioch) was created on 5 September 1938 with France's support. Following an agreement between Turkey and France on 23 June 1939, the territory was annexed by Turkey on 23 July of the same year. The Sanjak of Alexandretta's change of status concerned Woolley, who wrote in a letter to Seyrig, dated 15 December 1936: "I expect to be coming out early in March. At present we examine the newspapers eagerly to find out what is going to happen about the Sanjak, hoping that nothing will happen."

80   Patrick Maxime Michel

lesquelles le Service des Antiquités choisit librement, ce qui protège aussi bien le fouilleur que l'Etat. Votre principe, au contraire, consiste à faire deux parts qui correspondent à votre idée—peut-être juste d'ailleurs—des intérêts respectifs de deux musées. Cette procédure, qui supprime la liberté du choix de l'Etat, est contraire à la loi.[22]

From Woolley's perspective, the excavations had yielded a rather large number of Attic pottery shards, the majority of which could be more compelling and evocative in the showcases of Antioch's new museum, whereas only a few pieces were truly of interest to the British Museum. Woolley had therefore sorted out the shards that interested the British Museum from the rest, then attempted to provide appropriate counterparts for Antioch, "always giving the first choice to Antioch."[23] He even explains that he left pieces in Antioch without equivalents for the British Museum.

According to Dunand, the lot chosen for the British Museum had greater worth than the lot left in Antioch, for the following reasons:

- there were several fragments of a neck;
- there were two fragments of a beautifully painted cup;
- there was a group of fragments which made possible the restitution of a third of a "Kertch" type crater.

According to Woolley's writings, however, the most complete objects had been left to the museum of Antioch, which would certainly need them for its showcases, whereas the shards were of greater interest to the studies that were to be conducted in London. This was clearly also the Mutassarif's opinion. Even so, Woolley had made the offer to Dunand to transfer the "Kertch" type crater[24] into the lot for Antioch.[25]

Seyrig's position, meanwhile, remained clear: he considered that Woolley had influenced the Mutassarif by pressuring him to reverse Dunand's choice. On that account, Seyrig asked for a written confirmation from the latter. The Mutassarif, S. E. Hysni Bey El-Barazi, answered Mr Meyrier, *délégué-général* of the Haut-Commissaire à Alexandrette, on 8 July 1936:

J'ai l'honneur de vous faire connaître qu'en effet il est exact que je me suis rendu à Suédieh à la demande du fouilleur pour voir sur place des antiquités découvertes et ainsi être à même de ratifier en toute connaissance de cause le partage effectué par Monsieur DUNAND.

Il est également bien exact et mérite d'être cité que j'ai confirmé ce dernier archéologue dans les lots qu'il a constitués comme j'ai approuvé aussi la part

22. Letter from Seyrig to Woolley, 22 August 1936.
23. Letter from Woolley to Robert Parr, 23 July 1936.
24. See http://www.britishmuseum.org/research/collection_online/collection_object_details.aspx ?objectId=416697&partId=1&place=34443&object=24016%7C21884&matcult=16099&page=1 (accessed 9 February 2017).
25. Letter from Woolley to Robert Parr (23 July 1936). Woolley had indeed asked Parr, the British consul in Aleppo at the time, to intercede with Seyrig on his behalf.

The Sharing Out of Antiquities in Syria During the Interwar Period　81

qu'il a choisi [sic!] pour le musée d'Antioche sauf en ce qui concerne la céramique grecque.

Il n'est toutefois pas bien conforme à la réalité que je me suis contenté de renverser seulement les lots des vases grecques (parce que le lot destiné au fouilleur m'a paru plus avantageux au Musée).

J'ai fait plus encore car j'ai obtenu de Sir Léonard Woolley (mais non pas sans difficulté) d'ajouter au lot que j'ai cru de voir réserver au Musée deux autres vases à ne pas dédaigner dont un assez grand et très intéressant et de grande valeur pour le Musée et pour l'Etat comme me l'a affirmé d'ailleurs Sir Léonard Woolley avec toute franchise.

Ceci étant je maintiens donc que le lot réservé par Monsieur Dunand à l'Etat modifié comme dit ci-dessus en ce qui concerne la céramique grecque seulement est tout à fait plus avantageux pour notre Musée.

The sharing out was finally handled through several exchanges and arrangements, as another letter from Seyrig to Woolley, dated 22 August 1936, reveals:

Une fois le partage fait sur ces bases, je ne suis pas opposé à certains échanges comme vous l'avait déjà dit Dunand. Pour me permettre de juger de l'opportunité de ces échanges, je vous serais reconnaissant de me faire connaître le plus exactement possible quelles sont, parmi les pièces attribuées par Dunand au Musée d'Antioche, celles que vous tiendriez à voir attribuer au Musée britannique, et quelles pièces vous seriez disposé à abandonner en échange.

It took several more months for the final catalog to be compiled by Woolley, judging by his letter to Seyrig attached with the catalog and dated 15 December 1936, as well as by Seyrig's answer dated 18 January 1937, in which he suggested several more exchanges and formally requested certain objects.

Meanwhile, the items had been sent to London with the mention "for study," implying that everything was to return to Syria before the final sharing out. Nevertheless, Woolley had organized an exhibition in London in early December 1936, so as to display the findings of Al-Mina to the public eye (Figure 5.1).[26] "Last week we opened here a temporary exhibition of the objects found in the course of the season; there has not been much time to do so much as I should have wished in the way of repairs, but still the things make a very good show."[27]

The quality of the exhibition and of its objects was later observed by Miss Evans, who mentioned it to Seyrig. As a matter of fact, Seyrig congratulated Woolley for this exhibition in his answer on 18 January 1937. According to the British Museum's online catalog, the archaeological findings from Al-Mina finally joined the British Museum's collections in 1955.[28]

---

26. A radiogram had urgently been sent to Seyrig because the objects intended for the exhibition in London were still in Alexandretta on 13 September 1936, see Figure 5.1 here.

27. Letter from Woolley to Seyrig, 15 December 1936.

28. See https://www.britishmuseum.org/about_us/departments/greece_and_rome/history_of_the _collection/the_twentieth_century.aspx (accessed 9 February 2017).

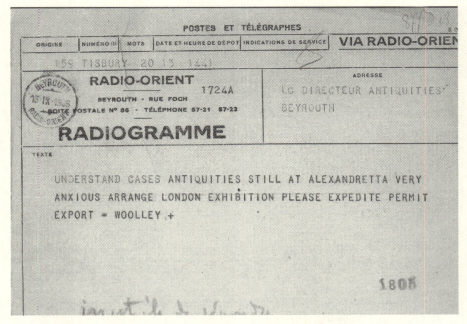

FIGURE 5.1. Radiogram sent by Woolley to Seyrig on 13 September 1936. Fonds Maurice Dunand, Patrimonial and administrative archives of the University of Geneva, CH UNIGE/aap/65/2011/21

In sum, the case of the sharing out of Al-Mina findings after the dig in March 1936 allows us to better understand how the sharing out of objects operated, but it especially highlights the relations between three big names of Oriental archaeology in the twentieth century.

The sharing out was done according to strict rules[29] which were meant to ensure an equal division. This division enabled the creation of museum collections in the Near East, as well as the expansion of those in Europe. The excavator had to sort through the objects and prepare two lots. Thereafter a delegate, an expert from the Service des antiquités, chose which lot would go to the Syrian state. Lastly, the Mohafez formalized the decision.

This episode, which could seem anecdotal, depicts Seyrig as director of the Service des antiquités, Woolley, the excavator of Ur, and Dunand, the excavator of Byblos, to whom we owe this exceptional documentation. As an expert and delegate of the Service des antiquités, Seyrig carefully safeguarded all written letters, as well as photographs and the catalog of objects. As it so happens, from 1940 on, he would be the director of the Service des antiquités himself.

One last detail in this correspondence deserves emphasis: the concession of the excavation of Tell Atchana. In his letter dated 2 September 1936, Woolley asked Seyrig

---

29. Regarding the regulation of antiquities in the Levant during the mandate, see for example bylaw N° 166 LR from 7 November 1933, pertaining to antiquities and published in Beirut in 1935. Chap. II, sec. I, article 4: "Sous réserve des dispositions prévues par le présent règlement, les droits dont les antiquités font l'objet sont régis par les lois de droit commun en vigueur dans les Etats sous Mandat."

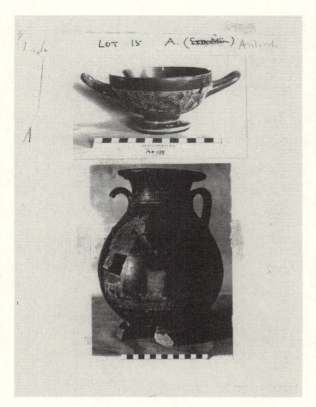

FIGURE 5.2. Excerpt of the catalog of objects compiled by Woolley (lot A). Fonds Maurice Dunand, Patrimonial and administrative archives of the University of Geneva, CH UNIGE/aap/65/2011/21

for permission to excavate Tell Marouche:[30] "You will, I hope, be pleased to hear that the Trustees of the British Museum have voted a handsome nucleus for the fund for excavations next spring; I hope to finish the Mina site and to make a good start at Atchana. Might I have the formal permit for excavations on the latter site, i.e., Tell Marouche,[31] as I think it is also called on the map of the Survey?" Thus, we learn that a second and final dig was envisaged for Al-Mina in spring 1937, and that Woolley would then be able to excavate ancient Alalakh. Indeed, Seyrig granted him the concession: "Pour ce qui est de la concession, elle sera accordée immédiatement, et vous en recevrez prochainement l'acte. Je vous serais reconnaissant de le signer sans retard:

---

30. "When Sir Leonard Woolley decided in 1935 to launch a field project in the northern Levant he surveyed forty mounds along the Amuq and the Orontes Delta. Having selected four sites, he received permission to excavate on of them (al-Mina) and to dig *sondages* at three other sites including Tell Atchana. In the following year he conducted the first season at the site of Tell Atchana, a short ten-day mission in which two trenches were excavated. It was during that period of time that Woolley gave attention to the name of the site, noting that 'on the French maps the mound is named Marouche and the tiny hamlet on its eastern end is called Atchana; Marouche is the name of somewhat larger village half a mile away. Local use is divided between two names, but on the whole Atchana seems the more generally employed'" (Woolley 1936, 126 n. 2), quoted by Sumaka'i Fink 2008, 165.

31. An Arabic name; Sumaka'i Fink 2008, 165 n. 1: "Many of the sites in the Amuq (Amik in Turkish) carry both Turkish and Arabic names. Some of the names are translations from Arabic to Turkish names, homophonic to the Arabic name. I believe that this is the case with the Turkish name Varışlı, used today to denote the Atchana village as well as a larger village across the main road, north of the Antakya-Aleppo highway. It is most probable the Varışlı stands for the Arabic Marouche."

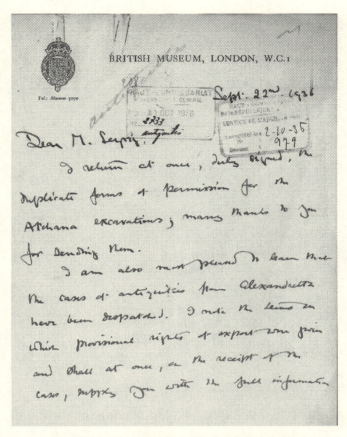

FIGURE 5.3. Handwritten letter from Woolley to Seyrig dated 22 September 1936, London. Fonds Maurice Dunand, Patrimonial and administrative archives of the University of Geneva, CH UNIGE/aap/65/2011/21

étant donné qu'en principe les objets d'un site ne peuvent être soumis à partage qu'en vertu d'une concession, le partage de vos trouvailles d'Atchana n'a pu avoir lieu que pour une tolérance, que je serais heureux de régulariser."[32]

On 22 September, Woolley wrote to Seyrig.

Dear M. Seyrig,
I returned at once, duly signed, the duplicate forms of permission for the Atchana excavations; many thanks to you for sending them (Figure 5.3).[33]

The concession was granted, and excavations began on the site of Alalakh in 1937. In this case too, the issue of the sharing out remained central, and even before the beginning of the excavations, Seyrig reminded Woolley of the requirement of official concession before proceeding with the sharing out of antiquities.

32. Letter from Seyrig to Woolley, 11 September 1936.
33. Handwritten letter from Woolley to Seyrig, 22 September 1936.

Appendix

Inventory of letters from the case:

20 June 1936	letter from Woolley to Seyrig, Sueidia (Al-Mina)
24 June 1936	letter from Woolley to Seyrig, Sueidia (Al-Mina)
29 June 1936	letter from Seyrig to Woolley, Beirut
30 June 1936	letter from Mr Meyrier (administration of the Service des antiquités) to the *délégué-adjoint* of the Haut-Commissaire pour le Mohafazat d'Alexandrette
8 July 1936	letter from S. E. Hysni Bey El-Barazi to the *délégué-adjoint* of the Haut-Commissaire pour le Mohafazat d'Alexandrette
11 July 1936	accompanying letter from the *conseiller-adjoint* of the Haut-Commissariat, *délégué-adjoint* of the Haut-Commissaire pour le Sandjak d'Alexandrette (this letter accompanied that of the Mohafez El-Barazi, addressed to Mr Meyrier)
23 July 1936	letter from Woolley to Robert Parr, London
4 August 1936	accompanying letter from Parr to Seyrig, Aleppo (this letter accompanied the copy of Woolley's letter to Parr from 23 July)
22 August 1936	letter from Seyrig to Woolley, Beirut
2 September 1936	letter from Woolley to Seyrig, London
11 September 1936	letter from Seyrig to Woolley, Beirut
13 September 1936	radiogram from Woolley to Seyrig, London (Figure 5.1)
22 September 1936	letter from Woolley to Seyrig, London (Figure 5.3)
15 December 1936	letter from Woolley to Seyrig, London
18 January 1937	letter from Seyrig to Woolley, Beirut

REFERENCES

Beazley, J. D. 1939. "Excavations at Al Mina, Sueidia III: The Red-figured Vases." *The Journal of Hellenic Studies* 59:1–44.

Elayi, J. 1987. "Al-Mina sur l'Oronte à l'époque perse." Pages 249–66 in *Phoenicia and the East Mediterranean in the First Millennium B.C.* Edited by E. Lipinski. Leuven: Peeters.

Graham, J. A. 1986. "The Historical Interpretation of Al Mina." *Dialogues d'histoire ancienne* 12:51–65.

Gran-Aymerich, E. 2007. *Les chercheurs du passé 1798–1945: Aux sources de l'archéologie.* Paris: CNRS Editions.

Kienle, E., ed. 2012. *Henri Seyrig (1895–1973). Actes du Colloque tenu les 10 et 11 octobre 2013 à la Bibliothèque nationale de France et à l'académie des Inscriptions et Belles-Lettres.* Syria Supplément III. Beirut: Institut français du Proche-Orient.

Lane Fox, R. 2008. *Travelling Heroes in the Epic Age of Homer.* London: Allen Lane.

Lehmann, G. 1996. *Untersuchungen zur späten Eisenzeit in Syrien und Libanon. Stratigraphie und Keramikformen zwischen ca. 720 bis 300 v. Chr.* Altertumskunde des Vorderen Orients 5. Münster: Ugarit-Verlag.

Michel, P. M. 2008. "Le Fonds d'archives Maurice Dunand à l'Université de Genève." *Anabases* 8:243–53.

Sumaka'i Fink, A. 2008. "Levantine Standardized Luxury in the Late Bronze Age: Waste Management at Tell Atchana (Alalakh)." Pages in 165–95 in *Bene Israel: Studies in the*

86   Patrick Maxime Michel

Archaeology of Israel and the Levant During the Bronze and Iron Ages in Honour of Israel Finkelstein. Edited by A. Fantalkin and A. Yassur-Landau. Leiden: Brill.
Woolley, L. 1936. "Tal Atchana." *The Journal of Hellenic Studies* 36:125–32.
———. 1937. "Excavations near Antioch." *Antiquaries Journal* 17:1–15.
———. 1938. "Excavations at Al Mina, Sueidia I and II." *The Journal of Hellenic Studies* 58:1–30, 133–70.
———. 1953. *A Forgotten Kingdom.* London: Penguin.

CHAPTER 6

"Die Assyriologie nicht weiter unberücksichtigt bleiben dürfte": On the (Non-)Existence of Assyriology at the German University in Prague (1908–1945)

Luděk Vacín and Jitka Sýkorová

ACCORDING TO THE MASTER NARRATIVE of Assyriology in Czechia, it all began upon the return of Bedřich Hrozný from Vienna to Prague and his appointment as Professor of Cuneiform Studies and History of the Ancient Orient at Charles University in 1919.[1] Assyriology then thrived for decades at the university department founded by Hrozný as well as at the independent Oriental Institute established three years later.[2]

The dominance of Hrozný and his school (notably Lubor Matouš, Josef Klíma, and Vladimír Souček) in the historiography of Assyriology in Czechia clearly hinges on the spectacular achievements of the decipherment of the Hittite language, the excavations at Kültepe, and subsequent numerous publications and studies of predominantly Hittite and Old Assyrian material.

However, this straightforward and exclusive story about Czech Assyriology eclipsed the lives and work of other scholars, Czech and German alike, who taught ancient Near Eastern languages in the Czech lands and published their Assyriological research in the first half of the twentieth century. Some of them were active not only alongside Hrozný but had offered Assyriological classes and published significant studies years before Hrozný's appointment. In fact, the true beginning of Czech Assyriology can currently be traced back to 1906 and, surprisingly enough, outside of Prague.[3]

In this essay, we will describe the history of German Assyriology in Prague. Even though never institutionally established, the field was represented there by three outstanding scholars between 1908 and 1945. Two of them spent only limited time in Prague, and both are well known to every student of cuneiform cultures. However, the one who introduced Assyriology to the German academic milieu in Prague, and who continued to teach it throughout the investigated period, is almost entirely forgotten.

Authors' note: This chapter is an output of project No. 15-04166Y funded by the Czech Science Foundation (GA ČR). We would like to thank the staff of the National Archive (NA), the Archive of Charles University (AUK), and the National Museum—Náprstek Museum of Asian, African, and American Cultures (NpM) in Prague for assistance in locating the pertinent archival sources and for permission to publish reproductions of some of those. We are also indebted to Martin Dekarli for providing us with a copy of Kisch 1975, and to Michal Topor for a copy of his recent monograph relevant to this study (Topor 2015).

1. For a solid account of Hrozný's life and work, see now the studies in Velhartická 2015 and particularly Svatoš 2015.

2. See, e.g., Zbavitel 1959, 22–25, 44–46.

3. Research on the Czech predecessors and contemporaries of Hrozný is currently well underway and will be published elsewhere in due course.

Special attention will be paid to a failed attempt at establishing a chair of Assyriology at the Faculty of Arts of the German University between 1922 and 1929, which, if successful, may have changed the global history of the field. We will then follow the development of the Department of Semitic Philology at that faculty until February 1945, when the graduation of a peculiar doctoral candidate with his thesis on an Assyriological topic effectively marked the end of German cuneiform studies in Prague.

The Divided University and Available Sources on German Assyriology in Prague

Essentials About the Partition of Prague University

The University of Prague, founded in 1348 by decree of the king of Bohemia and later (1355) Holy Roman Emperor Charles IV as the first institution of its kind north of the Alps, became a predominantly German place of learning after the incorporation of the Czech lands into the Habsburg Empire in 1526 at the latest.

Only in 1848 was instruction in the Czech language allowed. Toward the end of the 1860s, the interest in Czech classes increased considerably, as did the number of Czech lecturers. The nation that finally got the opportunity for higher education in its own language began to build its intellectual elite at the domestic university founded half a millennium ago to that end.

At the time of growing tension between the Czechs and Germans, the German academic community resolved that it would have been best to split the university into two parts, one for each nation. However, the Czechs demanded that the split be carried out at a later date, once there were enough Czech teachers for all key disciplines and the students had relevant textbooks in the Czech language.

Early in the 1880s, the request of the Germans that the University of Prague be divided was discussed in the Austro-Hungarian parliament, and on 11 April 1881 Emperor Franz Joseph I issued a decree to that effect which was finally implemented by the Viennese government at the beginning of 1882. Both universities should have used the name Charles'-Ferdinand's. The partition of Prague University came into effect in the winter semester of 1882 and remained in effect until the German University was closed on 18 October 1945 by decree of Czechoslovak President Edvard Beneš.

Professors could decide which part of the university they wanted to be affiliated with. Their institutes and departments automatically followed suit. Even though the German University was very well equipped, both in terms of staff and facilities—most professors of the united university continued to teach at the German part, which also kept most of the clinics, departments, institutes, libraries, and the archive—interest in German lectures steadily declined. The Czech University had more students than the German one simply because the Czech population always constituted the majority in the Czech lands, and the students no longer had to learn German in order to be able to enter the university.

Both universities tended to ignore each other, and their relationships were limited to necessary official and professional communication (e.g., international conferences). This situation was in favor of the Czechs, who tried to promote their mother tongue in

"Die Assyriologie nicht weiter unberücksichtigt bleiben dürfte"   89

all academic and cultural areas where the German language had been used by default in the past. In view of the age-old tension between the two nations, both universities understood the proclaiming and promoting of the interests of their own nation as their "national duty" during much of the time of their coexistence.

As a consequence of this development, the German academic community became ever more isolated beyond the context of the Czech lands. Viewed from the centers of German learning and culture, such as Berlin, Munich, or Vienna, the German University in Prague was considered "provincial" and "low-grade," and therefore unattractive not only for German-speaking students, but also for academics from East Central Europe who generally preferred Vienna, Leipzig, or Berlin. For some of them, Prague was even "overly Jewish," as many members of the German-speaking community in Prague were Jews. Frequently, German junior academics used an appointment in Prague merely as a "stepping stone," while for senior scholars it constituted an "interchange junction" on their journey to a better and more respected position elsewhere. All those factors significantly contributed to the long-term instability and variability of faculty at the German University in Prague.[4]

Essentials About the Relationship of the German University and Czechoslovak Authorities

After the fall of the Habsburg Empire and the establishment of the Czechoslovak Republic in autumn 1918, the German University in Prague came under the administration of new authorities, particularly the Ministry of Education and National Enlightenment (Ministerstvo školství a národní osvěty, henceforth MŠANO). Generally, no essential changes in the higher education system took place in the "First Republic" (1918–1938) period, and the new state basically replicated the tried and tested Habsburg system concerning the internal management of universities, their relationship to state authorities, and the status of faculty and students.[5]

In 1919, the Czechoslovak parliament passed a bill on the salaries and status of university professors. A year later they also passed a language act to regulate the management of public institutions like schools run in languages of the minorities (including German), and in 1926 another bill on state administration was passed, again stipulating the wages of university professors. Those legal norms defined the pay of the German University teaching staff, their status as state employees, and the rules for liaison between the German University and Czechoslovak authorities.[6]

The bill of 1919 guaranteed autonomy to all universities, thus the state virtually did not interfere with their matters at all. Appointments of new professors took place according to previous norms and customs. A faculty set up a special committee that prepared a proposal for filling the position with a primary candidate and several alternatives. The board of professors then voted on the proposal and, if approved, the

---

4. In general, this section draws on the studies of the history of Charles University between 1848 and 1918 in Havránek and Pousta 2001, 71–174. Regarding the German University, it builds on Hlaváčková, Míšková and Pešek 2001. See further the important essays in Neumüller 1984 and Lemberg 2003.

5. See the valuable comparative study of the humanities at Universities of Leipzig, Vienna, and Prague, Konrád 2007.

6. Konrád 2007, 191.

proposal was submitted to the MŠANO which informed the president of the Republic. Candidates were then formally approached. If any of them agreed to take up the position, the president appointed the candidate as professor.

Yet, a very different and much more complicated situation arose if a candidate from abroad was proposed, which proves to have been quite important for the attempts to appoint an Assyriologist at the German University, as will be shown later in this essay. The new Czechoslovak Republic generally preferred inland candidates. According to Czechoslovak laws, a university professor was an employee of the state, and the state was not much interested in employing foreigners. In such cases, the process of appointment could be quite complex and protracted, as the MŠANO requested information on the political and personal credentials of the candidates from the Ministry of Foreign Affairs, sometimes even from the Ministry of the Interior.[7]

Furthermore, if a foreign professor wanted a position in Prague, he must have met an essential condition, which was to acquire Czechoslovak citizenship (just like he would have had to become a citizen of Austria-Hungary before). This was one of the main reasons why foreign candidates showed little interest in a professorship in Prague after early in the 1920s; to become a Czechoslovak citizen also meant to be conscripted into the Czechoslovak military.

All this constituted a disadvantage particularly for the German University which strove to compete with universities in Germany and Austria. As it was difficult to appoint professors only from the ranks of the German-speaking minority in Czechoslovakia, who could also get a position in Germany or Austria, the German University was immensely interested in attracting foreign academics.[8]

However, there was another significant obstacle: the salary level. Professors were paid from the state budget and their salaries were regulated by special laws, setting them apart from the rest of state employees. Further, some old Austrian legal norms were still in effect which allowed for granting higher salary on an individual basis. In general, the wages of university professors were the highest in comparison with other state officials (except judges of higher courts of law), and their advance on the salary scale was the fastest. Wages could be increased even beyond the salary scale.

Still, the wages of professors of the German University could not compare with the income of professors from Germany or Austria, while a newcomer to Prague had to start at the lowest salary grade, which was a huge problem for many. The necessity to obtain Czechoslovak citizenship together with a considerable salary drop were the main reasons why professors from Germany were usually not willing to take up a position in Prague.[9]

On the other hand, we must take into account the security, economic, and social situation in Germany at the time. The German economy was ruined by the war indemnities imposed on the country by the victorious powers after World War I. The huge unemployment rate, poverty, devaluation of currency, the feelings of betrayal and national disgrace all resulted in both leftist and rightist political radicalism, riots, and outright chaos in many parts of the country. In contrast, Prague was a safe place in the newly established republic that was economically very much on the rise.

7 Konrád 2007, 192–93.
8 Konrád 2007, 194.
9. Konrád 2007, 196–97.

As the Prague-born law historian Guido Kisch fittingly put it in his memoirs:

Am 13. November 1923 kostete ein Dollar in Berlin 840 Milliarden Mark. In Prag entwickelten sich dagegen die Verhältnisse nach Gründung der Tschechoslowakischen Republik durch den ersten Präsidenten Thomas Masaryk weitaus günstiger. Die germanistische Professur an der Deutschen Universität war dort noch immer vakant. Die Regierung wollte sie lieber durch einen gebürtigen Prager besetzt sehen, als einen der zahlreichen Bewerber aus Deutschland berufen, welche von den in der Tschechoslowakei sich stabilisierenden politischen und günstiger entwickelnden wirtschaftlichen Verhältnissen angezogen wurden.[10]

This shows that despite the disadvantages described above, in the political and economic circumstances of the day, Prague could be a promising place for academics from the German-speaking countries, yet hardly for established full professors. As we shall see later on, faculty committees selected suitable candidates apparently with such considerations in mind, i.e., from among academics whose career was still at the outset, or whose current position was somewhat unstable. Thus, the majority of foreign candidates who did get a position in Prague came shortly after their *Habilitation* or having obtained an associate professorship (*ausserordentliche Professur*). With a full professorship, Prague offered them social security at a well-equipped university along with high status in a vibrant city where Germans were in the minority but could develop their social and cultural life as they pleased. For some of the candidates, these factors outweighed all the obstacles recounted above.[11]

Finally, we must mention the so-called *Lex Mareš* of 19 February 1920 regarding the relationship of the two Prague universities. The German University perceived this law as unjust toward the German minority. Indeed, the law did complicate the relationship of the German University toward the Czechoslovak state because it proclaimed the Czech University as the only successor to the medieval institution. Accordingly, the Czech University was renamed "Charles University," while the German one was from then on called the "German University." The consequences of this decision became most pungent in a dozen years, when, inspired by the developments in Germany, the German students and some academics began to use their university as an arena of nationalist, if not outright National Socialist politics.[12]

Available Sources on German Assyriology in Prague

After the preliminary passages introducing major points of the context in which the story of German Assyriology in Prague took place, a few words should be said about the crucial source material which substantiates the following narrative.

Available sources can be divided into three groups: (1) academic, (2) administrative, and (3) private, with a certain degree of overlap between all groups. Even though there are considerable gaps in the documentation, and many sources do not reveal information desirable for historical research which invites some reading between the

10. Kisch 1975, 79.
11. Konrád 2007, 198, 200–201, 203–4.
12. Konrád 2007, 205–7.

lines and speculation, it is possible to draw a coherent picture of the history of Assyriology at the German University in Prague by combining material from all source groups.

1. The academic sources are kept in the Archive of Charles University (AUK) in Prague. The ravages of World War II have left most of the dossiers of individual faculties of the German University in a fragmentary state, particularly the personal files, which could be remedied at least in the case of deceased academics by using obituaries found in official publications of the university. On the other hand, the dossier of the Department of Semitic Philology at the Faculty of Arts is comparatively well preserved, including the proceedings of the selection committees set up to appoint a new professor, i.e., some of the key material for this essay. These files allow us to closely follow the development of the department for most of the investigated period. As for Assyriological teaching at the German University, the fully preserved series of syllabi published by the university constitute an indispensable source of information.
2. Sources of administrative or official nature are kept in the National Archive (NA) in Prague. The crucial ones are documents on appointments of professors issued by both the Habsburg and Czechoslovak administrations. An essential dossier is the MŠANO files on the selection of a new professor at the Department of Semitic Philology. Those documents add important information to that gleaned from the corresponding files kept in the AUK, while they reveal the viewpoint of the ministry in some detail as well. Another significant body of archival sources are the documents which the police authorities of the Habsburg, Czechoslovak, and Nazi governments kept on the individuals who played a role in the history of German Assyriology and Semitic philology in Prague. Those files include passport applications with personal data (and photographs), population registry sheets, and similar records that add important bits of information to the whole story.
3. There are only a few relevant sources of private nature, kept in the Náprstek Museum of Asian, African, and American Cultures (NpM) in Prague as part of a large collection of correspondence addressed to Hrozný. Particularly the letter from Benno Landsberger to Hrozný, edited in this chapter, provides immensely important insights into the attempt to appoint an Assyriologist at the Department of Semitic Philology in 1922. Useful passages from the memoirs of the Prague-born law historian Guido Kisch (1975), and from the brief autobiography of the historian of cuneiform law Paul Koschaker (1951) can also be counted among the private sources for this study.

Needless to say, information from archival sources will be complemented with relevant data from secondary literature as applicable. Since full references to the archival sources used are very complex, the long titles of individual items often blending Czech and German expressions followed by various abbreviations and numbers, we decided to assign a siglum to each item. The sigla will be used in the footnotes, while full references are given in the chart at the end of the chapter.

A Survey of Assyriological Teaching and Research at the German University

The history of Assyriology at the German University in Prague will be described chronologically, beginning with two scholars from the Theological Faculty, where the interest in ancient Near Eastern cultures was first recast into actual teaching and research.

Assyriology at the German Theological Faculty

As in many other cases in the German-speaking cultural area, German (Roman Catholic) theologians in Prague became interested in Assyriology in the wake of the "Babel-Bibel-Streit," culminating in 1902–1904 with three lectures given by Assyriologist Friedrich Delitzsch, revolving around the question of the influence of Babylonian culture, literature, and religion on the Old Testament.[13]

Perhaps surprisingly, the response to Delitzsch's bold conclusions in Roman Catholic circles was milder than in Protestant and Jewish environments,[14] and many Catholic scholars began to seriously study Assyriology either for apologetic reasons or just to become well versed in the discipline then perceived as intimately related to biblical studies and the linguistics of Old Testament languages.

Josef Rieber (Figure 6.1) belonged to the former category. Born on 22 January 1862 in Bečov nad Teplou (Petschau) in the western part of the region of the Czech lands that bordered Germany—a place inhabited predominantly by Germans which came to be known as the *Sudetenland*—Rieber went on to study theology in Prague (1883–1887). Ordained as a priest in 1887, he fulfilled his pastoral duties for several years, at the same time pursuing his doctoral studies in theology. Having graduated in 1892, he taught canon law and Semitic languages at the Theological Faculty and became associate professor in those fields in 1897. He spent the year 1898 at the universities of Leipzig, Halle, and Berlin deepening his knowledge of the Bible and Semitics. Subsequently, Rieber was appointed Professor of the Old Testament and Semitic Languages at the Theological Faculty of his alma mater, where he taught Old Testament exegesis, Hebrew, Aramaic, Syriac, Ethiopic, and Arabic until his retirement in 1932. He frequently served as dean or vice-dean of the Theological Faculty and was elected Rector Magnificus of the German University for the academic year 1905–1906. He died on 5 December 1934.[15]

Although Rieber published a comparative study on the "Flood" in Semitic literatures as early as 1897, he extensively worked on Assyriological topics only at the time of the "Babel-Bibel-Streit." Having published a paper on the importance of the Tell el-Amarna cuneiform texts first, he commented on the Babel-Bibel controversy itself, devoting also his inaugural lecture as rector of the university to the same topic.[16] The latter essay with the programmatic title "The Modern Fight over the Bible" betrays

---

13. For details on the controversy see Lehmann 1994, Johanning 1988, Shavit and Eran 2007, 156–352.

14. See Johanning 1988, 203–17.

15. AUK Rieber, NA Rieber. See also Hahn 2000, and the lists of rectors, vice-rectors, deans, and vice-deans of the German University in Havránek 1997, 343–47 and Havránek and Pousta 1998, 587–89.

16. See Rieber 1897, 1903, 1904, and 1905.

FIGURE 6.1. Josef Rieber (1862–1934), Professor of the Old Testament and Semitic Languages. Source: AUK Rieber

his position as a defender of biblical truth against the findings of Assyriology, which he was nevertheless very well versed in.[17]

Even though an expert in various Semitic languages, well acquainted with and interested in the advances and results of Assyriological research, Rieber never taught cuneiform languages, nor did he publish any work in the field of Mesopotamian philology proper. That was to be the task of his disciple, the only true Assyriologist among the German academics in Prague.

Franz Xaver Steinmetzer (Figure 6.2a–b) was born on 12 January 1879 in Dubá (Dauba) in the northern part of the *Sudetenland* into the family of a physician. He moved to Prague for his high school studies, where he then continued his education at the Theological Faculty of the German University. Ordained as a priest in 1901, he fulfilled pastoral duties for a year in Bečov nad Teplou (Petschau), the hometown of his teacher Rieber, after which he was called back to Prague to pursue doctoral studies.[18] He graduated in January 1905 with a dissertation, supervised by Rieber, entitled "Illustratur sententia trita: In V.T. prophetae, sacerdotes necnon reges ungebantur (Explaining the Known Statement: In the Old Testament Were the Prophets, Priests, and even Kings Anointed)."[19]

From winter semester of 1905 until the summer semester 1907, Steinmetzer studied with Adolf Erman, Eduard Meyer, Adolf von Harnack, and particularly with Friedrich Delitzsch in Berlin. He frequented the lessons in Oriental languages and literatures

17. See Shavit and Eran 2007, 199 n. 11 where Rieber's surname is erroneously spelled as Lieber.
18. See NA Steinmetzer Passport, Makariusová 2008.
19. AUK Steinmetzer.

FIGURE 6.2a–b. Franz Xaver Steinmetzer (1879–1945), Professor of Biblical Studies and New Testament Exegesis (and Assyriology) in 1922 and 1932. Source: NA Steinmetzer Passport

both at the university department and at the *Institut Judaicum*.[20] As a result, he published a detailed analysis of the deuterocanonical book of Judith.[21]

In the winter semester of 1907, Steinmetzer gave lessons on Hebrew antiquity, the grammar of biblical Hebrew, Arabic grammar, and the grammar of Ethiopic at the Theological Faculty of his alma mater in Prague.[22] In 1908 Steinmetzer completed his *Habilitation* at the Theological Faculty and received a secondary school professorship at the theological seminary in Litoměřice (Leitmeritz) in the *Sudetenland* region, northwest of Prague.[23]

However, already in autumn 1908 he was back in Berlin for further studies with Delitzsch. Under his supervision, Steinmetzer completed, and in May 1909 successfully defended, a dissertation entitled "Die Schenkungsurkunde des Königs Melišihu an seinen Sohn Marduk-aplam-iddina: Umschrift, Übersetzung und Erklärung in Zusammenhang mit den übrigen sogen. 'Grenzsteinen,'"[24] thereby obtaining his doctorate in Assyriology. The cuneiform cultures were from that point on at the center of Steinmetzer's research.[25]

20. See Makariusová 2008, Topor 2015, 224, 229, 239, 245.
21. Steinmetzer 1907.
22. See Topor 2015, 246.
23. See Makariusová 2008.
24. See Topor 2015, 264. The work was published as Steinmetzer 1910b.
25. Cf. his monograph comparing the birth and childhood of Christ with Babylonian mythology, Steinmetzer 1910a.

96   Luděk Vacín and Jitka Sýkorová

It is no wonder, then, that the emperor resolved to appoint the thirty-one year old gifted, versatile, and prolific scholar as Associate Professor of Biblical Studies and New Testament Exegesis at the Theological Faculty of the German University in Prague effective from 1 October 1910.[26] The appointment as full professor followed shortly thereafter, effective from 1 November 1912.[27] We find it noteworthy with respect to Steinmetzer's self-perception as a scholar that while the appointment documents do not mention Assyriology at all, in documents issued by the university he is sometimes referred to as Professor of New Testament (Exegesis) and Assyriology,[28] which is a combination that may raise the eyebrows of many an advocate of interdisciplinary approach in the humanities even today! Obviously, he wished to be acknowledged as an Assyriologist, and deservedly so.

Steinmetzer offered Assyriological classes for the first time in the summer semester of 1908 and continued to teach the discipline along with New Testament exegesis until summer semester 1942. The only break in his Assyriological teaching was World War II, during which he continued to offer his New Testament courses. As becomes clear from the list of his Assyriological classes in Appendix 1, Steinmetzer mastered virtually all areas of contemporary Assyriology, with a focus on cuneiform languages (particularly Akkadian), (comparative) mythology, and Babylonian and Assyrian economic, legal, and monumental texts.

Being at the intersection of the latter two categories, the Babylonian *kudurru* inscriptions became his favorite topic. All his major scholarly publications after his appointment are devoted to the *kudurru*s.[29] Steinmetzer's research on that topic culminated with the publication of his magnum opus in 1922, a monograph on the *kudurru*s which remained the standard work until the recent publication of the comprehensive study by Susanne Paulus.[30]

As a specialist on the *kudurru* inscriptions, Steinmetzer was invited to contribute his lexicographical material to the preliminary files for the *Assyrian Dictionary* of the Oriental Institute of the University of Chicago, which he did.[31] Steinmetzer's merits in Assyriology further granted him membership in the Oriental Institute in Prague and a place in the editorial board of its journal *Archiv orientální* (see Figure 6.3).[32]

---

26. NA Steinmetzer Appointment: "An den Privatdozenten an der deutschen Universität in Prag und Professor an der theologischen Diözesanlehranstalt in Leitmeritz Dr. theol. Franz Steinmetzer. Seine k. u. k. Apostolische Majestät haben mit Ah. Entschließung vom 21. August 1910 Sie zum ausserordentlichen Professor des Bibelstudiums und der Exegese des neuen Testamentes an der deutschen Universität in Prag mit den systemmäßigen Bezügen und der Rechtswirksamkeit vom 1. Oktober 1910 allergn. zu ernennen geruht." The file also contains Steinmetzer's own handwritten CV and a detailed proposal for his appointment dated 31 January 1910 which are important sources of information on his life and career up to that date.

27. NA Steinmetzer Appointment: "Ich ernenne den ausserordentlichen Professor Dr. Franz Steinmetzer zum ordentlichen Professor des Bibelstudiums und der Exegese des Neuen Testamentes an der theologischen Fakultät der deutschen Universität in Prag. Wien, am 1. Oktober 1912. Franz Joseph m.p."

28. See, e.g., AUK Classes 36, 21.

29. Cf. Steinmetzer 1912, 1915, 1918, 1920a, 1920b, 1927, and 1936.

30. See Steinmetzer 1922, and the assessment of the work in Paulus 2014, 3. The bibliographic data in Paulus 2014, 906 shows that she used all relevant works by Steinmetzer.

31. Cf. Pešek et al. 1998, 188. See Gelb 1964, xiii and xxiii.

32. Pešek et al. 2001, 247–48, Makariusová 2008. Sadly, Steinmetzer's merits did not warrant him an entry in the RlA.

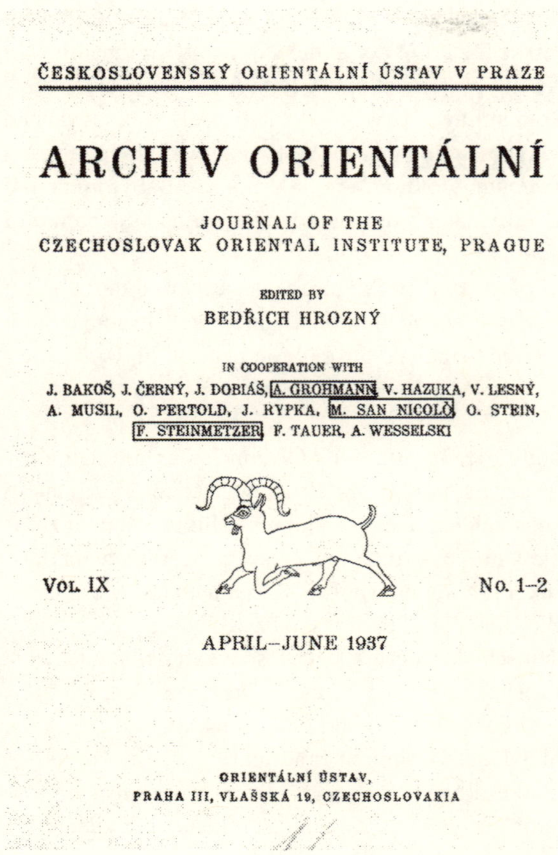

"*Die Assyriologie nicht weiter unberücksichtigt bleiben dürfte*" 97

FIGURE 6.3. Title page of a 1937 issue of *ArOr* with our *dramatis personae* highlighted. Source: Digital Library of the Czech Academy of Sciences (http://www.digitalniknihovna.cz/knav)

ČESKOSLOVENSKÝ ORIENTÁLNÍ ÚSTAV V PRAZE

ARCHIV ORIENTÁLNÍ

JOURNAL OF THE
CZECHOSLOVAK ORIENTAL INSTITUTE, PRAGUE

EDITED BY
BEDŘICH HROZNÝ

IN COOPERATION WITH

J. BAKOŠ, J. ČERNÝ, J. DOBIÁŠ, A. GROHMANN, V. HAZUKA, V. LESNÝ,
A. MUSIL, O. PERTOLD, J. RYPKA, M. SAN NICOLÒ, O. STEIN,
F. STEINMETZER, F. TAUER, A. WESSELSKI

Vol. IX   No. 1–2

APRIL–JUNE 1937

ORIENTÁLNÍ ÚSTAV,
PRAHA III, VLAŠSKÁ 19, CZECHOSLOVAKIA

Since wars always make suffer the most those who deserve it the least, Steinmetzer died in July 1945 in a transit camp near the town of Slaný not far from Prague whilst awaiting expulsion to Germany like almost all the other Czechoslovak Germans.[33]

Assyriology at the German Faculty of Law and Political Science

While from the perspective of our time it may seem a little odd to find cuneiform scholarship at a *Rechts- und Staatswissenschaftliche Fakultät*, it was certainly not unusual in the first half of the past century, when some law historians decided to anchor their research in the rich reservoir of cuneiform legal and business texts, not much exploited up to that point. For that endeavor they were well armed with knowledge of Roman law and the rapidly developing Graeco-Roman papyrology. Two pioneers of that interdisciplinary branch of ancient Near Eastern studies worked at the German University in Prague between 1909 and 1935.

Paul Koschaker, the actual founder of cuneiform law history, was born on 19 April 1879 in Klagenfurt. He graduated as Doctor of Jurisprudence at the University of Graz

33. The precise date and circumstances of his death cannot be ascertained. A note in Czech in NA Steinmetzer Register states laconically: "July 1945, died at labor in Slaný—date unknown."

in 1903. After further study of law and legal history in Leipzig, he got a *Habilitation* in Graz in 1905. He was appointed associate professor at the University of Innsbruck in 1908 but, attracted by the offer of a full professorship, he left for Prague a year later.[34]

Appointed as *Ordinarius* of Roman Law,[35] Koschaker taught only courses related to that field.[36] However, most of his research work in the Prague period was already devoted to *Keilschriftrechtsgeschichte*, yielding a monograph on Babylonian and Assyrian warranty law which, in Koschaker's own words, determined the nature of his research for the rest of his career.[37]

Koschaker had fond memories of his time in Prague, as is clear from the relevant passage in his autobiography which may sound "politically incorrect" to some, but it gives an idea how a German academic perceived the environment of the *Dreivölker-stadt* Prague at the time:

> Schon zum Frühjahr 1909 folgte die Berufung als Ordinarius an die dama-
> lige deutsche Universität in Prag. Es mochte für einen deutschen Alpenlän-
> der bedenklich erscheinen, in das von nationalen Kämpfen erfüllte Böhmen zu
> gehen ... doch blicke ich auf die Jahre 1909–1914, die ich in Prag verbrachte, mit
> besonderer Befriedigung zurück. Prag war eine geistig regsame Stadt, wie auch
> die Čechen geistig und wirtschaftlich die Elite der slawischen Nationen Öster-
> reichs waren. Was die kleine deutsche Minderheit betraf, so ergab sich dasselbe
> schon daraus, daß sie zum großen Teil aus Juden bestand, deren Familien, schon
> seit langem in Prag ansässig, weitgehend assimiliert und hoch kultiviert waren,
> so daß die Juden als Träger des Deutschtums in Prag galten. Damit scheint
> es mir zusammenzuhängen, daß es keinen ausgesprochenen Antisemitismus
> gab. ... So war Prag reich für mich an persönlichen und anregenden Beziehun-
> gen. ... Die Arbeits-, insbesondere die Bibliotheksverhältnisse waren in dem
> großen Prag natürlich wesentlich günstigere, zumal die Universitätsbibliothek
> beiden Universitäten, der deutschen und der čechischen, gemeinsam war.[38]

Even though he obviously enjoyed living and working in Prague, Koschaker belonged among the young scholars for whom the full professorship in that city was essentially a stepping stone to a better employment elsewhere in the German cultural area.[39]

---

34. On Koschaker's career see Müller 1982, Petschow 1983, Ries 1979, San Nicolò 1953. For a recent study on Koschaker, see Neumann 2012, and particularly Beggio 2018.

35. NA Koschaker Appointment. The appointment effective from 1 April 1909 seems to have been conditioned in some way—perhaps because of the youth of the new *Ordinarius*—because on 23 October 1911 Koschaker asked for confirmation of his teaching position stating that three years have already passed since his appointment. His professorship was confirmed on 7 February 1912.

36. See the syllabi of the Faculty of Law and Political Science in AUK Classes 5–8.

37. Koschaker 1911. In his short autobiography, Koschaker (1951, 113) states: "So ist ... ein Buch ent-standen, das für Jahre und im Grunde bis heute weitgehend meine Forschung bestimmen sollte."

38. Koschaker 1951, 112.

39. Arguably the most famous example is the physicist Albert Einstein whose short stay at the German University as full professor (spring 1911 to autumn 1912) falls within Koschaker's Prague period. Unlike Koschaker, Einstein considered the atmosphere in Prague as stiff and self-congratulatory to the point of ridiculousness, particularly in comparison with the liberalism and democracy of Switzerland, where he returned as full professor after the Prague interlude which had not been pointless as it did bolster his career in practical terms. See Schulmann 2005, 159.

"Die Assyriologie nicht weiter unberücksichtigt bleiben dürfte" 99

Already in August 1914 he asked to be relieved of his post, which the emperor approved on 19 September, and Koschaker left the university by the end of that month.[40]

Subsequently, he worked at the universities of Frankfurt am Main (1914–1915), Leipzig (1915–1936), Berlin (1936–1941), and Tübingen (1941–1946). The twenty-one years he spent in Leipzig were decisive for his research on cuneiform legal history. In Leipzig he could rely on the philological knowledge and acumen of Landsberger in particular. Koschaker kept teaching even after his retirement. He was visiting professor in Munich (1946–1947), Halle (1948), Ankara (1949–1950), and Bonn (1951). He died on 1 June 1951.[41] After Koschaker's departure from Prague in 1914, his chair remained vacant for several years until it was taken up by a law historian influenced by Koschaker's work.

Mariano San Nicolò was born on 20 August 1887 in the town of Rovereto in South Tyrol into the family of a regional high court judge of noble birth.[42] He studied law in Graz, having graduated in 1911 as Doctor of Jurisprudence.[43] He spent the years 1911–1913 at Leopold Wenger's *Seminar für Papyrusforschung* in Munich, where he prepared the first volume of his *Ägyptisches Vereinswesen zur Zeit der Ptolemäer und Römer* which secured him the *venia legendi* for Roman Law at the University of Graz in 1913.[44]

Yet, shortly after he commenced teaching, San Nicolò had to join the Austro-Hungarian military, and spent much of the war as an officer in Albania. At Koschaker's suggestion he turned to cuneiform law history and taught himself the cuneiform script as well as the Akkadian language during those years.[45]

San Nicolò was appointed as Associate Professor of Roman Law at the German University in Prague effective from 1 October 1917.[46] However, as he was still in the army, he could not take up the post until winter semester of 1918, and his situation was somewhat unclear even then because the monarchy had fallen and the Czechoslovak Republic was just being established in autumn 1918.[47] Nonetheless, San Nicolò quickly settled down in Prague and soon started teaching Roman law. Just like Koschaker, he never offered Assyriological courses.[48] As of 1 October 1920, the president of Czechoslovakia appointed him as full Professor of Roman Law, in which capacity he worked at the German University for the next fifteen years.[49] His first substantial

40. NA Koschaker Appointment.
41. See Petschow 1983 and Ries 1979.
42. Ries 2005, 430.
43. Steinwenter and Falkenstein 1955, 494 and Ries 2005, 430.
44. Steinwenter and Falkenstein 1955, 494, Ries 2005, 430, and Pfeifer 2009, 24.
45. Steinwenter and Falkenstein 1955, 494–95, Ries 2005, 430, and Pfeifer 2009, 24.
46. NA San Nicolò Appointment.
47. AUK San Nicolò. The preserved personal file in the university archive contains a number of letters and statements from San Nicolò to military, government, and university authorities and back, dating to this period.
48. See the syllabi of the Faculty of Law and Political Science in AUK Classes 9–22.
49. AUK San Nicolò. Unfortunately, most of the remaining documents in the personal file for the whole fifteen-year period are limited to financial matters (requests for subsidies, remunerations; grants for purchase of books, subsidies for printing costs of major publications, bursaries for research and conference travels), housing problems, etc., which have little bearing on a historical reconstruction of San Nicolò's life and work in Prague.

100 Luděk Vacín and Jitka Sýkorová

work from the realm of cuneiform legal history appeared already two years after his appointment as *Ordinarius*.[50]

It was about the same time when San Nicolò's political convictions began to show as well. It was certainly not unusual for a professor of the German University to be politically active, particularly in the sense of "defending" the cultural identity of the German minority in Czechoslovakia. In fact, a number of academics and some of the rectors—especially the Church Historian August Naegle (in office 1918–1920 and again in 1929–1930) among the latter—very much cherished national sentiments and did not hesitate to show their disdain for the new state where they felt "besieged."[51]

However, most of the nationalistic excesses were from early on instigated by the radical German Student Union (*Deutsche Studentenschaft*), the statutes of which openly stipulated that "non-Aryans" were not allowed to become members. The majority of the professors who had overcome the shock of the loss in World War I and gradually accepted the new reality of coexistence with the Czechs in a state not ruled by the German minority, attempted to tame the passions, at least until the years of economic crisis and the Nazi takeover in Germany. Moreover, until the early 1930s, anti-Semitism was gaining ground much more slowly at the German University in Prague than at universities in Germany and Austria.[52]

Still, it must be noted that some professors supported the student union and their anti-Semitic tirades virtually from the beginning, San Nicolò among them.[53] In the wake of the "Steinherz Affair,"[54] the Prague-born law historian Kisch was invited to teach at the German University in 1924, when San Nicolò was dean of the Faculty of Law and Political Science. According to Kisch's memoirs:

> Den Gegensatz . . . bildete allein der mir bis dahin unbekannte Vertreter des römischen Rechts, Mariano San Nicolò, der im Jahre 1924 das Dekanat der rechts- und staatswissenschaftlichen Fakultät bekleidete. Wie schon sein Name erkennen läßt, war er italienischer Nationalität [*sic*!], zwar ein Schüler von Paul Koschaker [*sic*!], gerierte sich aber stramm deutschnational und entschieden antisemitisch. . . . Ich war ein willkommenes Objekt seiner von mir nicht provozierten Angriffe. Während alle anderen Mitglieder des Lehrkörpers meiner

---

50. San Nicolò 1922.
51. See Pešek et al. 2001, 245.
52. Pešek et al. 2001, 245–47.
53. Pešek et al. 2001, 247, 252 and Konrád 2007, 209.
54. In July 1922, Professor Samuel Steinherz was elected Rector Magnificus of the German University, which provoked riots of the *Deutsche Studentenschaft*, petitions (also from the citizens of towns and villages in the *Sudetenland*), and appeals in the press demanding Steinherz's immediate resignation. As the turmoil intesified, Steinherz decided to step down, but the MŠANO refused his resignation. With the support of the MŠANO, several unions of liberal-minded German students, the academic senate, and a number of the professors, the situation eventually calmed down. See Pešek et al. 2001, 247 and Konrád 2007, 207–8 with further literature. Cf. the latest biography of the student activist and organizer of the riots, Kleo Pleyer, in Fahlbusch, Haar, and Pinwinkler 2017, 601: "Er studierte danach an der Deutschen Universität in Prag Philosophie, Slawistik und Germanistik und organisierte den 'grenzvölkischen Kampf' der deutschen Studentenschaft. Als der jüdische Professor Samuel Steinherz zum Rektor der Deutschen Universität gewählt wurde, reagierten die zahlreichen völkisch orientierten Studenten mit Drohungen und scharfer antisemitischer Hetze gegen die angebliche 'Verjudung' der Universität. Pleyer war im November 1922 massgeblich an einem Studentenstreik und der Besetzung von Universitätsgebäuden beteiligt."

"Die Assyriologie nicht weiter unberücksichtigt bleiben dürfte"

schwierigen Situation Verständnis entgegenbrachten, nahm er jede Gelegenheit wahr, mir seine Gehässigkeit zu zeigen. Mit großer Geduld bemühten sich Fakultät und Ministerium, mich in Prag zu halten. Nicolò dagegen drängte mich ständig zu einer schleunigen endgültigen Entscheidung, wozu er amtlich keineswegs befugt war. Wiederholt kam es zu unerfreulichen Aussprachen.... So sah ich mich denn veranlaßt oder vielmehr gedrängt, schon Ende Oktober der Fakultät und dem Ministerium meinen Entschluß mitzuteilen, wieder nach Halle zurückzukehren.[55]

San Nicolò's political outlook would become very vocal once he was elected rector of the German University for the years 1931–1933. In the meantime, he continued his research on cuneiform law history which resulted in groundbreaking publications, particularly of a large body of Neo- and Late Babylonian legal and administrative texts, with the philological collaboration of Arthur Ungnad.[56] In 1932 he began publishing a long series of significant essays on Babylonian legal history under the summary heading "Parerga Babylonica," most of which appeared in the journal of the Prague Oriental Institute, *Archiv orientální*.[57] San Nicolò was member of the editorial board of *Archiv orientální* even after he left Czechoslovakia (see Figure 6.3). In the early 1930s, he also supervised the research of Josef Klíma, a Czech law historian who had begun his studies of cuneiform cultures with Hrozný, and who, besides San Nicolò, had studied with Koschaker and Landsberger in Leipzig. Klíma published a book on Old Babylonian inheritance law in 1940, and eventually became one of the leading specialists in cuneiform legal history.[58] In view of all this, the ambivalence between San Nicolò's scholarly integrity and his political convictions is remarkable.[59]

In his inaugural lecture as Rector Magnificus of the German University (see Figure 6.4), San Nicolò duly emphasized the importance of the research in Babylonian legal history based on meticulous scrutiny of the cuneiform sources.[60] While the substantial obituaries published shortly after his death praise San Nicolò's supposedly great diplomatic skills in the difficult years of his tenure as rector,[61] the reality seems to

---

55. Kisch 1975, 83, 110.

56. San Nicolò 1931a, San Nicolò and Ungnad 1929–1935.

57. For the individual items see the bibliography in Seidl 1956, 13–14.

58. See the introduction in Klíma 1940, v–vi: "Einen besonderen Dank muß ich an dieser Stelle Sr Magn. Herrn Prof. M. San Nicolò aussprechen, der mich systematisch in das Studium der vorderasiatischen keilschriftlichen Rechtsquellen eingeführt und auf die Möglichkeit einer tieferen Bearbeitung des babylonischen Erbrechtes hingewiesen hat. Schon von Anfang an hat er viel Zeit meinen Untersuchungen geschenkt und bei der Lösung mancher Probleme geholfen."

59. See also the letter which San Nicolò sent to Hrozný already from Munich, on 12 July 1937: "Ich hätte aber noch eine Bitte an Sie, nämlich ob Sie nicht für mich zur Besprechung in Ihrer Zeitschrift das soeben erschienene Buch von Landsberger, Die Serie ana ittišu … anfordern möchten. Der Grund warum ich mich an Sie wenden muss, ist der, dass hier Arbeiten von Juden von den Zeitschriften nicht gerne angezeigt werden. Das Buch ist aber für uns Rechtshistoriker so wertvoll, dass wir es auch anzeigen müssen." NpM San Nicolò. According to San Nicolò's bibliography in Seidl 1956, 14–17, he never published a review of Landsberger's book.

60. San Nicolò 1931b.

61. Steinwenter and Falkenstein 1955, 502: "In Prag wurde San Nicolò durch das Vertrauen seiner Kollegen für das Studienjahr 1931/32 und wieder für 1932/33 zum Rektor gewählt und hat unter denkbar schwierigen Verhältnissen die ihm anvertraute Hochschule mit diplomatischem Geschick, aber auch in gefahrvoller Lage mit persönlichem Mut geleitet. Es war begreiflich, daß er sich nach Ablauf dieser

FIGURE 6.4a–b. Mariano San Nicolò (1887–1955), Professor of Roman Law on an official portrait as Rector Magnificus of the German University, and an invitation card to his inauguration sent to the dean of the Theological Faculty of the Czech University in Prague. Sources: AUK Photo-archive; AUK Invitation

have been somewhat different.[62] As pointed out by Maximilian Schreiber in his study on the history of the University of Munich (San Nicolò's next place of employment) in the Third Reich period:

> Tatsächlich trat ... San Nicolò als strammer Verfechter der deutschen Interessen und früher Unterstützer der nationalsozialistischen Studenten während seiner

---

Sturmjahre nach ruhiger wissenschaftlicher Arbeit sehnte." Even more blatantly Seidl 1956, 9: "1931 wurde er in einer Zeit, als die Ära des älteren Masaryk mit ihrem Streben nach Ausgleich zwischen den verschiedenen Nationen des tschechoslowakischen Staates einer Periode der politischen Spannungen wich, zum Rektor der deutschen Universität Prag gewählt. In der Verwaltung dieses Amtes bewies er ungewöhnliche diplomatische Geschicklichkeit."

62. See Pešek et al. 1998, 186.

"*Die Assyriologie nicht weiter unberücksichtigt bleiben dürfte*" 103

Rektoratszeit in Prag von 1931 bis 1933 in Erscheinung. Sein damaliges Verhalten als Wegbereiter des Nationalsozialismus, indem er sich für inhaftierte Angehörige des NS-Studentenbundes einsetzte, die Berufung von jüdischen, aus Deutschland emigrierten Professoren verhinderte und allein marxistischen Studentengruppen verbot, Flugblätter in der Universität zu verteilen, wurde auch in einschlägiger völkischer Literatur über "Prag und das Reich" hervorgehoben. Siehe dazu Wolfgang Wolfram von Wolmar, Prag und das Reich. 600 Jahre Kampf deutscher Studenten, Dresden 1943, 610–632.[63]

Moreover, during the German gymnastics festival at Žatec (Saaz) in the western part of the *Sudetenland* in July 1933, the leading ideologues of the fragmented (and eventually banned) Sudeten-German nationalist parties Rudolf Jung and Hans Krebs approached San Nicolò with the suggestion that he become the leader of a united *Sudetendeutsche Volksfront* of all non-Marxist German political parties in Czechoslovakia.[64] He refused this, at the time, still precarious honor, pointing to Konrad Henlein, the leader of the German Gymnastics Union (*Deutscher Turnverband*), as the "man of the future."[65]

Henlein founded the Sudeten-German Homeland Front (*Sudetendeutsche Heimatfront*, later *Sudetendeutsche Partei*) on 1 October 1933. The party was pivotal in the process leading to the Munich Agreement signed by the representatives of Germany, Britain, France, and Italy on 30 September 1938, after which the *Sudetenland* was annexed to the Third Reich, and the rest of Czechoslovakia remained helpless against future Nazi aggression.

San Nicolò left the perhaps too hot ground of the Czechoslovak capital long before that day. Having refused offers from Freiburg and Zürich,[66] he replaced one of his mentors Wenger at the University of Munich, the capital of the Nazi movement. Although the obituaries present his appointment in 1935 as a natural generation change of pupil for teacher,[67] scholarly merit was apparently not the decisive factor in San Nicolò's obtaining of Wenger's chair:

Furthermore, between 1933 and 1939, all professors of the Munich law faculty were replaced, and by men who had either been NSDAP members before 1933 or

---

63. Schreiber 2008, 218 n. 16.

64. See Pešek et al. 1998, 186. Note that Rudolf Jung (from Plasy/Plass near Plzeň/Pilsen) was the mastermind of Nazi political doctrine. He actually coined the term "National Socialism." Gebel 2000, 28: "Rudolf Jung, der ideologische Vordenker der Partei, veröffentlichte 1919 eine programmatische Schrift unter dem Titel 'Der nationale Sozialismus. Seine Grundlagen, sein Werdegang und seine Ziele.' Sie wurde von Hitler nicht nur gelesen und zur Lektüre weiterempfohlen, sondern hatte möglicherweise einen starken Einfluß auf das Parteiprogramm der NSDAP und auf Hitlers 'Mein Kampf.' Aus dieser Vorgänger- und Vordenkerschaft der DNSAP zogen die Mitglieder und vor allem ihre Führer wie z. B. Rudolf Jung und Hans Krebs Selbstvertrauen und einen gewissen Führungsanspruch—auch gegenüber der reichsdeutschen NSDAP. Jung wagte es sogar, 'Hitler als ersten Ideologen der Bewegung in Frage zu stellen.'" See also Gebel 2000, 28 n. 15. A comprehensive study on Jung is yet to be written.

65. Luh 1988, 208: "Hans Krebs wandte sich hierauf an Prof. Marian San Nicolo, den Rektor der Prager deutschen Universität, um den populären und geachteten Wissenschaftler dazu zu bewegen, eine Zusammenfassung aller Sudetendeutschen zu einer 'Außerparlamentarischen Front' zu versuchen. San Nicolo, von Henlein geladener Ehrengast beim Saazer Turnfest, lehnte allerdings ab und verwies Hans Krebs auf den jungen Verbandsturnwart: Er sei der Mann der Zukunft."

66. Steinwenter and Falkenstein 1955, 502, Ries 2005, 430.

67. Steinwenter and Falkenstein 1955, 502, Seidl 1956, 9–10.

had joined in 1937. Despina remembers the return of Leopold Wenger, professor of Roman and German civil law, to his homeland of Vienna in the spring of 1935, as being a dismissal. He was ... a highly respected scholar, who presented his students with a critical assessment of Caesar's personality.... Wenger's place was taken by Mariano San Nicolo, former rector of the German University of Prague, who enjoyed the approval of the Reich authorities.[68]

In September 1938, the month of the "Munich Crisis" in Czechoslovakia, San Nicolò hosted in Munich a group of "refugee" academics from the German University in Prague.[69] In autumn 1940, San Nicolò stood for election as rector of Munich University. He did not succeed but the reasons for supporting him given by those who voted for him are worth quoting: "Als Begründung führten sie an, 'dass Prof. San Nicolò in der Zeit schwersten nationalen Kampfes Rektor der Deutschen Universität Prag' gewesen sei und sich 'um diesen Deutschen Außenposten' große Verdienste erworben habe."[70]

During the war, San Nicolò was twice secretary of the Bavarian Academy of Sciences; in 1944–1945 he was its president. At the end of 1945, the military authorities dismissed him from the chair of Roman and German Civil Law, but he was reappointed at the beginning of 1948, and in the years 1952–1953 he was elected rector of the University of Munich. He died on 15 May 1955.[71]

A pioneer of cuneiform law history who has left to Assyriology a voluminous legacy of lasting value—a good deal of which came into being in Prague of the "First Republic" period of Czech history—San Nicolò is one of the examples showing that scholarship and politics do not go together very well.

Attempts to Appoint a Professor of Assyriology at the German University

Let us now take a look at the development of Near Eastern studies at the Faculty of Arts of the German University, seemingly the most appropriate place for Assyriology. Indeed, attempts had been made to fill a vacant chair of Semitic philology there with an Assyriologist, but in the end it was never to happen. The reasons are elusive and difficult to infer from available documentation, nevertheless we will try to offer plausible explanations against the background of the political climate of the time and the subsequent development of the department, which seems to betray the motives of the key characters of the story.

68. Georgiadou 2004, 308–9.
69. Míšková 2001, 257.
70. Schreiber 2008, 218.
71. Ries 2005, 430, Pfeifer 2009, 24. The obituaries from the 1950s downplay San Nicolò's role in the brownish administration of the Bavarian Academy, and his temporary dismissal after the war, which is typical of the forgetful discourse in Germany of the day (see, e.g., Ellinger 2006, 443–44). Seidl 1956, 10: "Auch als Präsident der bayerischen Akademie der Wissenschaften wurde er Nachfolger seines Lehrers Wenger. Die diplomatische Geschicklichkeit, die er in Prag gezeigt hatte, blieb ihm in den politisch so schwierigen Jahren treu. Der zweite Weltkrieg freilich schien alles zu zerstören." Steinwenter and Falkenstein 1955, 503: "Zu allem kam noch eine zwei Jahre dauernde Entlassung aus Gründen, die sich nachher als nicht stichhaltig erwiesen, so daß ihm 1952 wieder die Rektorswürde übertragen wurde, die dieses Mal mit der Bürde der Wiederaufbauarbeit an der schwer geschädigten Münchener Universität verbunden war."

FIGURE 6.5. Max Grünert (1849–1929), Professor of Semitic Languages and Literatures. Source: AUK Grünert A

A Survey of Near Eastern Studies at the Faculty of Arts up to 1922

The most important representative of Near Eastern studies at the Faculty of Arts prior to the fall of the Habsburg Empire was Max Grünert (1849–1929), from Most (Brüx) in the western part of the *Sudetenland*. Grünert studied in Vienna and Leipzig. Particularly in Leipzig he acquired consummate knowledge of Arabic, Persian, and Turkish under the guidance of the *Altmeister* of Arabic studies, Heinrich Leberecht Fleischer. Having graduated in 1876, he completed a *Habilitation* for Oriental languages at the German University in 1877. He was appointed as full Professor of Semitic Languages and Literatures in 1892 (Figure 6.5),[72] acted as Rector Magnificus of the German University from 1910 to 1911,[73] and taught in Prague until his official retirement on 1 April 1921. Yet, Grünert kept offering courses in Arabic, Persian, and Turkish philology as an honorary professor and head of the second *Lehrkanzel* of the department until his death in 1929. According to the obituary by Adolf Grohmann, he did so out of "Lust und Liebe" for teaching but that may not have been the only motive, as we shall see later on.[74]

Significantly, already in the years 1893–1894 Grünert co-authored an elaborate proposal for the establishment of a Department of Oriental Philology comprising all branches of Semitic, Egyptian (including Coptic), Sanskrit, all phases of Persian and Armenian, as well as the Turkic languages. In the list of languages to be taught at

---

72. See AUK Grünert A, Anonymous 1957.
73. See AUK Grünert B.
74. AUK Grünert A, 22.

FIGURE 6.6. Isidor Pollak (1874–1922), Professor of Semitic Philology. Source: AUK Pollak

the proposed department, he also included: "ostsemitisch: die Sprache der assyrisch-babylon. Keilinschriften."[75] The Austro-Hungarian administration did not accept the proposal, though, and the philology of Oriental languages was further on represented by individual professors, or chairs (*Lehrkanzeln*).

One of those was formally occupied since 1917 by Isidor Pollak (1874–1922), a specialist in medieval Jewish and Arabic philosophy (Figure 6.6) who had studied Hebrew, Arabic, and Syriac in Prague and Berlin, and who, after graduating from Prague (1899) and undertaking a short service in the university library, had obtained the *venia legendi* for Semitic languages and literatures in 1904. His actual appointment as *ausserordentlicher Professor* with a special focus on north Semitic occurred only shortly before his untimely death, though.[76]

Specifically, in March 1920 with Grünert's retirement in sight, a faculty committee consisting of Grünert, Moriz Winternitz (Professor of Indology), and Reinhold Trautmann (Professor of Slavonic Studies), came up with another proposal, this time comprising only the Semitic—"die Sprache der assyrisch-babylonischen Keilinschriften" is mentioned in this document as well—and "Islamic" languages, with a focus on the latter. Having pointed out that other universities had two or three chairs for the different branches of Semitics, the committee suggested that Grünert's full professorship be complemented with an associate chair. This was approved by the collegium of professors and a letter was sent to the MŠANO.[77]

75. The proposal is preserved in the dossier NA Semitics Professorships.
76. AUK Pollak. See also NA Pollak Passport.
77. AUK Semitics Professorships. Note the perhaps reproachful sigh in the committee report: "Tatsächlich bestehen an den meisten Universitäten für das Gebiet der semitischen Philologie zwei Professuren,

FIGURE 6.7. Adolf Grohmann (1887–1977), Professor of Semitic Philology and Islamic Studies. Source: NA Grohmann Citizenship

At the end of April 1920, the committee members changed their mind and suggested that not one but two associate professorships should be added to Grünert's *Ordinariat*, specifying the scholarly focus as follows: "Das Ordinariat soll die Bezeichnung führen: 'Professur für semitische Philologie und Islamforschung,' Das 1. Extraordinariat: 'Professur für semitische Philologie mit besonderer Berücksichtigung des Hebräischen und Aramäischen,' Das 2. Extraordinariat: 'Professur für arabische Paläographie und Kulturgeschichte des Orients.'"[78] The committee also proposed specific candidates for each position: August Haffner (Professor of Semitics in Innsbruck), Isidor Pollak (Titular Associate Professor in Prague), and Adolf Grohmann (Adjunct Professor of Near Eastern Languages and Antiquity in Vienna).

In mid-February 1921, Grünert, supported by the board of professors, sent a reminder to the MŠANO.[79] Although further relevant documentation is missing, the proposal could hardly be acceptable for the ministry, as it would have entailed considerable costs for two new jobs beyond the valid systemization of professorial positions. Instead, a compromise was made and Grünert's chair was divided into two associate professorships in 1921, one taken up by Isidor Pollak and the other one by Adolf Grohmann (1887–1977), already then an eminent scholar in the field of Arabic philology and papyrology, who came to Prague from Vienna (Figure 6.7).[80]

---

an manchen (wie z. B. in Berlin, Leipzig und der tschechischen Universität in Prag) sogar deren drei."
   78. AUK Semitics Professorships, Kommissions-Bericht zur Besetzung der Lehrkanzel für "Semitische Philologie," 29 April 1920.
   79. NA Semitics Professorships.
   80. See NA Grohmann Register, AUK Grohmann. For a study on Grohmann see Reinfandt 2013, here 252.

The Failed Attempt to Appoint an Assyriologist in 1922 and Its Consequences

With Pollak's sudden death on 7 January 1922, one of the chairs became vacant. Already by the end of January the faculty elected a committee of four scholars who should have suggested suitable candidates for filling the position again. The committee, joined by Grünert as consultant, prepared a detailed report for the board of professors, written down by Grohmann and dated 28 June 1922.[81] (For an edition of the document see Appendix 2, No. 1 in this essay with Figures 6.11–6.12.)

While two years previously it had been suggested that Grünert's professorship be divided into three chairs, two of which would be devoted specifically to Arabic and Islamic material, and the remaining chair to Hebrew and Aramaic, this time the situation was radically different, at least according to the report. Assyriology came to the fore in this proposal as a "so important branch of north Semitic philology that should no longer remain ignored." Even though the reasons given by the committee certainly do make sense,[82] perhaps the most plausible explanation why Assyriology was to be suddenly considered that important would be the gradual international acknowledgment of Hrozný's decipherment of Hittite, and thus the excellent reputation of the professor from the Faculty of Arts of the Czech University in Prague, for whom the German Faculty of Arts had no adequate counterpart.

This inference seems supported by the statement of the committee "that the History of the Ancient Orient is not represented in Prague, while its representation in the framework of Assyriology would be almost a matter of course." It is understandable that a committee of the German University did not take into account the more and more respected decipherer or other competent Assyriologists from their Czech competitor. Strikingly, though, this statement blatantly ignores Steinmetzer, an accomplished Assyriologist and full professor at the Theological Faculty since 1912. As we shall see later on, Steinmetzer's Assyriological classes were attended by Grohmann's students as well, thus the committee members must no doubt have been aware of his teaching and research, particularly considering that Steinmetzer's most important work appeared the very same year. Therefore, the decision to hire their own Assyriologist seems to betray not only the indifference, if not outright rivalry, between the Faculties of Arts and Theology (certainly not only then and there), but also the wish of the committee members to get a strong counterpart to Hrozný.

The selection of scholars chosen by the committee also points into that direction. In accordance with the general strategy of the German University to attract academics who were not yet established as full professors but whose career was promising, the committee suggested Arno Poebel as primary candidate, Hans Bauer and Erich Ebeling as equal first alternatives, and Hans Ehelolf as second alternative. There is little need to go into much detail about the importance of those scholars for the progress of cuneiform studies.[83]

---

81. The handwritten document is in the dossier AUK Semitics Professorships.

82. See particularly the italicized passage in Appendix 2, No. 1, 1.

83. On Poebel see Edzard 2003, Weidner 1959–1960, and the detailed CV in Appendix 2, No. 1. On Bauer see Wehr 1953, and the detailed CV in Appendix 2, No. 1. On Ebeling see Weidner 1954–1956, 1959, and the detailed CV in Appendix 2, No. 1. On Ehelolf see the detailed CV in Appendix 2, No. 1.

"Die Assyriologie nicht weiter unberücksichtigt bleiben dürfte" 109

Particularly Poebel, whose experience and work above all on the grammar of Sumerian is praised in the proposal, would have been an excellent counterpart to Hrozný. Not only because of his knowledge and a number of important publications, but also because of "his close relationship with American universities, opening a prospect of an active work at the cultural sites of ancient Babylonia, which must be considered as especially valuable for German science under the current circumstances."[84] This may be taken as a reaction to Hrozný's plans for Czechoslovak excavations in the Middle East which he published in 1920 under the title "Nové úkoly orientální archeologie (New Tasks of Oriental Archaeology),"[85] eventually accomplishing some of them in 1924–1925.[86]

The proposal was approved by the collegium of professors of the Faculty of Arts on 6 July 1922, and a letter from the dean was sent five days later to the MŠANO, so that negotiations with the candidate(s) could begin (see Figure 6.8). The reaction of the ministry was negative but logical in view of the current situation at the department:

> Professor Emeritus Dr. Grünert was entrusted with substituting 5 hours of lectures in Semitic philology ... and in addition ∴ Dr. Adolf Grohmann is teaching there too. Therefore, as long as Prof. Dr. Grünert is able to teach, there is no need to hurry with filling the chair of Semitic Philology vacated after the death of Prof. Dr. Pollak—who had been appointed to the position vacated by the retirement of Dr. Grünert—particularly in view of the fact that candidates proposed by the board of professors come from Germany. Prof. Dr. Grünert was entrusted with substituting the lectures after Prof. Dr. Pollak's death. Thus, it is suggested that the file be deposited ad acta for the time being.[87]

This begs the question of how serious the proposal of the selection committee to hire an Assyriologist really was meant to be. That the MŠANO would not be happy about candidates from Germany must have been well known to all members of the committee. Although it was not ruled out that a candidate from abroad would eventually be appointed, as shown by the example of Grohmann himself,[88] the ministry wanted to know first if there really were no suitable candidates from Czechoslovakia.[89] Further, the retired professor Grünert apparently could not resist his "Lust und Liebe" for teaching before the selection committee was even set up. The emeritus effectively took back the position of his deceased successor, earning remunerations for classes in addition to his pension.[90] It thus appears that the two specialists in Islamic languages and cultures, Grünert and Grohmann, only formally approved of the idea of hiring

84. See the italicized passage in Appendix 2, No. 1, 8.

85. Hrozný 1920. For a study of this programmatic document see Hadler 2012.

86. See chapters 7–11 in Velhartická 2015.

87. NA Semitics Professorships, Praha—německá universita—fakulta filosofická—návrh na obsazení stolice semitské filologie, 17 November 1922.

88. Even the requirement that the candidate become Czechoslovak citizen may not have been that urgent, for Grohmann acquired the citizenship as late as 25 April 1928. See NA Grohmann Citizenship.

89. See the next section.

90. For documents on the remunerations and other financial issues of the department see AUK Semitics Finances and AUK Semitics.

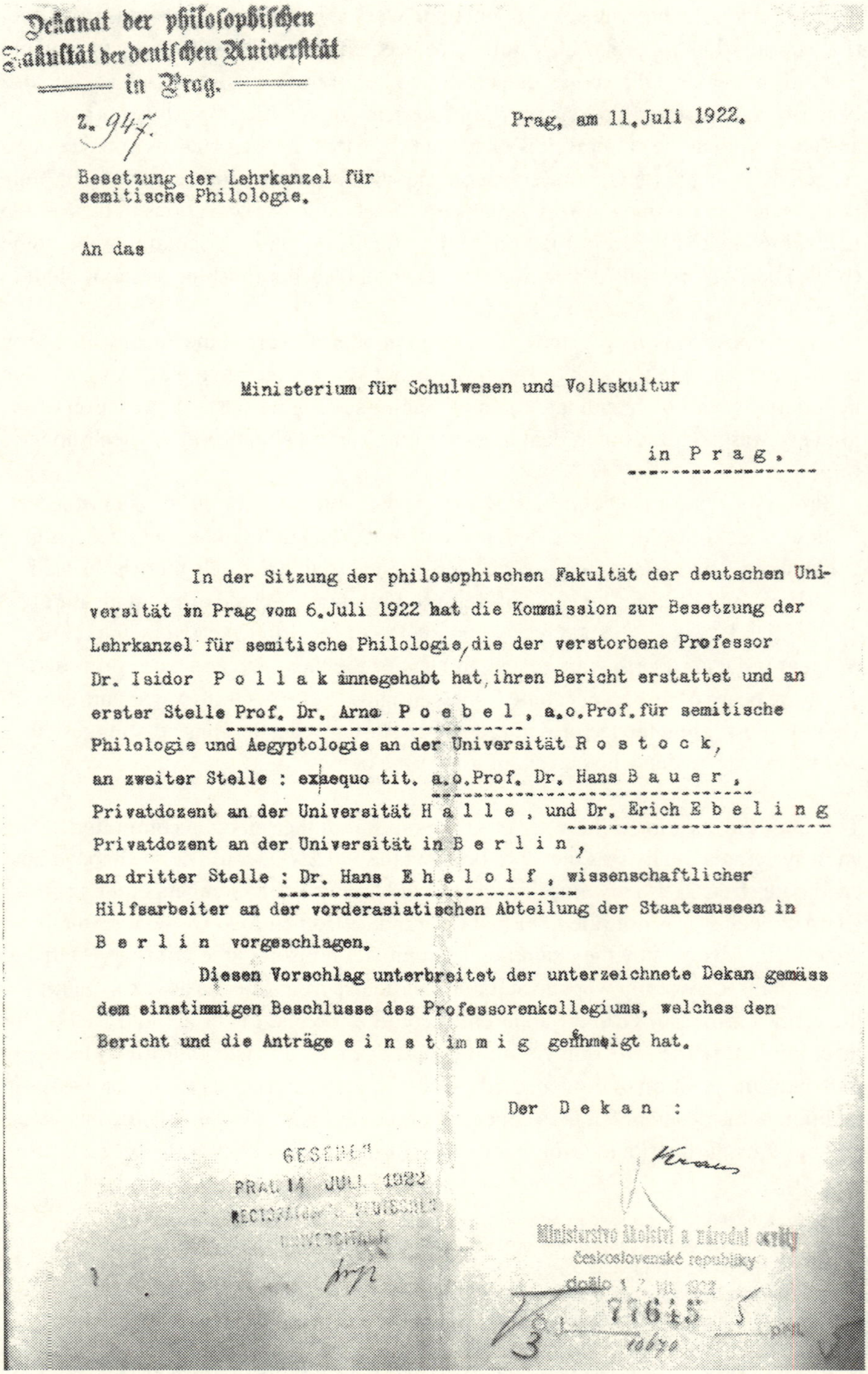

DeRanat der philosopsischen
Fakultät der deutschen Universität
in Prag.

Z. 947.

Prag, am 11.Juli 1922.

Besetzung der Lehrkanzel für
semitische Philologie.

An das

Ministerium für Schulwesen und Volkskultur

in P r a g .

        In der Sitzung der philosophischen Fakultät der deutschen Uni-
versität in Prag vom 6.Juli 1922 hat die Kommission zur Besetzung der
Lehrkanzel für semitische Philologie, die der verstorbene Professor
Dr. Isidor P o l l a k innegehabt hat, ihren Bericht erstattet und an
erster Stelle Prof. Dr. Arno P o e b e l , a.o.Prof.für semitische
Philologie und Aegyptologie an der Universität R o s t o c k ,
an zweiter Stelle : exaequo tit. a.o.Prof. Dr. Hans B a u e r ,
Privatdozent an der Universität H a l l e , und Dr. Erich E b e l i n g
Privatdozent an der Universität in B e r l i n ,
an dritter Stelle : Dr. Hans E h e l o l f , wissenschaftlicher
Hilfsarbeiter an der vorderasiatischen Abteilung der Staatsmuseen in
B e r l i n vorgeschlagen.
        Diesen Vorschlag unterbreitet der unterzeichnete Dekan gemäss
dem einstimmigen Beschlusse des Professorenkollegiums, welches den
Bericht und die Anträge e i n s t i m m i g genehmigt hat.

                                Der D e k a n :

                                    Kraus

GESEHEN
PRAG 14 JULI 1922
RECTORAT...DEUTSCHEN
UNIVERSITÄT

Ministerstvo školství a národní osvěty
československé republiky
došlo 12. VII. 1922
77645
10670

FIGURE 6.8. Letter from the dean of the Faculty of Arts of the German University to the Ministry of Education of the Czechoslovak Republic, inviting the ministry to initiate negotiations with the chosen candidates for the vacant chair of Semitic philology. Source: NA Semitics Professorships

"Die Assyriologie nicht weiter unberücksichtigt bleiben dürfte"

an Assyriologist which they agreed on with the other three members of the selection committee.

This conclusion is supported by the fact that there was an Assyriologist interested in the position who met all the academic as well as administrative requirements for the appointment, yet his name does not occur in the preserved official documentation at all: Benno Landsberger. Were it not for his letter to Hrozný from 25 January 1922 (edited in Appendix 2, No. 2 with Figure 6.13), i.e., precisely a day before the selection committee was elected (see Appendix 2, No. 1, 1), we would never know about his interest in the vacant chair of Semitic Philology in Prague.

Apart from the content, the diction of Landsberger's letter to Hrozný is unusually polite, even obsequious, showing that the brilliant young Assyriologist who had recently obtained the *venia legendi* in Leipzig was quite keen to get the Prague position.[91] Yet, his plea for interventions from Czech scholars may seem a little shortsighted, because, even though both Hrozný and Alois Musil spent decades in Viennese academia,[92] it is hard to imagine that the German University would listen to their advice, particularly if the unspoken purpose of the proposal was to find a counterpart to Hrozný. Nonetheless, what was perhaps really fatal is revealed by the following statement from the letter: "Vorläufig habe ich mich an San Nicolo gewendet, Zimmern hat an Grünert geschrieben."

While Grünert had mentioned Assyriology in all his proposals since 1894, he actually seems to have been more interested in fulfilling the teaching obligations of the late Pollak and getting paid for it at this point, than in heeding interventions from Landsberger's Leipzig mentor. Further, in view of San Nicolò's open anti-Semitism and the fact that the "Steinherz Affair" would break out later that year, accompanied by the riots of the German Student Union, it apparently was not a good idea for a Jewish academic to strive for a professorship in Prague at that time. It certainly was not a good idea to ask San Nicolò for help in that matter. These factors seem to explain why Landsberger was not even mentioned by the selection committee.

They become even more flagrant in view of the fact that must have been known to both Grünert and San Nicolò, namely that as a native of Frýdek in the Czech part of Silesia, Landsberger automatically became Czechoslovak citizen in 1918.[93] Thus, given his academic merit together with his status as a domestic candidate, Landsberger would have been a perfectly acceptable choice for the MŠANO, had the committee suggested him in the proposal.[94]

---

91. See UAL Landsberger, 2: "10. 7. 1920: Habilitation Leipzig."

92. Alois Musil (1868–1944), an extraordinary figure in the history of Arabic and Islamic studies, was at that time Professor of Auxiliary Sciences of the Orient and Modern Arabic at the Czech University in Prague. His legacy is the subject of the research and other activities of the Czech Academic Society of Alois Musil (ASAM), http://www.aloismusil.cz/index.php/english (accessed 12 July 2017).

93. Landsberger dropped Czechoslovak citizenship as late as 1926, exchanging it for German, or more precisely, Saxonian citizenship, which he was legally obliged to do after accepting an associate professorship in Leipzig. See SOkA Landsberger.

94. On the other hand, it seems that although Heinrich Zimmern recommended Landsberger for the Prague professorship, he did not really want him to leave Leipzig, as the two "promotions" of Landsberger during that very year may indicate: "9. 2. 1922: Lehrauftrag f. Assyriologie; 9. 6. 1922: Assistent am Semitistischen Institut Leipzig." Yet, Landsberger had to wait almost three more years for the associate professorship in Leipzig. See UAL Landsberger, 2.

The attempt to appoint an Assyriologist at the German Faculty of Arts in Prague in 1922 was therefore futile. In fact, as available sources seem to show, it may have been devised from the outset to end up as a failure. Already in June 1922, the board of professors sent a request to the MŠANO for establishment of a Department of Oriental Philology which included a draft of the statutes. Those statutes explicitly mentioned the focus on Islamic studies, and suggested that the department consist of two "divisions": "Die erste Abteilung umfasst die semitischen Sprachen in Verbindung mit Kulturgeschichte des Orients, sowie Geschichte der islamischen Völker und ihrer Hilfswissenschaften, die zweite Abteilung die Turko-Tartarischen und das Alt-Mittel- und Neupersische."[95] Each division should have its own director, obviously Grohmann for the first and Grünert for the second. As directors of those divisions, both professors would be entitled to special remunerations, the department would get an annual institutional allowance, and more money would be spent on enlarging the library. All this was approved by the MŠANO already in August 1922. Therefore, it is no wonder that the ministry took the almost simultaneous proposal for appointment of an Assyriologist as pointless.

After Grohmann's promotion to full Professor of Semitic Philology with a Special Focus on South Semitic Languages and the Cultural History of the Near East, effective from 31 December 1923,[96] the scholarly orientation of the new department on Islamic studies was a given. Before long, the collegium of professors of the German Faculty of Arts asked the MŠANO for approval to change the broadly conceived name of the Department of Oriental Philology to the Department of Semitic Philology and Islamic Studies (*Seminar für semitische Philologie und Islamkunde*). The ministry approved of the change in 1925.[97]

The proposal to fill the vacant chair of Pollak with an Assyriologist was not forgotten, but became an occasionally used tool of academic politics. For instance, on 16 July 1924 the dean of the German Faculty of Arts sent a reminder to the MŠANO that the vacant chair had not yet been filled, emphasizing that H. Bauer had been appointed full professor at the University of Halle in the meantime, but it would have still been possible to appoint Poebel, Ebeling, or Ehelolf (Landsberger is not mentioned, of course).[98]

The reaction of the MŠANO to this silent accusation that it was the ministry's fault that the position had not yet been filled, is worth quoting: "The board of professors presses for the settlement of the proposal to fill the chair of Semitic Philology. This demand cannot be taken into account for the following reasons: Semitic philology is sufficiently represented in full Prof. Dr. Grohmann, and it would be pointless to fill the vacant associate chair with another Semitist. . . . It seems that this demand is made because of a certain jealousy against Grünert's substituting the lessons, and the remuneration associated with that."[99]

---

95. NA Semitics Professorships.

96. See the appointment letter addressed to the Minister of Education and signed by President T. G. Masaryk in NA Grohmann Appointment.

97. AUK Semitics, NA Semitics Professorships.

98. AUK Semitics Professorships, NA Semitics Professorships.

99. NA Semitics Professorships, Praha—německá universita—fakulta filosofická—návrh na obsazení stolice semitské filologie, 29 July 1924.

"Die Assyriologie nicht weiter unberücksichtigt bleiben dürfte"

While the MŠANO obviously did not mind that Grünert continued teaching as the head of the second division of the recently established department, it seems to have been well informed that some influential person at the German Faculty of Arts did not like it. If so, the reminder had nothing to do with Assyriology, of course. In any case, Grünert had no intention to step down and finally enjoy his retirement. Let us imagine for a moment what would have happened if he did retire.

First, the faculty would have had to persuade the MŠANO that there was no suitable domestic candidate (i.e., Landsberger) and to explain to the ministry the differences between a Semitist and an Assyriologist. Second, Poebel would have had to accept the salary and the condition to become Czechoslovak citizen. If all this had worked out, the history of Assyriology would have been very different indeed. Who would have taught Samuel N. Kramer Sumerian, then?[100] And how would the reconstruction of Sumerian literature in the past century have proceeded? Those are some of the questions that come to mind while thinking of this strange Prague episode that Poebel most likely had no idea about.[101]

Resuming our reconstruction of historical reality now, we must mention that in those years there had been a student at the German Faculty of Arts who was to become a brilliant Semitist whose works, particularly on Arabic chemistry and alchemy, have considerable influence to this day, but who actually began his career as an Assyriologist.

Paul Kraus, born on 11 December 1904 in Prague entered the Faculty of Arts of the German University in the winter semester of 1923.[102] He attended classes offered by Grohmann, like "Die Kunst des alten Orients," "Arabische Papyruskunde," and "Geschichte der aethiopischen Literatur," and Grünert, like "Erklärung des Buches Ruth" and "Türkisch." In the summer semester of 1924, he continued studying Arabic, Ethiopic, and Turkish with Grohmann and Grünert but he also attended Steinmetzer's "Neubabylonische Geschäftsurkunden" and "Assyrische Inschriften." His further studies with Grohmann included "Altorientalische Kunst," "Arab. Paläographie," "Landeskunde von Arabien," "Koranlektüre," "Ausgewählte Kapitel aus d. arab. Grammatik" in winter semester 1924, and ended in summer semester 1925 with the continuation of courses in "Arab. Paläographie" and "Landeskunde von Arabien." The winter semester of 1925 was the last period of his enrollment at the German University in Prague, but he attended no more classes in Semitics.[103]

Kraus pursued his studies further in Jerusalem and Damascus, returning to Europe in 1927. He obtained his doctorate in Berlin under the supervision of the distinguished Assyriologist Bruno Meissner in 1929. Published in two volumes in 1931–1932, his dissertation, a critical edition of some 130 Old Babylonian letters published in facsimile drawings in *VS* 16, shows great meticulousness and maturity.[104] The sub-

---

100. For Kramer's appreciation of the deep influence that Poebel had on him see Chapter 3 in Kramer 1988, 34–41.

101. At least, that is what the only preserved piece of relevant evidence suggests. A postcard from Poebel to Hrozný dated 15 August 1922, i.e., from the time when he was first selected for the position, speaks of scholarly matters only. It contains no hint to Poebel's possible appointment in Prague. See NpM Poebel.

102. See NA Kraus.

103. See AUK Kraus.

104. Kraus 1931–1932.

stantial and thorough glossary at the end of the book was worked into the preliminary files of the *CAD*.[105] At the end of the introduction, a moving connection to Prague occurs: "Ich widme das Buch dem Andenken meines Onkels Isidor Pollak, Professors der semitischen Philologie an der deutschen Universität in Prag, der mir die ersten wissenschaftlichen Anregungen gab."[106]

Paul Kraus (Figure 6.9), having eventually achieved groundbreaking accomplishments in the field of Arabic philology and the early history of Islamic science, committed suicide on 12 October 1944 in Cairo.[107]

A New Attempt to Fill the Chair of Semitic Philology in 1929

Although there are sporadic indications that the Berlin Professor of Iranian and Armenian Philology, Josef Marquardt, may have been in play for Pollak's chair in 1923–1924 too, this possibility seems to have never been seriously considered either.[108] Born in 1864, Marquardt was approaching retirement age, after all.

Thus, since mid-1924, the status quo at the Department of Semitic Philology and Islamic Studies seems to have been undisturbed by any other attempts to fill Pollak's chair. Grünert and Grohmann continued teaching, and asking for additional funds for books, etc.[109] Further, Grohmann received funding from the Oriental Institute in Prague to visit the famous collection of papyri in Vienna during the summer vacations in those years. He became a fellow of the Oriental Institute in 1927 and was a member of the editorial board of its journal *Archiv orientální* (see Figure 6.3).[110]

In 1928 Grohmann asked the MŠANO to allow the establishment of a librarian position at the department, stating that his student Karl Jahn had volunteered to work in that capacity for free since winter semester 1927.[111] The request was rejected at that time and again ten years later for budgetary reasons,[112] which was not unusual. Libraries of many institutes at both the Czech and German universities were taken care of by student volunteers who were happy if the ministry approved a small bursary for them. Nonetheless, the annual institutional allowance for the department was doubled in January 1928, so the MŠANO may have assumed that the department had enough money to pay a student for library services.[113]

---

105. Kraus 1931–1932, 2.107–209. See Gelb 1964, xi.

106. Kraus 1931–1932, 1.viii. While we were not able to confirm the familial relationship of both scholars on the basis of available documents, there seems to be evidence that Pollak was a member of the Kraus household during Kraus' childhood. See NA Pollak Register.

107. For more information on Kraus, particularly on his work in Arabic and Islamic studies, see Brague 1994, Kraemer 1999, Ščrbačić 2013. Since Ludmila Hanisch (2001, viii, 48–49) bewails the impossibility of getting a picture of Kraus in her book of portraits of exiled Orientalists, we publish here three photos of Kraus for the benefit of all interested scholars. Note that Kraus signed the earliest photo using the Czech form of his first name, Pavel. Like many members of the German-speaking Jewish community in Czechoslovakia, he too was bilingual. He remained Czechoslovak citizen until his death.

108. AUK Semitics Professorships, NA Semitics Professorships.

109. AUK Semitics Finances. For instance, Aufteilung der Extradotation pro 1926 unter den beiden Direktoren (18 November 1926), Ansuchen um eine ausserordentliche Dotation pro 1927 (16 January 1927).

110. AUK Grohmann, Reinfandt 2013, 252–53 n. 9.

111. AUK Semitics, Bestellung eines Bibliothekars, 25 January 1928.

112. NA Semitics Professorships, Praha—německá universita—filosofická fakulta—zřízení místa knihovníkova v semináři pro semitskou filologii, 15 June 1938.

113. AUK Semitics, Evidenz der Institute (Seminar f. semit. Philologie u. Islamkunde).

FIGURE 6.9a–c. (*top left, bottom left, top right*) Three photos of Semitist and Islamic scholar Paul Kraus (1904–1944) from Prague (1923), Jerusalem (1927), and Berlin (1929). Source: NA Kraus

On 10 February 1929 the Honorary Professor of Semitic Languages and Literatures, Max Grünert, died. The situation at the department thus became essentially the same as in the Austro-Hungarian times. The faculty had only one full professor of Semitic philology. Already on 5 March 1929, the board of professors elected a committee entrusted with the task of selecting suitable candidates for the additional vacant *Extraordinariat*. While the reasoning in the new very detailed report seems well grounded, one cannot resist the impression that the proposals from 1920–1922 are used here to blame the MŠANO for deliberate idleness, and that Grohmann picked the conditions for the new selection in such a way that only an Islamic scholar would come into consideration:

> Der Vorschlag der Fakultät zur Besetzung der vakanten Lehrkanzel für Hebräisch und Aramäisch einschliesslich der Assyriologie ist bis zum heutigen Tage nicht realisiert worden. Wenn die dadurch entstandene Lücke nicht in jenem Ausmasse für die Fakultät fühlbar geworden ist, wie zunächst zu befürchten stand, so ist dies dem Umstande zuzuschreiben, dass Prof. Dr. Max Grünert als Professor honorarius eine ausgedehnte Lehrtätigkeit entfaltete und neben Kollegien über nordsemitische Philologie auch Vorlesungen über Türkisch und Persisch gehalten hat. Hiermit war gleichzeitig ein Gebiet bestritten, das an allen deutschen Universitäten immer grössere Bedeutung erlangt hat und das auch an der tschechischen Universität in Prag durch zwei Lehrkanzeln vertreten ist.... Eine befriedigende Lösung der Frage wäre eigentlich nur durch zwei Professuren zu erzielen.... Da aber durch die inzwischen eingesetzte Systemisierung zwei neue ausserordentliche Lehrkanzeln neben dem bereits bestehenden Ordinariate ... kaum Aussicht auf Verwirklichung haben, musste sich die Kommission mit einem Kompromiss begnügen.... Da nur ein Extraordinariat zur Zeit in Frage kommt, war der Kreis der Vorzuschlagenden von vornherein enger gezogen und konnte sich nur auf jene Gelehrten erstrecken, die nicht in Besitze eines wirklichen Extraordinariats sind. Aus demselben Grunde konnte aus dem Vorschlage der Fakultät vom 28. Juni 1922 nur der an letzter Stelle genannte Privatdozent Dr. Hans Ehelolf in Berlin in Betracht kommen.[114]

Formally true to the previous proposal, Grohmann made it clear this time that no Assyriologist was really wanted. After all, in 1929 it was too late to catch up with Hrozný, and Grohmann quite understandably preferred some colleague from his own discipline. Thus, even though two Assyriologists are suggested in the new proposal, their position in it indicates that their chance to have been appointed was very low:

> Zufolge dessen bringt die Kommission dem Professorenkollegium folgende Reihenfolge in Vorschlag:
> 1. primo et aequo loco Hans Ehelolf und Franz Täschner.
> 2. secundo et aequo loco Theodor Menzel und Theodor Seif.
> 3. tertio loco Theo Bauer.[115]

Ehelolf was taken over from the previous proposal of 1922 and put in front but together with Täschner, Associate Professor of Semitics and Islamic Studies in Münster. Menzel was Associate Professor of Islamic Philology in Kiel. Seif obtained his *Habilitation* in Turkology and Islamic studies in Vienna in 1924, and had good relations

---

114. AUK Semitics Professorships, NA Semitics Professorships, Kommissionsbericht über die Besetzung der II. Lehrkanzel für orientalische Philologie, 14 June 1929.

115. AUK Semitics Professorships, NA Semitics Professorships, Kommissionsbericht über die Besetzung der II. Lehrkanzel für orientalische Philologie, 14 June 1929.

"Die Assyriologie nicht weiter unberücksichtigt bleiben dürfte" 117

with Grohmann.[116] Finally, the Assyriologist Theo Bauer obtained his *venia legendi* in Munich in 1925.[117]

Just like seven years previously, all candidates were from Germany or Austria, and the proposal contained no justification for why a domestic candidate could not be selected. Therefore, difficulties with the authorities were to be expected. Indeed, in 1929, Czechoslovak authorities were increasingly worried about appointing professors with potentially hostile political outlook at the German University, which was gradually becoming a primary stage for German nationalist politics in Prague.

The MŠANO could dismiss the proposal outright on formal grounds considering that Grünert's original *Ordinariat* had been divided into two associate professorships, one of which became an *Ordinariat*, and therefore there was no reason to keep the additional associate professorship after Grünert's death. Yet, the department consisting of two divisions already existed, and thus the ministry began to check the credentials of the candidates suggested in the new proposal.

That was done in collaboration with the Ministry of Foreign Affairs and the Ministry of the Interior. It was a long process accompanied by agitated correspondence between government authorities and the faculty.[118] The dean, at that time Grohmann himself, specified that he wanted Täschner for the position and that there really was no suitable domestic candidate. The Ministry of the Interior was not satisfied with that justification, while the Ministry of Foreign Affairs was gathering information on all the candidates in the meantime. Although the authorities eventually had no objections against the candidates, some of them were no longer available (Ehelolf and Menzel). In the end, the whole matter seems to have been put to rest by the Ministry of the Interior which by the end of 1932(!) still insisted that "the chair cannot be filled with a foreign citizen unless there is a persuasive proof that there are no domestic candidates, along with an explanation of the reasons that lead the board of professors to selecting foreigners for the vacant chair."[119]

History of the German University Department of Semitic Philology (1930–1945)

Grohmann eventually remained the only Professor of Semitic Philology at the German Faculty of Arts. He had to substitute for the classes of the late Grünert, for which the MŠANO granted him financial compensation already in October 1931.[120] He continued with his research, for which he kept demanding more money.[121] For instance, in 1937 he asked for a grant to obtain a piece of equipment indispensable for his work which

---

116. See Reinfandt 2013, 253 n. 8.

117. On Bauer see Weidner 1957–1958.

118. Relevant documents are kept in the dossier NA Semitics Professorships.

119. NA Semitics Professorships, Statement of the MŠANO and the Ministry of the Interior, 29 November 1932.

120. AUK Semitics, Evidenz der Institute (Seminar f. semit. Philologie u. Islamkunde), AUK Semitics Finances, AUK Grohmann.

121. Between 1930 and 1939 he spent several months every year in Cairo to work on Arabic papyri kept in the Egyptian Library. See Ellinger 2006, 219.

FIGURE 6.10. Karl Jahn (1906–1985), Adjunct Professor of Islamic Languages in Connection with the History and Cultural History of Persia and the Turkic Peoples. Source: NA Jahn Register

he wanted to purchase in Cairo, namely a typewriter with Arabic characters that cost a third of the annual institutional allowance. The MŠANO reimbursed the costs days before the Munich Agreement was signed.[122]

Over the years, Grohmann was also able to bring up a scholar who would take up the second division of the department (Figure 6.10). Karl Jahn (1906–1985) was born in the capital of Moravia, Brno (Brünn). He studied with Grohmann and Grünert, but also with Steinmetzer and the Czech Iranologist Jan Rypka in Prague. In 1929 he went to Leipzig to further study Arabic, Assyriology, and Hittitology. Having obtained his doctorate in Prague in 1931 with the thesis "Studien zur arabischen Epistologie," he went to Berlin for advanced studies of Central Asian languages and history. Jahn began teaching Turkish as lecturer at the German University in Prague in October 1936. He also passed state exams for librarians and from February 1938 worked in the university library, which was his only paid job for the time being.

Focusing on the history of the Il-khanid rule in Iran, Jahn edited the section of the monumental chronicle of Mongol history *Jāmeʿ al-tawārīḵ* that deals with the reign of the Il-khan Maḥmud Ḡāzān. He presented that critical edition from manuscripts in Istanbul, London, Paris, and Vienna as his *Habilitationsschrift* to the faculty in Prague in May 1938. He was awarded the *venia legendi* for Islamic Languages in Connection with the History and Cultural History of Persia and the Turkic Peoples in June of that year, the *Habilitation* was confirmed in March 1939.[123]

Following the establishment of the Protectorate of Bohemia and Moravia in the spring of 1939 and the closure of the Czech University in autumn 1939—whose Rector Magnificus was Hrozný at the time—both Grohmann and Jahn quickly conformed to the new order.

The "Aryanization" of the German University was already in full swing. In comparison to universities in Germany where that process had begun in 1933, the German University in Prague was "Aryanized" quite quickly, just in a few months. The deans

---

122. AUK Semitics Finances, NA Semitics Professorships.
123. NA Jahn Register, AUK Jahn, NA Jahn Personal Information Sheet, Bruijn 2008.

"*Die Assyriologie nicht weiter unberücksichtigt bleiben dürfte*"

of individual faculties promptly dismissed Jewish teaching staff and students. Consequently, the number of teachers at the university shrank by 34 percent. Apart from that, the process of Nazification (*Gleichschaltung*) was most successful at the Faculty of Arts, where more than half of the teaching staff were members of the Nazi Party already before 1939. The vacant positions were filled with academics from the *Reich*. In 1939 the German University was put under the administration of the Reich Ministry of Education, which completed and legalized the institution's "Aryanization."[124]

Both Grohmann and Jahn were members of the NSDAP by that time. Formerly, they had been members of the *Sudetendeutsche Partei* which merged with the NSDAP in November 1938.[125] Grohmann was also member of the paramilitary party organization National Socialist Motor Corps (*Nationalsozialistisches Kraftfahrkorps*), and the German Union of University Teachers (*Deutsche Dozentenschaft*). In addition, he belonged to the ranks of the German Culture Union (*Deutscher Kulturverband*). Further, both scholars were members of the Union of Germans in Bohemia (*Bund der Deutschen in Böhmen*).[126]

Accordingly, their activities at the university were not limited to research and teaching their usual classes like "Einführung in die Grundzüge der islamischen Rechtswissenschaft mit Übungen an Rechtsurkunden," "Grundzüge der arabischen Epigraphik und Paläographie mit Übungen an Inschriften und Papyri," "Neuarabisch für Anfänger," "Lektüre arabischer und äthiopischer Texte" (Grohmann), "'Die islamische Welt' im Mongolen-Zeitalter," "Lektüre leichter türkischer Texte," "Die persische Geschichtsschreibung. Mit Textproben" (Jahn).[127] They also lectured on "Die geschichtlichen Grundlagen der Judenfrage" (Grohmann),[128] "Die historischen Grundlagen der Judenfrage. II. (Zusammen mit Priv.-Doz. Dr. Karl Jahn),"[129] "Die rassischen und geschichtlichen Grundlagen der Judenfrage" (Grohmann),[130] and "Die türkischen und mongolischen Völkerschaften Rußlands" (Jahn).[131]

Both were rewarded for this service with secure positions when Hitler appointed Grohmann "unter Berufung in das Beamtenverhältnis auf Lebenszeit zum ordentlichen Professor im Reichsdienst," and the Reich Ministry of Education appointed Jahn as adjunct professor: "Sie sind … Beamter auf Widerruf geworden."[132] In 1942 the ministry sent Jahn to work in the library of the *Deutsche Morgenländische Gesellschaft*

---

124. See Konrád 2007, 271–72, 274, 351. For a detailed study of the German University during World War II, see Míšková 2007.

125. Grohmann became member of the NSDAP in December 1938 (No. 6652055), Jahn in April 1939 (No. 7165101). See Ellinger 2006, 38.

126. NA Grohmann Personal Information Sheet, NA Jahn Personal Information Sheet.

127. AUK Classes 36.

128. AUK Classes 30, 31.

129. AUK Classes 34–35.

130. AUK Classes 33, 62–63, and AUK Classes 37. Note Reinfandt's (2013, 258) claim that Grohmann also taught Hebrew to members of the SS in Prague. However, the work he refers to (Potthast 2002, 331) obviously mentions the lectures listed above ("Vorlesungen zu jüdischen Themen"), and states that they may have had SS audience as well, for which there is no evidence, since Grohmann did not offer those lectures at all in the period covered by the source used by Potthast (2002, 351 sub 65). The source in question is AUK Classes 38.

131. AUK Classes 37.

132. Ellinger 2006, 162–63.

120   Luděk Vacín and Jitka Sýkorová

in Halle.[133] A year later he was sent to the Netherlands as an interpreter for a unit of Azerbaijanis put to work on German fortifications. In 1948 he began teaching at the University of Utrecht, and from 1951 he taught at the University of Leiden as well.[134]

While it has been noted in the literature that Grohmann was instructed already in March 1941 "eine 4.000 Bände umfassende jüdische Bibliothek in Mähr.-Ostrau zu besichtigen und gegebenenfalls ... zu übernehmen" for his department,[135] the Prague archives reveal his involvement in another similar case later that year: "Vom Sicherheitsdienst ... wird der Universität die Bibliothek der jüdischen Kultusgemeinde in Olmütz zur Verfügung gestellt. Die Bücher sind von Professor Grohmann als wertvoll und als ein willkommener Zuwachs für das orientalische Seminar bezeichnet. ... Die Bibliothek umfasst etwa 700 Buchwerke und ist in Olmütz sichergestellt."[136]

In addition to plundering libraries left behind by the victims of the Nazi "final solution," Grohmann became director of the Oriental Institute in Prague, taken over from the Czechs by Nazi administration, and appended to the Reinhard Heydrich Foundation (*Reinhard-Heydrich-Stiftung*). This organization, established on 25 July 1942, was named in memory of the *Reichsprotektor* in Bohemia and Moravia, and the main architect of the Holocaust. Heydrich had been attacked on 27 May by two Czechoslovak paratroopers sent from Britain by the government-in-exile. He died on 4 June. The foundation that bore his name was supposed to become a vehicle of theoretical elaboration of Nazi policies of ethnic cleansing and Germanization of the Czech lands, eastern, and southeastern Europe.[137]

Moreover, Grohmann belonged to a group of professors from the German University who joined the initiative to educate soldiers of the Third Reich military (*Vortragsdienst*). In May 1940 he came up with the following topics: "1. Das Aegypten von heute mit Lichtbildern, 2. England und die Palästinafrage, 3. Der Kampf zwischen Frankreich und England um den arabischen Raum, 4. Die rassischen und historischen Grundlagen der Judenfrage 2–3 Vorträge," and noted his readiness to give his lectures "in und ausserhalb Prags und im Reiche."[138] Later he lectured on "1. Der Kampf um den arabischen Raum, 2. Das moderne Ägypten, 3. England und die Palästinafrage, 4. Ägypten und die britische Politik, 5. Der Islam als Religion und Weltanschauung."[139]

Regarding Grohmann's activities and behavior during the war, scholars have pointed out his disturbing dismissal of his colleagues' Schaade und Rathjens intervention on behalf of the Orientalist Hedwig Klein shortly after her deportation to Auschwitz-Birkenau on 11 July 1942. Grohmann did not believe "dass eine weitere

---

133. Ellinger 2006, 163.

134. Bruijn 2008.

135. Ellinger 2006, 163.

136. AUK Library, Bibliothek der jüdischen Kultusgemeinde in Olmütz, 26 July 1941. The preserved list of the books also contains a work by Grohmann's erstwhile colleague under the number "797 Pollak I. Prof. Dr. Vom jüd. Sein und Werden."

137. See Potthast 2002, 329–31. Among the main points of the foundation's research agenda was "a) totale Erforschung des Tschechentums in rassenkundlicher, psychologischer, volkswissenschaftlicher und historischer Hinsicht und b) Erforschung und Darstellung des Panslawismus" (Potthast 2002, 330–31). In detail, Wiedemann 2000.

138. AUK Lectures.

139. AUK Lectures, 28 March 1943.

"Die Assyriologie nicht weiter unberücksichtigt bleiben dürfte" 121

Mitarbeit der Genannten in Frage kommt, schon aus Prestigegründen."[140] Klein, the thirty-one year old doctor of Islamic studies, was murdered at Auschwitz.

Grohmann was ready to help other threatened scholars, though. Toward the end of the war he welcomed in Prague a "refugee" student from Berlin. According to the brief CV preserved in the Prague archives, Abdel Halim El-Naggar, born on 4 September 1908 in Cairo, studied Islamic theology and Arabic literature at al-Azhar University in his hometown. In 1934 he came to Germany to learn the German language and further study Semitic philology.[141]

What El-Naggar forgot to mention in his CV, however, were his activities in Berlin since 1940. At that time, he worked for the German Foreign Office and the Ministry of Propaganda. He published a journal in Arabic for Middle Eastern audiences to stir them up to support the Third Reich. In 1942 El-Naggar became the director of Nazi short-wave broadcasts to the Middle East.[142]

When the Grand Mufti of Jerusalem, Haj Amin al-Husseini, fled to Germany in 1941, where he resided in a villa in the Krumme Lanke neighborhood of Berlin until early 1945,[143] he collaborated with El-Naggar on the broadcasts which articulated the shared belief of SS leadership, al-Husseini, and El-Naggar that Nazism and Islam had common values and enemies, particularly the Jews. It was El-Naggar who founded the Islamic Central Institute (*Islamisches Zentralinstitut*) which provided the relations of Muslims in Germany to the Third Reich with an institutional backing.[144]

In January 1945, El-Naggar submitted a dissertation entitled "Akkadische Briefe des Archivs von Boghazköi" to the Faculty of Arts of the German University.[145] The rather modest thesis was "supervised" by Grohmann, and contains editions of selected pieces of diplomatic correspondence between the Hittite state, Egypt, Babylonia, and Assyria made from the autographs in *KBo* 1 and *KUB* 3. The transliterations and translations are accompanied by short introductions and a few philological notes, and one may ask if that would be enough for obtaining a doctorate at a different time and place, particularly if compared with, for instance, Kraus' (1931–1932) similarly conceived, but magisterial edition of Old Babylonian letters.

The report on the thesis was written by the only German scholar in Prague competent to do so, Steinmetzer. He may have not known (or asked) who El-Naggar was, but he knew that El-Naggar had studied with Ebeling in Berlin,[146] and he generally regarded the thesis as satisfactory. After all, Steinmetzer most likely did not wish to get into a conflict with Grohmann at a time when the upcoming defeat of the Third Reich was crystal clear. This seems to be suggested by the cautiously phrased critical remarks in his report:

140. See Ellinger 2006, 70.
141. AUK El-Naggar, Lebenslauf.
142. Breitman and Goda 2010, 20.
143. See Breitman and Goda 2010, 19.
144. See Breitman and Goda 2010, 20 and 31 n. 15.
145. AUK El-Naggar. See also Výborná, Havránek, and Kučera 1965, 134, sub 43.
146. AUK El-Naggar, Bericht über die Doktorarbeit des Herrn stud. phil. Abdel Halim El-Naggar mit dem Titel: "Akkadische Briefe des Archives von Boghazköi," 24 January 1945: "Sein Lehrer, Erich Ebeling, der sich vielfach mit der keilinschriftlichen Briefliteratur beschäftigt hat, hat dem Verfasser das nötige Rüstzeug auf den Weg gegeben."

Allerdings ist hier zu berücksichtigen, daß gelegentlich durch die uns heute nicht erreichbaren Fortschritte der assyriologischen Forschung kleine Verbesserungen sich als notwendig ergeben können. Dabei handelt es sich aber um einen Mangel, der jeder wissenschaftlichen Arbeit der Kriegszeit mehr oder minder anhaftet. Daher wäre dem Verfasser zu empfehlen, bevor die Arbeit in Druck gelegt wird ... die während der letzten Jahre erschienene assyriologische Literatur zur Rate zu ziehen und gegebenen Falles Aenderungen oder Verbesserungen anzubringen.[147]

The "supervisor" appended the following note to Steinmetzer's report: "Ich schließe mich dem Gutachten Prof. Steinmetzers an. Notevorschl.(?) sehr gut. Dr. Grohmann,"[148] and El-Naggar was awarded the doctorate on 17 February 1945 with the mark "gut."[149]

A couple of weeks later, on 6 March 1945, Grohmann asked "um Dienstbefreiung für die Zeit vom 15. 3. bis 20. 4. 1945 zwecks Durchführung eines mir erteilten Forschungsauftrages im Rahmen der Reinhard Heydrich-Stiftung und des Orientalischen Instituts,"[150] which was a pretext for his flight and the removal of his private library to Austria.[151]

Steinmetzer, on the other hand, died in July in a transit camp where he had been waiting together with other Germans for their expulsion from Czechoslovakia (see above). Thus, the story of German Assyriology in Prague came to an end that hardly needs any more comment.

---

147. AUK El-Naggar, Bericht über die Doktorarbeit des Herrn stud. phil. Abdel Halim El-Naggar mit dem Titel: "Akkadische Briefe des Archives von Boghazköi," 24 January 1945.

148. AUK El-Naggar, Bericht über die Doktorarbeit des Herrn stud. phil. Abdel Halim El-Naggar mit dem Titel: "Akkadische Briefe des Archives von Boghazköi," 24 January 1945.

149. AUK Register. The newly graduated doctor was still resident in Prague in October 1945, as testified by NA El-Naggar, which is a record of a fine imposed on him for failing to ask for an extension of his residence permit. His next fortunes are not known to us.

150. Ellinger 2006, 73.

151. For Grohmann's fortunes after the war see Reinfandt 2013, 260–66.

Appendix 1

Assyriological Classes of F. X. Steinmetzer at the Theological Faculty of the German University in Prague, 1908–1945

Title	Year	Source
Die Weltschöpfung in der Bibel und in der Keilschriftliteratur	1908	AUK Classes 1
Assyrisch für Anfänger[a]	1908	AUK Classes 2
Assyrische Inschriften[b]	1908	AUK Classes 3
Die Geburtsgeschichte Christi und der babylonische Mythenkreis	1909	AUK Classes 4
Babylonische Parallelen zum Leben Jesu	1909	AUK Classes 5
Christus und Gilgamesch	1910	AUK Classes 6
Einführung in die assyrische Schrift und Sprache	1911	AUK Classes 7
Leichte assyrische Inschriften	1914	AUK Classes 8
Lesung und Erklärung neubabylonischer Rechtsurkunden	1918	AUK Classes 9
Erklärung alt- und mittelbabylonischer Plastiken	1922	AUK Classes 10
Erklärung assyrischer Plastiken	1922	AUK Classes 11
Neubabylonische Geschäftsurkunden	1924	AUK Classes 12
Das babylonische Weltschöpfungslied	1925	AUK Classes 13
Lesung und Erklärung des Chammurapi-Kodex	1925	AUK Classes 14
Inschriften Asurbanapals	1926	AUK Classes 15
Neuere Ausgrabungen im Zweistromland	1930	AUK Classes 16
Assyrisch für Vorgeschrittene	1932	AUK Classes 17
Bilder aus der Kultur des alten Babyloniens	1932	AUK Classes 18
Bilder aus der babylonischen Kulturgeschichte	1933	AUK Classes 19
Assyrische Inschriften für Fortgeschrittene	1934	AUK Classes 20
Sumerische Inschriften	1934	AUK Classes 21
Neubabylonische Rechtsurkunden	1935	AUK Classes 22
Ausgewählte Stücke aus der babylonisch-assyrischen Kulturgeschichte	1935	AUK Classes 23
Die Hettiter, ihre Sprache und Schrift	1936	AUK Classes 24
Ausgewählte Stücke aus der Kulturgeschichte Vorderasiens	1936	AUK Classes 25
Bilder aus der Geschichte des Zweistromlandes	1937	AUK Classes 26
Lichtbildervortrag über die Kultur des Zweistromlandes	1937	AUK Classes 27
Lichtbildervortrag über die Kultur des Zweistromlandes. II. Teil	1938	AUK Classes 28
Lichtbildervortrag über einzelne Partien der Kulturgeschichte Babyloniens	1938	AUK Classes 29
Die Kultur des Zweistromlandes. (Mit Lichtbildern.)	1939	AUK Classes 30
Assyrisch für Anfänger	1941	AUK Classes 31
Assyrische Inschriften	1941	AUK Classes 32
Assyrisch für Anfänger	1941	AUK Classes 33

[a] This course was offered regularly throughout the documented period, except some terms during World War II.

[b] This course was offered regularly throughout the documented period, except some terms during World War II.

124   Luděk Vacín and Jitka Sýkorová

Appendix 2

Edition of Selected Documents

No. 1

[Report of the Selection Committee for the appointment of a Professor of Semitic Philology at the Faculty of Arts of the German University in Prague, 8 pages, handwritten, dated 28 June 1922, see Fig. 11, italics ours, source: AUK Semitics Professorships; a typewritten version with negligible differences is preserved in the dossier NA Semitics Professorships, see Fig. 12]

Bericht

der Kommission zur Besetzung der Lehrkanzel des verstorbenen Prof. Dr. I. Pollak

An das Professorenkollegium der philosophischen Fakultät der deutschen Universität in Prag

Bereits bei der Schaffung der Lehrkanzel des verstorbenen Professors Dr Isidor Pollak, die die Semitische Philologie mit besonderer Berücksichtigung des Hebräischen und Aramäischen zum Gegenstande hatte, hatte sich die Fakultät von dem Gesichtspunkte leiten lassen, dass das gewaltig angewachsene Gebiet der Semitischen Philologie im Interesse eines gedeihlichen Betriebes, der allen wissenschaftlichen Anforderungen nachkommen soll, am besten dahin zu teilen sei, daß das Nordsemitische—Hebräisch und Aramäisch-Syrisch, ebenso wie das Südsemitische, Arabisch-Aethiopisch mit seinem ganzen Komplex von Dialekten seinen besonderen Vertreter erhält. Wenn die in der Sitzung vom 26 Jan 22 gewählte unterzeichnete Kommission, der Prof. Honor. Dr. M. Grünert als beratendes Mitglied beigezogen wurde, nun vor der Aufgabe steht, Vorschläge für die durch Professor I Pollaks Tode freigewordene Kanzel zu erstatten, so mußte sie sich vor allem von der Erwägung leiten lassen, das durch Prof Pollak vertretene Gebiet der nordsemitischen Sprachen nach den Erfordernissen der Wissenschaft auszubauen und dabei *ergab es sich von selbst, daß ein so wichtiger Zweig der nordsemitischen Philologie, wie die Assyriologie, nicht weiter unberücksichtigt bleiben dürfte. Haben heute doch die meisten deutschen Universitäten der Assyriologie eigene Kanzeln eröffnet. Dazu kam noch, dass die Geschichte des alten Orients in Prag noch keinen Vertreter hat und ihre Vertretung im Rahmen der Assyriologie sich doch fast von selbst ergibt. Die Kommission ist nun der Ansicht, daß im Interesse der Pflege dieser wichtigen Gebiete die Besetzung der Kanzel Prof. Pollaks dahin erfolgen solle, daß neben dem Hebräischen und Aramäisch-Syrischen auch die Assyriologie vertreten werde.* Damit würden die gelehrten orientalistischen Disziplinen [*page 2*] eine höchst wertvolle Ergänzung und Abrundung ihres Gebietes erhalten, zumal ja die sogenannten islamitischen Sprachen, Türkisch und Persisch in Prof. M. Grünert einen berufenen Vertreter gefunden haben und dem Inhaber der Kanzel für arabische Paläographie und Kulturgeschichte des Orients zugleich die Pflege des ganzen Gebietes der Südsemitischen Philologie obliegt. Aus diesen Erwägungen hat sich die Kommission die Aufgabe gestellt, Persönlichkeiten namhaft zu machen, die die Nordsemitische Philologie in Verbindung mit der Assyriologie zu vertreten im Stande sind und gestattet sich, der Fakultät folgende Herren in Vorschlag zu bringen.

[*crossed out*]
Primo loco: Prof. Dr. Arno Poebel, a.o. Professor der semitischen Philologie und Aegyptologie an der Universität Rostock
Secundo loco ex aequo: Tit. a.o. Prof. Dr. Hans Bauer, Privatdozent an der Universität Halle
Dr. Erich Ebeling, Privatdozent an der Universität Berlin
Tertio loco: Dr. Hans Ehelolf, wissenschaftlicher Hilfsarbeiter an der vorderasiatischen Abteilung der Staatsmuseen in Berlin.

Arno Poebel wurde am 26. Jan. 1881 als Sohn des Zimmerpoliers Philipp Poebel in Eisenach in Thüringen geboren, studierte in Heidelberg, Marburg, Zürich, Jena und Berlin Theologie und Philologie und zwar indogermanische Sprachen (Gothisch, Althochdeutsch, Sanskrit) ebensowohl wie Semitische. Nach Ablegung des Doktorexamens wurde Poebel 1905 von der Universität von Pennsilvanien in Philadelphia USA zum Harrison Research Fellow in Assyriology gewählt und arbeitete gemeinsam mit Hilprecht an den Ausgrabungsfunden von Nippur und im Auftrage der Universität 1907 auch im Osmanischen Museum in Konstantinopel. 1910 habilitierte er sich in Breslau für semitische Sprachen und erhielt im selben Jahre die venia legendi für altorientalische Geschichte, 1911 und 1912 folgte er einer Einladung der Johns Hopkins University in Baltimore, um daselbst Vorlesungen über altorientalische Geschichte zu halten, 1913 u. 1914 einer Aufforderung des Universitätsmuseums in Philadelphia, die dort befindlichen historischen und grammatischen Keilschrifttexte in der Sprache von Sumer und Akkad herauszugeben u. zu bearbeiten. 1919 wurde er von Breslau als a.o. [*page 3*] Professor für Semitische Philologie und Aegyptologie nach Rostock berufen, wo er noch gegenwärtig tätig ist.

Die ausserordentlich zahlreichen Arbeiten Poebel<s> umfassen das ganze Gebiet der Assyriologie sowohl nach der historischen, als auch der philologischen Richtung und behandeln auch philologische Themen allgemein semitistischen Inhalts. Aus der letzteren Gruppe sei im Besonderen auf die Besprechung von H. Bauers Aufsatz „die Tempora im Semitischen" verwiesen, die Poebel zu einer Vorarbeit über den Bau der semitischen Sprachen ausgestaltet hat. In philologischer Richtung hat Poebel vor allem der Grammatik des Sumerischen seine Kraft gewidmet und die Wissenschaft verdankt ihm hier fast so viel wie Alles, was an neuen Erkenntnissen erschlossen wurde. Nicht minder wichtig ist die Herausgabe der zahlreichen und schwierigen sumerischen Rechtsurkunden, die Poebel übersetzt hat, sowie seine Ergänzung der Lücke von Hamurhapis Gesetz. Die Geschichte des alten Babylonien dankt Poebel nicht nur die Aufdeckung des Verhältnisses der ersten beiden Dynastien von Babylon sowie den Nachweis der Reihenfolge der Könige von Agade, sondern auch die wichtigen Texte und Untersuchungen zur altbabylonischen Geschichte. Poebel ist heute unstreitig die erste Autorität auf diesem Gebiete. Seine Vorlesungen umspannen das ganze Gebiet des Nordsemitischen: Hebräische Lektüre und Grammatik, Syrisch, Kanaʻanäische Inschriften, Phoenizische Inschriften, Biblisch-Aramäisch. Auf dem Gebiete der Geschichte des alten Orients liegen die Vorlesungen über Königsannalen,

126 Luděk Vacín and Jitka Sýkorová

Geschichte Babyloniens und Assyriens, Geschichte des alten Orients bis zur Perserzeit, ausserdem las Poebel über babylonisch-assyrische Grammatik, babylonische u. akkadische Texte, sumerische Texte, Geschichte der Keilschrift, über den Bau der semitischen Sprachen, sumerische Grammatik, Litteratur Babyloniens u. Assyriens, die babylonische Kultur und ihr Einfluß auf die europäischen Kulturvölker, die babylonische Religion und ihr Verhältnis zur israelitischen und griechischen, orientalische Erzählungskunst, Arabisch für Anfänger, die Diebsgeschichten in 1001 Nacht. Auch die Aegyptologie [*page 4*] vertritt Poebel in seinen Vorlesungen, sodaß nun auch dies Gebiet an unserer Universität wieder gepflegt werden könnte.

Hans Bauer wurde am 16. Jan. 1878 zu Grasmannsdorf bei Bamberg als Sohn eines Landwirts geboren, studierte Theologie, dann in Berlin und Leipzig semitische Sprachen, promovierte 1910 zu Berlin, verbrachte dann 1911 ein halbes Jahr zu Studienzwecken in Aegypten und Syrien, habilitierte sich 1912 in Halle, wo er gegenwärtig einen Lehrauftrag für Assyriologie inne hat. Gleich Poebel hat sich auch Bauer nicht auf das semitische Sprachgebiet beschränkt, sondern auch indogermanische Sprachen und sogar das Chinesische in den Kreis seiner Untersuchungen gezogen. Seine Hauptwerke liegen insgesamt auf philologischem Gebiete; so seine Dissertation über die Entstehung der semitischen Tempora und ihre Ausgestaltung in den Einzelsprachen, die ein viel erörtertes Problem auf ganz neue Grundlagen stellte, ferner eine Reihe von Untersuchungen zur semitischen Sprachgeschichte, die in der Zeitschrift der deutschen morgenländischen Gesellschaft und in der Zeitschrift für Assyriologie erschienen. Besonders wertvoll ist hier seine Erklärung der Flexion des sogenannten schwachen Verbums. Den Abschluß seiner philologischen Studien bildet die gemeinsam mit P. Leander in Götheborg herausgegebene, groß angelegte historische hebräische Grammatik des Alten Testaments, deren erster Band Laut-u.-Formenlehre eben mit der 3ten Lieferung abschloß. Bauers Arbeit ist hier die historische Einleitung, die Darstellung der Tempuslehre und der Nominalbildung, seine Ideen beherrschen das ganze Buch, ihm dankt es die Erkenntnis vom Mischcharakter der hebräischen Schriftsprache, die zahlreichen Probleme der Laut-u.-Formenlehre überraschend einfach erklärt. Auch der semitischen Epigraphik hat Bauer wesentliche Dienste geleistet. So ist die Inschrift Königs Kalamu in ihrem Verständnis durch Bauer entschieden gefördert worden und auch das Verhältnis dieses Regenten zum assyrischen Großkönig hat erst Bauer richtig aufgefasst. Neben der neuhebräischen Litteratur hat sich Bauer auch eingehend mit der Assyriologie beschäftigt. Er hat sie nicht nur in seinen Arbeiten stets berücksichtigt, sondern auch [*page 5*] zu den Tellel-Amarnabriefen wertvolle Bemerkungen beigesteuert. Seine Habilitationsschrift „die Dogmatik al-Ghazâlis nach dem 2ten Buche seines Hauptwerks" beschäftigt sich mit islamischer Philosophie, die ja auch die Hauptdomäne unseres verstorbenen Kollegen I. Pollak gewesen <ist>, und auf diesem Gebiete liegt auch seine bedeutendste jüngste Arbeit Islamische Ethik, von der bis jetzt 3 Bände von zusammen mehr als 400 Seiten vorliegen. Seine Vorlesungen umfassten historische Grammatik des Hebräischen, semitische Epigraphik und Assyriologie.

Erich Ebeling, geboren am 21. Nov. 1886 zu Berlin, studierte orientalische und klassische Philologie an der Universität Berlin, promovierte hier 1908 und erwarb bereits

"Die Assyriologie nicht weiter unberücksichtigt bleiben dürfte" 127

im nächsten Jahre die facultas docendi für Hebräisch und die klassischen Sprachen. Dieser Erfolg verschaffte ihm eine Studienrats-(Oberlehrer)stelle am Humboldt-Gymnasium in Berlin, an dem er noch jetzt wirkt. 1919 habilitierte er sich für Assyriologie an der Universität Berlin. In dieser Disziplin hat Ebeling eine geradezu staunenerregende Produktivität erreicht, die umso höher zu werten ist, als der Betrieb an der Mittelschule ihm 24 Wochenstunden zur wissenschaftlichen Arbeit entzieht. Bereits in seiner Dissertation „das Verbum der El-Amarna Briefe" gelang es ihm, die vorhebräische Gestalt des Kanaʿanäischen Verbums festzustellen und damit einen wichtigen Baustein in das Gebäude der historischen semitischen Grammatik einzufügen. Durch diese Arbeit wurde Prof. Knudtzon in Christiania, der Herausgeber der Tell el-Amarnabriefe auf Ebeling aufmerksam und übertrug ihm die Abfassung des Glossars zu dieser Ausgabe, das 1915 erschien und gegen 200 Seiten umfasst. 1911/12 konnte Ebeling in Paris und London die Vorarbeiten für seine Publikationen assyrischer Keilschrifttafeln anlegen u. bei dieser Gelegenheit auch syrische Handschriften in den Kreis seiner Untersuchungen einbeziehen. Im Auftrage der preussischen Akademie der Wissenschaften hat er im selben Jahre die Katalogisierung der Keilschrifttexte aus Assur übernommen, denen in der Hauptsache noch jetzt seine Arbeit gewidmet ist. Von diesen Texten sind bis jetzt 6 Hefte, in Ganzen 414 Seiten unter dem Titel [*page 6*] Keilschrifttexte aus Assur religiösen Inhalts <erschienen>, zwei weitere Hefte werden demnächst erscheinen und die letzten beiden Hefte, die den zweiten Band mit 480 Seiten abschließen, sind unter der Presse. Neben einer ganzen Anzahl kleineren Aufsätze hat Ebeling die Früchte seiner Beschäftigung mit den Assurtexten in 2 größeren Arbeiten niedergelegt, in den „Quellen zur Kenntnis der babylonischen Religion I, II" (Mitteil. der vorderasiat. Gesellschaft XXIII 1918, 160 SS.) und „das babylonische Weltschöpfungslied" 1921. Die religiösen Texte aus Assur, eine umfangreiche Arbeit, konnten leider noch nicht gedruckt werden. Die Kollegien Ebelings umfassen assyrische und sumerische Grammatik, religiöse Keilschrifttexte, das altassyrische Gesetz, Quellen zur Babylonischen Religionsgeschichte, sumerische Keilschrifttexte. An ungedruckten Arbeiten liegen vor: Texte medizinischen Inhalts, die Prof. Sudhoff in Leipzig Ebeling abtrat, Das Aramäische in den Pehlewîideogrammen, Handschriftliches Material zum Achiqarromane in Syrischer Sprache, vormasoretische Materialien zur hebräischen Grammatik, die Terminologie der syrischen Ärzte.

Hans Ehelolf ist am 30. Juli 1891 zu Hannover als Sohn des Lehrers Ehelolf geboren, studierte 1910 in Marburg und 1911 in Leipzig, 1911–14 wieder in Marburg orientalische Philologie, wo er 1914 das Rigorosum bestand. 1915 wurde er als wissenschaftlicher Hilfsarbeiter an der vorderasiatischen Abteilung der Berliner Museen angestellt, deren Verbande er auch jetzt angehört, 1921 wurde er von der philosophischen Fakultät der Universität Königsberg zur Habilitation aufgefordert und ihm zugleich ein Lehrauftrag für Keilschriftforschung zugesichert, aus pekuniären Gründen konnte er aber dieser Aufforderung nicht entsprechen. 1919 stand Ehelolf auf der Vorschlagsliste zur Besetzung der Kanzel Prof. Ungnads und wurde auch nach Meissners Abgang von Breslau in den Vorschlag für die Besetzung dieser Lehrkanzel aufgenommen. ~~Ebelings~~ Ehelolfs Arbeiten behandeln das Gebiet der Assyriologie sowohl nach der [*page 7*] philologischen als auch der rechtshistorischen Seite. Seine Dissertation erörterte ein Wortfolgeprinzip im Assyrisch-Babylonischen (Leipziger Semitist. Studien VI.3 1916), eine

Reihe kleinerer Arbeiten ist den assyrischen Vokabularen, dem altassyrischen Kalender und jüngeren Erscheinungen in der assyriologischen wissenschaftlichen Litteratur gewidmet. Überaus wertvoll ist seine Übersetzung des altassyrischen Rechtsbuchs zu der Paul Koschaker eine Einleitung geschrieben hat und bereits zur Hälfte gedruckt sind die Kappadokischen Tontafeln der Berliner Museen. Es ist ein Beweis von ganz besonderem Vertrauen und wissenschaftlicher Anerkennung von Seiten der berufenen Gelehrten, daß bei Umgestaltung der Orientalistischen Literaturzeitung Ehelolf die Vertretung des ganzen Gebietes der Keilschriftforschung übertragen wurde. Ehelolf hat einen weiten Gesichtskreis und beherrscht neben der Assyriologie eine ganze Reihe von Sprachen; nicht nur das Hebräische und Aramäische, mit welchen letzterer Sprache er sich im Oriente in Dêr ez-Zôr, wo das Syrische noch von den Nestorianern gesprochen wird, beschäftigte, auch Pehlewi, Sanskrit und Chinesisch sind ihm nicht fremd. Seine verantwortungsvolle Tätigkeit am Museum erschließt ihm zudem ein wissenschaftliches Material, das nur selten Gelehrten in so reichem Maße zur freien Verfügung steht und befähigt ihn, auch für die Lehrtätigkeit aus dem Vollen zu schöpfen. Dabei besitzt er nach dem übereinstimmenden Urteile von Jensen, Littmann und O. Weber eine ganz ausgezeichnete Lehrgabe.

[*crossed out*]
Die Kommission gestattet sich nun, ihre nach eingehenden mehrmaligen Beratungen gefassten, oben niedergelegten Vorschläge der Fakultät mit der Bitte um ~~wohl~~wollende Befürwortung beim Ministerium für Schulwesen und Volkskultur zu unterbreiten.

[*crossed out*]
Prag. am 28. Juni 1922.

[*page 8*]
Von den ~~genannten~~ erwähnten Herren hat die Kommission an erster Stelle Prof. Dr. Arno Poebel genannt, der bereits eine lange akademische Tätigkeit hinter sich hat und dessen zahlreiche, wertvolle Arbeiten das gesamte Gebiet der Assyriologie umfassen. *Seine engen Beziehungen zu Amerikanischen Universitäten eröffnen zudem die Aussicht auf eine aktive Betätigung an den Kulturstätten des Alten Babylonien, die unter den gegenwärtigen Verhältnissen für die deutsche Wissenschaft als besonders wertvoll bezeichnet werden muß.*
An zweiter Stelle bringt die Kommission ex aequo Dr. Hans Bauer und Dr. Erich Ebeling in Vorschlag, die jeder für sich eine ausgesprochene wissenschaftliche Individualität darstellen.
An dritter Stelle nennt die Kommission Dr. Hans Ehelolf, der zwar noch nicht habilitiert ist, aber durch seine wertvollen wissenschaftlichen Arbeiten die volle Gewähr für den Lehrberuf mit sich bringt und sich bereits einen geachteten Namen in der in ihm vertretenen Wissenschaft erworben hat.

Prag den 28 Juni 1922

[*signatures*]

"Die Assyriologie nicht weiter unberücksichtigt bleiben dürfte" 129

Rzach[152]
Swoboda[153]
Winternitz[154]
Grohmann[155]

Mit Beilage der Verzeichnisse der Arbeiten

152. Alois Rzach (1850–1935), Professor of Classical Philology (1887–1923).
153. Heinrich Swoboda (1856–1926), Professor of Greek Antiquity and Epigraphy (1899–1926).
154. Moriz Winternitz (1863–1937), Professor of Indology and Ethnology (1911–1934).
155. Adolf Grohmann (1887–1977), Professor of Semitic Philology and Islamic Studies (1923–1945); see also above.

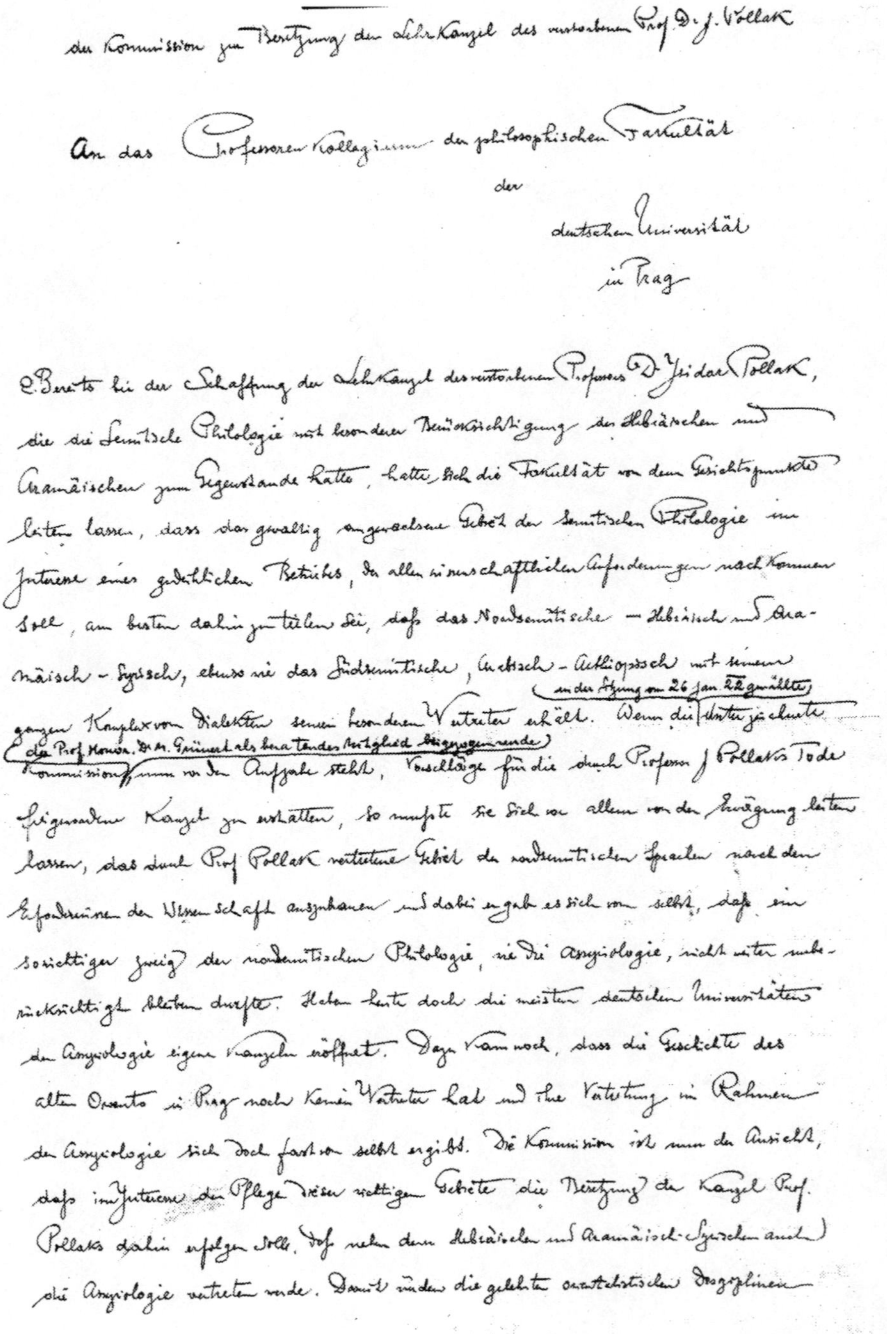

FIGURE 6.11a. The first page of the handwritten version of Document No. 1. Source: AUK Semitics Professorships

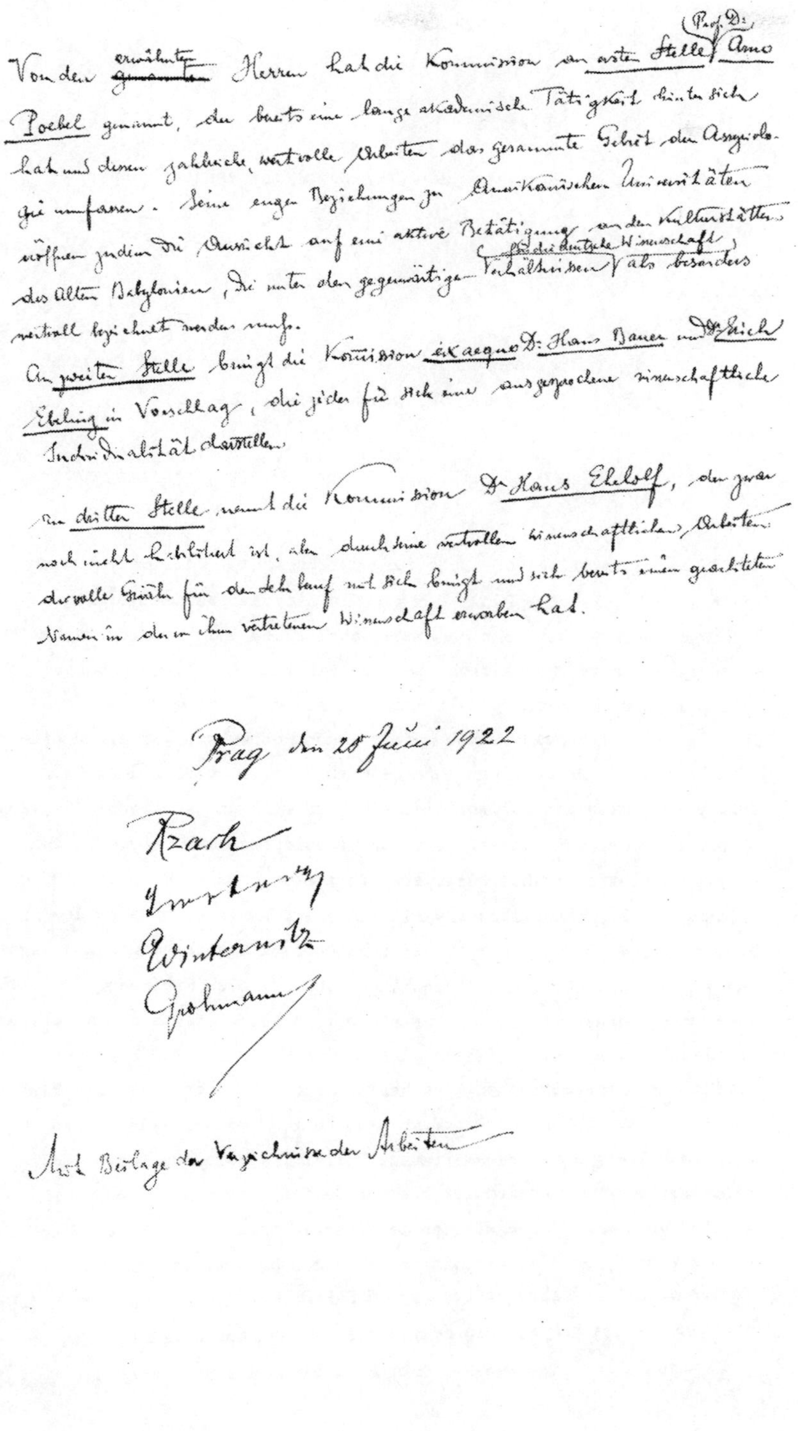

"Die Assyriologie nicht weiter unberücksichtigt bleiben dürfte"   131

FIGURE 6.11b. The last page of the handwritten version of Document No. 1. Source: AUK Semitics Professorships

Luděk Vacín and Jitka Sýkorová

Bericht

der Kommission zur Besetzung der Lehrkanzel des verstorbenen
Prof.Dr. J. Pollak .

An das

Professorenkollegium der philosophischen Fakultät
der deutschen Universität

in Prag .

Bereits bei der Schaffung der Lhrkanzel des verstorbenen
Professors Dr. Isidor Pollak , die die semitische Philologie
mit besonderer Berücksichtigung des Hebräischen und Aramäischen zum
Gegenstande hatte, hatte sich die Fakultät von dem Gesichtspunkte
leiten lassen, dass das gewaltig angewachsene Gebiet der Semitischen
Philologie im Interesse eines gedeihlichen Betriebes, der allen wissenschaftlichen Anforderungen nachkommen soll, am besten dahin zu
teilen sei, dass das Nordsemitische - Hebräisch und Armäisch - Syrisch,
ebenso wie das Südsemitische,Arabisch-Aethiopisch mit seinem ganzen
Komplex Dialekten seinen besonderen Vertreter erhält. Wenn die in der
Sitzung vom 26.Jänner 1922 gewählte unterzeichnete Kommission der Prof.
honror. Dr. M. Grünert als beratendes Mitglied beigezogen werde,
nun vor der Aufgabe steht, Vorschläge für die durch Professor J. Pollak's
Tode freigewordene Kanzel zu erstatten , so musste sie sich vor allem
von den Erwägung leiten lassen , das durch Prof. Pollak vertretene
Gebiet der nordsemitischen Sprachen nach den Erfordernissen der Wissenschaft auszubauen,und dabei ergab es sich von selbst, dass ein so
wichtiger Zweig der nordsemitischen Philologie, wie die Assyriologie,
nicht weiter unberücksichtigt bleiben dürfte. Haben heute doch die
meisten deutschen Universitäten der Assyriologie eigene Kanzeln eröffnet,
Dazu kam noch, dass die Geschichte des alten Orients in Prag noch keinen
Vertreter hat und ihre Vertretung im Rahmen der Assyriologie sich doch
fast von selbst ergibt. Die Kommission ist nun der Ansicht, dass im
Interesse der Pflege dieser wichtigen Gebiete die Besetzung der Kanzel

FIGURE 6.12a. The first page of the typewritten version of Document No. 1. Source:
NA Semitics Professorships

Lehrtätigkeit aus dem Vollen zuschöpfen. Dabei besitzt er nach dem übereinstimmenden Urteile von Jensen, Littmann und O. Weber eine ganz ausgezeichne Lehrgabe.

Von den erwähnten Herren hat die Kommission an ersten Stelle Prof. Dr. Arno P o e b e l genannt, der bereits eine lange akademische Tätigkeit hinter sich hat und dessen zahlreiche, wertvolle Arbeiten das gesamte Gebiet der Assyriologie umfassen. Seine engen Beziehungen zu Amerikanischen Universitäten eröffnen zu dem die Aussicht auf eine aktive Betätigung an den Kulturstätten des alten Babylonien, die unter den gegenwärtigen Verhältnissen für die deutsche Wissenschaft als besonders wertvoll bezeichnet werden muss.

An zweiter Stelle bringt die Kommission ex aequo Dr. Hans B a u e r und Dr. Erich E b e l i n g in Vorschlag, die jeder für sich eine ausgesprochene wissenschaftliche Individualität darstellen.

An dritter Stelle nennt die Kommission Dr. Hans E h e l o l f , der zwar noch nicht habilitiert ist, aber durch seine wertvollen wissenschaftlichen Arbeiten die volle Gewähr für den Lehrberuf mit sich bringt und sich bereits einen geachteten Namen in der in ihm vertretenen Wissenschaft erworben hat.

Prag, am 28. Juni 1922.

R z a c h m.p. S w o b o d a m.p.
W i n t e r n i t z m.p. G r o h m a n n m.p.

Mit Beilagen der Verzeichnisse der Arbeiten.

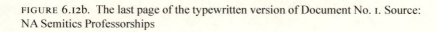

FIGURE 6.12b. The last page of the typewritten version of Document No. 1. Source: NA Semitics Professorships

No. 2

[Letter from Benno Landsberger to Bedřich Hrozný, 2 pages, handwritten, dated 25 January 1922, see Fig. 13, source: NpM Landsberger]

Leipzig, Südstr. 3.
25/1 · 22.

Hochverehrter Herr Professor,

Dass Sie sich gelegentlich der in Prag eingetretenen Vakanz meiner erinnert haben, hat mich sehr gefreut. Meinen besten Dank dafür! Ich wollte übrigens eben in der gleichen Angelegenheit mich wieder an Sie wenden. Für eine Fürsprache beim Ministerium werde ich Ihnen sehr dankbar sein. Was für Absichten die philos. Fakultät hat, weiss ich nicht, werde es aber bald in Erfahrung bringen. Ich möchte natürlich nichts versäumen und werde wohl in den nächsten Wochen in Prag bei den Herren, welche Einfluss auf die Wiederbesetzung haben, vorsprechen. Vorläufig habe ich mich an San Nicolo gewendet, Zimmern hat an Grünert geschrieben. Ich vertraue, dass auch Sie, sehr verehrter Herr Professor, wenn Sie etwas in Erfahrung bringen oder einen zweckdienlichen Wink für einen meinerseits zu unternehmenden Schritt geben können, mir freundlichst Mitteilung davon machen. Das letzte Mal hatte ich ja wenig Glück mit meinen Interventionen, doch war der Zeitpunkt verspätet, auch ich damals erst im Stadium der Habilitation. So könnten jetzt meine Chancen besser sein, denn ich weiss wirklich nicht, wer sonst noch für diesen Posten in Betracht käme. Haben Sie vielleicht schon mit Prof. Musil darüber gesprochen? Meiner Dankbarkeit für Ihre Freundlichkeit, die Sie mir bei früherer Gelegenheit reichlich bewiesen, seien Sie versichert!

Übrigens werde ich wahrscheinlich als Nachfolger Peisers nach Königsberg einen Ruf erhalten, doch ist es noch sehr unsicher, ob ich diesen [*page 2*] annehmen würde, denn die Bezahlung ist sehr schlecht, auch die Bibliotheksverhältnisse traurig.

Für eine Fortsetzung Ihres „Getreides" besteht wohl keine Aussicht,[156] ich habe Ihnen in einem demnächst erscheinenden Artikel über NÍĜ.ḪAR.RA[157] [*in cuneiform*] und Verwandtes etwas ins Handwerk gepfuscht. Dagegen dürfen wir wohl bald meine Hethitica erwarten, insbesondere die Übersetzung des Gesetzes, von dem auch Zimmern, in Gemeinschaft mit einem Indogermanisten, eine Übersetzung wagen will.

So danke ich Ihnen bestens, empfehle mich Ihnen und Ihrer Frau Gemahlin bestens
als Ihr
ganz ergebener

B. Landsberger

---

156. A reference to Hrozný 1913.

157. A reference to Landsberger 1922 where he suggested a meaning "fine flour" (*Feinmehl*) for this sequence. See also *CAD* S 107 s.v. *samādu*.

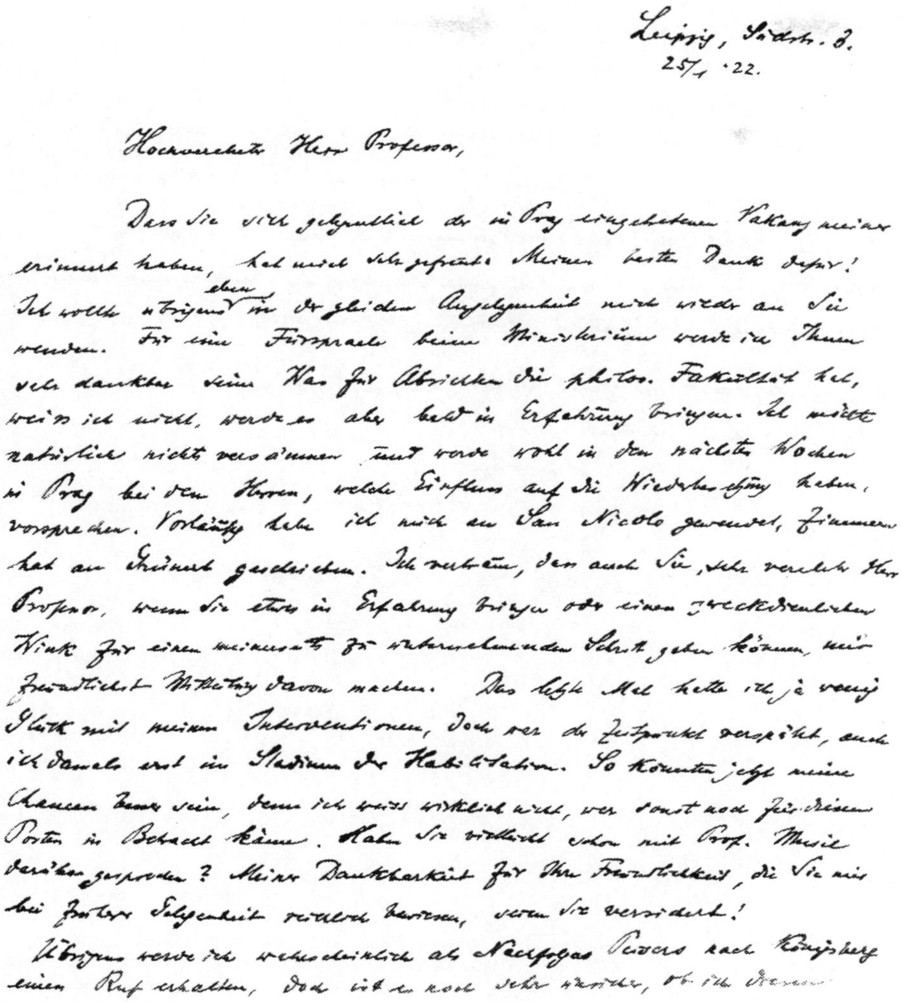

Leipzig, Sidonienstr. 8.
25/1 '22.

Hochverehrter Herr Professor,

Dass Sie sich gelegentlich der in Prag eingetretenen Vakanz meiner erinnert haben, hat mich sehr gefreut. Meinen besten Dank dafür! Ich wollte übrigens eben in der gleichen Angelegenheit mich wieder an Sie wenden. Für eine Fürsprache beim Ministerium werde ich Ihnen sehr dankbar sein. Was für Absichten die philos. Fakultät hat, weiss ich nicht, werde es aber bald in Erfahrung bringen. Ich möchte natürlich nichts versäumen und werde wohl in den nächsten Wochen in Prag bei den Herren, welche Einfluss auf die Wiederbesetzung haben, vorsprechen. Vorläufig habe ich mich an San Nicolò gewendet, Zimmern hat an Grünert geschrieben. Ich vertraue, dass auch Sie, sehr verehrter Herr Professor, wenn Sie etwas in Erfahrung bringen oder einen zweckdienlichen Wink für einen meinerseits zu unternehmenden Schritt geben können, mir freundlichst Mitteilung davon machen. Das letzte Mal hatte ich ja wenig Glück mit meinen Interventionen, doch war der Zeitpunkt verspätet, auch ich damals erst im Stadium der Habilitation. So könnten jetzt meine Chancen besser sein, denn ich weiss wirklich nicht, wer sonst noch für diesen Posten in Betracht käme. Haben Sie vielleicht schon mit Prof. Musil darüber gesprochen? Meiner Dankbarkeit für Ihre Freundlichkeit, die Sie mir bei früherer Gelegenheit reichlich bewiesen, seien Sie versichert!

Übrigens werde ich wahrscheinlich als Nachfolger Peisers nach Königsberg einen Ruf erhalten, doch ist es noch sehr unsicher, ob ich diesem

FIGURE 6.13a. Reproduction of Document No. 2. Source: NpM Landsberger

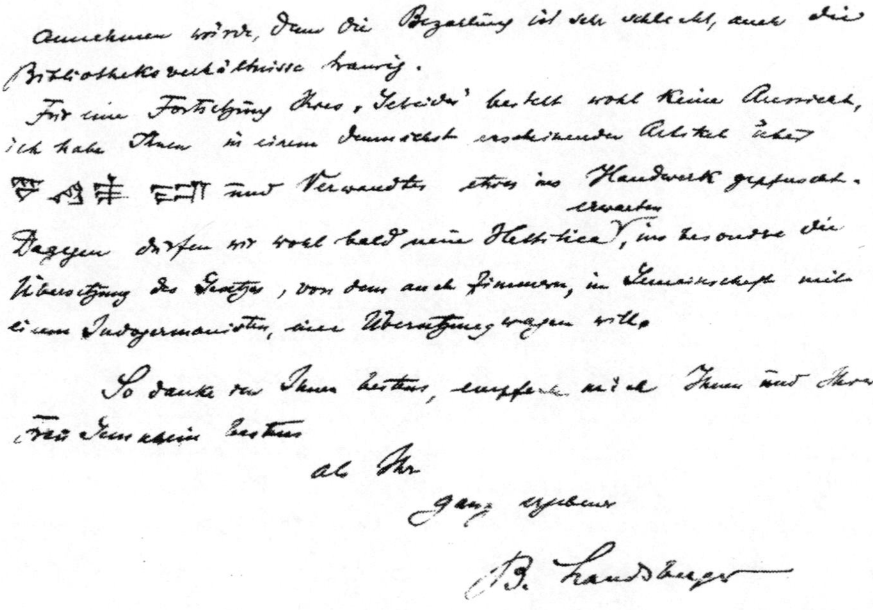

FIGURE 6.13b. Reproduction of Document No. 2. Source: NpM Landsberger

"Die Assyriologie nicht weiter unberücksichtigt bleiben dürfte" 137

Reference Key to Archival Sources

Siglum	Source(s)
AUK Classes	Archiv Univerzity Karlovy (Archive of Charles University in Prague), fond Úřední tisky Německé univerzity v Praze (1881) 1882–1945; Seznamy přednášek (Ordnungen der Vorlesungen) 1882/1883–1940, Archivní řada, ka. 1, inv. č. 37, Ordnung der Vorlesungen an der k.k. deutschen Karl-Ferdinands-Universität zu Prag im Sommersemester 1908, p. 70 (= 1–2) / inv. č. 38, Wintersemester (= WiSe) 1908–1909, p. 74 (= 3) / inv. č. 39, Sommersemester (= SoSe) 1909, p. 56 (= 4) / inv. č. 40, WiSe 1909–1910, p. 5 (= 5) / inv. č. 41, SoSe 1910, p. 56 (= 6) / inv. č. 43, SoSe 1911, p. 5 (= 7) / inv. č. 49, SoSe 1914, p. 66 (= 8) / ka. 2, inv. č. 58, WiSe 1918–1919, p. 8 (= 9) / inv. č. 65, Ordnung der Vorlesungen an der deutschen Universität in Prag im Sommersemester 1922, p. 4 (= 10) / inv. č. 66, WiSe 1922–1923, p. 4 (= 11) / inv. č. 69, SoSe 1924, p. 4 (= 12) / inv. č. 71, SoSe 1925, p. 4 (= 13) / inv. č. 72, WiSe 1925–1926, p. 4 (= 14) / inv. č. 74, WiSe 1926–1927, p. 4 (= 15) / inv. č. 82, WiSe 1930–1931, p. 4 (= 16) / inv. č. 85, SoSe 1932, p. 5 (= 17) / inv. č. 86, WiSe 1932–1933, p. 5 (= 18) / inv. č. 88, WiSe 1933–1934, p. 6 (= 19) / inv. č. 89, SoSe 1934, p. 6 (= 20) / inv. č. 90, WiSe 1934–1935, p. 6 (= 21) / inv. č. 91, SoSe 1935, p. 6 (= 22) / inv. č. 92, WiSe 1935–1936, p. 6 (= 23) / inv. č. 93, SoSe 1936, p. 6 (= 24) / inv. č. 94, WiSe 1936–1937, p. 6 (= 25) / inv. č. 95, SoSe 1937, p. 6 (= 26) / inv. č. 96, WiSe 1937–1938, p. 6 (= 27) / inv. č. 97, SoSe 1938, p. 6 (= 28) / inv. č. 98, WiSe 1938–1939, p. 6 (= 29) / inv. č. 99, SoSe 1939, p. 6 (= 30) / Multiplikáty, ka. 11, inv. č. 416, 1. trim. 1941, Deutsche Karls-Universität Prag. Personal- und Vorlesungsverzeichnis, p. 35 (= 31) / inv. č. 417, Deutsche Karls-Universität Prag. Gegründet 1348. Personal- und Vorlesungsverzeichnis, SoSe 1941, p. 34 (= 32) / inv. č. 418, WiSe 1941–1942, p. 34 (= 33) / ka. 9, inv. č. 269, WiSe 1939–1940, Deutsche Karls-Universität in Prag: Vorlesungsverzeichnis, p. 34 (= 34) / inv. č. 270, 1. trim. 1940, p. 40 (= 35) / ka. 11, inv. č. 415, 3. trim. 1940, p. 60 (= 36) / inv. č. 419, SoSe 1942, Deutsche Karls-Universität Prag. Gegründet 1348. Personal- und Vorlesungsverzeichnis, p. 65 (= 37) / inv. č. 420, WiSe 1942–1943, p. 79 (= 38).
AUK El-Naggar	Archiv Univerzity Karlovy (Archive of Charles University in Prague), fond Filozofická fakulta Německé univerzity v Praze (Philosophische Fakultät der Deutschen Universität in Prag), Spisový materiál (1857) 1882–1945; Disertace (Dissertationen), Abdel Halim El-Naggar, sign. H VII, inv. č. dis. 291/V 43.
AUK Grohmann	*Ditto*; Personální záležitosti vyučujících a zaměstnanců, Grohmann Adolf, Dr.phil., o.ö. Professor, ka. 49, inv. č. 504, sign. P I/4.
AUK Grünert A	Archiv Univerzity Karlovy (Archive of Charles University in Prague), fond Úřední tisky Německé univerzity v Praze (1881) 1882–1945; An Stelle der feierlichen Inauguration des Rektors der deutschen Karl-Ferdinands-Universität in Prag für das Studienjahr 1928–1929, ka. B35, inv. č. 498—Nachrufe: Adolf Grohmann, "Dr. Max Grünert, o. ö. Professor der semitischen Sprachen und Literaturen," pp. 21–24.

138   Luděk Vacín and Jitka Sýkorová

Siglum	Source(s)
AUK Grünert B	*Ditto*; Die feierliche Installation des Rectors der k. k. deutschen Carl-Ferdinands-Universität in Prag für das Studienjahr 1894/1895–1911/1912, ka. B34, inv. č. 495—"Das Gebet im Islâm. Rektoratsrede gehalten in der Aula der k. k. deutschen Karl-Ferdinands-Universität in Prag von Prof. Dr. Max Grünert am 27. Oktober 1910," pp. 17–38.
AUK Invitation	Archiv Univerzity Karlovy (Archive of Charles University in Prague), fond Katolická teologická fakulta 1891–1981; Děkanát, ka. 13, inv. č. 138.
AUK Jahn	Archiv Univerzity Karlovy (Archive of Charles University in Prague), fond Filozofická fakulta Německé univerzity v Praze (Philosophische Fakultät der Deutschen Universität in Prag), Spisový materiál (1857) 1882–1945; Personální záležitosti vyučujících a zaměstnanců, Privatdozent Dr. Karl Jahn, ka. 54, inv. č. 556, sign. P III/20.
AUK Kraus	*Ditto*; Katalogy posluchačů (Ordentl. Hörer/Philosophen) 1923–1926, Paul Kraus (*11. Dezember 1904).
AUK Lectures	*Ditto*; Přednášky pro Wehrmacht (Vortragsdienst militärischer Wehrbetreuung) 1940–1944, ka. 95, inv. č. 1070, sign. V II.
AUK Library	*Ditto*; Převzetí knihovny olomoucké židovské obce knihovnou orientalistického semináře (soupis knih) 1941, ka. 66, inv. č. 826.
AUK Photoarchive	Archiv Univerzity Karlovy (Archive of Charles University in Prague), fond Fotoarchiv (1887)–2013; Marian San Nicolò, profesor římského práva, rektor Německé univerzity roku 1931–1932 a 1932–1933, foto J. Smit.
AUK Pollak	Archiv Univerzity Karlovy (Archive of Charles University in Prague), fond Úřední tisky Německé univerzity v Praze (1881) 1882–1945; An Stelle der feierlichen Inauguration des Rektors der Deutschen Karlsuniversität in Prag für die Studienjahre 1918/1919–1928/1929, ka. B34, inv. č. 497—Würdigung der in den Studienjahren 1920–1921 bis 1926–1927 verstorbenen Professoren der Deutschen Universität in Prag: Max Grünert, "Dr. Isidor Pollak, ao. Professor der semitischen Philologie," pp. 18–19.
AUK Register	Archiv Univerzity Karlovy (Archive of Charles University in Prague), fond Sbírka matrik Německé univerzity v Praze; Matrika doktorů Německé univerzity v Praze (Doktorenmatrik der Deutschen Universität in Prag) 1940–1945, inv. č. 7, p. 326.
AUK Rieber	Archiv Univerzity Karlovy (Archive of Charles University in Prague), fond Úřední tisky Německé univerzity v Praze (1881) 1882–1945; Bericht über das Studienjahr 1934–1935 der Deutschen Universität in Prag erstattet von Prorektor Prof. Dr. Otto Grosser. Universität und Weltanschauung von Prof. Dr. Karl Hilgenreiner, Rektor 1935/36, ka. B37, inv. č. 499—Nachrufe: Wenzel Stoderl, "Josef Rieber, 22. I. 1862–5. XII. 1934," pp. 21–25.
AUK San Nicolò	Archiv Univerzity Karlovy (Archive of Charles University in Prague), fond Právnická fakulta Německé univerzity v Praze (Rechts- und Staatswissenschaftliche Fakultät der Deutschen Universität in Prag), Spisový materiál (1857) 1882–1945; Personální záležitosti vyučujících a zaměstnanců, San Nicolò Mariano, nezprac. (unprocessed personal file).

Siglum	Source(s)
AUK Semitics	Archiv Univerzity Karlovy (Archive of Charles University in Prague), fond Filozofická fakulta Německé univerzity v Praze (Philosophische Fakultät der Deutschen Universität in Prag), Spisový materiál (1857) 1882–1945; Seminář pro orientální filologii (Seminar für orientalische Philologie) 1922–1928, ka. 66, inv. č. 819.
AUK Semitics Finances	*Ditto*; Seminář pro orientální filologii (Seminar für orientalische Philologie, Seminar für semitische Philologie und Islamkunde)—dotace, stipendia 1922–1940, ka. 66, inv. č. 821, sign. J 5.
AUK Semitics Professorships	*Ditto*; Semitská/orientální filologie (Lehrkanzel für semitische Philologie, Orientalische Lehrkanzel) 1920–1930—zřízení nových profesur; obsazení profesury po smrti I. Pollaka; obsazování profesury 1929, ka. 66, inv. č. 823.
AUK Steinmetzer	Archiv Univerzity Karlovy (Archive of Charles University in Prague), fond Teologická fakulta Německé univerzity v Praze (Theologische Fakultät der Deutschen Universität in Prag) (1809) 1891–1945; Disertační práce teologické fakulty Karlo-Ferdinandovy university v Praze 1809–1881 a teologické fakulty býv. Německé university v Praze (1882) 1891–1945, Franz Steinmetzer, inv. č. 87, sign. 43.
NA El-Naggar	Národní archiv (National Archive in Prague), fond Policejní ředitelství Praha II—všeobecná spisovna—1941–1950; ka. 1, sign. A 2/11, Abdel Halim El-Naggar.
NA Grohmann Appointment	Národní archiv (National Archive in Prague), fond Ministerstvo školství a kultury, Praha—osobní spisy; ka. 40, sign. Grohmann Adolf.
NA Grohmann Citizenship	Národní archiv (National Archive in Prague), fond Policejní ředitelství Praha II—všeobecná spisovna—1931–1940; ka. 6088, sign. G 901/6, Grohmann Adolf.
NA Grohmann Personal Information Sheet	Národní archiv (National Archive in Prague), fond Ministerstvo vnitra I—prezidium, Praha—fond 225; ka. 1110, sign. 225-1110-3/57,76.
NA Grohmann Register	Národní archiv (National Archive in Prague), fond Policejní ředitelství Praha II—evidence obyvatelstva; sign. Grohmann Adolf 1887.
NA Jahn Personal Information Sheet	Národní archiv (National Archive in Prague), fond Úřad říšského protektora, Praha—fond 114; ka. 207, sign. 114-209-7/14.
NA Jahn Register	Národní archiv (National Archive in Prague), fond Policejní ředitelství Praha II—evidence obyvatelstva; sign. Jahn Karel 1906.
NA Koschaker Appointment	Národní archiv (National Archive in Prague), fond Ministerstvo kultu a vyučování Vídeň; ka. 130, inv. č. 18, sign. 5 Prag Jus-Professoren A-Z, Koschaker Paul, Dr.
NA Kraus	Národní archiv (National Archive in Prague), fond Policejní ředitelství Praha II—všeobecná spisovna—1931–1940; ka. 7953, sign. K 4308/5, Kraus Paul.
NA Pollak Passport	*Ditto*—1921–1930; ka. 2834, sign. P-1748/17, Isidor Pollak.
NA Pollak Register	Národní archiv (National Archive in Prague), fond Policejní ředitelství Praha I—všeobecná registratura—1901–1913; ka. 6175, sign. P-662/205, Isidor Pollak.
NA Rieber	Národní archiv (National Archive in Prague), fond Policejní ředitelství Praha II—všeobecná spisovna—1931–1940; ka. 10076, sign. R-1083/14, Josef Rieber.

Siglum	Source(s)
NA San Nicolò Appointment	Národní archiv (National Archive in Prague), fond Ministerstvo kultu a vyučování Vídeň; ka. 131, inv. č. 18, sign. 5 Prag Jus-Professoren A-Z, San Nicolò Mariano, Dr.
NA Semitics Professorships	Národní archiv (National Archive in Prague), fond Ministerstvo školství Praha; ka. 1080, inv. č. 1536, sign. 4 II $_2$, Seminář orientální 1922–1932—zřízení nových profesur; obsazení profesury po smrti I. Pollaka.
NA Steinmetzer Appointment	Národní archiv (National Archive in Prague), fond Ministerstvo kultu a vyučování Vídeň; ka. 126, inv. č. 15, sign. 5 Prag Theologie-Professoren E-S, Steinmetzer Franz, Dr.
NA Steinmetzer Passport	Národní archiv (National Archive in Prague), fond Policejní ředitelství Praha II—všeobecná spisovna—1931–1940; ka. 11091, sign. S-5903/3, Steinmetzer Franz.
NA Steinmetzer Register	Národní archiv (National Archive in Prague), fond Policejní ředitelství Praha II—evidence obyvatelstva; sign. Steinmetzer F.
NpM Landsberger	Národní muzeum—Náprstkovo muzeum asijských, afrických a amerických kultur (National Museum—Náprstek Museum of Asian, African and American Cultures in Prague), fond Hrozný Bedřich (1879–1952), Konvolut přijaté korespondence: H–O; ka. 2, Landsberger B., sign. ar. Hroz. 2/1-275.
NpM Poebel	*Ditto*, Konvolut přijaté korespondence: P–Z; ka. 3, Poebel A., sign. ar. Hroz. 3/1-128.
NpM San Nicolò	*Ditto*; ka. 3, San Nicolò M., sign. ar. Hroz. 3/1-288.
SOkA Landsberger	Státní okresní archiv (State District Archive) Frýdek-Místek, fond Archiv města Frýdek; ka. 210, inv. č. 764, Spis o propuštění ze státního svazku—Benno Landsberger.
UAL Landsberger	Universitätsarchiv Leipzig, Personenakten/Personalakten; sign. PA 0676, Landsberger, Benno (accessible online for registered users at http://www.recherche.archiv.uni-leipzig.de/Dokument/anzeigen/235988).

REFERENCES

Anonymous. 1957. "Grünert Max." Page 89 in *Österreichisches Biographisches Lexikon 1815–1950*. Vol. 2/6. Vienna: Verlag der Österreichischen Akademie der Wissenschaften. http://www.biographien.ac.at/oebl_2/89.pdf (accessed 12 July 2017).

Beggio, T. 2018. *Paul Koschaker (1879–1951): Rediscovering the Roman Foundations of European Legal Tradition*. 2nd ed. Heidelberg: Universitätsverlag Winter.

Brague, R. 1994. "Paul Kraus: Person und Werk (1904–1944)." Pages vii–xiii in *Paul Kraus: Alchemie, Ketzerei, Apokryphen im frühen Islam. Gesammelte Aufsätze*. Edited by R. Brague. Hildesheim: Georg Olms.

Breitman, R., and N. J. W. Goda. 2010. *Hitler's Shadow: Nazi War Criminals, U.S. Intelligence, and the Cold War*. Washington, D.C.: National Archives and Records Administration. https://archive.org/details/bub_gb_SpMVUEXINRQC (accessed 12 July 2017).

Bruijn, J. T. P. de. 2008. "Jahn, Karl Emil Oskar." Pages 391–92 in *Encyclopaedia Iranica*. Vol. 14/4. Edited by E. Yarshater. New York: Encyclopaedia Iranica Foundation. http://www.iranicaonline.org/articles/jahn-karl-emil-oskar (accessed 12 July 2017).

Edzard, D. O. 2005. "Poebel, Arno." Page 593 in *Reallexikon der Assyriologie*. Vol. 10. Edited by D. O. Edzard. Berlin: de Gruyter.

Ellinger, E. 2006. *Deutsche Orientalistik zur Zeit des Nationalsozialismus 1933–1945*. Edingen-Neckarhausen: Deux Mondes.

Fahlbusch, M., I. Haar, and A. Pinwinkler, eds. 2017. *Handbuch der völkischen Wissenschaften: Akteure, Netzwerke, Forschungsprogramme*. 2nd exp. and rev. ed. Berlin: de Gruyter.

Gebel, R. 2000. *"Heim ins Reich!" Konrad Henlein und der Reichsgau Sudetenland (1938–1945)*. 2nd ed. Veröffentlichungen des Collegium Carolinum 83. Munich: R. Oldenbourg.

Gelb, I. J. 1964. "Introduction." Pages vii–xxiii in *The Assyrian Dictionary of the Oriental Institute of the University of Chicago*. Vol. 1, *A Part 1*. Edited by A. L. Oppenheim and E. Reiner. Chicago: The Oriental Institute.

Georgiadou, M. 2004. *Constantin Carathéodory: Mathematics and Politics in Turbulent Times*. New York: Springer.

Hadler, F. 2012. "Graben wie die Großen in Kleinasien: Ein frisch berufener Prager Professor umreißt mit weltpolitischen Argumenten sein archäologisches Karrierefeld." Pages 206–13 in *Kultur und Beruf in Europa*. Edited by I. Löhr, M. Middell, and H. Siegrist. Stuttgart: Steiner.

Hahn, E. 2000. "Rieber, Josef." Pages 415–16 in *Biographisches Lexikon zur Geschichte der böhmischen Länder*. Vol. 3. Edited by F. Seibt, H. Lemberg, and H. Slapnicka. Munich: R. Oldenbourg.

Hanisch, L. 2001. *Ausgegrenzte Kompetenz: Porträts vertriebener Orientalisten und Orientalistinnen 1933–1945*. Halle: OWZ.

Havránek, J., ed. 1997. *Dějiny Univerzity Karlovy*. Vol. 3, *1802–1918*. Prague: Univerzita Karlova/Karolinum.

Havránek, J., and Z. Pousta, eds. 1998. *Dějiny Univerzity Karlovy*. Vol. 4, *1918–1990*. Prague: Univerzita Karlova/Karolinum.

———. 2001. *A History of Charles University*. Vol. 2, *1802–1990*. Prague: Univerzita Karlova/Karolinum.

Hlaváčková, L., A. Míšková, and J. Pešek. 2001. "The German University 1882–1918." Pages 163–74 in *A History of Charles University*. Vol. 2, *1802–1990*. Edited by J. Havránek and Z. Pousta. Prague: Univerzita Karlova/Karolinum.

Hrozný, B. 1913. *Das Getreide im alten Babylonien: Ein Beitrag zur Kultur- und Wirtschaftsgeschichte des alten Orients, I. Teil. Mit einem botanischen Beitrage von Dr. Franz von Frimmel: "Über einige antike Samen aus dem Orient."* Vienna: A. Hölder.

———. 1920. "Nové úkoly orientální archeologie." *Naše doba* 27(7):484–90.

Johanning, K. 1988. *Der Bibel-Babel-Streit: Eine forschungsgeschichtliche Studie*. Frankfurt am Main: Peter Lang.

Kisch, G. 1975. *Der Lebensweg eines Rechtshistorikers: Erinnerungen*. Sigmaringen: Jan Thorbecke.

Klíma, J. 1940. *Untersuchungen zum altbabylonischen Erbrecht*. Prague: Orientalisches Institut.

Konrád, O. 2007. "Humanitní obory v době nacionálního socialismu. Srovnání universit v Lipsku, Vídni a v Praze." PhD diss., Charles University Prague.

Koschaker, P. 1911. *Babylonisch-assyrisches Bürgschaftsrecht: Ein Beitrag zur Lehre von Schuld und Haftung*. Berlin: Teubner. https://www.archive.org/details/babylonischassyr00koscuoft (accessed 12 July 2017).

———. 1951. "Autobiographie." Pages 105–25 in *Österreichische Geschichtswissenschaft der Gegenwart in Selbstdarstellungen*. Vol. 2. Edited by N. Grass. Innsbruck: Universitätsverlag Wagner.

Kraemer, J. L. 1999. "The Death of an Orientalist: Paul Kraus from Prague to Cairo." Pages 181–223 in *The Jewish Discovery of Islam: Studies in Honor of Bernard Lewis*. Edited by M. Kramer. Tel Aviv: The Moshe Dayan Center for Middle Eastern and African Studies, Tel Aviv University.

Kramer, S. N. 1988. *In the World of Sumer: An Autobiography*. 1st paperback ed. Detroit: Wayne State University Press.

Kraus, P. 1931–1932. *Altbabylonische Briefe aus der Vorderasiatischen Abteilung der Preussischen Staatsmuseen zu Berlin*. 2 vols. Leipzig: Hinrichs.

Landsberger, B. 1922. "Zur Mehlbereitung im Altertum." *Orientalistische Literaturzeitung* 25:337–44.

Lehmann, R. G. 1994. *Friedrich Delitzsch und der Babel-Bibel-Streit*. Orbis Biblicus et Orientalis 133. Göttingen: Vandenhoeck & Ruprecht.

Lemberg, H., ed. 2003. *Universitäten in nationaler Konkurrenz: Zur Geschichte der Prager Universitäten im 19. und 20. Jahrhundert*. Veröffentlichungen des Collegium Carolinum 86. Munich: R. Oldenbourg.

Luh, A. 1988. *Der Deutsche Turnverband in der Ersten Tschechoslowakischen Republik: Vom völkischen Vereinsbetrieb zur volkspolitischen Bewegung*. Veröffentlichungen des Collegium Carolinum 62. Munich: R. Oldenbourg.

Makariusová, M. 2008. "Steinmetzer, Franz Xav." Page 197 in *Österreichisches Biographisches Lexikon 1815–1950*. Vol. 13. Vienna: Verlag der Österreichischen Akademie der Wissenschaften. http://www.biographien.ac.at/oebl (accessed 12 July 2017).

Míšková, A. 2001. "The German University during the Second World War." Pages 257–62 in *A History of Charles University*. Vol. 2, *1802–1990*. Edited by J. Havránek and Z. Pousta. Prague: Univerzita Karlova/Karolinum.

———. 2007. *Die Deutsche (Karls-)Universität vom Münchener Abkommen bis zum Ende des Zweiten Weltkrieges: Universitätsleitung und Wandel des Professorenkollegiums*. Prague: Karolinum.

Müller, M. 1982. "Paul Koschaker (1879–1951). Zum 100. Geburtstag des Begründers der Keilschriftrechtsgeschichte." *Altorientalische Forschungen* 9:271–84.

Neumann, G. 2012. "Paul Koschaker in Tübingen (1941–1946)." *Zeitschrift für Altorientalische und Biblische Rechtsgeschichte* 18:23–36.

Neumüller, M., ed. 1984. *Die Teilung der Prager Universität 1882 und die intellektuelle Desintegration in den böhmischen Ländern*. Bad Wiesseer Tagungen des Collegium Carolinum 12. Munich: R. Oldenbourg.

Paulus, S. 2014. *Die babylonischen Kudurru-Inschriften von der kassitischen bis zur frühneubabylonischen Zeit: Untersucht unter besonderer Berücksichtigung gesellschafts- und rechtshistorischer Fragestellungen*. Alter Orient und Altes Testament 51. Münster: Ugarit-Verlag.

Pešek, J., A. Míšková, P. Svobodný, and J. Janko. 1998. "Německá univerzita v Praze v letech 1918–1939." Pages 181–212 in *Dějiny Univerzity Karlovy*. Vol. 4, *1918–1990*. Edited by J. Havránek and Z. Pousta. Prague: Univerzita Karlova/Karolinum.

———. 2001. "The German University of Prague 1918–1939." Pages 245–56 in *A History of Charles University*. Vol. 2, *1802–1990*. Edited by J. Havránek and Z. Pousta. Prague: Univerzita Karlova/Karolinum.

Petschow, H. P. H. 1983. "Koschaker, Paul." Pages 213–14 in *Reallexikon der Assyriologie*. Vol. 6. Edited by D. O. Edzard. Berlin: de Gruyter.

Pfeifer, G. 2009. "San Nicolò, Mariano." Pages 24–25 in *Reallexikon der Assyriologie*. Vol. 12. Edited by M. P. Streck. Berlin: de Gruyter.

Potthast, J. B. 2002. *Das jüdische Zentralmuseum der SS in Prag: Gegnerforschung und Völkermord im Nationalsozialismus*. Frankfurt am Main: Campus.

Reinfandt, L. 2013. "The Political Papyrologist: Adolf Grohmann (1887–1977)." Pages 251–69 in *Sources and Approaches across Disciplines in Near Eastern Studies: Proceedings of the 24th Congress, Union Européenne des Arabisants et Islamisants, Leipzig 2008*. Orientalia Lovaniensia Analecta 215. Edited by V. Klemm and N. al-Shaʿar. Leuven: Peeters.

Rieber, J. 1897. "Über Flutsagen und deren Beziehung zu den semitischen Flutberichten I, II." *Der Katholik: Zeitschrift für katholische Wissenschaft und kirchliches Leben* 15:65–84, 154–72. http://www.digizeitschriften.de/dms/toc/?PID=urn%3Anbn%3Ade%3Absz%3A21 -dt-6185 (accessed 12 July 2017).

———. 1903. "Die El-Amarna-Tafeln und ihre geschichtliche Bedeutung." *Die Kultur* 4(3):161–77.

———. 1904. "Zum Babel-Bibel-Streit in der jüngsten Zeit." *Sammlung gemeinnütziger Vorträge* 315:191–207.

———. 1905. *Der moderne Kampf um die Bibel: Rektoratsrede des Prof. Dr. Josef Rieber, gehalten in der Aula der Deutschen Karl-Ferdinands-Universität in Prag am 16.*

November 1905. Prague: J. G. Calve'sche k. u. k. Hof- und Universitäts-Buchhandlung (Josef Koch).

Ries, G. 1979. "Koschaker, Paul." Pages 608–9 in *Neue Deutsche Biographie*. Vol. 12. https://www.deutsche-biographie.de/pnd118565621.html#ndbcontent (accessed 12 July 2017).

———. 2005. "San Nicolò, Mariano." Pages 430–31 in *Neue Deutsche Biographie*. Vol. 22. https://www.deutsche-biographie.de/gnd10198104X.html#ndbcontent (accessed 12 July 2017).

San Nicolò, M. 1922. *Die Schlußklauseln der altbabylonischen Kauf- und Tauschverträge: Ein Beitrag zur Geschichte des Barkaufes*. Münchener Beiträge zur Papyrusforschung und Antiken Rechtsgeschichte 4. Munich: Beck.

———. 1931a. *Beiträge zur Rechtsgeschichte im Bereiche der keilschriftlichen Rechtsquellen*. Instituttet for sammenlignende kulturforskning. Serie A: Forelesninger 13. Oslo: H. Aschehoug & Company.

———. 1931b. *Römische und antike Rechtsgeschichte: Rektoratsrede des Rektors Prof. Dr. Marian San Nicolò, gehalten in der Aula der Deutschen Universität zu Prag am 23. November 1931*. Prague: Selbstverlag der Deutschen Universität. http://www.historische-kommission-muenchen-editionen.de/rektoratsreden/pdf/Prag_1931_Cori_San_Nicolò_röm._u._antike_Rechtsgeschichte.pdf, pp. 53–78 (accessed 12 July 2017).

———. 1953. "Paul Koschaker 19. 4. 1879–1. 6. 1951." *Bayerische Akademie der Wissenschaften Jahrbuch* 1952:163–65.

San Nicolò, M., and A. Ungnad. 1929–1935. *Neubabylonische Rechts- und Verwaltungsurkunden*. Vol. 1/1–5: Rechts- und Wirtschaftsurkunden der Berliner Museen aus vorhellenistischer Zeit. Leipzig: Hinrichs.

Schreiber, M. 2008. *Walther Wüst: Dekan und Rektor der Universität München 1935–1945*. Beiträge zur Geschichte der Ludwig-Maximilians-Universität München 3. Munich: Herbert Utz.

Schulmann, R. 2005. "Einstein's Swiss Years." Pages 156–60 in *Albert Einstein: Chief Engineer of the Universe. One Hundred Authors for Einstein*. Edited by J. Renn. Berlin: Max Planck Institute for the History of Science.

Ščrbačić, M. 2013. "Von der Semitistik zur Islamwissenschaft und zurück—Paul Kraus (1904–1944)." *Simon Dubnow Institute Yearbook* 12:389–416.

Seidl, E. 1956. "Mariano San Nicolò (1887–1955)." *Zeitschrift der Deutschen Morgenländischen Gesellschaft* 106:7–17.

Shavit, Y., and M. Eran. 2007. *The Hebrew Bible Reborn: From Holy Scripture to the Book of Books. A History of Biblical Culture and the Battles over the Bible in Modern Judaism*. Studia Judaica 38. Translated by C. Naor. Berlin: de Gruyter.

Steinmetzer, F. X. 1907. *Neue Untersuchung über die Geschichtlichkeit der Juditherzählung: Ein Beitrag zur Erklärung des Buches Judith*. Leipzig: Rudolf Haupt.

———. 1910a. *Die Geschichte der Geburt und Kindheit Christi und ihr Verhältnis zur babylonischen Mythe: Eine religionsgeschichtliche Untersuchung*. Neutestamentliche Abhandlungen 2/1–2. Münster: Aschendorff.

———. 1910b. "Eine Schenkungsurkunde des Königs Melišichu." *Beiträge zur Assyriologie* 8:1–38.

———. 1912. "Babylonische Parallelen zu den Fluchpsalmen." *Biblische Zeitschrift* 10:133–42, 363–69.

———. 1915. "Die Sinnbilder auf dem Grenzstein des Nazi-Marutaš." Pages 62–71 in *Festschrift Eduard Sachau zum siebzigsten Geburtstage gewidmet von Freunden und Schülern*. Edited by G. Weil. Berlin: G. Reimer.

———. 1918. "Über den Grundbesitz in Babylonien zur Kassitenzeit. Nach den sog. Grenzsteinen dargestellt." *Der Alte Orient* 19:3–32.

———. 1920a. "Bemerkungen zu den babylonischen Grenzsteinurkunden." *Orientalistische Literaturzeitung* 23:145–54.

———. 1920b. "Bemerkungen zu den babylonischen Grenzsteinurkunden (Schluss)." *Orientalistische Literaturzeitung* 23:193–205.

144 Luděk Vacín and Jitka Sýkorová

———. 1922. *Die babylonischen Kudurru (Grenzsteine) als Urkundenform*. Studien zur Geschichte und Kultur des Altertums 11. Paderborn: F. Schöningh.

———. 1927. "Eine Bestallungsurkunde Königs Šamaš-šumi-ukîn von Babylon." Pages 319–24 in Ἐπιτύμβιον. *HEINRICH SWOBODA dargebracht*. Reichenberg: Gebr. Stiepel.

———. 1936. "Zur Datierung undatierter Grenzsteinfragmente." *Orientalia* 5:347–48.

Steinwenter, A., and A. Falkenstein. 1955. "Mariano San Nicolò†." *Zeitschrift der Savigny-Stiftung für Rechtsgeschichte* 72:493–503.

Svatoš, M. 2015. "The Academic Career of Bedřich Hrozný at Charles University." Pages 140–47 in *Bedřich Hrozný a 100 let chetitologie (and 100 Years of Hittitology)*. Edited by Š. Velhartická. Prague: Národní galerie.

Topor, M. 2015. *Berlínské epizody. Příspěvek k dějinám filologie v Čechách a na Moravě 1878–1914*. Prague: Institut pro studium literatury.

Velhartická, Š., ed. 2015. *Bedřich Hrozný a 100 let chetitologie (and 100 Years of Hittitology)*. Prague: Národní galerie.

Výborná, M., J. Havránek, and K. Kučera. 1965. *Disertace pražské university 1882–1945*. Vol. 2, *Německá universita*. Sbírka pramenů a příruček k dějinám University Karlovy 3. Prague: Universita Karlova/Státní pedagogické nakladatelství.

Wehr, H. 1953. "Bauer, Hans." Page 639 in *Neue Deutsche Biographie*. Vol. 1. https://www.deutsche-biographie.de/pnd131435701.html#ndbcontent (accessed 12 July 2017).

Weidner, E. 1954–1956. "Erich Ebeling." *Archiv für Orientforschung* 17:481–82.

———. 1957–1958. "Theo Bauer." *Archiv für Orientforschung* 18:229–30.

———. 1959. "Ebeling, Erich." Pages 220–21 in *Neue Deutsche Biographie*. Vol. 4. https://www.deutsche-biographie.de/pnd116320885.html#ndbcontent (accessed 12 July 2017).

———. 1959–1960. "Arno Poebel." *Archiv für Orientforschung* 19:264–65.

Wiedemann, A. 2000. *Die Reinhard-Heydrich-Stiftung in Prag (1942–1945)*. Dresden: Hannah-Arendt-Institut für Totalitarismusforschung. http://www.hait.tu-dresden.de/dok/bst/Heft_28_Wiedemann.pdf (accessed 12 July 2017).

Zbavitel, D. 1959. *Die Orientalistik in der Tschechoslowakei*. Prague: Orbis.

PART II

Intellectual History and Ancient
Near Eastern Studies: Some Case Studies

CHAPTER 7

Notes on the History of the Historiography of Cuneiform Mathematics

Carlos Gonçalves

> Most Assyriologists had by then become accustomed to consider tablets containing too many numbers in place-value notation "a matter for Neugebauer" (Høyrup and Damerow 2001, viii)

THIS PAPER IS A SURVEY of the history of the efforts that researchers have made in order to decipher and understand part of the mathematical knowledge of the ancient Near East, namely cuneiform mathematics.

It is always useful to remember that although the history of the research is very recent—having begun in the years around 1900—cuneiform mathematics is quite ancient, dating to a time span that encompasses the end of the fourth millennium BCE and the very beginning of the first millennium CE. Also, if researchers are located mainly in present-day Europe and United States, the object of study was a phenomenon situated in ancient Syria, Iraq, and Iran, in the areas traditionally called Mesopotamia and Elam. Additionally, if research has been carried out mainly in German, English, and French, cuneiform mathematics was produced in Sumerian and Akkadian. It is quite a feat indeed that it has been possible to understand so much of this form of knowledge.

When writing this paper, I tried to keep in mind that my readers would include not only the dozen or so professional researchers that have been working in the field of the history of cuneiform mathematics in the last decades, but hopefully also people interested in the history of this field as a point of comparison with other efforts to understand historical aspects of the ancient Near East, other mathematical traditions, or as a case study in the history of historiography. Furthermore, given the growing interest in the history of cuneiform mathematics among teachers of mathematics and researchers in ethno-mathematics—at least in my country—I assume that the paper will be read also by people that want to take historiographical contents into the math classroom. In order to be accessible to this hopefully enlarged audience, it seemed to me that large parts of the paper should be above all descriptive. Thus, when describing works dealing with the mathematics of ancient Mesopotamia, its history, and the history of its writing, I hope to convey a lively image of the field to the readers.

Author's note: This article benefitted from a fellowship at the Paris Institute for Advanced Studies (France), with the financial support of the French state managed by the Agence Nationale de la Recherche, program "Investissements d'avenir" (ANR-11-LABX-0027-01 Labex RFIEA+).

148   Carlos Gonçalves

The paper is structured in the following way. Because the history of historiography has already been for a long time a preoccupation of professional historians, I considered it useful to develop a number of distinctions regarding levels of history, such as history as what happens in the course of time and history as an intellectual effort. Although the distinctions are not complex, they contain some subtleties whose consequences are important for my exposition.

Next, I survey previous efforts to describe and analyze the history of the historiography of cuneiform mathematics. This will give the reader an idea of the chronological development of the historiography of cuneiform mathematics, its main concerns and, most importantly, how some of its practitioners see the field.

My own contribution to the theme follows this description. In this section I tried to provide the reader a number of indications regarding an issue that has been growing in importance, namely, how to approach cuneiform mathematics from a social perspective. The production in the field shows that not only the answers to the question of the social place of mathematics in the ancient Near East differ from each other, but also that researchers have approached the whole issue with different strategies and interests. The final section summarizes the whole argument and includes a few additional remarks, with the aim of reinforcing the questions dealt with and giving further explanation for why they are formulated in the way I propose.

At this point I should mention a few very important items that compose the universe of the historiography of cuneiform mathematics, in addition to what I will analyze in this paper. Their absence is the result of a painful decision I thought it was necessary to make, so that the present paper could be self-contained and kept within a reasonable size limit.

The first one is the historiography of the kind of mathematics one finds in proto-cuneiform texts.[1] Secondly, historians of mathematics continue to work on the edition of texts. The literature includes the publication of new tablets as well as some new treatments of material published before the developments that have taken place in the field in the last decades.[2] Finally, there is much interesting research in course of publication as the result of research programs carried out recently.[3]

Useful Distinctions: History, Historiography, History of Historiography, and so on

The terms and expressions appearing in the title of this section are prone to much confusion, for they involve differentiations so subtle that in many environments some of their daily uses are interchangeable. Besides, I have been noticing too that different national or disciplinary research communities employ them in different ways. For

---

1. As in the groundbreaking Nissen, Damerow, and Englund 1993.

2. See Proust 2007, Proust 2008, Friberg 2007, Gonçalves 2015, Friberg and Al-Rawi 2016.

3. In particular, the newly created collection "Why the Sciences of the Ancient World Matter" (http://www.springer.com/series/15657), edited by Karine Chemla, Agathe Keller and Christine Proust and published by Springer, will be gradually publishing results of the ERC project "Mathematical Sciences in the Ancient World" (https://sawerc.hypotheses.org/). It is certain that after these publications a new historiographical assessment of the field will be welcome.

these reasons, I believe it is useful that I explain to the reader how I employ each of them.

To begin with, *history* is a word I use to speak of the body of human activities along the flow of time. I emphasize *human activities*, for I am not dealing with other kinds of histories, such as the geological history of the earth or the history of the universe. History, in this paper, is always related to human beings. The first consequence of this standpoint is that, as time seems to go by in the same way everywhere (although it can be felt differently), every community or people have history in the sense that I employ the term. The second consequence is that it is possible to speak of specialized histories if one pays attention only to some delimited set of related phenomena, such as history of colonial Brazil, history of women, history of social movements, and, of course, history of cuneiform mathematics.

In the course of history (in the sense just defined), there have been many people who devoted themselves to transforming history into something that could be remembered, investigated or interpreted, thus giving birth to a large range of possibilities: written and oral productions, but also painting, singing, dancing, as well as photography and cinema. Of all those possibilities, in this paper, I am interested in the written practices, and they will always be referred to here as historiography.

Accordingly, I will speak of the *history of cuneiform mathematics* (that is to say, a certain body of human activities related to mathematics in the ancient Near East) and the *historiography of cuneiform mathematics* (the effort to describe, explain, and understand all this history).[4] The important thing to keep in mind is that if, on the one hand, history is the body of what happened to human beings along time, historiography refers to academic, intellectual, and also political efforts that have history as their object.

We can speak, as already mentioned, of histories of specific related phenomena that happened in the human realm, and the history of cuneiform mathematics is one example. As a matter of fact, lots of human activities in principle could be thought of as pertaining to a specialized history. This has a very important consequence. Take the writing of the history of cuneiform mathematics, that is to say, the *historiography of cuneiform mathematics*. This writing itself has a history and we can call it the *history of the historiography of cuneiform mathematics*.

These might seem moot distinctions, but they have powerful and interesting consequences. One of them is that they make it easier for us to see that, if the *historiography of cuneiform mathematics* has as its object all the mathematical knowledge and practices that belonged to the more than three millennia of the history of the cuneiform, the *history of the historiography of cuneiform mathematics* is a body of human events encompassing only some 150 years of efforts made by scholars trying to understand certain aspects of those millennia. An additional consequence of the highest importance in this paper is that one could write about the *history of the historiography of cuneiform mathematics*, and this would be an activity positioned in the field of the *historiography of the historiography of cuneiform mathematics*. This is an obvious consequence of the distinctions made above, although I admit the phrasing is somewhat appalling. In other words, the efforts to describe, explain, and understand the different ways that the historiography of cuneiform mathematics was produced over time (that is to say,

---

4. In other contexts, I have freely been using "history" as a wildcard for both meanings.

150   Carlos Gonçalves

the efforts to understand the history of historiography of cuneiform mathematics) are elements of the *historiography of the historiography of cuneiform mathematics*.

We could go on indefinitely to higher and higher levels of metalanguage, but it will not be necessary to do so. The immediate usefulness of these distinctions in the present paper is to enable me to split the exposition into two parts. I will examine first some of the previous efforts in the historiography of cuneiform mathematics. As stated in the introduction, this will enable the readers to get a glimpse of what some of the practitioners consider the most important issues in the history of the field. This is, by the way, a most traditional historiographical procedure: in analyzing some historical phenomenon, we should always try to understand the actors' categories (or the agents', depending on one's point of view about the degree of agency history allows us). In this case, as I am dealing with the history of the historiography of cuneiform mathematics, it makes sense to see what historians of mathematics themselves think of their field. After that I will examine works belonging to the historiography of mathematics that bring some new understanding to an issue that has grown in importance in the last decades: the problem of mathematics and society in Mesopotamia. As the reader will see, in order to do what they aim, these works often resort to the history of the historiography of cuneiform mathematics.

Distinctions of levels of history have often been made in the history of historiography. History and historiography are called H1 and H2 by Helge Kragh (1987), in his classic *An Introduction to the Historiography of Science.* The history of the historiography is referred to as H3 and its historiography is referred to as H4 in Rogério F. da Silva (2015).[5] Thus, the next two sections are dedicated to a survey of works produced at the H3 level, while the section thereafter deals with works in which levels H2 and H3 interact. In plain words, the latter are works in which the vision the authors have of the history of the field is of fundamental importance if one wants to understand her or his research procedures and goals.

A Survey of Previous Accounts of the Historiography of Cuneiform Mathematics

The following is a list of texts, ranging from a few paragraphs to full-length books, in which the historiography of cuneiform mathematics is analyzed. In chronological order, they are:

- a section of Marvin Powell's PhD dissertation (1971), "Sumerian Numeration and Metrology," describing a turning point for the study of ancient Mesopotamian metrology, namely the work of Franz Weissbach (1907);
- an article by Jens Høyrup (1996) dealing, among other things, with the history of the first two massive editions of mathematical cuneiform texts by Otto Neugebauer (1935–1937) and François Thureau-Dangin (1938), as well as with the productive rivalry that these two men had;

---

5 The tradition of the history of historiography in the Brazilian academic setting is a rich one, and it constitutes one of the ways to critically understand how Brazilian historiography interacts with European historiographies. In this regard, see also Novais 2005.

- the preface of Høyrup and Peter Damerow's (2001) book, where the authors explain how a series of workshops held in Berlin, in the 1980s and 1990s, involving the Altorientalisches Seminar und Seminar für Vorderasiatische Altertumskunde at the Freie Universität Berlin, the Max Planck Institute for Human Development and Education and the Max Planck Institute for the History of Science, was formed to deal with the history of cuneiform mathematics;
- two chapters of Elanor Robson's (2008) book on the social history of cuneiform mathematics, namely the presentation of "Scope, Methods, Sources" (Chapter 1) and the "Epilogue" (Chapter 9), which discuss, among other things, the reception of the historiography of cuneiform mathematics in the secondary literature of the history of mathematics;
- the introduction of Grégory Chambon's (2011) book on the measurement practices in ancient Syria, tracing the history of the ways historians of mathematics and Assyriologists investigated certain aspects of metrological systems in ancient Mesopotamia;
- a paper I wrote in Portuguese to historians of science, where I tried to describe the succeeding different styles in the history of the historiography of cuneiform mathematics (Gonçalves 2012);
- chapter 5 of my book (Gonçalves 2015) on the Tell Harmal tablets, which briefly relates some practices of the historiography of mathematics with those of archaeology and the making of critical editions;
- Robert Middeke-Conlin's PhD dissertation (2015), where the author makes efforts to explain how outsiders from Assyriology studying mathematical texts had an impact in the field and, reciprocally, how the field was open and receptive to outsiders;
- and, finally, a book edited by Alexander Jones, Christine Proust, and John Steele (2016), offering a series of essays on the figure of Neugebauer, of which the chapters written by Høyrup (2016) and by Duncan Melville (2016) try to outline a general view of what led to Neugebauer's and Thureau-Dangin's achievements and what happened after that.

These texts constitute the object for a history of the different ways of writing the history of the historiography of cuneiform mathematics, and they differ in relation to their moment of production, academic setting, and theoretical approach. As a consequence, always with these examples in mind, I would like to suggest that there is no rigid or predefined standpoint for one to engage with the history of the historiography of cuneiform mathematics. Each of us in the above list departed from specific academic trajectories, institutional settings, and questions to produce our contributions to the historiography of cuneiform mathematics.

The list also shows that levels H2 and H3 highly interfere with each other. This should be no surprise, because the way one sees the historiography of cuneiform mathematics (H3) is not independent from the way one practices it (H2). For a very comprehensive but not updated bibliography on cuneiform mathematics, see Melville's website, *Mesopotamian Mathematics*.[6]

---

6. See http://it.stlawu.edu/~dmelvill/mesomath/biblio/bigbib.html (accessed 19 September 2019).

152   Carlos Gonçalves

From the above list, three papers were written with the explicit goal of being autonomous texts on the history of the historiography of cuneiform mathematics, Høyrup (1996, 2016) and Melville (2016). They all belong to the H3 level, and I will briefly summarize and comment on them below. Among the remaining works, there are some that discuss the history of the historiography of mathematics (a discussion at the H3 level) in order to make clear what they intend to offer as a contribution to the field (a contribution in the H2 level). Accordingly, a summary and a few comments on the discussions contained in Robson (2008), Chambon (2011), and Middeke-Conlin (2015) constitute part of the section entitled "Mathematics and other Spheres of Life."

A Sketchy Exercise in the Historiography of the Historiography of Cuneiform Mathematics

The three article-length texts dealing with the history of the historiography of cuneiform mathematics are Høyrup (1996, 2016) and Melville (2016), of which the latter two appeared in the same collective work edited by Jones, Proust, and Steele (2016). It is worth taking a detailed look at them because they offer a very stable framework from which to discuss the history of the historiography of cuneiform mathematics.

In very general lines, Høyrup (1996), which has four sections and a postscript, offers a tentative periodization of the historiography of cuneiform mathematics. The main concern is to discuss the ways of and the reasons for a split between the humanist Assyriologist and the scientist historian of mathematics in the treatment of cuneiform mathematics. The "Heroic Era, 1930 to 1940" (section 1 of the article) would have been a period marked by efforts to "crack the codes"[7] of cuneiform mathematics, that is to say, to understand the contents of the advanced mathematics of cuneiform tablets. In order to do that, it was necessary that the texts were analyzed by scholars with thorough mathematical knowledge and this would explain the slight advantage that Neugebauer (who published the first massive collection of mathematical texts in 1935–1937) had over Thureau-Dangin (who published almost the same tablets in 1938). After the initial breakthroughs, other scholars would give their contributions, among them "Assyriologists with less exhaustive mathematical competence."[8] Another characteristic of the period was a tendency to identify the whole of cuneiform mathematics to Babylonian mathematics, because of the large predominance of Old Babylonian texts known at the time. Finally, the study of cuneiform mathematics in this period was also affected by issues that were important for the research on other mathematical traditions, like the pertinence of calling ancient mathematics "algebra" and the insistence in fitting every local tradition into a general history of mathematics. In this way, Babylonian mathematics was seen as the cradle of algebra. In the same way, it was compared with the Greek, medieval, and Arabic mathematical traditions. All in all, the section conveys the idea that the emphases of the period were directed mainly to the technical aspects of mathematics per se. Interest in the relationship of mathematics to the lives of people was not an issue, even though scholars tried to understand texts

7. Høyrup 1996, 5.
8. Høyrup 1996, 5.

Notes on the History of the Historiography of Cuneiform Mathematics   153

that were "concerned with practical problems involving metrological conversions, norms for work, etc."[9]

The following decades would have marked "The Triumph of Translations, 1940 to 1975,"[10] defined by a tendency for authors to dismiss the original texts and rely only in translations, mainly modernizing translations formulated in formal, symbolic algebraic language. The reliance on modernized translations was accompanied by evaluations of cuneiform mathematics as if it was conceptualized as modern mathematics, leading some authors to believe that Mesopotamians had, for instance, knowledge similar to trigonometry and logarithms. Not surprisingly, this tendency is found mainly in general histories of mathematics and in the secondary literature. However, even the specialist resorted to it, as exemplified by the edition of *Cuneiform Mathematical Texts* by Neugebauer and Abraham Sachs (1945), although they were not as careless as the authors of general histories of mathematics. The period saw also the publication of the *Textes mathématiques de Suse* by Evert Bruins and Marguerite Rutten (1961), and the article explains how the nasty temperament of Bruins made it difficult for the field to keep a healthy discussion about this important material, which is a much more serious matter if we take into account the many errors in Bruins's analysis of the tablets from Susa. Finally, the period was also the stage for internal dissonances of the field of the history of mathematics, with impact on the historiography of cuneiform mathematics. This entailed Michael Mahoney's critique of the use of the term algebra to refer to cuneiform mathematics, Arpád Szabó's rejection that the Greeks might have known of Babylonian algebra (which he accepted), and the fierce critique of Sabetai Unguru (1975) on the modernization of Greek mathematics as a factor of awareness even for those working with cuneiform mathematics that the "orthodox interpretation was an orthodoxy."[11]

The studies in the history of cuneiform mathematics were, however, at a standstill, and "A Fresh Start from the Sources through New Approaches, 1971 Onwards"[12] was made possible by the work of three scholars. Powell's (1971) PhD dissertation took up "systematic study of the topic [that is, metrology] in a way which would ultimately connect it again to the global field of mathematical thought and techniques," and one of the consequences it had is that "he brought the badly neglected third millennium back into focus," showing "that Mesopotamian mathematics had to be seen in historical development."[13] In other works, Powell made other contributions: especially, by establishing a new *terminus ante quem* for the invention of the sexagesimal place value notation,[14] namely the twenty-first century BCE, he connected the development

9. Høyrup 1996, 9.
10. Høyrup 1996, section 2.
11. Høyrup 1996, 17.
12. Høyrup 1996, section 3.
13. Høyrup 1996, 17.
14. Sexagesimal Place Value Notation (SPVN) is a way of denoting numbers developed probably during Ur III period and highly frequent in Old Babylonian mathematical tablets. Its main characteristics are that (1) it is used without accompanying measurement units, a trait that has led researchers to call the numbers represented in this notation "pure" or "abstract" numbers, in opposition to numbers with measurement units; (2) it represents floating values, not absolute value, which is admittedly a difficult feature to assimilate in the way that, for instance, a vertical wedge stands equally for 1 or for 60 or for 1/60 (to mention only these values).

154   Carlos Gonçalves

of this system with the needs of the bureaucracy of the Ur III state (Powell 1976). He also analyzed school mathematical exercises, thus showing that this kind of source was important too for a history of mathematics. The second and third scholars of this era, according to Høyrup (1996), were Denise Schmandt-Besserat and Jöran Friberg. The work of the former relating calculi (tokens) to proto-cuneiform symbols[15] was nuanced by the latter, who also extended the chronological scope for the study of cuneiform mathematics. The remainder of this section of Høyrup's (1996) paper is dedicated to analyzing the impact of the Berlin Workshop on "concept development in Babylonian mathematics."[16] The participants of the workshop were Marvin Powell, Jöran Friberg, Peter Damerow, Robert Englund, Hans Nissen, Jens Høyrup, and others.[17]

In the final section of his paper, Høyrup tries to detect possible trends within the many apparently disparate developments, what he entitles "The Present Situation." The first part of his very compact conclusion is that the approaches and the dialogue among the approaches being carried out at that moment "made it possible to see the function of the token-system and its role in the emergence of script, mathematical notations and mathematical conceptualizations in the light of general cognitive psychology and anthropological state formation theory, and to integrate the insights thereby obtained with what else is known about the specific development of social structure and culture in early Mesopotamia and its Near Eastern surroundings."[18] Similarly, "an integration of mathematics into general history and culture had been achieved for later periods." The two conditions that allowed this phenomenon, according to Høyrup (1996), were the demise of the idea of a timeless mathematics and a new interest by Assyriologists in mathematical issues, which he exemplifies mainly with Karen Rhea Nemet-Nejat's (1993) book, *Cuneiform Mathematical Texts as a Reflection of Everyday Life in Mesopotamia* (see below).

Høyrup's "As the Outsider Walked in the Historiography of Mesopotamian Mathematics Until Neugebauer" (2016) is part of the collection of papers edited by Jones, Proust, and Steele (2016) on the life and works of Neugebauer. The text starts with a description of the "Background"[19] of the work on "Properly Mathematical Tablets,"[20] which in some way resumes preoccupations Høyrup had dealt with twenty years before in the 1996 paper I have just commented on. The last decades of the nineteenth century witnessed the establishment of Assyriology, while researchers like Jules Oppert, Edward Hincks, Vincent Scheil, François Thureau-Dangin, and others made some steps toward the understanding of metrology and the sexagesimal notation (despite some drawbacks, such as an interpretation of the table of reciprocals tainted by esoteric positions).[21] This was mainly achieved by taking into account actual measurements of archaeological remains and by studying numerical tables and administrative texts. In the first three decades of the twentieth century, mathematical tablets

---

15. Høyrup (1996) is here referring to papers published by Schmandt-Besserat in the 1970s.
16. Overlapping in this way with Høyrup and Damerow 2001, that I mentioned above.
17. Høyrup 1996, 19.
18. Høyrup 1996, 21.
19. Høyrup 2016, 165–68.
20. Høyrup 2016, 168–69.
21. Høyrup 2016, 168.

Notes on the History of the Historiography of Cuneiform Mathematics

containing "word problems"[22] entered the scene, and their decipherment combined difficulty and astonishment, the latter provoked by the realization that cuneiform mathematics included something equivalent to the resolution of second-degree equations. The following two sections of Høyrup (2016) are dense. They first compare Ernst F. Weidner's and Neugebauer's readings and translations of a same text;[23] then Carl Frank's and Neugebauer's readings and translations of another text.[24] These comparisons show a number of improvements Neugebauer was able to bring to previous efforts. All in all, Høyrup's analyses of these "Confronted Readings" [25] constitute a convincing argument that Thureau-Dangin "was thus mistaken when believing in a kind of division of labour, where he was going to take care of terminology and grammar and Neugebauer of the substance."[26] It is also noteworthy that in relation to the issue of the place of mathematics in society, this moment is characterized by a few unconnected insights: for instance, that the mathematical texts "go far beyond the practical concerns of surveying and accounting" and that Seleucid tables were produced by "a representative of a large family of priests known since long from other texts from the Seleucid epoch."[27]

The section "The Sexagesimal System" in Høyrup's (2016) article, despite the title, is not restricted to the sexagesimal system: it begins with an explanation of the somewhat tortuous way that led to the understanding of terms that refers to a pair of reciprocals (namely *igûm* and *igibûm*). The bulk of the section is dedicated to comments on the publications by Neugebauer and Thureau-Dangin in which they tried to explain the nature and the origin of the sexagesimal system. Especially when commenting on Neugebauer's publications, Høyrup points out that Neugebauer's views were connected to what was then available to him (at that time).[28] The following section explains how each of these concrete spotty developments fit into a larger system ("Neugebauer's Project").

The last section of Høyrup's paper (2016), that tackles the difficult task of explaining "Why Neugebauer, Why Göttingen," offers some insights about the nature of the perceived division between Assyriology and the history of mathematics (what I call here historiography of cuneiform mathematics) from the point of view of the practitioners of the latter. As already mentioned, this perceived division is a constant theme in the production of the field.

We move on to another publication. "After Neugebauer: Recent Developments in Mesopotamian Mathematics" is the title of a paper published by Melville (2016), also a part of the collective work edited by Jones, Proust, and Steele (2016).

The first section of Melville's paper summarizes the long process of understanding the number system and its origins, structure, and use. It deals with Mesopotamian measuring systems and with the sexagesimal numeration. The author focuses

---

22. "Word problem" is an expression used by historians of mathematics in general to refer to texts in which one finds a statement of a problem and sometimes its solution.

23. Høyrup 2016, 169–75.

24. Høyrup 2016, 175–81.

25. Høyrup 2016, 169–81.

26. Høyrup 2016, 181.

27. Høyrup 2016, 181.

28. Høyrup 2016, 183–84. This is, by the way, a very good example of historiographical sensitiveness applied to the work of former historians of mathematics.

156 Carlos Gonçalves

on issues such as the origin of the sexagesimal place value notation and how the work of historians of mathematics dealt with sources coming from different periods: Old Babylonian, Uruk, Fara, the Sargonic period and Ur III. If the origin of the sexagesimal place value system was in the beginning a central concern for researchers, its use and structure became later a recurrent theme for investigation, mainly because each group of new sources created new questions. In this regard, the discussion about how to pass from the side of a square to its area and how to pass from its area to its side in relation to texts from the Sargonic period shows clearly how sources evoke new research problems.

The second section of Melville's paper, "Arithmetic and Table Texts," presents the developments of the historiography of cuneiform mathematics that led to the understanding of the origin and the use of metrological tables, that is, tables that associate measurement values and abstract numbers. This development gathered together research about the Old Babylonian curricular setting in general, as in the publications by Niek Veldhuis (1997), Steve Tinney (1998), and Andrew George (2005), with research more strictly focused on the Old Babylonian mathematical curriculum, such as in the works by Robson (2002, 2004) and Proust (2007). Melville (2016) also explains the headway that was made in the understanding of regional variances of terminology and techniques, beginning with a chapter written by Albrecht Götze (1945) on the "Akkadian Dialects of the Old Babylonian Mathematical Texts," as a part of Neugebauer and Sachs's (1945) edition of *Mathematical Cuneiform Texts*, and culminating in some way with a chapter in Høyrup's (2002) book on "The 'Finer Structure' of the Old Babylonian Corpus." This culmination also includes other publications, such as Friberg (2000), dealing with the corpus from Ur, and Isma'el and Robson (2010), dealing with mathematical tablets from the area of the Diyala. The third topic taken up by Melville is that of "Word Problems."[29] Problems may range from a simple situation, such as calculating the area of a rectangle from its given sides, to more difficult tasks, such as finding the sides of a rectangle given its area and the sum of its dimensions, to really difficult tasks involving complex mathematical properties. The understanding of these texts has been completely modified by the geometrical interpretation proposed by Høyrup, which appears especially in his 2002 book as a result of a research program he had carried out for some twenty years. Tablets may contain from one to several word problems, with or without solution, pertaining to the same theme or not, and all these variations have led to a few proposals for classification that do not always reach a consensus among historians of cuneiform mathematics. A final issue related to word problems is their use. This is still a point open to debate, highly dependent upon the type of tablet one analyzes.

Having summarized these three papers, I would like to make some comments. Although I believe this is not the place to develop a sociology of these fields and their relationship, I should at least comment that, as an intellectual field, the historiography of mathematics has had to fight for its legitimacy on many different fronts, namely,

---

29. The expression "word problem" is widely used in mathematics teaching and education, meaning "verbal descriptions of problem situations wherein one or more questions are raised the answer to which can be obtained by the application of mathematical operations to numerical data available in the problem statement" (Lerman 2014, 642).

Notes on the History of the Historiography of Cuneiform Mathematics 157

with mathematics, history of science, and history. This peculiar situation is, in my opinion, a factor that permeated the vision of the field brought by the three papers and its relation to neighboring intellectual enterprises. In this respect, Høyrup's (2016) article offers a goldmine for those that would like to better understand how complex the task of assigning historiographical meaning to cuneiform mathematical texts was and how easy it is to capitulate to the delusional attitude of considering the whole process just a "matter for mathematicians." In the same context, the rich correspondence that Neugebauer exchanged with other researchers working on the history, philology, and archaeology of the ancient Near East[30] suggests that, strictly speaking, Neugebauer was not being a mathematician while conducting his studies on cuneiform mathematics.

The tension between the historiography of mathematics and mathematics appear in an extremely gentle manner in Melville's (2016) paper, by way of the incorporation of historiographical research in the "tertiary literature, the history of mathematics textbooks where the Babylonians get their half-hour in the sun."[31] It may help to clarify that such textbooks are read mainly by students and teachers of mathematics. As a consequence, the way they depict cuneiform mathematics is representative of the care and the interest with which the historiography of cuneiform mathematics is received by large sectors of the mathematical community. The tension between the two disciplinary communities has already been the object of many publications, an example being the aforementioned critique of Unguru to a certain way of practicing the historiography of Greek mathematics. Other less acrimonious and reactive expositions of the problem and related issues can be found in Joan Richards (1995) and Ivor Grattan-Guinness (2004).

In terms of research concerns that have been keeping the historiography of cuneiform mathematics busy, these three mentioned papers touched many important points: accounting for the development of the sexagesimal place value system, deciphering of the technical terms, understanding of the techniques, the formulation of a useful text typology, and the efforts to associate mathematics to other spheres of life in Mesopotamian societies. The last of these items deserves further development and is the central motivation for the exposition in the next section.

Mathematics and Other Spheres of Life—A Contribution to the History of the Historiography of Cuneiform Mathematics (Emphasis Is on Society)

Put in simple terms, this section aims at surveying how the historiography of mathematics has dealt with the problem of mathematics and society. This problem has been approached according to different views on fundamental issues: what is society, what were the Mesopotamian societies, what possibilities do the documentation allow us?

In what follows, some of the works I mention also offer some explicit remarks on the history of the historiography of cuneiform mathematics. They are Robson (2008),

---

30. As shown by Proust 2016.
31. Melville 2016, 237.

158   Carlos Gonçalves

Chambon (2011), and Middeke-Conlin (2015). In them, as noted above, the positions of the authors in relation to the history of the historiography of cuneiform mathematics (that is, level H3) are relevant to their historiographical approach (that is, level H2). The remaining works mentioned in this section, namely, Nemet-Nejat (1993) and Høyrup (2002), are not explicit about their positioning in relation to the history of the historiography, but all of them contributed to the issue of mathematics and society.

I begin with Nemet-Nejat's (1993) book, *Cuneiform Mathematical Texts as a Reflection of Everyday Life in Mesopotamia*. The book opens with a few observations on the "Economic Dimensions of Cuneiform Mathematics" (chapter 1), a suggestive title indicating that one of the general historiographical problems of cuneiform mathematics is a little more than simply embedding mathematical texts in an economic context or framework. Rather, by recognizing its "economic dimensions," the author depicts cuneiform mathematics as constitutive of the economic. The chapter is devoted to summarizing research results about the usage of various types of numbers and representations to count, measure, and calculate. Emphasis is put into the fact that bookkeeping, counting, the development of cities, and the administration of large institutions are intermingled processes and phenomena, because in the "third millennium political and economic changes ... required the development of a complex notation system in record keeping in order to handle both very large and very small numbers."[32] The chapter, though, is extremely concise. It is followed by a "Survey of Mathematical Training for Scribes" (chapter 2), also extremely concise, dedicated to quoting excerpts from *eduba* texts in which mathematical issues are present.[33] The general goal is to make clear that mathematics was a school subject in Mesopotamia. Chapter 3 offers a classification of mathematical texts: table texts, coefficient lists, and problem texts. In both chapters 2 and 3, Nemet-Nejat (1993) brings plenty of bibliographical items. Problem texts are divided in two categories: "(1) algebraic/geometric problems; and (2) practical problems, that is, problems concerned with the *realia* of Mesopotamian life."[34] The author recognizes that the "boundaries are not hard and fast" and that "tablets may contain both categories of problems." The main goal of the book, however, is to survey a series of everyday life topics that pop up in problem texts, for instance: bricks and brickworks, canals and irrigation, *maḫiru* (price equivalency), interest, buying and selling, wood placed on top of a wall, and a pole or reed leaning against a wall.[35] The main part of the book is an "Analysis of the Practical Problem Texts" (chapter 4), in which each topic is subject to a dual scheme: a "discussion," in which all problems known at the time the book was written are listed and briefly summarized, and a "summary," in which the author comments on philological and vocabulary issues, groups problems that are similar within the category, and quotes the general bibliography of the topic. The summaries provide a thematic overview of what one needs to know in order to understand the usage of each topic in mathematical problem texts. Yet summaries are very concise, and each of them could in principle be expanded to an entire book. The discussion is analytic, and the summary is synthetic.

---

32. Nemet-Nejat 1993, 4.
33. These are compositions describing the life in ancient schools, known in Sumerian as *eduba*. Some of these texts were copied by Old Babylonian students as part of their Sumerian training. See George 2005.
34. Nemet-Nejat 1993, 21.
35. Nemet-Nejat 1993, 24.

Høyrup's (2002) *Lengths, Widths and Surfaces* also deals with the issue of cuneiform mathematics and society, although this is not the main theme of the book. There are two chapters of interest, the first of which is "The Historical Framework" (chapter 8). In it, Høyrup links scribes and administration to mathematics, taking into account a series of phenomena from the administrative sphere that may have had an impact on the way mathematics was practiced. For example, the administrative reform carried out by king Šulgi, inducing the development of "several mathematical tools" and the "new social system" of the Old Babylonian period, gave room to an "individualism" that expressed itself in ways that included a "supra-utilitarian mathematical competence."[36]

However, not all of mathematics had to do with the state and the administration of the main institutions. According to Høyrup (2002), "The Origin and Transformation of Old Babylonian Algebra" (chapter 10), the fact that algebra equates to the tradition of problems on lengths, widths, and surfaces (by the way, the title of the book) and the techniques to solve them can be explained only by assuming a non-scholastic tradition of proto-algebraic riddles. The argument is made in two steps. By examining later mathematical traditions (medieval, Indian, and Arabic), Høyrup draws our attention to the fact that these traditions also show some of the riddles present in Old Babylonian mathematics, without, however, presenting the full set of properties involving general operations with length, widths, and surfaces found in the Old Babylonian period. This would point to a common ancestry to these riddles and not to a transmission of Old Babylonian algebra to later mathematical traditions. This common ancestry is then supposed to be a "non-school or 'lay' tradition."[37] The second part of the argument is made by looking at what came before Old Babylonian mathematics: the result is that the proto-algebraic riddles incorporated into the mathematics of the Old Babylonian period that formed some substratum upon which the Old Babylonian algebra was developed could not have come from the Ur III or the Sargonic scholastic mathematical knowledge.[38] An external, lay tradition is required to explain the seeds of the Old Babylonian algebra: the lay surveyors mathematics is then assumed to be the missing point.[39]

We move on now to 2008, when Eleanor Robson's book, *Mathematics in Ancient Iraq: A Social History*, came to light. In "The Subject: Ancient Iraq and its Mathematics" (the first section of the first chapter of her book), the author weaves a number of considerations concerning the history of the historiography of cuneiform mathematics. These are almost all derived from Høyrup's (1996) article, which I commented on above. However, there are some additions that are worth mentioning, in order to illustrate how rich the history of historiography can be. The first one is the role of interpersonal relationships in the development of the field. Bruins difficult temperament, according to Robson,[40] was one of the reasons why the field of Babylonian mathematics was "stifled"; the other reason was "Neugebauer's renown for scholarly excellence." These factors were so strong that, only with Bruins's and Neugebauer's

36. Høyrup 2002, 314–15.
37. Høyrup 2002, 374.
38. Høyrup 2002, 378.
39. Høyrup 2002, 378–80.
40. See also Høyrup 1996, 29 nn.51 and 52.

160   Carlos Gonçalves

deaths in 1990, some room to accommodate new approaches became available.[41] The new approach at that moment was Høyrup's works.

This is, in my opinion, a point of great relevance: the historiography of cuneiform mathematics (as any historiography) is carried out by human beings and the relationships these human beings establish among themselves are a fundamental component of any understanding of the field. I would add that one should also take into account the institutional settings of each participant, in order to understand the constraints to which they are subject. Anyway, the lesson is that, if I may summarize the point in this way, one must be attentive to other humans.

One should look in the same way at the individuals producing the historiography of cuneiform mathematics in order to get a wide understanding of this production. The emphasis of Robson's book lies in the effort to connect the mathematics of the tablets to the individuals that wrote and used them and to the context to which they belonged. As an example of this possibility, she examines one small square tablet from Nippur and states that understanding that its text brings a mathematical problem in which one must calculate the area of a square from its side is only one part of the investigator's task. In order to connect it to its contexts, it is necessary to take into account additional information. In this case, it is the information about the specific locus of the excavation where the tablet was exhumed that helps one understand that it was an exercise performed by someone that was learning mathematics.[42]

The same principle is emphasized in the "Epilogue" (chapter 9 of her book): that is, "to consider cuneiform mathematics not as a single closed, abstract system but as a complex of ideas and practices that are best understood when contextualised within the social, intellectual, and political history of the ancient Middle East."[43] This principle is clearly employed in the explanation of what Robson calls "metrological justice," a concept she resumes in the "Epilogue."[44] The relation between justice and metrology, therefore, between context and mathematics, is epitomized in the following two excerpts: "Early Mesopotamian kingship was constructed on the intertwined ideals of piety, military might, and justice. And justice—'making straight'—was conceptualised through fairness and equality. Equality could be measured and measurement was the key to ensuring justice." And then "in solving abstruse puzzles about measured space, the true scribe demonstrated his or her technical capability and moral fitness for upholding justice and maintaining social and political stability on behalf of the king."[45] This equation of justice and metrology leads to the supposition that "mathematics never really caught on in the wider Middle East, presumably because it had little relevance to local counting systems, metrologies, or political ideologies."[46]

The following section of the "Epilogue," entitled "Ancient Mathematics in the Modern World," describes how cuneiform mathematics has been represented in the general literature of history of mathematics. In order to follow Robson's description,

41. Robson 2008, 7.
42. Robson 2008, 17–26.
43. Robson 2008, 263.
44. Robson 2008, 265–67.
45. Robson 2008, 266.
45. Robson 2008, 267.

it is useful to know that there is a huge gap between what professional researchers in history of mathematics do and what writers of general history of mathematics books write. It is not that all historians are equal, or that all general expositions of history of mathematics make the same distorted simplifications. Yet, there is a gap.

I would like to say that, amazing as it is, historians of mathematics in general, and historians of cuneiform mathematics in particular, are not mathematicians in the sense that it is not our business to prove theorems, to exhibit counterexamples, or to extend theories. Our job, instead, is to know what mathematicians and the like have been doing the last, let us say, six millennia, and how they related to the societies they belonged. This is indeed a complex issue, and its manifestations vary from country to country. Having said that, I can get back to Robson's (2008) description of the treatment that general histories of mathematics give to cuneiform mathematics:[47]

- More often than not, cuneiform mathematics has been compared with ancient Greek mathematics in order to establish some sort of hierarchy, in which Greek mathematics would occupy a higher position as more complex, more theoretical, more abstract, more developed;
- a canon of what is found of cuneiform mathematics in the general expositions of the history of mathematics was established following Neugebauer's *The Exact Sciences in Antiquity* (1952) and Asger Aaboe's *Episodes from the Early History of Mathematics* (1964). This canon "led Old Babylonian mathematics to be viewed through the lens of early Greek mathematics, whose received image was at that point no less partial;"[48]
- history of mathematics is completely impersonal;
- the received image of cuneiform mathematics was coherent with the attitude of the West toward the so-called Orient as described in Edward Said's *Orientalism* (1978) and the postcolonial literature that followed.

One important issue in the research on the history of cuneiform mathematics is presented as "Inside Ancient Mathematics: Translation, Representation, Interpretation," focusing on the developments brought by the work of Høyrup.[49] The starting point for his approach is the concept of "conformal translation," that is to say, a translation that renders different words in the original by different words in the end language. As an example, different verbs for "addition," such as *kamārum* and *waṣābum*, should be rendered into translations by different words, in this case "to heap" and "to append." A second characteristic of Høyrup's approach is the use of diagrams containing squares and rectangles to represent and interpret cuneiform mathematics, instead of previous scholars's use of algebraic notation. Robson's is a very careful presentation of these principles in action. Specifically, she gives examples of how Høyrup's approach can produce a new interpretation of what numbers are in word problems: "arithmetical numbers turn out to have dimension: they are particular lengths and

47. Robson 2008, 268–74.
48. Robson 2008, 272.
49. Robson 2008, 274–84.

areas that are manipulated very physically."[50] Furthermore, she exemplifies how this approach allows one to notice important differences between the mathematics from the Old Babylonian period and that of the Seleucid period as far as word problems are concerned: if in the former squares and rectangles can be cut and pasted, in the latter the emphasis falls on the possibility of making multiple copies of these figures. Finally, she relates this advancement in the historiography of cuneiform mathematics to a new attitude toward translation that had already been employed in the study of ancient Greek mathematics.

The excerpts I commented upon from Robson's book show what I consider a very important characteristic of the historiography of cuneiform mathematics nowadays: an acute awareness that our practice as historians of mathematics depend on (1) our understanding of the history of our field as much as of the history of cuneiform mathematics itself, and (2) we should have a word as to how the production we make is appropriated by the secondary literature of the history of mathematics in general and by textbooks. The book also channels some of the very important discussion held in relation to what limits and requirements were expected from the historiography of mathematics in general, in order that it could meet present standards, such as the critique of presentism and anachronism, a need to overcome the dichotomy of the internal versus the external, the use of the results of social, cultural, and political history, the understanding of the Eurocentrism of some of the older research in the area, and a sensitiveness to issues of gender, to mention only these.

Chambon's (2011) book *Normes et pratiques: L'homme, la mesure et l'écriture en Mésopotamie* is a study about measurement practices in a specific region during a specific time in ancient Mesopotamia. The geographical framework is called "ancient Syria," which is established by the very nature of the historical problem being investigated.[51] In the south of Mesopotamia, the representation of units of measurement and their deployment in the first half of the second millennium BCE followed previous practices (namely, those from Ur III) almost without absorbing anything from arriving peoples, like the Amorites. In the North, however, some sets of documents show a very clear adherence to the "vernacular expressions" (that is to say, local, non-Sumerian expressions). The documentation used by Chambon comes mainly from the ancient cities of Nabada (Tell Beydar), Mari (Tell Hariri), and Ebla (Tell Mardikh), three vertices of an imaginary triangle in the map, going from east to west, oscillating from north to south and back to north, approximately coinciding with the territory of present-day Syria, hence the motivation to call it "ancient Syria." In order to deal with this issue, that is to say, in order to understand the historical processes at work, the author looks at a larger span of time, from the middle of the third millennium BCE to the thirteenth century BCE.

In the section entitled "A Historiographical Point," Chambon briefly sketches some traits of how the issue of measure has been dealt with by historians. In one tendency, historians are interested in converting ancient measurement to modern equivalencies in order to assess the order of magnitude of goods and commodities, as well as the amount of bounty from war and other things in ancient societies. This gives us

---

50. Robson 2008, 278.
51. Chambon 2011, 15–18.

some understanding of the orders of magnitude of the amounts that were mobilized in ancient societies. However, since the 1970s, according to the author, new trends have entered the historiography. That is the moment when historical metrology is born and from which, in the 1980s, a shift of interest was produced, from a technical history of metrology to a social history of metrology. As Chambon comments, the phenomenon "found echo in Assyriology too, thanks to the works by N. Parise and C. Zaccagnini."[52] As regards the historiography of mathematics, a similar shift was felt too, but somewhat "delayed in time," according to the author. While in the so-called founding works by Neugebauer and Thureau-Dangin, and also in much of what followed, the interest was concentrated in technical and arithmetical aspects of metrology, from the 1990s the publications in the field began to deal with the "human and social framework in which mathematical and metrical practices were developed," as well as how they were theorized in educational settings.[53] Chambon refers here explicitly to works by Robson (2008) and Proust (2007).

After recognizing that the "complexity of the procedures of each discipline makes it difficult to produce a complete historiographical exposition," Chambon states that he will focus on three specific issues: "the problem of center and periphery, the question of the metric norm, and the interpretation of royal reforms regarding weights and measures in ancient Mesopotamia."[54]

As regards the question of center and periphery, Chambon refutes the idea that there was a center of Mesopotamian culture that imposed on the region referred to as ancient Syria its metrological system. Instead, in ancient Syria the absorbed metrological material from other regions was combined with local practices. The second issue is also central to the argument of the book: a critique of the scholarly tradition of comparative metrology that tries to establish simple arithmetical relations between the elements of various metrological systems from different regions and times, thus assuming (even if not overtly) that there exists some suprahistorical organizing principle governing specific concrete metrological systems, from which follows a critique of the methods and aims of the comparative metrology. One particular consequence of that standpoint is an opening to accept that more than one standard might have existed for the same measure in the same place and time. Another consequence is a distinction between imposed standards (imposed by kings, for instance) and consensual standards, obtained as an agreement, for the sake of practicality.[55] All of that goes in accordance with a development toward a conception of standard that is dependent on its social context of use: weights found in places of commercial activities would not be the same thing as weights found in tombs.[56]

An additional useful distinction discussed by Chambon concerns the study of standards: one possible approach is based on the existence of a physical measurement of each thing that could only be approximated by the ancients due to their technical limitations. Another approach, the one that is supported by the book, is concerned above all with the reasons why in given contexts given values became standard. The second

52. Chambon 2011, 24, always my translation from the French original.
53. Chambon 2011, 24–25.
54. Chambon 2011, 25.
55. Chambon 2011, 35.
56. Chambon 2011, 37.

164   Carlos Gonçalves

approach is also related to a greater attention to archaeological sources and the study of coherent sets of epigraphic sources, like archives, whereas the first approach has the tendency of grouping together sources scattered in space and time.[57]

The last issue is that of the metrical reforms. Chambon offers a critique of the interpretation arising from an assumption that there existed the idea of standard in certain moments of the history of ancient Mesopotamia, and that this standard could be set by the king. This is clear in the supposed metrical reformation conducted by king Ur-Namma, a reformation whose reality is by the way dependent upon a reading of the prologue of the law collections attributed to him that itself could be problematized, as the author shows.[58]

A final methodological point is important in order to understand Chambon's approach. It is a distinction between standardization of a value for a unit of measurement, which is dependent on social and cultural variability of its use, and the standardization of the way this unit of measurement is written, which is dependent of practices located in the setting of scribal culture. The proposal of the book can then be stated more clearly: to study $sila_3$, one of the most commonly used capacity measures[59] in cuneiform texts, in a vast geographical area, in a vast chronological scope. Regional variations are not to be understood as deviations from a standard; rather, regional variations must be understood as local expressions of local needs, usages, measures in the context of negotiations.[60]

Chambon's book exemplifies two present trends in the historiography of cuneiform mathematics. First, Mesopotamia is not accepted anymore by the historiography of cuneiform mathematics as a homogeneous entity and, for this reason, it makes sense for researchers to focus on specific regions within restricted timespans. Even if we still resort to data from a somewhat general background or to a possible mathematical "stream of tradition," the field now has enough material to deal with the diversity of mathematical knowledge and practices. Second, the historiography of cuneiform mathematics is not isolated from other disciplines in terms of methodological preoccupations. Chambon's book shows this clearly when dealing with the traditions of a "comparative metrology" and the new trends of the studies of ancient metrologies. The lessons from other fields can be imported and adapted to the study of cuneiform mathematics.

A recent contribution throwing a new perspective on the issue of mathematics and society is the Middeke-Conlin's (2015) PhD dissertation. The first aspect of the text I would like to underline is the author's account of the interaction between historians of mathematics and Assyriology. As the reader is now aware (see above), this is a recurrent preoccupation of the field. However, as I will show presently, there are alternative ways of looking at the issue.

Middeke-Conlin is concerned with the history of Assyriology and the reception of the history of mathematics in it. In a section entitled "Early Assyriology:

57. Chambon 2011, 37–38.
58. Chambon 2011, 38–40.
59. A survey of metrological units in use in Mesopotamia is in progress at the CDLI Wiki under the entry "Numbers & Metrology," http://cdli.ox.ac.uk/wiki/doku.php?id=numbers_metrology.
   However, work of reference for the topic is still Powell (1987–1990).
60. Chambon 2011, 42.

The Formation of a Field of Research" (focusing on research before the turn of the twentieth century), Middeke-Conlin states that the emphasis in Assyriological research at this moment was in chronology and antiquities, while the study of literary texts had less importance. The study of context was practically non-existent, and rule texts (when studied) were always thought of as isolated pieces.[61]

Before going on, it is worth noticing that these characteristics have frequently been ascribed to the work of historians of cuneiform mathematics in particular, and to historians of mathematics in general, with a tone implying that this is not good historiographical research. Maybe the example from the history of Assyriology, as described above, could teach us that the interesting issue is not to know if a determined historiographical practice is legitimate or not, but to try to connect that practice to other practices of the same moment in time.

Anyway, a wider interest in texts began to appear in publications after the turn of the century, and this is exemplified for Middeke-Conlin by Hermann Hilprecht (1906), when texts started to receive a finer-grained classification and were tentatively assigned to specific places of provenance.[62]

The section of Middeke-Conlin's text entitled "Outsiders Brought in: New Approaches to Textual Analysis" corresponds to the period from the end of the First World War to the 1960s. A shift in historiography happens, moving from interest in chronological texts and year dates to economic texts. Interesting for my purposes here is the fact that Middeke-Conlin characterizes this period as one in which "classics and biblical perspectives begin to be supplanted by outside perspectives such as economic theory and mathematics."[63] A distinctive trait of Middeke-Conlin's report about the history of Assyriology is the way the historiography of mathematics is viewed. While in Høyrup's and Melville's articles (see above) the reason for the entrance of outsiders in Assyriology are presented from the point of view of the outsiders, Middeke-Conlin's text, on the contrary, is presented from the point of view of those already in the field. With the new emphasis on textual analysis, the range of texts submitted to scrutiny was considerably enlarged. I would say that at this moment Assyriology established a *total research program* in the sense that all texts are interesting for historiography. According to Middeke-Conlin,

> in this period of textual analysis, Assyriology saw brilliant works in such areas as mathematics, chemistry, lexicography, and literature that attested to the high level of Babylonian learning and culture *as a uniform society* with *uniform traditions*. Thus we see the famous study of Otto Neugebauer in his *Mathematische Keilschrifttexte* ... as well as his work with Abraham Sachs in the famous 1945 publication of *Mathematical Cuneiform Texts* ... or we can look to the work of François Thureau-Dangin and his *Textes mathématiques babyloniens*. ... These works held a significant impact on Assyriology as they created an awareness of a pre-Greek mathematical culture in ancient Mesopotamia.[64]

61. Middeke-Conlin 2015, 36–37.
62. Middeke-Conlin 2015, 38.
63. Middeke-Conlin 2015, 40.
64. Middeke-Conlin 2015, 41.

166   Carlos Gonçalves

To me this is a piece of the account that was lacking. That Neugebauer and Thureau-Dangin worked in different ways and established a positive competition is a phenomenon that connects with the desire in Assyriological milieus to understand all types of texts in as much detail as possible, even if some of the practitioners would specialize in certain textual genres. That outside influences were desired can be seen too in the historiography of economics. In order to evidence this, Middeke-Conlin turns to the development that is contained in the works by Schneider and Deimel, presenting the temple–state theory, and in the rival state–economy theory of Koschaker, that is to say, in the efforts to understand ancient Mesopotamia from the economic point of view. Middeke-Conlin states that "classicism and biblical studies are no longer the center of discussion with these works, and are replaced with economic theories from outside sources. Indeed, we see in this a distinctly relativist, almost Weberian model of economic activity in which a 'moral peasant' is presupposed for these models to work. Thus, we see traces of economic theory as well as cultural anthropology in Assyriological works, a great change from the classical models prescribed by the early authors on Mesopotamian history."[65]

The 1960s, finally, would see the whole issue from a new perspective, presented by the problem of the archive: "Thus, the nature of an archive is viewed as important to any textual study because it delimits the role this archive played in society around it."[66] This was an important point in the critiques that Gelb and Diakonoff made of the state–temple theory. This questioning of the reach of the conclusions we might obtain from a specific archive can be rephrased as an awareness of the heterogeneity of ancient Mesopotamia. In relation to cuneiform mathematics, though, historians of mathematics were not always able to translate this awareness into practical results; the presence of Götze's chapter in the book by Neugebauer and Sachs (1945) is a token of the seriousness of the problem.

It is in this context that Middeke-Conlin tries to describe the process that led "from uniformity to variation."[67] He describes the history of the historiography of lexical material up to Veldhuis (1997), in which there is a consistent preoccupation to show that lexical lists varied chronologically and geographically. This approach is then compared with that of Proust's (2007) reconstruction of the curriculum of mathematics. Both in Veldhuis's and in Proust's studies, each canonical text is canonical only in relation to a specific moment in time and a specific space.

Middeke-Conlin moves on then to a discussion of "current trends in Assyriology."[68] One of these trends is represented by "archival studies." [69] The other trend underlies the possibility of bringing "unity out of variety" [70] in the study of ancient Mesopotamia. This is visible in both the publications on more administrative aspects of ancient Mesopotamia and on publications dealing with cuneiform mathematics. In relation to the historiography of cuneiform mathematics, Middeke-Conlin points out three trends: (1) giving attention to the mathematical texts themselves, especially by being careful

65. Middeke-Conlin 2015, 40.
66. Middeke-Conlin 2015, 41.
67. Middeke-Conlin 2015, 42.
68. Middeke-Conlin 2015, 47.
69. Middeke-Conlin 2015, 47.
70. Middeke-Conlin 2015, 50.

enough to translate ancient vocabulary into a modern language keeping all the vocabulary distinctions (the conformal translation) and by assuming a geometric, almost visual reasoning subjacent to the mathematical texts (the cut-and-paste geometry), a trend whose paradigm appears in Høyrup's (2002) book; (2) focusing on the role of numbers in texts and attempts to account as much as possible in relation to their use, leading to the hypothesis that there were numerical procedures going on outside a text, such as in Proust's (2000) assumption of the existence of an abacus to perform certain calculations; and (3) making efforts to assess the impact of mathematics on economic texts, such as in the works of Nemet-Nejat (1993), Robson (1999), and Friberg (2001).[71]

Both in the analysis of studies dealing with administrative issues and with mathematics, Middeke-Conlin underlies that researchers do not see Mesopotamia any more as a homogeneous entity. If chronological and geographical variations had already begun to be accepted in the previous period of the historiography, this period incorporated social and professional variations too. The issue of variety versus unity is closely linked to the distinction between "history from above" and "history from below," the well-known expressions used to talk about much of the historiography produced during the twentieth century, but taken here in the context of Assyriological studies, especially as found in the historiographical study by Van de Mieroop (1999). It seems that when viewed from below, Mesopotamia is much more likely to show all its variety of practices.[72]

Additional Remarks

I hope that the previous exposition has made a few points clear which, in my opinion, are relevant for anyone trying to approach the field, either as someone who wants to learn more about cuneiform mathematics and its history or as someone who wants to do research on the history of cuneiform mathematics.

First, as the reader may have noticed, trends in the historiography of cuneiform mathematics are tied to individuals. This is due, in my opinion, to the fact that the number of researchers that were or that are active in the area can be counted on the fingers of two hands. Also, researchers have been scattered in many different institutions, which in their turn provide very different challenges and peer interaction. Although the way these institutional settings have left their mark on the historiography of mathematics is still a subject to be investigated, these differences should be taken into account in any evaluation of the field.

Also important is the perceived dichotomy between the work of historians of mathematics and Assyriologists. I emphasize "perceived dichotomy," because I do not believe that the works analyzed above were able to bring convincing arguments. All that they can bring are some personal testimonies, plus the weird episodes involving a socially problematic Bruins. None of the studies present consistent sociological research regarding this difference. In addition, in the studies I rehearsed in previous

---

71. Middeke-Conlin 2015, 51–52.
72. Middeke-Conlin 2015, 50–51.

168   Carlos Gonçalves

sections, opinions vary. This is not to say that the issue is nonexistent, but only that the method to present it is not convincing enough.

Anyway, what one could say is that (1) the interaction between so-called Assyriologists and so-called historians of mathematics is an appealing issue from the point of view of the historiography of mathematics; (2) the works of the "first decipherers," Neugebauer and Thureau-Dangin mainly, was not the result of sheer will of these men to decipher, but a need of the field, as Middeke-Conlin suggests; and (3) in spite of everything, this perceived dichotomy has a positive side, as it seems to be a great motivation for historians of mathematics to reassess the possibilities and the aims of their research.

Borrowing a concept from the very different context of postcolonial studies, the concept of contact zone, one could wonder if the historiography of cuneiform mathematics, instead of suffering from this dichotomy, is in fact highly productive because of it.[73] If one of the properties of knowledge is its circulation, this is valid too for historiographical knowledge, even for historiographical knowledge about cuneiform mathematics. Historiography of mathematics exists in a place where different academic traditions meet, where historiographical and mathematical knowledge have mingled and circulated. It is no surprise thus that the labels "mathematician," "historian of mathematics," and "Assyriologist" have had to be constantly renegotiated.

A further point that I would like to underline is represented by the efforts of the field to deal with the issue of mathematics and society. I would like to draw the readers' attention to the fact that the expression "mathematics and society" does not necessarily entail the assumption that mathematics has its existence outside society and that sometimes it finds some practical applications in society. Instead, the problem at issue is (1) how to formulate good questions involving mathematics and society and (2) how to give appropriate answers to these questions.

The previous sections show a number of possibilities: to study the general issue of scribal education where mathematics had a place; to study specific archives and accept the questions these archives admit as possible ones; to study specific areas and periods; to summon general concepts such as state or ideology and try to fit the mathematical evidence in their frameworks; to account for non-written transmissions of mathematical knowledge and practices; and to study error and approximation in order to detect how mathematical knowledge circulated through different sectors of the same society.

None of these possibilities is in principle better that the others. In practice, each researcher is able to evaluate how the documentation at hand, the questions, and the answers engage with each other. There is no such thing as a perfect historiographical method; after all, historiography has a history too.

REFERENCES

Aaboe, A. 1964. *Episodes from the Early History of Mathematics*. Washington, D.C.: Mathematical Association of America.
Bruins, E. M., and M. Rutten. 1961. *Textes mathématiques de Suse*. Mémoires de la mission archéologique en Iran 34. Paris: Geuthner.

73. See, for instance, Raj 2013.

Chambon, G. 2011. *Normes et pratiques: L'homme, la mesure et l'écriture en Mésopotamie. I. Les mesures de capacité et de poids en Syrie Ancienne, d'Ébla à Émar.* Gladbeck: PeWe-Verlag.

Friberg, J. 2000. "Mathematics at Ur in the Old Babylonian Period." *Revue d'Assyriologie* 94:97–188.

―――. 2001. "Bricks and Mud in Metro-mathematical Cuneiform Texts." Pages 427–58 in *Changing Views on Ancient Near Eastern Mathematics.* Berliner Beiträge zum Vorderen Orient 19. Edited by J. Høyrup and P. Damerow. Berlin: Dietrich Reimer.

―――. 2007. *A Remarkable Collection of Babylonian Mathematical Texts.* Manuscripts in the Schøyen Collection. Cuneiform Texts I. New York: Springer.

Friberg, J., and F. N. H. Al-Rawi. 2016. *New Mathematical Cuneiform Texts.* New York: Springer.

George, A. R. 2005. "In Search of the é.dub.ba.a: The Ancient Mesopotamian School in Literature and Reality." Pages 127–37 in *An Experienced Scribe Who Neglects Nothing: Ancient Near Eastern Studies in Honor of Jacob Klein.* Edited by Y. Sefati et al. Bethesda: CDL Press.

Gonçalves, C. 2012. "Notas sobre a recepção da matemática mesopotâmica na historiografia." *Educação Matemática Pesquisa* 14(3):322–35.

Götze, A. 1945. "The Akkadian Dialects of the Old Babylonian Mathematical Texts." Pages 146–51 in *Mathematical Cuneiform Texts.* American Oriental Series 29. Edited by O. Neugebauer and A. Sachs. New Haven: American Oriental Society.

―――. 2015. *Mathematical Tablets from Tell Harmal.* New York: Springer.

Grattan-Guinness, I. 2004. "The Mathematics of the Past: Distinguishing Its History from Our Heritage." *Historia Mathematica* 31:163–85.

Hilprecht, H. V. 1906. *Mathematical, Metrological, and Chronological Tablets from the Temple Library of Nippur.* Philadelphia: Department of Archaeology, University of Pennsylvania.

Høyrup, J. 1996. "Changing Trends in the Historiography of Mesopotamian Mathematics: An Insider's View." *History of Science* 34:1–32.

―――. 2002. *Lengths, Widths, Surfaces: A Portrait of Old Babylonian Algebra and Its Kin.* New York: Springer.

―――. 2016. "As the Outsider Walked in the Historiography of Mesopotamian Mathematics Until Neugebauer." Pages 165–95 in *A Mathematician's Journeys: Otto Neugebauer and Modern Transformations of Ancient Science.* Edited by A. Jones, C. Proust, and J. Steele. New York: Springer.

Høyrup, J., and P. Damerow, eds. 2001. *Changing Views on Ancient Near Eastern Mathematics.* Berliner Beiträge zum Vorderen Orient 19. Berlin: Dietrich Reimer.

Isma'el, K. S., and E. Robson. 2010. "Arithmetical Tablets from Iraqi Excavations in the Diyala." Pages 151–64 in *Your Praise is Sweet: A Memorial Volume for Jeremy Black from Students, Colleagues and Friends.* Edited by H. D. Baker, E. Robson, and G. G. Zólyomi. London: British Institute for the Study of Iraq.

Jones, A., C. Proust, and J. M. Steele, eds. 2016. *A Mathematician's Journeys: Otto Neugebauer and Modern Transformations of Ancient Science.* New York: Springer.

Kragh, H. 1987. *An Introduction to the Historiography of Science.* Cambridge: Cambridge University Press.

Lerman, S., ed. 2014. *Encyclopedia of Mathematics Education.* New York: Springer.

Melville, D. J. 2016. "After Neugebauer: Recent Developments in Mesopotamian Mathematics." Pages 237–63 in *A Mathematician's Journeys: Otto Neugebauer and Modern Transformations of Ancient Science.* Edited by A. Jones, C. Proust, and J. Steele. New York: Springer.

Middeke-Conlin, R. 2015. "The Making of a Scribe: How Rounding Numbers Was Expressed in the Scribal Curriculum and Adapted for Administrative Purposes." PhD diss., Université Paris Didedot.

Nemet-Nejat, K. R. 1993. *Cuneiform Mathematical Texts as a Reflection of Everyday Life in Mesopotamia*. American Oriental Series 75. New Haven: American Oriental Society.

Neugebauer, O. 1935–1937. *Mathematische Keilschrifttexte, I–III*. Berlin: Springer.

———. 1952. *The Exact Sciences in Antiquity*. Princeton: Princeton University Press.

Neugebauer, O., A. Sachs, and A. Götze. 1945. *Mathematical Cuneiform Texts*. American Oriental Series 29. New Haven: American Oriental Society.

Nissen, H., P. Damerow, and R. K. Englund. 1993. *Archaic Bookkepping*. Chicago: University of Chicago Press.

Novais, F. A. 2005. *Aproximações. Estudos de História e Historiografia* (*Approximations. Studies of History and Historiography*). São Paulo: Cosac Naify.

Powell, M. 1971. "Sumerian Numeration and Metrology." PhD diss., University of Minnesota.

———. 1976. "Antecedents of Old Babylonian Place Notation and the Early History of Babylonian Mathematics. *Historia Mathematica* 3:417–39.

———. 1987–1990. "Maße und Gewichte." Pages 457–516 in *Reallexikon der Assyriologie*. Vol. 7. Edited by D. O. Edzard. Berlin: de Gruyter.

Proust, C. 2000. "La multiplication babylonienne: La part non écrite du calcul." *Revue d'histoire des mathématiques* 6:293–303.

———. 2007. *Tablettes mathématiques de Nippur*. Paris: De Boccard.

———. 2008. *Tablettes mathématiques de la collection Hilprecht. Avec la collaboration de Manfred Krebernik et Joachim Oelsner*. Texten und Materialen der Hilprecht Collection 8. Wiesbaden: Harrassowitz.

———. 2016. "Mathematical and Philological Insights on Cuneiform Texts: Neugebauer's Correspondence with Fellow Assyriologists." Pages 207–35 in *A Mathematician's Journeys. Otto Neugebauer and Modern Transformations of Ancient Science*. Edited by A. Jones, C. Proust, and J. Steele. New York: Springer.

Raj, K. 2013. "Beyond Postcolonialism . . . and Postpositivism: Circulation and the Global History of Science. *Isis* 104(2):337–47.

Richards, J. 1995. "The History of Mathematics and l'esprit humain: A Critical Reappraisal." *Osiris* 2nd series 10:122–35.

Robson, E. 1999. *Mesopotamian Mathematics 2100–1600 BC: Technical Constants in Bureaucracy and Education*. Oxford Editions of Cuneiform Texts 14. Oxford: Clarendon.

———. 2002. "More than Metrology: Mathematics Education in an Old Babylonian Scribal School." Pages 325–65 in *Under One Sky: Astronomy and Mathematics in the Ancient Near East*. Alter Orient und Altes Testament 297. Edited by J. M. Steele and A. Imhausen. Münster: Ugarit-Verlag.

———. 2004. "Mathematical Cuneiform Tablets in the Ashmolean Museum, Oxford." *SCIAMVS—Sources and Commentaries in Exact Sciences* 5:3–65.

———. 2008. *Mathematics in Ancient Iraq: A Social History*. Princeton: Princeton University Press.

Said, E. 1978. *Orientalism*. New York: Pantheon.

Silva, R. F. da. 2015. "A História da Historiografia e o Desafio do Giro Linguístico" (The History of Historiography and the Challenge of the Linguistic Turn). *História da Historiografia* 15:377–95.

Thureau-Dangin, F. 1938. *Textes mathématiques babyloniens*. Leiden: Brill.

Tinney, S. 1998. "Texts, Tablets and Teaching: Scribal Education in Nippur and Ur." *Expedition* 40(2):40–50.

Unguru, S. 1975. "On the Need to Rewrite the History of Greek Mathematics." *Archive for History of Exact Sciences* 15(1):67–114.

Van de Mieroop, M. 1999. *Cuneiform Texts and the Writing of History*. London: Routledge.

Veldhuis, N. 1997. "Elementary Education at Nippur: The Lists of Trees and Wooden Objects." PhD diss., University of Groningen.

Weissbach, F. H. 1907. "Über die babylonischen, assyrischen und altpersischen Gewichte." *Zeitschrift der Deutschen Morgenländischen Gesellschaft* 61:379–402.

Websites:

CDLI Wiki, "Numbers & Metrologie." http://cdli.ox.ac.uk/wiki/doku.php?id=numbers_metrology (accessed 12 April 2018).

Mesopotamian Mathematics. http://it.stlawu.edu/~dmelvill/mesomath/ (accessed 12 April 2018).

CHAPTER 8

Feudalism and Vassalage in Twentieth-Century Assyriology

Emanuel Pfoh

FEUDAL AND VASSAL RELATIONSHIPS have been rather ubiquitous and generally accepted models for arranging and interpreting economic and political data from the ancient Near Eastern/Southwest Asian world[1] in twentieth-century Assyriology. Terms like "feudalism," "feudal," and "fief" are found widely in oriental scholarship up to the 1980s, describing territorial and/or political control by means of economic exploitation or asymmetrical exchange. Terms like "vassalage" and "vassal" have instead had a longer validity and are still used, although in a somewhat loose manner, to denote political subordination mediated by personal oaths or treaties between two parties, kingdoms, states, etc.[2] The Assyriological historiography on these subjects, however, have seldom made the epistemological arrangement of these concepts explicit, or assessed the obvious question of how these concepts, stemming in fact from medieval European historical phenomena and experiences, are utterly appropriate for ancient Southwest Asian socioeconomic and sociopolitical realities.

The present contribution is far from exhaustive in its coverage of examples, in its engagement with the details and particularities of land-tenure, and in its attention to political subordination in ancient Southwest Asia. Rather, it aims at conceptually surveying, in a selective manner, the most salient cases in order to review and revisit the issue and to evaluate the ultimate usefulness of the aforementioned concepts from a critical perspective.[3]

Author's note: I must express sincere gratitude toward both of the editors of this volume, not only for their kind invitation to contribute, but especially for their patience, advice, and support. This paper was written during a research stay at the Oriental Institute (University of Chicago), April–June 2017, funded by the Fulbright Commission and Argentina's National Research Council (CONICET). I thank Prof. J. D. Schloen for having directed my attention to the recent PhD thesis by J. M. Burgin, relevant for this research.

1. "Southwest Asia" has become in recent times a less subjective and ideologically charged term for what is usually (and still) called the "ancient Near East," but also the "Middle East." Cf. Scheffler 2003.

2. Here the notable "Vassal Treaties of Esarhaddon" are illustrative of the sociopolitical image; cf. *ANET*, 534–41.

3. I have already addressed this revision, although very briefly and focusing on Syria-Palestine, in Pfoh 2013 and 2016, 108–19. Arguments from these treatments are reproduced and expanded here.

Finding Feudalism and Vassalage

Feudalism and vassalage have been two sides of the same coin in Western twentieth-century ancient Near Eastern studies.[4] Although both phenomena were not always evident at the same time, indications of the existence of one of them was assumed most of the time to express the necessary existence of the other part. In other words, the socioeconomic structure of the fief had its counterpart in a sociopolitical order arranged in a suzerain–vassal dichotomy.[5]

In this view, one of the first clear examples of feudalism as a socioeconomic system was found in ancient Mesopotamia, coming from the city of Nuzi (Yorghan Tepe) in northern Iraq. During the excavations of the site between 1925 and 1934, some 7,000 tablets in the Akkadian language of both public and private character (on legal, economic, and administrative matters) were found, dating back from the Late Bronze Age, covering some five generations (ca. 1475–1350 BCE) and offering many details on domestic and "family" economic transactions, apart from notices on the political relationships between Assyria, Mittani, and Arrapḫa.[6] Already in 1942, Hildegard Lewy offered an interpretation of the references to the *ilku* (a tax, payed some times in goods, some other in service or labor) in the textual data as related to feudal obligations, similar to those of medieval Europe, especially in relation to the attested phenomenon of legal adoptions in lands transferences.[7] In effect, Lewy, commenting on the deeds of one Nuzian family, as they were recorded in the tablets, observes:

> Like Teḫiptilla himself, all the members of his family to whom the administration of crown-land in the various subdistricts of the Nuzi region was entrusted are known to have possessed large estates, especially in and near the town of Turša. That these estates were subject to *ilku* charges is shown, e.g., by the passage NV 492, ll. 22 ff. which speaks of the service to be rendered by one of Teḫiptilla's grandsons in return for a property consisting of fields, houses, and a threshing place. Thus, the position of these men has a double aspect: on the one hand, they were responsible for the military organization of their sector and exerted, as we have seen, in their subdistricts powers similar to those used by the royal minister Teḫiptilla in the whole Nuzi region; but since, on the other hand, they were themselves compelled to render feudal service in return for

---

4. Soviet ancient Near Eastern historiography, up through the mid-twentieth century, did not consider feudalism as a historical and theoretical possibility within the Marxist scheme of succession of modes of productions, favoring a slave-based socioeconomic reality for pre-Hellenistic Southwest Asia. In the 1960s, with the notable figure of Igor Diakonoff, the two-sector model (palace and village community, a variant of Marx's Asiatic mode of production) appeared as a theoretical way to explain feudal-like structures and relations (cf. Schloen 2001, 187–94 and, especially, Burgin 2016, 13–24).

5. Especially during the first half of the twentieth century, the historiography of ancient Egypt (which shall not be treated here), when addressing the intermediate periods, deployed also feudal terminology and concepts to explain political fragmentation and provincialization. See, notably, Pirenne 1936. A similar criticism to the one applied to Assyriological understandings of feudalism may be directed toward such ancient Egyptian feudalism. See, further, Coulborn 1956.

6. See further the recent evaluation in Maidman 2010.

7. Cf. also, and earlier, Pfeiffer 1922.

174   Emanuel Pfoh

the use of the vast portions of crown-land under their control, they recall the grand vassals of better known feudal states in later history, as, e. g., those of the Carolingian Empire.[8]

For Lewy, not only the internal organization of Nuzian society was anchored in a feudal socioeconomic structure, but also the external political relationships with higher powers, like Arrapḫa or Mittani.[9] Furthermore, Lewy made explicit her close comparison between European feudalism and the Nuzian one as the main framework of her interpretation of the textual data from Nuzi: "In view of the parallels which we drew previously between the feudal institutions of the Mitannian Empire and those under the Carolingians in France, one may compare the act of 'bowing down' to the Mitannian king with the *serment de fidélité* taken by the grand vassals of Charlemagne and his successors."[10]

By the middle of the twentieth century, this interpretation, although with minor variations, was accepted as sociopolitical normality for many situations of ancient Southwest Asia, in which granting of lands in exchange for military or political service were observed. For example, and as a chapter in a collected volume on feudalism in history, Burr Brundage—curiously not an ancient Near Eastern scholar, but originally a historian of pre-Hispanic America—authored an article in 1956 investigating the phenomenon in ancient Mesopotamia and Iran, which is especially representative of this general outlook on the feudal Near East.[11] Brundage is cautious in his analytical comparison and offers a serious historical interpretation of feudal clues in the then available textual and archaeological data. In general, Brundage finds some hints of feudalism in ancient Mesopotamian and Iranian history, especially in those periods of weak state control of the land and its peoples. For the Amorite period, he notes that

> we cannot overlook the fact, however, that the Amorite kings of the First Babylonian Dynasty had created a group of military dependents who were at times granted certain immunities in their persons. At the same time they were professional officers in the royal army, and the estates they held did not confer on them governmental or jurisdictional prerogatives. We might remove the dilemma by assuming that some of the elements of feudalism were present in the Old Babylonian period, but were disparate and muted by the stringent and unrelaxed exercise of the central power.[12]

Regarding the Kassite period, Brundage notes, too, the existence of possible factors of a feudal regime, notably royal charters of immunity:

---

8. Lewy 1942, 14–15. This understanding is currently, and naturally, profoundly challenged. Maidman (2010, 10) has stated: "Whatever economic regime characterized Nuzi and Arrapḫa at large, it was not feudal, and not solely (or even predominantly) communal (if it was communal at all); rather it was essentially private. Landlords consisted of individuals, families, royal retainers, even the palace itself. But private landlords they were and they remained." See further on this issue Maidman 2010, 163–227.

9. Lewy 1942, 318–34.

10. Lewy 1942, 332 n. 1. Cf. n. 53 below.

11. Further on Iranian feudalism, see Widengren 1969.

12. Brundage 1956, 96.

the king would give over such rights upon the lands in question as the collections of various levies, assessments and taxes, the *corvée* upon the dikes and canals, water and pasture rights, and the right of military protection. We are also informed that these benefices became hereditary, at least in some cases. One benefice in particular was in litigation under the crown for the duration of three reigns. In this instance we can see that the king could bestow the estate if the owner died without issue, or if there were a dispute over ownership. Yet apparently the crown was not powerful enough to secure reversion, except to grant the benefice out again.

Cities, and of course villages, were also from time to time parceled out as benefices to deserving officials, generally without immunity from military service. Such grants may have been subject to recall by the crown. It should be noted that this was in the later period when the Kassite kings were deified. Here at least was the fiction of unity in the state, and perhaps a fair amount of the substance.

We do not know what were the *personal* relationships which bound together benefice-holder and king, and we can therefore state nothing definite concerning Kassite vassalage (or other form of dependency if the word vassalage is not justified) as it was conceived apart from benefice-holding. Possibly as time went on there was a general loosening of the feudalistic elements in Kassite society—this is an assumption we make as a corollary of what seems to be the gradual strengthening of the central power.[13]

Moving on in time and space, in the particular case of the kingdom of Ḫatti, the existence of a feudal-like relation in the internal organization seemed to be confirmed especially by one key feature: the presence of a powerful king, to whom officials had to swear loyalty, who granted lands in return, and who also replicated this practice toward the exterior of the polity. Conquered kings also had to swear an oath of loyalty to the Hittite king as a proper means of political subordination.[14] Regarding this last situation, Hittite rule implied essentially a formal political exchange—an unequal exchange in reality—between the subjects and the king, and this exchange was recognized in both its material and symbolic aspects. The usual procedure consisted of the celebration of a treaty of political alliance and subordination between the Hittite king and the subject king, including a series of seemingly symmetrical clauses established between the parties, and at times marriage alliances as well, which up until the 1970s, were taken to express some form of feudalism.[15] Expressing this precisely view, a classical formulation of ancient Near Eastern feudalism was provided by Erich Ebeling's (1971) entry "Feudalismus" in the *Reallexikon der Assyriologie*, finding clear examples of feudal structures in Kassite Babylonia, Ḫatti, Mittani, Assyria, and ancient Iran. In particular, the Hittite social structure portrayed by Ebeling consisted of the king and the aristocracy (landowners and courtiers) at the top of a hierarchical pyramid, then the freemen (merchants and priests), semi-free men (warriors, craftsmen, and farmers), and slaves (meaning State administration):

13. Brundage 1956, 98 (emphasis original). See further Sommerfeld 1995, 488–90.

14. See Cornelius 1972, but contrast especially with Haase 1968 for a rebuttal of these ideas. Burgin (2016, 6–13, 24–28) provides the more recent evaluation of this historiographic development in Hittitology.

15. See further the discussion in Pfoh 2016, 108–19.

Auch in Ḫatti ist die Gesellschaftsform als feudal zu bezeichnen. An der Spitze stehen der König und der Adel (Grundbesitzerund Hofwürdenträger, hett. *panku*). Diese letzteren stehen zum König im Verhältnis des Lehensträgers zum Lehensherrn, allerdings mit bemerkenswerten Rechten auch gegenüber dem König. Auf den weiteren Stufen der Staatspyramide nach unten hin stehen die Freien (Kaufleute und Priester), Halbfreie (Krieger, Handwerker und Bauern) und schließlich die Sklaven (s. Ḫatti, Staatsverwaltung). Allerdings lockert sich in der jüngeren Periode die Strenge der Unterschiede zwischen den einzelnen Schichten. Aus dem Feudalstaat wird allmählich ein Beamtenstaat.[16]

Dealing with a more peripheral region, Albrecht Alt understood too the socio-politics of subordination in Syria-Palestine, both in the Bronze and Iron Ages (ca. 3300–600 BCE), essentially, if not exclusively, in terms of vassalage, as can be appreciated by browsing through his numerous essays collected in the three-volume *Kleine Schriften*.[17] Some years later, and building on Alt's studies, Giorgio Buccellati offered a sociopolitical typology for Bronze and Iron Ages Syria-Palestine in his *Cities and Nations of Ancient Syria* from 1967 that still is found widespread among ancient Levant studies. In this study, Buccellati conceived of a historical sequence of *territorial states* for the Bronze Age polities of the Levant, and *national states* for the Iron Age. Beyond the analytical nature of this typology, and regarding political dynamics, subordination was also understood by Buccellati as basically constituting vassalage.[18] Actually, as J. D. Schloen observed, until the 1960s such a model crafted from medieval feudalism was deployed in any treatment of the ancient Near East to describe Old Babylonian society, Kassite Babylonia, Middle Assyrian society, Nuzi and the kingdom of Arrapḫa, the Hittite kingdom and its empire, and Middle and Late Bronze Age Syria-Palestine.[19] This model would basically assert, once again, that the king granted lands ("fiefs"), eventually becoming hereditary estates, to his men ("vassals"), who would in return be at his service (expectedly, through a sworn bond of "fealty"). Those receiving the land may divide it in order to be exploited by their own servants. The resulting scheme was in fact a kind of hierarchy of feudal appearance, but one that actually lacked—when seen from a proper historical comparison—the juridical and political framework of European feudalism, which depended on the contract between free men with institutionalized rights and duties for both parties, something actually non-existent in Southwest Asia, at least in pre-Hellenistic times.[20]

From the field of medieval studies, however, the situation of feudal relations outside of the European framework had already been tackled and confronted after the mid-twentieth century. Perhaps most famously, the French medievalist Robert Boutruche reviewed, in a synthetic two-volume work entitled *Seigneurie et féodalité*,

16. Ebeling 1971, 54–55.

17. Cf. Alt 1953a, 99–111, 217–25, 248–52; 1953b, 39–54, 69–72, 152–60, 228–38; 1959, 7–10, 43–44, 100–104, etc.

18. Cf. Buccellati 1967, 30, 34, 44–56, 109, 139, 161–62, 215.

19. Schloen 2001, 187–94.

20. The feudal model had also, during the late 1970s and early 1980s, some diffusion—yet not equal acceptance—in Old Testament studies when referring to Late Bronze Age Canaan. See, notably, Gottwald 1979, 391–400.

the interpretations of the existence of feudal institutions and practices in the ancient Near East.[21] Relevant for the present treatment is Boutruche's treatment of the Mesopotamian, Levantine, and Hittite situations of feudalism. According to Boutruche:

> La "féodalité hammourabienne" a été mise à l'honneur parce que, sans se préoccuper assez de la nature des liens personnels et réels, ses inventeurs ont opposé aux biens patrimoniaux et assimilé à des fiefs les terres qui, selon le code d'Hammourabi, rétribuaient des fonctions publiques et des services militaires durant le temps où ils étaient exécutés. Or, il s'agissait là d'une forme de paiement temporaire à des agents qui, même dotés d'immunités, dépendaient directement de l'État. À cette époque, la Babylonie était une monarchie centralisée dont le chef, représentant de Dieu sur cette terre, gardait entre ses mains les principaux pouvoirs. Il contrôlait l'administration centrale ainsi que les chefs des gouvernements provinciaux, veillait à ce que les dotations foncières attachés à une fonction ne fussent pas dissociées de cette dernière, ni transformées en biens héréditaires.
>
> L'affaiblissement de la monarchie babylonienne sous les successeurs d'Hammourabi eut pour conséquence le glissement des tenures et de certaines fonctions vers l'hérédité, ainsi qu'une exécution imparfaite des charges, laissées par leurs titulaires à des remplaçants. Mais il n'est pas prouvé que des relations proprement vassaliques aient existé entre le roi et les grands, ni entre les diverses couches de l'aristocratie.[22]

Further, regarding the Ugaritic evidence from the archives of Ras Shamra, Boutruche commented on the organization of the kingdom:

> Organisation qualifiée aussitôt de féodale ... L'auteur voit dans le fief une concession faite "par la puissance publique." D'une part, nous dit-il, le roi distribuait des terres auxquelles étaient attachés des services d'ordre surtout économique: hébergement des gens de guerre, livraison de denrées et d'animaux domestiques au Palais. ... Leurs titulaires pouvaient les aliéner librement, et peu importait la personne du preneur pourvu que les services fussent exécutés. C'était la "féodalité foncière." D'autre part, le souverain rétribuait de nombreux agents en leur donnant pour la durée de leur charge la jouissance de certains biens. Ils formaient la "féodalité de fonctions."—Abus de langage éclatants! Il y a, dans le premier cas, des tenures chargées d'humbles tâches économiques, dans le second cas des terres servant à l'entretien des agents de l'État. Le roi les concédait sans exiger au préalable un serment de nature privée. Elles n'étaient pas des fiefs, ni leurs titulaires des vassaux.[23]

Boutruche continued his revision addressing the Hittite case also, in which he deems "feudality" to have had more success in the specialized historiography:

---

21. Boutruche 1968, 240–57.
22. Boutruche 1968, 242–43.
23. Boutruche 1968, 243–44 n. 5.

178   Emanuel Pfoh

Plus qu'en Égypte ou qu'en Babylonie, des liens personnels de fidélité ont couru à travers l'État hittite. Ils rattachaient au grand roi ses guerriers professionnels, dotés de tenures, ses gouverneurs de province, les chefs héréditaires des royaumes protégés, largement autonomes, les chefs également héréditaires, et souvent recrutés dans la famille royale, des royaumes sujets où le souverain installait des hommes à lui, qui rappelaient les *vassi dominici* de l'empire carolingien. Ce roi n'était pas absolu. Les textes font état, dans l'Ancien Empire, d'une assemblée de la caste dirigeante qui se réunissait périodiquement non seulement pour lui renouveler sa fidélité et jurer de le servir, mais pour recevoir de lui le serment de respeter ses privilèges. Enfin, sous l'Ancien comme sous le Nouvel Empire, la loyauté des dépendants avait pour contrepartie l'engagement pris par le roi de venir à leur aide en cas de besoin. Cet appareil éveille des images si familières que des historiens de la société hittite l'ont représenté comme une société féodale parfaite.[24]

However, in this case, the conditions of feudality were still lacking in Boutruche's opinion:

L'organisation Hittite offre avec nos liens de dépendance d'évidentes analogies qui, pourtant, ne doivent pas faire illusion. L'une des sources essentielles, le Code hittite, fait surtout état des rapports entre le roi et ses subordonnés immédiats. Noués par des serments périodiquement renouvelés, que scellait une invocation aux dieux, et suivis du versement d'un tribut, ils unissaient non pas des vassaux à un seigneur, mais des chefs de protectorat à une puissance protectrice, des princes apanagés et de hautes fonctionnaires à un souverain. Ils avaient un caractère public beaucoup plus que privé. Enfin, les offices et les domaines concédés étaient dépourvus des éléments qui entraient dans la nature complexe du fief. De contexture fragile, l'empire hittite fut pour une part centralisé, dans les régions soumises directement au roi, et pour une part fédéral. Il ne semble pas avoir été féodal en raison du prestige attaché à une royauté d'essence divine, dont le représentant était déifié après sa mort, du maintien de la loi dont il était le gardien, de l'importance des villes, où vivait l'aristocratie, des ressources que le pouvoir monarchique tirait notamment de l'économie commerciale et qui lui permettaient d'entretenir une administration et une forte armée. La société le fut moins encore. On cherche vainement un étagement de vassaux et d'arrière-vassaux, de fiefs et d'arrière-fiefs. En tout cas, la documentation n'a pas conservé la trace de relations féodo-vassaliques entre personnes privées.[25]

Following these insights, it should be clear by now that Hittite treaties, in spite of having in appearance a notable similitude with Frankish feudal–vassal bonds, did not actually imply the essential particularities of the European feudal concession. First of all, the lord–vassal bond was a private affair in feudalism, while in Ḫatti the treaty

24. Boutruche 1968, 244–45.
25. Boutruche 1968, 245–46.

with foreign subjects—although a personal relationship between two kings—was a public political matter. Furthermore, and on legal grounds, there was legislation on the nature of the European feudal order between lords and vassals, and each party could have appealed to it in a dispute. This was nonexistent in the Hittite Empire, as the legal terms of the sociopolitical transaction represented by the treaty were actually personal: those of the Hittite king. And, as another notable French medievalist, Marc Bloch, asserted in his monumental work *Feudal Society*: "Vassal homage was a genuine contract and a bilateral one. If the lord failed to fulfil his engagements he lost his rights."[26] Hittite treaties hardly fall then into this presentation of "lord–vassal" treaties and, therefore, their historical understanding as expressions of Hittite feudalism and vassalage is in fact misleading and anachronistic.

Of course, this is not a novelty, having in mind that in the field of Hittitology, the notion of Hittite feudalism had already been criticized in the 1970s, especially by Alfonso Archi (1977) and Fiorella Imparati (1982, 1983). Both authors proposed considering the general layout of the organization of the Hittite kingdom appealing to the two-sector model or the Asiatic mode of production—but that is quite another discussion.[27] Imparati concludes her contribution to the *Reallexikon der Assyriologie* on feudalism among the Hittites by noting that "the adoption of a typically feudal terminology to designate certain institutions of the Hittite state may misrepresent the features proper to this society."[28]

The demise of the presence of "feudal relations" as a part of ancient Near Eastern society in the scholarship of the 1980s—notably in Hittitology[29]—did not prevent, of course, later researchers from continuing to use concepts like "fief" or "vassalage" for addressing evidence of royal grants or political subordination. To date, the most comprehensive treatment of feudalism in ancient Southwest Asia is the lengthy synthesis by Sophie Lafont (1998), published in an anthology of cases of feudalism in world history. Lafont correctly distinguishes the notion of "fief" from "feudalism," noting that "le fief n'est ainsi qu'une variante occasionnelle du système général des tenures, couramment pratiqué par des institutions—l'État ou le temple—comme mode de rémunération de ses dépendants."[30] Further, she defends the use of the term "fief,"

---

26. Bloch 1962, 172.

27. See notably here Archi 1977, 16: "Dunque, in ultima analisi, esistevano [in the Hittite kingdom]: *a)* terre controllate dai liberi, che erano tenuti a fornire al Palazzo delle *corvées*; *b)* terre del Palazzo, amministrate direttamente da esso, messe a coltura mediante le *corvées* dei liberi e in parte mediante servi; *c)* terre del Palazzo assegnate a un LÚ ILKI o a dipendenti dell'amministrazione palatina, che disponevano talvolta di mano d'opera servile. È quindi il Palazzo che ha il predominio del sistema economico, e di fronte gli stanno le comunità. Manca una clase di signori terrieri. Ai funzionari dell'amministrazione statale potevano essere assegnati dei benefici, ai quali però non erano strettamente connessi i servizi richiesti, ed il cui sfruttamento era assicurato da lavoranti non subordinati da vincoli di carattere personale o politico. Che all'interno di alcuni possedimenti chi formava la mano d'opera avesse appezzamenti di terra con cui mantenersi, rientra nel medesimo sistema di remunerazione. Comunque, alcuni addetti del Palazzo erano retribuiti non singolarmente, ma per categorie. La concessione di tale benefici è un tratto comune a molti stati antichi e dell'Oriente medievale, e non costituisce di per sé un elemento feudale." A key positive revaluation on the Asiatic mode of production for the ancient Near East is Zaccagnini 1981. See further Burgin 2016, 32–50.

28. Imparati 1983, 547.

29. See Burgin 2016, 1–97.

30. Lafont 1998, 517.

as well as of the idea of "feudalism," for addressing some socioeconomic realities in the ancient Near East. It is useful here to quote extensively from Lafont's study:

> Il reste que l'usage du mot lui-même "fief" n'est pas forcément un anachronisme au Proche-Orient. . . . Le concept de féodalité est soumis à un sémantisme beaucoup plus tyrannique qui exclut toute signification neutre, synonyme de "phénomène du fief". Au contraire, les deux définitions classiquement admises, et qui sont utilisées dans les travaux orientalistes, ont une connotation tantôt économique tantôt politique. La première, issue des théories marxistes, fait de la féodalité le stade intermédiaire entre la société esclavagiste et le capitalisme. Ce modèle, transposé dans la sphère proche-orientale, dépeint un système dans lequel le roi, propriétaire suprême de la terre dans son royaume, concède des tenures à ses dépendants en échange de leurs services. C'est en réalité une organisation palatiale ou domaniale de la société qui est ainsi décrite. La seconde approche met l'accent sur le phénomène politique qui consiste en un détournement des prérogatives de puissance publique au profit d'agents administratifs. C'est précisément l'absence de tels comportements dans l'Orient cunéiforme qui conduit souvent à nier l'existence de fiefs et de la féodalité. Même si l'ampleur des usurpations de pouvoir, attestés à plusieurs époques de l'histoire mésopotamienne, est difficile à tracer faute de sources explicites, *il reste que de tels détournements sont caractéristiques du régime seigneurial: l'exercice des droits régaliens est concevable, théoriquement, dans le cadre d'un alleu.* Une autre approche, plus sociologique, de la féodalité, consisterait à chercher la répétition de comportements calqués sur la vassalité dans des domaines où le fief n'apparaît pas. Cette perspective se révèle plus fructueuse: plusieurs aspects de la vie politique mésopotamienne se comprennent en référence à un lien personnel, établi selon des formes particulières et solennelles, et impliquant la fidélité et la loyauté d'une partenaire par rapport à l'autre. Parler de "phénomène du fief" serait à cet égard impropre, puisque la tenure militaire est absente de ces engagements d'homme à homme. *L'expression "féodalité" est finalement la mieux adaptée pour qualifier ce genre de situation où le rapports individuels sont organisés hiérarchiquement autour des obligations respectives de chacun.* Il faut toutefois éviter de généraliser cette conclusion à toutes les époques et à tous les milieux. *Le phénomène est documenté au IIe millénaire, dans les royaumes syriens du XVIIIe siècle et à l'apogée de la domination hittite au XIVe siècle, et il intervient soit dans les rapports entre le roi et ses sujets, soit dans les relations internationales. Il n'est pas attesté à l'échelon privé, entre particuliers.* De même que le fief est un accessoire de la notion de tenure, la féodalité—au sens retenu plus haut—est une donnée occasionnelle dictée par les circonstances culturelles et historiques. C'est une réponse ponctuelle et non pas une construction pérenne.[31]

After such a theoretical departure, it is difficult nonetheless to find clear cases in which feudalism presents itself as the correct concept to interpret the textual data, as Lafont

---

31. Lafont 1998, 518–19. The emphasis is mine.

herself shows in the rest of her study. Not much evidence of "fiefs" is to be found in third-millennium-BCE Sumer and Akkad. For the first half of the second millennium BCE, Lafont assesses the evidence from the Amorite kingdoms and, although some evidence of fiefs might be found, it seems to have been a rather minor aspect of Old Babylonian society,[32] noting herself also that "le mot 'fief,' utilize systématiquement par certains auteurs, n'est pas toujours appropriée"[33] for Babylonia and Syria during the first half of the second millennium BCE.[34] In the case of the kingdom of Mari, Lafont finds personal bonds of vassalage both at the interior of the polity (political loyalty to the king is rewarded with land) as well as toward the exterior, within a framework of a hierarchy of personal dependence.[35] In this sense, what appears to be "feudal" in Mari is the bond of political dependence, which Lafont—along with most Assyriologists—calls vassalage.[36] For the second half of the second millennium BCE, Lafont surveys again the relevant data and concludes that there is not sufficient evidence for finding proper feudalism among the Kassites,[37] the Assyrians,[38] or the Hittites,[39] within their own societies. The smaller kingdoms of Nuzi and Ugarit possess no proper evidence of feudalism in their socioeconomic arrangements either, apart from their external relationships of subordination toward greater polities.[40] For

32. "En premier lieu, les concessions foncières sont bien attestées à l'époque paléo-babylonienne, mais le fief n'est qu'un aspect de ce système et ne constitue pas une catégorie juridiquement distinguée des autres formes de tenures. On a considéré que l'attribution d'une terre avait d'abord une visée économique: le roi chercherait moins à obtenir un service, par exemple militaire, qu'à faire entretenir et exploiter le domaine de la couronne. En réalité, il s'agit plutôt pour le roi de procurer à ceux qui travaillent pour le compte du palais un mode rémunération alternatif au système des rations. En second lieu, la dépendance personnelle des individus dans une organisation complexe et hiérarchisée est bien documentée à un niveau officiel, c'est-à-dire principalement entre États. La fidélité est en effet l'une des pièces essentielles des stratégies politiques royales dans les relations internationales, reposant sur un agencement mouvant d'alliances vassaliques" (Lafont 1998, 537–38).

33. Lafont 1998, 538.

34. Lafont 1998, 538–59.

35. Lafont 1998, 559–70.

36. "Le lien personnel de dépendance était donc fondamental pour comprendre les relations internationales complexes de cette période. Chacun faisait partir d'une chaîne de rapports hiérarchisées; l'autonomie des souverains n'existait pas" (Lafont 1998, 565). In his superb translation of the epistolary documents from Mari, Durand 1997, 458–60 makes frequent use of the notion of "vassal" and "vassalage" to refer to political subordination. This use, however, is nowhere justified or conceptually defined in his study in order to find out or clarify how or to what extent the vassal of a king of Mari was a different political creature than, for instance, a Carolingian vassal.

37. "Il est difficile de parler de féodalité kassite.... Il n'y a pas non plus de fiefs, juridiquement distincts d'autres formes de tenures, à cette période" (Lafont 1998, 577).

38. "Force est de constater, en l'état actuel de la documentation, que ces dignitaires n'étaient pas liés à la royauté par un engagement personnel de fidélité; leur charge n'était pas concédée par un contrat privé, mais bel et bien attribué par le roi, dans un cadre strictement public. Autrement dit, il n'y avait pas de superposition entre les fonctions administratives et le lien d'homme à homme, typique de la féodalité occidentale carolingienne" (Lafont 1998, 589).

39. "L'existence de fiefs est ... plausible, encore que, comme ailleurs au Proche Orient, la tenure militaire ne puisse être distinguée des nombreuses autres formes de concessions foncières. On observera cependant que l'organisation militaire et surtout l'équipement incombaient au pouvoir central. La parcelle attribuée aux soldats garantissait ainsi leur entretien mais non leur armement. Au surplus, la couronne n'exigeait pas de ses tenanciers une fidélité et un engagement personnel comparables à ceux du vassal envers son seigneur.... Au total, ces données incitent à rejeter l'appellation 'féodale' pour l'organisation politique hittite: les fiefs n'entrent pas dans un système d'alliances personnelles et de protection d'un faible par un plus puissant" (Lafont 1998, 593–94).

40. "La situation politique d'Ugarit ne peut être qualifiée de véritablement féodale. Les tenures concédées par le roi étaient parfois des fiefs, parfois des censives, pouvant être assortis d'exemptions et tendant à

182   Emanuel Pfoh

the first millennium BCE, Lafont finds the evidence for feudalism in Assyria lacking as well,[41] while she, however, confidently speaks of "les fiefs achémenides" for
fifth-century-BCE Mesopotamia.[42] All in all, she concludes that "la féodalité comme
phénomène politique n'est pas attestée pour cette époque."[43]

In sum, Lafont's treatment of the question of feudalism in the ancient Near East,
while certainly being one of the best assessments of the matter to date, exposes a common interpretative strategy in current Assyriological studies when dealing with the
issue: even when European medieval feudal relationships are not to be found anymore
in recent approaches to socioeconomic aspects, the political side of the relationship
still lingers on as a conceptual tool. Any bond of political subordination between two
polities is consequently read through the grammar of medieval vassalage, or at least
its practical aspects, and the question is certainly not that the concept might not be
fully useful for certain situations,[44] but rather that other analytical models, stemming
from sociology and anthropology, should also be explored and considered.

Assessing the Nature of Political Subordination

An explicit definition of "vassal/vassalage" has never been thoroughly offered in
twentieth-century Assyriology (and Hittitology and Egyptology, for that matter). The
term seemed to be self-evident, and a proper comparative discussion of its relationship
to European feudalism is even rarely found in current ancient Near Eastern historiography. On some occasions, a caveat is made noting that ancient Near Eastern vassalage
is of course not the same phenomenon as medieval European vassalage.[45] However,

devenir héréditaires. Mais les notions de lien personnel, de soumission hiérarchique et de réseau de fidélité
ne sont pas documentées dans les sources. Elles apparaissent en revanche dans les relations internationales,
à l'examen des traités diplomatiques conclus entre Ugarit et ses voisins, notamment le Hatti" (Lafont 1998,
608).

41. "Quelques fiefs, une 'industrie' militaire et un recours ponctuel à l'engagement de fidélité envers
le pouvoir central: ces éléments sont trop disparates pour qu'on puisse y voir les prémisses d'une société
féodale. Au Ier millénaire, la vassalité ne fut qu'une modalité de la politique expansionniste assyrienne.
Elle n'est pas attestée à l'échelon des personnes privées, ni encouragée par l'État. Le roi voulait seulement
s'assurer sporadiquement le soutien de ses sujets, sans faire de cette fidélité un véritable mode de gouver-
nement" (Lafont 1998, 619).

42. Since "le bénéficiaire doit fournir une prestation soutenant l'armée royale, qu'elle consiste en
une participation active aux expéditions royales ou en une somme d'argent" (Lafont 1998, 623; see further on this Cardascia 1983, 1995, and compare also with Engels 2011 for a later period: the end of the
Seleucid Empire). Lafont nonetheless later (1998, 626) notes the following: "On ignore en revanche si
les feudataires étaient des vassaux du roi, autrement dit des individus ayant prêté foi et hommage à leur
seigneur-souverain."

43. Lafont 1998, 627.

44. See the relevant considerations about this already in Cahen 1960; see also Strayer and Coulborn
1956.

45. Although critical of the feudal model for the Hittite kingdom (see n. 27 above), Archi had stated in
the same study: "La parola 'vassallaggio' (e 'vassallo'), largamente usata dagli orientalisti per esprimere
questi rapporti di dipendenza, sembra ancora la più adatta. Essa non deve assolutamente implicare condizioni proprie dell'Europa medievale" (1977, 17). See also more recently Devecchi 2015, 12 n. 2: "Parlare
di vassallaggio e vassalli in relazione al sistema politico e gerarchico ittita è chiaramente un anacronismo,
mutuato dal sistema medievale ed entrato in uso quando lo stato ittita veniva concepito come una struttura
feudale. ... Nonostante l'imprecisione di questi termini, si continua convenzionalmente a usarli per indicare
la condizione di subordinazione di un sovrano nei confronti del Gran re ittita."

such caveats do not ultimately avoid the problems of the continuing deployment of anachronistic terminology nor overcome its interpretative effects. Vassalage is essentially used to denote political subordination; yet, the connotative aspect of this usage of the term infiltrates—willingly or not—ancient Near Eastern realities with medieval features, political assumptions, and behavioral expectations. One way to resolve this problem is perhaps to employ a more neutral terminology, like *subordination*, instead of vassalage. Furthermore, on some occasions, *patronage* (and its reverse, *clientship*) is a more suitable concept to describe and analyze the particularities of a political subordination organized through personal means of domination, even at a regional (so-called "international") level of authority of a great king over a small king. True, patronage and clientelism draw their terminology from the Roman system involving a *patronus*, a *cliens*, and a *clientela*, and one could object that this replacement is nothing but an exchange of one anachronism with another. However, unlike vassalage in general historical studies, patronage/clientelism does possess an analytical autonomy widespread in current anthropology, sociology, history, and political science,[46] which actually allows for a better interpretation of particular situations of political subordination, like some of what we find in the ancient Near East.[47]

Subordination treaties in the ancient Near East made room for personal relationships between the parties, and reciprocity—although, as already noted, asymmetrical—was an essential part of the sociopolitical bond: for example, the Hittite king protected the subject king militarily, exempted him from certain tributes, and guaranteed his dynasty on the throne. The subject king, in return, had to assist the Hittite king militarily and protect him against any enemy, give any service required of him, and be loyal to his person (not to his office). This arrangement, aside from expanding the Hittite Empire, assured the internal governance of the subject king's kingdom and the external protection by the Hittite king. In general, Hittite treaties said nothing about what will happen if the Hittite king transgresses the oath, as a lord–vassal relationship would require it. Also, the fact that the Hittite king is the one who imposes the bond and the arrangement for the exchange of assistance and loyalty, from one king to another (not between kingdoms!),[48] clearly indicates *personal* rather than impersonal

46. On this see, for instance, Roniger 1983 and the vast literature on patronage and clientelism quoted and discussed therein. Feudalism and clientelism coexisted indeed in the European Middle Ages (see, for instance, Mączak 1988), and one should profit from analyzing both sociopolitical systems in order to clarify the general features of political dependence in ancient Near Eastern societies. Some scholars have argued that feudal–vassal relations are a form of patronage (Blok 1969, 367–69; Montgomery 2007, 565–67). This identification, however, ignores the constitutive features of, and differences between, institutional feudalism/vassalage and non-institutional patronage.

47. And perhaps, instead of vassalage, ancient Near Eastern inter-polity subordination and alliance could be better compared to Roman foreign *clientelae:* see Rich 1989; and the considerations in Johne 2015. See also the comparison between Hittite and Roman imperialism in Altman 2008. An initial survey of patronage in the ancient Near East and its appropriateness is found in Westbrook 2005; but cf. Pfoh 2009 for a reappraisal of Westbrook's perspective.

48. In this respect, McCarthy (1978, 51) had already noted regarding the so-called Hittite vassal treaties: "One might almost wonder if these are truly treaties. They are so one-sided in making demands almost exclusively on the lesser prince that they must have been more or less imposed on him. Where was the element of freedom and consent essential to any binding agreement? Still, we must conclude that these texts were true treaties [!]. The vassal may not have been entirely willing to accept his position, but only a relative freedom is required. Perhaps he was consenting to the lesser of two evils, submission rather than war or at least the continued threat of war, but nonetheless he was consenting."

or bureaucratic dynamics of empire management. Interstate subordination is then a personal affair between the royal houses under the Hittite rule and the Hittite king himself.

In spite of some structural differences, this insight applies also, for instance, to first-millennium-BCE Assyrian rule of Syria-Palestine: the Assyrian king imposed a submission treaty with the defeated or surrendered local king, through which a certain political reciprocity was established—favoring always the Assyrian party, which guaranteed *de facto* the bond (the gods, as in the Hittite case, were also witnesses to the relationship of subordination). However, in Hittite treaties, the contractual formalism expressed a parity between the parties that was *only* apparent; in reality it did not exist. In Assyrian treaties, the subordination of the lesser king was rather explicit. Political subordination in both cases is thus expressed by means of alliance, although an unequal alliance: the Hittites imposed treaties on kings in the periphery of their kingdom; the Assyrians imposed treaties or pacts (*adû*) and loyalty oaths on the subject kings from conquered lands, but also on officers from the kingdom's own administration.[49] These treaties or pacts enforced the subordinate party to loyally protect and assist the Assyrian king—or the crown prince—and never to desert him or betray him, under the threat of a divine punishment materialized in the form of the Assyrian army. From a comparative and historical perspective, it is difficult again to see how this kind of relationship could be characterized precisely as "vassalage," other than in a very superficial manner, or as actually expressing some kind of *external* feudalism in sociopolitical terms—and I emphasize the word *external* here since a kind of *internal* feudalism had already been proposed in ancient Near Eastern historiography for Assyria during the fifteenth century and for Ḫatti in the fourteenth century.[50]

Another main objection to the assumed vassalage relationship is that the political rights—if we may call them that—of the lesser party were not explicit in the treaties, as is the case in medieval feudal bonds. Instead the relationship is dependent on the personal will and judgment of the king establishing the treaty, as stated above. And even though a group of gods acted as witnesses to the treaty and ensured that the parties acted accordingly, we may assume that the superior party (the Hittite or the Assyrian king) would have most probably acted according to the needs of the kingdom's *Realpolitik* and, therefore, the favor of the gods limited in practice the political autonomy and agency of the lesser party. Political authority rested ultimately with the overlord's person.

Considering therefore the aforementioned examples of subordination to foreign powers, the model of *patron–client relationships*, or *political patronage*, as it is documented in the ethnographic and ethno-historical records of the Mediterranean and the Middle East, appears to be much more appropriate than vassal relationships, as it enhances significantly our interpretation of the sources and our understanding

---

49. See further Holloway 2002, 217–419, who deploys the model of patron–client relationships to analyze the internal and external articulation of power in the Neo-Assyrian Empire. Holloway, however, makes extensive use in his study of terminology like "vassal state/s" without discussing in depth the question of vassalage and clientelism, apart from noting in a footnote: "'vassal' and other legal expressions drawn from European feudalism should be eschewed because of their heavy freight of anachronistic political and social infrastructures" (Holloway 2002, 99 n. 78).

50. For Assyria, see Garelli 1967; for Ḫatti, see Goetze 1957.

of power dynamics. In general, patron–client relations imply the following: (1) it is a personalized and reciprocal, although necessarily asymmetrical, relationship between two individuals; (2) the greater party, the patron, imposes the conditions under which resources, goods and/or assistance will be exchanged with the lesser party, the client; and (3) there is no institutionalized set of rules external to the dyadic relationship telling the parties how to behave, but rather expectations of behavior, probably due to the structural fragility of patronage bonds.[51]

Departing now from this brief characterization, we certainly find traces of patron–client bonds in both Hittite and Assyrian treaties, usually interpreted as reflecting vassalage: in both cases, it is imposed "from above" a particular mode of sociopolitical bonding; in both cases, a set of asymmetrical reciprocal exchanges are accorded, mostly favoring the superior party; in both cases, the superior party—having the monopoly of coercion in the relationship[52]—governs the whole political situation. Thus, Hittite or Assyrian treaties should not be considered the ultimate "legal" warrant of a situation, enforcing strict political subordination, but rather its celebration, that is, *the enhancement of the effective control over the subjected party in symbolic and ideological terms*.[53] As stated above, patronage relations are not institutionalized in society and, therefore, the presence of written treaties connoting patronage bonds would appear prima facie paradoxical. Nonetheless, if we stress the celebrative and performative aspects of treaties, rather than their supposedly prescriptive or normative status with respect to sociopolitical practice, this problem is solved effectively. The treaty is then to be seen as an ideological component of material rule over a defeated king, with a symbolic impact as important as the profane and material factors articulating the subordination of the defeated king. The treaty seems in effect to be the symbolic means by which a great king expresses his effective (ontological) rule and supremacy over foreign and conquered polities embodied in the subordinated lesser kings.[54]

Finally, Hittite and Assyrian rule represented kind of monopoly of coercion over their conquered territory. However, these great polities chose or needed to carry out their rule through treaties, imposing what may be named "forced patronage"—forced indeed, since a regular or standard patron–client relation requires some degree of consent by the client—probably as a strategic means to assure the periphery of their

---

51. Once again, as the bibliography on the subject is rather vast. I refer only to Roniger 1983 for the sake of convenience (further bibliography and discussion is to be found in Westbrook 2005; and especially in Pfoh 2016, 123–37).

52. Weber (1978, 54) considers the "monopoly of the legitimate use of physical force" as the key element in defining a state. I rather use the concept of monopoly of coercion in this context to characterize the ultimate factor that exerts political order in society.

53. When discussing feudalism and symbolism, the extraordinary study by Jacques Le Goff on the symbolic ritual of vassalage comes immediately to mind (1976). Yet again, one should not hasten to make analogies between the ancient Near East and European realities in the Middle Age. As noted, the medieval ritual of vassalage was performed by two free men "where one man places his clasped hands between the hands of another as a gesture of submission, and declares himself to be the 'man' of the person facing him, and they kiss each other on the mouth in a gesture of friendship [cf. Bloch 1961, 145–46]. From everything we know as Hittitologists, such a scene would be entirely alien to Hittite culture and completely insufficient as a contract between the king and his vassal, which had to be defined and then sworn before the assembled gods" (Burgin 2016, 44 n. 90).

54. See Pfoh 2016, 115.

kingdoms with buffer-polities, lowering considerably the logistical and operative costs of the material means of dominion (both in people and resources) and defense of the territory. But beyond the reasons offered for the use of treaties and oaths in the rule of conquered lands in Syria-Palestine,[55] I may propose that the recognition of a certain political autonomy—though considerably restricted—for the local small kingdoms in the case of Hittite and Assyrian rule reveals a particular expression of political behavior, one that inscribed subordination precisely under the rules of *patron–client relationships*; in other words, this relationship expressed subordination in the form of *political clientelism* rather than vassalage. In this view, and from an ancient Southwest Asian native perspective, terms like ÌR or *'bd* in treaties and epistolography of inter-polity relationships during the second and first millennia BCE, but also on texts dealing with internal affairs of a kingdom, should be read as expressing certainly political servitude and personal submission in the sense of clientage.[56] This, of course, does not necessarily mean that "client" is the first and only meaning of ÌR and *'bd*, but instead that, in certain contexts, it is in fact a more appropriate meaning for denoting political subordination—and it is certainly a much more appropriate rendition than "vassal."

Conclusion

All historiography is the product of its own time, as it is usually stated. Feudalism and vassalage were concepts already at hand for twentieth-century Assyriology—especially during the first half of the century—easily available from medieval studies, and rapidly useful for assessing the vast amount of empirical data coming from excavations and its deciphering in the late nineteenth and early twentieth centuries. The urgent necessity to incorporate such an amount of textual information resulted in a detriment to the proper theoretical development on political theory in Assyriological historiography until the 1960s.[57] Since then, however, social and cultural anthropology and sociology, comparative history and ethnography, together with other social scientific approaches, have broadened the field in order to reach a better and more precise knowledge about ancient Southwest Asian societies and their native worldviews.[58] We should look at the notable efforts of our predecessors in this light, to attempt a correct understanding of economic and political subordination in ancient Southwest Asia and its representation in twentieth-century ancient Near Eastern historiography. In this light also, it is the duty of younger generations not to perpetuate the misconceptions of our elders. Thus, the use of adjectives and concepts like "feudal/feudalism," "vassal state/kingdom," or "vassalage" in ancient Near Eastern studies, if undefined or

55. On treaties and oaths in the ancient Near East, see for instance the now classic perspectives in Weinfeld 1976, McCarthy 1978, and Tadmor 1982. Cf. also Liverani 1990 and Zaccagnini 1990. I am aware of more recent treatments on the topic, but these older studies are especially relevant for thinking about patronage and other forms of political subordination or submission.

56. See further the thorough terminological discussion on slave, servant, vassal, and client in Loretz 2003, who unfortunately does not appeal to any insights from sociological or anthropological research.

57. A question already tackled in Liverani 1966.

58. See Kramer 1962 (which, in spite of the article's title, has little of proper cultural anthropology in it—at least not in the professional fashion of the discipline); and especially the pioneering insights in Gelb 1967, 1980, Zaccagnini 1973, and the collected studies in Liverani 2004.

theoretically unjustified when employed, creates a serious risk of filling in the gaps in our knowledge with anachronistic situations and misleading interpretations. A change in terminology, or better, a precise and conscious deployment of well-crafted and explicit analytical models and concepts, implies then a redefinition of the studied data and a new—hopefully, better—understanding of the economic, political, and social circumstances at different periods of the history of the ancient Near East/Southwest Asia.

REFERENCES

Alt, A. 1953a. *Kleine Schriften zur Geschichte des Volkes Israel.* Vol. 1. Edited by M. Noth. Munich: Beck.

———. 1953b. *Kleine Schriften zur Geschichte des Volkes Israel.* Vol. 2. Edited by M. Noth. Munich: Beck.

———. 1959. *Kleine Schriften zur Geschichte des Volkes Israel.* Vol. 3. Edited by M. Noth. Munich: Beck.

Altman, A. 2008. "Hittite Imperialism in Perspective: The Hittite and the Roman Treatment of Subordinate States Compared." Pages 377–96 in *Ḫattuša—Boğazköy. Das Hethiterreich im Spannungsfeld des Alten Orients. 6. Internationales Colloquium der Deutschen Orient-Gesellschaft 22.–24. Marz 2006, Würzburg.* Edited by G. Wilhelm. Wiesbaden: Harrassowitz.

Archi, A. 1977. "Il 'feudalesimo' ittita." *Studi Micenei ed Egeo-Anatolici* 18:7–18.

Bloch, M. 1961. *Feudal Society, I: The Growth of Ties of Dependency.* London: Routledge.

———. 1962. *Feudal Society, II: Social Classes and Political Organization.* London: Routledge.

Blok, A. 1969. "Variations in Patronage." *Sociologische Gids* 16:365–78.

Boutruche, R. 1968. *Seigneurie et féodalité. Le premier âge: Les liens d'homme à homme.* 2nd ed. Paris: Aubier.

Brundage, B. C. 1956. "Feudalism in Ancient Mesopotamia and Iran." Pages 93–119 in *Feudalism in History.* Edited by R. Coulborn. Princeton: Princeton University Press.

Buccellati, G. 1967. *Cities and Nations of Ancient Syria: An Essay on Political Institutions with Special Reference to the Israelite Kingdoms.* Studi Semitici 92. Rome: Istituto di Studi del Vicino Oriente, Università di Roma.

Burgin, J. M. 2016. "Aspects of Religious Administration in the Hittite Late New Kingdom." PhD diss., University of Chicago.

Cahen, C. 1960. "Au seuil de la troisième année: Réflexions sur l'usage du mot de 'féodalité.' À propos d'une livre récent." *Journal of the Economic and Social History of the Orient* 3:2–20.

Cardascia, G. 1983. "Lehnwesen. B. In der Perzerzeit." Pages 547–50 in *Reallexikon der Assyriologie.* Vol. 6. Edited by E. Weidner and W. von Soden. Berlin: de Gruyter.

———. 1995. "Le fief dans la Babylonie achéménide." Pages 59–84 in *Hommage à Guillaume Cardascia.* Edited by S. Lafont. Nanterre: Université Paris X—Nanterre.

Cornelius, F. 1972. "Das Hethiterreich als Feudalstaat." Pages 31–34 in *Gesellschaftsklassen im Alten Zweistromland und in den angrenzenden Gebieten; XVIII. Rencontre assyriologique internationale, München, 29. Juni bis 3. Juli 1970.* Edited by D. O. Edzard. Munich: Akademie der Wissenschaften.

Coulborn, R. 1956. "A Comparative Study of Feudalism." Pages 185–420 in *Feudalism in History.* Edited by R. Coulborn. Princeton: Princeton University Press.

Devecchi, E. 2015. *Trattati internazionali ittiti.* TVOA 4. Brescia: Paideia.

Durand, J.-M. 1997. *Les documents épistolaires du palais de Mari.* Vol. 1. LAPO 16. Paris: Éditions du Cerf.

188   Emanuel Pfoh

Ebeling, E. 1971. "Feudalismus." Pages 54–55 in *Reallexikon der Assyriologie*. Vol. 3. Edited by E. Weidner and W. von Soden. Berlin: de Gruyter.

Engels, D. 2011. "Middle Eastern 'Feudalism' and Seleucid Dissolution." Pages 19–36 in *Seleucid Dissolution. The Sinking of the Anchor*. Edited by K. Erickson and G. Ramsay. Wiesbaden: Harrassowitz.

Garelli, P. 1967. "Le problème de la 'féodalité' assyrienne du XVe au XIIe siècle av. J.-C." *Semitica* 17:5–21.

Gelb. I. J. 1967. "Approaches to the Study of Ancient Society." *Journal of the American Oriental Society* 87:1–8.

———. 1980. "Comparative Method in the Study of the Society and Economy of the Ancient Near East." *Rocznik Orientalistyczny* 41:29–36.

Goetze, A. 1957. *Kleinasien*. Handbuch der Altertumswissenschaft 3.1.3. 2nd rev. ed. Edited by A. Alt et al. Munich: Beck.

Gottwald, N. K. 1979. *The Tribes of Yahweh: A Sociology of the Religion of Liberated Israel, 1250–1050 B.C.E.* Maryknoll, NY: Orbis.

Haase, R. 1968. "Herrscher und Beherrschte im Hatti-Reich." *Recueils de la Société Jean Bodin* 23:87–100.

Holloway, S. W. 2002. *Aššur is King! Aššur is King! Religion in the Exercise of Power in the Neo-Assyrian Empire*. Culture and History of the Ancient Near East 10. Leiden: Brill.

Imparati, F. 1982. "Aspects de l'organisation de l'État Hittite dans les documents juridiques et administratifs." *Journal of the Economic and Social History of the Orient* 25:225–67.

———. 1983. "Lehnwesen s. a. Feudalismus, *ilku*. A. Bei den Hethitern." Pages 543–47 in *Reallexikon der Assyriologie*. Vol. 6. Edited by E. Weidner and W. von Soden. Berlin: de Gruyter.

Johne, K.-P. 2015. "Klienten, Klientenstaaten und Klientenkönige bei den Germanen." Pages 225–42 in *Amici—socii—clientes? Abhängige Herrschaft im Imperium Romanum*. Berlin Studies of the Ancient World 31. Edited by E. Baltrusch and J. Wilker. Berlin: Edition Topoi.

Kramer, S. N. 1962. "Cultural Anthropology and the Cuneiform Documents." *Ethnology* 1:299–314.

Lafont, S. 1998. "Fief et féodalité dans le Proche-Orient ancien." Pages 517–630 in *Les féodalités*. Edited by E. Bournazel and J.-P. Poly. Paris: Presses Universitaires de France.

Le Goff, J. 1976. "Le rituel symbolique de la vassalité." Pages 679–788 in *Simboli e Simbologia nell'Alto Medioevo*. Settimane di studio del Centro italiano di studi sull'alto Medioevo 23. Spoleto: Centro Italiano di Studi sull'Alto Medioevo.

Lewy, H. 1942. "The Nuzian Feudal System." *Orientalia* NS 11:1–40, 209–50, 297–349.

Liverani, M. 1966. "Problemi e indirizzi degli studi storici sul Vicino Oriente antico." *Cultura e scuola* 5:72–79.

———. 1990. "Terminologia e ideologia del patto nelle iscrizioni reali assire." Pages 113–147 in *I trattati nel mondo antico: Forma, ideologia, funzione*. Edited by L. Canfora, M. Liverani, and C. Zaccagnini. Roma: L'Erma di Bretschneider.

———. 2004. *Myth and Politics in Ancient Near Eastern Historiography*. Studies in Egyptology and the Ancient Near East. London: Equinox.

Loretz, O. 2003. "Ugaritisch *ʿbd* 'Sklave, Diener, Vasall': Eine Studie zu ug.-he. *ʿbd ʾlm* ‖ *bn ʾmt* (KTU 1.14 III 22-32a et par.) in der juridischen Terminologie altorientalischer Verträge." *Ugarit Forschungen* 35:333–84.

Mączak, A., ed. 1988. *Klientelsysteme im Europa der Frühen Neuzeit*. Munich: Oldenbourg.

Maidman, M. P. 2010. *Nuzi Texts and Their Uses as Historical Evidence*. Atlanta: SBL.

McCarthy, D. J. 1978. *Treaty and Covenant: A Study in Form in the Ancient Oriental Documents and in the Old Testament*. 2nd ed. Analecta Biblica 21a. Rome: Biblical Institute Press.

Montgomery, J. D. 2007. "The Structure of Norms and Relations in Patronage Systems." *Social Networks* 29:565–84.

Pfeiffer, R. H. 1922. "On Babylonian-Assyrian Feudalism (*ilku*)." *The American Journal of Semitic Languages and Literatures* 39:66–68.

Pfoh, E. 2009. "Some Remarks on Patronage in Syria-Palestine during the Late Bronze Age." *Journal of the Economic and Social History of the Orient* 52:363–81.

———. 2013. "Loyal Servants of the King: A Political Anthropology of Subordination in Syria-Palestine (ca. 1600–600 BCE)." *Palamedes: A Journal of Ancient History* 8:25–41.

———. 2016. *Syria-Palestine in the Late Bronze Age: An Anthropology of Politics and Power*. Copenhagen International Seminar. London: Routledge.

Pirenne, J. 1936. "La féodalité en Égypte." *Revue de l'Institut de Sociologie* 16:15–36.

Rich, J. 1989. "Patronage and Interstate Relations in the Roman Republic." Pages 117–35 in *Patronage in Ancient Society*. Edited by A. Wallace-Hadrill. London: Routledge.

Roniger, L. 1983. "Modern Patron–Client Relations and Historical Clientelism: Some Clues from Ancient Republican Rome." *European Journal of Sociology* 24:63–95.

Scheffler, T. 2003. "'Fertile Crescent,' 'Orient,' 'Middle East': The Changing Mental Maps of Southwest Asia." *European Review of History* 10:253–72.

Schloen, J. D. 2001. *The House of the Father as Fact and Symbol: Patrimonialism in Ugarit and the Ancient Near East*. Studies in the Archaeology and History of the Levant 2. Winona Lake: Eisenbrauns.

Sommerfeld, W. 1995. "Der babylonische 'Feudalismus.'" Pages 467–90 in *Vom alten Orient zum Alten Testament*. Alter Orient und Altes Testament 240. Edited by M. Dietrich and O. Loretz. Neukirchen-Vluyn: Neukirchener.

Strayer, J. R., and R. Coulborn. 1956. "The Idea of Feudalism." Pages 3–11 in *Feudalism in History*. Edited by R. Coulborn. Princeton: Princeton University Press.

Tadmor, H. 1982. "Treaty and Oath in the Ancient Near East: A Historian's Approach." Pages 127–52 in *Humanizing America's Iconic Book*. Edited by G. M. Tucker and D.A. Knight. Chico: Scholars Press.

Weber, M. 1978. *Economy and Society: An Outline of Interpretive Sociology*. Edited by G. Roth and C. Wittich. Berkeley: The University of California Press.

Weinfeld, M. 1976. "The Loyalty Oath in the Ancient Near East." *Ugarit Forschungen* 8:379–414.

Westbrook, R. 2005. "Patronage in the Ancient Near East." *Journal of the Economic and Social History of the Orient* 48:210–33.

Widengren, G. 1969. *Der Feudalismus in alten Iran. Männerbund—Gefolgswesen—Feudalismus in der iranischen Gesellschaft im Hinblick auf die indogermanischen Verhältnisse*. Cologne: Westdeutscher Verlag.

Zaccagnini, C. 1973. *Lo scambio dei doni nel Vicino Oriente durante i secoli XV–XIII*. Orientis Antiqvi Collectio 11. Roma: Centro per le Antichità e la Storia dell'Arte del Vicino Oriente.

———. 1981. "Modo di produzione asiatico e Vicino Oriente antico. Appunti per una discussione." *Dialoghi di archeologia* NS 3:3–65.

———. 1990. "The Forms of Alliance and Subjugation in the Near East of the Late Bronze Age." Pages 37–79 in *I trattati nel mondo antico: Forma, ideologia, funzione*. Edited by L. Canfora, M. Liverani, and C. Zaccagnini. Roma: L'Erma di Bretschneider.

CHAPTER 9

Nation Building in the Plain of Antioch from Hatti to Hatay

Eva von Dassow

THE ANCIENT PAST SERVES both as a screen on which to project the ideas and preoccupations of the present and as a repository of material to support present day claims. One of the ideas that motivated much of twentieth-century history is the concept of an organic unity conjoining race, culture, and political aspirations, so that all persons and populations may be defined and classified under the sign of an identity cast in such terms. This concept has been deployed as an organizing principle of the nation-state, as grounds for allocating territory to people or removing people from it, for programs euphemistically termed ethnic cleansing, and, above all, for sorting people into racial categories. The same ideology was applied to the past: it supplied an all-purpose conceptual framework for explaining ancient history, just as it did for justifying modern political decisions. Thus, the history of the ancient Near East, which was being unearthed during the very period this ideology developed, came to be told as a story of distinct peoples. They were called races before that word acquired negative connotations, and nations before that word came to be associated more with the state than with genealogy, and they were usually labeled according to languages. For language was the only means of identification ready to hand in ancient texts, and languages were imagined to correspond to races of men.

These putative ancient peoples—the Sumerians, Akkadians, Amorites, Hittites, and so forth—were construed as collective historical actors, and to each were ascribed not only shared ancestry and a language but qualities of mind and character, a "spirit" inherited along with a physical type that might be identified in skeletal remains. Homelands have been sought for them, too, geographical points of origin for these hypothetical transhistorical descent groups. Their migrations, actions, and interactions have been posited as the mechanisms of historical and cultural change.[1] Their presence is detected in ceramics, burial practices, and every other material trace of cultural practice, as well as in the languages of writing and in onomastica. Yet all of these phenomena depend on factors that have nothing to do with race or biological identity. Notwithstanding the invalidity of every element of the conceptual framework just outlined, it has not been banished from scholarship; on the contrary, it still furnishes

---

1. To give but one example of this mode of historiography, Albrecht Götze (1936) relates ancient Near Eastern history as a succession of peoples: first Sumerians, then Semites, subdivided into Amorites, Babylonians ("bekannt als Beispiel des homo oeconomicus"; 1936, 3), and Assyrians, whose distinct trajectory is explained by the infusion of "Indogermanen," specifically Hittites in the west and Hurrians, ruled by Aryans, in the east (1936, 29–33). On peoples as collective historical actors, or "characters in historiographical narratives," see now Wiedemann 2017 (published after this article was written).

190

the armature of our discourse about the ancient world, albeit the notion of race has been replaced by more permeable analytic categories.

Since its discovery in the 1930s, Alalakh has played a prominent role in constructing racialized narratives of ancient Near Eastern history. This mode of historiography climaxed with the identification in the Alalakh tablets of a handful of Indo-Aryan names and words, in particular the Hurrianized word *maryanni* that was adopted to denote nobility, data that were rapidly deployed in the invention of a master race that was imagined to have swept into the Near East upon horse-drawn chariots, founding the kingdom of Mittani and imposing its dominion on a passive mass of Hurrians and Semites. The Aryan myth lives on to this day, albeit drained of the concept of "blood" in most of its present hypostases.[2] Less pernicious, but arising from the same conceptual ground, is the search to determine the composition of the population of a place based on the personal names attested in the texts found there. Ann Draffkorn Kilmer's 1959 dissertation, "Hurrians and Hurrian at Alalakh," is an example of this line of inquiry. Hers is one of a cluster of onomastic studies produced in the mid-twentieth century, all animated by the same guiding idea: a philological approach that posits language as a proxy for ethnicity. This idea represents the intellectual offspring of racial essentialism that survived the overt disavowal of race as the basis of social and political domination. The problem inherent in such studies becomes evident in Emmanuel Laroche's prefatory remarks to his 1966 work, *Les noms des Hittites*. Laroche recognizes that people and their languages mix, yet he nevertheless seems to imagine that if it were possible to recover a state prior to mixing, one would find pure populations marked by their language as if by DNA. The governing idea is revealed in his closing question: he asks, "who were the aboriginal people established in northern and central Mesopotamia before the Semitic invasion,"[3] as if Semitic were a species of humans rather than a family of languages!

Building Nations

It is self-evident that language is acquired, not inherited, and a moment's consideration yields the observation that many factors motivate the choice of names. Derivation from the name-users' language may not even be the default option (as the naming practices of English speakers demonstrate). Anthropological research, moreover, shows that language may relate to heritable group membership in a variety of ways, that ethnicity is elective—even tribe membership is elective—and that such group identities are deliberately created, reproduced, and altered, far from being simply hereditary and immutable.[4] Yet in ancient Near Eastern studies, the notion of language as the identifying mark of a distinct people has persisted in the ongoing endeavor to

---

2. On the Aryan myth, see the book by that title by Léon Poliakov (1971), who describes the sources and historical development of this ideology. On the rise and progress of the Aryan myth in ancient Near Eastern studies (apparently unknown to Poliakov), see von Dassow 2008, 68–90, esp. 77–81, focusing on the use of data drawn from the Alalakh tablets.

3. Laroche 1966, 16.

4. On these issues see Kamp and Yoffee 1980, esp. 87–88 and 95–96, and von Dassow 2008, 69, with references cited there.

map ethnicities onto time and space using the languages of people's names and texts as proxies for their putative identities. The assumptions underlying this approach operate in a double sense on the study of the past in the present tense.

First, although we no longer speak of race, we continue to describe the past in terms of distinct peoples who acted in history and who may be detected in its archaeological remains. At Tell Atchana, for example, the material culture and textual records suggest to us a society at the intersection of cultures, mirroring the city's position betwixt great kingdoms, at the nexus of routes leading from mountains to plains and interior to sea.[5] In the texts found at the site, we seek people's identity through language, in the artifacts through form and style. Language in writing and the languages of names are treated as trace markers of ethnic identity, political affiliation, and cultural affinity, yielding an image of a polyglot realm where speakers of Hurrian, Semitic, Indo-Aryan, and Anatolian languages mingled, layering putatively distinct populations into the society of Alalakh as they layered elements of distinct languages into the texts produced there. Today's preferred concepts of cultural hybridity and diversity only seem to transcend the essentialism of an earlier day, inasmuch as they depend on the assumption that prior to miscegenation people formed a taxonomy of discrete genera. Too seldom is the question asked whether the ancient people who are the subjects of our studies identified themselves by the labels we assign them. Did the people of Alalakh, for example, conceptualize their identity as we do, in terms of the languages of their onomastica and analogous features of their material culture? The texts found there give no reason to believe that they did.

Second, the remains of ancient cultures are claimed as the heritage of modern nation-states. This strategy was pioneered by colonial powers in the Middle East. The ideological tools employed to create the nation-states of Europe were imported to the Orient: the identification of race with nation as the basis for sovereignty and communal self-determination; the attribution of territory to nations on the basis of putative historical rights; the idea that language was key to nationality, thus to reifying political claims—these misbegotten spawn of Enlightenment rationalism were carried aboard the project of modernization to the Ottoman Empire.[6] There, inasmuch as the idea of freedom took the form of national liberation, it required the creation of nations. Where races had not been before, they had to be constructed, using language, physiognomy, religion, or whatever other features were available, and historical lineages had to be found for them. Those who had never known an ethnic identity had to acquire one. In order to constitute states free of European domination it was necessary to mimic Europe, not only by adopting the paraphernalia of modernity, but above all by imagining into existence entities that could both command people's allegiance and form the basis for asserting political and territorial claims. These ideas influenced Mustafa Kemal before he became Atatürk, and they proved their value for the project of building

---

5. See for example Yener 2013, 12 and 2014, 63.

6. The genealogy of these ideas, the paths they took into the Ottoman world, and the ways they developed to form Turkish nationalism are outlined by Michel Gilquin in his history of the Sanjak of Alexandretta's transformation into the province of Hatay (Gilquin 2000, esp. 26–27, 33–34, and 44–49), and by Andrew Mango in his biography of Atatürk (2002; his discussion of these issues is diffused throughout the book, e.g., 2, 9, 40, 65, 75, 96, and 210–11). Both authors remark on how deeply out of accord with the pluralism of Ottoman society the new European ideology was.

a nation.[7] History, as well as people, territory, and language, had to be refashioned accordingly. The quest for a secular identity rooted in the territory of the new nation led to inventing "une turquité nouvelle, mythique, cherchant ses racines en Anatolie, chez les Hittites en particulier," as Michel Gilquin observes.[8] In 1931, Mustafa Kemal charged the nascent Turkish Historical Society with writing a new history that would account for all the nameable populations that had in the past inhabited territory that was now Turkey's, retroactively adopting Hittites, Phrygians, even Sumerians—anyone who had once lived in lands that came within the orbit of Ottoman rule—as Turkish forebears.[9] Thus, archaeological remains too served to support the Republic of Turkey's political claims at a time when those claims were still new and still under threat.

The ideology of Turkish nationalism that developed in the early twentieth century accorded fully with that propounded by European powers (and would-be masters of erstwhile Ottoman lands), who envisioned a future Middle East consisting of homogeneous nation-states defined according to racial, linguistic, and sectarian criteria—like their vision of Europe.[10] This vision entailed imagining a past along the same lines. Just as there should once have been an Indo-European homeland before the carriers of Indo-European languages spread over the continents, there should once have been a Slavic homeland and heritable identity, and a Turkic one likewise, anchored in land, language, and heritage.[11] Just as there should once have been an Israel defined by genealogy, to whom God granted an ideal territory, there should likewise have been an Assyria, inhabited by an Assyrian people endowed with martial vigor and a will to dominate like the imaginary Aryans with whom some Orientalists wished to identify them.[12] And there should likewise have been a distinct Hittite population, an offshoot of the supposed Indo-European one, endowed with social and spiritual traits and recognizable on the ground by the material and linguistic artifacts of their presence.

7. Mango (2002, esp. chapter 2) describes the stages of education and career during which Mustafa Kemal and his cohort became acquainted with European rationalism and nationalism.

8. Gilquin 2000, 46.

9. This historiographic endeavor is discussed by Mango (2002, 493–94) in a chapter that explains how the scientific racism of the early twentieth century influenced the writing of Turkish history, and by Cagaptay (2006, 48–54), who describes the racial and linguistic contents of the Turkish history thesis, with ample quotations from its proponents. Its initial application to the ancient past is represented in a speech given by Avram Galanti at the first meeting of the Turkish Historical Society, the proceedings of which were published in 1933, in which he itemizes peoples of the ancient Near East, mentioning their supposed racial descent and affiliation of their languages, citing the work of Leonard Woolley among others. I thank Wesley Lummus, graduate student in the Department of History at the University of Minnesota, for providing me the reference to Galanti's speech and making an English translation of it, as well as for the reference to Mango's biography of Atatürk.

10. Gilquin (2000, 45–46) comments that the 1920 Treaty of Sèvres (which required the government in Istanbul to renounce all non-Turkish territories, thus making it necessary to define what was a Turkish territory) revealed "une certaine vision du monde, d'États-nations à population relativement homogène, comme seule issue à la 'question d'Orient'"; in the course of war, Mustafa Kemal came to adopt "cette conception homogenéisante et jacobine de la nation, issue de la Révolution française."

11. See Mango 2002, 494–96 for an outline of how theories linking homeland and migration to language and race were transposed from the Indo-European to the Turkish language families, and of the historical context that generated such "wayward product[s] of rationalism" as the new Turkish historiography and the "Sun-Language Theory." As Mango puts it, "linguistic engineering reflected cultural engineering" (p. 494).

12. The idea that Assyrians were (part) Aryan was propounded by Wolfram von Soden (1937, esp. 23–27), as well as Götze (1936; see above, n. 1), to name two. Through a similar application of racial genealogy Jesus of Nazareth had already been made Aryan by Friedrich Delitzsch and his disciples, who indirectly included Adolf Hitler; see Vidal 2015, 74–77.

194   Eva von Dassow

From Hatti to Hatay in the Plain of Antioch

Even before its ancient name was known, Alalakh was enlisted in the project of inscribing national identities onto the past. In 1935 Leonard Woolley arrived in the Sanjak of Alexandretta seeking a site to excavate in the midst of political competition between Britain and France, as mandatory powers, and the republic of Turkey. Woolley came to this region, he said, in search of evidence for interactions linking the Aegean and the Near East. He first excavated at coastal sites, where he saw Greek presence in the pottery finds; then he fixed on Tell Atchana, where the loveliest local pottery spoke to him of Minoan influence.[13] So the site already provided the kind of evidence he sought. To back up his interpretation, he adduced a legend recorded by the early Byzantine chronicler John Malalas, according to which the Greek hero Kasios founded a town on the coast, "peopled it with Cretans and Cypriotes," and married the local princess Amyke (= Amuq): Tell Sheikh Yusuf on the coast must be the town Kasios founded, for there (based on the pottery) "we have found the Cypriotes and suspect the Cretans," and at Atchana "we have found the Cretans."[14] Woolley found these Cretans in the Minoan features he saw in Atchana ware, the painted pottery that he recognized as a local variety of Nuzi ware and identified as "Hurrian." Meanwhile, excavations at Atchana revealed construction methods that he considered Hittite, as well as yielding seals and impressions of seals inscribed in what were then known as Hittite hieroglyphs.[15] These discoveries proved to Woolley the Hittite character of the place, while also proving its Aegean connections. Having begun to excavate the Level IV palace, he described it as "the earliest Hittite building yet known to us—that it should properly be called Hittite is, I think, proved by its resemblance in every point of construction and technique to the Hittite buildings of a later date—and it is interesting to observe how closely allied it is to the Cretan buildings of the Minoan Age."[16] The Amuq was, after all, thought to have been called Hattina in the Neo-Assyrian period (when the Assyrians called all the lands west of the Euphrates Hatti); only decades later was this reading corrected to Patin, a name that may derive from Palistin, the newly-discovered early Iron Age kingdom whose creation reflects an influx of some kind from the Aegean.[17]

---

13. See Woolley 1936b, his report on the first season of excavations at al-Mina and Tell Atchana, and also Woolley 1937, a report focusing on excavations at the coastal sites of Tell Sheikh Yusuf, Sabouni, and Al-Mina.

14. Woolley 1937, 13–14.

15. For the Hittite identity of the architecture and the Hurrian identity of Atchana ware—both (supposedly) inflected with Cretan features—and for the objects inscribed in Hittite hieroglyphs (including a strainer), see Woolley 1938, 8–11, 19–20, and 1939a, 16–19, 31–32.

16. Woolley 1938, 28. See further Woolley 1939a, 16–17 and 31–32, where he defends his application of the label "Hittite." It is worth noting the terms in which he argues for it, against Sidney Smith's objection on narrowly linguistic grounds (to wit, the language written in "Hittite hieroglyphs" was not Hittite), by citing Smith's own explanation that the modern usage of "Hittite" derives from its usage in the Bible, as well as in Egyptian and Assyrian records, to refer to people originating from or residing in lands once under the rule of Hatti.

17. The correction of Hattina to Patin was made by Hawkins (1974, 81), to whom is also due the discovery of the kingdom of Palistin, based largely on inscriptions found in the temple of the storm god at Aleppo. These are published in Hawkins 2011, with discussion of the Aegean connections and the possible transformation of the name into Patin(a) (2011, 52).

But Tell Atchana also surprised Woolley with quantities of cuneiform tablets, which at that time were somewhat unexpected in Mesopotamia's western periphery, as Syria was considered to be. The tablets made known that the city's ancient name was Alalakh and its territory was Mukiš. This made it possible to integrate the site into the history of the ancient Near East, in particular the history of Hatti, for Suppiluliuma I had subjugated Mukish in the course of conquering Mittani, and centuries before that, Hattusili I had destroyed Alalakh in the course of extinguishing the great kingship exercised by Aleppo.[18] Texts helped Woolley construct tales (sometimes fanciful) about the archaeological remains, which he labeled with the designation of the people to whom he attributed them; these designations usually referred to language, while his attributions were usually based on features of material culture. Thus strata, structures, and finds acquired Hittite identity, or Hurrian, Minoan, or even Egyptian identity.[19] (Egyptian rule of the city at one time or another could not but be assumed as fact, notwithstanding that evidence suggesting any such thing is exiguous.) Yet the tablets were written by and about people who mostly bore Semitic and Hurrian names, and very few Hittite ones (while they did not attest Egyptian rule at all).

In the meantime, while excavations at Alalakh progressed, negotiations were underway over the political status of the Sanjak of Alexandretta. Through a series of agreements and disputes among representatives of the mandatory powers, the nascent Turkish state, and the yet-to-be-formed Syrian one, this territory had become a political football.[20] The 1921 Ankara Agreement between France and Turkey, which was incorporated into the 1923 Treaty of Lausanne, stipulated that a "special administrative regime" should be established for the district of Alexandretta, that provision should be made for the "cultural development" of its Turkish inhabitants, and that the Turkish language should have "official recognition" (article 7).[21] This treaty stipulation was subsequently interpreted by the Turkish government as if it recognized not only the Turkish affiliation of some part of the region's population, but Turkey's interim "cession" of the territory while the frontiers of a future Syrian state remained to be determined.[22] The representatives of the future Syria and their state-in-waiting's French

18. For the history of Alalakh during the periods represented by Woolley's levels VII–IV see von Dassow 2008, 12–64. The periods represented by Woolley's levels IV–I have been reinterpreted, and the periodization revised, in accord with evidence from the current excavations under the direction of Aslıhan Yener. This evidence and the new periodization are presented in the second volume publishing the excavation results (Yener, Akar, and Horowitz, eds. 2020). See also von Dassow in press.

19. See the citations in n. 15 above, as well as Woolley's report on the 1939 season, in which he describes Yarim-Lim's palace, frescoes, and a porphyry lamp as Minoan (or Cretan) in style or manufacture (1948, 5, 14). Woolley sought Egyptian dominion over Alalakh during levels VII and V (see, e.g., 1955, 383–84, 386, 389–91, 395).

20. The political transfiguration of the Sanjak of Alexandretta into a Turkish province has been the subject of many accounts. One of the earliest is surely that of Majid Khadduri (1945), written when the events that transpired were within recent memory and composed on the basis of interviews as well as documentary sources. The story is related at greater length by Gilquin (2000), who provides the pertinent documents in appendices. Soner Cagaptay (2006, 116–21) describes the manipulation of historical identities in the service of claiming the territory for Turkey. Dilek Barlas (2014) gives what appears to represent an official Turkish account of events.

21. Quoted by Khadduri 1945, 407.

22. See the statement issued by the Turkish government in 1936 referring to "the sovereignty conditionally relinquished by Turkey over the Alexandretta and Antioch districts," and the telegram of the foreign minister Rüstü Aras referring to "the territories of Alexandretta, Antioch, and dependencies conditionally ceded by Turkey," quoted by Khadduri (1945, 412).

mandatory guardians interpreted the matter otherwise; the French foreign minister objected that "detaching from the Syrian State a Sanjak which belongs to it" would contravene France's mandatory obligations.[23] The Turkish view presumably rested on the theory that the Republic of Turkey was the natural heir to the Ottoman estate, a theory not shared by France or by the Arabs of Syria.[24] The differences of interpretation were repeatedly contested following the Lausanne treaty as the several parties' power, and their will to exercise it, waxed or waned. Among other factors, having previously won control of Cilicia, in 1926 Turkey lost Mosul to the state of Iraq then in formation.[25] The conclusion in 1936 of the Franco–Syrian Treaty, by which France's mandate would terminate and Syria would become independent, provided the occasion for Turkey to raise its claim to the Alexandretta district anew.[26]

Intent on compensating for the loss of Mosul with another win, Atatürk bent his last political energies on the acquisition of the Sanjak of Alexandretta for Turkey, and by then France and Britain were ready to concede.[27] Arab representatives of the future Syrian republic, meanwhile, were not in a position to negotiate effectively, much less to defend their claims.[28] In 1936 the Turkish government argued for the Sanjak's independence, on the premise that its inhabitants (in particular its Turkish population) should have the right to govern themselves (i.e., should not be attached to the Syrian state), against France's sound counterarguments.[29] In 1937, with the prospect of intra-European war threatening France and Britain, Turkey won from the League of Nations an agreement guaranteeing the Sanjak's independence, under an arrangement guaranteed to be unworkable: the territory would be independent, it would have no army, its foreign affairs would be in Syria's hands, and France, Turkey, and Syria would jointly undertake its defense; meanwhile Turkish would be an official language.[30] The territory would moreover have "a legislative Assem-

23. See the statement of the French foreign minister Yvon Delbos, as well as the statement of the Secretary General of the League of Nations upon referral of the dispute to that body, quoted by Khadduri (1945, 411–12).

24. Contrast the statement of Khadduri, "in order to carry out the provisions of the Ankara Agreement, the French High Commissioner in Syria issued an *arrêté* on March 4, 1923, by virtue of which the Sanjak of Alexandretta was attached to the state of Aleppo, but had its own council" (Khadduri 1945, 408), with those of Barlas: "following Lausanne, Ismet Pasha criticized the fast-changing governments of France, who had been entrusted with the administration of Hatay within Syria under their mandate, as though it was a part of it, in complete violation of the agreement"—anachronistically using Hatay to designate a territory that would not bear this name until many years later—and, "consequently, France united the Sanjak of Alexandretta with the state of Aleppo" (Barlas 2014, 23).

25. The role of Cilicia in Turkey's line of argument is evident in Foreign Minister Rüstü Aras's speech to the Council of the League of Nations in December 1936, and in the French representative's response, quoted by Khadduri 1945, 413–14. The role of Mosul is mentioned by Khadduri (1945, 406) and Barlas (2014, 25). How the dispute over Mosul was decided in favor of Iraq is described in some detail by Pursley (2015), under the subheading "Iraq and Turkey" in the second part of a two-part article. Pursley examines the fallacies and motivations involved in invoking the Sykes-Picot map to construct the narrative of "artificial states" created by European agency in Part 1, and in Part 2 she discusses how the borders of Iraq and its neighbors were actually created not by mandatory powers drawing arbitrary lines on a map but through contestation, negotiation, and strife involving the agency of local actors in spite of European wishes.

26. Khadduri 1945, 408–9; Barlas 2014, 27.

27. On Atatürk's role, see especially Mango 2002, 506–9; also Khadduri 1945, 410, 416.

28. See Khadduri 1945, 409, 418 n. 40, 420.

29. See Mango 2002, 507; Barlas 2014, 27. The arguments and counterarguments are delineated by Khadduri 1945, 411–15.

30. Khadduri 1945, 417–20; Mango 2002, 509.

Nation Building in the Plain of Antioch from Hatti to Hatay 197

bly representing the various elements of the population"; accordingly, the population was divided on partly ethnic and partly sectarian criteria for the purpose of elections, preparations for which Turkey interrupted with appeals to the League of Nations.[31] In 1938, what Turkey meant by independence became clear: when elections were at last held, they produced results indicating that since 1936 "the Turkish percentage of the population had apparently increased from about 40 percent to over 60 percent of the total," and the assembly's new president declared the territory "liberated from tyranny."[32] According to the theory of political liberty adopted from the ideology of the French Revolution, sovereignty proceeded from the people, so the population was Turkified to the requisite degree. This had been done by declaring the Arabic-speaking Nusayris (or Alawites), who constituted almost 30% of the population according to 1936 figures, to be "Eti Türkleri" (Hittite Turks, using the form Eti borrowed from French "Héthéen"), concocting a Hittite genealogy for them as well as for the territory in dispute.[33] The Sanjak of Alexandretta was recreated as the Republic of Hatay, a new name that simultaneously bespoke Hittite and Turkish identity: Hatay was said to be the territory's Neo-Hittite name, or else it derived from Khitay, the name of a Turkic population that ruled central Asia in bygone centuries (and yielded the name Cathay that Europeans once learned as a designation for China).[34] The ambiguity accords with the appropriation of Hittites as proto-Turks.

Woolley had attributed Hittite identity to Alalakh, and Alalakh to Hatti. He concluded his report on the 1938 excavation season at Tell Atchana by arguing in favor of identifying the level IV palace as Hittite, and closed with the statement, "it seems to me probable that Shubbiluliuma's conquest of North Syria in the 14th century aimed merely at forcing into the Hittite confederacy, centred on Hattushash, those Syrian city-states which, so far as one element of their population was concerned, were already and had long been Hittite."[35] With the substitution of Atatürk for Suppiluliuma, Ankara for Hattusa, and Turkish for Hittite, this sentence would describe events underway at the moment Woolley wrote. In 1939 Woolley found the statue of Idrimi, inscribed with the tale of a prince descended from the royal house of Aleppo who established himself as king at Alalakh and campaigned successfully against Hatti; by then Hatay had been annexed to Turkey.[36] The annexation has never been recognized by the Syrian state, which includes the Sanjak of Alexandretta on its map even today.

---

31. Khadduri 1945, 418–22, quotation from 418; see also Cagaptay 2006, 119–20.

32. Khadduri 1945, 422–23 n. 59; see also Mango 2002, 509, Barlas 2014, 31 n. 4. No account is given by these authors of how the proportion of Turks in the population increased; see next note.

33. The figures are given by Cagaptay (2006, 117–18, 121), who explains the measures taken to produce a Turkish majority in the region. One was to redefine the Nusayris as "Eti Türkleri": books were written claiming that the Sanjak had been Hittite and the Nusayris descended from "Alpine Hittites." Moreover, claims were made that they had spoken Turkish until their persecution by Sultan Selim II. For information on this subject I am grateful to Ilgi Gercek (personal communication).

34. Cagaptay cites Agop Dilaçar's claim that the "Sancak's name had been Hatay in the Neo-Hittite period," which, along with this author's pseudo-anthropological arguments, provided the basis for asserting that the territory and its inhabitants were Hittite, ergo Turkish (2006, 118). This claim is reflected by Khadduri 1945, 423 n. 63. However, Mango writes that Atatürk "decided to call [the territory] Hatay, after Khitai, the name of a medieval grouping of Turkic (or perhaps Mongol) tribes . . . Hatay also brought to mind the Hittites, the Turks' ancestors in Anatolia according to Atatürk's view of history" (Mango 2002, 507).

35. Woolley 1939a, 33 (reporting on the 1938 season).

36. Khadduri 1945, 423–24; cf. Barlas 2014, 33. The discovery of Idrimi's statue was first announced in Woolley 1939b.

198   Eva von Dassow

A curious footnote to the entanglement of archaeological work at Alalakh with the politics of the day is the role of Woolley's foreman Hamoudi. Hamoudi, whom Woolley held in the highest esteem, had worked with him first at Carchemish, then at Ur, and now at Atchana. In his memoir *Spadework*, Woolley relates anecdotes about how Hamoudi dealt with tensions between Arab and Turkish workmen at the site, when in 1936 the region that would soon become Hatay came to be contested between Syria and Turkey.[37] Woolley tells how on one occasion Hamoudi used clever rhetoric to defuse potential conflict between the workmen, and on another he organized them into competitive teams to get the work done, assigning Arabs to be Turks and vice versa, in a game with Hatay as the prize; both teams won. After the war, Woolley writes, Hamoudi's eldest son Yahia took over as foreman, "because his father was really too old for the work and also was a member of Parliament and had to attend the sittings," presumably referring to the parliament of the newly independent Syrian republic.[38]

Idrimi in Historiography

Woolley wove dramatic tales about Idrimi, his statue, and its discovery. Since then the story of Idrimi has been retold in virtually every treatment of the ancient Near East, for it is the only source that supplies a narrative to bridge the gap at the transition from Middle to Late Bronze Age. It has also been subjected to numerous textual and literary analyses, which tend to cast doubt on its historicity, as does the statue's archaeological context.[39] Even if it was indeed a mortuary monument set up at Idrimi's behest, the moment of its inscription was necessarily much later than all but the last of the events it records. Idrimi has thus carried the burden of speaking for the mid-second millennium, when it is uncertain whether the statue and the story even speak for him.

Recently, Jean-Marie Durand has recast Idrimi as an Amorite prince and reinterpreted the statue inscription under the influence of eighteenth-century Mari.[40] He explains every motif and every incident as an instance of Amorite practice (even if comparanda can be found across world cultures), fashioning for every word an entire scenario or an element of social order, with reference to Mariote examples (even when the sense of the text is plain without adding this layer to the tale, and even

37. Woolley 1953, 113–16.
38. Woolley 1953, 116. At this time, it cannot have been the parliament of Hatay. In his report on the 1946 season Woolley writes that he had to carry on without Hamoudi, "who, owing to trouble caused by a mistake regarding his identity, was forbidden by the Government to enter Turkey until it was too late" (1950, 1), while in his memoir it was Yahia who in 1948 could not enter the country due to "some misunderstanding about his Syrian passport" (1953, 116). Woolley's accounts do not always square with each other. I thank Nicolo Marchetti for the reference to *Spadework* and to Hamoudi serving in parliament.
39. For the history of interpretation see von Dassow 2008, 23–45 with references there.
40. Durand 2011. His reading of the text departs on many points from the treatments of previous scholars, none of whom has noticed "l'omniprésence du thème de la tribalité" that for Durand best shows "le lien entre l'époque amorrite et celle d'Idrimi" (2011, 110). Interestingly, tribalism is not one of the characteristics attributed to the people designated mar-tu or *amurrûm* according to the study of Lorenzo Verderame (2009, esp. 13–14), who critiques the scholarly construction of a persistent ethnicity under those terms, while acknowledging the emergence of Amorite identity in the early second millennium (2009, 28).

at the price of stretching the sense).[41] Durand's exegesis depends not only on reading the text through the lens of the Mari letters but on treating it as the unmediated output of its ostensible author—as if Idrimi himself chose every word and the result reflects his very thoughts. (Too hastily Durand dismisses the arguments that both the statue and its inscription postdate their subject, perhaps considerably.) Accordingly, it must have been Idrimi's idea to have this text written, initially on a tablet before eventual transfer to the statue, and his motive can be found in the penultimate lines: his entire purpose was the restoration of the cult at Alalakh and especially the rites for the ancestors, for which Durand uses the word *kispum*, as if we were still in the realm of Yamhad.[42] In his view we are, in effect. Durand justifies drawing upon the "ancient Amorite documentation" to expound the career, goals, and inscription of Idrimi by asserting that the Late Bronze Age is the latter phase of the Amorite period, which "does not really end until, with the arrival of the Aramaeans in the Near East, a new world is established at the turn of the twelfth century before our era."[43] Never mind that people who became Aramaean were likely descended from those who had been Amorite; the habit persists of attributing historical change to named populations and their movements, and periodizing the past accordingly.

While in some respects Durand's *interpretatio Amoritica* could be right, his application of it to the inscription on Idrimi's statue begs the question whether Idrimi himself, or his contemporaries, would have called him Amorite. Neither the statue inscription nor any other source identifies Idrimi by a gentilic. The same is true of his descendants; in fact, the same is true of almost all of the thousands of individuals attested in the Alalakh tablets. There is very little evidence to suggest by what gentilics any of the people who dwelt at Alalakh would have identified themselves, or how they would have been identified by their contemporaries, except for immigrants and the occasional Sutean.[44] We might like to label the people of Alalakh and periods of their history Amorite, Hurrian, Hittite, or the like, but the sources do not confirm that any of them called themselves by such ethnicons or that they were called so by others. This indicates that our ethno-linguistic categories do not apply to our subjects—that is, these categories are not valid for the region of Alalakh and its populations.

41. For example, the theme of the wanderer in quest of a new domain is "well documented in the Amorite epoch," as is that of the "good vassal" (Durand 2011, 99, 108). Membership in a *bīt abim* made one a citizen, "son of (city X)," and among citizens there were ranks, of which the "middle" rank is attested only in the Idrimi inscription (in l.11: TUR, GAL, and MURUB₄). When Idrimi's family, whose *bīt abim* was at Aleppo, took refuge with their maternal kin at Emar—their *mahraštum*, in Mariote terms—he became a *wardum* ("slave") in the proper Amorite sense of someone "descended" into another's service and not assimilated into the body politic (2011, 111–15). The fellow expatriates from Yamhad whom Idrimi met at Ammiya were "habitants," *ašbū*, meaning "un groupe sociale." Moreover, they formed a community of mercenaries, sa(g).gaz (derived from the root *šgš*), to be distinguished from *hapiru*, "exile." Surely Idrimi—whose family in Mariote terms were not *hapirū* but *halqānu*—did not have a romantic notion of sharing the life of brigands with the sa(g).gaz at Ammiya (2011, 104–5).

42. Durand 2011, 117, 127. Among elements that may raise the eyebrows of those familiar with Tell Atchana is the statement that Alalakh seems to have been an abandoned town when Idrimi chose it for his city (p. 117).

43. Durand 2011, 96.

44. For example, persons are identified by Canaanite origin in AT 48 and 181, and several texts record persons identified as Sutean (von Dassow 2008, 127 n. 80; 139–40).

What about the stories that Woolley and his successors, up to Durand and ourselves, have projected onto Alalakh? Upon examination, fissures appear between the narrative derived from sources external to Alalakh and the indigenous textual and archaeological material, fissures that are signaled by the appearance of an outside power.

The tablets found thus far at Tell Atchana were produced almost exclusively by the royal administration, and almost exclusively in two narrowly circumscribed periods, during each of which an intrusive dynasty implanted itself at Alalakh.[45] In the seventeenth century BCE Abban, king of Aleppo, installed a cadet branch of his lineage as Alalakh's ruling house, which probably went under when Hattusili I destroyed the city four generations later. Then in the fifteenth century Idrimi, claiming origins from the Aleppine royal lineage, established himself at Alalakh as king, founding a dynasty that may have ended with his grandson Ilimilimma. Before and between these two episodes, the city and the surrounding region were, on present evidence, anepigraphic. After Idrimi's dynasty or its successor gave way to Hittite conquest, the defeated city gave up writing again; the written records extant from the period of Hittite rule, few and brief though they are, pertain to the rulers and their associates. The defunct kingdom itself, now called by the name of Mukish, fades from history as if on purpose.

This pattern should shape our understanding of Alalakh's political and social history, starting with the nature of the state that was sometimes based at this city. Was Alalakh the locus of political authority in periods other than those represented by written records? What was the nature of the polity during the anepigraphic periods, and was it completely displaced by the intrusive rulers? How did the communities comprising this polity relate to the ruling authority? How would these people, the ones who made and used the pottery and burials, who built the place, and who are recorded in the tablets, have told the history they experienced? Would they perhaps have remembered the period between Hattusili's departure and Idrimi's arrival as a happy interlude of self-rule? Would they have told of their valor in the wars they fought under Idrimi's son Niqmepa? Would they have pointed with pride at the citadel they rebuilt again and again after Ilimilimma's defeat circa 1400, and regarded the fortress we have called Hittite as the monstrous memorial of an occupying power? The scarcity of legible evidence from these very people makes any answers inferential at best, but such questions must be posed nevertheless, if only to delineate the contours of what we cannot know in order to contextualize correctly what little we can.

Ideas of Genealogy and Genealogy of Ideas

To explain the past by reference to ethnic groups that did not demonstrably exist as such can only skew the story. Yet the idea that language and material culture reliably mark distinct populations, each possessing an explicit identity thus conceived, retains its hold on scholarship. To give one further example, a single phrase in an inscribed funerary stela recently found at Zincirli, ancient Sam'al, has inspired elaborate disquisitions on the ethnic composition, religious beliefs, and political history of the

---

45. The observation that the use of writing at Alalakh is correlated with the city's subordination to a foreign power is developed by van Soldt (2012, 110).

city during the Iron Age. The stela belonged to a man with a Luwian name spelled KTMW, it was inscribed alphabetically in a local Northwest Semitic language, and its text refers to "my soul (*nbš*) that is in this stela." In reporting on the discovery, David Schloen and Amir Fink assert that this phrase reflects "Hittite/Luwian (and more generally 'Indo-European') conceptions of the afterlife, in which the soul is released from the body by means of cremation," contrasting with "the traditional West Semitic conception that one's soul resides in one's bones after death."[46] The absence of human remains nearby indicates that the deceased was likely cremated, they say, and cremation was "an Indo-European practice generally regarded as abhorrent in the Semitic world"; this statement is supported only by a broad reference to the Hebrew Bible and by declaring cremation burials found in the Levant to be associated with Mittanian, Hittite, or Luwian dominion.[47] Would the inhabitants of Jabesh-Gilead then be disqualified as Semites because they cremated the bodies of Saul and his sons (1 Sam 31:11–13)? For Schloen and Fink, the transition from Luwian to Semitic writing in the region means regime change, the use of both Luwian and Semitic names by kings of Sam'al indicates the persistence of Luwian identity, and Luwian influence is manifest in the emulation of Neo-Hittite style "even by non-Luwian rulers."[48] Although they sometimes take care to specify "Luwian-speaking" or "Semitic-speaking," speech readily turns into ethnicity as they describe people, their ideas, and their possessions as Semitic, Luwian, Aramaean, or Amorite—even a rampart may be Amorite—and conclude that the evidence shows "coexistence and mutual cultural adaptation of people of diverse ethnic origins."[49] But these ethnic origins are a present-day postulate based only on the languages of names, which need not signify the name-bearers' genealogy, and on the languages of inscriptions, which may reflect the training of scribes rather than the choice of their employers. Even if one were to read "cultural" everywhere Schloen and Fink write "ethnic" or "ethnolinguistic," the interpretation they build upon the phrase "my soul that is in this stela"—since contested by other scholars—ignores the fact that it was general practice among ancient Near Eastern cultures, regardless of language, to make an image as an embodiment for a soul.[50]

46. Schloen and Fink 2009, 11. No sources are cited for these conceptions.

47. Schloen and Fink 2009. They further suggest that the deceased included the phrase at issue to inform those "unacquainted with the old Luwian traditions and theology," who might consider that "in the West Semitic tradition, cremation serves to extinguish the soul." Are the inscription's ancient or modern readers being addressed here? Cremation was not so unfamiliar to the "Semitic world," however. Tenu (2005, 40), surveying the incidence of cremation in Syria and beyond, comments on the propensity to attribute this practice to exogenous populations—Sea Peoples, Hittites, Hurrians—and suggests, based on the distribution of the evidence, that it could instead be "an Aramaean funerary practice."

48. Schloen and Fink 2009, 8. Without irony, they then admonish scholars to distinguish "Neo-Hittite as an architectural or artistic style from 'Neo-Hittite' (i.e., Luwian) political or ethnic affiliation."

49. Schloen and Fink 2009, 9. Cf. Bonatz 2014, 242; he describes funerary monuments like the stela of KTMW as "a vivid expression of the cultural symbiosis in the Aramaean and Luwian city-states." For an earlier critique of writing ethnicity into the evidence, focusing on the nature of Aramaization with particular reference to Sam'al, see von Dassow 1999. On the same subject, see most recently Tamur (2017), who focuses on the construct of "Aramaean style" in sculpture.

50. Noteworthy among treatments of KTMW's funerary inscription that revise or nuance Schloen and Fink's interpretation are those of Sanders 2012 and Hawkins 2015. Sanders interprets the text in light of Qatabanian funerary inscriptions in which *nfs* denotes "funerary monument," and emphasizes that "there is no reason to give [the key terms] ethnic significance" (2012, 26). Hawkins interprets *nbš* as a translation

More fundamentally, the idea that there exists an Indo-European concept of the soul, to be differentiated from a Semitic one, evinces the same mode of thinking that prevailed a century ago and yielded pronouncements like this one by S. A. Cook: "The Semite must personify; law and order in the Universe must be embodied in or associated with an anthropomorphic god, and Semitic anthropomorphism is sometimes of the crudest."[51] Cook and his fellow contributors to the first edition of the *Cambridge Ancient History* shared a "scientific" concept of race as the carrier of mental as well as physical character, and of racial genealogies as manifest in linguistic ones. In the same work, H. R. Hall attributes the development of Egyptian civilization to "the infiltration into Egypt from Syria of an alien race ('Armenoids'), who brought to the Nile-land a higher brain-capacity than that of the native Hamitic population," as their skulls testify. And Stephen Langdon, discussing the origins of Mesopotamian civilization, writes that "all the evidence suggests that a dolichocephalic race speaking agglutinative languages descended upon Iran, Mesopotamia and the shores of the Persian Gulf probably from the then fertile plains of central Asia before 5000 B.C. Of this race, the Sumerians ... were by far the most talented."[52] The sort of evidence he means would include skulls and skull measurements collected by Felix von Luschan in the late nineteenth century for the purpose of defining the races that inhabited western Asia in antiquity.[53] He concluded that the entire region was originally inhabited by a "hypsi-brachycephalic" race, represented by the Hittites. Then an invasion of dolichocephalic Semites commenced around 4000 BCE, followed two millennia later by xanthrochrous Nordic types exemplified by the Aryans of Mittani. To illustrate the admixture of Hittite and Semite, von Luschan presents, as if they were photographs of human specimens, sculptures he excavated at Zincirli.

Statements identifying people by cranial type sound absurd today, but the endeavor to affix cultural to biological identity continues, nowadays using the toolkit of genetics. One recent example of research on the genetics of ancient populations is a study of ancient Egyptian mummy genomes, based in part on samples from the Felix von Luschan Skull Collection, which found that, compared with modern Egyptians, the ancient population studied had closer genetic affinity to populations of the modern Levant

---

of Luwian *atri-*, "person, soul" in its denotation "likeness, image." Thus, the key phrase refers to the image of KTMW on the stela. See also Suriano 2014; Archi 2016, 38–39.

51. Cook 1923, 203. This statement appears in a section of a chapter entitled "The Semites" that treats Semitic "temperament and thought," the relation of which to language Cook discussed in the preceding section, explaining, for example, that "the Semitic languages have retained throughout all time ... their most distinctive features, and this persistence corresponds to a certain temperament which is best seen among the desert peoples. The facts have led to the theory of Arabia as the original home of the Semites and of the Arabian (Bedouin) mind as the representative of Semitic thought" (1923, 186).

52. Hall 1923, 261, 263; Langdon 1923, 364–65. R. Campbell Thompson commences the subsequent chapter, "Isin, Larsa, and Babylon," by writing of how, "if eastern Turkestan did cradle the Sumerian forerunners, it was a harsher foster-mother that brought them to adolescence. The Sumerian died out where the Semite throve" (1923, 464), and it is clear he does not mean this metaphorically. The notion of a "dynastic race" from Central Asia invading both Sumer and Egypt had a long life in scholarship, perpetuated by Gadd 1960, for example, in his contribution to a volume honoring Woolley.

53. Von Luschan 1911. His anthropometric ideas remained long in vogue. Gelb, for example, still wrote of Sumerians as "a round-headed type" in 1960 (1960, 262). Evans has recently discussed the use of craniometry in the racial classification of Sumerians, situating this practice in the development of racial science that associated physiognomic traits with moral and cultural ones (2012, 15–45).

than Africa south of the Sahara.[54] This finding is likely to inspire some consumers of the study to revive the notion that ancient Egyptian civilization was the creation of an invasive, non-African race, disregarding the historical and cultural information considered by the researchers as well as their caution against overgeneralizing from their results.[55] Another recent example is a project announced by Aaron J. Brody and Roy J. King, who open by posing the question, "who were the ancient Israelites," proposing that it can be answered by investigating their biology, i.e., the DNA of skeletal remains found in the southern Levant, along with that of present-day Jews.[56] Notwithstanding the authors' caveat regarding the uses of such research, the idea that the identity of Israel resides in Israelite chromosomes is problematic.

How then to refer to people of the past, without projecting onto them identities they might not have recognized and without construing cultural or political affinity in mock-genetic terms?[57] Gentilics like Israelite and Sumerian are after all necessary to our discourse, if we do not care to speak always in circumlocutions. One way to avoid slipping from linguistic into gentilic designations is to refer to "(language X)-speakers" (as Schloen and Fink occasionally do), when we know people used a certain language but cannot know how they identified themselves. Often, however, the evidence warrants attributing neither a particular language nor a gentilic identity to the people who produced it. We ought then to explain what we intend by an apparent gentilic, specifying for example whether Hittite is meant to refer to inhabitants of Hatti, speakers of Hittite, members of the political community constituted by the kingdom of Hatti, or what. Otherwise it is too easy to read race, by another name, into history.

Woolley participated in the racial historiography of his age, with an interesting difference. When he was about to commence excavations at Tell Atchana, he gave a lecture at the Royal Society of Arts in which he argued that the Sumerians succeeded in creating the earliest known civilization because they were "a hybrid people. No nation," he continued, "has ever done anything much so long as it was pure-blooded. That is, of course, theoretical and a dangerous theory to hold in a modern world."[58] We may want to commend Woolley for promoting miscegenation as the fount of civilization in 1936, while bearing in mind that his theory depended on the same concept of race that was the foundation of far more dangerous theories.[59] He begins his lecture by outlining how efforts to identify the Sumerian type in art foundered, and then he proceeds to identify the three races that mixed to make Sumerians

---

54. Schuenemann et al., 2017. The work was widely featured in the popular press immediately upon publication, not always with the nuance and precision of its authors.

55. Fear of Western scholars (again) depriving Egypt of its own past probably underlies the negative reaction reported by el-Aref 2017, a reaction that exhibits the conflation of cultural with genetic identity.

56. Brody and King 2015.

57. I am grateful to Lucia Mori for posing this question, when I gave a version of the present paper at the Università di Roma La Sapienza (5 February 2016).

58. Woolley 1936a, 552. For reference to this article I thank Lorenzo Verderame.

59. Should it be protested on behalf of Woolley and his contemporaries that they could hardly be faulted for holding the ideas current in their day, it must be noted that the fallacy of these very ideas was exposed at that very time by Jacques Barzun, who wrote *Race: A Study in Modern Superstition* in 1937, then supplemented this work with an essay that undid racial thinking with logic while cauterizing it with the sarcasm it deserves (Barzun 1939).

by tracing their genealogy in the material culture of prehistoric Mesopotamia and Iran. First come the makers of Ubaid pottery, who were part of "a great Asianic or Iranian cultural unit." In Mesopotamia these Ubaid people were almost wiped out by the Flood and suffered "spiritual decadence."[60] But their decline was reversed by the influx of new people of two kinds, represented by two new kinds of pottery, one from Anatolia and one from Syria. "That gives us three nations mixed together in the Euphrates valley," Woolley writes, "and we can draw out a sort of family tree of who the real Sumerians were" on the basis of both their sculpture and their skulls: examination of the skulls reveals "an astonishing mixture of cranial types," but "it is the intermediate types that predominate," and this corresponds to the sculpture, in which "the individual racial types are unmistakable," while in many instances Semitic, Sumerian, and Anatolian elements are mixed.[61] Woolley continues his demonstration by pointing to evidence of the unmixed types, in artifacts and architecture, and tracing the lines of descent through which this cultural material generated Sumerian civilization. But more research is needed, he says, to discover to what extent Sumerian art "was indebted respectively to the Caucasian and the Semite," for "we do not know what the people in Anatolia and Northern Syria were like in their early and uncontaminated state: there has not been enough excavation."[62] Indeed, perhaps the "dynamic centre for the growth of civilization" was not in Mesopotamia, but rather both east and west "may be found to have been indebted to the people of the important geographical knot on the lower Orontes."[63] So Woolley went to the Plain of Antioch to excavate one of his three races that hybridized to become Sumerians.

From Present to Past and Back

Though racism has never been extirpated, indeed it is resurgent in many countries, it is almost universally decried in academe and in the value systems modern states publicly espouse. Were we to examine our scholarship or our politics, however, we would find the premises of racial thinking still shaping interpretation and policy. The assumption that culture and character are properties of genealogically coherent populations, that they are in effect genetic attributes of human races (however classified—white and black, Jew and Aryan, Arab and Turk, Western and Middle Eastern) remains encoded in the conceptual operating system even of countries that, like the United States, are founded on the radically opposite principle of a nation as the product of elective affinity regardless of sect, language, biological heritage, or other elements of personal origin and identity. Whether or not we use the word "race," the idea that people's identity is determined by birth—not education or other factors—and that language, creed, and biological descent are the predicates of national belonging, are part of our cultural heritage. Racial science sprang from the rationalism of Western modernity. So did the notion that people's political freedom is conditional on their categorization

60. Woolley 1936a, 555.
61. Woolley 1936a, 557.
62. Woolley 1936a, 563.
63. Woolley 1936a, 564.

by nation, generating the "fantasy of ethnosectarian homogeneity as the foundation of stable statehood," as Sara Pursley puts it in her critique of the narrative of Iraq as an artificial state.[64] This was the conceptual framework that European powers attempted to impose, and native nationalists adopted, in refashioning the former Ottoman Empire against the grain of its historical pluralism. This was also the conceptual framework that was retrojected onto the ancient Oriental past. Thus, for example, Anton Moortgat asserted in 1950 that the Assyrians of the early second millennium BCE were pure-blooded, and therefore motivated to win freedom from domination by foreigners of mixed blood, and this was their first step toward realizing their ambition of world domination.[65] The logic of this kind of thinking is the logic of "ethnic cleansing"—that is, of apartheid and genocide. Pursley points out that the vision of homogeneous ethnosectarian states that Western powers tried to implement in the Middle East starting in the early twentieth century has at last begun to be realized in the twenty-first by the Islamic State and kindred movements,[66] abetted by state parties. The violence this ideology has done and continues to do in the present hardly needs mention. We can at least avoid perpetrating it on the past.

Acknowledgments

This article is based on a paper first presented at a conference celebrating the fifteenth anniversary of the Alalakh excavations under the direction of K. Aslıhan Yener, held at the new Hatay Archaeology Museum in Antakya, 10–12 June 2015. I presented a subsequent version of the paper in a seminar, "Carteggi e archivi di studiosi: lingua e razza" (4–5 February 2016), which was part of a series treating the intellectual history of ancient Near Eastern studies, organized by Agnès Garcia-Ventura and Lorenzo Verderame at the Università di Roma La Sapienza. I thank the organizers for inviting me to participate in the seminar and to contribute to the present volume. I wrote this article during my tenure of a National Endowment for the Humanities Postdoctoral Fellowship at the American Academy of Rome in 2016, and I gratefully acknowledge the support provided by this award.

REFERENCES

Archi, A. 2016. "Luwian Monumental Inscriptions and Luwians in Northern Syria." Pages 16–47 in *Audias fabulas veteres: Anatolian Studies in Honor of Jana Součková-Siegelová.* Edited by Š. Velhartická. Leiden: Brill.

64. Pursley 2015, under the subheading "Ethnosectarian Visions." In the same paragraph, Pursley observes that, "when Iraq was created after World War I, the notion that states should strive for ethnic homogeneity was a new one and far from universally accepted."

65. The rulers of the Old Assyrian state were the only ones "denen nicht fremdes Blut in den Adern floß," accordingly they were "völkisch berechtigt" to liberate Babylonian cities from the rule of Elamites and West Semites, "auch mögen sie schon . . . eine Weltherrschaft geplant haben" (Moortgat 1950, 287–88). These are among the passages cited by Larsen 1976, 65–66 in examining the history of interpretation of Ilušuma's declaration that he established the *addurārum* of the Akkadians.

66. Pursley 2015, under the subheading "Ethnosectarian Visions."

Aref, N. el-. 2017. "Not out of Africa?" *Ahram Online* 10 June 2017. http://english.ahram.org
.eg/NewsContent/9/40/270666/Heritage/Ancient-Egypt/Not-out-of-Africa.aspx (accessed
30 June 2017).

Barlas, D. 2014. "Hatay in the Early Republican Era in Turkey." Pages 20–33 in *Unutulmuş
Krallık: Antik Alalah'ta Arkeoloji ve Fotoğraf* (*The Forgotten Kingdom: Archaeology and
Photography at Ancient Alalakh*). Edited by M. Akar and H. Maloigne. Istanbul: Koç Uni-
versity Press.

Barzun, J. 1937. *Race: A Study in Modern Superstition*. New York: Harcourt, Brace and
Company.

———. 1939. "The 'Race Mind' to End Mind." Pages 144–65 in *Of Human Freedom*. Edited
by J. Barzun. Boston: Little, Brown.

Bonatz, D. 2014. "Art." Pages 205–53 in *The Aramaeans in Ancient Syria*. Edited by H. Niehr.
Leiden: Brill.

Brody, A. J., and R. J. King. 2015. "Genetics and the Archaeology of Ancient Israel."
The Ancient Near East Today 3(6). http://asorblog.org/2015/06/12/genetics-and-the
-archaeology-of-ancient-israel/ (accessed 8 July 2015).

Cagaptay, S. 2006. *Islam, Secularism, and Nationalism in Modern Turkey: Who Is a Turk?*
London: Routledge.

Cook, S. A. 1923. "The Semites." Pages 181–237 in *Cambridge Ancient History*. Vol. 1, *Egypt
and Babylonia to 1580 B.C.* 1st ed. Edited by J. B. Bury, S. A. Cook, and F. E. Adcock.
Cambridge: Cambridge University Press.

Dassow, E. von. 1999. "Text and Artifact—A Comprehensive History of the Aramaeans."
Near Eastern Archaeology 62:247–51.

Draffkorn, A. 1959. "Hurrians and Hurrian at Alalah: An Ethnolinguistic Analysis." PhD diss.,
University of Pennsylvania.

Durand, J.-M. 2011. "La fondation d'une lignée royale syrienne: La geste d'Idrimi d'Alalah."
Pages 94–150 in *Le jeune héros: Recherches sur la formation et la diffusion d'un thème
littéraire au Proche-Orient ancient.* Orbis Biblicus et Orientalis 250. Edited by
J.-M. Durand, Th. Römer, and M. Langlois. Fribourg: Academic Press.

Evans, J. M. 2012. *The Lives of Sumerian Sculpture: An Archaeology of the Early Dynastic
Temple*. Cambridge: Cambridge University Press.

Gadd, C. J. 1960. "The Spirit of Living Sacrifices in Tombs." *Iraq* 22:51–58.

Galanti, A. 1933. "Speech in the First Afternoon Session of the First Turkish Historical Congress." Pages 445–52 in *Birinci Türk Tarih Kongresi, Konferanslar Müzakere zabıtları.*
Istanbul: Devlet Matbaası.

Gelb, I. J. 1960. "Sumerians and Akkadians in their Ethno-Linguistic Relationship." *Genava*
NS 8:258–71.

Gilquin, M. 2000. *D'Antioche au Hatay: L'histoire oubliée du Sandjak d'Alexandrette*. Paris:
L'Harmattan.

Götze, A. 1936. *Hethiter, Churriter und Assyrer. Hauptlinien der vorderasiatischen Kulturentwicklung im II. Jahrtausend v. Chr. Geb.* Oslo: H. Aschehoug & Co.

Hall, H. R. 1923. "The Union of Egypt and the Old Kingdom." Pages 257–98 in *Cambridge
Ancient History*. Vol. 1, *Egypt and Babylonia to 1580 B.C.* 1st ed. Edited by J. B. Bury,
S. A. Cook, and F. E. Adcock. Cambridge: Cambridge University Press.

Hawkins, J. D. 1974. "Assyrians and Hittites." *Iraq* 36:67–83.

———. 2011. "The Inscriptions of the Aleppo Temple." *Anatolian Studies* 61:35–54.

———. 2015. "The Soul in the Stele?" Pages 49–56 in *Tradition and Innovation in the Ancient
Near East: Proceedings of the 57th Rencontre Assyriologique Internationale at Rome,
4–8 July 2011.* Edited by A. Archi. Eisenbrauns: Winona Lake.

Kamp, K., and N. Yoffee. 1980. "Ethnicity in Ancient Western Asia During the Early Second
Millennium B.C.: Archaeological Assessments and Ethnoarchaeological Prospectives."
BASOR 237:85–104.

Khadduri, M. 1945. "The Alexandretta Dispute." *American Journal of International Law*
39:406–25.

Langdon, S. H. 1923. "Early Babylonia and Its Cities." Pages 356–401 in *Cambridge Ancient History*. Vol. 1. *Egypt and Babylonia to 1580 B.C.* 1st ed. Edited by J. B. Bury, S. A. Cook, and F. E. Adcock. Cambridge: Cambridge University Press.

Laroche, E. 1966. *Les noms des Hittites*. Études linguistiques 4. Paris: Klincksieck.

Larsen, M. T. 1976. *The Old Assyrian City-state and Its Colonies*. Copenhagen: Akademisk Forlag.

Lauinger, J. 2015. *Following the Man of Yamhad: Settlement and Territory at Old Babylonian Alalah*. Culture and History of the Ancient Near East 75. Leiden: Brill.

Luschan, F. von. 1911. "The Early Inhabitants of Western Asia." *Journal of the Royal Anthropological Institute of Great Britain and Ireland* 41:221–44.

Mango, A. 2002. *Atatürk: The Biography of the Founder of Modern Turkey*. Woodstock, NY: Overlook.

Moortgat, Anton. 1950. "Geschichte Vorderasiens bis zum Hellenismus." Pages 193–505 in *Ägypten und Vorderasien im Altertum*. Edited by A. Scharff and A. Moortgat. München: Bruckmann.

Poliakov, L. 1971. *The Aryan Myth: A History of Racist and Nationalist Ideas in Europe*. Translated by E. Howard. New York: Basic Books.

Pursley, S. 2015. "'Lines Drawn on an Empty Map': Iraq's Borders and the Legend of the Artificial State (Parts 1, 2)." *Jadaliyya* 2–3, June. http://www.jadaliyya.com (accessed 8 December 2015).

Sanders, S. L. 2012. "Naming the Dead: Funerary Writing and Historical Change in the Iron Age Levant." *Maarav* 19:11–36.

Schloen, J. D., and A. S. Fink, A. S. 2009. "New Excavations at Zincirli Höyük in Turkey (Ancient Sam'al) and the Discovery of an Inscribed Mortuary Stele." *BASOR* 356:1–13.

Schuenemann, V. J. et al. 2017. "Ancient Egyptian Mummy Genomes Suggest an Increase of Sub-Saharan African Ancestry in Post-Roman Periods." *Nature Communications* 8, 15694.

Soden, W. von. 1937. *Der Aufstieg des Assyrerreichs als geschichtliches Problem*. Leipzig: Hinrichs.

Soldt, W. H. van. 2012. "Why Did They Write? On Empires and Vassals in Syria and Palestine in the Late Bronze Age." Pages 103–13 in *Theory and Practice of Knowledge Transfer: Studies in School Education in the Ancient Near East and Beyond*. Publications de l'Institut historique-archéologique néerlandais de Stamboul 121. Edited by W. S. van Egmond and W. H. van Soldt. Leiden: Nederlands Instituut voor het Nabije Oosten.

Suriano, M. J. 2014. "Breaking Bread with the Dead: Katumuwa's Stele, Hosea 9:4, and the Early History of the Soul." *Journal of the American Oriental Society* 134.3: 385–405.

Tamur, E. 2017. "Style, Ethnicity and the Archaeology of the Aramaeans: The Problem of Ethnic Markers in the Art of the Syro-Anatolian Region in the Iron Age." *Forum Kritische Archäologie* 6:1–72.

Tenu, A. 2005. "La pratique de la crémation en Syrie: Un usage marginal?" *Ktema* 30:37–46.

Thompson, R. C. 1923. "Isin, Larsa and Babylon." Pages 464–93 in *Cambridge Ancient History*. Vol. 1. *Egypt and Babylonia to 1580 B.C.* 1st ed. Edited by J. B. Bury, S. A. Cook, and F. E. Adcock. Cambridge: Cambridge University Press.

Verderame, L. 2009. "mar-tu nel III millennio: Fonti e interpretazioni." *Rivista degli studi orientali* NS 82:229–60.

Vidal, J. 2008. *State and Society in the Late Bronze Age: Alalah under the Mittani Empire*. Studies on the Civilization and Culture of Nuzi and the Hurrians 17. Bethesda: CDL Press.

———. 2015. "Adolf Hitler, Friedrich Delitzsch y el antisemitismo en los estudios bíblicos." *Historiae* 12:65–80.

———. In press. "Alalah between Mittani and Hatti." *Asia Anteriore Antica* 2.

Wiedemann, F. 2017. "The Aryans: Ideology and Historiographical Narrative Types in the Nineteenth and Early Twentieth Centuries." Pages 31–59 in *Brill's Companion to the Classics, Fascist Italy, and Nazi Germany*. Brill's Companions to Classical Reception 12. Edited by H. Roche and K. N. Demetriou. Leiden: Brill.

208   Eva von Dassow

Woolley, L. 1936a. "The Racial Elements in Sumerian Art History." *Journal of the Royal Society of Arts* 84:552–64.

———. 1936b. "Tal Atchana." *Journal of Hellenic Studies* 56:125–32.

———. 1937. "Excavations near Antioch in 1936." *Antiquaries Journal* 17:1–15.

———. 1938. "Excavations at Tal Atchana, 1937." *Antiquaries Journal* 18:1–28.

———. 1939a. "Excavations at Atchana-Alalakh, 1938." *Antiquaries Journal* 19:1–33.

———. 1939b. "A New Chapter of Hittite Sculpture Opens." *Illustrated London News* 9:28.

———. 1948. "Excavations at Atchana-Alalakh, 1939." *Antiquaries Journal* 28:1–19.

———. 1950. "Excavations at Atchana-Alalakh, 1946." *Antiquaries Journal* 30:1–21.

———. 1953. *Spadework: Adventures in Archaeology.* London: Lutterworth.

———. 1955. *Alalakh: An Account of the Excavations at Tell Atchana in the Hatay, 1937–1949.* Oxford: The Society of Antiquaries.

Yener, K. A. 2013. "New Excavations at Alalakh: The 14th–12th Centuries BC." Pages 11–35 in *Across the Border: Late Bronze-Iron Age Relations Between Syria and Anatolia.* Edited by K. A. Yener. Leuven: Peeters.

———. 2014. "Re-examining and Re-imaging the Past: The Woolley and Yener Excavations at Alalakh." Pages 46–65 in *Unutulmuş Krallık: Antik Alalah'ta Arkeoloji ve Fotoğraf* (*The Forgotten Kingdom: Archaeology and Photography at Ancient Alalakh*). Edited by M. Akar and H. Maloigne. Istanbul: Koç University Press.

Yener, K. A., M. Akar, and M. Horowitz, eds. 2020. *Tell Atchana, Alalakh.* Vol. 2, *The Late Bronze II City (2006–2010 Excavation Seasons).* Istanbul: Koç University Press.

PART III

From Our Stories to the History
of Ancient Near Eastern Studies

CHAPTER 10

The Historiography of Assyriology in Turkey: A Short Survey

Selim Ferruh Adalı and Hakan Erol

THE 2017 HOLLYWOOD FILM *Wonder Woman* stars a superhuman Amazonian woman who in one scene deciphers the enemy's coded book. The code is a mixture of Ottoman and "Sumerian" (actually Neo-Assyrian!) scripts. The fact is far from the fiction, however: cuneiform studies were not on the research agenda of Turkish scholars until the Republic of Turkey was founded. Nonetheless, antiquarian and archaeological interest in the Near East and its cuneiform artefacts is attested among the Turkish elite of the Ottoman Empire starting from the second half of the nineteenth century, especially after the discovery of Assyrian cities and the historical heartland of the Assyrian Empire in northern Iraq during the mid-to-late nineteenth century.[1] Interest in ancient history—especially Homer and the ancient Greek philosophers—did otherwise exist among members of the Ottoman elite and scholars, attested at least since the time of Mehmed II (1432–1481).[2] Their classification of world history relied on the rise and fall of dynasties and with geographical groupings before the nineteenth century. Deeper interaction with European historiography brought about attempts to classify world history according to great periods as "ancient," "medieval," and "new."[3]

Members of the Ottoman administration oversaw several European and American archaeological expeditions at sites under the sovereignty of the Ottoman State. European collectors and excavators did encounter resistance from local inhabitants when they tried to take away artefacts and monuments which had become part of their daily life.[4] The Ottoman administrative prerogative, however, was to allow European expeditions and excavations. In some cases, the officials would intervene only if there was a perceived economic factor, such as gold or silver among the antiquities.[5] Eventually, however, sensitivity grew among the Ottomans elites to try to protect antiquities against their easy extraction. The result of this sentiment, coupled with the need to have a Muslim as director of the Imperial Museum (*Müze-i Hümayun*; modern day Istanbul Archaeological Museums) during the time of Abdulhamit II (r. 1876–1909), resulted in the appointment of the polymath Osman Hamdi Bey as director of the

---

Authors' note: We are grateful to Ali Çifçi for bibliographical support and to Fahri Dikkaya for discussing Çelik's monograph. The historiographical treatment of Turkish archaeology by Tekin 2017 and the recent biography of Benno Landsberger by Vacín and Sýkorová 2018 were not available to us during the preparation of the present study.

1. Çelik 2016. For the discoveries, see Smith 1875, Larsen 1994.
2. Uslu 2015, 169–73.
3. Karateke 2013. We are grateful to Metin Atmaca for drawing attention to this work.
4. Anderson 2015.
5. Süel 2017, 139.

Istanbul Museum in 1881. The emphasis on the Islamic character of the Ottoman state under Sultan Abdülhamit II was accompanied by Ottoman reform of institutions according to European standards. Trying to modernize and equip Ottoman society in the face of Europe, the Ottoman elite wrote about and embraced ancient Greek civilization, therefore rejecting European exclusion of the Ottomans from the history of civilizations.[6] Hellenistic, Roman, and Byzantine antiquities emphasized the Ottoman Empire's connection with Europe and, therefore, their collection in the Ottoman Imperial Museum can also be seen in such a context.[7] A school, named *Asar-ı Atika Mektebi* (School of Antiquities), was planned in 1874 to train archaeologists. Its law was passed in 1875, but the plan did not materialize.[8] Bey led the collection of artefacts and initiated formal Turkish archaeological research up to 1910.[9] It was through his efforts especially that during this process a significant number of cuneiform tablets were brought to the Istanbul. The *Asar-ı Atika Nizamnamesi* (Antiquities Regulation), the first of which was promulgated in 1874, defined all antiquities within Ottoman territory as state property to be distributed among the excavator, the landowner, and the state. This led to the sharing of key corpus of cuneiform texts such as those from Assur, Nippur between the Istanbul Museum and Berlin or Philadelphia. The second regulation in 1884 prohibited all export of antiquities and placed all archaeological activities under the Ministry of Education.

The Search for Origins in Anatolia and Assyriology in Turkey: What Is the Relation?

After the World War I and following the Turkish war of liberation under the leadership of Mustafa Kemal Atatürk, the Republic of Turkey was founded in 1923. Atatürk placed great emphasis on education, which he considered a fundamental driving force in the development of Turkish society. The republic aimed at forming a modern Western society.[10] In the first decades of the newly founded republic, there was a nationwide mobilization in the field of education, as was the case in many other fields. In this context, plenty of students were sent to the European countries, available education institutions were overhauled, and new institutions were founded. The study of Assyriology and Hittitology were instituted in Turkey at this time of great mobilization.

The establishment of Assyriology and Hittitology were the result of the efforts of Atatürk, who provided refuge to Jewish and German scholars under persecution in Nazi Germany. Following the agreement on 6 July 1933 with the *Notgemeinschaft Deutscher Wissenschaftler im Ausland* (the organization formed by some of the scholars under persecution), granted by Atatürk through initial communication of Professor Albert Malche of Geneva, 1,202 scholars and artists migrated to Turkey between 1933 and 1945, including world renowned economist Fritz Neumark and pathologist Philipp

---

6. Uslu 2015, 105–7.
7. Topçuoğlu 2013, 2015, 2017; we are grateful to Oya Topçuoğlu for sharing her papers in progress.
8. Akçay 2013, 24.
9. Uslu 2015, 123–35; Eldem 2004.
10. Atakuman 2008, 216.

Schwartz.[11] Neumark wrote: "In a country which at first was alien, but soon became more and more our second homeland, my first feeling is a deep and sincere gratitude to the Turkish Republic, which offered not only shelter, but also adequate working conditions to so many German refugees, at a time when for most of us life-threatening conditions prevailed in our country of origin."[12]

The historiography of cuneiform studies in Turkey took root thanks to the initial work especially by Benno Landsberger, Hans Gustav Güterbock, and Fritz Rudolf Kraus, who, after arriving following Atatürk's acceptance of scholars into Turkey, grounded Assyriology and Hittitology in Turkey (Çığ 1988). Atatürk and the young Turkish Republic supported and facilitated their work. It is therefore critical *not* to directly connect the history of Assyriology and Hittitology in Turkey with an anachronistic view of Turkey's queries of Turkish ethnicity in ancient history, Anatolian origins and antiquity in the 1930s, and the alternative forms of Anatolianism debated in archaeology and other areas in the subsequent decades. These ideas have only indirect influence on certain aspects of cuneiform historiography in Turkey; they are not the driving factors. The same is the case with historiography in Turkey in general, which continues to focus on the Ottoman and Turkish Republic periods with texts as the primary (if not the only) source (İnalcık 2013). Turkey's political elite in the 1930s did not enforce their ideas on the foreign scholars employed in Ankara and Istanbul. Neither did they, however, shy away from trying to explore Turkish origins for the people, seeking independence in all areas of political, economic, ideological, and cultural life following the Turkish war of liberation against occupying foreign powers. In the 1930s, the new Turkish state was trying to develop its national identity in the face of denigration and cultural rejection from Europe. Looking from today's globalizing world, some of the specific attempts to view the Hittites or Sumerians as Asian migrants with possible connections to a Turkish ethnogenesis may appear outdated. Such views are best interpreted within their own early historical context, bearing in mind that even at the time major Turkish historians, such as Mehmed Fuad Köprülü, distanced themselves from these attempts. Köprülü focused on medieval Turkish history (Dressler 2017). Turkey was trying to become a modern nation—and modernity had its own Eurocentric definition in the 1920s and 1930s. It was inevitable that early twentieth-century Western diffusionist approaches to ethnic and historical origins provided the earlier models for Turkey in trying to explore its own roots.

According to these diffusionist models, civilization developed from ancient Greek and Roman civilizations and the West inherited this civilization, spreading it through the age of discoveries and industrialization. Turkey sought to assert itself within the history of civilizations and determine its place among "civilized" nations. It was believed in these decades that a revision of world history, based genuinely on discoveries and facts unbeknownst to the West that the latter would otherwise be unaware or treat with prejudice, could help Turkey in relation to its nation-building process, national unity, and its place in the international society of states. Hence, Atatürk set on a quest for historical and archaeological evidence. He himself had read several references in the late-nineteenth and early-twentieth centuries about the Sumerians and the

---

11. Çığ 1988, 211–13.
12. Neumark 1980, 19, quoted and translated in Çığ 1988, 212.

Hittites and their "Turanian" and Asian connections.[13] In the case of the Sumerians, the term "Turanian" and sometimes even "Scythian," referring to the agglutinative character of their language, was used since 1850s, especially by Rawlinson.[14]

Archaeological interpretations and explorations were carried out by the means of the Turkish Historical Institute (*Türk Tarih Kurumu*), Turkish Language Institute (*Türk Dil Kurumu*), and other scholarly platforms (Aytürk 2009). The Turkish Hearths' Committee for the Study of Turkish History (*Türk Ocakları Türk Tarihi Tetkik Heyeti*), founded in 1930 under Atatürk's instructions, produced the General Themes of Turkish History (*Türk Tarihinin Ana Hatları*) dated again 1930.[15] Members of the Committee were Afet İnan, Yusuf Akçura, and several other leading Turkish scholars. This work, and later its reduced version (General Themes of Turkish History—The Introduction Section [*Türk Tarihinin Ana Hatları—Methal Kısmı*]), suggested that the Turks were of Central Asian origin and were diffused to parts of the world because of climatic conditions in their original homeland. The same committee continued as the Society for the Study of Turkish History (*Türk Tarihini Tetkik Cemiyeti*) in 1931, later becoming the Turkish History Institute (*Türk Tarih Kurumu*) (İnan 1953). The historical thesis was accompanied by the Sun-Language Theory (*Güneş-Dil Teorisi*) that was rejected by the mid-1930s (Aytürk 2004).

The Hittites as heirs to Anatolia as a people of Asian origins were one of the possibilities investigated as to how Turkish history could relate to some of the periods before the Greeks and the Romans. As mentioned above, this was in part a reaction against the derogatory Western perception of the Turks as late comers in Anatolian history. Furthermore, however, the Turkish history thesis was an experiment designed to achieve a common national past and identity among citizens of the Turkish Republic, and here archaeology drew more attention when compared to linguistics or Near Eastern philology (Atakuman 2008). The museum of Hittite artefacts (later the Museum of Anatolian Civilizations) and other planned scientific work, like the newly excavated Hittite sites and artefacts, aimed to exhibit and promote the Hittites as one of the civilizations of Anatolia, contributing to the building of identity and belonging for the new Turkish nation-state and identity in ways also to connect modernizing Turkey to European culture (Topçuoğlu 2017). Signalling this, for example, is the naming of modern economic institutions, state sponsored corporations, as *Etibank* (i.e., Hittite bank, based on the French pronunciation of the word "Hittite" as *l'hittite* with the loss of the initial consonant in French pronunciation as borrowed in early modern Turkish) and *Sümerbank* (Sumer bank, from the Sumerians).

Another approach to Turkish history vis-à-vis Anatolia, known for example under the names *memleketçilik* ("homelandism") or *Anadoluculuk* (Anatolianism), and going back to an 1869 book *Les Turcs anciens et modernes* by Mustafa Celaleddin Pasha, proposed territorial kinship based on the notion of a fatherland and a nationalist narrative based on Anatolian history and the Anatolian peasant. Advocates of this point of view included Remzi Arık and Zübeyir Koşay, who took important roles in the development and administration of the Hittite museum, the Turkish Historical

---

13. Lenormant 1881, Conder 1898, and Barenton 1932 cited in Çığ 1988, 213–14 and Meydan 2010, 206–7.
14. Kramer 1963, 20.
15. Cagaptay 2004, Dinler 2017, İnan et al. 1931; an accessible reprint is available in Usta 2014.

Institute, and the excavations at the site of Alacahöyük. Arık's books and articles were even distributed by the state press, since advocates of this kind of Anatolianism still posited the possibility of Turkish elements and their various connections with pre-Islamic Anatolian civilizations.[16] Yet another alternative, this time to Anatolianism, emerged during the 1950s and 1960s. Bedri Rahmi, Eren and Sabahattin Eyüboğlu, Mina Urgan, Cevat Şakir Kabaağaçlı ("the Fisherman of Halicarnassus"), and Azra Erhat wrote of their "blue voyages" along the Aegean coast. Dubbed "Blue Anatolia," their movement focused on Anatolia without an attempt to posit Turkish connections or origins for certain ancient peoples, focusing on the Anatolian origins of Western civilization and also the significance of studying classical civilizations as part of Anatolian civilizations.[17]

The Trajectory of Turkish Assyriology

It may be posited that Turkish Assyriology, as mentioned briefly above, interacted with differing forms of Anatolianism debated in archaeology and elsewhere at least in part, although there is no concrete evidence that their impact was so great. Having Anatolia as a primary research agenda of Turkish Assyriology can partly be explained by the availabilities of primary sources in Turkey and partly by the interest in Anatolia on the part of Turkish scholars. One should note, however, that there are many cuneiform texts available for study in Turkey, not only from Anatolian sites such as Kültepe and Boğazköy, but there are also many tablets in the Istanbul Museum, collected under Ottoman law from different parts of Mesopotamia (Özkan 2017). The distribution of work is in part determined by the way cuneiform expertise developed from the outset more in the areas of Old Assyrian studies and Hittitology in Turkey.

The first university of the new Turkish Republic was founded in Ankara, the capital city, called Ankara University, and its first faculty was the Faculty of Languages and History-Geography, which was found on 22 June 1935. The first lecture was given on 9 January 1936. According to the faculty records and a national newspaper (*Ulus Gazetesi*, 7 January 1936), in the first stage, five German scholars were employed in this faculty. Among them were Landsberger (as an Assyriologist) and Güterbock (as a Hittitologist), who were assigned to research and lecture in their areas of expertise.[18] Accordingly, Assyriology and Hittitology in Turkey was initiated in 1935 by the those scholars who were invited from Germany in order to found these departments at Ankara University within the Faculty of Languages and History-Geography, the first educational institution of the young republic. It is worthy of respect that the government of the newly established republic gave special importance to the field of Assyriology, which was a relatively new discipline, despite so many difficult problems suffered by the country.

Professor Sedat Alp, one of the first students who was sent to Germany by the Turkish Ministry of Education to learn ancient history and archaeology (and who during his

16. Gur 2010, 17–19.
17. Gur 2010, 20–30.
18. Bilici 2016, 236–37.

stay in Germany wrote to Cevat Dursunoğlu of the ministry asking instead to train in Hittitology at the University of Leipzig),[19] had mediated between Turkish authorities and Landsberger for his position in the Faculty of Languages and History-Geography, which was about to be founded in Ankara. During his education in Leipzig, Alp had learned that his teacher in Akkadian and Sumerian, Landsberger, had been dismissed from his position in the university as part of a law related to the civil servants, enacted 7 April 1933 by the Nazi regime in Germany. Alp contacted the Turkish authorities regarding Landsberger's situation, and they offered him the position in Ankara. Landsberger accepted this offer with one condition: he requested a library for the departments of Sumerology and Hittitology and suggested the library of his teacher, the late Heinrich Zimmern. Zimmern's library was put on the market by his wife (Alp 1997, 2–3.). Landsberger's condition was accepted and he was assigned as a professor to the Department of Sumerology at the Faculty of Languages and History-Geography, with a salary of 600 Turkish liras, signing a contract with the representative of Turkey's Ministry of Culture in Berlin on 22 October 1935. It must be noted here that, during this period, "Assyriology" was officially named "Sumerology" in Turkey under the leadership of Atatürk. Unlike the discovery of the Assyrian kingdom in northern Iraq when the field took on the name "Assyriology" in Europe and America in the nineteenth century, the time of the field's establishment in Turkey coincided with a great interest in the Sumerians.

Landsberger worked for thirteen years in Ankara University's Department of Sumerology. Conditions in Turkey slowly changed after Atatürk's demise in 1938. His professorship was removed by a law that was enacted 6 July 1948, and he resigned when his agreement finished on 15 October 1948. He then started to work at the Oriental Institute in Chicago. Similarly, Güterbock had worked as a researcher and lecturer at Ankara University's Department of Hittitology for about twelve years in the context of his contract with the Turkish Government signed 26 October 1935.[20]

During thirteen years of his work in Ankara, Landsberger educated Turkish students in the field of Assyriology by giving Sumerian and Akkadian lessons for about twenty hours per week besides his scientific studies.[21] Landsberger taught his students and was able to research at the same time. Among students of Assyriology, especially Kemal Balkan, Emin Bilgiç, Kadriye Yalvaç, and Mebrure Tosun distinguished themselves. Those first Turkish Assyriologists concentrated mainly on Akkadian, especially on the Old Assyrian dialect, besides Sumerian. The main reason for this tendency is that the majority of the sources under study are Old Assyrian texts from Kültepe/Kanesh, which is located on the northeast of modern Kayseri in central Anatolia. The official Turkish excavations in Kültepe began in 1948 under Tahsin Özgüç and all the texts that have been unearthed there have been preserved in Ankara, in the Museum of Anatolian Civilizations, as well as the Kayseri Museum (earlier tablets from before the 1948 excavations are in the Istanbul Museum or in private collections). Initially, those newly discovered Kültepe texts were studied mostly by Balkan, one Landsberger's prominent students. For instance, the famous letter of Anum-hirbi which includes the

19. Süel 2017, 142.
20. Bilici 2016, 239–40, Süel 2017, 145.
21. Bilici 2016, 238.

problems that took place between two rival Anatolian city-states was published by him in 1957 (Balkan 1957). On the other hand, the systematic publication of these texts that belonged to the private archives of individual Assyrian merchants started late, beginning only after the foundation of The Publication Committee of Kültepe Tablets in 1983 by Emin Bilgiç, one of the first Turkish Assyriologists. From that point, over ten volumes have been published by the Turkish Historical Institute, mostly by the members of this committee of both Turkish and foreign researchers, and most of the texts are still in the process of publication.

Muazzez İlmiye Çığ and Hatice Kızılyay, who are among the earliest graduates of Ankara University's Department of Hittitology, also with training from the Departments of Sumerology and Archaeology,[22] were appointed to the Istanbul Archaeological Museums after graduation in 1940. There, Çığ and Kızılyay worked first with Fritz R. Kraus who had started in the Istanbul Museum archives in 1937, and later they worked with Samuel Noah Kramer who came to Turkey for a longer period in 1951.[23] Kızılyay and Çığ worked in the Istanbul Museum until 1972 and Hatice Kızılyay retired in 1969. Çığ authored and contributed to significant publications of Hittite texts in the Istanbul Museum, Old Babylonian legal texts from Nippur (with Kraus), Neo-Sumerian texts from Nippur (with Kızılay), and a range of other texts, cataloguing also around 74,000 tablets over the years.[24] Approximately two decades after her retirement, Çığ translated one of Kramer's monographs, *History Begins at Sumer* (1990), published by the Turkish Historical Institute. Çığ later went on to wiote popular books which compared the Bible, the Qur'an, and Mesopotamian literary sources, as well as her views about the relation between Sumerian and Altaic languages (Çığ 2013). Her publications became widely popular and resonated with a public interest in the origins of Abrahamic religions as well as Turkish origins. There is currently a range of publications positing a connection between Turkish and Sumerian.[25]

Among the names of the second generation of Turkish Assyriologists from Ankara University, Veysel Donbaz, Hüseyin Sever, and Cahit Günbattı are deemed as prominent because of their knowledge of the field and publications. These scholars primarily focused on the Old Assyrian Kültepe texts and have made important publications. As curator and later chief curator at the Istanbul Archaeological Museums, Donbaz has also published texts from a range of periods,[26] such as administrative documents from the Middle Assyrian period (Donbaz 1976), Old Babylonian tablets from Kish (Donbaz and Yoffee 1986), Neo-Babylonian economic texts (Donbaz and Stolper 1997), and two Neo-Assyrian stelae shedding light on the history of Adad-nirari III (Donbaz 1990). Cahit Günbattı has published very important texts, such as a legendary text which includes the achievements of Sargon, the king of Agade (Kt j/k 97) (Günbattı 1997), two separate treaties between Assur and Kanesh (Kt oo/k 6) and Assur and Hahhum (Kt oo/k 10) (Günbattı 2004), a *līmum* list (Kt o1/k 287) that substantially illustrates the chronology of the period (Günbattı 2008), and a letter (Kt o1/k 217) from

22. Öztürk 2002, 32.

23. Öztürk 2002, 77–78. For Kramer's own account of his experiences in Istanbul, see Kramer 1986. We are grateful to Sanna Aro for drawing attention to Kramer's autobiography.

24. Çığ 1988, 215–16; Öztürk 2002, 181–88.

25. For a collection, see Yıldırım 2017, 117–21.

26. Dönmez 2010, xv–xxiii.

the envoys of the city of Assur to Hurmeli the king of Harsamna, which demonstrates the late Colony period (Günbattı 2014).

Sebahattin Bayram, Salih Çeçen, and İrfan Albayrak are among the third generation Turkish Assyriologists who are still working at the department of Sumerology in the Faculty of Languages and History-Geography in Ankara University. These academics teach and research especially on the Old Assyrian Kültepe texts. Their approach is to publish the Old Assyrian texts within their archival contexts, hence a philological approach in dialogue with archaeology. The approach to historiography remains essentially focused on the publication of primary sources, a great need in Turkey. The focus on publishing texts is also attested in other areas of modern Turkish historiography, with methodologies of social history influenced from the annals school, by leading historians such as Mehmed Fuad Köprülü, Ömer Lütfi Barkan, and Halil İnalcık.[27]

Turkish scholars trained in Ankara, Istanbul, or overseas in the recent years have also contributed to the growing interdisciplinary dialogue of Assyriology, and they continue their academic life in various departments in Turkey and abroad. Due to reasons of space it will not be possible to summarize all of their works, and some pertinent references will herewith be provided. Hittitology in Turkey developed around the same time as Assyriology, with contributions initially from Alp, Güterbock, and Bossert.[28] Ali and Belkıs Dinçol led Istanbul University's Department of Hittitology with many publications and projects,[29] and currently their students, Metin Alparslan, Meltem Doğan-Alparslan, and Hasan Peker are Hittitologists recognized in Turkey and abroad. Aygül Süel, Ahmet Ünal, Yasemin Arıkan, Cem Karasu, Turgut Yiğit, and Oğuz Soysal are among the established Turkish names in Hittitology. Critical readings of Assyrian and Anatolian history and discourses by means of adding non-textual evidence are offered for example by Mehmet-Ali Ataç (Ataç 2010), Ömür Harmanşah (Harmanşah 2013), and Kemalettin Köroğlu (Köroğlu 2016). We emphasize of course that this does not by any means exhaust the list of Turkish scholars in these fields or related ones.[30]

Concluding Remarks

We are very grateful to the editors for accepting our paper as it was prepared under considerable pressure of time and delivered much beyond the requested deadline. Our purpose has been to provide a survey of a relatively less explored area in the history of cuneiform studies. We recognize the survey is incomplete; this is not only due to the pressure of time, but also because there is much more documentary evidence that can shed new light into this area as well as other areas of Turkish history, historiography, and archaeology. It is hoped in any case that the short survey in the present volume will provide at least some insight into and further impetus for understanding

---

27. Sönmez 2012, İnalcık 2013; I am grateful to Selim Tezcan for drawing attention to this book.
28. Doğan-Alparslan 2017; Süel 2017.
29. Alparslan, Doğan-Alparslan, and Peker 2007, xix–xxviii; Jean 2007.
30. Note for example that Urartian studies in Turkey, based primarily on archaeological research, was influenced early on by Russian scholarship, which emphasized the role of the state in Urartian political and economic structure. This is marked especially in the 1970s and 1980s (Çifçi 2017, 8).

the history of cuneiform studies in Turkey, also triggering perspectives as to future intellectual and scholarly dialogue among Assyriologists within and outside their scientific community.

REFERENCES

Akçay, Y. 2013. "Türkiye'deki Hiyeroglif Çalışmaları ve Hurûf-ı Berbâiyye Tercümesi." *Dil ve Edebiyat Araştırmaları* 7:21–9.

Alp, S. 1997. "Asur Ticaret Kolonileri Çağı'nda Kaneš/Neša'da Hititlerin Varlığı ve Yoğunluğu, Bilimsel bir Oluşumunu Öyküsü." *Archivum Anatolicum* (*Emin Bilgiç Anı Kitabı*) 3:1–17.

Anderson, B. 2015. "'An Alternative Discourse': Local Interpreters of Antiquities in the Ottoman Empire." *Journal of Field Archaeology* 40:450–60.

Ataç, M.-A. 2010. *The Mythology of Kingship in Neo-Assyrian Art*. Cambridge: Cambridge University Press.

Atakuman, Ç. 2008. "Cradle or Crucible: Anatolia and Archaeology in the Early Years of the Turkish Republic (1923–1938)." *Journal of Social Archaeology* 8:214–35.

Aytürk, İ. 2004. "Turkish Linguists Against the West: Origins of Linguistic Nationalism in Atatürk's Turkey." *Middle Eastern Studies* 40:1–25.

———. 2009. "H. F. Kvergić and the Sun-Language Theory." *Zeitschrift der Deutschen Morgenländischen Gesellschaft* 159:23–44.

Balkan, K. 1957. *Mama Kralı Anum-hirbi'nin Kaniş Kralı Warşama'ya Gönderdiği Mektup*. Ankara: Türk Tarih Kurumu.

Barenton, H. de. 1932. *L'origine des langues, des religions et des peoples*. Paris: Libraire Orientale et Américaine.

Bilici, Z. K. 2016. "Dil ve Tarih-Coğrafya Fakültesi ve Eğitim Öğretimde Alman Bilim Kadrosu (1936–1970)." Pages 235–68 in *İkinci Vatan ve Ankara Üniversitesi (1933–1970)*. Edited by K. Karakütük. Ankara: Ankara Üniversitesi.

Cagaptay, S. 2004. "Race, Assimilation and Kemalism: Turkish Nationalism and the Minorities in the 1930s." *Middle Eastern Studies* 40:86–101.

Celaleddin, M. 1869. *Les Turcs anciens et modernes*. Istanbul: Courrier d'Orient.

Çelik, Z. 2016. *About Antiquities: Politics of Archaeology in the Ottoman Empire*. Austin: The University of Texas Press.

Çifçi, A. 2017. *The Socio-Economic Organisation of the Urartian Kingdom*. Leiden: Brill.

Çığ, M. İ. 1988. "Atatürk and the Beginnings of Cuneiform Studies in Turkey." *Journal of Cuneiform Studies* 40:211–16.

———. 2013. *Sumerliler Türklerin Bir Koludur. Sumer-Türk Kültür Bağları*. Istanbul: Kaynak Yayınları.

Conder, C. R. 1898. *The Hittites and their Language*. New York: Dodd, Mead and Co.

Dinler, M. 2017. "The Knife's Edge of the Present. Archaeology in Turkey from the Nineteenth Century to the 1940s." *International Journal of Historical Archaeology*. https://doi.org/10.1007/s10761-017-0446-x.

Doğan-Alparslan, M. 2017. "The Foundation of Hittitology in the Istanbul University." Pages 145–56 in *The Discovery of an Anatolian Empire: A Colloquium to Commemorate the 100th Anniversary of the Decipherment of the Hittite Language*. Edited by M. Doğan-Alparslan, A. Schachner, and M. Alparslan. Istanbul: Türk Eskiçağ Bilimleri Enstitüsü.

Donbaz, V. 1976. *Ninurta-tukulti-Aššur Zamanına ait Orta Asur İdarî Belgeleri*. Ankara: Türk Tarih Kurumu.

———. 1990. "Two Neo-Assyrian Stelae in the Antakya and Kahramanmaraş Museums." *Annual Review of the Royal Inscriptions of Mesopotamia Project* 8:4–24.

Donbaz, V., and M. M. Stolper. 1997. *Istanbul Murašû Texts*. Istanbul: Nederlands Historisch-Archaeologisch Instituut het Nabije Oosten.

Donbaz, V., and N. Yoffee. 1986. *Old Babylonian Texts from Kish Conserved in the Istanbul Archaeological Museums*. Malibu: Undena Publications.

Dönmez, Ş. 2010. *Veysel Donbaz'a Sunulan Yazılar. DUB.SAR É.DUB.BA.A. Studies Presented in Honour of Veysel Donbaz*. Istanbul: Ege Yayınları.

Dressler, M. 2017. "Mehmed Fuad Köprülü and the Turkish History Thesis." Pages 245–53 in *Ölümünün 50. Yılında Uluslararası M. Fuad Köprülü Türkoloji ve Beşeri Bilimler Sempozyumu (21–22 Kasım 2016) Bildirileri*. Edited by F. Turan, E. Temel, and H. Korkmaz. Istanbul: Kültür Sanat Basımevi.

Eldem, E. 2004. "An Ottoman Archaeologist Caught Between Two Worlds: Osman Hamdi Bey (1842–1910)." Pages 121–49 in *Archaeology, Anthropology and Heritage in the Balkans and Anatolia: The Life and Times of F. W. Hasluck, 1878–1920*. Edited by D. Shankland. Istanbul: The Isis Press.

Günbattı, C. 1997. "Kültepe'den Akadlı Sargon'a Ait Bir Tablet." *Archivum Anatolicum* 3:131–55.

———. 2004. "Two Treaty Texts Found at Kültepe." Pages 249–68 in *Assyrian and Beyond: Studies Presented to M. T. Larsen*. Publications de l'Institut historique-archéologique néerlandais de Stamboul 100. Edited by J. G. Dercksen. Leiden: Nederlands Instituut voor het Nabije Oosten.

———. 2008. "An Eponym List (KEL G) from Kültepe." *Altorientalische Forschungen* 35:103–32.

———. 2014. *Harsamna Kralı Hurmeli'ye Gönderilen Mektup ve Kaniš Kralları*. Ankara: Türk Tarih Kurumu.

Gur, A. 2010. "Political Excavations of the Anatolian Past: Nationalism and Archaeology in Turkey." Pages 1–38 in *Controlling the Past, Owning the Future: The Political Uses of Archaeology in the Middle East*. Edited by R. Boytner, L. Swartz Dodd, and B. J. Parker. Tucson: Arizona University Press.

Harmanşah, Ö. 2013. *Memory in the Ancient Near East*. Cambridge: Cambridge University Press.

İnalcık, H. 2013. "Türkiye'de Modern Tarihçiliğin Kurucuları." Pages 179–96 in *Türkiye'de Tarihyazım*. Edited by V. Engin and A. Şimşek. Istanbul: Yeditepe Yayınevi.

İnan, A. 1953. *Gazi M. Kemal Atatürk ve Türk Tarih Kurumu*. Ankara: Türk Tarih Kurumu.

İnan, A., et al. 1931. *Türk Tarihinin Ana Hatları—Methal Kısmı*. Istanbul: Devlet Matbaası.

Jean, E. 2007. "Lettre à Ouvert pour Belkıs et Ali." Pages 1–12 in *Belkıs Dinçol ve Ali Dinçol'a Armağan (Festschrift in Honour of Belkıs Dinçol and Ali Dinçol)*. Edited by M. Alparslan, M. Doğan-Alparslan, and H. Peker. Ege Yayınları: Istanbul.

Karateke, H. T. 2013. "The Challenge of Periodization. New Patterns in Nineteenth Century Ottoman Historiography." Pages 129–54 in *Writing History at the Ottoman Court: Editing the Past, Fashioning the Future*. Edited by H. E. Çıpa and E. Fetvacı. Bloomington: Indiana University Press.

Köroğlu, K. 2016. "Archaeological Evidence for the Provincial System of the Neo-Assyrian Empire in Anatolia." Pages 309–20 in *The Provincial Archaeology of the Assyrian Empire*. Edited by J. MacGinnis, D. Wicke, and T. Greenfield. Cambridge: McDonald Institute for Archaeological Research.

Kramer, S. N. 1963. *The Sumerians. Their History, Culture, and Character*. Chicago: The University of Chicago Press.

———. 1986. *In the World of Sumer: An Autobiography*. Detroit: Wayne State University Press.

Larsen, M. T. 1994. *The Conquest of Assyria: Excavations in an Antique Land 1840–1860*. London: Routledge.

Lenormant, F. 1881. *Histoire ancienne de l'orient jusqu'aux guerres médiques*. Paris: A. Lévy.

Meydan, S. 2010. *Atatürk ve Türklerin Saklı Tarihi*. İstanbul: İnkılap.

Neumark, F. 1980. *Zuflucht am Bosporus: Deutsche Gelehrte, Politiker und Künstler in der Emigration 1933–1953*. Frankfurt am Main: Knecht.

Özkan, S. 2017. "Türkiye Müzelerinde Korunan Çivi Yazılı Tabletler (Cuneiform Tablets Preserved in Museums of Turkey)." Pages 173–92 in *Prof. Dr. Recep Yıldırım'a Armağan*. Edited by P. Pınarcık et al. Ankara: Bilgin Kültür Sanat Yayınları.

Öztürk, S. 2002. *Çivi Çiviyi Söker. Muazzez İlmiye Çığ Kitabı*. Istanbul: Türkiye İş Bankası Kültür Yayınları.

Smith, G. 1875. *Assyrian Discoveries: An Account of Explorations and Discoveries on the Site of Nineveh, during 1873 and 1874*. New York: Scribner, Armstrong & Co.

Sönmez, E. 2012. "Annales Okulu'nun Türkiye'deki Tarih Araştırmalarına Etkisi." Pages 253–65 in *Mehmet Fuat Köprülü*. Edited by Y. K. Taştan. Ankara: Kültür ve Turizm Bakanlığı Yayınları.

Süel, A. 2017. "Cumhuriyet ve Hititoloji." Pages 139–46 in *The Discovery of an Anatolian Empire. A Colloquium to Commemorate the 100ᵗʰ Anniversary of the Decipherment of the Hittite Language*. Edited by M. Doğan-Alparslan, A. Schachner, and M. Alparslan. İstanbul: Türk Eskiçağ Bilimleri Enstitüsü.

Tekin, H. 2017. *Tarihöncesinde Mezopotamya: Yeni Yaklaşımlar, Yeni Yorumlar ve Yeni Kronoloji*. Ankara: Bilgin Kültür Sanay.

Topçuoğlu, O. 2013. "Istanbul Archaeological Museums and Turkey's View of Collecting and Displaying Near Eastern Antiquities." Paper presented at the American Schools of Oriental Research Annual Meeting, Baltimore.

———. 2015. "Identities on the Move: Archaeological Museums of Istanbul and Ankara and their Role in the Formation of Ottoman and Turkish National Identities." Paper presented at the North American Theoretical Archaeology Group Conference, New York.

———. 2017. "From 'Our ancestors the Hittites' to the Steppes of Central Asia: Political Uses of the Past in Turkey from the 19ᵗʰ Century to Today." Paper presented at the Society of Biblical Literature Annual Meeting, Boston.

Uslu, G. 2015. "Homer, Troy and the Turks: Heritage and Identity in the Late Ottoman Empire 1870–1915." PhD diss., University of Amsterdam.

Usta, R. 2014. *Türk Tarihinin Ana Hatları. Kemalist Yönetimin Resmî Tarih Tezi*. Istanbul: Kaynak Yayınları.

Vacín, L., and J. Sýkorová. 2018. *The Unknown Benno Landsberger: A Biographical Sketch of an Assyriological Altmeister's Development, Exile, and Personal Life*. Wiesbaden: Harrassowitz.

Yıldırım, M. N. 2017. *Babil Kulesi'nde Buluşalım, Dünya Dilleriyle Tanışalım*. Istanbul: Demkar Yayınevi.

CHAPTER 11

Ancient Near Eastern Studies and Portuguese Academia: A Love Affair Under Construction

Isabel Gomes de Almeida

FOR MODERN WESTERN SOCIETIES, the ancient world comprised between the banks of the Mediterranean Sea, the Nilotic territory, and the Near East always stood as a fascinating place where some of the roots of present-day civilization are found. Though the allure for antiquity was always felt within Western societies and academia, the nineteenth century stands as a special period where this appeal increased, due largely to the Orientalism movement.[1] In fact, as is well-known, the profound interest for everything that was "Oriental" and, at the same time, "ancient" impelled the development of archaeology and philology, among other disciplines, which in turn allowed for an academic rediscovery of ancient civilizations and cultures. Consequently, history gained a new vigor, widening its subject matter both in time and space. A new era for humanities and social sciences began, where interdisciplinary work and critical reflection within different and new fields were cultivated.

Throughout the twentieth century, this tendency deepened with the development of multiple schools of thought that still influence the craft of the historian to this day. During this time, Near Eastern studies, along with other fields, gradually claimed their vital place within Western academia. The twentieth century saw the rise of multiple schools and research units focused on the specialized analysis of the linguistic, archaeological, and iconographic data left by the historical actors that once dwelt in the ancient Near East.

Portuguese society and academia also felt the attraction for this ancient Orient. However, due to its own historical context and historiographical development, throughout the late nineteenth and twentieth centuries most Portuguese scholars did not focus their research on Near Eastern studies, leading to a rather small academic production on that subject when compared to the research outputs of other countries. Yet, due to the efforts of some Portuguese biblical scholars, who from the 1970s onward drew their attention to the east Semitic world, the Near East slowly began to appeal to more researchers and students. A timid love affair came to light during the next decades, fueled in recent years by the members of the research group Antiquity

---

Author's note: This paper had the support of CHAM (FCSH/NOVA-UAc) through the strategic project sponsored by FCT (UID/HIS/04666/2013). The author is a researcher of CHAM & DH, FCSH, Universidade NOVA de Lisboa.

1. Note that I am referring to the movement itself, and not the historiographical concept and/or trend. About interpretations on the latter, see for instance Said 1978 or Spivak 1988.

222

and its Reception, which integrates CHAM—Centre for the Humanities of FCSH, Universidade NOVA de Lisboa, and University of the Azores.[2]

In the following pages, I propose to stress three fundamental aspects. First, I present the motives that led Portuguese historiography to somehow resist the intense magnetism of the ancient Near East. Second, I highlight the work of the Portuguese predecessors in the field from the 1970s onward. And finally, I bring forward the work currently being developed that opens the possibility for a new chapter on the romance between Portuguese academia and the Near East.

An Outlook of the Portuguese Historical and Historiographical Contexts

The Academic Necessity to Revisit Portuguese History

On 28 May 1926 there was a military *coup d'état* that led to the establishment of a dictatorial regime in Portugal, which was consummated with the formulation and approval of a new constitution in 1933. This new regime, *Estado Novo*, lasted until the 25th of April Revolution, also known as "Carnation Revolution," in 1974. The long period of *Estado Novo*, a fascist regime, had a profound impact in many spheres, including academia.[3]

The discipline of history, as others, was used to legitimate the dictatorial agenda, namely by highlighting certain episodes of the Portuguese history, while casting a shadow over other periods. To give just a few examples, the medieval "birth of the nation," the construction of the overseas empire, and the "heroes" of the so-called Portuguese *gesta* were eulogized, while nineteenth-century liberalism and the First Portuguese Republic were neglected. An episodic and propagandistic history was thus promoted, which considerably incapacitated Portuguese historians from following the new critical approaches developed during those decades. The scholars who tried to resist were removed from universities, and many were forced into exile to continue their unrestricted academic work.[4]

Unsurprisingly, when *Estado Novo* was deposed there was a renewal within Portuguese humanities and social sciences, recognizing the need to revisit what was produced in the previous decades. Concerning the discipline of history, from the 1980s onward there was a profound historiographical shift regarding medieval, early modern, and contemporary studies, which aimed to fill the existing theoretical and methodological gaps.[5] The academic impact was remarkable, leading to the creation or reformulation of schools (like the School of Social Sciences and Humanities of UNL—NOVA FCSH, founded in 1977), undergraduate courses, masters and doctorate programs, and, consequently, research units. The academic independence that was

---

2. CHAM is an inter-university research unit that connects scholars from the Universidade NOVA de Lisboa (UNL) and from the University of the Azores (UAc). See http://www.cham.fcsh.unl.pt/ (accessed 15 September 2017).

3. About the events that led to the formation of this new regime and its different aspects, see Rosas 1994.

4. On Portuguese historiographical development and its context, see Torgal, Mendes, and Catroga 1998.

5. Mattoso 2011, 12.

gained after 1974 finally allowed for the much-needed intense debate among scholars from different theoretical backgrounds.[6] These sometimes rather tenacious discussions were (and still are) extremely fruitful, contributing to the creation of international networks and interdisciplinary projects. A high level of academic productivity was thus achieved, originating solid and state-of-the-art schools of thought regarding Portuguese history.

Given this context, it comes as no surprise that the research and teaching focus of the latest generations of historians, archaeologists, and other humanists and social scientists was not the Near East. Nevertheless, antiquity was appealing, especially as it concerns the ancient Mediterranean world.

Portuguese Academia and Classical Studies

As already mentioned, from the nineteenth century onward, the ancient world, namely the Oriental one, attracted numerous scholars from a wide range of disciplines. However, most Portuguese scholars who focused on antiquity were focused on the classical heritage. This circumstance can be explained by two main reasons. On the one hand, the scholastic tradition in European universities impelled the development of classical studies. Hence, Portuguese universities integrated this trend by displaying an intense scholarly interest in ancient Greek and Latin cultures, literatures, and languages. On the other hand, the strong Roman presence on the Portuguese territory prompted archaeological work to focus on that ancient period, and consequently the development of linguistic and historical research about it. A quick overview of the Portuguese humanities panorama in Lisbon and Coimbra highlights this tendency.[7]

In Lisbon, the Department of Classical Studies (DEC), which belongs today to the School of Arts and Humanities of the University of Lisbon (FLUL), is one of the direct heirs of the first nineteenth-century efforts to increasing the academic interest in the ancient Greek and Roman worlds. In 1859, D. Pedro V, Portuguese monarch at the time, supported the creation of a graduate course in humanities at the Royal Academy of Sciences where Latin and Greek literatures were taught from the very beginning. Later on, Latin philology and a course on Greek language were added to its *curricula*, stimulating the increase of students in the field.

After the Portuguese Republican Revolution occurred on 5 October 1910, the government proceeded to enact several educational reforms, which brought about the creation of the first schools of humanities in Portugal.[8] In 1911, the aforementioned FLUL was founded, integrating the classical scholars and the classical courses previously taught at the Royal Academy of Sciences. Decades later, in 1966, the Centre for Classical Studies (CEC) was created with the aim of developing research work in the

6. Regarding the motives underneath the beginnings of the Portuguese overseas expansion, João Paulo Oliveira e Costa evokes the strong dispute between scholars who looked for political and religious causes and the ones "who argued for the primacy of economic" ones; see Costa 2011, 593.

7. I am not disregarding the contributions of other Portuguese universities to classical studies. There are several researchers affiliated with other institutions that profoundly contribute to the development of this field. However, since the present paper does not intend to detail this specific field, I choose to highlight these two universities given their long and specialized academic tradition.

8. On the evolution of the educational system in Portugal, see the different contributions in Proença 1998.

field. From then onwards, the department and the research unit joined efforts, intertwining teaching and research. At present, DEC offers three undergraduate courses, a masters degree, and a doctorate program in classical studies. As for CEC, it has four main lines of research: "(Con)textual approaches to Classical Antiquity," "Texts and Culture from Late Antiquity to Humanism," "Asian Wisdom," and "Classical roots and European Identity." The combined activities of the two made FLUL an academic reference on the subject both nationally and internationally.

The School of Arts and Humanities of the University of Coimbra (FLUC) took a similar path.[9] Also created in 1911, it soon became eminent within the fields of literature, philosophy, and history, among others. Some of the most important figures of the twentieth-century Portuguese culture panorama are among its *alumni*. Concerns antiquity, FLUC saw the birth of the Institute of Classical Studies in 1944, a scientific and pedagogic department that aims to establish a link between teaching and research regarding Greek and Latin languages, literatures, and cultures and their permanencies throughout time. Since 1947, this institute is responsible for the edition and publication of the journal *Humanitas* and since 1984, of the journal *Boletim de Estudos Clássicos*.

The Institute of Classical Studies works closely with the Department of Languages, Literatures, and Cultures of FLUC, which at the present time offers an undergraduate course, a masters degree, and a doctorate program in classical studies. At the same time, the institute crosses the bridge with the Centre of Classical and Humanistic Studies (CECH), a research unit founded in 1967.[10] CECH has had a vital importance within the field of philology, actively contributing to the development of linguistic, literary, and cultural knowledge on ancient Greece and Rome as well as neo-Latin studies. Nowadays, CECH is structured in five different research groups: "Greek Studies," "Latin Studies," and "Renaissance Studies," "Rational Hermeneutics," and "Semantics and Pragmatics of Art," which emphasizes the hermeneutic dialogue between antiquity and modernity with a laboratorial dimension.

This rather prosperous panorama on classical studies within the Portuguese universities is enriched with the plentiful archaeological work focused on the Roman period beginning in the nineteenth century. Hundreds of sites displaying Roman material have been identified throughout the Portuguese territory,[11] which impelled the creation of several archaeological nucleuses, enhancing museum collections pertaining to this ancient period. The amount of Roman data (epigraphic, iconographic, ceramic, etc.) allowed for academic specialization in the field, currently attracting more students and researchers every year.

From this general overview, it is fair to say that both the recent Portuguese historical context and the significant tradition of in classical studies coalesced to overshadow Near Eastern studies. Yet, the strong appeal of the Orient remained irresistible to some of us.

---

9. About the history of FLUL, see http://www.uc.pt/en/fluc/apresentacao/history_faculty (accessed 15 September 2017).

10. About CECH, see http://www.uc.pt/en/iii/research_centers/CECH/apresentacao (accessed 15 September 2017).

11. There are currently over 9,300 Roman archaeological sites of different typologies identified by the Direcção Geral do Património Cultural (DGPC), the Portuguese institute that has the custody for the cultural patrimony in Portugal. For an index of the Roman archaeological sites in Portugal, see http://arqueologia .patrimoniocultural.pt/index.php?sid=sitios (accessed 15 September 2017).

Portuguese Predecessors in Near Eastern Studies

The Birth of a Specialized Field

The Portuguese presence in Asia, from the sixteenth century onward could have prompted an early modern academic interest in Near Eastern antiquity. In fact, many court officials and clerical scholars of the time, who were en route from or to the Portuguese State of India, passed through this area, writing about the ancient ruins they came across with in their travel journals. These were frequently published, and they circulated in the cultural and academic Portuguese scene of the time. For instance, the Franciscan friar Gaspar de São Bernardino, who travelled through Persia, Mesopotamia, and Palestine between 1605 and 1607, published his travel journal in 1611.[12] His book contains several references to the ancient city of Babylon and its famous tower, which he mistakes with another ancient ruin located 8 leagues from Bagdad (probably the Birs Nimrud ziggurat ruins).[13]

Yet, these accounts did not endure or raise a great deal of interest in the academic sphere apart from the teaching of Hebrew, Syriac, and Arabic at the University of Coimbra during the eighteenth century. As Nunes Carreira stated, the Portuguese contribution to ancient Near East philology and archaeological during the early modern and modern periods was rather scarce, despite the long-lasting presence in the Orient.[14]

Indeed, it was only in the last quarter of the twentieth century that Near Eastern studies started out to be systematically promoted, due primarily to the intensive work of some Portuguese biblical scholars. The teaching and research efforts of António Augusto Tavares (1929–2016),[15] José Nunes Carreira, José Augusto Ramos, and Francolino Gonçalves (1943–2017)[16] prompted the first specialized courses on ancient Semitic languages, literature, and culture within Portuguese universities. Their place as the precursors of the field in Portugal should thus be recognized.

It is fair to say that the late António Augusto Tavares was the pioneer who established and developed Near Eastern studies in Portugal. Having studied at the École Biblique et Archéologique Française (EBAF) in Jerusalem during the late 1950s, Tavares was among the first Portuguese scholars to attended specialized classes on Near Eastern archaeology. Given that EBAF promoted field trips for their students, Tavares gained a profound knowledge about the archaeological sites dated to antiquity and located in Israel, Jordan, Syria, and Iraq. Later on, after finishing his degree, Tavares was invited by Jean Perrot to work as his assistant at the Beersheba excavations. In an interview given by Tavares to *Res Antiquitatis—Journal of Ancient History*, he stated that his experiences at EBAF made him "comprendre que je devrais me laisser tomber amoureux de l'histoire de l'antiquité orientale qui aller marquer ma destinée d'un goût qui n'allait pas disparaître et qui serait irrépressible."[17]

---

12. This account has been published in a modern edition (Bernardino 1953). On the life of this friar, see Carreira 1985.

13. Carreira 1983.

14. Carreira 1983, 181.

15. See http://www.fcsh.unl.pt/media/noticias/falecimento-de-antonio-augusto-aguiar (accessed 15 September 2017).

16. See http://www.agencia.ecclesia.pt/noticias/nacional/igreja-faleceu-frei-francolino-goncalves -biblista-portugues/ (accessed 15 September 2017]).

17. Caramelo and Sales 2010, 223.

After completing his doctorate in Rome,[18] Tavares returned to Portugal in the 1970s where he began a brilliant teaching career, first at Universidade Católica Portuguesa (UCP) and later at FLUL. In 1977, the recently founded NOVA FCSH invited him to join the history department where he actively participated in the organization of the history undergraduate course, creating a curricular unit about the societies, cultures, and civilizations of the pre-classical world. This was a complete novelty in Portuguese universities, leading to the creation of the first chair in Oriental antiquity, which he occupied. Two years later, in 1979, Tavares founded the Institute of Oriental Studies, the first Portuguese research unit focused on this field. From the start, the goals of the Institute were ambitious: to create a specialized research library, to organize colloquiums and conferences on specific themes regarding the Orient and the ancient world, to publish the proceedings of these academic meetings (which came to light in the series *Estudos Orientais*, coordinated by Tavares), and to provide courses on oriental languages (such as modern and ancient Hebrew, Arabic, ancient hieroglyphic Egyptian, Akkadian, and also Korean, Japanese, and Mandarin). Gradually, all these goals were achieved, forever changing the Portuguese academic landscape on ancient and oriental history.

It should be noted that the aforementioned institute was renamed in 1982 as Oriental Institute of UNL, and recently, in 2014, it was integrated into CHAM-Centre for the Humanities. The work inaugurated by Tavares in the late 1970s is being continued by his direct heirs in this interdisciplinary research unit.

During the 1980s, Tavares sought the collaboration of French scholars like Jean Perrot, Pierre Amiet, Paul Garelli, Francis Joannés, Pierre Villard, and Pascal Vernus, inviting them to participate in conferences held at NOVA FCSH and in other Portuguese research and teaching institutions. This fruitful collaboration allowed for the creation of the first Portuguese masters program focused on the pre-classical world in 1989.

Besides his work at NOVA FCSH, Tavares also collaborated with Universidade Aberta (UAb), the only public distance education university in Portugal founded in 1988. He wrote a study guide about pre-classical civilizations, which was widely well received by the public.[19] His intense academic productivity engaged themes relevant to Hebrew studies (1976), ancient Egypt and Mesopotamia (1998), and even the Hittite world (1990).

Tavares' remarkable teaching and research efforts encouraged a whole new generation of students to choose ancient Mesopotamia and ancient Egypt as a postgraduate area within the field of history. This seminal work was paralleled by José Nunes Carreira, who developed a similar career at FLUL.

Having graduated in theology at the Pontificia Università Gregoriana (PUG) Rome in 1960, Nunes Carreira continued his studies in Italy, receiving another graduate degree in Oriental and biblical sciences from the Pontificio Istituto Biblico (1963). The following year he went to Jerusalem where he specialized in Semitic languages

---

18. Tavares received his PhD at the Pontificia Università San Tommaso d'Aquino, Rome, with a thesis on the modern exegesis of the patristics, with a special focus on Matt 1:5, under supervision of J. Salguero (Tavares 1972).

19. Tavares 1995.

228 Isabel Gomes de Almeida

at the EBAF. Returning to PUG, Nunes Carreira completed his doctorate in 1968 with a thesis that analyzed the philological development of the book of Isaiah and its interpretation by Francisco Foreiro, a sixteenth century Portuguese Dominican friar.[20]

During the 1970s, Nunes Carreira consolidated his research work in biblical studies with intense academic attention to exegetical themes. Back in Portugal, his teaching activity started at the UCP (1974–1978), continuing at UAc (1978–1984). In this institution he began to teach courses related to ancient Mesopotamia and ancient Egypt, a path he would continue from 1984 until his retirement in 2004 as a full professor at FLUL. In 1986, he created the Oriental Institute of FLUL, a research unit focused on ancient history. In the same year, Nunes Carreira established a close collaboration with Emanuel Bouzon from the Pontifícia Universidade Católica in Rio de Janeiro, creating a masters program on history and culture of the pre-classical world, which would began in 1990.[21]

In the following years, he published a book on the theme "History before Herodotus," in order to highlight the Sumerian, Semitic, Egyptian, and Hittite contributes to historiographical notions in antiquity.[22] Then, he again returned to the early modern period, publishing several books and papers on sixteenth- and seventeenth-century Portuguese travelers who crossed the Near and Middle East. Undoubtedly, these works emphasized reception studies regarding the ancient Near and Middle East.[23]

At the same institution (FLUL) another Portuguese biblical scholar developed a comparable work to the ones detailed above. José Augusto Ramos, having graduated in theology at the Institut Catholique de Toulouse (1969), continued his studies at the Pontificio Istituto Biblico in Rome, where he graduated in oriental and biblical sciences (1972). Back in Portugal, he received his doctorate in ancient history at FLUL, with a thesis focused on philological aspects of the ancient Hebrew language.[24]

One can say that the learning and teaching of ancient oriental languages is one of his great academic passions, having taught courses on Hebrew, Akkadian, Aramaic, Phoenician, Ugaritic, and Syriac. It should be noted how singular his contribution to the linguistic field is, given that some of these courses were first (and sometimes only) taught by him in Portugal.

Another of his strong academic interest relates to the history of religions, namely the ancient Semitic religious systems.[25] Responsible for a Portuguese translation of the Bible,[26] Ramos' research focus goes beyond the monotheistic world. One of the lines of research he has been following concerns the divine figure of Baal, and through him the identification and analysis of the alterity frontier between the Hebrew and the Canaanite cultures.[27]

20. Carreira 1974.

21. Later, he also wrote a guide for the students of the field (Carreira 1992a).

22. Carreira 1993. Later on, Carreira published a volume dedicated to the literary tradition of Mesopotamia (2002), helping to further spread the knowledge on the contribution of this civilization to cultural history.

23. For instance, Carreira 1992b, 1996.

24. Ramos 1989.

25. Ramos 2001

26. Ramos 1993.

27. For instance, Ramos 2000.

Full professor at FLUL, Ramos also collaborated with UCP, where he taught courses and seminars related to the ancient Semitic world. At present, though an emeritus professor, he continues his work as an advisor and researcher devoted to the development of ancient Near Eastern studies in Portugal.

The work developed within the Portuguese academic scene by these eminent figures was frequently aided by the late Francolino Gonçalves. A Dominican friar ordained in 1968, Gonçalves received his doctorate in oriental philology and history at the Université Catholique de Louvain in 1986. Professor at EBAF from 1975 on, his research revolved around the literary and political dimensions of ancient Near Eastern prophetic traditions.[28] On numerous occasions, Gonçalves collaborated with his colleagues and friends, including teaching seminars at the postgraduate courses on the ancient Near East and participating in the postgraduate juris both in FLUL and NOVA FCSH. Moreover, he was always available to help and guide researchers who visited EBAF, sharing with them its profound knowledge on the ancient world.

These four scholars were, thus, the forerunners of a new school of thought in Portugal, focused on the Near East and with a strong Orientalist inclination. Their immense contribution to Portuguese academia was soon consolidated with the specialized work of their students.

A New Generation of Specialized Scholars

In the late 1990s and early 2000s, the first solid academic fruits of the intense labor of the aforementioned scholars flourished, as new researchers presented their research in the field. At FLUL, António Ramos dos Santos presented a doctoral dissertation about the first millennium BCE economy of ancient Babylon in 1999, supervised by Bouzon.[29] Later, Ramos dos Santos became a professor at the same institution, continuing his line of research on socioeconomic themes.[30] His activities at FLUL are a strong contribution that continues the work promoted in the previous decades.

Also in 1999, another of Nunes Carreira's students, Maria de Lurdes Palma, received her masters degree with a dissertation on Assyrian royal ideology.[31] Continuing this line of research, Palma received her doctorate in 2004 with a thesis focused on the reign of Tiglath- pileser I.[32] Presently, she persists on her research path, focusing on the history of Assyria.[33] It should be noted that she is also a member of the editorial committee of *Cadmo Journal* (FLUL).

As for NOVA FCSH, under the guidance of Tavares, a new generation of researchers bloomed, having the pre-classical world as their main focus. For instance, in 1993 José das Candeias Sales received his masters degree in the history of pre-classical civilizations at this institution, with a dissertation supervised by Tavares that compared Akkadian and Egyptian royal ideologies.[34] Later on, Candeias Sales specialized in

28. See, for instance, Gonçalves 2003, 2006–2007, and 2008.
29. Santos 1999.
30. Santos 2003.
31. Palma 1999.
32. Palma 2004.
33. For instance, see Palma 2007, 2010.
34. Sales 1997.

Egyptology, having received his doctorate at the UAb in 2002. Nowadays, he teaches ancient history courses at this university where he is also pro-rector for lifelong learning and cultural extension.

The contacts Tavares established with French academia enriched these results, given that some scholars from this country supervised doctoral thesis. This was the case of Maria Helena Trindade Lopes, who focused on the importance of the name in the New Kingdom of Egypt and received her doctorate in Egyptology in 1995, with a dissertation supervised by Tavares and Pascal Vernus.[35] Trindade Lopes continues her research and teaching career at NOVA FCSH, where at the moment she is a full professor. Responsible for the supervision of several doctoral dissertations in Egyptology, Trindade Lopes continues to promote a specialized path inaugurated by Tavares.

Concerning Near Eastern studies, Francisco Caramelo, the present dean of NOVA FCSH and a full professor at the same institution, can be considered the direct heir of Tavares. Caramelo received his doctorate in 2001, presenting a thesis focused on the translation and interpretation of the Mesopotamian prophetic *corpora*, which was also supervised by Pierre Villard.[36] Having learned ancient Semitic languages, first with the already mentioned Portuguese scholars, and later at Oxford, London, and Lyon, Caramelo's work on the philological, literary, and cultural fields regarding ancient Mesopotamia established him as the successor of all the efforts detailed above.[37]

In the early 2000s, Caramelo began a fruitful collaboration with Juan Luis Montero Fenollós, among other Spanish scholars. This relationship resulted in the creation of the first Portuguese–Spanish archaeological project in the Near East, focusing on the region of Deir ez-Zor, Syria. The "Proyecto Arqueológico Medio Éufrates Sirio" (PAMES 2005–2011), co-directed by the two, opened the opportunity for postgraduate students to participate in its expeditions and in the subsequent laboratory work.[38] The results of PAMES were presented in several national and international conferences and published in several books.[39]

In close connection with PAMES, Caramelo also coordinated a research project (2008–2011) funded by Fundação para a Ciência e Tecnologia (FCT), the national agency which funds scientific projects in Portugal, entitled "Border and Territory in the Middle Euphrates during the Middle Assyrian period (13th century BC)."[40] Within its research outputs should be stressed the masters dissertation of Diogo Paiva, supervised by Caramelo, about the Middle Assyrian expansion in the reign of Tukulti-Ninurta (2012).[41]

Unfortunately, given the political and military crisis that struck Syria in the spring of 2011, PAMES, like so many others archaeological projects, ended abruptly. Yet, it was an experience that profoundly fueled the love-affair between Portuguese academia and this field of studies.

---

35. Lopes 1995.

36. Caramelo 2002.

37. See for instance Caramelo 2004, 2007, 2010, and 2011.

38. Valério 2011.

39. On the works published about PAMES, see for instance Montero Fenollós and Al-Shbib 2008, Caramelo, Montero Fenollós, and Masó 2011, and Montero Fenollós 2015.

40. See, for instance Caramelo 2012; and Caramelo, Montero Fenollós, and Tenu 2012.

41. Paiva 2012.

Current Lines of Research

Since 2010, NOVA FCSH has been occupying a more relevant place regarding research on the Near East, a situation directly connected with the dynamism of its doctorate program, the research unit CHAM, and the work of the research group "Antiquity and its Reception."

In the academic year of 2009–2010, the doctorate program of history in this institution went through a reformulation, which created a more intertwined path for PhD candidates in the area. By having mandatory specialized seminars with colleagues who focus on different chronological and spatial contexts in the first year of their research, history PhD candidates are impelled to discuss theoretical and methodological approaches diachronically. This new doctoral program configuration enriches the historiographical debate among junior scholars and prompts new lines of research. In 2009–2010, there were four PhD candidates in ancient history on this program who closely connected and worked with fellow candidates in medieval, early modern, and modern history.

The members of this group, Luís Duque, Marcel Paiva do Monte, Maria de Fátima Rosa, and myself, were supervised by Caramelo, who had already supervised their masters dissertations on themes related to the history of ancient Mesopotamia. They all intended to follow subjects matters related to the cultural and religious spheres, having all received a scholarship from the FCT.

Duque graduated in Archaeology at NOVA FCSH and later received his masters degree at the same institution in the history of religions (2009), with a dissertation on the religious and symbolic themes and concepts on some examples of Neo-Assyrian glyptic.[42] For his doctorate, Duque deepened this topic by widening the scope of its *corpora*. He is currently finishing his dissertation, having participated in several national conferences and scientific meetings.

Graduating in history at NOVA FCSH, Paiva do Monte received his masters degree in ancient history from FLUL (2010), with a dissertation about the *adê* treaties as political and juridical instruments in Assyrian imperial construction.[43] He was supervised by Ramos dos Santos and Caramelo. In 2017 he received his doctorate from NOVA FCSH, with a thesis entitled "Idea and Presence: The Image of the King and the Symbolic Construction of Neo-Assyrian Imperial Space (10th–7th centuries BCE)."[44]

Rosa also graduated in Archaeology at NOVA FCSH, with a final report on Mesopotamian glyptic. She then pursued her studies at FLUL, receiving her masters degree (2010) under the supervision of Ramos dos Santos and Caramelo. Her dissertation focused on the political project of Zimri-Lim in Mari (1775–1762 BCE).[45] The Mariotic context was, likewise, in the horizon of her doctorate, which she received in 2015 from NOVA FCSH, completing a dissertation on the perception of order and the conscience of time in Mari in the Old Babylonian period (nineteenth and eighteenth centuries BCE).[46]

---

42. Duque 2009.
43. Monte 2010.
44. Monte 2017.
45. Rosa 2010.
46. Rosa 2015.

In the past few years, Rosa has been developing her postdoctoral project on the reception of ancient Near East by early modern and modern Western societies. Having learned ancient languages with Ramos and Caramelo, she has been teaching Akkadian courses for undergraduate students at NOVA FCSH. Rosa and I worked in close collaboration, which had already resulted in the creation of an optional course about the perceptions of antiquity in early modern narratives and in the elaboration of an interdisciplinary project, RAR—Reception, Appropriation, Representation—Western Rhetorical Discourses on the Ancient Orient (1799–1939), which is now taking its first steps.

As for me, I graduated in history with a minor in Asian history at NOVA FCSH, where I also received my masters and doctoral degrees in ancient history, both supervised by Caramelo. I have tried to connect both the history of religions and history of women by analyzing the feminine stereotypical images displayed by Inanna/Ištar in the *Epic of Gilgameš* and *The Descent of Inanna/Ištar to the Netherworld* in my masters dissertation (2009).[47] For the doctorate, I widened this topic, presenting in 2015 a dissertation on the construction of the divine figure of Inanna/Ištar between the end of the fourth millennium and the beginning of the second millennium BCE.[48]

Since 2009, I have been teaching undergraduate and postgraduate courses on ancient Mesopotamian history, culture, and religion, as well as courses related to ancient Asia (namely the Silk Road in antiquity and the development of the ancient Chinese civilization) at NOVA FCSH. In the past few years, Caramelo, Rosa, and I have been teaching and supervising postgraduate students of the masters program in History—civilizations of the Middle East and ancient Asia.

In 2017, Rosa and I joined efforts with fellow postdoctoral colleagues at CHAM, Maria Dávila and Carla Alferes Pinto, who are working on late medieval and early modern Portuguese contexts, on a common research interest: the history of women.[49] We created a summer course at NOVA FCSH on the historiographical, theoretical, and methodological aspects of this topic, presenting new diachronic approaches to it. In the fall of 2017, another course was taught by us at the same institution, aiming to develop the interdisciplinary debate among students and fellow colleagues on feminine governance throughout time. We also prepared a cycle of conferences for the doctorate program in history, which was held during the first semester of 2018. The close connection with Alferes Pinto and Dávila opens up new research possibilities also on receptions studies related to the ancient Near East. At the same time, and given that we were all integrated into the reformulated doctoral program at NOVA FCSH, this team work actively displays the benefit of encouraging dialogue between historians from different contexts. At the end of 2017, we proposed the creation of a new thematic line, "History of Women and Gender" within CHAM, aiming to impel a wider discussion among scholars of this research unit.[50]

---

47. Almeida 2009.

48. Almeida 2015. See also Almeida 2012.

49. Davila's postdoctoral project is entitled "Gender, Space, and Power: Representations of Female Authority at the Portuguese Court (1438–1521)." As for Alferes Pinto, she is working on a postdoctoral project entitled "The Allure of Things. The Consumption of Artistic Objects by the Infantas and Queens Avis-Beja (1430–1577)."

50. See http://www.cham.fcsh.unl.pt/lintem_show.aspx?lintem=9 (accessed 15 January 2018).

On another level, and since the abrupt end of PAMES, Caramelo and Fenollós have been joining efforts to develop a new archaeological project in the Near East. In 2015, they started a fruitful dialogue with the Directorate of Excavation and Museum of the Ministry of Tourism and Antiquities of Palestine, which led to some first prospective expeditions at Khirbet Rabud in 2016, and later at Tell el Far'ah. A Portuguese–Spanish team, led by Caramelo and Fenollós, prepared the first campaign at Tell el Far'ah (October 2017), which included archaeologists of CHAM and of NOVA FCSH.[51] This project reopened the possibility for Portuguese presence in international archaeological projects on the Near East, prompting further academic work in the field.

The multi and interdisciplinary character of CHAM promotes both critical debate and the projects mentioned above. With more than 400 researchers at present, CHAM assembles junior and senior scholars within the fields of history, archaeology, art history, philosophy, literary studies, and philology, with a timeline that goes from antiquity to the nineteenth century. CHAM is divided into different research groups connected by several thematic lines. This configuration was achieved in 2014, when CHAM merged with the Oriental Institute and with another NOVA FCSH research unit, the Centre for the History of Culture (CHC).

Between 2010 and 2014, there was a first moment in the life of the research group that focused on ancient Mesopotamia and its reception through time. The previously mentioned PhD candidates were among its initial members. One of the more important results achieved during this period was the creation of *Res Antiquitatis—Journal of Ancient History*, due largely to the editorial efforts of Caramelo and Marcel Paiva do Monte.

After the 2014 merge, the group was reconfigured with the integration of scholars who were previously affiliated with the Oriental Institute, namely the Egyptologists and those who were affiliated with CHC, especially researchers focused on classical studies. From then on, the group "Antiquity and its Reception" assembled junior and senior scholars to work on different ancient historical and cultural contexts (Mesopotamia, Egypt, biblical, Mediterranean, Greek, Roman, and Hellenistic). Together, we aim to strongly develop research in reception studies of antiquity in Portugal, from a multidisciplinary perspective.

In 2017 NOVA FCSH held the first section of a colloquium in this field, organized by Caramelo, Rosa, and me. It brought together national and international scholars, stimulating a rich debate.[52] The proceedings of this colloquium were published in a thematic dossier of *Res Antiquitatis* in 2020.

Interestingly, the coordination of this research group is now in the hands of Trindade Lopes, who, like Caramelo, initiated her path in ancient history due to the combined actions of Tavares, Nunes Carreira, Ramos, and Gonçalves. Their one-time pupils are now the cornerstone of ancient history in Portugal, driving a new generation of scholars into the next step of the love-affair between antiquity and Portuguese academia.

---

51. See https://www.youtube.com/watch?v=XQQ4kU7BUiA (accessed 15 February 2018]).
52. See http://www.cham.fcsh.unl.pt/ac_actividade.aspx?ActId=515 (accessed 15 September 2017).

REFERENCES

Almeida, I. 2009. "O carácter do 'Divino Feminino' na Literatura Mesopotâmica: Inanna/ Ištar- personificação divina do imaginário feminino." MA diss., Universidade NOVA de Lisboa.

———. 2012. "The Descent to the Netherworld: A Comparative Study on the Inanna/Ištar Imagery in the Sumerian and Semitic Texts." Pages 91–100 in *Séptimo Centenario de los Estudios Orientales en Salamanca*. Edited by A. Agud et al. Salamanca: Ediciones Universidad de Salamanca.

———. 2015. "A construção da figura de Inanna/Ištar na Mesopotâmia: IV–II milénios a.C." PhD diss., Universidade NOVA de Lisboa.

Bernardino, G. de São. 1953. *Itinerário da Índia por Terra até à Ilha de Chipre*. Lisboa: Agência Geral do Ultramar.

Caramelo, F. 2002. *A Linguagem profética na Mesopotâmia (Mari e Assíria)*. Cascais: Patrimonia.

———. 2004. "As fórmulas de maldição na Mesopotâmia: uma proposta de análise." Pages 99–103 in *Percursos do Oriente Antigo. Homenagem a José Nunes Carreira*. Edited by J. A. dos Santos, L. Araújo, and A. R. dos Santos. Lisboa: Instituto Oriental—FLUL.

———. 2007. "Relações entre o Templo e o Palácio no período neo-assírio: Duas concessões reais ao templo de Aššur." Pages 271–75 in *Rumos e escrita da História. Estudos em homenagem a A. A. Marques de Almeida*. Edited by F. Reis. Lisboa: Edicões Colibri.

———. 2010. "La religion babilónica. El triunf del dio Marduk." Pages 167–77 in *Torre de Babel Historia y Mito*. Edited by J. L. Montero Fenollós. Murcia: Museo Arqueologico de Murcia.

———. 2011. "Visões da Antiguidade nos Comentarios de Don García de Silva y Figueroa." Pages 345–66 in *Estudos sobre Don García de Silva y Figueroa*. Edited by R. Loureiro and V. Resende. Lisboa: CHAM.

———. 2012. "L'expansion médio-assyrienne au Moyen Euphrate syrien: Le contexte international, l'affirmation de l'Assyrie et la problématique de la frontière." Pages 133–41 in *Du village néolithique à la ville syro-mésopotamienne*. Edited by J. L. Montero Fenollós. Ferrol: Universidad de Coruña.

Caramelo, F., J. L. Montero Fenollós, and F. Masó. 2011. *De Uruk a Bizancio. Arqueologia e Historia Antigua en la cuna de la civilización*. Ferrol: Proyecto Arqueológico Medio Éufrates Sirio.

Caramelo, F., J. L. Montero Fenollós, and A. Tenu. 2012. "L'empire assyrien au XIIIe siècle av. J.-C.: Tell Qabr Abu al-'Atiq sur le moyen Euphrate." Pages 143–61 in *Du village néolithique à la ville syro-mésopotamienne*. Edited by J. L. Montero Fenollós. Ferrol: Universidad de Coruña.

Caramelo, F., and J. C. Sales. 2010. "Interview d'António Augusto Tavares." *Res Anqituitatis—Journal of Ancient History* 1:217–29.

Carreira, J. N. 1974. *Filologia e Crítica de Isaías no Comentário de Francisco Foreiro (1522?–1581). Subsídios para a História da Exegese Quinhentista*. Coimbra: Gráfica de Coimbra.

———. 1983. "Portugal e a moderna orientalística." *Arquipélago. Ciências humanas* 5:179–95.

———. 1985. "Frei Gaspar de S. Bernardino: Um exegeta 'itinerante.'" *Didaskalia* 15:345–55.

———. 1992a. *Introdução à História e Cultura Pré-Clássica: Guia de Estudo*. Mem-Martins: Edições Europa-América.

———. 1992b. *Do Preste João às ruínas da Babilónia. Civilizações Orientais na Literatura Portuguesa de Viagens*. Lisboa: Comunicação.

———. 1993. *História antes de Heródoto. Historiografia e ideia de História na Antiguidade Oriental*. Lisboa: Edições Cosmos/Instituto Oriental.

———. 1996. *Outra face do Oriente. O Próximo Oriente em relatos de viagem*. Mem-Martins: Edições Europa-América.

———. 2002. *Literaturas da Mesopotâmia*. Lisboa: Centro de História da Universidade de Lisboa.

Costa, J. P. O. 2011. "The Beginnings of the Portuguese Overseas Expansion." Pages 591–606 in *The Historiography of Medieval Portugal c. 1950–2010*. Edited by J. Mattoso. Lisboa: Instituto de Estudos Medievais.

Duque, L. 2009. "A glíptica Neo-Assíria- Iconografia, Temas e Conceitos." MA diss., Universidade NOVA de Lisboa.

Gonçalves, F. 2003. "Concepção deuteronomista dos profetas e sua posteridade." *Disaskalia* 33:73–96.

———. 2006–2007. "Deux systèmes religieux dans l'Ancien Testament: De la concurrence à la convergence." *Annuaire de l'École Pratique des Hautes Études. Section des sciences religieuses* 115:117–22.

———. 2008. "Fundamentos da mensagem moral dos profetas bíblicos." *Cadmo* 18:9–29.

Lopes, M. H. T. 1995. "Os nomes próprios no império Novo." PhD diss., Universidade NOVA de Lisboa.

Mattoso, J. 2011. "Medieval Studies in Portugal: An Overview." Pages 12–24 in *The Historiography of Medieval Portugal c. 1950–2010*. Edited by J. Mattoso. Lisboa: Instituto de Estudos Medievais.

Monte, M. P. 2010. "Os tratados adē- instrumentos políticos e jurídicos na construção imperial assíria (sécs VIII–VII a.C.): Entre a continuidade e a singularidade." MA diss., Universidade de Lisboa.

———. 2017. "Ideia e Presença: A imagem do rei na construção simbólica do espaço imperial neo-assírio (séculos IX–VII a.C.)." PhD diss., Universidade NOVA de Lisboa.

Montero Fenollós, J. L., ed. 2015. *Asirios en el Medio Éufrates: La Cerámica Medioasiria de Tell Qabr Abu Al-'Atiq en su Contexto Histórico-Arqueológico*. Ferrol: Universidade de Coruña.

Montero Fenollós, J. L., and S. al-Shbib, eds. 2008. *La Necrópolis Bizantina de alla s-Sin (Deir Ez-Zor, Siria). Memorias del Proyecto Arqueológico Medio Éufrates Sirio*. Madrid: Consejo Superior de Investigaciones Científicas.

Paiva, D. 2012. "A expansão meso-assíria no reinado de Tukulti-Ninurta I." MA diss., Universidade NOVA de Lisboa.

Palma, M. L. 1999. "Poder e imagem: A idealização do rei na historiografia assíria— de Samsi-Adad I a Tiglat-pileser I." MA diss., Universidade de Lisboa.

———. 2004. "Tiglat-Pileser I e o seu tempo: A guerra, as leis e a ideologia: contributos para a sua análise." PhD diss., Universidade de Lisboa.

———. 2007. "Esposas e concubinas na legislação meso-assíria." *Cadmo* 17:27–53.

———. 2010. "Taram-kubi: Uma mulher de negócios no período paleo-assírio." *Cadmo* 20:267–94.

Proença, M. C., ed. 1998. *O Sistema de Ensino em Portugal. Séculos XIX e XX*. Lisboa: Edições Colibri.

Ramos, J. A. 1989. "O Sufixo Verba Não-Acusativo em Hebraico Antigo." PhD diss., Universidade de Lisboa.

———. 1993. *Bíblia Sagrada. Tradução em Português Corrente*. Lisboa: Sociedade Bíblica.

———. 2000. "Baal, o que é um deus?" *Cadmo* 10:197–223.

———. 2001. "Os Sacerdotes na História das Religiões, como Mediadores do Sagrado." *Bíblica* 10:35–54.

Rosa, M. F. 2010. "O projecto político de Zimri-Lim (1775–1762 a.C.)." MA diss., Universidade de Lisboa.

———. 2015. "A percepção da ordem e a consciência do tempo em Mari no período paleo-babilónico (seculos XIX e XVIII a.C.)." PhD diss., Universidade NOVA de Lisboa.

Rosas, F., ed. 1994. *O Estado Novo:1926–1974*. História de Portugal 7. Lisboa: Editorial Estampa.

Said, E. 1978. *Orientalism*. New York: Pantheon Books.

236 Isabel Gomes de Almeida

Sales, J. C. 1997. *A ideologia Real Acádica e Egípcia. Representações do Poder Político Pré-Clássico*. Lisboa: Editorial Estampa.

Santos, J. R. 1999. "O sector 'privado' na economia da Babilónia recente (626–539 a.C.): O modelo fundiário e o modelo comercial." PhD diss., Universidade de Lisboa.

———. 2003. *A Babilónia dos Caldeus Uma caracterização socioeconómica*. Lisboa: Edições Colibri.

Spivak, G. C. 1988. *Selected Subaltern Studies*. Oxford: Oxford University Press.

Tavares, A. A. 1972. "Estudo de Mt. 1,25 na tradição patrística e nas perspectivas da exegese actual." PhD diss., Pontificia Università San Tommaso d'Aquino, Rome.

———. 1976. "Palavras hebraicas e hebraísmos na língua Portuguesa." *Disdakalia* 6:95–121.

———. 1990. "Instituições dos hititas em Hebron no contexto do Médio Oriente." *Didaskalia* 2c:189–97.

———. 1995. *Civilizações Pré-Clássicas—Guia de Estudo*. Lisboa: Universidade Aberta.

———. 1998. *Impérios e propaganda na Antiguidade*. Lisboa: Editorial Presença.

Torgal, L. R., J. A. Mendes, and F. Catroga. 1998. *História da História em Portugal. Séculos XIX–XX*. 2 vols. Lisbon: Temas & Debates.

Valério, M. F. G. 2011. "A presença meso-assíria no Médio Eufrates: O contributo da cerâmica de Tall Qabr Abu al-'Atiq (Deir ez-Zor, Síria)." MA diss., Universidade NOVA de Lisboa.

CHAPTER 12

Near Eastern Archaeology and the Czech-Speaking Lands

Petr Charvát

ALL IN ALL, THE STORY of Near Eastern archaeology in the Czech-speaking lands is marked by ups and downs following irregularly after one another. The opportunities of the great founding period of Alois Musil (1868–1944) and Bedřich Hrozný (1879–1952) came to naught with the Nazi occupation and then with the communist regime. No serious undertaking abroad materialized from 1948 to 1989, save for the ill-fated Mongolian expedition of the Archaeological Institute of the Czechoslovak Academy of Sciences at Prague of 1958. At that time, Czech scholars strove to preserve the sum of knowledge then available, especially in the university courses, and grasped for whatever opportunities friendly academics and institutions abroad offered them. It was only after 1990 that new challenges could be properly answered and that a new generation of young and enterprising explorers took up management of the discipline.

Currently, four fully constituted expeditions operate in the Orient. Oriental archaeology now disposes of an institutional base, a thing unheard of in its history on Czech-speaking territory, at the Masaryk University of Brno, and lectures in Near Eastern archaeology make up a component of the Masaryk University archaeological curriculum. With the recent appointment of Karel Nováček to the Palacký University of Olomouc, the successor of the institution where Musil had once studied, Czech Oriental archaeology has returned to its own original birthplace. Let us hope that this is a good omen for its future.

Beginnings in the Days of Empire

The term "Czech-speaking lands" may puzzle the readers of this article. However, the fact that the historical provinces of Bohemia, Moravia, and Silesia changed their state affiliation several times during the twentieth century[1] makes a summary name difficult. Therefore, it seemed most appropriate to me to resort to a neologism which, in my view, best describes the historical reality of a nation that all too frequently constituted one of the balls in a great game of domination in central eastern Europe.

---

1. Just for the sake of completeness: From the Kingdom of Bohemia as a member land of the Habsburg Austro-Hungarian Empire *via* the two Czechoslovak Republics (1918–1938 and 1938–1939), the Nazi-ruled *Protektorat Böhmen und Mähren* (1939–1945), the Czechoslovak- and Czechoslovak Socialist Republic (1945–1960 and 1960–1989), the Czech and Slovak Federal Republic (1989–1992), up to the present-day Czech Republic (since 1993).

We owe the debt of gratitude for conditions allowing for the birth of true Near Eastern archaeology to no lesser a personage than His Apostolic Majesty, the Austro-Hungarian emperor Franz Joseph I (1830–1916), under the protection and ultimate sponsorship of whom the first explorers from our part of Europe challenged the faraway mountains, plains, steppes, and deserts of the region in which the first civilizations of humankind had been born. The role of the founding father of Czech, or rather Moravian, Oriental archaeology falls to Alois Musil (1868–1944).[2] He studied Catholic theology in Olomouc, Moravia, where he showed a keen interest in Near Eastern languages. He was ordained priest in 1891, having obtained a doctoral title in 1895.

His first trip to the Orient, where he worked at the Dominican École biblique in Jerusalem and then at the Jesuit Université St. Joseph in Beirut, took him to Palestine, Egypt, and present-day Jordan, where he also visited the famous ruins of Petra in 1895–1898. Musil won his spurs by the discovery of a "desert castle" Qusayr ʿAmra (1898), an Umayyad structure of the early eighth century with frescoes showing historical, courtly, and mythological motifs, including a rich array of human figures. The discovery seemed so surprising that Musil was at first accused of a hoax and had to prove the truth of his assertions. Returning to ʿAmra in 1900–1901 in the company of an expert painter, he had the frescoes copied, which brought forth firm arguments in favor of his discovery.

The following expedition (1902) took him to the northern Hejaz where he made the first detailed map of the region, publishing it in 1906. This time it was, of course, the Austro-Hungarian army who demonstrated a keen interest in Musil's activities.

In 1908–1909, Musil turned ethnologist and spent almost a year with the Rwala nomads, pasturing their herds in the territories of present-day Syria, Jordan, Iraq, and Saudi Arabia. In 1910 another mapping campaign followed, during which Musil made a map of regions along the Hejaz railway in northwestern Saudi Arabia.

Musil left a copious bequest of documents visualizing his journeys throughout Near Eastern historical and archaeological sites. He did not excavate but he carried out surface surveys, measured and mapped the sites and their architectural monuments, and photographed extensively. He thus left precious documentation of a host of sites, including such major localities as Dura Europos, itself constituting a source of our present-day knowledge of the archaeological heritage of the Near East prior to 1914.

Having attempted unsuccessfully to keep the nomad tribes of the Near East on the Ottoman-Austrian side, Musil assisted Austro-Hungarian interests in the Great War by accompanying the Habsburg expedition to the Holy Land in 1917. This last-ditch attempt to save Habsburg political influence in the Mediterranean failed, and it also constituted the final act of Musil's engagement on Near Eastern soil.

As from 1920, Musil taught courses of Arab history, ethnology, and culture at Charles University, Prague. He published extensively and became a sort of a symbolic figure linked with the Arab world at home. Thanks to the support of Thomas Garrigue Masaryk, first president of the Czechoslovak Republic, Musil was able to prepare an English version of *Oriental Explorations and Studies*, a summary report on his Oriental activities in six volumes, including the much appreciated book *The Manners and*

---

2. Veselá 2012.

Customs of the Rwala Bedouins, cited even today, during trips to the United Kingdom and the United States in 1923–1924 and 1926–1927.[3]

The second founding personage of Near Eastern archaeology of this country, Bedřich (Friedrich, Frédéric) Hrozný (1879–1952), gained world renown as decipherer of the Hittite language.[4] Son of an evangelical pastor from central Bohemia, he exhibited a talent for languages from his early youth. His studies in the Vienna University furnished him with knowledge of most of the Near Eastern languages, dead or living, and he made himself known by his studies of Semitic languages and especially of cuneiform texts. He came into contact with Near Eastern archaeology as early as the year 1904, when Ernst Sellin entrusted him with the second millennium cuneiform tablets excavated at Tell Taʾannek.[5]

In 1912, the Deutsche Orient-Gesellschaft hired Hrozný for the study and publication of the tablets written in cuneiform but in an unknown language, excavated at the sites of Boghazköy by the expedition directed by Hugo Winckler and Theodor Macridy Bey in two campaigns (1906–1907 and 1911–1912). Hrozný set to work immediately, and in 1915 he formulated a hypothesis to the effect that the language of the Boghazköy tablets belonged to the Indo-European family, choosing to call it Hittite. His full publication appeared in 1917 and it brought him at first doubts and objections, but subsequently acknowledgment, gratitude, and admiration.

After his transfer from the University of Vienna to Prague in 1919, Hrozný pondered the possibility of his own archaeological excavations in the Near East. The opportune moment came in 1924 when Hrozný, having gathered a considerable sum of money donated not only by authorities of state including President Masaryk, but also by a number of institutional and private sponsors, launched into the enterprise.

Having been at first refused permission to dig by the new Turkish government, he came over to Syria, then under the government of the French Republic, and in 1924–1925 he excavated two sites in western Syria: Sheikh Saʿad (also Šayh Saʿd or Markaz) and Tell Erfad or Rifaʾat.[6] Sheikh Saʿad rewarded Hrozný with a Hellenistic temple building on an earlier terrace, a group of statuary of the same time period, and copious small finds.[7] Tell Erfad contributed a first-millennium "Hittite administrative building," rampart fragments, and numerous small finds including items of terracotta sculpture, pottery, glass, metal,[8] and stone.[9] Coin finds from Erfad come from the times of Antiochus VII and XII, Septimius Severus, and Galerius Maximianus up to Constantine the Great, the earliest item found here dating to 175 BCE.[10]

A capital discovery awaited Hrozný at the Anatolian site of Kültepe, ancient Kaneš. Having at first attacked the impressive tell on the site without the expected results, he later found out that the findspot of the so-called Cappadocian tablets, cuneiform

---

3. A part of the documentary bequest of Musil has been digitalized and is accessible at http://aloismusil .htf.cuni.cz (accessed 4 January 2017). On Musil's engagement in the First World War see also Gellner 1994.

4. See most recently Velhartická 2015.

5. Sellin 1906; Niemann 2012, 151–52 n. 843 with references.

6. On the sites see Lehmann 2002 s.v.

7. See most recently Bouzek 1990, 1999, Bouzek et al. 2008, Nováková 2006, 150.

8. Nováková 1979.

9. Boháč et al. 1998, Boháč and Bouzek 1999, Nováková 1971.

10. Lehmann 2002, s.v. On later British excavations at the site see Nováková 2006, 152.

documents which had earlier appeared on the antiquities' market, was situated in the tell's piedmont area. He opened excavations there immediately and reaped a rich harvest of 1,034 Old Assyrian texts.[11] Hrozný's last trip took him to Turkey in 1934. This time he focused on inscriptions in hieroglyphic Hittite, which he copied from their original immobile and mobile carriers.

Fluctuat nec mergitur: Czech Archaeology Outside Europe, 1950–1981

An intermission of almost a quarter of a century followed after 1934. The next protagonist of Near Eastern archeology in what was then Czechoslovakia, Bohumil Soudský (1921–1976), became attracted to the discipline during the Second World War.[12] Having passed his secondary school examinations in 1941, he became a seminarian of the Premonstratensian Order chapter of canons at Strahov in Prague. He studied in the Archiepiscopal Theological Institute, namely theology, Oriental archaeology, Hebrew, and Akkadian languages. He enrolled in the Charles University in 1945 and, profiting from an offer of a French government scholarship, went to France where he dedicated himself to Oriental studies at the École Pratique des Hautes Etudes (Section des sciences religieuses et historiques) and École du Louvre (some courses he did at the École des langues orientales de l'Institut Catholique, Université de Sorbonne) in 1946–1948. He completed his university studies in Prague in 1950 by writing a doctoral dissertation on the earliest agricultural civilizations of southwestern Asia.[13] This was the first major work on Oriental archaeology written in the Czech language.

For a long time after 1952, Soudský worked in the Archaeological Institute of the Czechoslovak Academy of Sciences in Prague (Archeologický ústav ČSAV Praha). He opened the first large-scale excavations on the Neolithic site of Bylany by the city of Kutná-Hora in central Bohemia and was the first archaeologist in this country to apply mathematical methods to post-excavation treatment of archaeological finds. In 1969 he went first to the university of Saarbrücken and then in 1970, to the Université de Sorbonne in Paris, where he continued his Neolithic pursuits by initiating a series of large-scale excavations of Neolithic sites along the Aisne river. He died prematurely of a cardiac problem in 1976, missing his fifty-fifth birthday by four days.

Soudský was the first Oriental archaeology specialist of Bohemia who knew perfectly well the materials and problems of the discipline. Thanks to the understanding of the direction of Department of Archaeology of Charles's Philosophical Faculty (present-day Ústav pravěku a rané doby dějinné, Filozofická fakulta UK Praha), he regularly taught courses on the earliest agricultural civilizations of southwestern Asia, and his deep insight, the extent of his knowledge, and the overwhelming vigor with which he drove the facts into the heads of the amazed students fascinated us all. His role is chiefly that of a transmitter of Oriental archaeology issues which he introduced and established in the Archaeology syllabus of Charles University, Prague.

---

11. Nováková 2006, 153 with references, Atici et al. 2014. On the publication of Kaneš texts see http://cdli.ucla.edu/collections/prague/prague_cz.html (accessed 5 July 2016).

12. Charvát and Demoule 1999 s.v.

13. Soudský 1950. The text is now online at https://www.academia.edu/39094612/Bohumil_Soudsk%C3%BD_Nejstar%C5%A1%C3%AD_zem%C4%9Bd%C4%9Blsk%C3%A9_civilizace_v_p%C5%99edn%C3%AD_Asii_The_oldest_agricultural_civilization_in_Asia (accessed March 19, 2020).

Near Eastern Archaeology and the Czech-Speaking Lands 241

In 1958, Soudský visited Iraq for a short study tour, having brought back a small collection of study materials which he used for teaching purposes. Petr Charvát saw this collection in 1968 and remembers seeing painted (Ubaid-culture?) sherds and a brick fragment with inscription of Gudea of Lagaš (2141–2124 BC). The present whereabouts of this collection are unknown.

In terms of our topic, the Czechoslovak–Mongolian expedition of 1958, directed by Lumír Jisl, occupies a special place.[14] Though this was not exactly the Near East, Czechoslovak archaeologists of the Archaeological Institute of the Czechoslovak Academy of Sciences in Prague did, for the first time, try out a complete operation in a faraway land, focusing on a problem which, though of extraordinary significance in international terms, lacked a direct bearing on the early history of the Czech-speaking lands. The archaeological team sent out to Mongolia, under the terms of Czechoslovak aid to this country, located and excavated the tomb of Kültegin, a major personage of the Second Turkish kaganate (685–732). For the very first time, Jisl's expedition secured safe data on the forms of funerary architecture of elites of the Second Turkish kaganate, including sculptural decoration, and documented written sources, namely stone stelae with inscriptions in Chinese and Turkic languages. Unfortunately, the expedition ended in disaster, as all the members fell sick and had to seek medical aid due to bad sanitary conditions. This fact strongly discouraged the Czechoslovak archaeological authorities from similar undertakings and the situation had dire consequences for future operations of this kind outside Europe.

In the Czech-speaking lands, the 1960s represented the second "golden age" of Near Eastern archaeology. In the years 1966 and 1968, Radomír Pleiner of the Archaeological Institute of the Czechoslovak Academy of Sciences in Prague (1929–2015), already a noted specialist in prehistoric technical matters and especially metallurgy, participated in British and American expeditions to Iran and Afghanistan.[15] These included the first surface surveys of southern Iran, organized by a Harvard University archaeological team directed by Carl Lamberg-Karlovsky. Three years later, in 1971, he spent six months in the USA on an internship, at the Massachusetts Institute of Technology and the Universities of Chicago and California. However, the prevailing political conditions barred him from participation in the successful excavations at the Iranian site of Tepe Yahya, organized by Lamberg-Karlovsky since 1972.

Unfortunately, this second "golden age" ended very soon. Jisl died in 1969. Soudský went first to Germany and then to France in 1969. Pleiner was unable to leave the country for longer-term undertakings after 1971. Another pause of ten years followed.

Czech Archaeology in Sri Lanka, 1981–1993

In 1981, the UNESCO organization approved a "Cultural Triangle Project," an operation of documentation, conservation, and presentation of the major historical monuments of Sri Lanka (Ceylon). The three major sites of this project—Anuradhapura, Sigiriya, and Polonnaruwa—formed a roughly triangular area in the midst of the island, hence the name "Cultural Triangle Project." All the member states of the

14. See most recently Šmahelová 2014.
15. Cleere et al. 2015; see also Arab 2010; Crew and Hošek 2015.

242   Petr Charvát

UNESCO were asked to contribute, and the government of the then Czechoslovak Socialist Republic chose to send out experts. A "task force" of three explorers, formed for this purpose, included Jan Bouzek of Charles University, Jiří Břeň of the Prague National Museum, and Petr Charvát, and subsequently also Martin Kuna, both of the Prague Archaeological Institute of the Czechoslovak Academy of Sciences. The group, based at Anuradhapura, the island's ancient capital, advised the excavation and conservation teams operating at the first-millennium CE monastic site of Abhayagiri Vihara in four campaigns in 1982–1985, just before the island sunk into the tempests of civil war.[16] The Czechoslovak team supervised preventive archaeological excavations required in places where major conservation works were to reach underground. Its members proposed a pottery chronology for the monument, reaching from third century BCE to twelfth century CE, and identified a number of items imported to the island. These included Roman glass and coins, Islamic glass items, and a number of pottery imports from the Near East, of the Parthian, Sasanian, and early Islamic epochs. After the ninth century CE, most of the imported pottery came from Chinese workshops.

A New Takeoff: 1989–2000

Both the veterans of archaeological research and representatives of a new generation of scholars quickly grasped the new opportunities offered by political changes after the year 1989. In 1989, Charvát took part in the excavations of the British Archaeological School in Iraq, directed by Roger Matthews, at the prehistorical site of Jemdet Nasr by Baghdad, findspot of the second most ancient group of cuneiform texts (around 3000 BCE) in the 1920s.[17] Prague's "mother of Czech Oriental archaeology," the Archaeological Institute of the Czechoslovak Academy of Sciences (present-day Archeologický ústav Akademie věd České republiky v Praze, v. v. i.), has also engaged its researchers in Turkey. In accordance with the tradition of this institution, Ivan Pavlů, successor of Soudský, and his colleague Jaroslav Řídký participated in the post-excavation treatment of finds from the sites of Güvercinkayasi (Chalcolithic age, Aksaray region, organized by Sevil Gülcur) and Tepecik—Çiftlik (Neolithic, Niğde region, organized by Erhan Bıçakçı) under the patronage of the University of Istanbul, providing information on a wider perspective of comparative studies of Anatolian and central European developments in prehistory.[18]

The next Czech archaeological campaign in the Orient came along in 1996, when, thanks to the intrepid Jan Bouzek, a team of specialists from Charles University and the Oriental Institute (Academy of Sciences of the Czech Republic, Prague) joined the international archaeological group operating a series of preventive excavations prior to the rebuilding of the municipal area of the city of Beirut, devastated by the long-term Lebanese civil war (1975–1990).[19] The Czech concession, bearing the designation Bey

---

16. Bouzek et al. 1986, Bouzek et al. 1993, Charvát 1993.
17. Matthews 1990.
18. Pavlů et al. 2007, Řídký 2009.
19. For subsequent Czech explorations in the area, see Charvát 2015.

069, opened a plot in Beirut's central space, the *Place des Martyrs*. Bouzek's team laid bare a long sequence of habitation structures beginning the in third century BCE and ending in the seventh century CE. In the Middle Ages and later, the local ground was used for dumping rubbish, then as a garden of the famous Druze emir named Fakhruddin (1572–1635),[20] and, ultimately, as a site of an Ottoman *suq* in the nineteenth century.[21]

In 1996, the forty-third Rencontre Assyriologique Internationale was held in Prague. Jesús Gil Fuensanta, a participant from the Universidad Autónoma de Madrid, suggested to Charvát the possibility of participating in the Spanish–Turkish–U.S. excavations at Tilbes Höyük (Sanlıurfa province, southeastern Turkey). Charvát accepted, and the Tilbes Höyük excavations of 1997–2000 became one of the first ports of entry for Czech archaeologists into the Orient. The archaeological work at Tilbes and related sites resulted in a fruitful international cooperation, chiefly with the Spanish side, to which Inna Mateicucová (Masaryk University, Brno), Petr Květina, Jaroslav Řídký, and Filip Velímský (all three from the Archaeological Institute, Academy of Sciences of the Czech Republic) all contributed in their turn (for a bibliography of Czech participation in the project see Appendix).

The site itself, a tell 12m high and 6 hectares in extent, is now under water due to the Birecik dam. The local occupation started somewhere in the Late Chalcolithic, probably before LC 3 (= Middle Uruk). The tell consists mainly of third-millennium BCE materials. Occupation ceased sometime in the Middle Bronze Age here, and the site was deserted for about a millennium. Renewed human presence may have started in Late Assyrian times, and definitely materialized in the Achaemenid and Hellenistic periods. Some Parthian and Roman material is present. A ruin of a small rectangular structure on the hilltop may be medieval, and possibly belonged to one of the guard posts of the Mamluk forces in the Levant and southeastern Anatolia.

Alive and Well: Czech Non-European Archaeology, 2000–2017

In the third millennium CE, undertakings of Czech archaeological research in the Near East burst to full bloom. In 2001, a team from Charles University, directed by Ladislav Stančo, went to Uzbekistan to discuss the possibility of excavations at the site of Jandavlattepa in the Sherabad oasis, historically speaking located in northwestern Bactria (present-day Surkhandarya region, southern Uzbekistan). A full Czech–Uzbekistani field operation, covering the years 2002–2006, ensued out of this initial move.[22]

---

20. Gorton 2014.

21. Bouzek 2002a, 2002b, Bouzek and Musil 2008. On Fakhruddin, see Hourani 2010, 921–32 and Gorton 2013. Just for the sake of pleasure, let us listen to the description of Fakhruddin's palace by an English traveler named Henry Maundrell of 1695: "The emir Faccardine had his chief residence in this place.... At the entrance of it is a marble fountain, of greater beauty than is usually seen in Turkey. The palace within consists of several courts, all now run much to ruin; or rather perhaps never finish'd. The stables, yards for horses, dens for lions and other savage creatures, gardens, &c. are such as would not be unworthy of the quality of a prince in Christendom ... but the best sight that this palace affords, and the worthiest to be remember'd, is the orange garden.... One cannot imagine any thing more perfect in this kind" (Gorton 2014, 26). Excavations of the garden yielded levelling layers containing earlier rubbish, and stone-lined pits as tree beds.

22. Abdullaev and Stančo 2011.

The site, a fortified urban agglomeration consisting of a citadel and a lower town (*shahristan*), is situated in a fertile plain watered by the Sherabad River, on an overland route linking ancient Sogdiana and Bactria. The local settlement reaches back into the Late Bronze Age (end of second millennium BCE), but structures visible on the site now probably started in the early third century CE and continued into early fifth century CE. The coins indicate the initial link with the Kushan Empire of India, followed by an epoch of Kushano-Sasanian orientation. The latter period of time seems to be one of impoverishment, the extinction of long-distance contact, and a certain encapsulation of the site as against the surrounding world.

During the years 2008–2011, the Jandavlattepa excavations gave way to a systematic surface survey of the Sherabad district of southern Uzbekistan, leaning on the knowledge of material gathered before. Finds of these campaigns fall into the Graeco-Bactrian, Kushan, Kushano-Sasanian and High Middle Ages (tenth to thirteenth centuries CE), ending as late as the nineteenth century CE.

In the course of the 1990s, Inna Mateiciucová, an archaeology graduate of the Masaryk University of Brno, had gathered extensive excavation experience in working with Dutch and German archaeological teams in Syria (Tell Sabi Abyad, Tell Mozan). Building upon this foundation, she opened up her own excavations in 2005, choosing the site of Tell Arbid Abyad within the concession of our Polish colleagues at the Tell Arbid site in the upper Khabur Area of northern Syria. This happened due to the magnanimity of Professor Piotr Bieliński of Warsaw University, who generously ceded to Mateiciucová a part of his own claim. The Brno University team worked at the site of Tell Arbid Abyad, situated some 35km from the Syrian town of Qamishli, intermittently from 2005 to 2011.[23]

Tell Arbid Abyad, some 12km east of Chagar Bazar, is a small mound approximately 2m high, covering about 0.5 hectares. Finds and structures identified on the site belong to Late Neolithic, Early Bronze Age, Iron Age, and Islamic epochs. Its chief interest, however, lies in the structures left behind by the Late Neolithic proto-Halaf and Early Halaf culture of the early sixth millennium BCE. The site yielded architectural remains, pottery, stone tools, sealing fragments, tokens, and other objects dating to that time period.

In 2006, an archaeological expedition of the University of West Bohemia in Plzeň (Pilsen) opened an exploration of the citadel of the north Iraqi city of Erbil.[24] The expedition, organized in cooperation with the Salahuddin University of Erbil, documented especially surface finds from the slopes of the famed Citadel of Erbil (10 hectares in extent). Except for a group of Middle Paleolithic artefacts, probably used as pavement stones, its members gathered a collection of some 7,000 pottery fragments. These range from Late Ubaid and Late Chalcolithic ages, with major groups belonging to the Neo-Assyrian and Hellenistic periods, down to the Islamic epoch (twelfth to fourteenth centuries CE). In 2007, the Czech team carried out a complete architectural survey of the building layout of the citadel of the Late Ottoman period and twentieth century.[25]

23. Gregerová et al. 2013, Mateiciucová 2010; Mateiciucová et al. 2009, Mateiciucová et al. 2012; see also Cruells, Mateiciucová, and Nieuwenhuyse 2017.

24. Nováček et al. 2008.

25. Nováček 2008.

The subsequent campaigns of 2009 and 2010 saw intense surface explorations verifying hypotheses of the municipal development of Erbil suggested by the evaluation of earlier air photos. The city was found to have been enclosed by a massive rampart fortification of the Assyrian (?) period. This original protection received subsequent refurbishment by means of a wall fortification system of the Islamic period (seventh to thirteenth century CE). In both cases, the municipal area included amounted to some three square kilometers.

A minor survey focused on the site of Tell Baxçan on the southwestern edge of Erbil, some 4km from the Erbil citadel. The presence of the cultures of Hassuna, Halaf, and Nineveh V, together with Middle Assyrian, Late Assyrian, and Islamic materials has been observed.[26]

A specific operation targeted the ruins known as al-Qubahan *madrasa* in Amadiya or Amedi. The architectural complex, dating from the twelfth to the fourteenth century, consisted of a large congregation hall, and service and entry buildings making up a four-sided complex with oblong internal court. The presence of thirteenth to nineteenth century archaeological materials has been established.[27]

In 2013–2015, a project of Nováček´s team concentrated on the early urban history of the central Tigris and northeastern Mesopotamia (Adiabene) in the Islamic period (sixth to seventeenth century CE). Although the long-term continuity and high degree of resilience against political changes seems to be the most distinctive feature of the local urban landscape, the life periods of central places in Adiabene might have varied considerably. Several towns might have been abandoned or lost urban status within periods that are generally considered times of stability and prosperity (Mahoze/Tell Mahuz in the ninth century, al-Sinn and Hadīthat al-Mawsil in the twelfth century.[28] As a bonus of these investigations, surface finds from Uruk culture, Neo-Assyrian, Hellenistic, and Parthian dates came forth at least in one site.[29]

In 2011–2019, Filip Čapek and David Rafael Moulis of the Evangelical Theological Faculty at Charles University, Prague participated in the excavations of the Israeli sites of Khirbet Kheiyafa, Tel Azekah, and Tel Motsah. Tel Azekah, a fortified town, was already in existence in the Middle Bronze Age at the latest. Later it became a border fortress of the Kingdom of Judah, attacked and destroyed first by the Assyrians in the 8th century BCE and then by the Babylonians in the 6th century BCE (Čapek 2016). Tel Motsa in the vicinity of Jerusalem is the only temple of the megaron type (originally a simple hall with a rectangular ground plan and one entrance in one of the shorter walls) from the Iron Age with some remarkable cultic finds (Čapek 2019; see also Čapek's website at https://web.etf.cuni.cz/ETFN-449.html).

Czech archaeology attained the farthest limit of the ancient Near East in 2012 when Jiří Unger of the Archaeological Institute (Academy of Sciences of the Czech Republic) participated in excavations of the Mes ʿAynak area (Logar Province) in Afghanistan, an extensive area of deposits of copper, in which recent prospecting and mining activities brought to light a series of Buddhist monasteries dating to the first through

---

26. Nováček et al. 2013.
27. Nováček and Sůvová 2011, Nováček 2012.
28. Nováček and Melčák 2016.
29. Nováček and Melčák 2016, 103, Makhmur al-Qadima.

the ninth century CE.[30] The features investigated date from second to ninth centuries CE, and could possibly represent part of a mining settlement enclosed in a rampart wall.

The Czech engagement at Mes ʿAynak resulted in the travel of a selected group of items deposited at the National Museum of Afghanistan in Kabul to Prague, to be shown in a special exhibition at the National Museum in 2016.[31] Most of the objects represented finds from the site of Mes ʿAynak. These exhibits included stone and clay statuary, a hoard of jewelry of precious metals and stones of the third through fifth century CE found at Mes ʿAynak in 2012, a group of silver tableware vessels in Sasanian style, utility objects, cosmetic accessories, coins, and various other artefacts. Impressions of textile in which the objects were wrapped, and even of lace, survived on some, trapped by corrosive products. Sculpture items of painted clay were analyzed for the origin of the pigments, which were shown to come both from the site and to have been imported from afar. The finds underwent scientific analyses and conservation, and precious technical data was secured.

For the sake of completeness, this survey must be rounded out with reference to the activities of Charles University's Institute of Classical Archaeology, and especially its Director, Peter Pavúk, since 2013. Having worked with the Manfred Korfmann expedition at Troy in 1995–2006 as Member of the *"Graduierten Kolleg" Anatolien und seine Nachbarn*, Eberhard-Karls Universität Tübingen, Pavúk rendered service to Oriental archaeology as an expert on second-millennium archaeology of the Aegean, Troad, and western Anatolia.[32]

All Is Well When the End Is Well?

All in all, the story of Near Eastern archaeology in the Czech-speaking lands is marked by ups and downs following irregularly after one another. The opportunities of the great founding period of Musil and Hrozný came to naught with the Nazi occupation and then with the communist regime. No self-standing undertaking abroad materialized in 1948–1989, save for the ill-fated Mongolian expedition of the Archaeological Institute of the Czechoslovak Academy of Sciences. At that time, Czech scholars strove to preserve the sum of knowledge then available, especially in the university courses, and grasped whatever opportunities friendly academics and institutions abroad offered them. It was only after 1990 that new challenges could be properly answered and that a new generation of young and enterprising explorers took up the management of the discipline.

At the time being, four fully constituted expeditions operate in the Orient: the Uzbekistan team of Stančo, the Syrian group of Mateiciucová, and the Iraqi Kurdistan "task force" of Nováček as well as the Israeli colleagues Filip Čapek and David Rafael Moulis. Oriental archaeology now disposes of an institutional base, a thing unheard of in its history on Czech-speaking territory: the Department of Prehistoric

---

30. Unger 2013.
31. Stančo 2016.
32. Pavúk 2014, 2015.

Archaeology of the Near East of the Institute of Archaeology and Museology, Faculty of Philosophy, Masaryk University of Brno (Oddělení pravěké archeologie Předního Východu, Filozofická fakulta MU Brno).[33] The first BA theses have been submitted[34] and PhD dissertations have been defended both in Prague[35] and in Plzeň/Pilsen.[36] With the recent appointment of Karel Nováček to the Palacký University of Olomouc, the successor of the institution where Musil once studied, Czech Oriental archaeology returned to its own original birthplace. Let us hope that this is a good omen for its future.

Appendix

Bibliography of contributions pertaining to participation of Czech archaeologists in the Tilbes Höyük and neighboring excavations

Charvát, P. 2001. "Tilbes Höyük v provincii Sanliurfa, jihovýchodní Turecko (The Site of Tilbes Höyük, Sanliurfa Province, Southeastern Turkey)." Pages 5–9 in *Orientalia Antiqua Nova—Sborník z mezinárodního vědeckého kolokvia, konaného v Plzni dne 9. února 2001*. Edited by I. Budil and P. Charvát. Plzeň: ZČU Plzeň.

Charvát, P., and J. Gil Fuensanta. 2001. "Seals and Seal Impressions from Tilbes Höyük, South-Eastern Turkey (1996–1999)." *Archív orientální* 69:559–70.

Fuensanta, J. Gil, E. Algorri, E. Bucak, and P. Charvat. 2002. "Trabajos de la Misión Arqueológica Española en Turquía (VII): El proyecto Tilbes 2001." *Boletín de la Asociación Española de Orientalistas* 38:233–47.

Fuensanta, J. Gil, E. Bucak, and P. Charvat. 2002. "La Misión Arqueológica Española en Turquía 2000." *Revista de Arqueología del siglo XXI* 23:32–39.

Fuensanta, J. Gil, M. S. Rothman, P. Charvat, and E. Bucak. 2002. "Tilbeş Höyük Salvage Project Excavation." Pages 131–44 in *T. C., Kültür Bakanlığı, Anıtlar ve Müzeler Müdürlüğü, 23.Kazı Sonuçları Toplantısı, 1. cilt, 28 Mayis–01 Haziran 2001*. Ankara: Kültür Bakanlığı Milli Kütüphane Basımevi.

Fuensanta, J. Gil, P. Charvát, and E. Bucak. 2000. "1998 and 1997 Salvage Survey and Excavations at Tilmusa, Tilöbür and Tilvez Höyük." *Orient-Express—Notes et Nouvelles d'Archéologie Orientale* 2000/4:89–91.

———. 2001. "1999 Salvage Survey and Excavations at Tilmusa, Tilobur and Tilvez Hoyuk." *Orient-Express—Notes et Nouvelles d'Archéologie Orientale* 2001/1:3–5.

———. 2002. "2000 Surtepe Höyük Salvage Excavation Report." Pages 197–204 in *T. C., Kültür Bakanlığı, Anıtlar ve Müzeler Müdürlüğü, 23.Kazı Sonuçları Toplantısı, 1. cilt, 28 Mayis–01 Haziran 2001*. Ankara: Kültür Bakanlığı Milli Kütüphane Basımevi.

———. 2002. "2000 Salvage Excavations at Surtepe, Tilbes and Tilvez (Birecik Dam)." *Orient Express—Notes et Nouvelles d'Archéologie Orientale* 2002/3:74–76.

———. 2002. "2001 Salvage Survey and Excavations at Surtepe, Tilbes and Tilvez (Birecik Dam)." *Orient Express—Notes et Nouvelles d'Archéologie Orientale* 2002/4:100–103.

Fuensanta, J. Gil, P. Charvat, E. Bucak, M. A. Jimenez, P. Kvetina, and F. Velimsky. 2003. "2001 Surtepe Höyük Salvage Excavations Report." Pages 105–12 in *T. C., Kültür Bakanlığı, Anıtlar ve Müzeler Müdürlüğü, 24.Kazı Sonuçları Toplantısı, 1. cilt, 27–31 Mayis 2002*. Ankara: Kültür Bakanlığı Milli Kütüphane Basımevi.

---

33. See https://classics.phil.muni.cz/en/pane/praveka-archeologie-predniho-vychodu (accessed March 19, 2020).
34. E.g. Koubková 2015.
35. Vaškaninová 2013, Belaňová 2015.
36. Král 2016.

248 Petr Charvát

Fuensanta, J. Gil, P. Charvat, E. Bucak, R. M. Molina, and M. A. Jimenez. 2003. "2001 Tilves and Tilvez Höyük Salvage Excavations Report." Pages 369–76 in *T. C., Kültür Bakanlığı, Anıtlar ve Müzeler Müdürlüğü, 24.Kazı Sonuçları Toplantısı, 1. cilt, 27–31 Mayis 2002*. Ankara: Kültür Bakanlığı Milli Kütüphane Basımevi.

Fuensanta, J. Gil, in cooperation with P. Charvát. 2004. "Trabajos de la Misión Arqueológica Española en Turquía (IX): El proyecto Tilbes, 2003." *Boletín de la Asociación Española de Orientalistas* 40:267–83.

———. 2005. "Trabajos de la Misión Arqueológica Española en Turquía (X): El proyecto Tilbes, 2004." *Boletín de la Asociación Española de Orientalistas* 41:345–57.

———. 2006. "Trabajos de la Misión Arqueológica Española en Turquía (XI): El proyecto Tilbes, 2005." *Boletín de la Asociación Española de Orientalistas* 42:41–58.

———. 2007. "Trabajos de la Misión Arqueológica Española en Turquía (XIII): El proyecto Tilbes, 2007." *Boletín de la Asociación Española de Orientalistas* 43:25–53.

Fuensanta, J. Gil, and P. Charvat. 2005. "Halafians and Ubaidians: The Case of Tilbes Höyük in Birecik (Southeastern Turkey)." Pages 123–33 in *Ethnicity in Ancient Mesopotamia, Papers Read at the 48th Rencontre Assyriologique Internationale, Leiden, 1–4 July 2002*. Edited by W. H. van Soldt, R. Kalvelagen, and D. Katz. Leuven: Peeters.

———. 2005. "Birecik achéménide et l'âge du Fer IIIB dans le Sud-Est anatolien." Pages 151–73 in *L'archéologie de l'empire achéménide: nouvelles recherches. Actes du colloque organisé au Collège de France par le "Réseau international d'études et de recherches achéménides" (GDR 2538 CNRS), 21–22 novembre 2003*. Persika 6. Edited by P. Briant and R. Boucharlat. Paris: Éditions de Boccard.

Fuensanta, J. Gil, P. Charvat, and E. Crivelli. 2008. "The Dawn of a City. Surtepe Höyük Excavations, Birecik Dam Area, Eastern Turkey." Pages 97–112 in *Proceedings of the 5th International Congress of the Archaeology of the Ancient Near East (3–8 April 2006)*. Vol. 2. Edited by J. M. Córdoba et al. Madrid: Centro Superior de estudios sobre el Oriente Próximo y Egipto.

Fuensanta, J. Gil, and E. Crivelli Montero, in cooperation with P. Charvát. 2008. "Trabajos de la Misión Arqueológica Española en Turquía (XIV): El proyecto Tilbes, 2008." *Boletín de la Asociación Española de Orientalistas* 44:233–49.

Fuensanta, J. Gil, A. J. Trapero, E. Crivelli, P. Charvát, and V. Toscano. 2009. "Visión antropológica de los rituales prehistóricos en el Éufrates (parte I)." *Boletín de la Asociación Española de Orientalistas* 45:225–48.

REFERENCES

Abdullaev, K., and L. Stančo. 2011. *Jandavlattepa—The Excavation Report for Seasons 2002–2006*. Vol. 1. Prague: Charles University in Prague/Karolinum Press.

Arab, R. 2010. "Iran Survey 1968: Iranian Artefacts at the Institute of Archaeology, UCL." http://www.ucl.ac.uk/iransurvey/index.php (accessed 6 January 2017).

Atici, L. et al., eds. 2014. *Current research at Kültepe-Kanesh, An Interdisciplinary and Integrative Approach to Trade Networks, Internationalism and Identity*. Journal of Cuneiform Studies, Supplemental Series 4. Atlanta: Lockwood Press.

Belaňová, P. 2015. "Staroveký šperk Strednej Ázie a jeho vztahy k umeniu šperkárov antického Stredomoria" (Ancient Jewellery of Central Asia and its Relations to the Jewellers' Art of Ancient Mediterranean). PhD diss., Charles University, Prague.

Boháč, L. et al. 1998. "Hellenistic and Roman Finds from Bedřich Hrozný's Excavations at Tell Erfad, Syria, Parts I–II." *Eirene* 32:122–57.

Boháč, L., and J. Bouzek. 1999. "Hellenistic and Roman Finds from Bedřich Hrozný's Excavations at Tell Erfad, Syria, Part III and Addenda." *Eirene* 35:47–60.

Bouzek, J. 1990. "La sculpture romaine des fouilles de Bedřich Hrozný à Sheikh Sa'ad." *Etudes et Travaux* 15:87–92.

————, ed. 1993. *Ceylon Between East and West: Anuradhapura, Abhayagiri Vihara, 1981–1984. Excavations and Studies*. Prague: Charles University Press.

————. 1999. *Corpus Signorum Imperii Romani, Czech Republic I: Roman Sculpture from Syria and Asia Minor in Czech Collections*. Prague: Charles University Press.

————. 2002a. "Czech Excavations in Beirut, Martyrs' Square (Bey 069), Sondage A, Part I, General Survey: Pottery and Other Small Finds of Hellenistic, Early Roman and Medieval Periods, Glass and Metal Objects." *Eirene* 38:7–166.

————. 2002b. "Czech Excavations at Beirut, Martyrs' Square, Part II: Architecture, Survey of Layers and Deposits, Addenda to Part I—The Lamps." *Studia Hercynia* 6:41–106.

Bouzek, J., et al. 1986. "The Chronology of the Local Pottery and Other Finds Uncovered in the SW Sector of the Abhayagiri Vihara (Asnuradhapura, Sri Lanka)." *Archeologické rozhledy* 38:241–62.

————. 2008. "Sheikh Sa'ad, A Preliminary Report on the Project of Publication of Hrozný's Digs." *Studia Hercynia* 11:98–100.

Bouzek, J., and J. Musil. 2008. "Czech Excavations at Beirut, Martyrs Square, Part III." *Studia Hercynia* 12:5–79.

Čapek, F. 2016. "Continuing Cooperation between the Prague Theology Faculty and Tel Aviv University." *Czech Protestant News*, November 29, 2016. http://e-bulletin.cz/eng/2016/11/29/continuing-cooperation-between-the-prague-theology-faculty-and-tel-aviv-university. Accessed March 19, 2020.

————. 2019. "A Temple Full of Questions." *Spotlight Forum* 6, 10–12. https://web.etf.cuni.cz/ETFN-449-version1-a_temple_full_of_questions_2019.pdf (accessed March 19, 2020).

Charvát, P. 1993. "External Contacts of Sri Lanka in the 1st Millennium A.D. (Archeological evidence from Mantai)." *Archív Orientální* 61:13–29.

————. 2015. "Archeologický výzkum Bedřicha Hrozného na Šech Sa´adu v Sýrii." Pages 150–60 in *Bedřich Hrozný a 100 let chetitologie—Bedřich Hrozný and 100 Years of Hittitology*. Edited by Š. Velhartická. Prague: Národní galerie v Praze.

Charvát, P., and J.-P. Demoule. 1999. "Soudský, Bohumil (in Czech)." In *Kdo byl kdo—Čeští orientalisté, afrikanisté a iberoamerikanisté (Who Was Who—Czech Orientalists, Africanists and Ibero-Americanists)*. Prague: LIBRI. http://www.libri.cz/databaze/orient/list.php?od=s&count=10&start=1 (accessed 5 January 2017).

Cleere, H., et al. 2015. "In memoriam—Prof. PhDr. Radomir Pleiner, DrSc." *The Crucible (HMS News)* 88:10–11.

Crew, P., and J. Hošek, comps. 2015. "Radomír Pleiner 1929–2015: A Celebration of His Life and Work." *Historical Metallurgy* 49 (1). https://archeoindustrysites.com/sites/default/files/pdf/radomir-pleiner-1929-2015-a-celebration-of-his-life-and-work-in-historical-metallurgy-491-2015-pp-1.pdf (accessed October 10, 2019).

Cruells, W., I. Mateiciucová, and O. Nieuwenhuyse, eds. 2017. *Painting Pots—Painting People: Late Neolithic Ceramics in Ancient Mesopotamia*. Oxford: Oxbow.

Gellner, E. 1994. "Lawrence of Moravia." *Times Literary Supplement* 19 August: 12–14.

Gorton, T. 2013. *Renaissance Emir: A Druze Warlord at the Court of the Medici*. London: Quartet Books.

————. 2014. "Lebanon's Renaissance Prince." *Aramco World* 65:26. http://archive.aramcoworld.com/issue/201404/lebanon.s.renaissance.prince.htm (accessed 7 January 2017).

Gregerová, M. et al. 2013. "Rethinking the Making of the Late Neolithic Pottery: An Example of Tell Arbid Abyad (Northeast Syria)." Pages 305–14 in *Interpreting the Late Neolithic of Upper Mesopotamia, Leiden, March 2009: Papers on Archaeology of the Leiden Museum of Antiquities (PALMA)*. Edited by O. P. Nieuwenhuyse et al. Turnhout: Brepols.

Hourani, A. 2010. "New Documents on the History of Mount Lebanon and Arabistan in the 10th and 11th Centuries H. Beirut." https://archive.org/stream/NewDocumentsOnThe HistoryOfMtLebanonAndArabistanInThe10thAnd11th/NewDocumentsOnTheHistory OfMountLebanonAndArabistanInThe10thAnd11thCenturiesH.AlexanderHourani#page /n921/mode/2up (accessed 7 January 2017).

250   Petr Charvát

Koubková, H. 2015. "Fine Ware Ninevite 5 Pottery from Khabur Basin Project." BA thesis, Masaryk University Brno. http://is.muni.cz/th/415501/ff_b/?lang=en (accessed 10 January 2017).

Král, P. 2016. "Krajina v zázemí asyrských metropolí" (Landscape in the Hinterland of Assyrian Metropolises). PhD diss., University of Pilsen.

Lehmann, G. 2002. *Bibliographie der archäologischen Fundstellen und Surveys in Syrien und Libanon.* Deutsches Archäologisches Institut, Orient-Abteilung, Orient-Archäologie 9. Rahden: Verlag Marie Leidorf.

Mateiciucová, I. 2010. "Tell Arbid Abyad—A New Late Neolithic Site in the Upper Khabur Basin, NE Syria: The Preliminary Report." Pages 411–22 in *Proceedings of the 6th International Congress on the Archaeology of the Ancient Near East (ICAANE), May, 5th–10th 2008.* Edited by P. Matthiae. Wiesbaden: Harrassowitz.

Mateiciucová, I., et al. 2009. "Geophysical Survey at Archaeological Sites in Northeastern Syria." *ArchéoSciences* 33:111–13.

———. 2012. "Surface Survey and Geophysical Prospection in the Micro-region of Tell Arbid, NE Syria: A Preliminary Report." Pages 17–32 in *Proceedings of the 7th International Congress on the Archaeology of the Ancient Near East (ICAANE), London, April, 12th–16th 2010.* Edited by R. Matthews and J. Curtis. Wiesbaden: Harrassowitz.

Matthews, R. J. 1990. "Excavations at Jemdet Nasr, 1989." *Iraq* 52:25–39.

Niemann, H. 2012. "Ernst Sellin: Powerful in His Time; A Sketch of the Life and Work of an Old Testament Scholar, and Pioneer in Biblical Archaeology from Mecklenburg." Pages 131–63 in *Ernst Sellin—Alttestamentler und Archäologe.* Beiträge zur Erforschung des Alten Testaments und des Antiken Judentums 58. Edited by U. Palmer. Frankfurt am Main: Peter Lang.

Nováček, K. 2008. "Architektura citadely v Arbílu—Předběžná zpráva o druhé sezóně výzkumu citadely v roce 2007 (Architecture of the Erbil Citadel—A Preliminary Report on the Second Season of Investigation of the Citadel in 2007)." *Orientalia Antiqua Nova* 8:60–83.

———. 2012. "Čeští archeologové v Kurdistánu (Czech Archaeologists in Kurdistan)." Pages 11–30 in *Stopy (v) šafránu.* Edited by P. Písařová and K. Šašková. Plzeň: Západočeská univerzita v Plzni.

Nováček, K., and M. Melčák. 2016. "The Medieval Urban Landscape in Northeastern Mesopotamia (MULINEM): First Two Years of the Project." Pages 95–105 in *9th ICAANE, Basel 2014, Proceedings.* Vol. 3. Edited by R. A. Stucky, O. Kaelin, and H. P. Mathys. Wiesbaden: Harrassowitz.

Nováček, K., and Z. Sůvová. 2011. "Zangi-Period Architecture in Iraqi Kurdistan. Medrese Qubahan at Amêdi ('Amadīya)." *Zeitschrift für Orient-Archäologie* 4:176–210.

Nováček, K., et al. 2008. "Research of the Arbil Citadel, Iraqi Kurdistan, First Season—Výzkum citadely v Arbilu (irácký Kurdistán), první sezona." *Památky archeologické* 99:259–302.

———. 2013. "A Medieval City within Assyrian Walls: The Continuity of the Town of Arbīl in Northern Mesopotamia." *Iraq* 75:1–42.

Nováková, N. 1971. *Terres cuites de Tell Erfad, I–II.* Anthropological Papers of the Náprstek Museum Prague 2. Prague: Náprstek Museum.

———. 1979. "La statuette de bronze de Tell Erfad." *Archiv Orientální* 47:100–102.

———. 2006. "Les recherches archéologiques de Bedřich Hrozný au Proche Orient." Pages 149–57 in *L'état, le pouvoir, les prestations et leurs formes en Mésopotamie ancienne, Actes du Colloque assyriologique franco-tchèque, Paris, 7–8 novembre 2002.* Edited by P. Charvát et al. Prague: Univerzita Karlova v Praze, Filozofická fakulta.

Pavlů, I., et al. 2007. "Grinding Stones and Handstones from the Chalcolithic Site of Güvercinkayasi (1996–2004)." *Anatolia Antiqua* 15:17–48.

Pavúk, P. 2014. *Troia VI-Früh und Mitte. Keramik der Grabungen 1988–2002.* Studia Troica Monographien 3. Bonn: Rudolf Habelt.

———. 2015. "Between the Aegeans and the Hittites: Western Anatolia in the 2nd Millennium BC." Pages 81–114 in *NOSTOI: Indigenous Culture, Migration and Integration in the Aegean Islands and Western Anatolia during the Late Bronze and Early Iron Ages*. Edited by N. C. Stampolidis, Ç. Maner, and K. Kopanias. Istanbul: Koç University Press.

Řídký, J. 2009. "Fragmentation and Secondary Use of the Manos and Metates from the Tepecik–Çiftlik Site in Central Turkey." Pages 140–49 in *My Things Changed Things. Social Development and Cultural Exchange in Prehistory, Antiquity and the Middle Ages*. Edited by P. Maříková-Vlčková, J. Mynářová, and M. Tomášek. Prague: Institute of Archaeology of the Academy of Sciences of the Czech Republic, v. v. i.

Sellin, E. 1906. *Eine Nachlese auf den Tell Ta'annek in Palästina, nebst einem Anhange von Friedrich Hrozný: Die neuen Keilschrifttexte von Ta'annek*. Denkschriften der Kaiserlichen Akademie der Wissenschaften, phil.-hist. Klasse 52/3. Vienna: Alfred Holder.

Šmahelová, L. 2014. "Kül-Tegin památník. Turkický kaganát a výzkum československo-mongolské expedice v Chöšöö–Cajdam 1958 (Kül-Tegin Monument. Turkic khaganate and Research of the First Czechoslovak–Mongolian Expedition in Khöshöö Tsaidam 1958)." PhD diss., Charles University, Prague.

Soudský, B. 1950. "Nejstarší zemědělské civilisace v Přední Asii." *Obzor prehistorický* 14:5–162.

Stančo, L., ed. 2016. *Afghanistan—Rescued Treasures of Buddhism*. Prague: National Museum.

Unger, J. 2013. "Preliminary Findings and Results from Sites 005 and 034." Pages 19–34 in *Recent Archaeological Work in Afghanistan—Preliminary Studies on Mes 'Aynak Excavations and Other Field Works*. Kabul: Délégation archéologique française en Afghanistan.

Vaškaninová, V. 2013. "Umenie sz. Anatólie v achajmenovskej dobe a jeho vzťahy s gréckym a perzským umením (The Art of North-Western Anatolia in the Achaemenid-Persian Period and Its Relations with the Greek and Persian Art)." PhD diss., Charles University, Prague.

Velhartická, Š., ed. 2015. *Bedřich Hrozný a 100 let chetitologie—Bedřich Hrozný and 100 Years of Hittitology*. Prague: Národní galerie v Praze.

Veselá, M. 2012. "Alois Musil (1868–1944): Archaeology of Late Antiquity and the Beginning of Islamic Archaeology in the Middle East." PhD diss., Université de Paris I Panthéon-Sorbonne and Západočeská univerzita v Plzni.

CHAPTER 13

Tintin in Mesopotamia: The Story of Belgian Assyriology (1890–2017)

Katrien De Graef

THE FOLLOWING SHORT OVERVIEW presents a general picture of the origin and development of Assyriological studies in Belgium. The main focus lies on Belgian scholars involved in Assyriology *stricto sensu*, being "the science or study of the history, language, and antiquities of ancient Assyria and Babylonia" as defined in the Merriam-Webster online dictionary.[1] Ancient Near Eastern Archaeology, Semitics, Hittitology, Elamitology, and other related subfields will be mentioned when appropriate, but they are not the subject of this overview.

This overview of Belgian Assyriologists is limited to persons who have been or are employed by the different Belgian universities, as enumerating all of their students would lead too far. For evident reasons, I will not list all publications by Belgian Assyriologists mentioned in this overview—their bibliographies can be found in their *Festschrifts* or on the websites of their universities—but restrict myself to the main names, specialties, and places that make up the story of Belgian Assyriology.[2]

"Explorers on the Moon":[3] The First Steps in Belgian Assyriology from Leuven to Liège

In Belgium, Assyriology officially started in 1890, when at the then French-speaking Catholic University of Leuven (Université Catholique de Louvain), canon Albinus Van Hoonacker (1857–1933),[4] a doctor in theology, who had been teaching "critical history of the Old Testament" (*histoire critique de l'Ancien Testament*) as well as an introductory course of biblical Hebrew, started teaching "Assyrian" (*Assyrien*). He probably was an autodidact as far as cuneiform was concerned and his focus lay on the contributions of Assyriology to biblical exegesis and "critical history," but some of his publications can be considered "purely" Assyriological, such as those on the Cyrus cylinder or on the annals of Assurbanipal in volumes 24, 25, and 28 of the *Zeitschrift für Assyriologie*.

---

1. See https://www.merriam-webster.com/dictionary/Assyriology (accessed 15 September 2017).

2. I would like to thank M. Tanret, Ö. Tunca, P. Talon, J. Tavernier, L. Colonna d'Istria, and K. Abraham for providing me with information.

3. Originally published by Hergé in Tintin magazine as *On a marché sur la Lune* (1952–1953).

4. See Naster 1978, 9–11 and Schelkens 2008.

252

In 1927, upon the retirement of Van Hoonacker, canon Gonzague Ryckmans (1887–1969)[5] was appointed as his successor for the "Assyrian" course. Ryckmans had obtained a PhD in philosophy at the Catholic University of Leuven in 1908 and had also studied Hebrew and Arabic. He spent three years at the École Biblique de Jérusalem (1911–1914) where he also studied Akkadian with Father Dhorme. His PhD in Assyriology was complete, but the First World War interrupted matters, and it was only in 1919 that he obtained the degree of Doctor in Semitic Languages.[6] Although he continued to teach and work on Assyrian, as shown by the publication of his *Grammaire accadienne* in 1938, his main specialty was South Arabian epigraphy. In 1936, an Oriental Institute (Institut orientaliste/Instituut voor Oriëntalisme) was created and added to the Faculty of Humanities.

In 1938, a student of Ryckmans, Paul Naster (1913–1998), obtained his PhD in Oriental philology and history,[7] after which he went on to Prague where he studied Akkadian and Hittite with the Czech Hittitologist Bedřich Hrozný. From 1945 to 1958, canon Robert De Langhe (1911–1963), another student of Ryckmans who had written a PhD in theology on Ugaritic texts and their connections with the biblical world,[8] taught Akkadian in Leuven. From 1958 onwards, Naster, who was active as an Assyriologist but whose main interest and publications lay in the field of numismatics, took over the teaching of Akkadian.

At the Université de Liège, Assyriology was introduced by Jules Prickartz (1886–1975). During his studies in classical languages at the Catholic University of Leuven he developed an interest in Semitic languages and, after obtaining his PhD in classical languages in 1907, he spent two years at the École Biblique de Jérusalem and one year at the Institute of Semitic Languages in Leipzig under the direction of Heinrich Zimmern.

In 1914 he started his career at the University of Liège in the Faculty of Arts where he taught history of the ancient Orient and Assyriology, two courses created at his instigation. Under his impulse, all courses concerning the languages of the Orient were grouped in the Higher Institute of History and Oriental Literatures (Institut supérieur d'histoire et de littératures orientales) created in 1922 and attached to the Faculty of Arts. Within this institute he taught courses concerning Assyriology as well as comparative grammar of the Semitic languages. His scientific work, now largely forgotten, concerned the relationship between Sumerian, Semitic, and Indo-European languages.[9]

At his initiative the University of Liège acquired a small collection of cuneiform tablets in order to show original documents to the students, which were bought between 1925 and 1930 by his student Georges Dossin who was sent to Paris in order to buy them.[10]

---

5. See Irvine 1970, Naster 1978, 11–13, and https://www.kaowarsom.be/fr/notices_ryckmans_gonzague (accessed 15 September 2017).

6. Ryckmans 1919.

7. Naster 1938.

8. De Langhe 1945.

9. See https://orbi.ulg.ac.be/bitstream/2268/119736/5/4.%20Jules%20Prickartz_noticenecrologique_1886-1975.pdf (accessed 15 September 2017).

10. See Limet 1973, 13 n. 2.

"The Blue Lotus":[11] A Breakthrough in Belgian Assyriology—Georges Dossin[12]

The real bloom of Belgian Assyriology occurred when Dossin came on the scene. Dossin (1896–1983) was born in Wandre near Liège in a family of industrialists. He studied classical languages at the University of Liège where he obtained his first PhD in 1921. The classes he took with the recently appointed Prickartz opened up the world of Assyriology for him. From 1922 to 1923 he went to study in Paris with Charles Fossey and Vincent Scheil at the Collège de France and the École Pratique des Hautes Études where he also met François Thureau-Dangin whom he would accompany during archaeological missions in Syria later on. In 1923 he completed a second PhD, this time in languages and literatures of the Orient.

Already in the following year he started his long career at the University of Liège, where he taught various courses in ancient Near Eastern art history and archaeology (1924–1935) and was later appointed full professor of Assyriology and comparative grammar of Semitic languages (1951–1966). He also taught art history of Asia Minor at the Royal Institute of Art History and Archaeology of Brussels (1924–1945) and various courses in Akkadian, Assyro-Babylonian languages, and history at the Institut des Hautes Études de Belgique in Brussels (1929–1939 and 1945–1955) and the then-French-speaking Free University of Brussels (1935–1941 and 1946–1951).

He was not only active as a teacher and a prolific researcher but visited the Near East, accompanying Thureau-Dangin in his excavations of Arslan-Tash (1928) and Tell Ahmar (1929–1931) in Syria, and undertaking in 1931 a trip through Syria, Iraq, and Persia. He then worked on and published texts from the French excavations in Susa,[13] and published two volumes of letters dating to the Old Babylonian period.[14]

When André Parrot discovered ancient Mari in 1933, its plentiful archives were first entrusted to Thureau-Dangin but soon passed to Dossin. Dossin became the Mari epigraphist for twelve years from 1937 to 1966. His publications began already in 1937 and continued in a vast and steady flow until 1978.[15] It is not the place here in this brief overview to cite all his publications, but let it suffice to state that they have been foundational for Assyriology in such domains as history, philology, and religion. In view of the enormity of the task, he created a team in Belgium with his students Jean-Robert Kupper and André Finet and in France with Raymond Jestin, Jean Bottéro, Maurice Birot, and Georges Boyer. Although Mari certainly was the focus of his research, he published on a number of other topics, reaching as far as the Luristan bronzes.[16]

He was a founding member of the Groupe François Thureau-Dangin and one of the fathers of the Rencontre Assyriologique Internationale. It is no exaggeration to state

---

11. Originally published by Hergé in *Le Petit Vingtième* as *Le Lotus bleu* (1934–1935).

12. See Finet 1977a, Duval 1983, Birot 1984, Kupper 1984, 1985, Servais 2012, and https://www.kaowarsom.be/fr/notices_dossin_georges (accessed 15 September 2017).

13. Dossin 1927.

14. Dossin 1933, 1934.

15. An overview of all published Mari texts, including those by Dossin and his team, can be found at http://digitorient.com/wp/wp-content/uploads/2012/04/Bibliographie_des_textes_de_Mari_j1936_2016.pdf (accessed 15 September 2017).

16. A bibliography of Dossin compiled by P. Talon can be found in Dossin 1983.

that he was for four decades one of the leading figures of not only Belgian Assyriology, but Assyriology in general.

In 1976, a foundation was created by Dossin's four disciples—Jean-Robert Kupper, Henri Limet, André Finet, and Léon De Meyer—and the art historian and archaeologist, professor at the Flemish Free University of Brussels,[17] and conservator at the Royal Museums of Art and History, Denyse Homès-Frédéricq. The main aim was to contribute to the development of Assyriological studies in Belgium. In honor of their teacher, this was called Fondation Assyriologique Georges Dossin/Assyriologische Stichting Georges Dossin,[18] later renamed Assyriological Center Georges Dossin for administrative reasons.

Main activities of the foundation are lectures organized in the Royal Museums of Art and History, seat of the foundation, as well as the publication of the periodical *Akkadica* since 1977. Members of the foundation are the Belgian Assyriologists, but it is also open to the general public. Lectures are still given twice each year, the periodical *Akkadica* plus was created, aimed at interested non-specialists, and a yearly trip is organized to places in connection with the ancient Near East.[19]

"Cigars of the Pharaoh":[20] The Disciples of Georges Dossin—Liège, Brussels, and Ghent

University of Liège

Jean-Robert Kupper (1920–2009)[21] studied history at the Free University of Brussels and was introduced to Assyriology by Dossin, who taught not only in Liège but also at the ULB. In 1946, Kupper was awarded a PhD in Oriental Philology and History and, in line with his teacher, he would make Mari one of his main scientific interests. After stays in Rome and Paris, he was research assistant at the Oriental Institute of Chicago from 1949 to 1951, where A. Leo Oppenheim, Benno Landsberger, and Ignace J. Gelb were the leading figures. It is there that he conceived the idea to study the nomads at the time of Mari. This study became his "special PhD" (*doctorat spécial*) in 1956.[22] In 1964 he took part in the excavations of Mari and in 1967, he succeeded to Dossin at the University of Liège where he taught Assyriology as well as the art history and archaeology of the ancient Near East until 1985.

Henri Limet (1924–2009)[23] studied classical languages and Oriental history and languages at the University of Liège, for which he received both his masters degree (*diplôme de licence*) in 1946. For a long time (1949–1967) he taught Latin in a secondary school near Liège. During this time, he researched metalworking in Sumer during

---

17. The originally French speaking Free University of Brussels (Université Libre de Bruxelles or ULB) was split up into a French speaking one (Université Libre de Bruxelles or ULB) and a Flemish one (Vrije Universiteit Brussel or VUB) in 1969.

18. See Finet 1977c and http://www.akkadica.org/fondationdossin.htm (accessed 15 September 2017).

19. See http://www.akkadica.org (accessed 15 September 2017).

20. Originally published by Hergé in *Le Petit Vingtième* as *Les Cigares du Pharaon* (1932–1934).

21. See Durand 2009 and Tunca 2009a.

22. Kupper 1957.

23. See Tunca 2009b.

256   Katrien De Graef

the third dynasty of Ur for which he was awarded a PhD in 1956.[24] With this, his fame spread as the only Belgian Sumerologist. Ten years later, in 1966 he was awarded his "special PhD" (*doctorat spécial*) for his study on Sumerian anthroponymy at the time of the third dynasty of Ur.[25] After a period of two years at the National Fund for Scientific Research (Fonds national de la recherche scientifique), which allowed him to devote himself completely to research, he started his career at the University of Liège in 1969, where, as a lecturer and later associate professor, he was able to further develop Sumerology. In 1985, he succeeded Kupper and took over the course of art and archaeology of the ancient Near East until his own retirement in 1989.

Free University of Brussels

Assyriology came to the Free University of Brussels when Dossin was appointed lecturer there in 1946. In 1951, when he resigned to be appointed professor at the University of Liège, his student André Finet (1921–2007)[26] succeeded him in Brussels. Finet studied classical philology and Hebrew at the Free University of Brussels and worked several years in a family company after his studies. When Dossin came to Brussels, Finet studied Akkadian with him, together with Léon De Meyer and Kupper. Finet became Dossin's assistant in Brussels, and he too followed in the footsteps of his master and specialized in Old Babylonian, more specifically the Mari documentation. His particular interest in grammar determined the subject of his PhD on the grammar of Mari texts, which he obtained in 1956.[27] He undertook excavations at Tell Kannas (Syria) where he uncovered the temple district of an Uruk period settlement. These excavations continued until 1974, when the site was inundated due to the big dam on the Euphrates.

A special mention must be made of the Institut des Hautes Études de Belgique, founded in 1894 and linked to the Free University of Brussels, which organized lectures at university level, international colloquia, and courses not given in the universities. These courses are accessible to all and are free. Dossin lectured there between 1929 and 1939 and between 1945 and 1955. After him, his student Finet took over and he kept doing this until 2004. At present, two of Philippe Talon's students, Véronique Van der Stede and Cynthia Jean are lecturers of Akkadian at the Institute.

University of Ghent

Assyriology arrived at the University of Ghent with the appointment of Léon De Meyer (1928–2006).[28] He had studied classical languages in Ghent but developed an interest in the ancient Orient. While teaching in a secondary school, he continued his studies at the Free University of Brussels where he took the courses taught by Dossin. As such, he became Dossin's youngest disciple, after Kupper, Limet, and Finet. Dossin directed him not to Mari, but to another region on which he had worked previously:

24. Limet 1960.
25. Limet 1968.
26. See Talon 2008.
27. Finet 1956.
28. See Thibau 1994 and Anonymous 2006.

Elam. In the meantime, Louis Van den Berghe, who had been appointed Professor of Ancient Near Eastern Archaeology at Ghent University took him as his assistant in 1958. He wrote a PhD on the Akkadian of the Susa contracts with Dossin as supervisor and was awarded the title of doctor in 1960.[29] His work drew the attention of Roman Ghirshman, director of the French excavations at Susa (Iran), and he was asked to work as an epigrapher there. He worked in Susa from 1963 to 1968. In 1965 De Meyer was appointed professor in Ghent and with him Assyriology really started at this university.

In 1970 he began his own excavations in Iraq, at the site of Tell ed-Dēr. Together with the archaeologist Hermann Gasche innovative research was undertaken. This yielded the largest Old Babylonian private archive found *in situ*, the archive of Ur-Utu, as well as a number of groundbreaking studies in the historical geography and landscape reconstruction of this region. Apart from his scientific work, De Meyer was elected Dean of the Arts Faculty from 1982 to 1984 and Rector of Ghent University from 1985 to 1993, the time of his retirement.

"King Ottokar's Sceptre":[30] The Students of Dossin's Disciples—Liège, Brussels, Ghent, and Leuven

University of Liège

Önhan Tunca (1947–) studied art history and archaeology as well as Oriental literatures and languages at the University of Liège, where he was assistant to Kupper and was awarded a PhD in art history and archaeology in 1982.[31] After two years at the University of Ghent as scientific collaborator of De Meyer, a year in Germany on a stipend from the Humboldt Foundation spent in the service of Bartel Hrouda at the Institut für Vorderasiatische Archäologie of the University of Munich, and a year at the University of Liège as scientific collaborator of Limet, he became professor and director of the Institut d'histoire et d'archéologie de l'Orient ancien at the University of Strasbourg II (1987–1990). In 1989, he succeeded Limet and started his career as lecturer and later full professor at the University of Liège, where he worked until his retirement in 2012, teaching archaeological as well as Assyriological courses.

Tunca participated in several excavations, both in Syria (Ras Shamra, Tell Brak, and Terqa) and Iraq (Tell ed-Dēr), before starting his own excavations in Syria in Tell Amarna (1990–2000) and Chagar Bazar (1999–2011). His numerous publications show him to be an accomplished archaeologist with a solid Assyriological knowledge.

Free University of Brussels

Philippe Talon (1952–) studied Oriental philology and history as well as art history and archaeology at the French speaking Free University of Brussels[32] with Finet.

---

29. De Meyer 1962.

30. Originally published by Hergé in *Le Petit Vingtième* as *Le Sceptre d'Ottokar* (1938–1939).

31. Tunca 1984.

32. After the division of the Free University of Brussels in a French speaking one (ULB) and a Flemish one (VUB) in 1969, no courses in Assyriology were taught at the Flemish one. However, archaeology

After his studies, he became assistant in the Groupe d'Informatique et Traitement Automatique of the Arts Faculty headed by Jacques-Henri Michel until 1993. In the meantime, he was awarded the title of doctor in 1982 for his research on a group of Mari texts,[33] thus continuing the line of Dossin and Finet. In 1993, he succeeded Finet, first as lecturer and later as full professor. Until the mid 1980s, he worked on the Mari documentation, after which his interests broadened toward the intellectual history of Mesopotamia with studies on literature and religion. His edition of the great mythological text *Enūma eliš* must be mentioned in this regard.[34] Apart from text publications and studies of cuneiform documents he also published on Syriac texts.

Talon participated as epigrapher in the Tell Beydar excavations from 1993 to 2000 and published a number of the texts found there. He retired in October 2017 and, sadly, the Assyriological curriculum has subsequently come to an end at the Free University of Brussels.

University of Ghent

Michel Tanret (1946–) first studied romance languages and then Oriental languages and history at the University of Ghent. He taught for several years in secondary schools and became an assistant in the Department of Historical and Comparative Pedagogics at Ghent University in 1978. Two years later, he became assistant of De Meyer. In 1981, he was awarded the title of Doctor in Oriental Languages and History with a PhD on the scribal exercise tablets from the Ur-Utu archive.[35] Since 1982, when De Meyer became dean of the Arts Faculty and later on rector of Ghent University, he was entrusted with the whole Assyriological curriculum, first as lecturer and later as full professor, until his own retirement in 2011.

Tanret participated as epigrapher to the excavations at Tell ed-Dēr from 1980 until 1991, when work had to be stopped because of the Gulf War. His research and publications focus on the socioeconomic history of the Old Babylonian period, more specifically the twin cities Sippar-Jaḫrūrum (Abu Ḥabbah) and Sippar-Amnānum (Tell ed-Dēr), as well as on sealing practice and exercise tablets. During the fifteen years from 1996 to 2011, he coordinated the inter-university program "Greater Mesopotamia: Reconstruction of its Environment and History," combining (geo)-archaeological, historical, and philological research at the Universities of Ghent, Leuven, and Liège, and the Royal Belgian Institute of Natural Sciences.

The Catholic University of Leuven and Louvain-la-Neuve

In 1968, the originally French speaking Catholic University of Leuven was divided in two independent universities, a Flemish one (Katholieke Universiteit Leuven) in Leuven and a French speaking (or Walloon) one (Université Catholique de Louvain) in the newly established campus Louvain-la-Neuve in Ottignies.

---

of the ancient Near East was taught at the VUB, first by Louis Speleers, then by Van den Berghe, Denyse Homès-Frédéricq, and currently by Eric Gubel.

33. Talon 1985.
34. Talon 2005.
35. Published in a reworked version in Tanret 2002.

The German Herbert Sauren (1934–) was appointed as professor of Sumerian in both institutions and of Akkadian in Louvain-la-Neuve, while Naster continued to teach Akkadian in Leuven. Naster was succeeded by Edward Lipinski (1930–), a specialist in comparative Semitic linguistics, Old Aramaic, and Phoenician who also taught Akkadian.

From 1978 on, Karel Van Lerberghe (1947–),[36] a student of De Meyer at Ghent University, where he obtained his PhD in 1980 with a study of a group of texts from the Ur-Utu archive,[37] became assistant of Lipinski and took over the Assyriological part of his teaching. After his studies in Ghent, he became a research assistant at Leiden University with the renowned Fritz R. Kraus before being called to Leuven, where he became lecturer and later full professor.

Only with Van Lerberghe did Assyriology become a full-fledged discipline in Leuven. He is a specialist of the Old Babylonian period, focusing on socioeconomic texts of which he published a great number, but he also taught archaeology of the ancient Near East and participated in excavations before leading his own. He co-authored a number of publications with his wife, Gabriella Voet, who, as an archaeologist, specialized in the study of ancient seals.

In Louvain-la-Neuve, Assyriology started with the arrival of Sauren from Germany. He had been awarded a PhD at the University of Heidelberg in 1966 with a study on the topography of the Umma Province according to documents dating to the third dynasty of Ur.[38] In Louvain-la-Neuve, he taught a wide range of languages written in cuneiform, Sumerian, Babylonian, Assyrian, Hittite, and Ugaritic, to which were added languages using alphabetical writing from Yemen to Damascus, from southern Egypt to Hatra and Palmyra. Sauren is a scholar of wide interests with publications on a wide range of topics, including numerous Assyriological publications.

In 1976, his student René Lebrun (1943–)[39] was awarded a PhD in Hittitology[40] at the Université catholique de Louvain. Later on, Lebrun was appointed full professor in Hittitology and Assyriology in Louvain-la-Neuve and in Hittitology at the Institut catholique de Paris.

"Prisoners of the Sun":[41] The Current Situation in Belgian Assyriology—Liège, Ghent, Leuven, and Louvain-la-Neuve

University of Liège

In 2012, Laurent Colonna d'Istria (1980–) succeeded Tunca. He studied history at the University of Lyon II Lumière and was awarded the title of doctor there with a study on Bronze Age Middle Euphrates Valley cultural traditions in 2009.[42] He was research assistant and then postdoctoral researcher in the department led by Antoine Cavigneaux

---

36. See Boiy et al. 2012b.
37. Van Lerberghe and Voet 1991.
38. Sauren 1966.
39. See Naster 1978, 14–15 and Degrève and Gérard 2009.
40. Lebrun 1976.
41. Originally published by Hergé in Tintin magazine as *Le temple du Soleil* (1946–1948).
42. D'Istria 2009, see http://www.theses.fr/2009LYO20108 (accessed 15 September 2017).

260   Katrien De Graef

at Geneva University from 2006 to 2012, and he participated in various excavations in Syria (Tell Ashara/Terqa, Tell Masaikh, and Tell Hariri/Mari). He is a specialist of the *šakkanakku* period in Mari and now participates as head of the Belgian team in the French excavations at Qara Dagh (Iraqi Kurdistan).

University of Ghent

In 2011, Tanret was succeeded by Katrien De Graef (1976–). She studied Oriental languages and cultures in Ghent, became an assistant in this department in 1999, and was entrusted by De Meyer with the study of a group of texts from Susa for her PhD. She was awarded the title of doctor in 2004.[43] She participated in Tunca's excavations at Chagar Bazar in Syria and undertook several study missions to Iran. She studies and publishes on the socioeconomic history of third- and second-millennium Susa and Old Babylonian Sippar.

Catholic University of Leuven

In 2012, Van Lerberghe was succeeded by Kathleen Abraham (1963–), who studied languages and civilizations of the ancient Near East and biblical studies at the University of Leuven and took Akkadian classes with Van Lerberghe. She was awarded her PhD in Hebrew and Semitic Languages at Bar Ilan University (Israel) in 1993 with a study on first-millennium cuneiform texts, supervised by Aaron Skaist. She was postdoctoral researcher at Beer Sheva University (Israel) and later lecturer at Bar Ilan University where she became professor in 2012. Abraham is a specialist of the socioeconomic history of first-millennium Babylonia with a keen interest in Babylonian juridical history, bilingualism, and Jewish and other minorities in Babylonia.

Catholic University of Louvain-la-Neuve

In 2008, Jan Tavernier (1971–), who studied ancient history and languages and civilizations of the ancient Near East at the Catholic University of Leuven with Van Lerberghe, where he was awarded his PhD on Old Iranian personal names and loanwords in 2002,[44] succeeded Lebrun as professor of Assyriology and Hittitology in Louvain-la-Neuve. He studied Indo-European comparative linguistics with Petr Vavroušek in Prague and Elamite and Old Persian with Matthew Stolper in Chicago. He studies and publishes mainly on Elamite and Old Persian linguistics and history.

"Tintin in America":[45] Belgian Assyriologists Abroad

A number of Assyriologists who were trained in Belgium went and made career abroad. The most famous one is no doubt bestselling author and history professor at

43. De Graef 2005, 2006.
44. Tavernier 2007.
45. Originally published by Hergé in *Le Petit Vingtième* as *Tintin en Amérique* (1931–1932).

the prestigious Columbia University in New York, Marc Van De Mieroop (1956–). He started his studies in Assyriology at the Catholic University of Leuven with Sauren, after which he went to Yale to study with William W. Hallo, where he was awarded his PhD in Assyriology in 1983. He has published on various aspects of ancient Near Eastern, Egyptian, and world history and historical methodology.

Another student of Sauren at the Catholic University of Leuven, Herman Vanstiphout (1941–2019)46, who wrote his PhD on the literary traditions about the destruction of Ur in 1975, became a renowned specialist of Sumerian literature. He taught Semitics and Assyriology at the University of Groningen in the Netherlands until his retirement in 2006.

Caroline Waerzeggers (1975–) studied Oriental languages and cultures at the University of Ghent with Tanret, where she was awarded her PhD on Neo-Babylonian texts in 2001. She was lecturer in ancient Near Eastern history in the Free University of Amsterdam and the University College of London and is currently Professor of Assyriology in Leiden University (The Netherlands), where she is directing an ERC project on the rise of the Persian Empire.

"Land of Black Gold":[47] A Belgian School of Assyriology?

Although there is no real Belgian School of Assyriology, a kind of academic genealogical tree can be drawn, showing the Assyriologists who trained at and/or are working at Belgian universities, considering as "fathers" their *Doctorväter*, going back to Dossin and his four disciples.[48]

It is remarkable to observe that Dossin himself and three of disciples all started out with classical studies, the exception being Kupper who first studied history. Although they also studied other languages than Akkadian, none of them came from biblical or theological studies, contrary to their early predecessors in Leuven who were in some cases even canons.

As to the date of the introduction of Assyriology in Belgium, this is somewhat debatable. The first course of Akkadian was taught by Albinus Van Hoonacker at the then French speaking Catholic University of Leuven in 1890. However, one could very well argue that full-fledged Assyriology, with extensive study and publication in the field only came with Van Lerberghe in 1978. At the University of Liège, the first course of Akkadian was taught by Prickartz in 1914, but here too one could argue that full-fledged Assyriology started in Liège only when Dossin started teaching there in 1924. The same goes for the then-French-speaking Free University of Brussels, where Dossin started teaching in 1935. At the University of Ghent, Assyriology started in 1965 with the appointment of De Meyer, one of Dossin's disciples.

---

46. This chapter was written in 2017, but in 2019, the regrettable news of Herman Vanstiphout's death reached the author and editors.

47. Originally published by Hergé in *Le Petit Vingtième* (unfinished, 1939–1940) and Tintin magazine (1948–1950) as *Tintin au pays de l'or noir*.

48. Only Assyriologists having (had) tenured positions in universities are included in this academic genealogy, without taking into account all other pre- and postdoctoral trainings and affiliations that enriched some of them.

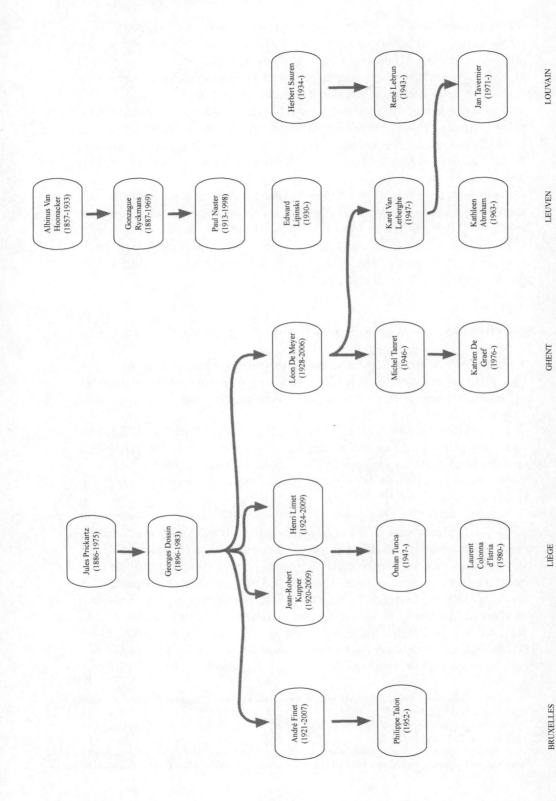

FIGURE 13.1. Assyriologists at Belgian Universities

REFERENCES

Anonymous. 2006. "Léon De Meyer (1928–2006)." *Akkadica* 127:105–7.

Birot, M. 1984. "Georges Dossin (1896–1983)." *Revue d'assyriologie* 78:1–5.

Boiy, T., et al., eds. 2012a. *The Ancient Near East, a Life! Festschrift Karel Van Lerberghe*. Orientalia Lovaniensia Analecta 220. Leuven: Peeters.

———. 2012b. "A Life in Ancient Near East is Something Not to Be Forgotten." Pages ix–xiii in *The Ancient Near East, a Life! Festschrift Karel Van Lerberghe*. Orientalia Lovaniensia Analecta 220. Edited by T. Boiy et al. Leuven: Peeters.

Bottéro, J. 1989. "André Finet." Pages vii–viii in *Reflets des deux fleuves. Volume de mélanges offerts à A. Finet*. Akkadica Supplementum 6. Edited by M. Lebeau and P. Talon. Leuven: Peeters.

Cannuyer, C., A. Degrève, and R. Gérard, eds. 2009. *Vin, bière et ivresse dans les civilisations orientales. Entre plaisir et interdit. Réne Lebrun in honorem*. Acta Orientalia Belgica 22. Louvain-la-Neuve: Société belge d'études orientales.

Colonna d'Istria, L. 2009. "Evolution des traditions culturelles dans la vallée du moyen Euphrate de la fin du Bronze ancien au début du Bronze moyen." PhD Diss., Université Lyon 2.

De Graef, K. 2005. *Les Archives d'Igibuni. Les documents Ur III du chantier B à Suse*. Mémoires de la délégation archéologique en Iran 54. Ghent: University of Ghent.

———. 2006. *De la dynastie Šimaški eu Sukkalmaḫat. Les documents fin PE II–début PE III du chantier B à Suse*. Mémoires de la délégation archéologique en Iran 55. Ghent: University of Ghent.

Degrève, A., and R. Gérard. 2009. "Bio-bibliographie de René Lebrun." Pages xi–xxviii in *Vin, bière et ivresse dans les civilisations orientales. Entre plaisir et interdit. Réne Lebrun in honorem*. Acta Orientalia Belgica 22. Edited by C. Cannuyer, A. Degrève, and R. Gérard. Louvain-la-Neuve: Société belge d'études orientales.

De Langhe, R. 1945. *Les textes de Ras Shamra-Ugarit et leurs rapports avec le milieu de l'Ancien Testament*. Universitas Catholica Lovaniensis 2. Gemboux: Duculot.

De Meyer, L. 1962. *L'accadien des contrats de Suse*. Iranica Antiqua Suppléments 1. Leiden: Brill.

Donceel, R., and R. Lebrun, eds. 1984. *Archéologie et religions de l'Anatolie ancienne: mélanges en l'honneur du professeur Paul Naster*. Homo religiosus I, 10. Louvain-la-Neuve: Centre d'histoire des religions.

Dossin, G. 1927. *Autres textes sumériens et accadiens*. Mémoires de la délégation archéologique en Perse 18. Paris: Leroux.

———. 1933. *Lettres de la première dynastie babylonienne*. Texts cunéiformes, Musées du Louvre 17. Paris: Geuthner.

———. 1934. *Lettres de la première dynastie babylonienne*. Texts cunéiformes, Musées du Louvre 18. Paris: Geuthner.

———. 1983. *Receuil Georges Dossin: mélanges d'Assyriologie (1934–1959)*. Akkadica Supplementum 1. Leuven: Peeters.

Durand, J.-M. 2009. "Jean-Robert Kupper (1920–2009)." *Revue d'assyriologie* 103:1–3.

Duval, P.-M. 1983. "Allocution à l'occasion du décès de M. Georges Dossin." *Comptes rendus des séances de l'Académie des Inscriptions et Belles-Lettres* 4:680–82.

Finet, A. 1956. *L'accadien des lettres de Mari*. Bruxelles: Académie royale de Belgique.

———. 1977a. "Monsieur Dossin." *Akkadica* 1:1–4.

———. 1977b. "A propos de l'assyriologie en Belgique." *Akkadica* 2:29–30.

———. 1977c. "Définition des objectifs de la Fondation assyriologique Georges Dossin/ Bepaling van de doelstellingen van de Assyriologische Stichting Georges Dossin." *Akkadica* 3:6–9.

Irvine, A. K. 1970. "Obituary: Gonzague Ryckmans." *Bulletin of the School of Oriental and African Studies* 33:374–77.

264   Katrien De Graef

Kupper, J.-R. 1957. *Les nomades de Mésopotamie au temps des rois de Mari*. Bibliothèque de la Faculté de Philosophie et Lettres de l'Université de Liège 142. Liège: Presses universitaires de Liège.

———. 1984. "In memoriam Georges Dossin." *Akkadica* 36:I–III.

———. 1985. "Notice sur Georges Dossin." *Annuaire de l'Académie Royale de Belgique* 1985:117–52.

Lebeau, M., and P. Talon, eds. 1989. *Reflets des deux fleuves. Volume de mélanges offerts à A. Finet*. Akkadica Supplementum 6. Leuven: Peeters.

Lebrun, R. 1976. *Samuha: foyer religieux de l'empire hittite*. Publications de l'Institut orientaliste de Louvain 11. Louvain-la-Neuve: Institut orientaliste.

Limet, H. 1960. *Le travail du métal au pays de Sumer au temps de la IIIe dynastie d'Ur*. Bibliothèque de la Faculté de Philosophie et Lettres de l'Université de Liège 155. Paris: Belles Lettres.

———. 1968. *L'Anthroponomie sumérienne dans les documents de la 3e dynastie d'Ur*. Bibliothèque de la Faculté de Philosophie et Lettres de l'Université de Liège 180. Paris: Belles Lettres.

———. 1973. *Étude de documents de la période d'Agadé appartenant à l'Université de Liège*. Bibliothèque de la Faculté de Philosophie et Lettres de l'Université de Liège 207. Paris: Belles Lettres.

Mazoyer, M., and O. Casabonne, eds. 2004a. *Antiquus Oriens. Mélanges offerts au Professeur René Lebrun*. Vol. 1. Paris: Kubaba-L'Harmattan.

———. 2004b. *Studia Anatolica et Varia. Mélanges offerts au Professeur René Lebrun*. Vol. 2. Paris: Kubaba-L'Harmattan.

Michalowski, P., and N. Veldhuis, eds. 2006. *Approaches to Sumerian Literature. Studies in Honour of Stip (H. L. J. Vanstiphout)*. Cuneiform Monographs 35. Leiden: Brill.

Naster, P. 1938. *L'asie mineure et l'Assyrie eu VIIIe et Vie siècles av. J.-C. d'après les Annales des rois assyriens*. Bibliothèque du Muséon 8. Leuven: Bureau du Muséon.

———. 1978. "De assyriologie aan de Universiteit te Leuven." *Akkadica* 6:8–16.

Quaegebeur, J., ed. 1982. *Studia Paulo Naster Oblata, II: Orientalia Antiqua*. Orientalia Lovaniensia Analecta 13. Leuven: Peeters.

Ryckmans, G. 1919. *Les formes nominales en babylonien. Étude de grammaire sémitique comparée*. Paris: Imprimerie Nationale.

Sauren, H. 1966. *Topographie der Provinz Umma nach den Urkunden der Zeit der III. Dynasty von Ur. Teil I: Kanäle und Bewässerungsanlagen*. Bamberg: K. Urlaub.

Schelkens, K. 2008. "Van Hoonacker, Albin-Augustin." *Biographisch-Bibliographisches Kirchenlexikon* 29:1485–91.

Servais, P. 2012. "DOSSIN Georges (Wandre, 1896–Liège, 1983)." Pages 329–30 in *Dictionnaire des orientalistes de langue français*. New revised and updated ed. Edited by F. Pouillon. Paris: Karthala.

Talon, P. 1985. *Textes administratifs des salles Y et Z du Palais de Mari*. Archives Royales de Mari 24/1–2. Paris: Recherches sur les Civilisations.

———. 2005. *The Standard Babylonian Creation Myth: Enūma Eliš*. State Archives of Assyria. Cuneiform Texts 4. Helsinki: The Neo-Assyrian Text Corpus Project.

———. 2008. "André Finet (1921–2008)." *Akkadica* 129:1–3.

Talon, P., and V. Van der Stede, eds. 2005. *Si un homme: Textes offerts en hommage à André Finet*. Turnhout: Brepols.

Tanret, M. 2002. *Per Aspera ad Astra. L'apprentissage du cunéiforme à Sippar-Amnānum pendant la période paleo-babylonienne tardive*. Mesopotamian History and Environment. Texts I 2. Ghent: University of Ghent.

Tavernier, J. 2007. *Iranica in the Achaemenid Period (ca. 550–330 BC). Lexicon of Old Iranian Proper Names and Loanwords, Attested in Non-Iranian Texts*. Orientalia Lovaniensa Analecta 158. Leuven: Peeters.

Thibau, R. 1994. "Ten geleide." Pages vii–ix in *Cinquante-deux réflexions sur le Proche-Orient ancien offertes en hommage à Léon De Meyer*. Mesopotamian History and Environment. Occasional Publications 2. Edited by H. Gasche et al. Leuven: Peeters.

Tunca, Ö. 1984. *L'architecture religieuse protodynastique en Mésopotamie*. Akkadica Supplementum 2. Leuven: Peeters.

————. 2009a. "Jean-Robert Kupper (22/1/1920–6/1/2009)." *Akkadica* 130:1–2.

————. 2009b. "Henri Limet (Huy 4/8/1924–Olne 18/8/2009)." *Akkadica* 130:III–12.

————, ed. 1990. *De la Babylonie à la Syrie, en passant par Mari: mélanges offerts à Monsieur J.-R. Kupper à l'occasion de son 70ᵉ anniversaire*. Liège: Université de Liège.

Tunca, Ö., and D. Deheselle, eds. 1996. *Tablettes et images aux pays de Sumer et d'Akkad: mélanges offerts à Monsieur H. Limet*. Liège: Université de Liège.

Van Lerberghe, K., and G. Voet. 1991. *Sippar-Amnānum. The Ur-Utu Archive*. Mesopotamian History and Environment. Texts I 1. Ghent: University of Ghent.

Van Waeyenbergh, H., and R. De Langhe, eds. 1963. *Mélanges Gonzague Ryckmans: miscellanea orientalia et biblica*. Bibliotheca ephemeridum theologicarum Lovaniensium 20. Leuven: Publications universitaires de Louvain.

CHAPTER 14

Assyriology in Iran?

Parsa Daneshmand

Defining Assyriology

The title of this paper might be one fraught with difficulties. For one thing, there is hardly a field of study in Iran at the present time that can be labelled as Assyriology; instead, there are scattered individual efforts, self-studied research, and erratic workshops run by a small number of genuine specialists. Although Iran is the birthplace of cuneiform decipherment,[1] Iranian universities offer no courses in Assyriology, nor is any local academic institute qualified to run a degree program in cuneiform studies.[2]

The aforementioned problem can be remedied by adding a question mark to the title of this paper. But significant issues remain. The term "Assyriology" is itself problematic because it covers a broad range of topics. Assyriology literally means the study of Assyria, yet the field is by no means restricted to Assyria. In his introduction to volume A/I of the *Chicago Assyrian Dictionary*, Ignace Gelb notes that in the early years of Assyriology the term "Assyrian" was used for the main Semitic language in Mesopotamia, as most cuneiform documents had been discovered in sites located in the land known as Assyria.[3] What Assyriology actually means, though, is the archaeological, historical, and linguistic study of ancient Mesopotamia (Iraq) and related cultures that also used cuneiform, like northeastern Syria, southeastern Turkey, and western Iran.[4] In other words, Assyriology is not merely one discipline, but a group of disciplines related to cuneiform that make frequent references to one another. An Assyriologist might be a specialist in the language, or archaeology, or history of the cuneiform world, but by no means is everyone who has worked on cuneiform materials an Assyriologist. Sir Max Mallowan might be better known as an archaeologist of ancient Near Eastern civilizations than an Assyriologist, to give one example.

A hallmark that distinguishes Assyriologists from other related specialists is training in ancient Mesopotamian languages, mainly Sumerian and Akkadian. Apart from Sumerology, Assyriology also embraces disciplines including Elamitology, Hittitology, Ugaritic, Urartian, and Old Persian studies.[5] However, experts in these fields are not always comfortable being known as Assyriologists. In the preface of *A Manual of*

---

1. Budge 1925, 11–52.
2. As will be discussed later, the situation is improving and there is genuine hope for a better future for cuneiform studies in Iran.
3. *CAD* A/I, vii.
4. Garelli 1972; Xifra and Heath 2015, 198.
5. Oppenheim 1977, 10.

Ugaritic, André Caquot asserts that "Ugaritology deserves to be considered an independent historical discipline, one to be mastered by itself and for itself, as distinct a field as Assyriology or Egyptology, even if it appears easier because of the profound affinities shown by Ugaritic with other long known Semitic languages."[6]

This might well also be acknowledged by specialists in Elamite, Hittite, and Urartian studies, unsettled by the obsessive attention given to Assyriology. For the purposes of this paper, however, I subsume all the aforementioned disciplines and subdisciplines within the category of Assyriology, or rather "cuneiform studies," with more focus on philological studies in Akkadian, Sumerian, and Elamite.

Cuneiform Education in Ancient Iran

Despite the lack of a modern academic branch of Assyriology in Iran, the cuneiform school and writing in Sumerian and Akkadian languages have a long tradition in Elam and Persia. The emergence of written materials started from around 3000 BCE in Iran when a native writing system, so-called Proto-Elamite—inspired by the ancient Mesopotamian Proto-cuneiform—was invented in Susa. As Jacob Dahl has noted, "Proto-Elamite seems to have disappeared relatively shortly after its invention" sometime between 3300 and 3000 BCE,[7] until a new system, known as Linear Elamite, appeared on a few dozen objects.[8] Other than these two native writing systems, hardly to be classified under cuneiform, from the late third millennium BCE onward, Elamites adopted the Mesopotamian cuneiform script for writing their royal and administrative documents in Akkadian and Sumerian.

Political and cultural links between Susa and Mesopotamia were the main reasons for such widespread use of the foreign script. In the late third millennium, the Akkadian successors of Sargon and later, the rulers of the third dynasty of Ur, seized Susa.[9] The inevitable consequence of occupation was the presence of Akkadian officials, bureaucrats, and their families at Susa, resulting in the "Akkadianization'" of the native population.[10] Akkadian names became common, even among ethnically non-Akkadian Elamites.[11] Alongside the ancient Mesopotamian languages, cuneiform script was used for writing the Elamite language.[12] Elamite cuneiform script was an adaptation of Mesopotamian cuneiform, which can be distinguished paleographically from that used in Akkadian texts. The Elamite language is an isolated one, completely unrelated to any well-known linguistic categorization.[13] The earliest attestation of writing in Elamite dates to the third millennium BCE, the latest, to the Achaemenid period.[14] Although after the Middle Elamite period, Elamite was more or less

6. Bordreuil and Pardee 2009, viii.
7. Dahl 2009, 24; 2013, 233; Englund 2004.
8. Dahl 2013, 257–59; 2009, 24–26.
9. Stolper 1992, 255.
10. Potts 2015, 101.
11. Potts 2015, 101.
12. Stolper 2004, 62–64.
13. There are scholarly efforts to connect Elamite to Dravidian languages (Khačikjan 1998, 3); but this hypothesis has not been welcomed by other specialists (Stolper 2004, 61).
14. Stolper 2004, 61–64.

FIGURE 14.1. A school tablet from Haft-Tappe. Photo by Javier Alvarez-Mon

preeminent, Akkadian continued to be written in the Iranian chancery until the end of the Achaemenid era.[15]

Akkadian texts found in Iran are characterized by significant peculiarities in all aspects of syntax, vocabulary, orthography, and logograms, which most likely was the result of local innovations among Iranian scribes.[16] Writing in Akkadian was not a decorative task, nor was it merely a way of acknowledging Akkadian as a *lingua franca*, but it was part of the everyday life of the Elamite population.[17] A significant number of Elamite royal inscriptions, economic and juridical texts, and a few literary texts, all from the early second millennium, are written in Akkadian.[18] Several thousand fragments and tablets found in Haft Tepe in categories including judiciary, daily business activities, school texts and omens, dating to the early Middle Elamite period, are also mainly written in Akkadian.[19] Although this trend had reduced by the late Middle Elamite period when writing in Elamite dominated royal and administrative texts, Akkadian continued to be the second most important language of the chancery (see Figure 14.1).[20]

In the Achaemenid period, Iranians invented a new cuneiform script with apparently no link with the cuneiform characters used to write Akkadian and Elamite.[21] Old Persian was an artificial script only for the Iranian language, mainly for royal

15. De Graef 2013.
16. Second-millennium divinatory texts from Susa and Haft Tepe are good examples of such idiosyncrasies. See Labat 1974, Herrero and Glassner 1993, 126–32, Daneshmand 2004. For an analysis of the non-normative Akkadian language of the Achaemenid royal inscriptions, see Daneshmand 2015.
17. For a description of the Akkadian texts unearthed in Iran, see De Graef 2013.
18. De Graef 2013, 270–73.
19. Negahban 1991, 102–12, De Graef 2013, 275.
20. For the photo, I am indebted to Javier Alvarez-Mon.
21. Stolper 2005, 19.

inscriptions. Only one administrative text in Old Persian is known to us.[22] Old Persian texts were strictly restricted for political purposes and carved in the center of trilingual inscriptions (Elamite, Old Persian, Akkadian). This standard was followed until the demise of the Achaemenid Empire. That even the last kings of Achaemenids (e.g. Artaxeres III, 358–338 BCE)[23] accompanied their royal inscriptions with Akkadian versions indicates the importance they attached to the language, even though by that time, Akkadian was no longer spoken. The consistency of inscribing Akkadian texts also implies the continuity of Akkadian training in the Iranian education system.

There are some theories on the *raison d'être* behind Akkadian writing in the Achaemenid period. The most common hypothesis highlights the political role of Persians after the conquest of Babylon, and that afterwards, Iranians took care to write in the local Mesopotamian language.[24] It is more likely, though, that by writing their inscriptions in Akkadian inside the palaces or at an invisible height, Achaemenid kings cleaved to the long tradition of writing in Akkadian initiated and followed by their Elamite predecessors.

Demise of Cuneiform in Iran

Neither cuneiform writing, nor the languages written in different cuneiform scripts including Old Persian, Elamite, and Akkadian, survived after the collapse of the Achaemenid Empire in Iran. Akkadian, of course, was still in use in Babylonia, and continued its life for three further centuries,[25] never reappearing in Iran. One reason, perhaps the most relevant one, as Jeremy Black pointed out, lay in "the loss of a native elite who valued" and acknowledged the writing.[26] The tradition of writing in cuneiform was closely associated with Achaemenid elites who supported sufficient numbers of scribes trained in Akkadian, Elamite, and Old Persian. Most of the population were not able to understand the script or the languages written in cuneiform, but trilingual inscriptions served as a display rather than practical texts.

By the arrival of Alexander, the Achaemenid Empire, the last powerful political system of the ancient world which continuously supported the cuneiform school, had collapsed. Thanks to the decline of a cuneiform education system, cuneiform scripts and languages represented by them disappeared in Iran. Written documents from the Parthian Empire scarcely record any reference to the Achaemenid dynasty,[27] while what we have from the Sassanian period bears little if any information about the Achaemenid kings, their monuments, and their history in general. Moreover, no direct evidence shows that the Sassanians were aware of the history of Persepolis, the hallmark of Achaemenid monumental constructions.

22. Stolper and Tavernier 2007.
23. Weissbach 1911, 131.
24. De Graef 2013, 279.
25. The last dateable cuneiform tablet was written in 75 CE, but cuneiform writing may have survived far longer than this date. See Geller 1997.
26. Black 2008, 65.
27. Shayegan 2011, 39.

FIGURE 14.2. The Palace of Darius I. Photo by the author

From the time of Shapur II (309–379 CE), two Pahlavi inscriptions are carved on the southern face of the east jamb of the doorway joining the main hall to the Palace of Darius (Tachara).[28] One text belongs to *Šāpur Sakānšāh*, Governor of Sistan and Sind, who travelled to those areas and visited Persepolis. The text gives a brief report of the royal visit of *Šāpur Sakānšāh* to the Palace of Persepolis, called "*Sad-Sotun*" (Hundred Columns): "He travelled on this road, between Istakhr and Sistan, and graciously came here to *Sad-Sotun*." As the text states, *Šāpur Sakānšāh* had a great feast at Persepolis, and "offered blessings to Shapur, the king of kings, to his own soul, and also to the one who had built this structure."[29]

The text provides not the faintest sign of whether the visitors had any knowledge of the history of the palace. However, its reference to offering prayer from a Zoroastrian king to the soul of the one who built the house may implicitly indicate that *Šāpur Sakānshāh* acknowledged that the founder of the palace was a Zoroastrian believer. The other inscription was engraved in Shapur II's honor decades later in his long reign by two nobles, but it provides no indication that they might have known about the palace and its founders (see Figure 14.2).[30]

Post-Sassanian Era: Two Narratives

After the Arab conquest of Iran, two narratives on the history of ancient Iran emerged, a pattern probably established in the Sassanian period. The first narrative, the Mazdayasnian or (with some considerations) Eastern narrative, gives exclusive weight to

28. Mousavi 2012, 81.
29. Daryaee 2000, 107–14; Mousavi 2012, 82.
30. Mousavi 2012, 81–82.

Assyriology in Iran 271

mythical, legendary, and historical figures linked to the Mazdaysnian (Zoroastrian) religion. This narrative is mostly attested to in Middle Persian texts and the Shahname (*Xwadāy Nāmag/ The Book of Lords*). The second narrative, termed here as the Western narrative, based essentially on Mesopotamian, biblical, Syriac, Hebrew, and Greek sources, covers most events and figures touched by the Eastern narrative, as well as mythical and historical figures cited in non-Mazdaysnian narratives.

Surviving Middle Persian texts copied or composed after the demise of the Sassanian dynasty constitute a major source of the first narrative. They offer a very brief reference to the Achaemenids. The narrative is limited to the story of a Persian king, introduced as *Dārāy*, the son of *Dārāy* (i.e. Darius III), who ordered that Avesta to be written and recorded in two copies. In this narrative, the other Achaemenid kings are completely ignored: "Darius, son of Darius commanded that two written copies of all of Avesta and the Zand [i.e., commentaries] as Zoroaster had received them from Ohrmazd, be housed; one in the *Šabīgān* treasury[31] and one in the Fortress of Writings."[32]

Another Middle Persian text repeats the same story, adding some hints on events after Alexander's invasion: "Thereafter, in the reign of Darius, son of Darius, Alexander the Keisar invaded from Rome, (and) came to Iran, and killed king Darius. He vanquished all the families of the lords, spiritual men, and nobles of Iran, and extinguished numerous fires. He seized (the Books) of the Mazdayasnian religion and the Zand, and sent them to Rome, and burnt the Avesta, (and) divided Iran among ninety householders" (see Figure 14.3).[33]

The reference to *Dārāy* (Darius III) in these Mazdayasnian texts may allude to a traditional narrative in which *Dārāy* was portrayed as a Zoroastrian king. The same pattern is followed in the *Shahname* composed by Ferdowsi, originally based on the *Xwadāy-Nāmag* (*The Book of Lords*), the official version of Iranian history. The story of *Dārāy* in the *Shahname*, despite some divergence from the official narrative,[34] follows rather the same framework:[35] it is briefly outlined in the Middle Persian texts and offers no reference whatsoever to other well-known Achaemenid kings, such as Cyrus. It is very unlikely that the Sassanians were ignorant of those historical figures, as there are explicit references to Iranian kings such as Cyrus, Darius, and Xerxes in the Old Testament and Syriac sources. Given that the political capital of Sassanians, Ctesiphon, was established along the Euphrates, and consequently Sassanian kings and their chancery were very much in the heart of Mesopotamia, we should expect that Sassanian kings and their scholars were not completely unaware of the history of

---

31. Shayegan 2011, 297 reads this word as *šāhīgān* (royal).

32. *dārāy ī dārāyan hamāg abestāg ud zand čiyōn zardušt az ohrmazd padīrift nibištag dō pačēn ēk pad ganj ī šabīgān ēk pad diz ī nibišt dāštan framūd* (Dreseden 1966, 511 II 1–8).

33. *pas andar xwadāyīh ī dārāy ī dārāyān aleksandar kēsar az hrōm dwārist ō ērānšahr āmad ud dārāy ī šāh ōzad hamāg dūdag ī xwadāyān mēnōg-mardān ud paydāgān ud ērānšahr abesīhēnīd ud was marag ātaxš afsārd dēn ī māzdēsnān zand stad ō hrōm frēstād ud abestāg sōxt ud ērānšahr pad nawad kadag-xwadāy baxt* (Bundahišn 33.14 = Anklesaria 1908 = TD 2 109 (214); Anklesaria 1956, 274–75; Bahar 2016, 140).

34. Shayegan 2011, 297.

35. Both the *Bundahišn* and the *Shahname* mention that *Dārāy* reigned fourteen years. Cf. Bundahišn 36 8 = Anklesaria 1956, 307, *Shahname* vol. 5:530 = Khaleghi Motlagh 2007.

272 Parsa Daneshmand

FIGURE 14.3. Bundahišn
(TD 2 109) = Anklesaria 1908

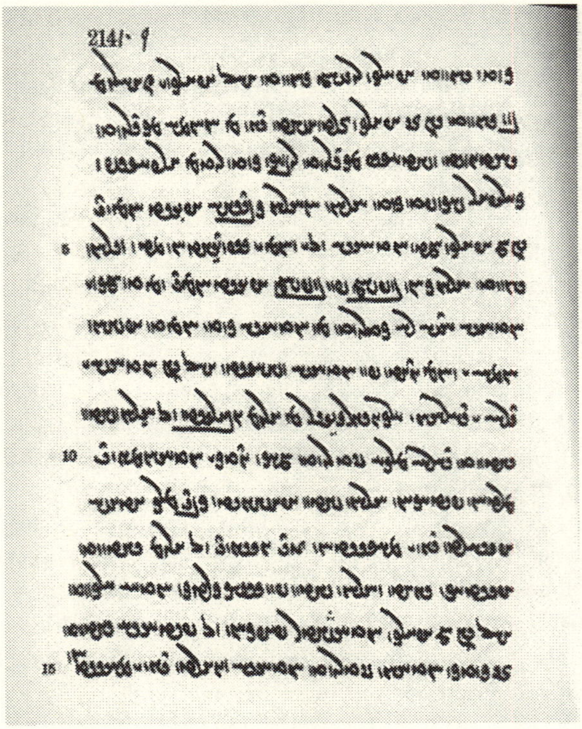

Achaemenid kings.[36] However, a religious filter may have blocked narratives related to the so-called non-Mazdayasnian kings.

The Western narrative, however, introduces historical figures absent from its Eastern counterpart. This narrative is discretely scattered across numerous sources surviving from before and after the Sassanians, documented by Iranian historians such as Ṭabari, Masoudi, and Balazori.[37] Ṭabari presents an amalgamated narrative of Kyrash (Kurash; Cyrus) and Darius:

فلما ملك بلتنشصر خلط فى أمره، فعزله بهمن وملّك مكانه على بابل و ما يتصل بها من الشأم و غيرها
داريوش ماذوىّ، المنسوب إلى ماذى بن يافث بن نوح عليه السلام حين صار الى المشرق، فقتل بلتنشصر،
و ملّك بابل و ناحيه الشأم ثلاث سنين. ثم عزله بهمن و ولّى مكانه كيرش غيلمىّ، من ولد غيلم بن سام
ابن نوح، الذى كان نزع الى جامر مع ماذى عندما مضى جامر الى المشرق؛ فلما صار الامر الى كيرش

36. The Syriac Apocalypse of Daniel dated to the first half of the seventh century, the end of the Sassanian Empire (Henze 2001, 15), provides an account of the reign of Gemath (Syr gmt, OP Gaumata) the magus who according to the Bisotun inscription, organized a rebellion to gain the control of the Achaemenid Empire. As Henze, the editor of this text pointed out, the only other reference to Gaumata in an ancient source is by Marcus Junianus Justinus, *Epitoma Historiarum Philippicarum Pompei Trogei* 9.4–23, where he is mentioned as Cometes (Henze 2001, 72 n. 40). Even Herodotus knows him only as Smerdis. That the story about Gaumata in the Bisotun inscriptinon shares common features with what is reported about Gemath the Magus in the Syriac Apocalypse of Daniel, indicates that the author of the Syriac text presumably had access to a Greek or Aramaic translation of the Bisotun inscription (Henze 2001, 72 n. 39; also see Shayegan 2012, 21–22).

37. For more details, see Bastani-Parizi 1967.

كتب بهمن إن يرفق ببنى إسرائيل، و يُطلق عليهم لهم النزول حيث أحبُّوا، و الرجوع إلى أرضهم، و أن يولّىَ عليهم مَن يختارونه، فاختاروا دانيال النبيّ عليه السلام، فولى أمرَهم، و كان مُلك كيرش على بابل و ما يتصل بها ثلاث سنين. [38]

When Belshazzar became king, he was perplexed in his affair. Then Bahman dethroned him, and in his place, he appointed Darius the Mede over Babylon and the neighboring regions of Sham (Syria) and other districts. He was attributed to Madhi, son of Japheth, son of Noah. He then killed Belshazzar, and ruled over Babylon and the region of Sham (Syria) for three years. Then Bahman dethroned him and, in his place, he appointed Cyrus the Elamite, a descendant of Elam, son of Shem, son of Noah, who had gone to Gomer with Madhi when Gomer went toward the east. When there came to Cyrus the matter, Bahman wrote to him to accompany the Israelites, to let them to settle wherever they liked, to return to their land, and to appoint whomever they chose to take charge of them. They chose the prophet Daniel, and he took charge of their affairs. Cyrus ruled over Babylon and the neighboring regions for three years (Ṭabari 652/1).[39]

This passage contains a very confused, weak narrative on several historical figures, mingled within the story of an almost unknown king, Darius the Mede, a literary figure mentioned in the book of Daniel.[40] However, there are traces of real events, such as linking Cyrus to Elam (Ghilam in the original text), and Cyrus' reign over Babylon. Moreover, the name of Darius is recorded in a well-known form from Hebrew and Syriac (*Dariyush*),[41] not its Iranian form, *Dārāy* or *Dārā*.

Despite these scattered references to the kings of the cuneiform era, the Eastern narrative was predominant. The stories of Cyrus, Darius, and other Achaemenid kings not regarded as Mazdayasnian were not popular among Iranians. The Sassanian official history hugely dominated other narratives. Persepolis was named *Takht-e Jamshid* (*The Throne of Jamshid*) after a legendary Iranian king, who is mentioned in the Gathas, the older part of Avesta.[42] The ancient necropolis embracing tombs of the Achaemenid king was called *Naghshe-Rostam* (*The Figure of Rostam*) after a legendary figure in the Eastern narrative.[43]

In all likelihood, any knowledge of the cuneiform texts had completely vanished in Iran. No serious attempt to decipher the meaning of the cuneiform inscriptions or the related sculptures is recorded in our extant documents. Travelers who visited Iran in those periods were not introduced to new ideas about the meaning of the ancient reliefs, but were probably satisfied by their personal observations or popular gossip or accepted superficial information. Muḥammad Abū'l-Qāsim Ibn Ḥawqal, an Arab Muslim writer, geographer, and chronicler, visited Iran in the late tenth century. In part of his well-known work, *Ṣūrat al-ʾArḍ* (*The Face of the Earth*), written in 977, he quoted a superficial interpretation of the sculptures of Darius I (see Figures 14.4–5):

38. Ibrāhīm 1966, 543.
39. My translation. See also Perlmann 1987, 49–50.
40. Dan 5:31.
41. See Budge 2013 and Henze 2001.
42. Mousavi 2012, 83. For different interpretations of the name Takhte Jamshid, see Wiesehöfer 1996, 229.
43. Wiesehöfer 1996, 227.

FIGURE 14.4. Bisotun sculpture

وأخبرني من رأى فى هذا الجبل على الغار من فوقه بمسيرةٍ بعيدةٍ صورة مكتبٍ و معلّم و صبيانٍ من حجارة، و بيد معلمهم كالسير يُومىء به لضرب الصبيان، و أنه رأى هناك مطبخاً و طبّاخه قائماً و قدوره منصوبةً على أثافٍ معمولةٍ منقوبةٍ، و بيد الطبّاخ مغرفة كل ذلك من حجارة.

Someone told me that in this mountain, above the cave, on an extended space, he had seen the representation of a school with a teacher and two children in stone; the teacher holds a lash in his hand to castigate the children. He also noticed a kitchen with his cook standing, some pots on a tripod, admirably shaped: the cook holds a spoon in his hand, and all this in stone.[44]

Until the nineteenth century, nothing changed—nobody so much as identified even the Sassanian reliefs at Naghshe-Rotam as belonging to the Sassanian kings, let alone the inscriptions and sculptures of the forgotten Achaemenid kings at Bisotun, Persepolis, and Pasargad. The first step toward a serious understanding of these inscriptions occurred only when the Danish expedition to Arabia took place in the late eighteenth century. Its only surviving member, Carsten Niebuhr, arrived in Persepolis in 1764, and stayed for three weeks, making careful copies of many inscriptions and cuneiform signs.[45] However, this proved a painstakingly process of trial and error, which would not bear results until the nineteenth century.

Cuneiform Studies in Modern Iran

The first to try cuneiform studies in Persian was the same scholar who deciphered the Bisotun inscription: Sir Henry Rawlinson. Rawlinson published the first part of his work containing the complete text of the Old Persian version, with a transliteration, two translations (one in Latin, the other in English), and two drawings of the sculpture

---

44. Ibn Hawghal 1964, 316–17 (my transaltion).
45. Wiesehöfer 1996, 230.

FIGURE 14.5. Darius' Tomb, Naghsh-e Rostam

on the rock.[46] Soon after publishing the English version, Rawlinson made a translation of the text in Persian, and sent it to Iran as a gift to Mohammad Shah, the King of Ghajar.[47] Shah immediately ordered his royal scribe, Lesan-al-Molk, to make a calligraphic copy of the translation, and write an introduction to it. The unique manuscript of this Persian translation is now kept in Iran's Centre of National Documents (see Figures 14.6–7).[48]

This constituted Iranians' first contact with cuneiform studies and the history of the Pre-Sassanian period.[49] Iranian historians and scholars of the Ghajar period had access to this translation, and quoted parts of it in their books.[50] Born in 1855, Forsat-al-dawle (Forsat), was the first Iranian to learn Old Persian. How he accessed primary cuneiform lessons is unclear, but he had a special talent in languages and mastered English and Arabic, while possessing basic knowledge of French and Hindu. He also worked on physics, geology, astronomy, painting, history, and music.

In his book *Āṯār-e ʿAjam* (*Antiquities of the Persians*), he presented a full, illustrated record of his visit to Iran's historical monuments. He also offered his translation of the Old Persian version of Achaemenid inscriptions and included drawings and photographs of the texts.[51] Some years later, he met Oscar Mann, the German orientalist, who crossed Iran, from Bushehr to the northwest, between 1901 and 1903. Forsat reviewed his knowledge of Old Persian with Mann. He prepared a manual of Old Persian and its cuneiform script, but publishers in Iran were not equipped with technical facilities for printing cuneiform characters. Thus, Forsat travelled to India and published *Dar sarf o nahv-e khatt-e Āriya* (*A Manual of Aryan Cuneiform*) in 1904, but

46. Budge 1925, 54.
47. Bahrami 2009, 104.
48. Bahrami has recently published Rawlinson's Persian translation (2009).
49. For the images, I am indebted to Askar Bahrami.
50. Bahrami 2009, 104.
51. Forsat-Al-Dawla 1998.

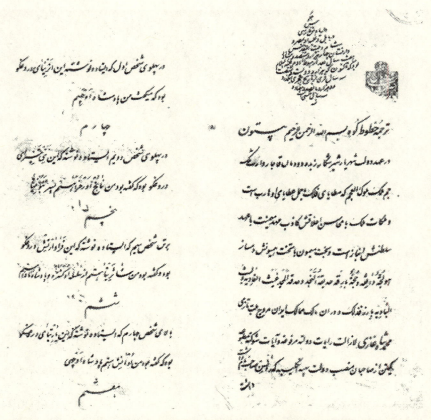

FIGURES 14.6 and 14.7. Two images of the calligraphic copy of the Persian translation (Bisotun inscription)

even he never displayed any interest in two other versions of Achaemenid inscriptions (see Figures 14.8–10).[52]

The first academic approach to the history of ancient Mesopotamia and Elam was set out in Hassan Pirnia's book. Graduating in Russia, Pirnia (1872–1935) was the top advisor in the cultural commission during the Reza Shah era. He was fluent in English, French, German, and Arabic, and had access to the most up-to-date studies. His book, *Tārikh-e Iran-e Bāstan* (*The History of Ancient Iran*), published in 1927, contains more than 3,000 pages, in which he cited a broad range of classical and modern texts.[53] He devoted a section to the history and civilization of ancient Mesopotamia.[54] For the first time, Iranian readers were introduced to the history of Sumer, Akkad, and Elam. He also provided a complete Persian translation of the Cyrus Cylinder (see Figure 14.11).[55]

52. For a comprehensive biography on Forsat, see Kasheff 1999, http://www.iranicaonline.org/articles/forsat-al-dawla.
53. Pirnia 2012.
54. Pirnia 2012, 103–26.
55. Pirnia 2012, 335–37 does not mention the source of his translation.

FIGURE 14.8. Forsat Shirazi (Salehi 2012, 3)

Yet despite Pirnia's efforts, ancient Mesopotamia and even Elam did not attract the attention of the new generation of Iranian intellectuals. Their main enthusiasm focused on ancient Iranian culture and related languages such as Old Persian, Avesta, and Middle Persian; even Elamite culture was not much welcomed even though it clearly belonged to the realm of Iranian civilization. However, over subsequent years, tendencies toward ancient Mesopotamia increased among Iranian scholars. *They Wrote on Clay* by Edward Chiera and *History Begins at Sumer* by Samuel Kramer were translated into Persian a few months after their publication in the United States. Chiera's work was the first ever source in the cuneiform studies field to be translated in Iran. Its translator, Ali Askar Hekmat, had some correspondence with George Cameron and Chiera's wife, obtaining their permission to publish the book in Persian (see Figures 14.12–13).

In the late 1950s, Majid Arfaee, a student of Persian literature, received an offer from the University of Pennsylvania (UPenn) to follow up on his research into ancient Iranian languages. However, his supervisor, Parviz Natel Khanlari, encouraged him to study Akkadian and Elamite instead. Arfaee did not pursue the Iranian studies course originally proposed and registered for a course in Assyriology at UPenn, where he started to learn Akkadian with Barry L. Eichler and Sumeiran with Åke W. Sjöberg.

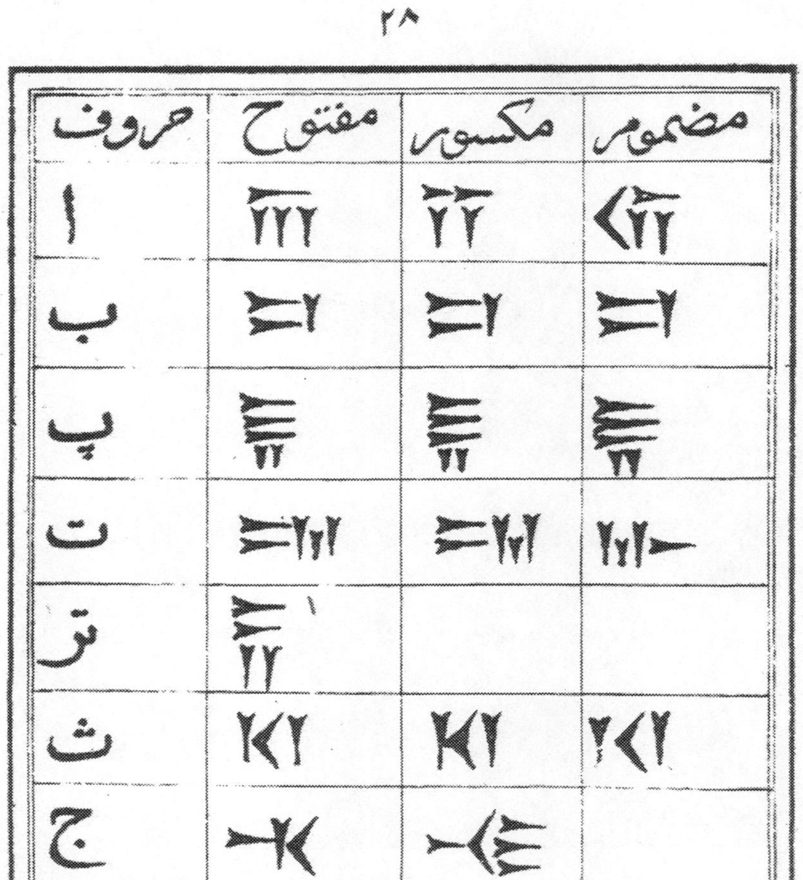

FIGURE 14.9. *A Manual of Aryan Cuneiform*. Courtesy of Askar Bahrami and Cyrus Nasrollahzadeh

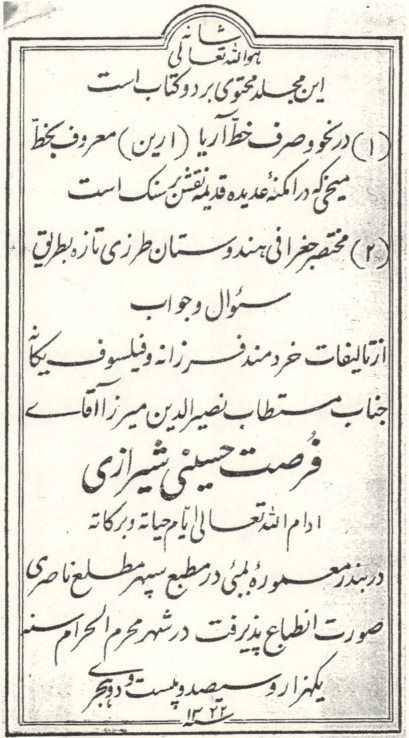

FIGURE 14.10. *A Manual of Aryan Cuneiform*. Courtesy of Askar Bahrami and Cyrus Nasrollahzadeh

FIGURE 14.11. (*top left*) Hassan Pirnia

FIGURE 14.12. (*top right*) The front cover of the Persian translation of *They Wrote on Clay*, translated by Ali Aghar Hekmat

FIGURE 14.13. (*bottom left*) Ali Aghar Hekmat

FIGURE 14.14. (*bottom right*) Majid Arfaee

After two years, Arfaee at last identified his main interest to be in Elamite, and therefore moved to Chicago, where he became Richard Hallock's only student. He also continued courses in Akkadian and Sumerian with A. Leo Oppenheim, Ignace Gelb, Samuel Kramer, Miguel Civil, Erica Reiner, John Brinkman, and Robert Biggs (see Figure 14.14).

When after ten years he returned to Iran, he found a job at the Academy of Art and Language in Tehran, where he tried to establish a Center of Assyriology. As a first step, he communicated with Blackwell and Harrassowitz and ordered a huge number of Assyriological publications. Yet despite having all tools necessary to initiate a course in Assyriology in Iran, no university showed an interest. Instead, Arfaee personally trained a handful of students who were keen on cuneiform studies. In recent years, The National Museum of Iran has established the Hall of Tablets, a center for studying cuneiform objects. For a couple of years, Arfaee was responsible for the hall, where he and a group of students organized and categorized thousands of tablets kept in the museum.

Some workshops and language classes have also been led by specialists in recent years as a response to the ever-increasing number of Iranian students and scholars interested in cuneiform studies. Several Iranian students have embarked on academic courses and degree programs in Assyriology at European universities. Although Assyriology has yet to find its way into Iranian universities, very gradually Iran is moving toward an academic approach both to it and to cuneiform studies.

REFERENCES

Anklesaria, B. T. 1956. *Zand-Ākāsīh: Iranian or Greater Bundahišn*. Bombay: The Rahnumae Mazdayasnan Sabha.

Anklesaria, T. D. 1908. *The Bûndahishn, a facs. of the TD MS. no. 2* (= TD 2). Byculla: The British India Press.

Bahar, M. 1982. *Bondahesh: Farnbagh Dādagī*. Tehran: Toos.

Bahrami, A. 2009. "Kohantarin bargardan-e katibe-ye Bisotun." *Ma'āref* 67:99–124.

Bastani-Parizi, E. 1967. "Kurosh dar revāyāt-e Irani." *Majallae-ye Barresihā-ye Tārikhi* 11:163–94.

Black, J. 2008. "The Obsolescence and Demise of Cuneiform Writing in Elam." Page 45–72 in *The Disappearance of Writing Systems: Perspectives on Literacy and Communication*. Edited by J. Baines, J. Bennet, and S. Houston. London: Equinox.

Bordreuil, P., and D. Pardee. 2009. *A Manual of Ugaritic*. Winona Lake: Eisenbrauns.

Budge, E. A. W. 1925. *The Rise & Progress of Assyriology*. London: M. Hopkinson & Co.

———. 2013. *The History of Alexander the Great: Being the Syriac Version of the Pseudo-Callisthenes*. Cambridge: Cambridge University Press.

Dahl, J. 2009. "Early Writing in Iran: A Reappraisal." *Iran* 47:23–31.

———. 2013. "Early Writing in Iran." Pages 233–62 in *The Oxford Handbook of Ancient Iran*. Edited by D. T. Potts. Oxford: Oxford University Press.

Daneshmand, P. 2004. "An Extispicy form Haft-Tappe." *Journal of Cuneiform Studies* 56:13–4.

———. 2015. "New Phraseology and Literary Style in the Babylonian Version of the Achaemenid Inscriptions." Pages 321–34 in *Tradition and Innovation in the Ancient Near East: Proceedings of the 57th Rencontre Assyriologique Internationale at Rome 4–8 July 2011*. Edited by A. Archi. Winona Lake: Eisenbrauns.

Daryaee, T. 2000. "Katibeye-Shāpur Sakānshāh dar Takht-e Jamshid." *Farhang* 37–38:107–114.

282   Parsa Daneshmand

De Graef, K. 2013. "The Use of Akkadian in Iran." Pages 263–82 in *The Oxford Handbook of Ancient Iran*. Edited by D. Potts. Oxford: Oxford University Press.

Dresden, M. J. 1966. *Dēnkart: A Pahlavi Text. Facsimile Edition of the Manuscript B of the K. R. Cama Oriental Institute Bombay*. Wiesbaden: Harrassowitz.

Englund, R. K. 2004. "The State of Decipherment of Proto-Elamite." Pages 100–149 in *The First Writing: Script Invention as History and Process*. Edited by S. D. Houston. Cambridge: Cambridge University Press.

Forsat-Al-Dawle. 1998. *Āṯār-e ʿAjam*. Edited by M. R. Fasai. Tehran: Amir-Kabir.

Garelli, P. 1972. *L'Assyriologie*. Paris: Presses Universitaires de France.

Geller, M. J. 1997. "The Last Wedge." *Zeitschrift für Assyriologie* 87:43–95.

Henze, M. 2001. *The Syriac Apocalypse of Daniel: Introduction, Text, and Commentary*. Tübingen: Mohr Siebeck.

Herrero, P., and J. J. Glassner. 1993. "Haft-Tépé: Choix de Textes III." *Iranica Antiqua* 28:128–32.

Ibn Ḥawqal, M. 1964. *Kītāb ṣūrat al-ard*. Beirut: Dār Maktabat al-Hayāh.

Ibrāhīm, M. Abū al-Faḍl. 1966. *Tārīkh al-Ṭabarī: Tārīkh al-rusul wa-al-mulūk*. al-Qāhirah: Dār al-Maʿārif.

Kasheff, M. 1999. "Forṣat-al-Dawla." http://www.iranicaonline.org/articles/forsat-al-dawla.

Khačikjan, M. 1998. *The Elamite Language*. Documenta Asiana 4. Rome: Consiglio Nazionale delle Ricerche Istituto per gli Studi Micenei ed Egeo-anatolici.

Khaleghi-Motlagh, D. 2007. *The Shahname (The Book of Kings)—Abu'l-Qasem Ferdowsi*. Vol. 5. Tehran: The Center for the Great Islamic Encyclopedia.

Labat, R. 1974. *Textes littéraires de Suse*. Mémoires de la Délégation archéologique en Iran 57. Paris: P. Geuthner.

Mousavi, A. 2012. *Persepolis: Discovery and Afterlife of a World Wonder*. Berlin: de Gruyter.

Negahban, E. O. 1991. *Excavations at Haft Tepe, Iran*. Philadelphia: University Museum, University of Pennsylvania.

Oppenheim, A. L. 1977. *Ancient Mesopotamia: Portrait of a Dead Civilization*. Chicago: University of Chicago Press.

Perlmann, M. 1987. *The History of al-Ṭabarī*. Vol. 4, *The Ancient Kingdoms*. Translated and annotated by M. Perlmann and S. Shaked. Albany: State University of New York Press.

Pirnia, H. 2012. *Tārikh-e Iran-e Bāstan* (I). Negah Publication: Tehran.

Potts, D. T. 2015. *The Archaeology of Elam: Formation and Transformation of an Ancient Iranian State*. New York: Cambridge University Press.

Salehi, M. H. 2012. *Ān Gohar-e Bi Hamtā (Negāhi be āsār-e mosavvar-e Forsat-Al-Dawle Shirazi)*. Tehran: Farhangestan Honar.

Shayegan, M. R. 2011. *Arsacids and Sasanians: Political Ideology in Post-Hellenistic and Late Antique Persia*. Cambridge: Cambridge University Press.

———. 2012. *Aspects of History and Epic in Ancient Iran, From Gaumāta to Wahnām*. London: Center for Hellenistic Studies, Trustees for Harvard University.

Stolper, M. W. 1992. "The Writing Record." Pages 253–78 in *The Royal City of Susa*. Edited by P. O. Harper, J. Aruz, and F. Tallon. New York: Metropolitan Museum of Art.

———. 2004. "Elamite." Pages 60–94 in *The Cambridge Encyclopedia of the World's Ancient Languages*. Edited by R. D. Woodard. Cambridge: Cambridge University Press.

———. 2005. "Achaemenid Languages and Inscriptions." Pages 18–24 in *Forgotten Empire: The World of Ancient Persia*. Edited by J. Curtis and N. Tallis. London: British Museum.

Stolper, M. W., and J. Tavernier. 2007. "An Old Persian Administrative Tablet form the Persepolis Fortification." https://oi.uchicago.edu/research/projects/persepolis-fortification-archive (accessed 1 January 2020).

Weissbach, F. H. 1911. *Die Keilschriften der Achämeniden*. Leipzig: Hinrichs.

Wiesehöfer, J. 1996. *Ancient Persian: From 550 BC to 650 AD*. London: Tauris.

Xifra, J., and R. L. Heath. 2015. "Reputation, Propaganda, and Hegemony in Assyriology Studies: A Gramscian View of Public Relations Historiography." *Journal of Public Relations Research* 27:196–211.

CHAPTER 15

Assyriology in China

Changyu Liu

BOTH MESOPOTAMIAN CIVILIZATION of West Asia and Chinese civilization of East Asia are considered among the earliest ones on earth. For Chinese scholars, there is a continued need to study this "lost civilization" of Mesopotamia by contributing to Assyriology. In the following essay, I will give a more detailed introduction and discuss the history and current state of Assyriology in China.

Premise

This first stage (before 1949) can be subdivided into three periods: that of the Ming and Qing Dynasties before the First Opium War (1680–1840), the late Qing Dynasty (1840–1912), and the Republic of China (1912–1949). Initially, Chinese scholars could not admit that there were civilizations other than Chinese civilization because the concept of the "Celestial Empire" or the "center of the world" was still prevalent. After the First Opium War (1840), they began to study Western civilization as well as that of ancient Mesopotamia by translating relevant books, visiting well-known museums (such as the British Museum and Musée du Louvre), and writing articles and books about the Mesopotamian civilization.

From the 1680 to 1840, during which time the Ming and Qing Dynasties ruled China, Jesuit missionaries who came to China in order to spread Christianity also brought some knowledge of ancient Mesopotamian civilization. For instance, the Italian Jesuit missionary Giulio Alenio (1582–1649) wrote a book in Chinese named *Zhifang Waiji* (*Chronicle of Foreign Lands*), which mentioned ancient Mesopotamian history, particularly the Tower of Babel and the Hanging Garden of Babylon. Unfortunately, knowledge about Mesopotamian history and geography did not spread easily in China because traditional Chinese scholars rejected external cultures.

China's defeat in the Opium War allowed more Chinese scholars to study Western culture, including Mesopotamian culture. For instance, Wei Yuan (1794–1857) in his well-known work *Haiguo Tuzhi* (*Illustrated Treatise on the Maritime Kingdoms*) mentioned Babylon. Furthermore, some Chinese scholars or officers saw cuneiform tablets and Mesopotamian antiquities while visiting museums in western Europe and the United States. For example, the merchant Li Gui (1842–1903) visited the British Museum in 1876 and saw cuneiform as "leaf-book and *zhongdingwen* (inscriptions on ancient bronze objects)." When Liang Qichao (1873–1929), the famous Chinese scholar and reformer of the late Qing Dynasty, lived in Chicago, he pointed out that

283

ancient Mesopotamian civilization was the origin of Greco-Roman civilization. What is more, a few books on Mesopotamian civilization were translated into Chinese and were introduced to China, such as a Japanese work *A History of Assyria and Babylon* written by Saburo Kitamura and translated into Chinese by Zhao Bizhen (1873–1956), which was thought as the first translated work in Chinese on ancient Mesopotamian history and culture.

During the Republic of China (1912–1949), more and more works and contributions on Mesopotamian civilization were introduced into China. Apart from translating many pertinent works in Chinese, a few Chinese scholars began to write their own works, both articles and books, related to Mesopotamian civilization. For instance, Chen Yujing (1898–1963) wrote an article "The Ancient Babylonian Codes" (1912), in which he introduced the well-known Code of Hammurabi. In 1938, Chilperic Edwards' work *The Hammurabi Code and the World's Earliest Laws* (1906) was translated into Chinese by Shen Dagui who also compared and contrasted it with the law of Moses. Furthermore, some scholars wrote works comparing Chinese civilization and Mesopotamia. Xu Qiu, for example, wrote an article "Garden of Huangdi and Hanging Garden of Babylon" (1931), which compared the ancient Chinese and Babylonian gardens.

To summarize, scholars in the late Qing Dynasty and the Republic of China introduced knowledge of ancient Mesopotamian history and culture into China but could not be said to have introduced Assyriology or Assyriological studies. The introduction of Assyriology as a discipline only came after the foundation of the People's Republic of China in 1949.

Foundation

The foundation of the People's Republic of China (PRC) in 1949 brought Chinese Assyriology and Mesopotamian studies into a new era. From 1949 to the 1984, Chinese Assyriology had a strong ideological Marxist bent due to influences from the Soviet Union. Between 1955 and 1957, the Soviet scholar A. N. Gladyshevskii lectured on ancient world history, including the history of ancient Mesopotamia, in training courses held at Northeast Normal University in Changchun, China. Soon afterwards, under the leadership of Lin Zhichun (1910–2007), recognized as the father of ancient world history and a pioneer of Assyriology, Egyptology, and classics in China, students and trainees undertook the translation of a great number of cuneiform documents following earlier Russian versions, such as Old Babylonian legal texts, the Middle Assyrian Laws, laws of the Neo-Assyrian period, and Neo-Babylonian legal texts. They also translated select Russian monographs and textbooks into Chinese, including V. V. Struve's *The Ancient Orient* (1955) and V. I. Avdiev's *History of the Ancient Orient* (1956). Apart from translating the works of Soviet orientalists into Chinese, some Chinese scholars of ancient history in particular began to debate the nature of the Old Babylonian society. Specifically, Tong Shuye (1908–1968) held the academic point of view that Old Babylonian society belonged to the beginning of the feudal society. Opposing him was Li Yongcai (1933–2013), who identified Old Babylonian society with the early stage of slave society. However, differing from both scholars' viewpoints was Lin Zhichun (1910–2007), who considered it unrealistic to discuss or debate the nature of the Old Babylonian society because there was not enough original material from ancient Mesopotamia available. Afterwards, these ideological debates were abandoned, as formally trained Assyriologists who could master the cuneiform evidence began to appear in China in the 1980s.

It was in 1984 that the Institute for the History of Ancient Civilizations (IHAC) was founded in Northeast Normal University, Changchun. A large number of books and journals on Assyriology (as well as Hittitology, Egyptology, and classics) were regularly bought for this institute through special funding made available by the Chinese Ministry of Education. Furthermore, a few Assyriologists were employed at this institute to teach Assyriology to Chinese undergraduates and postgraduate students. More importantly, an international journal, the *Journal of Ancient Civilizations* (*JAC*), was founded in 1986, which was regarded as the first academic journal on Assyriology (as well as Hittitology, Egyptology, and classics) in China and became the window of communication between Chinese Assyriologists and international scholars. The third great event was the emergence of the first generation of Assyriologists in China, most notably Yang Chi, Wu Yuhong, and Gong Yushu.

In 1987, Yang earned a PhD from the University of Chicago and then returned to IHAC, Northeast Normal University to teach. She was regarded as the first doctor of Assyriology in China and translated the Code of Hammurabi into Chinese directly from Akkadian cuneiform. Regrettably, she later left Assyriology and turned to a career in business. In 1993, Wu earned a PhD from the University of Birmingham in the United Kingdom and also returned to IHAC, Northeast Normal University to teach. His doctoral supervisor was Professor Wilfred George Lambert (1926–2011), under whom he completed a dissertation entitled "A Political History of Eshnunna, Mari and Assyria during the Early Old Babylonian Period (from the End of Ur III to the Death of Shamshi-Adad)." Wu's research interests involved various aspects of ancient Mesopotamia from the third millennium BCE to the first millennium BCE as well as slavery in ancient China and Mesopotamia. Afterwards, his research focused on reconstructing the Ur III administration, particularly the organization of Puzrish-Dagan (modern Drehem). Professor Wu is now retired from Northeast Normal University, but he has left a legacy of students at the masters and doctoral level who comprise most of the second generation of Assyriology in China, including Liu Jian, Guo Honggeng, Li Haifeng, and Qu Tianfu, and even extend to a third generations in Wang Guangsheng. These scholars are today teaching at various institutions throughout China, and many have become full or associate professors (see below). It is worth mentioning that the Swedish student Magnus Widell came to China, studied, and earned a PhD supervised by Wu in IHAC. Today he teaches Assyriology in the University of Liverpool, UK.

In 1994, Gong received a PhD from Ludwig-Maximilians-Universität Munich and went on to teach at Peking University, Beijing. His doctoral supervisor was Professor Dr. Dietz Otto Edzard (1930–2004). Professor Gong's research focuses on cuneiform writing and Sumerian literature. His two famous monographs, written in German, are *Studien zur Bildung und Entwicklung der Keilschriftzeichen* (1993) and *Die Namen der Keilschriftzeichen* (2000). Additionally, Gong wrote a number of works in Chinese related to Sumerian civilization and Near Eastern archaeology, such as *Exploring*

Sumerian Civilization (2001) and *History of West Asian Archaeology* (2002). Among the students whom Gong taught are Ouyang Xiaoli, Tang Jun, and Yin Ling.

Apart from Wu and Gong among the first generation of Assyriologists in China, there are additional scholars, including Li Zheng (Peking University), Yi Jianping, and Liu Jian (Chinese Academy of Social Sciences, CASS), who primarily focus on Hittitology, and Yu Dianli and Zheng Dianhua (both The Commercial Press), who focus on Old Babylonian society. They contributed to Assyriological developments in China in a variety of ways. To summarize, if one can say that the foundation of IHAC marks the formal foundation of Assyriology in China, then the first generation of Assyriologists in China are the pioneers and are key to the continued development of Assyriology in China.

Development

A significant development phase of Assyriology in China began during the turn of the twenty-first century and continues to the current day. This phase is the result of the cultivation of the first generation of Assyriologists in China. During this time, the main impetus has come from the second generation of Assyriologists, those scholars in universities or research institutions who hold the title of professor or associate professor and are roughly between 35 and 50 years of age. Most of them had been the masters or doctoral students of Wu or Gong, but they have since gone on to great achievements in their respective research areas. In the meantime, the development of Assyriology in China presents the following new features. First, there is a breadth of research interests and focus on different periods, including the Early Dynastic period (for Wang Xianhua), the Ur III dynasty (for Liu, the author of this essay), the Old Babylonian period (for Li), and the Neo-Assyrian period (for Guo). Second, many scholars have the background or experience necessary to be active abroad, including joining the International Association for Assyriology (IAA) or international cooperative projects (such as Cuneiform Digital Library Initiative, CDLI) and attending various international conference (such as Rencontre Assyriologique Internationale, RAI), which makes closer connection between Chinese scholars and scholars from Europe and the United States.

Among the second generation of Assyriologists in China, most used to be the doctoral students of Wu, including Guo (Chinese Academy of Social Sciences, Beijing, focusing on Neo-Assyrian period), Li (East China Normal University, Shanghai, Old Babylonian period), Qu Tianfu (Xiamen University, Xiamen, Neo-Assyrian period), Huo Wenyong (Shanxi Normal University, Xi'an, Old Babylonian to Neo-Assyrian period), and Yuan Zhihui (Tianjin Normal University, Tianjin, Amarna period). Furthermore, Tang Jun (Southwest Jiaotong University, Chengdu, linguistics) was the doctoral student of Gong. Both Zhang Wen'an (Shanxi Normal University, Xi'an, Mesopotamian mythology) and Zhou Hongxiang (Hanshan Normal University, Chaozhou, classics involving Assyriology) graduated and received PhD degrees from Beijing Normal University. In addition, a few scholars who earned PhD degree from universities in Europe or the United States are Wang Xianhua (Shanghai International Studies University, Shanghai, Early Dynasty and Old Akkadian period), who received a

PhD degree from Cambridge University and whose doctoral supervisor was Professor Nicholas Postgate, and Ouyang Xiaoli (Fudan University, Shanghai, Ur III period and Mesopotamian mathematics), who received a PhD degree from Harvard University and whose doctoral supervisor was Professor Piotr Steinkeller. The second generation of Assyriologists in China plays a very important role in the development and success of Assyriology. By carrying forward the tradition from the first generation, they make themselves masters of cuneiform writings (Sumerian, Akkadian, Hittite) and concentrate on one certain area, not only producing many high-quality academic monographs and works both in Chinese and foreign languages, but also writing many popular books and articles on ancient Mesopotamian civilization that popularize Assyriology for the general public.

Currently, the development of Assyriology in China is resulting in a third generation of Assyriologists, younger scholars whose average age is between twenty-five and thirty-five years old. They have recently received PhD degrees and are teaching in universities or research institutions, such as Chen Fei (Peking University, Beijing, Middle and Neo-Assyrian studies), Wang Guangsheng (Northeast Normal University, Changchun, Ur III studies), Wang Huan (Shanghai International Studies University, Shanghai, Hittitology), Jiang Jiayu (Capital Normal University, Beijing, Hittitology), Shi Xiaowen (Mudanjiang Normal University, Mudanjiang, Old Assyrian studies), Liu (the author, Zhejiang Normal University, Jinhua, in Ur III studies, particularly the Drehem administration, who earned a PhD degree from Ruprecht-Karls-Universität Heidelberg, Germany, and whose doctoral supervisor was Professor Dr. Markus Hilgert), and so forth.

Since the foundation of the IHAC in 1984 and of the *JAC* in 1986, Assyriology in China has gone through more than thirty years of history. During this relatively short period, Assyriological scholars and students in China have developed from one or two scholars to a large group, and they play an increasingly important role in international Assyriology. As a discipline, Assyriology is currently not classified as an independent subject in China, but instead is found in history departments in most Chinese universities, with the exception of foreign languages and literatures exclusively in Peking University. Apart from the RAI which Chinese Assyriological scholars occasionally attend, they more often attend the Annual Conference for the Study of Ancient World History in China.

REFERENCES

Alenio, Giulio. 2000. *Chronicle of Foreign Lands*. Translated by Xie Fang. Beijing: Zhonghua Book Company.

Avdiev, V .I. 1956. *History of the Ancient Orient*. Translated by Wang Yizhu. Beijing: SDX Joint Publishing Company. (Chinese)

Chen Yujing. 1912. "The Ancient Babylonian Codes." *Fazheng Zazhi* 2(1). (Chinese)

Gong Yushu. 1993. *Studien zur Bildung und Entwicklung der Keilschriftzeichen*. Hamburg: Verlag Dr. Kovac.

———. 2000. *Die Namen der Keilschriftzeichen*. Alter Orient und Altes Testament 268. Münster: Ugarit-Verlag.

Guo Honggeng, and Chen Dezheng. 2005. "General Introduction to Assyriological Studies in China." *World History* 5:121–28. (Chinese)

288   Changyu Liu

Kitamura, Saburo. 1902. *A History of Assyria and Babylon.* Translated by Zhao Bizhen. Shanghai: Shanghai Guangzhi Book Company. (Chinese)

Liu Changyu. 2017. *Organization, Administrative Practices and Written Documentation in Mesopotamia during the Ur III Period (c. 2112–2004 BC): A Case Study of Puzriš-Dagan in the Reign of Amar-Suen.* Beiträge zur Wirtschafts-, Rechts- und Sozialgeschichte des östlichen Mittelmeerraums und Altvorderasiens 3. Münster: Ugarit-Verlag.

Ouyang Xiaoli. 2013. *Monetary Role of Silver and Its Administration in Mesopotamia during the Ur III Period (c. 2112–2004 BCE): A Case Study of the Umma Province.* Biblioteca del Próximo Oriente Antiguo 11. Madrid: Consejo Superior de Investigaciones Científicas.

Struve, V. V. 1955. *The Ancient Orient.* Translated by Chen Wenlin and Jia Gang. Beijing: People Education Press. (Chinese)

Wang Xiaohua. 2011. *The Metamorphosis of Enlil in Early Mesopotamia.* Alter Orient und Altes Testament 385. Münster: Ugarit-Verlag.

Wei Yuan. 1999. *Illustrated Treatise on the Maritime Kingdoms.* Zhengzhou: Zhongzhou Ancient Books Publishing House. (Chinese)

Wu Yuhong. 1994. *A Political History of Eshnunna, Mari and Assyria during the Early Old Babylonian Period (from the Fall of Ur III to the Death of Samsi-Adad).* Changchun: IHAC.

———. 2003. "Assyriological Studies in China." *Collected Papers of History Studies* 3:101–4. (Chinese)

Xu Qiu. 1931. "Garden of Huangdi and Hanging Garden of Babylon." *Dixue Zazhi* 18(163). (Chinese)

Yang Chi, trans. 1992. *Code of Hammurabi.* Beijing: Higher Education Press. (Chinese)

CHAPTER 16

Looking for a Tell: The Beginnings of Ancient Near Eastern Archaeology at the University of Barcelona

Jordi Vidal

Del Olmo's Plan: The Beginnings of Ancient Near Eastern Studies in Barcelona

There was no discipline of ancient Near Eastern studies either in the Universitat de Barcelona (UB) nor indeed in any other Spanish university until the 1980s. When the archaeologist Pere Bosch Gimpera was appointed as professor of ancient history at the UB in 1916, he attempted to send some of his students (Salvador Espriu, Josep Gibert) abroad for ancient Near Eastern studies. The plan was that they would then return in order to create a new academic tradition in this subject.[1] Unfortunately, the fascist victory in the Spanish Civil War forced Bosch into exile in 1939, putting an end to his aims to promote ancient Near Eastern studies at UB. Just after the end of the Spanish Civil War (1936–1939), Henry Heras SJ, with the support of Martín Almagro and Lluís Pericot, both professors of the UB, tried to establish the so-called Instituto Ibérico-Oriental. It was an ambitious and bizarre project with the supposed aim of promoting the study of ancient cultures of the Mediterranean and also of Mesopotamia.[2] However, the Instituto Ibérico-Oriental was never created, and throughout the long period of Franco's dictatorship (1939–1975) ancient Near Eastern studies simply did not exist at the UB.

In 1971, Fernando Díaz Esteban,[3] professor of Hebrew language at the UB, founded the Instituto de Estudios Orientales (IEO) in Barcelona. With this Institute, Díaz Esteban intended to create, at last, an institution able to train Spanish scholars in the study of Oriental languages and cultures (both ancient and modern). However, this aim was never achieved due, according to Díaz Esteban, to the lack of adequate funding either from the university or the Spanish government. Hence IEO was an almost inactive institution between 1971 and 1986, offering only a few cycles of conferences on limited aspects of Oriental languages and cultures.[4]

The true founder of ancient Near Eastern studies at the UB was Gregorio Del Olmo. Del Olmo joined the UB in 1975 as professor of Hebrew language and literature.[5] At that

---

Author's Note: I am grateful to Wilfred G. E. Watson for his support in writing this article. Any mistakes, of course, are my own. This paper has been produced in the context of the research project HAR2017-82593-P (Ministerio de Economía y Competitividad).

1. Vidal 2016b, 2016c.
2. Garcia-Ventura and Vidal 2012.
3. See Spottorno, Sáenz-Badillos, and Del Olmo 1992 and Vidal 2013, 48–49 on Díaz Esteban.
4. Vidal 2016a, 9–20.
5. See Abad 2000; Molina, Márquez, and Sanmartín 1999–2000 and Vidal 2013, 45–47 on Del Olmo.

time, he believed that the introduction of ancient Near Eastern studies at the University required the implementation of three main projects: (1) the creation of a research institute devoted only to the study of the ancient Near East; (2) the foundation of a Spanish academic journal on this very topic; (3) the direction of an archaeological mission in Mesopotamia, able (a) to provide physical contact with the Near East and (b) to train a new generation of Spanish archaeologists specializing in the study of those cultures.[6]

The first project he was able to realize was the foundation of an academic journal. In 1983, the first volume of *Aula Orientalis* (*AuOr*), the journal of the IEO, was published. According to Del Olmo, *AuOr* was intended to publish papers by Spanish-speaking scholars in order to promote the development of the discipline in Spain.[7] Nevertheless, *AuOr* has modified this aim through the years, becoming an international journal, where 34% of the published papers are in English, 10% are in French, and 4% are in German or Italian.[8]

The second project undertaken by Del Olmo was the creation of a research institute. In 1987, he was elected as the new director of the IEO, due to the departure of Díaz Esteban to Madrid, where he was appointed as professor of Hebrew language and literature at the Universidad Complutense. Once in office, Del Olmo completely transformed the former IEO. It ceased to be an institute dedicated rather generically to Oriental culture, and became a true research institute, with a specialized library and a teaching program on Assyriology, Egyptology, Semitic studies, and Indo-European languages. Experts such as Miquel Civil, Fumi Karahashi, Rogelio Lemosín, Jesús López, Manuel Molina, Josep Padró, Éric Pirart, Joaquín Sanmartín, Wilfred Watson, Cornelia Wunsch, and, of course, Del Olmo, as well as other scholars, were in charge of training a young generation of students in these disciplines (e.g. Agustí Alemany, Juan Belmonte, Josep Cervelló, Lluís Feliu, Jaume Llop, Ignacio Márquez, Adelina Millet, Juan Carlos Oliva, Marcos Such, etc.). This process culminated in 1991 with the conversion of the former IEO into the current Institut del Pròxim Orient Antic (IPOA).[9]

Del Olmo's third project, concerning the archaeological mission, was finally achieved in 1989, after a long gestation process. The aim of this paper is to reconstruct and analyze the history of that process, making use of some unpublished documents kept in the Arxiu Històric del Institut del Pròxim Orient Antic (AHIPOA). The analysis of this documentation shows, among others, the social network which shaped the IEO's archaeological project, some of the working methods by the IEO's members, and the influence of the Syrian administration on the development of the project. In addition, it will provide some unpublished data on the site of Tell Maled.

Looking for a Tell: The Archaeology of Yamhad

In essence, the IEO was a research institute whose members were philologists, experts in language but not in ancient Near Eastern archaeology. This is why Del Olmo looked

6 Vidal 2016a, 115.
7 Del Olmo 1983, 8.
8 Vidal 2016a, 128.
9 Vidal 2016a, 21–47.

elsewhere for some archaeological guidance with regard to his project. In a letter that he sent to Paolo Matthiae on 23 November 1986 he remembered a previous meeting held in Paolo Xella's house in 1985. There, Del Olmo had told Matthiae about his plans to initiate an archaeological project in Syria and Matthiae had kindly offered to help. Del Olmo enquired to Matthiae for a tell where he could develop the mission. According to Del Olmo the tell must fulfil three requirements: it must (1) have easy access from a geographical point of view, (2) not raise technical difficulties from an archaeological point of view, and (3) have occupation levels of the second millennium BCE (the period to which Del Olmo was mainly devoted).[10]

After two months, Matthiae sent a reply to Del Olmo. His letter provided a considerable amount of archaeological information which helped Del Olmo to organize his project. Matthiae had advised him to choose a tell located in the region of Aleppo, more specifically in the area of Tell Rifa'at. The reasons given were that the zone offered logistical facilities, that it had hardly been explored by archaeologists, and that many sites from the Bronze Age and the Iron Age were located there, as had been demonstrated by the survey carried out by John Matthers in the late 1970s.[11] Matthiae especially emphasized the relevance of several settlements: Tell Aarane for Aramaean culture, and Tell Haylane, Tell Kaffine, Tell Qaramel, and Tell Karmine for the Early and Middle Bronze Ages. Moreover, according to him, an archaeological mission in the region of Aleppo would be particularly useful in order to settle two problems concerning both history and archaeology: to solve our ignorance of the archaeological features of the ancient kingdom of Yamhad, and to clarify the relations between Yamhad and Ebla, where Matthiae was working then.[12] Matthiae's comments highly conditioned the archaeological project of the IEO.

In 1987 Del Olmo submitted a research project to the Spanish Ministerio de Educación y Ciencia. Entitled "Misión Arqueológica de la Universidad de Barcelona," it reproduced Matthiae's proposal verbatim: "The main objective of the excavation project is to clarify the archaeological context of the kingdom of Yamhad/Halab/Aleppo. We know of its social and political relevance at the beginning of second millennium BCE from the Mari archives and, most recently, from the Tell Leylan texts. The kingdom was one of the great powers in Syria and remained active, with varying success, until the Aramaean period."[13] In his application, Del Olmo admitted that the final choice of the tell to be excavated by the IEO would be conditioned by a survey planned for 1988.

Del Olmo's project was accepted by the aforementioned Spanish office and was financed with the sum of €88,288.68 for the triennium 1988–1990. Therefore, the IEO was able to provide the minimum economic resources to undertake Del Olmo's third

10. Letter by Gregorio Del Olmo to Paolo Matthiae, 23 November 1986. Universidad de Barcelona/Facultad de Filología/08007 Barcelona/Catedrático: G. Del Olmo Lete. Typewritten text (AHIPOA: Folder *TQQ Documentación y correspondencia*, file 13).

11. Matthers et al. 1978; Matthers 1981.

12. Letter from Matthiae to Del Olmo, 24 January 1987. Dipartimento di Scienze Storiche Archeologiche e Antropologiche dell'Antichità. Università degli Studi di Roma "La Sapienza"/Il direttore/Piazzale Aldo Moro, 5—I. 00185 Roma. Typewritten text. Autograph signature (AHIPOA: Folder *TQQ Documentación y correspondencia*, file 13).

13. "Proyecto de investigación 1987" (AHIPOA: Folder *TQQ Documentación y correspondencia*, file 4).

292   Jordi Vidal

project for the development of ancient Near Eastern studies in Barcelona. Now, it was necessary to put it into practice on the ground.

Tell Maled

At this point it was imperative to appoint the archaeologist responsible for the project. Emilio Olávarri was the expert designated by Del Olmo. Olávarri had studied Near Eastern archaeology at the École Biblique et Archéologique Française in Jerusalem. He obtained his degree (Eléve Diplomé) in 1962 with a dissertation on Iron Age pottery, supervised by Roland de Vaux. In the early 1960s, he excavated several Palestinian and Jordanian settlements under the supervision of such prominent figures of biblical archaeology as Kathleen Kenyon, Diana Kirkbride, Peter Parr, and De Vaux himself. From 1964 to 1966 he had directed a Spanish archaeological project in the Moabite fortress of Khirbet Arair. Later he worked in other settlements such as Khirbet el-Medeineh (1978, 1982), Gerassa (1983–1984) and the fortress of Amman (1974–1982).[14] There is no doubt that Olávarri was the most experienced Spanish scholar on Near Eastern archaeology. His appointment as the director of the archaeological mission to be undertaken by the IEO was the obvious choice.

Between 19 and 29 March, a small team comprising Del Olmo, Olávarri, and Sanmartín carried out an archaeological survey in the Orontes Valley and the Wadi Quoueiq. They visited about thirty archaeological sites, and finally chose Tell Maled. The reasons put forward by Del Olmo to justify this choice have already been pointed out: it was a tell with easy access, of a reasonable size, and currently neither occupied nor used for agriculture. Moreover, the tell was within the boundaries of the ancient kingdom of Yamhad. Therefore, its excavation would fulfil the objective suggested by Matthiae and accepted by Del Olmo: to clarify the archaeological context of the kingdom of Yamhad.[15]

Stored in the archive of the IPOA is an unpublished report by Olávarri on Tell Maled, dated 7 April 1988. The report describes the main features of the site based on the data collected during the survey made between 25 and 26 March 1988.[16] It substantially supplements the previous brief description published by Matthers. According to Olávarri, Tell Maled was a site of notable strategic importance in the third and second millennia BCE, both from the military aspect and in terms of trade, since it lay on the routes from the Euphrates and central Syria to Anatolia. Subsequently, Olávarri described the main traits of the site. Tell Maled was 200m (north–south) by 300m (east–west) long. At its highest point it reached 25 meters above the surrounding plain. Olávarri also pointed out the existence of an eroded section at the bottom of the eastern slope of the tell, which revealed a section of the Early Bronze Age mudbrick wall.

Using the material collected on the surface of the site (pieces of flint and pottery fragments), Olávarri attempted a reconstruction of the occupation sequence of Tell Maled. The oldest phases would be PPNA and PPNB (eighth and seventh millennia

---

14. See González Echegaray and Menéndez 1999 and Vidal 2013, 83–85§ on Emilio Olávarri.
15. Del Olmo 1989, 271.
16. "Prospección en Tell Maled, Wuady Quoueiq" (AHIPOA: Folder *Informes anteriores*, file 3).

BCE). Material corresponding to these phases were carved flints, mostly located in the western slope of the tell. Olávarri admitted that only an archaeological excavation could determine whether those pieces corresponded to an occasional occupation of the site or whether they indicated a permanent settlement in Tell Maled.

Two fragments of small, handmade and burnished bowls testify to the possible existence of a Neolithic phase (sixth millennium BCE). A third phase (Late Neolithic— Chalcolithic, fifth millennium BCE) is shown by many fragments of painted Halaf pottery, both imported and local imitations. The fourth phase (Early Bronze Age I–III, 3100–2400 BCE) is documented by the finding of ledge-handles belonging to each of the three sub-phases. Most of the pottery fragments recovered on the surface belong to the final phases of occupation: Early Bronze Age IVa and IVb (2400–2000 BCE; pottery from this phase was very similar to pottery found in Ebla) and Middle Bronze Age I and II (2000–1600 BCE).

Olávarri concluded his report with a brief historical remark. He pointed out that Tell Maled was part of the kingdom of Yamhad in the Middle Bronze Age and was probably destroyed by a Hittite military campaign led by Hattusili I or Mursili I (ca. 1650 BCE). Afterwards, the site was completely abandoned, except for a brief occupation in the Byzantine period, indicated by a mosaic (still visible in 1988) located in the lower part of the southern slope.

Convinced of the convenience of excavating at Tell Maled, Del Olmo applied for permission to work on the site. The application was sent to the General Director of Antiquities in Syria, A. Bahnassi, on 25 April 1988.[17] Del Olmo specified his aim to undertake five to ten archaeological campaigns, with an estimated budget of $30,000. According to the project, the team was to be composed of himself (general director), Olávarri (archaeological director), Manuel Molina (archaeologist), Josep Sánchez Ferrer (architect), Miquel Civil, Joaquín Sanmartín, and Javier Teixidor (epigraphists).

The response to Del Olmo's application took almost five months to arrive. On 20 October 1988, the new General Director of Syrian Antiquities, Ali Abou Assaf, sent a letter to Del Olmo informing him that the excavation permit at Tell Maled had been denied.[18] The reason was that Syrian government would only grant new excavation permits for work in areas affected by the construction of the dams of Habur, Hassakeh, and Tishrin. That response put an end to the IEO archaeological project as planned by Del Olmo and Matthiae. The attempt to carry out a Spanish excavation contributing to a better archaeological knowledge of the kingdom of Yamhad had not succeeded.

Concluding Remarks: Qara Quzaq, the Only Option

After the response from Abou Assaf, there were two possibilities. Either completely give up the idea of attempting an excavation in Syria or change the objective and try

---

17. "Demande de Permis de fouille archéol. adréssé à la Direction Générale des Antiquités et des Musées de la République Arabe Syrienn (Damas)" (AHIPOA: Folder *Informes anteriores*, file 3).

18. Letter from Ali Abou Assaf to Del Olmo, 20 October 1988 (AHIPOA: Folder *Informes anteriores*, file 3).

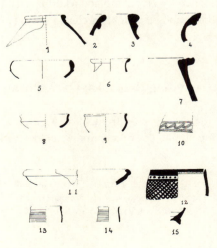

FIGURES 16.1–16.5. Unpublished report by Emilio Olávarri on Tell Maled

to excavate in any other site, with the main purpose of training Spanish students in Near Eastern archaeology. Del Olmo chose the second option.

Del Olmo sent a letter to Abou Assaf on 2 December 1988, expressing his interest in visiting the region of Tishrin to choose a new tell to carry out the excavations. On this occasion, the general director replied affirmatively to the request. A new team formed by Del Olmo, Olávarri, and Sánchez Ferrer visited the Tishrin area 19–26 June 1989. After surveying the region, studying the various possibilities, and receiving advice from the Syrian Directorate General of Antiquities, the Aleppo Museum, and the American archaeologists working at Tell Banat, Del Olmo and Olávarri chose Tell Qara Quzaq to carry out their archaeological project.[19] The mission from the University of Barcelona (with the support of the University of Murcia) excavated there during six campaigns (1989–1994). The scientific results of the excavations were published and are already well-known.[20] Moreover, as Del Olmo had planned, the excavation contributed to the training of a new generation of young Spanish archaeologists and Assyriologists. Therefore, thanks to the excavations at Qara Quzaq, Del Olmo was able to complete the last of the three projects he had devised in the 1970s to promote the development of ancient Near Eastern studies in Spain.

REFERENCES

Abad, M. 2000. "Gregorio del Olmo. Una vida dedicada al estudio del universo simbólico de los semitas occidentales." *Eridu* 4:20–4.

Del Olmo, G. 1983. "Sentido de un empeño." *Aula Orientalis* 1:7–15.

———. 1989. "Misión arqueológica de la Universidad de Barcelona en Siria." *Aula Orientalis* 7:269–77.

———, ed. 1994. *Qara Qūzāq—I. Campañas I–III (1989–1991)*. Sabadell: AUSA.

Del Olmo, G., J. L. Montero, and C. Valdés, eds. 2001. *Tell Qara Qūzāq—II. Campañas IV–VI (1992–1994)*. Sabadell: AUSA.

Garcia-Ventura, A., and J. Vidal. 2012. "El Instituto Ibérico Oriental (1938–1941). Un intento de introducción de los estudios sobre el Oriente Antiguo en España." *Archivo Español de Arqueología* 85:287–96.

González Echegaray, J., and M. Menéndez. 1999. "Presentación." Pages 11–13 in *De Oriente a Occidente. Homenaje al Dr. Emilio Olávarri*. Salamanca: Universidad Pontificia de Salamanca.

Matilla, G., et al. 2012. *Tell Qara Qūzāq—III. Campañas VII–XI (1995–1999)*. Sabadell: AUSA.

Matthers, J., ed. 1981. *The River Qoueiq, Northern Syria, and Its Catchment: Studies Arising from the Tell Rifa'at Survey 1977–1979.* Part 1. Oxford: BAR.

Matthers, J., et al. 1978. "Tell Rifa'at 1977: Preliminary Report of an Archaeological Survey." *Iraq* 40:119–62.

Molina, M., I. Márquez, and J. Sanmartín. 1999–2000. "Prefacio." *Aula Orientalis* 17–18:11.

Spottorno, M. V., A. Sáenz-Badillos, and G. Del Olmo. 1992. "*Curriculum Vitae* y publicaciones del Prof. Dr. D. Fernando Díaz Esteban." *Sefarad* 52:7–14.

Valdés, C. 2006. "Qara Qūzāq." Pages 153–54 in *Reallexikon der Assyriologie*. Vol. 11. Edited by M. P. Streck. Berlin: de Gruyter.

---

19. Del Olmo 1989, 273.

20. Del Olmo 1994; Del Olmo, Montero, and Valdés 2001; Matilla et al. 2012. See Valdés 2006 for an English abstract.

Vidal, J. 2013. *Diccionario biográfico del Orientalismo Antiguo en España*. A Coruña: Universidade da Coruña.

———. 2016a. *Historia del Instituto del Próximo Oriente Antiguo (1971–2012)*. Barcelona: Universitat de Barcelona.

———. 2016b. "La escuela de arqueología del Mediterráneo Oriental que no pudo ser. Aproximación a la figura de Josep Gibert i Buch." *Archivo Español de Arqueología* 89:181–91.

———. 2016c. "Salvador Espriu i l'Orientalisme Antic a Catalunya." *Butlletí de la Societat Catalana d'Estudis Històrics* 27:359–85.

PART IV

Current Prospectives, Future Perspectives

CHAPTER 17

Big Data, Big Deal: Use of Google Books Ngram Viewer and JSTOR *Data for Research* for Charting the Rise of Assyriology

Steven W. Holloway

Google Books Ngram Viewer

The Google Books Ngram Viewer project is a free, browser-accessible data mining tool that supports real-time complex queries of over 5.1 million Google digitized books. The dates of publication range from 1500 to 2008; there are no plans to include books published after 2008. The corpus contains over 500 billion words: 361 classified as English, 45 billion in French, 45 billion in Spanish, 37 billion in German, 35 billion in Russian, 13 billion in simplified Chinese, and 2 billion in Hebrew.[1] The data has been machine parsed into n-grams: single words (unigrams or 1-grams), two-word-phrase n-grams (bigrams), three-word-phrase n-grams (trigrams), 4- and 5-word n-grams.[2] Publication dates derive from the book metadata generated when they were scanned. The books scanned were provided by over forty major university and national and public libraries.[3] The full text of all the books in the corpus are unavailable due to copyright anxieties.[4] The complete Google Books Ngram corpus can be downloaded by anyone, but the books from which they were generated cannot be reverse-engineered (reconstructed) from the files since the n-gram files contain no bibliographic information that link them to the scanned books themselves.[5]

Limitations with using this dataset and text-mining tool for linguistic or cultural history research include errors in the image-to-text rendering process, known as optical character recognition (OCR), making for "dirty" n-grams;[6] the publication metadata

---

1. Michel et al. 2011, 176–80.

2. For technical details about Google's n-gram parsing, see http://storage.googleapis.com/books/ngrams/books/datasetsv2.html (accessed 29 June 2017).

3. See https://books.google.com/googlebooks/library/partners.html (accessed 29 June 2017).

4. See https://books.google.com/googlebooks/library/screenshots.html (accessed 29 June 2017).

5. The n-gram data consists of n-gram files (1-gram to 5-gram) in csv format, organized alphabetically, with the year, raw count of hits, and number of books that the n-gram occurs in. N-gram files were not generated for words or word phrases with fewer than 40 hits across the corpus. The original data files, generated in July 2009, contain massive numbers of OCR errors, especially for books printed prior to 1800. The files were regenerated in July 2012 from the original scans using improved OCR technology. For details about the process and for links to the raw files, see http://storage.googleapis.com/books/ngrams/books/datasetsv2.html (accessed 29 June 2017).

6. Example of bad OCR, a raw Google Books snippet for Priestly, *A New Chart of History* (1801): "About 1514 it was taken by Ismael Soft; and, after changing masters several' times, was at length finally conquered by the Turks in 16 37; BABYLONIsh Wn find Amraphel, king of Babylon, fighting under the

299

is subject to error;[7] and the fact that the originating corpus of books was assembled by librarians over centuries, working at around forty institutions, thus reflects their biases and purchasing limitations. Depending upon the research questions asked, many other limitations of the tool can be described, including the fact that it is comprised solely of books and does not include periodicals, broadsheets, epistles, inscriptions, and other text artifacts. The researchers who created the tool attempted to compensate for limitations one and two by regenerating the corpus in 2012, using more accurate OCR technology and excluded books with date of publication metadata that they identified as spurious. Librarian bias notwithstanding, the researchers responsible for the viewer estimate that the n-gram corpus of over 5.1 million scanned books represents roughly 4% of all books ever published.[8]

The basic operation of the tool is easy to master: a string of words, with or without limiting operators, is entered by the end user into a text field. The linguistic corpus (11 language options times 2 = 2009 and 2012) can be specified using a drop-down menu or entered directly into the search strings as a limiter. The search can be made case-insensitive by checking a box. The default date range of 1800–2000 can be modified. "Smoothing" (changing the raw publication count on either side of the dates displayed) can be turned off or set as high as 50. When the "Search lots of books" button is pressed, a plotted line chart is returned for a successful search, with the dates of publication on the x-axis, the frequency-adjusted percentage of books on the y-axis, and the term(s) printed at the end of its graph line. At the bottom of a successful search window are date-range hyperlinks to Google Books where the query terms occur. The researcher must not be misled by the live Google Books display—it may include magazines and other books scanned after July 2012 and may skip books used to generate the n-gram hits. Advanced queries support word inflection, part-of-speech specification, wildcards, and n-grams can be added, subtracted. or divided against each other.

JSTOR *Data for Research*

JSTOR was established in 1995 as a not-for-profit enterprise dedicated to digitizing and preserving academic journal content. The current iteration of JSTOR provides tiered access, including selective open access to some 10 million journal articles in over 2,400 periodical titles, 50,000 ebooks, and millions of primary objects in four collections, including nineteenth-century British pamphlets.[9] JSTOR claims to make accessible all of its journal titles from volume 1, issue 1 to the present embargo date through its standard search interface.

king of Elam in 19n'B.C. In 68t" (https://books.google.com/books?id=aBRXAAAAcAAJ&pg=PA68&dq=%22babylon%22&hl=en&sa=X&ved=oahUKEwjC5K-42-PUAhUGVD4KHUK-BgkQ6AEISjAH#v=onepage&q=%22babylon%22&f=false, accessed 29 June 2017).

7. For instance, Google Books metadata for George Rawlinson's 1859 Bampton Lectures lists the publication date as 1800 (https://books.google.com/books?id=iBoNAAAAYAAJ&source=gbs_navlinks_s, accessed 29 June 2017).

8. Michel et al. 2011. Google still espouses the figure of 129–130 million books *in toto*, and still plans on scanning them all.

9. What's In JSTOR: https://about.jstor.org/whats-in-jstor/ (accessed 27 May 2017).

JSTOR *Data for Research* (*DfR*) is a web service that facilitates sophisticated text mining of the entire JSTOR corpus, not just the subset of items subscribed to by a given institution or individual. Although the *DfR* website does not make its origins clear, by 2008, when *DfR* went live,[10] many large publishers who maintain research databases were being assailed by requests from researchers to provide access to their archives for text mining. In many cases they refused outright, in some cases they provided large data-dumps, and in some cases they created APIs (application profile interface, a means of database query that is usually more powerful and scalable than human-friendly browser sites) or authored text-mining affordances, like *DfR*. Despite the fact that anything published before 1923 is legally public domain material in the United States, and 1870 and earlier in some other countries, large-scale digitization projects like JSTOR and Google Books monetize their work-product in a variety of ways that makes straightforward access to the digital files en masse difficult, expensive, or impossible. *DfR* supports faceted searches of the entire JSTOR archive (journal articles and pamphlet collections), displaying results either as charts or bibliographic lists. It is also possible to download up to a thousand facet "hits" at a time. If a JSTOR resource has been assigned an open access status, or the researcher's JSTOR account includes access to the primary resource, the hyperlink in the title display will open a webpage reader with the corresponding document. If a researcher needs a dataset download with more than 1,000 word frequencies, citations, key terms, or n-grams, a request may be submitted to JSTOR using an online form.[11]

Single, compound phrase or Boolean searches are supported on all fields in JSTOR data, or can be limited by title, author, abstract, caption, key terms, or references. The search supports complex Boolean construction (example: (dur-sharrukin OR khorsabad) AND assyria). Boolean "AND" queries can be painlessly constructed by adding descriptors in the top search field, which act as limiters. For instance, "claudius rich" "1800–1900" nets 441 hits, mostly noise if you are searching for Claudius James Rich. Add "nineveh" and the 39 hits provide useful results. Queries are case insensitive—all queries should be submitted as lower-case constructs. The system cannot perform searches using non-ASCII characters (example: "aššur" pulls up both "assur" and "assurance"). The system supports wildcards (assyria? = "assyrian," assyria* = "assyria" "assyrian" "assyrians" "assyrianism"). Results are displayed as either a list

---

10. See https://support.jstor.org/additional-resources-student-and-faculty/2015/6/16/data-for-research-of-how-to-mine-jstor-data-easily-and-for-free (accessed 28 May 17).

11. JSTOR Labs is continuing research into text mining of the JSTOR corpus. "Topicgraph" (https://labs.jstor.org/topicgraph/) is a new online service that performs topic modeling of monographs using the JSTOR Thesaurus of 50,000 controlled vocabulary terms. The results are displayed as colored graphs organized by topic, chapter, and occurrence. Sliding a vertical line over the graph and clicking on it brings up the corresponding page of the book, with the terms selected algorithmically for the particular topic. The online demo site uses a small number of open access books, obviating the need to limit search results to Fair Use snippets like Google Books. You can upload a PDF document of your own to the service from your computer's file system. JSTOR Text Analyzer (https://www.jstor.org/analyze/) is another 2017 experimental service that can accept documents in many formats, analyze them using entity recognition routines, and generate matches from the entire JSTOR corpus. The results screen displays a series of "preferred" topics that can be weighted, removed, or replaced by ones of your own choosing. If an image file is uploaded, like a PDF, the service must use optical character recognition before it can process the text. The search results can be opened as PDF documents, provided that one has logged in with a valid JSTOR account.

of bibliographic hits, ordered by relevance, oldest to most recent, or most recent to oldest, or as a simple line graph that records the number of hits per publication year, and a bar graph with the algorithmically assigned subject groups. The search results are faceted by year of publication, content type, article type, key terms, journal title, publisher, author, language, reviewed work, reviewed author, page count, subject, subject group, discipline, and discipline group. Facets are added to a "Selection Criteria" field and can be removed singly or en bloc. All of the facet fields can be exported as cvs, JSON, or XML downloads. So, for instance, if I limit a search on "Elam AND Elamite" to the date range 1849–1900 and export the "Year of Publication" facet results as a cvs file, the results are listed in two columns, date of publication and number of hits per year. "Content type" facet export downloads a table consisting of two rows and two columns, content type (journal and pamphlet) and number of hits. For this project, I made use of the Year of Publication, Journal title, Author, Language, Reviewed work, and Reviewed author facets. "Article type" faceting was irrelevant, "Key terms" are algorithmically generated and use no stop words for any language other than English, "Publisher" is often anachronistic, "Page count" was irrelevant, and "Subject," "Subject group," "Discipline," and "Discipline group" are algorithmically generated classifications that often miss the mark entirely. JSTOR performs no manual or reliable machine authority work on author names, so the researcher may encounter the likes of "H. C. Rawlinson," "H. Rawlinson," and "Major Rawlinson" in the same author list—caveat emptor.

Ten Experiments Using Google Books Ngram Viewer and JSTOR *Data for Research* for Ancient Near Eastern Research

1. The Popularity of Things Egyptian, Assyrian, and Babylonian in English Publications, Based on Nineteenth-Century Books and Academic Periodicals

Google Books Ngram search string:

Egyptian:eng_gb_2012,Egyptian:eng_us_2012,Assyrian:eng_gb_2012,Assyrian:eng_us_2012,Babylonian:eng_gb_2012,Babylonian:eng_us_2012, smoothing default 3, date range 1800–1900, case-sensitive.

"Egyptian:eng_gb_2012" queries the dataset for the word "Egyptian" using the British English Ngram corpus that was generated in 2012.

JSTOR *DfR* searches:

"egyptian"	"1800–1900"	"English"	= 9753 hits
"assyrian"	"1800–1900"	"English"	= 2824 hits
"babylonian"	"1800–1900"	"English"	= 2385 hits

Most historians of the reception history of the ancient Near Eastern "know" that Egypt always attracted more writers than Mesopotamia, but the Ngram Viewer bears the observation out graphically, even correcting for American versus British monographic sources. The disparity in JSTOR *DfR* results is equally telling. The JSTOR *DfR* graphs for "egyptian," "assyrian," and "babylonian" are all weighted for the years 1880

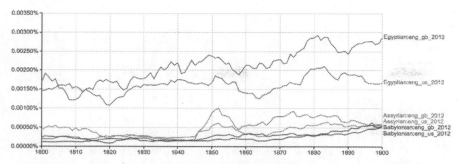

FIGURE 17.1. Google Books Ngram Viewer results graph for "egyptian" "assyrian" and "babylonian," 1800–1900

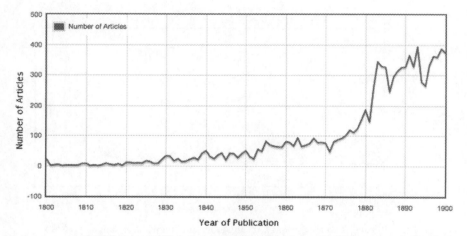

FIGURE 17.2. JSTOR *Data for Research* results graph for "egyptian" "1800–1900" "English"

through the end of the century, a pattern that recurs throughout much of the corpus. This appears to be a function of the rise of American periodicals devoted to Old Testament research and "the monuments," in titles edited by William Rainey Harper or his circle, together with a growing number of periodicals with sizable review sections.[12]

2. What to Call the Languages?

Google Books Ngram search string:
Babylonian language,Assyrian language,Akkadian language,Turanian language ,Sumerian language,Chaldean language, corpus English, smoothing default 3, date range 1840–1900, case-sensitive.

---

12. *Hebraica* (1884–95) becomes *American Journal of Semitic Languages and Literatures* (1895–1942); *Hebrew Student* (1882–83) becomes *Old Testament Student* (1883–89), which becomes *The Old and New Testament Student* (1889–92), which becomes *The Biblical World* (1893–1920), which becomes *American Journal of Theology* (1897–1920).

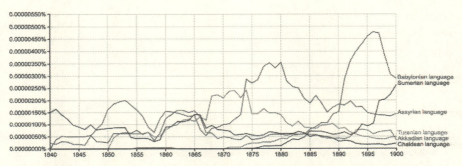

FIGURE 17.3. Google Books Ngram Viewer results graph for "Babylonian language" "Assyrian language" "Akkadian language" "Turanian language" "Sumerian language" "Chaldean language" English corpus, 1800–1900

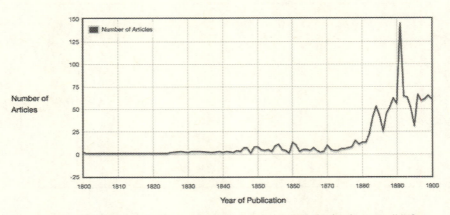

FIGURE 17.4. JSTOR *Data for Research* results graph for "babylonian language" "1800–1900" "English"

JSTOR *DfR* searches:
"babylonian language"	"1800–1900"	"English"	= 1347 hits
"assyrian language"	"1800–1900"	"English"	= 1528 hits
"akkadian language"	"1853–1900"	"English"	= 198 hits
"turanian language"	"1800–1900"	"English"	= 421 hits
"sumerian language"	"1874–1900"	"English"	= 143 hits
"chaldean language"	"1800–1900"	"English"	= 334 hits

The beginning dates for "akkadian language" and "sumerian language" of 1853 and 1874, respectively, indicate that *DfR* records no earlier occurrences of the terms. Unlike Ngram Viewer, JSTOR *DfR* does not support direct searching on phrases/poly-grams, so "babylonian language" will pull up instances of the exact phrase together with articles with "babylonian" and "language" located anywhere in the text, an annoying limitation.

What we term East Semitic "Akkadian" today was labeled "Assyrian" through most of the nineteenth century by dint of the spectacular reliefs excavated in Nineveh, Nimrud, and Khorsabad and the initial decipherment of the Neo-Assyrian royal inscriptions. The bigram "Babylonian language" overtakes "Assyrian language" as a monographic publication focus in 1890 (Ngram Viewer). The *DfR* "babylonian language" graph records almost 150 publications in 1891 as opposed to about fifty-five for "assyrian language," a fair correlation with the Ngram Viewer data. The burning "Sumero-Akkadian" question, with Assyriologists divided into the "Sumerists" and "anti-Sumerists" camps, died an empirical death by the end of the century, illustrated by the rise of "Sumerian" hits (Ngram Viewer and *DfR*).[13] The *DfR* graph for "akkadian language" shows twenty articles in 1893, the high point, with a steep decline the following years. "Turanian language" early on covered the little understood Sumerian as well as Hurrian and Kassite, among others, and would not be overtaken by "Sumerian language" according to the monographs analyzed by Ngram Viewer until 1892. "Chaldean" and "Babylonian" were virtually synonymous until the mid-1880s, as witness George Smith's "The Chaldean Account of the Deluge" (1873).[14]

3. *"Assyria"*

Google Books Ngram search string: Assyrie:fre_2012,Assyrien:ger_2012,Assyria: eng_gb_2012,Assyria:eng_us_2012, default smoothing 3, date range 1840–1900, case-sensitive.

JSTOR *DfR* searches:

"assyria"	"1800–1900"	"English"	= 1731 hits
"assyrie"	"1844–1900"	"French"	= 139 hits
"assyrien"	"1832–1900"	"German"	= 135 hits

American and British books "spike" publication in 1852 in the Ngram graph and two years later in the *DfR* results, presumably driven by the success of the publisher John Murray's mass marketing of A. H. Layard's engaging travelogues.[15] There is no such spike in French or German monographic sources in the Ngram results, but there certainly is a decided spike in French periodical coverage for 1855 in the *DfR* results. From 1856 to 1871 there is a pronounced "dip" in American monographic sources (Ngram Viewer), in comparison with the British, French, and German sources, perhaps a function of the relative paucity of academic training and scholarly communication in the United States for the period.[16] British sources in the Ngram Viewer results rise again in 1872–1881, the years matching publication of the first edition of *Records of the Past*, the first major collection of accessible English translations of ancient Near Eastern texts.[17] Contrast the Ngram results with the graphs generated by *DfR*, a tool that queries only mainline and upper crust periodicals and some scholarly pamphlet series. Savants, whether in France, Germany, Great Britain, or the United States, were collectively engaged in debating the historical, linguistic, and archaeological findings in the minuscule number of scholarly periodical organs available in mid-century

---

13. See, for example, Johnston 1893, 317–22.
14. Smith 1873, 213–34, 1876.
15. Bohrer 1993, 85–105, 2003, 132–67.
16. Foster 2006, 44–73.
17. Birch 1872–1881.

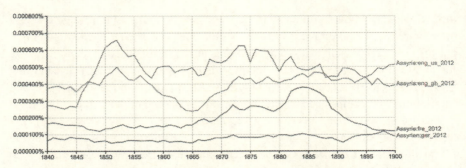

FIGURE 17.5. Google Books Ngram Viewer results graph for "Assyria" [American English and British English] "Assyrie" [French] "Assyrien" [German], 1800–1900

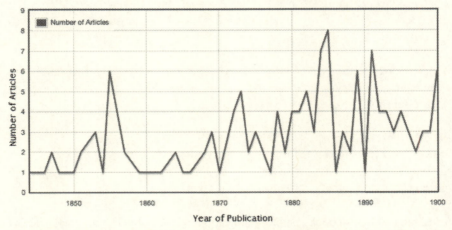

FIGURE 17.6. JSTOR *Data for Research* results graph for "assyrie" "1844–1900" "French"

Europe and America. English language sources climb decisively from 1881 on (*DfR*), a function of the Harper publications, an increasing numbers of academic journals in general, and the difference between monographic and periodical publication opportunities, it being harder at the time to convince a commerce-driven industry like the book trade that an academic title would bring in sufficient revenues to justify the risk.

4. "Nineveh" in English Versus "Ninive" in French and German Publications

Google Books Ngram search string: Nineveh:eng_us_2012,Nineveh:eng_gb_2012
,Ninive:fre_2012,Ninive:ger_2012, default smoothing 3, date range 1800–1900, case-sensitive.

JSTOR *DfR* searches:
"nineveh"	"1800–1900"	"English"	= 1225 hits
"ninive"	"1844–1900"	"French"	= 244 hits
"ninive"	"1852–1900"	"German"	= 79 hits
"nineveh OR ninevah OR ninive OR niniveh"	"1800–1900"	[no language facet]	= 1654 hits

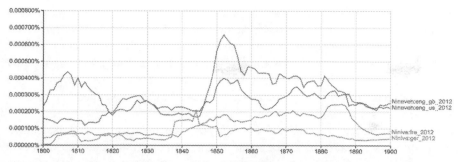

FIGURE 17.7. Google Books Ngram Viewer results graph for "Nineveh" [American English and British English] "Ninive" [French] "Ninive" [German], 1800–1900

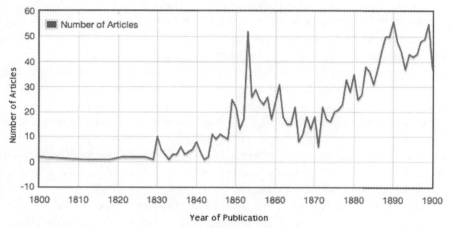

FIGURE 17.8. JSTOR *Data for Research* results graph for "ninive OR niniveh OR nineveh OR ninevah" "1800–1900"

Periodical publication counts for the first half of the nineteenth century, using the *DfR* graph for "ninive OR niniveh OR nineveh OR ninevah," spike dramatically in 1849 (25) and 1853 (52), not to be exceeded until 1890 (57) and 1899 (56), with additional spikes in 1861 (31), 1878 (33), 1880 (36), 1883 (38), and 1888 (50). The sensation surrounding Layard's publications in 1848–1853 account for the earlier spikes in publication, supporting F. M. Bohrer's observation that the costly, academic publication venues and inner-Francophone politics surrounding the circulation of the French excavation reports at Khorsabad did not generate public fascination corresponding to that experienced in England.[18] The spike in publications around 1861 is due to articles in *Revue Archéologique, Journal of the Royal Asiatic Society of Great Britain and Ireland,* Bristol Pamphlets (a JSTOR collection), and *Journal of the Royal Geographical Society of London* dealing with chronology, excavations, and linguistics. The 1878 peak includes erudite notices of British Museum acquisitions from Hormuzd Rassam's excavations as well as from the *British Medical Journal,* an allusion to a translated text by [George]

---

18. Bohrer 1998, 336–56.

308   Steven W. Holloway

Smith concerning Assyrian prisoners.[19] Richard Francis Burton, in a paper delivered to the Royal Society for the Encouragement of the Arts, Manufactures and Commerce, describes a set of ruins by analogy with those of Babylon, Nineveh, and Troy.[20] In 1880, Nineveh was cited in *The Art Amateur* (New York) four times, *The American Art Review* (Boston) four times, and four times in *The Art Journal* (New York), with two articles by Henry C. Rawlinson, including a note on the Cyrus Cylinder.[21]

By downloading the "Journal" facet for the entire century, we see at a glance that *Revue Archéologique* has by far the greatest number of hits (188), with a spike in 1844 in publications corresponding to the first year of publication and the early reports from Botta's excavations in Khorsabad. United Kingdom-based learned societies concerned with the orient show a title account with 202 aggregate hits.[22] Unsurprisingly, the graph for the *Journal of the Royal Asiatic Society of Great Britain and Ireland* spikes with the Layard publications in the 1850s. American Orientalist periodicals, including Harper's publications, account for 305 hits, the majority falling in the last twenty years of the nineteenth century when they began publication runs.[23] Several American titles devoted to archaeology and the arts garner a respectable number of hits (158), bespeaking the success of the visual "marketing" of the British excavations by John Murray press.[24] A number of British pamphlets in the collection have hits (139).[25] A curious outlier, *The Musical Times and Singing Class Circular*, nets fifty-two hits, with a graph that peaks in the early 1890s due to reviewers' enthusiasm for performances of the oratorio "The Repentance of Nineveh" by John Frederick Bridge. By faceting on any of these titles, the chronology and frequency of publications that use a form of "Nineveh" are immediately seen in graph form.

Ngram Viewer searching for "Nineveh" using the accepted spellings in English, French, and German sources does not display any 1850s "spike" for French or German sources, again probably a function of Layard/John Murray English-language press saturation. The anomalous peak in "Nineveh" in American publications 1802–1816 is inexplicable, unless it is either an artifact of OCR errors and scrambled publication metadata or the numbers are generated from the plethora of Bibles, sermons, and original British publications (re)printed in America at the time. There is no matching spike in the *DfR* results graph. This anomaly serves to highlight the limitations of the

19. Anonymous 1878, 319–20, Stone 1878, 935–36.

20. Burton 1878, 16–27.

21. Rawlinson 1880, 70–97.

22. *Journal of the Royal Asiatic Society of Great Britain and Ireland* (100), *Journal of the Royal Geographical Society of London* (71), *Transactions of the Royal Historical Society* (16), *The Journal of the Anthropological Institute of Great Britain and Ireland* (15).

23. *The Old Testament Student* (55), *The Biblical World* (51), *Journal of the American Oriental Society* (49), *The North American Review* (41), *Journal of the American Geographical Society of New York* (27), *The Old and New Testament Student* (26), *Hebraica* (24), *The American Journal of Semitic Languages and Literatures* (17), *The Hebrew Student* (15).

24. *The Journal of the Society of Arts* (71), *The American Journal of Archaeology and of the History of the Fine Arts* (32), *The Crayon* (26), *The Art Journal* (15), *The Decorator and Furnisher* (14).

25. Bristol Selected Pamphlets (49), Foreign and Commonwealth Office Collection (42), Cowen Tracts (25), Hume Tracts (23). My JSTOR subscription at James Madison University does not include access to these texts, so the contents are unknown to me.

Google data-mining tool; unlike JSTOR *DfR*, the actual page-level context of the raw data behind the n-grams is inaccessible.

5. "Babylon" in English, French, and German Sources

Google Books Ngram search string: Babylon:eng_gb_2012,Babylon:eng_us_2012 ,Babylone:fre_2012,Babylon:ger_2012, smoothing default 3, date range 1800–1900, case-sensitive.

JSTOR *DfR* searches:
"babylon"	"1800–1900"	"English"	= 2943 hits
"babylone"	"1800–1900"	"French"	= 430 hits
"babylon"	"1800–1900"	"German"	= 263 hits
"babylon*"	"1800–1900"	[no language facet]	= 7291 hits

A *DfR* search query for "babylon*" (babylon, babylonia, babylonians, babylonis, etc.) limited to 1800–1900, garnered 7,291 hits (6,626 periodicals, 665 pamphlets) in 216

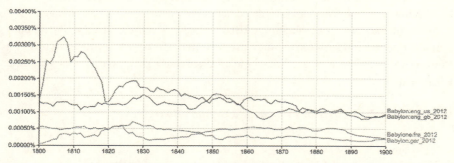

FIGURE 17.9. Google Books Ngram Viewer results graph for "Babylon" [American English and British English] "Babylone" [French] "Babylon" [German], 1800–1900

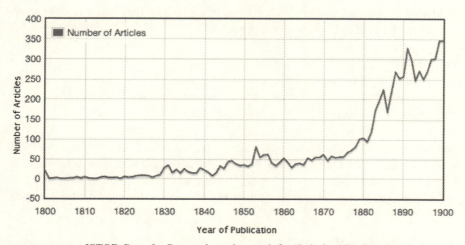

FIGURE 17.10. JSTOR *Data for Research* results graph for "babylon*" "1800–1900"

310   Steven W. Holloway

periodical titles. The Appendix lists the journal and pamphlet titles for the "babylon*" query hits in order of their frequency. Faceting on any title in the "babylon*" search brings up a graph with the number of hits per year for that title alone, making it extremely easy to visualize how the publication graph matches or contests our expectations for coverage on any given topic.

"Babylon/Babylonia/Babylonians/Babylonish" is a particularly complex set of terms to trace due to the multitude of signifiers, mostly negative, that the biblical entity could be attached to: Catholicism, Judaism, the Irish question, abolitionism, or corruption of the political agent of your choosing. It was also a staple in hymns, hence the 666 hits in *The Musical Times and Singing Class Circular* (1844–1900). Only 659 of these publications are signed, bespeaking the high percentage of anonymous pamphleteers and essayists using these code words. *DfR* metadata identifies 5,700 resources written in English, 685 in German, 839 in French, and fewer than ten each in Arabic, Dutch, Irish, modern Greek, Hebrew, Italian, Latin, Portuguese, Serbo-Croatian, Spanish, Syriac, and "undetermined," though more than one language descriptor can be assigned a single resource. The list of twenty-five authors whose works were reviewed are familiar names to those studying the rise of Assyriology in the last quarter of the nineteenth century: A. H. Sayce, Eberhard Schrader, P. Jensen, F. E. Peiser, Andrew Lang, François Lenormant, George Rawlinson, H. Winckler, L. W. King, T. K. Cheyne, and C. Bezold, among others.

With the exception of a "bump" in British English sources around 1851, monographic interest in Babylon is fairly proportionate from 1818 until 1900 (Ngram Viewer). On the bizarre 1802–1816 bubble in American monographs, see the caveat in example 4 above.

6. "Khorsabad" in English, French, and German Sources

Google Books Ngram search string:
(Khorsabad:fre_2012 * 6),(Khorsabad:ger_2012 * 6),Khorsabad:eng_gb_2012 ,Khorsabad:eng_us_2012, smoothing default 3, date range 1800–1900, case-sensitive. The "* 6" in the French and German search strings multiplies the number of hits by six in order to compensate in the results graph for the Google Books corpus superabundance of English language sources.

JSTOR *DfR* searches:
"khorsabad"   "1846–1900"   "English"   = 131 hits
"khorsabad"   "1844–1900"   "French"   = 101 hits
"khorsabad"   "1869–1900"   "German"   = 8 hits

Not unexpectedly, "Khorsabad" (Dūr Šarrūkin), the site of Sargon II's capital that was excavated by the French in 1842–1844 under Paul-Émile Botta (major publication in 1849–1850) and again in 1852–1855 by Victor Place (major publication in 1867), [26] spikes earlier in French sources, and peaks again in 1882–1887 with no later matching

---

26. Botta and Flandin 1849–1850, Place and Thomas 1867.

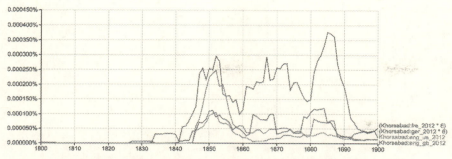

FIGURE 17.11. Google Books Ngram Viewer results graph for "Khorsabad" [American English, British English, French (enhanced for contrast), German (enhanced for contrast)], 1800–1900

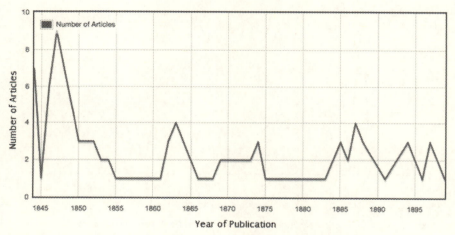

FIGURE 17.12. JSTOR *Data for Research* results graph for "khorsabad" "1844–1900" "French"

publication spike in English language sources (Ngram Viewer). A number of popular art and history survey works published in French probably accounts for this latter spike.[27] There is no 1880s spike in French language periodical publications (*DfR*).

7. *Visualizing the Popularity of Austen Henry Layard in American, British, German, and French Publications*

Google Books Ngram search strings:
Austen Henry Layard, A. H. Layard, corpus British English/American English/French/German, smoothing default 3, date range 1800–1900, case-sensitive.
Multiple discrete corpus searches were necessary because "A. H. Layard" cannot be searched using the syntax "A. H. Layard:eng_gb_2012."

27. For instance, Perrot and Chipiez 1884, Dumont 1884, Schlumberger 1883, and various editions of Maspero's *Histoire ancienne des peuples de l'orient*.

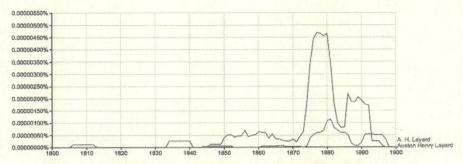

FIGURE 17.13. Google Books Ngram Viewer results graph for "Austen Henry Layard, A. H. Layard," French corpus, 1800–1900

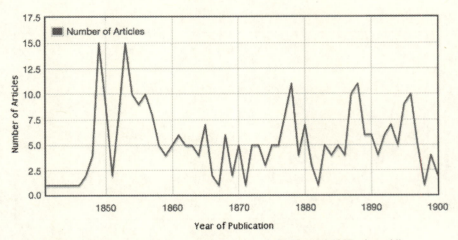

FIGURE 17.14. JSTOR *Data for Research* results graph for "layard AND nineveh" "1841–1900"

JSTOR *DfR* searches:

"layard AND nineveh"   "1841–1900"   [no language facet]   = 313 hits

Querying "a. h. layard" "austen henry layard" does not search trigrams like "a. h. layard," like Ngram Viewer. Adding "nineveh" to a Boolean search on the last name results in accurate discovery even if articles that might mention Layard without his deathless association with Nineveh are missed.

All four of the Ngram Viewer graphs for Layard are startlingly different, and they are different still from the *DfR* results graph. The American English Ngram graph bespeaks an interest in Layard's career during his "archaeological" phase and the close of his diplomatic career, which ended in 1880, but not in the period that he held various British political and diplomatic positions related to Spain. In British monographic sources, Layard's topicality waxed pretty steadily across his career arc. If there is any validity in the French corpus Ngram Vewer graph, French interest in his career skyrocketed while he was ambassador to the Ottoman Empire, 1877–1880.

German interest spiked during his archaeological exploits and again while he was First Commissioner of Works, 1868–1869, saddled with the thankless task of completing the Prince Albert Memorial Monument for Kensington Gardens. The "layard AND nineveh" *DfR* graph shows strong periodical publication spikes in 1849, 1853, 1877, 1888, and posthumously in 1896.

8. Comparison Between British English, American English, French, and German Sources Collocating Equivalent Expressions for "Decipher" and "Cuneiform"

Google Books Ngram search string:
(Entzifferung der Keilschriften:ger_2012 * 3),decipherment of the cuneiform:eng_gb_2012, decipherment of the cuneiform:eng_us_2012,(déchiffrer les inscriptions cunéiformes:fre_2012 * 3), smoothing default 3, date range 1800–1900, case-sensitive.

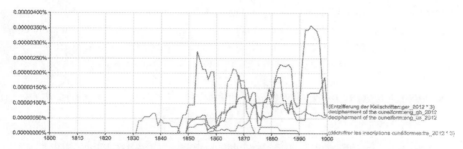

FIGURE 17.15. Google Books Ngram Viewer results graph for "Entzifferung der Keilschriften" [German, enhanced for contrast], "decipherment of the cuneiform" [American English and British English], "déchiffrer les inscriptions cunéiformes" [French, enhanced for contrast], 1800–1900

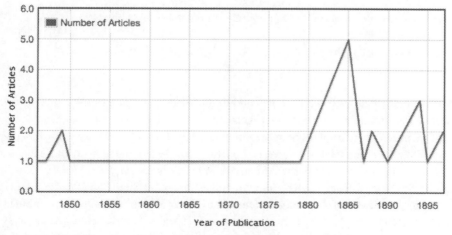

FIGURE 17.16. JSTOR *Data for Research* results graph for "dechiffrer AND inscriptions AND cuneiformes" "1846–1900" "French"

314   Steven W. Holloway

JSTOR *DfR* searches:

"decipherment AND cuneiform"	"1847–1900"	"English"	= 137 hits
"dechiffrer AND inscriptions AND cuneiformes"	"1846–1900"	"French"	= 26 hits
"entzifferung AND keilschriften"	"1859–1900"	"German"	= 7 hits

Since JSTOR *DfR* does not query trigrams and 4-grams in its database, successful queries that come close to the full phrases must be engineered using Boolean operators.

There are some surprises here. German, but not English usage, peaks in 1852, though the German sample is too small to draw meaningful conclusions about phrase usage (Ngram Viewer). French usage peaks between 1863 and 1870 (Ngram Viewer), whereas *DfR* indicates that more French articles published in 1885, a total of five, used "dechiffrer" "inscriptions," and "cuneiformes" than any other year. American usage peaks from 1874 to 1879; British usage peaks massively between 1882–1887 and 1892–1896 (Ngram Viewer), the latter closely matched by the corresponding *DfR* graph. The "contest" staged by the Royal Asiatic Society in 1857 to demonstrate that the "Assyrian language" had been deciphered did not convince everyone at the time, despite confident asseverations like "it is impossible at the present day, when the certainty of cuneiform decipherment is admitted on all hands, and the discoveries which continue to be made in it are accepted by all students of Asiatic lore."[28]

9. Comparison of the Equivalents for "Sennacherib" in English, French, and German Publications

Google Books Ngram search string: Sennacherib:eng_gb_2012,Sennacherib:eng_us _2012,(Sanherib:ger_2012 * 4),(Sanchérib:fre_2012 * 15), smoothing default 3, date range 1840–1900, case-sensitive.

JSTOR *DfR* searches:

"sennacherib"	"1844–1900"	"English"	= 401 hits
"sennacherib OR sanherib OR sancherib"	"1813–1900"	"French"	= 81 hits
"sennacherib OR sanherib OR sancherib"	"1853–1900"	"German"	= 23 hits

Sennacherib citations peak in French and English-language sources (Ngram Viewer) around 1855 (the John Murray factor). Another peak in English language sources occurs in 1873, probably a partial result of the reception of the first volume of *Records from the Past* (1872), with translations by W. H. Fox Talbot of the Bellino and Taylor Sennacherib cylinders, as well as Eberhard Schrader's *Die Keilinschriften und das Alte Testament* (1872). English language periodical sources for "sennacherib" in *DfR* rise sharply from 1882 to the end of the century, occurring for the most part in theology and biblical studies journals. Most of the French sources in *DfR* deal with inscriptions; 44 of the 81

---

28. Colebrooke 1865, vii. On the contest itself, see Anonymous 1857, 509–10; Royal Asiatic Society 1857.

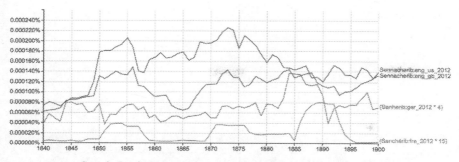

FIGURE 17.17. Google Books Ngram Viewer results graph for "Sennacherib" [American English and British English], "Sanchérib" [French, enhanced for contrast], "Sanherib" [German, enhanced for contrast], 1840–1900

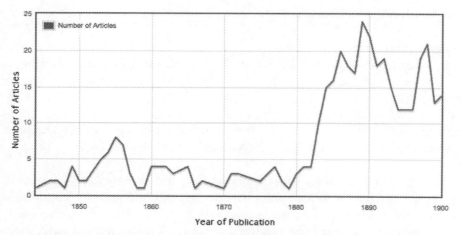

FIGURE 17.18. JSTOR *Data for Research* results graph for "sennacherib" "1844–1900" "English"

hits occur in *Revue Archéologique*. About half of the German *DfR* hits are in biblical studies, including references to the Jerusalem Siloam inscription found in 1880.

A *DfR* search query for "sennacherib" limited to publication dates between 1800 and 1900, yielded 477 hits in all languages, published in 70 periodical titles. Many of these will be familiar to seasoned historians of Assyriology: *Proceedings of the Royal Geographical Society of London, American Journal of Semitic Languages and Literatures, Zeitschrift des Deutschen Palästina-Vereins,* and *Journal of the Royal Geographical Society of London.* Others are likely to be terra incognita: *The Crayon, British Medical Journal, The Decorator and Furnisher,* and *International Journal of Ethics.*

Searching "sanherib" for the same period (1850 is the earliest publication) yields 43 hits, mostly German and French. In an 1897 issue of the *British Medical Journal*, C. F. Lehmann's interpretation of a Sennacherib relief scene as illustrating one of the earliest attestations of the art of massage is noted, an example of the diffusion of Assyriological "facts" into the field of medical history.[29]

29. Anonymous 1897, 147.

FIGURE 17.19. Google Books Ngram Viewer results graph for "Semiramis" and "Sammuramat," English corpus, "Sammuramat" enhanced for contrast, 1800–1900

10. Semiramis or Sammuramat?

Google Books Ngram search string:
"Semiramis,(Sammuramat * 8)," corpus English, smoothing default 3, date range 1800–1900, case-sensitive.

JSTOR *DfR* searches:
"semiramis"   "1800–1900"   [no language facet]   = 323 hits
"sammuramat OR sammu-ramat"   "1854–1900"   [no language facet]   = 19 hits

The perennially fascinating Greek legend of Semiramis, *femme forte* superstar of European literature, visual, and performing arts, figured heavily in early Assyriological attempts to correlate the classical received version of ancient Near Eastern history with emerging inscriptional and visual artifacts. The attempt to historicize the Semiramis of legend with Šammurāmat, regent and mother of the Assyrian king Adad-nirari III "caught on" in the 1870s, but never supplanted either the name Semiramis or her epic court, military, and monumental exploits in classical sources. The Ngram Viewer graph clearly depicts this parallel course in monographic sources, beginning in the 1870s. Most of the Google scanned books with "Semiramis," 1800–1840, deal either with the Greek legends or artistic renditions. Corresponding results in *DfR*, since the corpus is primarily academic periodicals, are far more likely to deal with the figure of Semiramis in classical or assyriological historiography than a Calderón de la Barca tragedy or a Rossini opera.[30]

Conclusions

Based on the hours spent putting Google Books Ngram Viewer (GBNV) and JSTOR *Data for Research* (*DfR*) through their paces, let me begin with some general pros and cons of the two tools, and finish with observations about their potential value for charting the history of Assyriology.

---

30. On the figure of Semiramis in art, history, and the pages of Assyriology see the incomparable Asher-Greve 2006, 322–73.

Pros of GBNV: The web service is free and works with any modern browser. Once the peculiarities of constructing successful queries are mastered, the tool is fast, robust, and functionally reliable. It uses n-grams (unigram through 5-gram), so it is possible to perform exact phrase lookups with as many as five collocated words. Multiple search strings can be entered as a single query, resulting in an easy-to-read color-coded line chart graph. "Trends" in linguistic usage are easy to spot. The graphs in whole or in part can be tweaked for legibility. All of the result sets are released under a CC-Attribution 3.0 license, so there are no permissions to obtain for publication or reuse.[31] GBNV is case sensitive and unicode-aware, so it is possible to run queries on complex diacritics and non-Roman fonts. The Google Books subset used to generate the Ngram corpus has been vetted, to some extent, for metadata accuracy.

Cons of GBNV: it is impossible to know with a certainty what books were used for any given search, meaning that there is no sure context available to check the meaningfulness of the result graphs generated. As a result, the smaller the sample, the more precarious any real-world conclusions drawn from this text-mining tool. The "bulge" in "Assyria" in American English sources during the first two decades of the nineteenth century, for instance, could constitute a significant machine-generated insight into the past, or it could be sheer noise—nothing in the tool supports a satisfactory conclusion. The bibliographic metadata is patently wrong in numerous cases. The OCR errors are legion and grievous. In most cases these errors will generate nonsense n-grams that will not enter any result sets, but in some cases they must, and every error means five fewer legitimate n-grams, at a minimum, are available for research per book. GBNV does not generate book counts per n-gram. That information is indeed in the raw n-gram dataset, but the tool cannot access it. The dataset covers mostly English language monographs, so non-English result sets must be used more cautiously.

Pros of *DfR*: The web service is free and works with any modern browser. The dataset runs from 1545 to 2014, consisting of over 9 million periodical articles and pamphlets. The bibliographically ordered faceting of the interface, combined with free text entry fields using Boolean operators, make it possible to drill down rapidly to the level of a single author, journal title, or language. The ability to download result sets as csv, XML, or JSON files can assist the advanced researcher in deeper analysis or publication. Even without a JSTOR subscription, the article or pamphlet titles behind a result set, containing basic bibliographic data, are immediately accessible. If JSTOR has elected to make a given article open access, or the researcher has subscription access to the database, then the full context of the data mining is available, the ultimate gift to exact scholarship. The importance of this last feature for salient research cannot be overestimated. The quality of the bibliographic metadata is extremely high. There are OCR errors in the corpus, but they are miniscule compared to those riddling Google Books.

Cons of *DfR*: The tool is slow at all times and frequently fails. At least it gives you a politely worded excuse when it crashes. Never anticipate a speedy and robust research session. The search does not support bigram and higher n-gram or phrase searches, so it is impossible to construct ironclad queries for "Austen Henry Layard," "Akkadian language," and the like. It is case-insensitive and it cannot deal with diacritics

---

31. See http://storage.googleapis.com/books/ngrams/books/datasetsv2.html (accessed 29 June 2017).

318   Steven W. Holloway

or unicode characters, making it dodgy to navigate diacritical fonts or non-Roman scripts. The result graphs can only display a single line chart, unlike the visually arresting complexity of GBNV. The bibliographic result sets can only be viewed ten items at a time. Not every Boolean operator construction works as advertised.

The text mining tools Google Books Ngram Viewer and JSTOR *Data for Research*, used with an understanding of the underlying technologies and skeptical discretion, can open doors to the history of Assyriology and the broader cultural reception of the discipline. Humanities researchers are accustomed to accessing subscription databases and plumbing the Internet for late-breaking archaeological postings and scattered scholarly communication. Data-mining Google Books and JSTOR is simply an extension of the research skills we already exercise in a digital age. GBNV is a powerful means of rapidly visualizing trends in word and phrase usage in monographic publications. The query language is taxing, but the About Ngram Viewer pages provide excellent how-to discussion and examples, and you can experiment with my search strings as pedagogical exercises.[32] GBNV is at its best in comparing different language corpora side-by-side in the same results graph. Nineteenth-century monographs are more likely to have indexes, very few of which figure in JSTOR periodicals, and popular press books are more likely to capture vernacular expressions. Given the profound limitations of the n-gram dataset's metadata and OCR errors, and the inaccessibility of the monographic context, however, I recommend that GBNV be used, judiciously, in conjunction with primary sources by seasoned researchers who already have a critical working understanding of their research topic. JSTOR *DfR*, coupled with full access to the database, complements GBNV monographic coverage and can correct for the more improbable result sets that will inevitably crop up.

JSTOR *DfR*, on its own, can function as a tool to quickly confirm, or put the lie to, expectations for the propagation of Assyriological primary publications through contemporary mainstream periodicals. The tool is uncommonly useful, however, in generating leads to the broad reception history of Assyriology as attested in contemporary professional periodicals. Racial anthropology, for example, can be mapped against Assyriology by combining search descriptors like "race" "turanian" "semit*" (=semite, semites, semités, semitic, semitique) with "sumer*" "assyri*" "babylon*" "sennacherib" and so forth. The latest, not necessarily the most trustworthy, "facts" about ancient medicine and Mesopotamia, for example, were seized upon by naïve authors in the likes of the *British Medical Journal*, *London Journal of Medicine*, and *Provincial Medical and Surgical Journal* (search "assyr*" OR "babylon*," "1800–1900," and limit results [over 10,000], by the journals in question). Art history, economics, military history, biblical studies, performing arts, political science, mathematics, and European identity politics can all be probed in relation to the rise of Assyriology using JSTOR *DfR* text mining.[33]

32. See https://books.google.com/ngrams/info (accessed 29 June 2017).

33. JSTOR *DfR* provides no graphical interface for limiting searches by nation of publication. Investigating a national timeline of diffusion of Assyriological "news" can, however, be managed by opening the primary texts through the results pages (only possible if JSTOR makes the resource available without subscription or if the researcher's institution covers the subscription). For instance, the first notice of Claudius James Rich's excavations at Babylon appear in an American periodical publication in 1815, with a substantial extract from his 1815 *Memoir on the Ruins of Babylon* printed in *The North American Review and*

JSTOR, comprised primarily of academic periodicals with no newsprint coverage, is a poor place to search for ephemeral popular cultural events, like Adam Forepaugh's "The Sublime Historic Bible Spectacle, Fall of Nineveh," a crowd-pleasing circus spectacle that was staged in Buffalo, Philadelphia, and Boston in 1892.[34] No vestige of it is to be found in *DfR*. *DfR* is an excellent place, however, to trace the long tail of reception history in contemporary professional periodicals and to chart major developments in excavations, decipherment, and text publication. It is also an effective biographical tool, though crafting an efficient search string that limits noise, like "layard AND nineveh," takes practice.[35]

Appendix: JSTOR *DfR* "Babylon*" Exported Publication List with Hits per Title, 1800–1900

Journal Title	Article Count
The Musical Times and Singing Class Circular	666
Revue Archéologique	432
The Biblical World	303
Science	271
Journal of the Royal Asiatic Society of Great Britain and Ireland	266
The Old Testament Student	255
The Jewish Quarterly Review	209
Hebraica	191
The North American Review	189
Revue Historique	183
Bristol Selected Pamphlets	150
Zeitschrift für Ethnologie	149
The Journal of the Society of Arts	147
The Old and New Testament Student	145
The American Journal of Archaeology and of the History of the Fine Arts	137
The American Journal of Philology	130
Historische Zeitschrift	130
Hume Tracts	130
Rheinisches Museum für Philologie	116
Cowen Tracts	113
The American Journal of Semitic Languages and Literatures	109
Journal of the American Oriental Society	109
LSE Selected Pamphlets	105

Miscellaneous Journal the following year; Storer 1815, 138, Rich 1816, 183–95. The next American citation occurs in a review of Layard's *Nineveh and Its Remains* (1849), Anonymous 1849, 110–42.

34. Long 2006, 365–80.

35. "jules oppert" nets 394 hits, mostly about the Assyriologist, since "oppert" is an uncommon name. For a common surname and given names like "edgar james banks," add a limiting keyword descriptor with Boolean operator AND: "edgar james banks AND babylonian" (317 hits).

The Journal of the Anthropological Institute of Great Britain and Ireland	99
The American Journal of Theology	95
The English Historical Review	88
Journal of the Royal Geographical Society of London	81
Foreign and Commonwealth Office Collection	78
Folklore	68
Hermes	64
Journal of Biblical Literature	62
The Hebrew Student	57
The Classical Review	56
L'Année sociologique (1896/1897–1924/1925)	54
American Journal of Archaeology	50
Revuassyarchorie	47
Zeitschrift des Deutschen Palästina-Vereins (1878–1945)	46
The Decorator and Furnisher	45
The Journal of Hellenic Studies	44
Revue Philosophique de la France et de l'Étranger	43
Journal of the American Geographical Society of New York	42
Zeitschrift für deutsches Altertum und deutsche Literatur	39
Transactions of the Royal Historical Society	38
The British Medical Journal	37
The Irish Monthly	37
Knowsley Pamphlet Collection	37
American Anthropologist	35
The Journal of American Folklore	33
Mnemosyne	33
Proceedings of the Royal Geographical Society and Monthly Record of Geography	32
The American Naturalist	31
The Catholic Layman	30
The Transactions of the Royal Irish Academy	30
The American Historical Review	29
The Geographical Journal	28
Journal of the Society of Biblical Literature and Exegesis	26
Proceedings of the Royal Geographical Society of London	26
T'oung Pao	26
The Crayon	25
Earl Grey Pamphlets Collection	24
Proceedings of the American Philosophical Society	23
The Monist	23
Bulletin of the Torrey Botanical Club	22
Proceedings of the Royal Irish Academy (1836–1869)	22
Transactions of the American Philological Association (1869–1896)	22
Amtliche Berichte aus den Königlichen Kunstsammlungen	21
The Illustrated Magazine of Art	19

Anthropological Review	18
Geographische Zeitschrift	18
Wilson Anti-Slavery Collection	18
Annual Report of the Trustees of the Metropolitan Museum of Art	17
International Journal of Ethics	17
Revuhistreli	17
Zeitschrift für deutsches Alterthum	17
Zeitschrift für die gesamte Staatswissenschaft/Journal of Institutional and Theoretical Economics	17
Zeitschrift für vergleichende Sprachforschung auf dem Gebiete der Indogermanischen Sprachen	17
The Art Amateur	16
Advocate of Peace (1847–1884)	14
The American Journal of Psychology	14
Hermathena	14
Proceedings of the Academy of Natural Sciences of Philadelphia	14
Transactions of the Ethnological Society of London	14
Romanische Forschungen	13
American Journal of Sociology	12
The Art Journal (1875–1887)	12
The Belfast Monthly Magazine	12
Modern Language Notes	12
Transactions of the American Philosophical Society	12
The American Art Review	11
The North-American Review and Miscellaneous Journal	11
Ulster Journal of Archaeology	11
Zeitschrift für neufranzösische Sprache und Literatur	11
Manchester Selected Pamphlets	10
PMLA	10
The Aldine	9
Journal of the Ethnological Society of London (1848–56)	9
Journal of the Statistical Society of London	9
Political Science Quarterly	9
The School Review	9
The Sewanee Review	9
Bulletin de la Société Royale de Botanique de Belgique/Bulletin van de Koninklijke Belgische Botanische Vereniging	8
The Dublin Literary Gazette	8
The Folk-Lore Journal	8
Jahrbuch der Königlich Preussischen Kunstsammlungen	8
Mind	8
Proceedings of the Royal Irish Academy. Polite Literature and Antiquities	8
The American Law Register and Review	7
Annanatumusewien	7
The Auk	7

The Journal of Speculative Philosophy	7
The Pennsylvania Magazine of History and Biography	7
The Philosophical Review	7
Proceedings of the Massachusetts Historical Society	7
The Advocate of Peace (1894–1920)	6
The Dublin Penny Journal	6
Harvard Studies in Classical Philology	6
Transactions of the American Art-Union	6
Transactions (Jewish Historical Society of England)	6
Transactions of the Royal Asiatic Society of Great Britain and Ireland	6
Zeitschrift für vergleichende Sprachforschung auf dem Gebiete des Deutschen, Griechischen und Lateinischen	6
Annals of the American Academy of Political and Social Science	5
The Annual of the British School at Athens	5
Bijdragen tot de Taal-, Land- en Volkenkunde van Nederlandsch-Indië	5
The Journal of Germanic Philology	5
Mitteilungen der Gesellschaft für jüdische Volkskunde	5
Philosophical Transactions of the Royal Society of London	5
Proceedings of the American Academy of Arts and Sciences	5
Proceedings of the Musical Association	5
The Collector	5
Transactions of the Society, Instituted at London, for the Encouragement of Arts, Manufactures, and Commerce	5
Watson's Art Journal	5
Association Medical Journal	4
Cosmopolitan Art Journal	4
The Economic Journal	4
Harvard Law Review	4
The Journal of the Polynesian Society	4
The Journal of the Royal Society of Antiquaries of Ireland	4
Revue d'Histoire littéraire de la France	4
The Scottish Antiquary, or, Northern Notes and Queries	4
Zeitschrift für Social- und Wirthschaftsgeschichte	4
The Collector and Art Critic	3
Journal of the Anthropological Society of London	3
The Journal of the Kilkenny and South-East of Ireland Archaeological Society	3
Journal of the Royal Statistical Society	3
Journal of the Society of Comparative Legislation	3
The New Path	3
Proceedings of the Royal Society of London	3
The Quarterly Journal of Economics	3
Revue de Métaphysique et de Morale	3
Rivintscisocdiau	3

Sammelbände der Internationalen Musikgesellschaft	3
Tijdschrift der Vereeniging voor Noord-Nederlands Muziekgeschiedenis	3
Zeitschrift für französische Sprache und Literatur	3
Abstracts of the Papers Printed in the Philosophical Transactions of the Royal Society of London	2
American Advocate of Peace (1892–1893)	2
L'Année épigraphique	2
Annual Reports of the Dante Society	2
Bulletin of the American Art-Union	2
The Folk-Lore Record	2
The Irish Penny Journal	2
Journal of Anthropology	2
The Journal of the Ethnological Society of London (1869–70)	2
Journal of Political Economy	2
The Journal of the Royal Historical and Archaeological Association of Ireland	2
Journal of the Straits Branch of the Royal Asiatic Society	2
Missouri Botanical Garden Annual Report	2
The Monthly Illustrator	2
Pädagogische Monatshefte/Pedagogical Monthly	2
Proceedings of the Royal Irish Academy (1889–1901)	2
Provincial Medical and Surgical Journal (1844–1852)	2
Publications of the Field Columbian Museum. Anthropological Series	2
Transactions of the Annual Meetings of the Kansas Academy of Science	2
Transactions of the Anthropological Society of Washington	2
Transactions and Proceedings of the American Philological Association	2
Transactions of the Moravian Historical Society	2
The Virginia Law Register	2
American Advocate of Peace (1834–1836)	1
The Advocate of Peace (1837–1845)	1
The Advocate of Peace and Universal Brotherhood	1
All Ireland Review	1
The American Advocate of Peace and Arbitration	1
American Art Illustrated	1
The American Art Journal (1866–1867)	1
The American Mathematical Monthly	1
Annual Publication of the Historical Society of Southern California and Pioneer Register, Los Angeles	1
Archiv für die civilistische Praxis	1
The Art Critic	1
The Art Union	1
The Assurance Magazine, and Journal of the Institute of Actuaries	1

324   Steven W. Holloway

The Belfast Magazine and Literary Journal	1
Botanical Bulletin	1
Botanical Gazette	1
Bouwsteenen	1
Bradley, His Book	1
Brush and Pencil	1
Bulletin of Miscellaneous Information (Royal Gardens, Kew)	1
The Cambro-Briton	1
The Course of Study	1
FinanzArchiv/Public Finance Analysis	1
Giornale degli Economisti	1
Journal of the American Geographical and Statistical Society	1
Journal of the Institute of Actuaries and Assurance Magazine	1
Journal of the New York Entomological Society	1
Memoirs of the American Academy of Arts and Sciences	1
The Modern Quarterly of Language and Literature	1
The National Magazine	1
Numchrjnumsoc	1
Philosophical Transactions of the Royal Society of London. A	1
Proceedings of the Royal Irish Academy. Science	1
Publications of the American Economic Association	1
Publications of the Astronomical Society of the Pacific	1
Revue d'histoire moderne et contemporaine (1899–1914)	1
Transactions of the American Entomological Society (1890–)	1
Transactions of the Modern Language Association of America	1
Transactions of the Kilkenny Archaeological Society	1
The Virginia Magazine of History and Biography	1
The William and Mary Quarterly	1

REFERENCES

Anonymous. 1849. "Review: Nineveh and Its Remains; With an Account of a Visit to the Chaldæan Christians of Kurdistan, and the Yezidis, or Devil-Worshippers; And an Inquiry into the Manners and Arts of the Ancient Assyrians by Austen Henry Layard." *The North American Review* 69:110–42.

———. 1857. "Assyrian Inscriptions." *Littell's Living Age* 54:509–10.

———. 1878. "Notes [Assyrian Antiquities]." *The Art Journal* NS 4:319–20.

———. 1897. "Literary Notes." *British Medical Journal* 1907:174–75.

Asher-Greve, J. M. 2006. "From 'Semiramis of Babylon' to 'Semiramis of Hammersmith.'" Pages 322–73 in *Orientalism, Assyriology and the Bible*. Hebrew Bible Monographs 10. Edited by S. W. Holloway. Sheffield: Sheffield Phoenix Press.

Birch, S., ed. 1872–1881. *Records of the Past: Being English Translations of the Assyrian and Egyptian Monuments*. 12 vols. London: Samuel Bagster.

Bohrer, F. N. 1993. "The Printed Orient: The Production of A. H. Layard's Earliest Works." Pages 85–105 in *The Construction of the Ancient Near East*. Culture and History 11. Edited by A. C. Gunter. Copenhagen: Akademisk Forlag.

———. 1998. "Inventing Assyria: Exoticism and Reception in Nineteenth-Century England and France." *Art Bulletin* 80:336–56.

———. 2003. *Orientalism and Visual Culture: Imagining Mesopotamia in Nineteenth-Century Europe*. Cambridge: Cambridge University Press.

Botta, P.-É., and E. Flandin. 1849–1850. *Monument de Ninive découvert et décrit*. 5 vols. Paris: Imprimerie Nationale.

Burton, R. F. 1878. "Midian and the Midianites." *Journal of the Society for the Arts* 27:16–27.

Colebrooke, E. 1865. "Proceedings of the Forty-Second Anniversary Meeting of the Society, Held on the 29th May, 1865." *Journal of the Royal Asiatic Society of Great Britain and Ireland* 1:i–xvi.

Dumont, A. 1884. *Terres cuites orientales et gréco-orientales: Chaldée, Assyrie, Phénicie, Chypre, et Rhodes*. Paris: Imprimerie Nationale.

Foster, B. R. 2006. "The Beginnings of Assyriology in the United States." Pages 44–73 in *Orientalism, Assyriology and the Bible*. Hebrew Bible Monographs 10. Edited by S. W. Holloway. Sheffield: Sheffield Phoenix Press.

Johnston, C. 1893. "The Sumero-Akkadian Question." *Journal of the American Oriental Society* 15:317–22.

Long, B. O. 2006. "The Circus." Pages 365–80 in *Blackwell Companion to the Bible and Culture*. Edited by J. F. A. Sawyer. Oxford: Blackwell.

Michel, J.-B. et al. 2011. "Quantitative Analysis of Culture using Millions of Digitized Books." *Science* 331(6014):176–82.

Perrot, G., and C. Chipiez. 1884. *Histoire de l'art dans l'antiquité*. Vol. 2, *Chaldée et Assyrie*. Paris: Hachette et Cie.

Place, V., and F. Thomas. 1867. *Ninive et l'Assyrie*. Paris: Imprimerie Impériale.

Rawlinson, H. C. 1880. "Notes on a Newly-Discovered Clay Cylinder of Cyrus the Great." *The Journal of the Royal Asiatic Society of Great Britain and Ireland* 12:70–97.

Rich, C. J. 1816. "From the Monthly Magazine for October. Extracts from a Memoir on the Ruins of Babylon, on the East Side of the Euphrates; By Claudius James Rich, Esq. Resident for the Honourable East India Company at the Court of the Pacha of Bagdad." *The North-American Review and Miscellaneous Journal* 2:183–95.

Royal Asiatic Society of Great Britain and Ireland, ed. 1857. *Inscription of Tiglath Pileser I., King of Assyria, B.C. 1150, as Translated by Sir Henry Rawlinson, Fox Talbot, Esq., Dr. Hincks, and Dr. Oppert*. London: J. W. Parker and Son.

Schlumberger, G. L. 1883. *Œuvres de A. de Longpérier ... réunies et mises en order.* Vol. 1, *Archéologie orientale*. Monuments arabes. Paris: Ernest Leroux.

Smith, G. 1873. "The Chaldean Account of the Deluge." *Transactions of the Society of Biblical Archaeology* 2:213–34.

———. 1876. *The Chaldean Account of Genesis, Containing the Description of the Creation, the Fall of Man, the Deluge, the Tower of Babel, the Times of the Patriarchs, and Nimrod: Babylonian Fables, and Legends of the Gods; from the Cuneiform Inscriptions*. New York: Scribner Armstrong & Co.

Stone, W. D. 1878. "Prison Dietaries." *British Medical Journal* 913:935–36.

Storer, J. 1815. "Miscellaneous and Literary Intelligence." *The North-American Review and Miscellaneous Journal* 2:135–42.

CHAPTER 18

The Future of the Past: How the Past Contributes to the Construction of Syrian National Identity

Ahmed Fatima Kzzo

HISTORY TELLS US ABOUT THE PAST. History can be affected by our own view of the past. Literally, the word "history" and "story" come from the same root.[1] However, the past is always presented in our present-day life in ways that can possibly influence our future. In such a way, the past contributes to the construction of the future or the identities of future generations. In every place in the world, legitimacy has its roots firmly anchored in the past. The legitimacy of property, the legitimacy of states, even the legitimacy of people's existence on specified land, can only be proven by referring back to some past act or event. Sometimes the narration of the past or history is reformed to overturn peoples' legitimate rights.

This paper attempts to analyze the role of the past in the construction of national identity in Syria. To achieve this goal, we will begin with the legislative items, since they form a framework within which institutions work.[2] The first step was thus to analyze the Syrian constitution because the constitution represents the basic law which gives the state its shape and identity. Second, antiquities law is also examined, as this law is specialized in objects which represent the cultural past. In the next step, I deal with institutions which are in direct contact with the people, such as museums and schools, that are considered to be the main resource for people to learn about their past or history. In the third step, I study the use of history by the political parties, which are manifestations of human common ideologies and orientations. Finally, some popular artworks are presented because they reflect the view of different ethnicities for history.[3]

The Past and Future in the Constitutions

Syria is the first Arab country to establish a constitution, drawn up by King Faisal in 1920. Although frequently modified and revised, this constitution is the base for successive iterations. At the end of the First World War in 1918, Prince Faisal bin Hussein

---

1. In Italian there is no different between "storia" (history) and "storia" (story). The same word is used to indicate history or story, instead, in Arabic *tārīḫ* means history. The word comes from *arraḫa*, meaning "to date." Its sense is far from story, novel, or tales, see *Lisān al-'Arab*, the dictionary of Ibn Manẓūr (1968, 58).

2. All quotes from the constitutions and textbooks are my translations.

3. I have given most of the Arabic titles—such as titles of textbooks and news titles—English translations, as this helps in understanding the ideology behind the titles. For the transliterations, I used Deutsches Institut für Normung (DIN) system except for personal names, which I have left in their common transliterations.

formed the first Arab government using Damascus as its capital. In 1920, a constitution that did not make any mention of any past cultural aspect was released. In fact, it only mentions that the king's religion should be Islam and that Arabic should be the language of the kingdom (articles 1 and 3).[4]

That said, archaeological antiquities played an important role very early, starting with the "Document of the French Mandate for Syria and Lebanon" (Anonymous 1923). In this document,[5] released by the League of Nations on 12 August 1922, article 14 deals with antiquities and excavation management. The article is the most detailed in the document. It calls upon the authorities to establish a law governing the study and trade in antiquities. That law was meant to ensure a level playing field for all the nationals of all the member states of the League of Nations with regard to excavations and archaeological research. Article 14 defines "antiquities" as any construction or any product of human activity earlier than the year 1700 CE. It contains a prohibition of export of antiquities without permission from the authorities. In addition, the article permits excavations only to the people who show sufficient guarantees of archaeological experience. As for the proceeds of the excavations, these may be divided between the excavator and the competent department in a proportion fixed by the department. If the division seems impossible for scientific reasons, the excavator shall receive a fair indemnity in lieu of a part of the find.

During the French mandate, a second Syrian constitution in 1930 was released. This constitution did not make any mention about the past. As for the constitution of Faisal, it stipulated that the religion of the president should be Islam but made no reference as to what the official language should be.

Four years after independence, a constitution was promulgated in 1950.[6] In this period there was a debate between different ideologies, particularly Islamists and liberalists, about what form the state should take. In this instance, as in the previous constitutions, Arabic was made the official language and Islam the religion of the president, in addition to the consideration that Islam should be "the main source for legislation." In the introduction to the constitution, it was also mentioned that the Syrian people should build this modern country on the basis of good morals that Islam and other heavenly religions reflect, fighting against all forms of atheism and moral decay.

In article 28, religious education was made obligatory in all phases of study, each religion being responsible for the teaching of its own faith. In the same article, the objective was specified as the construction of a strong, moral, God-fearing nation that was well educated and proud of its Arab heritage. The same article also prohibits any teaching which might be contrary to the goals mentioned in this article. For the first time, the protection of antiquities and archaeological sites was referred to. Article 28 explicitly explains that "the state shall protect antiquities, archaeological and heritage sites and objects of artistic, historical, and cultural value."

The constitution of 1973 was released under Ba'th Party rule as the "permanent constitution."[7] This document emphasized Arab history and the Arab socialist identity.

4. See http://ncro.sy/?p=3507 (accessed 25 August 2017).

5. Although this document is not part of the constitution, it can still be considered a basic law for Syria in this period.

6. See http://dustour.org (accessed 25 August 2017).

7. See http://ncro.sy/?p=3507 (accessed 25 August 2017).

Article 21, under the subsection Education and Cultural Principals, states as follows: "The education and cultural system aims to form a socialist nationalist Arab generation which is scientifically minded and attached to its history and land, proud of its heritage, and filled with the spirit of the struggle to achieve its nation's objectives of unity, freedom, and socialism, and to serve humanity and its progress."

This Constitution remained in force until 2012, when a new constitution was drawn up.[8] Although the Arab Socialist Ba'th Party remained the central governing power of the "Syrian Arab Republic," the constitution had altered in essence. Article 9 of the constitution of 2012 states: "The Constitution guarantees the protection of the cultural diversity of the Syrian society in all its components, and the multiplicity of its tributaries, as a national heritage which promotes the national unity in the framework of the territorial integrity of the Syrian Arab Republic." This constitution does not mention socialism or the aims of building an Arab socialist generation anymore. For the first time it declares the need to protect cultural diversity.

Article 32 restores part of article 28 of the constitution of 1950, adding "heritage sites." Article 32 states that "the state shall protect antiquities, archaeological, and heritage sites and objects of artistic, historical, and cultural value" (articles 9 and 32).

Antiquities Laws

Antiquity law number 166 was promulgated by the French authorities in 1933.[9] The law defines "antiquities" as all the products of human activity before 1700 AD (1107 Hijra), regardless of the civilization they belong to. Thus, the law makes no reference to any specific culture. The current law on antiquities was decreed in 1963 under the rule of the Ba'th Party.[10]

It was at this time that archaeological excavations witnessed a considerable development and spread all over the Syrian territory. The excavated sites pertained to various periods: Islamic, classical, pre-classical, and prehistoric. The law, like the law of 1933, does not differentiate between various local cultures. The law consists of seven chapters:

- General Definitions
- Fixed Antiquities
- Movable Antiquities
- Dealing in Antiquities
- Export of Antiquities
- Archaeological Excavations
- Penal Provisions

8. See http://parliament.gov.sy/arabic/index.php?node=5518&cat=423& (accessed 25 August 2017).

9. Other decrees related to antiquities were released in 1926. In 1927, laws for dealing with antiquities and their export were drawn up. Another was made in 1930 for historical monuments. Unfortunately, I could not find these decrees. However, law no. 166 of 1933 was drawn up for Syria and Lebanon and remains the Lebanese law of antiquities today.

10. Obviously, the law has had different legislative modifications, the last one in 1999.

In 1999, an important modification in the legislation for antiquities occurred. An official decree cancelled two chapters from the Syrian law:

- Trading with Antiquities
- Export of Antiquities

Museums and the Past

In Syria there are two national museums: the Museum of Damascus and the Museum of Aleppo. Both museums are considered to be national museums since each one focuses on a historical era of Syria: the Aleppo museum focuses on ancient Near Eastern civilizations and the Damascus Museum on classic and Islamic civilizations.

The National Museum of Damascus was founded by the Arab Academy of Damascus, which in its turn was formed in 1919, and the museum started to collect antiquities and display them in four rooms within the al-Madrasah al-ʿĀdiliyyah. Kurd Ali, the first director of the Academy, described the museum as the first "Arab museum" in Syria (Kurd Ali 1925, 170).

In 1936 a new building was erected near the Sultan Sulayman Mosque to house the national antiquity collection relating to the Greco-Roman and Islamic periods (Rossi 2011, 301). Additional wings were constructed in 1956 and 1975 (Ministry of Tourism and Syria 2006). The façade is different from the other neighboring historical Ottoman buildings as it is decorated with the stucco façade of Qaṣr al-Ḥīr al-Ġarbī which dates to the Umayyed Age.

The museum holds different sections:

- The prehistory section
- Old Syrian antiquities section
- Classical antiquity section
- Islamic antiquities section
- Modern art section (Assi 2012).

Contrastingly, the National Museum of Aleppo was founded in a small Ottoman palace in 1931. In 1966, a modern structure for the museum was built (Rossi 2011, 302). The façade of the museum recalls the façade of the temple-palace of Tell Halaf dating to the tenth century BCE.[11] The museum is particularly important for its ancient Near Eastern collection.

---

11. There was an international competition in 1956 for the museum building. Thirty-one projects were presented. The proposal of two Yugoslavian architects won the competition and the building was realized in 1966 (Hannura 2016). Instead, the proposal of the façade was presented by the previous director of antiquities and museum of Aleppo, Faisal Seirafi. The exhibition commission, which consisted of Abu al-Faraj al-ʿesh, Shawqi Shaʿth (director of antiquities and museum of Aleppo), Rabiʿ Dahman (engineer), Shafiq al-Imam, Wafa al-Dejani, and Faisal Seirafi, discussed the proposal with the participation of the architects: Georges Tchalenko and the Japanese, Yanshoba and later with Hisham Safadi, the German architect Ernst Heinrich, Einar von Schuler, and Eva Strommenger. Finally, the artist Wafa al-Dajani with the workman Maher Said al-Lahham completed the gypsum moulds. The engineer Rabiʿ Dahman supervised the structure

330 Ahmed Fatima Kzzo

The museum holds different halls (Sha'th 1991, 47):

- Prehistory
- Syrian antiquities from ancient Near East (fifth millennium BCE to 333 BCE)
- Syrian antiquities from the Greek, Roman, and Byzantine periods (333 BCE to 636 CE)
- Arab-Islamic antiquities (636 CE to ca. 1800)
- Modern art

It is clear that the division of museum parts is based on historical fact. Actually, in other Arab state museums, especially in Saudi Arabia, the division does not really concord to any historical period. The National Museum of Saudi Arabia, in Riyadh, is divided as follows:

- Man and Universe Hall
- Arab Kingdoms Hall
- Jahiliyya Era Hall
- The Prophet's Mission Hall
- Islam and the Arabian Peninsula Hall
- Exhibition Hall of Saudi First and Second State
- Exhibition Hall of the Kingdom's Unification
- The Hajj and the Two Holy Mosques Hall

It is clear that the division of the National Museum of Saudi Arabia is based on Islamic concepts. Jahiliyya means darkness or ignorance, and here the word is used to describe the period before Islam in order to bolster its importance (Kzzo 2016, 384–85).

History Textbooks and the Past[12]

The primary education system in Syria starts at the age of six and consists of twelve years divided into two levels: basic education (*al-Ta'līm al-asāsī*) which consists of *Ḥalaqah ʾūlā*, first circle (four years) and *Ḥalaqah ṯāniyyah*, second circle (five years), then *al-Ta'līm al-ṯānawy*, secondary education (three years), which has two separate education curricula: literary (*Adaby*) and scientific (*'ilmy*).

History starts to be taught during the third year of basic education, included in the social education textbook. By the seventh year of basic education, history starts to have a separate textbook. History remains part of the syllabus in the literary secondary

---

works. Then Abu Fahd al-Chalabi cast the statues and the artisan Abu Rasul engraved the statues (Sha'th 1973, 144–48).

12. During the writing of this article in September 2017 the Syrian Education Ministry altered the covers of some of its textbooks and was criticized for it. The cover of the history textbook for first secondary schools carries the image of Iku-Shamagan, king of Mari in the third millennium BCE. This image, and others were branded "scary." The Saudi news TV Alarabiya wrote on its website wrote two articles supporting these critiques (Faḍil 2017). It should be mentioned that in the Saudi textbooks there are no images of statues, since statues are considered to be pagan. See Kzzo 2016, 384 n. 7.

education. For the scientific secondary education, history stops at the second year. These books cover the history of the Arab world from ancient and pre-classic times until the present day and include a rapid overview of world history.[13]

Ancient Syrian culture starts to be taught at an early age in Syrian schools. Also, all the historical periods are clearly divided. Already in the third year some lessons about ancient civilizations contain artefact pictures with descriptions, such as the tablets from Ugarit, the statue of Ur-Nanshe, the temple singer from Mari etc. What stands out is how the ancient cultures of Ebla, Mari, Ugarit, the Sumerian culture, and Nabataeans are all grouped together in one chapter and entitled "The Ancient *Arab* Civilization in Levant, Iraq (Mesopotamia), and Arabian Peninsula"[14] (Figure 18.1). The ancient kingdoms of the Arabian Peninsula, Himyar, Kinda, Maʿin, and Sabaʾ are all included in Syrian textbooks.

Although the prehistoric periods are taught starting with the Paleolithic, the Mesolithic, and the Neolithic, etc., all reference to the human species is left out. Homo sapiens are only mentioned in the first year of secondary education textbooks.[15]

Comparisons between the syllabi of Syria and Saudi Arabia are revealing. In Syrian textbooks, communism comes under the title "the modern theories for the interpretation of history":

> Marx gives history a materialistic interpretation. He believes that historical progress comes from class conflict. In every historical era the economic relations dictate the life aspects of all the outcomes of social, political, and intellectual organizations. Man is the product of his own environment as well as being the maker of it. As a consequence, history formulates man and man formulates history. He is thus the machine and engine of evolution, which passes from primitive society, to slavery, to feudalism, to capitalism until it finally reaches socialism (Ministry of Education 2015a, 22).

In the second year of the Saudi Arabian secondary school, communism is entitled thus "communist invasion in Islamic countries":

> It is a revolutionary movement that denies all spiritual values. It attempts to cancel the difference between the social classes and establishes a society of workers and provides them all with the means of production. This movement appeared in Europe in the thirteenth century Hijra. Its philosophy was elaborated by the German Jew Karl Marx with the co-operation of his colleague Friedrich Engels. Communism promotes atheism and fights religions (Ministry of Education 2014, 142).

As it is clear, the goals of each education system are very far from one another.

---

13. It is worth noting that all the textbooks in the schools are designed and provided by the state. Private schools may add some textbooks to the syllabi, usually for languages.

14. Emphasis mine, Ministry of Education 2015b, 47.

15. Ministry of Education 2015a, 34.

FIGURE 18.1. Page 47 from the 5th Basic Education History textbook

Political Parties and the Past

Just before the end of French mandate, different political parties evolved, and after independence on 17 April 1946, these parties entered into the political life of the country. The forces driving them ranged from Islamic, communist, socialist, to Arab nationalist. In addition to these political currents, a new ideology was developed: that of Syrian nationalism.

The Syrian Social Nationalist Party was founded in 1932 by the Lebanese intellectual Antoun Saadeh (1904–1949). The party built its ideology around the cultural union of Syria. Obviously, what Saadeh had in mind was not the Syria we see today but the Great Syria, limited by its natural borders, that is, the Zagros Mountain in the east, the Taurus Mountains in the north, the Suez Canal in southwest, and the Arabian Desert in the south. This geographical area with the natural borders formed the Fertile Crescent, actually consisting of Syria, Lebanon, Jordan, Palestine, and Iraq, in addition to Cyprus which was considered to be the star of the Crescent. In the party constitution, this region is called *al-Hilāl al-Sūrī al-Ḥaṣīb wa Naǧmatahu Qubruṣ*, which means the Syrian Fertile Crescent and its Star, Cyprus.[16] During his conference in Buenos Aires in December 1939, Saadeh explained that the Second World War was a conflict between communism and nationalism; where the first was essentially materialist in viewpoint, the second was spiritual. He emphasized that the Syrian Social Nationalist Party did not really agree with either, since history could only be interpreted by combining the two viewpoints. In his book *The Rise of Nations* (*Nušū' al-'Umam*) in 1938, he denied religious view for the genesis of the humanity and adopted the evolution theory. He explained the rising of races and nations by scientific theories, based on discovering different human species such as neanderthal and homo heidelbergensis (Saadeh 1938). In his opinion, economic relations and interactions between the land and the inhabitants within a given specific geographic area would produce a homogenous culture. Thus, he refused the coupling of "nation" and "race." For him, the Syrian nation was historically rooted in interaction between different races. The Syrian nation was thus not composed of one race or dynasty but was a result of interaction between different populations that lived in this geographical area, including the Akkadians, Arameans, Assyrians, Amorites, Hittites, Canaanites, and Chaldeans (Saadeh 2011, 20–21).[17]

The party had an important role in Syria until the assassination of the Ba'thist Colonel Adnan al-Malki in 1955. Accused of being behind the assassination, the Syrian Social Nationalist Party was driven out of the country but continued its activities in Lebanon. Just after the election of Bashar Assad in 2000, the party officially returned to the country and now it is very active and has a minister in the government. However, it seems that the Syrian Social Nationalist Party is unique in that it treats the history of the region on the basis of archaeological studies and attempts to build an identity.

In his book *Orientalism and Orientalists*, published in 1949, Mustafa al-Siba'i (1915–1964), the founder of the Syrian branch of the Muslim Brotherhood, accuses Orientalism not only of having a colonialist goal, but also of attempting to revive dead cultures, such as pharaonic Egypt, Phoenicians in Syria, Lebanon, and Palestine, and Assyrian in Iraq. According to al-Siba'i, the creation of smaller identities, allows the colonialists to divide the Near Eastern populations and make them easier to control (1968, 23).[18]

The third main political orientation is communism, which was represented by the Syrian Communist Party, founded in 1923. With a Marxist-Leninist ideology, the party

16. The term "Fertile Crescent" was not invented by Saadeh, but was popularized by the American archaeologist James Henry Breasted in 1914, indicating the region extending from the south of Iraq to the north of Syria, including Lebanon, Jordan, and Palestine (Breasted 1914, 56).

17. Saadeh wrote the principles of the party in prison in 1935 and it has been republished many times, lastly in 2011.

18. Al- Siba'i critiques a lot the European scholars of Islam.

adopted a materialist view of history and so possesses no particular viewpoint on Syrian or Arab history.

Another important party which plays a huge role in Syria is the Ba'th Party founded in 1947, which is formally known as *Ḥizb al-Ba'ṯ al-'Arabī al-'Ištirākī* (Arab Socialist Ba'th Party). The word Ba'th, which literary means resurrection and rebirth, was heralded as a symbol of the rebirth of Arab civilization. The Ba'th Party took power in Syria, on 8 March 1963, at a time when the national identity started to take on a more pronounced Arab slant. The Ba'th Party had also succeeded in integrating Arabism with Islamism. The pre-classical cultures also were proclaimed to be ancient Arab cultures. It adopted the theory that the Sumerians, Akkadians, and Babylonians had originally migrated from the Arabian Peninsula, as we saw in the textbooks. This theory is recalled for Islamic history, in which Islam also is born in Arabian Peninsula and moved to Syria and Iraq.

Ethnicity and the Past

Syria consists of various ethnicities, so there are different views of history. Although the Syrian population learns the same history presented in the school textbooks, every ethnicity has its own particular view of history.

The Syriacs and Assyrians are two ethnic communities that live in northern and northeastern Syria. They both speak neo-Aramaic dialects. Both the Syriacs and modern Assyrians adopted the ancient Assyrian as their ancestors. After the archaeological discoveries in Iraq and Syria, in particular the cities of Nineveh, Assure, Khursabad, and Babylon, an Assyrian nationalist movement adopted these ancient cultures as products of its ancestries. This adoption lead to the appearance of various artistic works, specially by Assyrian-Syriac artists, that represent ancient Iraqi and Syrian cultures as belonging exclusively to their own heritage. One drawing (Figure 18.2) represents the suffering of Assyrian-Syriac people inflicted by different states like the USA, USSR, France, and the United Kingdom. The drawing portrays the flags of those countries which are bombing people. The Assyrian military leader in the First World War, Agha Petros[19] is represented in the drawing, backed by an Assyrian style building. He wears a cap with four horns, as well as the headdress of the winged human-headed bull of Khorsabad.[20]

A calendar (Figure 18.3) in 1978 displayed important figures who contributed to the founding of modern Assyrian nationalism in the early twentieth century, such as Naum Faiq (teacher and writer), Ashur Yousif (teacher), Petros (military leader), and others. Beside these figures there is Sargon of Akkad, represented by his copper head discovered in Nineveh and dating to around the twenty-third century BCE.

19. There is a biography about Petros entitled *Agha Petros. Sennacherib of the 20th Century*, written by Ninus Nirari in 1996. Describing Petros as the Sennacherib of the twentieth century seems appropriate for a military leader, as Sennacherib was leader of many military campaigns. In addition, the real name of the author is Ninus Anderios Yusef. Even the name of Ninus itself recalls the past as it is the name of the founder of the Assyrian capital, Nineveh, depending on Hellenistic historians. The author adopted as a second name the ancient Assyrian name, Nirari.

20. I am grateful to Issa Hanna for supplying me quality images and information about the figures presented in the art works.

The Future of the Past 335

FIGURE 18.2. The suffering of the Assyrian people and Agha Petros portrait

Another painting representing the Assyrian nation between its glorious past and disastrous present was executed in 1979 by the amateur artist, George Chanko. The painting called "Yemma Ator" or "Emo Othuroyoto" means "Assyrian Mother" (Figure 18.4).[21] The painting is divided into two parts. The left part represents Assyria's

21. It is necessary to mention that in Syriac, the word *umto* (nation) has the same root as *emo* (mother) (Costaz 2002, 11). Therefore, the artist may use a woman to present the past and present of nation. On Chanko see www.youtube.com/watch?v=XoIXNVZrWGY (accessed 9 September 2017).

FIGURE 18.3. Assyrian Syriac calendar

past, consisting of green steppes, two rivers (symbols of the Euphrates and Tigris), and a part of the Lamassu (winged human-headed bull). On the right of the picture, we can see desert, mountains, rocks, and rivers of blood. The woman's face is characterized by two aspects. The left part of her face, which belongs to the past, is young with loose black hair. On the right however, she is crying and has greasy braided hair which reflects her old age. In describing his painting, Chanko explains that on the right part, symbolizing the present, there is a dark sky which symbolizes the future of the Assyrians.

Yazidi is another small Syrian community which fights to save its culture. Although the Yazidis are considered to be the oldest religion in the Near East, it actually incorporates aspects from Zoroastrianism, Judaism, Christianity, and Islam. A fundamental difference between Yazidis and Islam, Judaism, and Christianity is the story of the creation of Adam and the role of Satan. Yazidis believe that when God created Adam out of clay, he asked the angels to kneel before Adam. All angels knelt except Satan. In the Islamic version, Satan refuses, saying that Adam is inferior to him, since he is created from fire, while Adam from clay. So, God cursed Satan. Instead, in Yazidism, Satan gave God a clever excuse. Satan told God that he does not kneel before anybody except God. For Satan's smart excuse, God makes him boss of all angels. Yazidis call Satan by the name Tawûsê Melek which means peacock of angels.

The Future of the Past 337

FIGURE 18.4. Emo Orthuroyoto, a painting presenting the Assyrian Nation by George Chanko

Yazidis have a standard representing Tawûsê Melek, consisting of a short pole topped by a peacock.[22] Also, Tawûsê Melek is represented by paintings. The most famous painting (Figure 18.5) was done in 1992 by Lauffrey Nabo, a Yazidi archaeologist from Syria. The painting has cuneiform script in order to give Yazidism more historical depth and authenticity as befitting an ancient Mesopotamian cult. The cuneiform script consists of syllables which belong to different chronological periods. In the white square, on the right side, is the word e_2-zi-di indicating "Yazidi." At the right of the white square, there is 7.bi which usually comes before the sign of the divinity to indicate a group of seven divinities or the seven demons (Sibitti/Sebēttu). On the left side, in vertical: en-zu ti-PI/WI-la-AH. The first big sign in white is AN (sky, heaven) or DINGIR which means God. The upper two syllables on the two sides of the peacock are: KAL/GURUŠ (strong, man) and IM.[23]

This representation of Tawûsê Melek would appear to be quite widespread among Yazidis. We found a mural (Figure 18.6) which could be in the city of Lalesh, the sacred city of Yazidis.

The second biggest community in Syria after the Arabs is the Kurds. Kurds have their own calendar. Newroz is the name given to the New Year's Day and it falls on 21 March. So, in the year 2017 CE we are in 2629 Kurdish year because the start of the Kurdish calendar is in 612 BCE when the Medes, in alliance with the Babylonians, conquered Nineveh.[24]

22. For more information see Joseph 1919, 156–57.
23. I would like to thank Lorenzo Verderame for his reading and explanation of these cuneiform scripts.
24. Actually, some Kurdish calendars take the year 2717, because their calendars start in 700 BCE which is the year when Medis was united, as cited by Herodotus. However, several scholars believe that Medis was unified in 625 BCE.

FIGURE 18.5. Painting of Tawûsê Melek by Lauffrey Nabo

Conclusions

It is remarkable that Arabism as a phenomenon does not appear with the rise of the Baʿth Party, but much earlier, as it is shown in the Syrian constitutions, starting with the constitution of the Kingdom of Syria in 1920, the constitution of 1950, and that of 1973. Indeed, it is still present in the constitution of 2012.

As regards the laws governing antiquities, it is clear that all artefacts are treated equally, independent of the culture they belong to. That said, the law of 1933 defines "antiquities" as any object dated to before 1700. The law thus excludes many items belonging to a large part of the Ottoman period. Then, in the law of 1963, the period was reduced yet further, defining antiquities as those objects which are at least two hundred years old.

A great deal about a museum's historiographical stance can be understood merely from glancing at its façade. The use of the Umayyad palace in Damascus speaks volumes of its orientation, while the tenth century BCE Aramaean temple-palace from Tell Halaf, fronting the National Museum of Aleppo, reveals a strong pre-classical interest.

In the Syrian educational system, explanations of all its ancient cultures abound, and include both Islamic and pre-Islamic. That said, they are all described as Arab. It is all the more difficult to find an appropriate name to classify these cultures, since both "Semitic" and "non-Semitic" civilizations existed in Syria. Their description as "ancient Syrian cultures" could be acceptable, but even with the name "Syria" we are slipping once again into a modern political context.

The pan-Arab views of the past create a fissure between the national identity desired by the state and the wishes of non-Arab ethnicities. It is noted that in every religious or ethnic community there is another view of the past. This view is transmitted from generation to generation, inside the community itself, and is often very distant from

FIGURE 18.6. Mural of Tawûsê Melek. mosttraveledpeople.com

the official state view of the past which is presented by the institutions. For example, in Syria there is a Mother's Day on 21 March as a national day, but Syrian Kurds do not celebrate it. For them, 21 March is the Kurdish new year, the Newroz which is a Kurdish national day.

Syria today is witnessing a war which is now more than eight years old. This war, in some aspects, has its roots in differing perspectives of the past, that is to say, between different Islamic currents, like Shiism and Sunnism. In addition, we have ISIS (Islamic State in Iraq and Syria) which presents the thorny issue of the creation of an ideal Islamic state. By wishing to restore old Islamic glories, ISIS has remained a prisoner of the past. This ideology is not able to live anywhere in particular in a country like Syria where different religious and ethnic communities coexist.

Finally, as already mentioned, in Syria there are a lot of different ancient cultures. The contemporary religious and ethnic diversity reflects this ancient cultural diversity. Although diversity and multiculturalism can be good things, extrapolating elements from the past in order to employ them in the construction of the future can cause problems. The solution, I believe, is to separate the past from the present. That does not mean ignoring Syria's past, but it does mean that all Syrians should learn about a past which is no longer part of the present, where conflicts are over and war no longer continues. They should accept all of this past as part of the wealth of their cultural heritage.

340   Ahmed Fatima Kzzo

REFERENCES

Al-Sibaʿi, M. 1968. *Al-ʾIstišrāq wa al-Mustašriqūn* (*Orientalism and Orientalists*). Al-Kuwait: Dar al-Bayan.

Anonymous. 1923. "Mandate Document (1922), French Mandate for Syria and Lebanon." *The American Journal of International Law* 17:177–82.

Assi, Hiba. 2012. "بدمشق الوطني المتحف" (The National Museum in Damascus). http://www .dgam.gov.sy/index.php?d=251&id=661 (accessed 17 December 2012).

Breasted, J. H. 1914. *Earliest Man, the Orient, Greece, and Rome*. Outlines of European History 1. Boston: Ginn.

Costaz, L., ed. 2002. *Syriac–English Dictionary*. Beirut: Dar El-Machreq.

Faḍil, ʿAhd. 2017. "ليس فيلم رعب . . بل أغلفة كتب تلاميذ سوريا" (It is Not Horror . . . It is Covers of Textbooks of Students of Syria). https://www.alarabiya.net/ar/arab-and-world/syria/2017 /09/09/ليس-فيلم-رعب-بل-أغلفة-كتب-تلاميذ-سوريا.html (accessed 9 September 2017).

Hannura, M. 2016. "تسعون عاماً على إنشاء متحف حلب الوطني" (Ninety Years from the Foundation of National Museum of Aleppo). *Tishreen Journal*. http://tishreen.news.sy/?p=64172 (accessed 24 December 2016).

Ibn Manẓūr. 1968. *Lisān al-ʿArab*. Beirut: Dar Sader.

Joseph, I. 1919. *Devil Worship. The Sacred Books and Traditions of the Yezidiz*. Boston: Richard G. Badger.

Kurd Ali, M. 1925. *Ḫuṭaṭ al-Šām*. Vol. 6. Damascus: Maktabt al-Nuri.

Kzzo, A. F. 2016. "The Ancient Past in the East, from the East: An Oriental Perspective (Syria, Saudi Arabia)." Pages 379–93 in *Proceedings of the 9th International Congress on the Archaeology of the Ancient Near East*. Vol. 1. Edited by O. Kaelin, R. Stucky, and A. Jamieson. Wiesbaden: Harrassowitz.

Ministry of Education, Saudi Arabia. 2014. *Aspects from the Civil and Political History of Muslims*. Academic year 2013–2014.

Ministry of Education, Syria. 2015a. *Civilizations History*. Academic year 2014–2015.

———. 2015b. *The Social Studies: Arab World in Asia*. Academic year 2014–2015.

Ministry of Tourism, Syria. 2006. *al-Mutḥaf al-Waṭany Bi Dimašq*. www.syriatourism.org /index.php?module=subjects&func=viewpage&pageid=1944 (accessed 21 March 2012).

Nirari, N. 1996. *Agha Petros. Sennacherib of the 20th Century*. Translated by F. Pola. San Diego: ND.

Rossi, M. 2011. "The Museum Display: Theoretical Implications." Pages 297–329 in *Archaeology of Cooperation Afis—Deinit and the Museum of Idlib. Activities in the Frame of the MEDA Project*. Studi di Archeologia Siriana 1. Edited by M. Rossi. Naples: Tilapia.

Saadeh, A. 1938. *Nušūʾ al-ʾUmam*. Vol. 3. http://antoun-saadeh.com/works/book/book3-2 (accessed 30 January 2020).

———. 2011. *Mabādiʾ al-Ḥizb al- Sūrī al-Qawmī al-ʾIǧtimāʿī wa Ġāyātuhu*. Beirut: Dar Fiker.

Shaʿth, S. 1972. "Reconstitution del la facade du Palais Temple à Tell Hallaf." *Annales Archeologiques Arabes Syriennes* 23:143–56 (Arabic).

———. 1991. *Ḥalab Tārīḫuha wa Maʿālimuhā al-Tārīḫiyyah*. Aleppo: Aleppo University.

Printed in the United States
By Bookmasters